Second Edition

Evaluation Roots

Second Edition

Evaluation Roots

A Wider Perspective of Theorists' Views and Influences

Editor
Marvin C. Alkin
University of California, Los Angeles

Los Angeles | London | New Delhi
Singapore | Washington DC

Los Angeles | London | New Delhi
Singapore | Washington DC

FOR INFORMATION:

SAGE Publications, Inc.
2455 Teller Road
Thousand Oaks, California 91320
E-mail: order@sagepub.com

SAGE Publications Ltd.
1 Oliver's Yard
55 City Road
London EC1Y 1SP
United Kingdom

SAGE Publications India Pvt. Ltd.
B 1/I 1 Mohan Cooperative Industrial Area
Mathura Road, New Delhi 110 044
India

SAGE Publications Asia-Pacific Pte. Ltd.
3 Church Street
#10-04 Samsung Hub
Singapore 049483

Acquisitions Editor: Helen Salmon
Editorial Assistant: Mayan White
Production Editor: Laureen Gleason
Copy Editor: QuADS Prepress (P) Ltd.
Typesetter: C&M Digitals (P) Ltd.
Proofreader: Victoria Reed-Castro
Indexer: Sheila Bodell
Cover Designer: Anupama Krishnan
Marketing Manager: Nicole Elliott
Permissions Editor: Adele Hutchinson

Copyright © 2013 by SAGE Publications, Inc.

All rights reserved. No part of this book may be reproduced or utilized in any form or by any means, electronic or mechanical, including photocopying, recording, or by any information storage and retrieval system, without permission in writing from the publisher.

Printed in the United States of America

Library of Congress Cataloging-in-Publication Data

Evaluation roots : a wider perspective of theorists' views and influences/editor, Marvin C. Alkin. — 2nd ed.

p. cm.
Includes bibliographical references and index.

ISBN 978-1-4129-9574-0 (pbk.)

1. Evaluation research (Social action programs) 2. Evaluation research (Social action programs)—History. I. Alkin, Marvin C.

H62.E853 2013 001.4—dc23 2011050635

This book is printed on acid-free paper.

14 15 16 10 9 8 7 6 5 4 3 2

CONTENTS

Editor's Introduction   viii

Acknowledgments   x

Part I. Introduction   1

  1. **Comparing Evaluation Points of View**   3
     Marvin C. Alkin

  2. **An Evaluation Theory Tree**   11
     Christina A. Christie and Marvin C. Alkin

Part II. Methods   59

  3. **Donald Campbell: The Accidental Evaluator**   61
     William R. Shadish and Jason K. Luellen

  4. **Roots, Cahoots, and Counsel**   66
     Robert F. Boruch

  5. **Causal Generalization: How Campbell and Cronbach Influenced My Theoretical Thinking on This Topic**   81
     Thomas D. Cook

  6. **The Educative Evaluator: An Interpretation of Lee J. Cronbach's Vision of Evaluation**   97
     Jennifer C. Greene

  7. **My Views of Evaluation and Their Origins**   106
     Peter H. Rossi

  8. **The Roots and Growth of Theory-Driven Evaluation: An Integrated Perspective for Assessing Viability, Effectuality, and Transferability**   113
     Huey T. Chen

  9. **Rooting for Evaluation: Digging Into Beliefs**   130
     Carol Hirschon Weiss

  10. **Multiple Routes: Evaluation, Assisted Sensemaking, and Pathways to Betterment**   144
     Melvin M. Mark and Gary T. Henry

  11. **Ralph W. Tyler's Contribution to Program Evaluation**   157
     George F. Madaus

Part III. Valuing	**165**
12. **Conceptual Revolutions in Evaluation: Past, Present, and Future** Michael Scriven	167
13. **Cost-Effectiveness Evaluation in Education** H. M. Levin	180
14. **Responsive Evaluation IV** Robert E. Stake	189
15. **Work Memoir—Ideas and Influences** Ernest R. House	198
16. **Making the World a Better Place Through Evaluation** Jennifer C. Greene	208
17. **The Roots of Fourth Generation Evaluation:** **Theoretical and Methodological Origins** Yvonna S. Lincoln and Egon G. Guba	218
18. **Social Transformation and Evaluation** Donna M. Mertens	229
Part IV. Use	**241**
19. **The CIPP Evaluation Model: Status, Origin, Development, Use, and Theory** Daniel L. Stufflebeam	243
20. **Using Evaluation to Improve Program Performance and Results** Joseph S. Wholey	261
21. **Evaluation Purposes, Perspectives, and Practice** Eleanor Chelimsky	267
22. **Context-Sensitive Evaluation** Marvin C. Alkin	283
23. **The Roots of Utilization-Focused Evaluation** Michael Quinn Patton	293
24. **Empowerment Evaluation: Learning to Think Like an Evaluator** David M. Fetterman	304
25. **The Transformational Power of Evaluation: Passion, Purpose, and Practice** Hallie Preskill	323
26. **Getting People Involved: The Origin of Interactive Evaluation Practice** Jean A. King	334
27. **Privileging Empiricism in Our Profession:** **Understanding Use Through Systematic Inquiry** J. Bradley Cousins	344
Part V. Evaluation Roots: A Wider Perspective	**353**
28. **A European Evaluation Theory Tree** Nicoletta Stame	355

29. **Australian and New Zealand Evaluation Theorists** *Patricia J. Rogers and E. Jane Davidson*	371
30. **Evaluation Theory: A Wider Roots Perspective** *Marvin C. Alkin, Christina A. Christie, and Anne T. Vo*	386

Online at www.sagepub.com/alkin2e:

31. **The Roots of Connoisseurship and Criticism: A Personal Journey**
    Elliott W. Eisner
32. **Evaluation Forms: Toward an Inclusive Framework for Evaluative Practice**
    John M. Owen

Author Index	394
Subject Index	401
About the Editor	412
About the Contributors	413

EDITOR'S INTRODUCTION

This book examines and compares current evaluation theoretical stances. The point of view of the book is that there is a relationship between evaluation theories in that theories proposed by theorists generally build on previous theoretical work. Furthermore, we consider the roots of evaluation in social science research methodology, social accountability, and epistemology. Seeing the way in which these evaluation "roots" grew over time into an evaluation theory tree, with different limbs for different evaluation theory orientations, helps provide a better understanding of evaluation theory.

In the two introductory chapters, the authors present an evaluation theory tree with three major limbs. The authors posit that evaluation theories are distinguished by the extent to which they place greatest emphasis on methods, valuing, or use. The extent to which a theory places highest priority on one or another of these dimensions determines its placement on a particular limb of the evaluation theory tree. Following the two introductory chapters, there are 25 chapters written by or about most of the major North American theorists in the field. Then there are two additional chapters—one describing evaluation theorists in Europe and another for Australia/New Zealand theorists.

The final chapter provides an examination of the two preceding chapters and incorporates these theorists onto the evaluation theorist tree presented in Chapter 2. The chapter authors were requested only that they address two areas: their own theories and their personal roots. Authors were asked to write a chapter of 10 to 15 pages in length. Most authors adhered to this limit, but some exceeded it. Editorial advice was occasionally given to authors, but ultimately, the chapters were accepted in the style used by the authors. Thus, writing styles differ from chapter to chapter. Some are very formal (akin to research papers), and others are more personal, capturing the influences and feelings of the authors. In many respects, the writing styles of the chapters provide further insights about each author. We see not only the author's view of evaluation, but also from the author's presentation style, we may gain a greater understanding of his or her perspective. Less formal styles dominate the volume.

The process of editing this book and reading all the chapters to provide comments to their authors has in many ways been confusing. Chapter authors have presented such an abundance of appealing ideas that one constantly finds oneself saying, "You're right." Each theorist may believe that his or her approach is the true nirvana. While I have theoretical prescriptive preferences, I nonetheless believe that there is validity in each of their models. In examining the theorists' views, readers will find not one but many chapters in which they find themselves saying, "Yes, yes, that makes sense." While I think that readers and practitioners are best advised to generally adhere to a particular model that makes the most intellectual sense to them, it is best to have a defining structure: a basic model or theory that one adheres to but that is potentially adaptable. It may be that some practitioners faced with a wide variety of very different contexts in which they will perform evaluations select the theoretical approaches that best fit these situations.

Theorists' views are constantly undergoing some change (as would those of practitioners who embrace a particular model or theory as their guiding framework). I addressed this in a chapter in which I discussed the many influences on an evaluator's changing prescriptive views (Alkin, 1991).

I anticipate that in reading this book, practitioners and theorists will find many appealing ideas that enhance their evaluation views and practice.

REFERENCE

Alkin, M. (1991). Evaluation theory development II. In M. McLaughlin & D. Phillips (Eds.), *Evaluation at quarter century* (90th yearbook of the National Society for the Study of Education). Chicago, IL: University of Chicago Press.

ACKNOWLEDGMENTS

My sincere thanks to the evaluation theorists who wrote chapters for *Evaluation Roots*. I am gratified by their willingness to participate in this project and to produce wise and lively essays within a relatively short time frame. It has been a joy to work with my colleague, Tina Christie, who enjoys, as much as I do, just sitting around and talking about evaluation theory. Likewise, Anne Vo has actively participated in and contributed to our theoretical discussions. Tarek Azzam provided substantial assistance on the tree as well. Celina Lee has been of assistance in providing editing, assorted comments, and administrative support. Iris Chen has assisted with clerical support.

My sincere thanks to SAGE editors whom I have dealt with over a 40-year period and who established for me an unparalleled standard of excellence, in particular Sara Miller (McCune), Mitch Allen, and C. Deborah Laughton. I would also like to acknowledge the fine work of Laureen Gleason, the production editor for this volume.

Thanks to my wife, Marilyn, for putting up with my obsession with "growing" a tree.

Marvin Alkin

SAGE Publications would like to thank the following reviewers who provided feedback on the first edition and participated in the development of the second edition: Susan Hunter, West Virginia University; Aron M. Kuntz, University of Alabama; and Linda B. Schrader, Florida State University.

PART I

INTRODUCTION

1

COMPARING EVALUATION POINTS OF VIEW

Marvin C. Alkin

When I first came to UCLA in 1964 as a new faculty member, I spent many hours in the office of a senior colleague, a man of great practical wisdom. I was fascinated by a giant clothespin that sat on his desk, crammed with papers and notes, which had a brass plate on top inscribed "New Ideas." I wondered about it and after many months had the courage to comment on it. Erick Lindman gently smiled and turned the clothespin over; on the other side was the inscription "Old Ideas Still Good."

It took several years for me to fully appreciate that sentiment. As I transitioned professionally into what many of us felt to be the "newly emerging" field of evaluation, I came to read the works of Ralph Tyler in connection with the evaluation conducted on the famous "Eight-Year Study" of progressive education. In Tyler (1942), I found many concepts that I recognized to be the basis of contemporary approaches to evaluation. Below is a sampling of statements from Tyler, followed by references to subsequent theoreticians in the field whose ideas show a striking parallel:

> Another important purpose of evaluation that is frequently not recognized is to validate the hypothesis upon which the education institution operates. (p. 492) (Theory-Based Evaluation? See Fitz-Gibbon & Morris, 1975; Chen, 1990)

> One purpose of evaluation is to make a periodic check on the effectiveness of the educational institution, and thus to indicate the points at which improvements in the program are necessary. (p. 492) (Formative Evaluation? See Scriven, 1967)

The participation of teachers, pupils, and parents in the processes of evaluation is essential to derive the maximum values from a program evaluation. They all have a stake in the educational program of the school or college. They can all contribute to the formation and classification of objectives, they are all in a position to obtain evidence about the progress pupils are making, they can all benefit from efforts to interpret the results of appraisal. (p. 497) (Stakeholders? See Stake, 1975. Participatory Evaluation? See Cousins & Earl, 1992)

A second basic assumption involved in evaluation is that the kinds of changes in behavior patterns in human beings which the school or college seeks to bring about are its educational objectives. . . . An educational program is appraised by finding out how far the objectives of the program are actually being realized. (pp. 495–496) (Goal Attainment Models? See Popham, 1975)

Clearly, many current ideas in evaluation had their foundation in this early writing on the subject. Likewise, many subsequent words of wisdom have had an enduring impact on the writings of other theorists. In reflecting on the insightful words on the other side of the clothespin, I felt perhaps that the inscription should have read "Old Ideas Revisited and *Enhanced*—But Still Good." To understand where we are in the field of evaluation today, it is important to revisit the old ideas—the roots—of evaluation and to see the way they were enhanced over time: the new growth, if you will.

THEORIES

In the following chapter, Christina Christie and I will talk about evaluation "theories." The reason why the word *theories* is in quotes is that while it is conventionally used in evaluation literature, in some ways, it would be more appropriate to use the term *approaches* or *models*. In this context, there are two general types of models: (a) a *prescriptive model*, the most common type, is a set of rules, prescriptions, prohibitions, and guiding frameworks that specify what a good or proper evaluation is and how evaluation should be done—such models serve as *exemplars*—and (b) a *descriptive model* is a set of statements and generalizations that describes, predicts, or explains evaluation activities—such a model is designed to offer an *empirical theory*. Regarding descriptive models, Henry and Mark (2003) and others have advocated for conducting research on evaluation. I applaud such efforts. But we are a long ways away from achieving such status. When (and if) we do, then the descriptive models would define what is to be appropriately "prescribed." Until then, however, we must rely on the prescriptive models generated by knowledgeable members of the evaluation community to guide practice.

Almost everyone who has written about educational evaluation has, in one way or another, made prescriptions. Some have spent more time systemizing their standards, criteria, and principles. A few have tried to defend or justify their prescriptions. None of the approaches is predictive or offers an empirical theory. That is, these "theories" have not been validated by empirical research. Thus, in the strictest sense, what we will refer to as "evaluation theories" do not fully qualify for that status. Nonetheless, we intentionally refer to them in that way to reflect their most common current usage, and similarly, we refer to those who have developed evaluation approaches and models as "theorists." In this volume, we identify theories by the name of the theorist prominently associated with it.

THEORISTS

Before we begin the process of discussing evaluation theorists, it is important to indicate the way in which we have distinguished various individuals prominent in evaluation. Obviously, all of those who have written about evaluation cannot be considered to have developed a unique evaluation theory (as we use the term here). While their contributions may nonetheless be quite significant, they are not theorists or model builders. We have chosen to categorize the primary writers in evaluation in four ways.

Some individuals have contributed very substantially to the basic research methodology that forms the essential foundation for much of the work in evaluation. These include people such as Donald Campbell, Julian Stanley, Thomas Cook, Matthew Miles and Michael Huberman, Robert Yin, and Anthony Bryk.[1] Of these individuals, we have written only about Donald Campbell in the discussion of theorists because of the unique impact of his methodological contributions. Let us refer to these individuals as *methodologists* who have influenced evaluation.

Another category of individuals we identify as *evaluation issue analysts.* Their work, while not necessarily associated with an evaluation model or theory, has very substantially assisted in the understanding of various aspects of evaluation. Individuals in this category would include Lois-Ellin Datta, Stewart Donaldson, Karen Kirkhart, Jonathan Morell, Michael Morris, Thomas Schwandt, William Shadish, Nick Smith, and many others.

An additional category of individuals we identify as *evaluation interpreters and teachers.* Individuals in this category might also be prominent analysts of evaluation (and many are), but they are distinguished by having written evaluation textbooks that, while not necessarily expounding a new theory, provide an important resource for teaching about evaluation and helping to interpret its nuances. Individuals in this category include, among many others, Michael Bamberger, Linda Mabry, and Jim Rugh (2011), Jody Fitzpatrick, James Sanders, and Blaine Worthen (2011), Rita O'Sullivan (2004), Emil Posevac and Raymond Carey (2007), and Liliana Rodriguez-Campos (2005). Some of these, arguably, might be considered theorists.

Finally, we have attempted to identify individuals who are definitively associated with a particular theoretical position on evaluation as *evaluation theorists.* These distinctions are difficult and perhaps subjective, since many in this category may not have presented a full theoretical exposition, but nevertheless, they appear to us to have proposed a particular evaluation orientation. Furthermore, some of those in the category denoted as "evaluation interpreters and teachers" might well be considered as theorists. Space limitations may be the only reason for their noninclusion in the "theorist" category.

One further note about the selection and inclusion of evaluation theorists. I have restricted my consideration of evaluators to those who speak about the field generically and whose writings are not restricted or focused on a specific field. For example, those who write only about evaluating health programs or education or social welfare have not been included. Furthermore, those who do not consider themselves as evaluators but exclusively assign another disciplinary designation to their name are also not generally included. (Some deviations from this rule are noteworthy—e.g., Donald Campbell.)

CATEGORY SYSTEMS

There have been many prior attempts to look at the ways in which various theoretic perspectives relate to each other. Earlier efforts have taken the form of category (or classification) systems. These simplified structures provided a way to identify a limited set of characteristics for grouping theories. Entries within a category are deemed to belong together in the sense that they can be judged to be similar with respect to the characteristic or configuration of characteristics that define that category. However, in making this judgment, the categorizer is selecting from the many aspects of the approach only those that are considered most essential. In many ways, this is similar to an artist's creation of a caricature, portraying someone or something by focusing on (even overemphasizing) its most prominent features. Among the earliest evaluation category systems were those provided by Worthen and Sanders (1973) and Popham (1975). Subsequently, category systems have been developed by House (1978), Glass and Ellett (1980), Alkin and Ellett (1985), Williams (1988), Shadish, Cook, and Leviton (1991), Alkin and House (1992), and others.

Category systems are of great value. By grouping theories within a category, frequently a new concept is introduced or an existing concept is reinforced. Thus, for example, Stufflebeam's context–input–process–product (CIPP) model and my Center for the Study of Evaluation (CSE) model of the early 1970s were defined as *decision management* (Worthen & Sanders, 1973) and *decision facilitation* (Popham, 1975), respectively. This provided an easily understood way for practitioners to think about and define their preferred approach to conducting evaluation.

Category systems also were an aid to theorists in understanding perceived relationships with other theorists. Placement within categories led theorists to question whether their views were being portrayed adequately (see Alkin, 1991). Since category systems dramatize those features presumed to be most prominent, illuminating those features and not others might provide discomfort to theorists. Theorists might not have seen certain emphases in their own work. The writing might have led to what they considered to be "misinterpretation."

Moreover, theorists' views are not fixed in time, as would seem to be implied by their published works. Theorists typically change their views over time, and their published work often lags behind these changes. Nonetheless, one's views as perceived by others (whether or not they are still held) have influenced theorists. Whatever the explanations for a perceived portrayal of a theorist's views, the perceptions provided by category systems may force theorists to reconsider their views and perhaps modify them.

While earlier category systems prior to the first edition of *Evaluation Roots* served evaluation well, they suffered from several deficiencies. These category systems failed to portray the historically derived relationships between theories. That is, they failed to show which theoretical formulations provided the intellectual stimulation for new theories (the "Old Ideas Revisited and Enhanced—But Still Good" notion). How might such relationships be depicted?

EVALUATION THEORY TREE

The guiding framework for the analyses in the *Roots* evaluation theory tree is provided by the comparative theory work of Alkin and colleagues (Alkin & Ellett, 1985; Alkin & House, 1992). As early as 1985, Alkin and Ellett maintained that all prescriptive theories must consider (a) the issues related to the methodology being used, (b) the manner in which data are to be judged or valued, and (c) the user focus of the evaluation effort. We represent relationships between theories in the form of an evaluation theory "tree," with each of the main branches representing one of these main dimensions: use, methods, judgment/valuing. Thus, each of the theorists is presented on the tree on a branch that we believe represents his or her main emphasis among these three. The distinction between evaluation models based on these three dimensions is not one based on exclusivity, or that only one model believes in the use of methodology and others do not. Rather, the category system is based on the relative emphasis within the various models. It might then be possible to ask this question: When evaluators must make concessions, what do they most easily give up and what do they most tenaciously defend (Alkin & Ellet, 1985)?

In the theory description in the first edition of this book (Alkin & Christie, 2004), we have attempted to place theorists in a position on the tree that best reflects the way in which they relate to other theorists of the same orientation. This caused some discomfort to various theorists. Carol Weiss, for example, indicated that she was satisfied with her placement but felt that, to some extent, she belonged on the "use" branch as well. David Fetterman, likewise, agreed with his placement but felt that it did not adequately represent his interest in "social justice." Jennifer Greene commented that Lee Cronbach is not fundamentally concerned about methods but that his placement on the "methods" branch was probably as good a representation as possible. Nonetheless, the process of categorizing in the form of an evaluation theory tree was helpful.

Furthermore, we have attempted to place theorists in a position that best reflects the way in which they relate to other theorists on the same branch. We considered the extent to which various theoretical ideas influenced the theory. This is sometimes historical, but not always so.

Indeed, we recognize this tree to be a drastic oversimplification of very complex relationships. "New" theoretical formulations are usually derived from a number of influences, both within the evaluation field (as the example of Tyler at the beginning of the chapter shows) and from external disciplines. By depicting the relationship between theorists and other evaluation writers with whom they share a common perspective, we capture only one dimension of the influences on their theoretical perspectives. Typically, this single characteristic is the main influence on each writer's work, but theorists differ in other respects. Clearly, theorists also are influenced by colleagues who have been identified on the basis of another main characteristic—that is, those who are on another branch of the theory tree. In *Evaluation Roots* (2004), I analyzed the evaluator influences from other branches of the tree based on the names identified by the theorists in their respective chapters. Carol Weiss, for example, identified Alkin, Guba, House, and Patton as theorists from other branches of the tree. Moreover, she indicated having been influenced by other evaluators not on the evaluation theory tree: Howard Freeman, Gene Glass, William Shadish, and others. Robert Stake identified Cronbach, Stufflebeam, and Tyler with other evaluators including Mike Atkin, David Hamilton, and Tom Hastings. Bradley Cousins identified Carol Weiss from another branch of the tree and other evaluators including Jennifer Greene and Michael Huberman.

Also, evaluators are stimulated in their thinking not only by the writing of other theorists in evaluation but also by a variety of other intellectual stimuli. Theorists from other disciplines, past and present, often provide insights and inspiration to those thinking about evaluation. An excellent case in point is provided by Ernest House's *The Logic of Evaluative Argument* (1977), which clearly shows the influence of early evaluation theorists such as Michael Scriven and Robert Stake but which also relies heavily on the work of two Belgian philosophers, Perelman and Olbrechts-Tyteca (1969) and on the work of Weizenbaum (1976). Numerous other examples will be provided in the chapters by the various evaluation theorists.

A WIDER PERSPECTIVE

This volume differs from the first edition in many ways. Most notable is the inclusion of more authors—a widening of the tree if you will. The field has changed, and Tina Christie and I felt the need to reflect this in the selection of authors. New invitations to participate have been extended to the North American authors Eleanor Chelimsky, Jennifer Greene, Henry Levin, Melvin Mark and Gary Henry, and Donna Mertens. Greene's work and that of Donna Mertens have become substantially more prominent and merited inclusion. Mark and Henry were not included in the first edition because we did not pay sufficient heed to their book with George Julnes. Eleanor Chelimsky had created an impressive model for evaluating national programs in her work at the GAO. Finally, it struck us that the inclusion of Henry Levin provided an evaluative dimension not otherwise represented—cost-effectiveness evaluation.

One American author, Elliot Eisner, previously represented by a chapter, will be discussed and placed on the tree but will not have a separate chapter. His chapter from the previous volume is available at the SAGE website for this book, www.sagepub.com/alkin2e.

It was my intention that this volume would be titled *Evaluation Roots: An International Perspective*. To attain this goal, a chapter summarizing evaluation theory in Europe was solicited from Nicoletta Stame, and this chapter was included. Another chapter summarizing work in Australia/New Zealand was prepared by Patricia Rogers with the assistance of Jane Davidson.[2] These are the two parts of the world where there has been the most evaluation work promulgated. To complete the international perspective, a third chapter was commissioned to briefly describe evaluation activity elsewhere in the world. Unfortunately, that author failed to produce a manuscript.[3] Thus, instead of a fully international perspective, I have produced *Evaluation Roots: A Wider Perspective of Theorists' Views and Influences.*

NOTES

1. Bryk might also be considered to belong in the theorist category for his contribution to the stakeholder evaluation model. We have not included him because his primary contributions have more significantly been to statistical methods than to evaluation theory.

2. A chapter by the Australian theorist John Owen, which appeared in the first volume, is likewise available at the SAGE website for this book, www.sagepub.com/alkin2e.

3. To partially address this issue, Fred Carden and I are developing an article focusing on evaluation in low- and middle-income countries, to appear in an issue of the *Journal of Multidisciplinary Evaluation.*

REFERENCES

Alkin, M. (1991). Evaluation theory development II. In M. McLaughlin & D. Phillips (Eds.), *Evaluation at quarter century* (pp. 91–112) (The 90th yearbook of the National Society for the Study of Education). Chicago, IL: University of Chicago Press.

Alkin, M., & Christie, C. (2004). An evaluation theory tree. In M. Alkin (Ed.), *Evaluation roots* (pp. 381–392). Thousand Oaks, CA: Sage.

Alkin, M., & Ellett, F. (1985). Evaluation models and their development. In T. Husèn & T. N. Postlethwaite (Eds.), *International encyclopedia of education: Research and studies* (Vol. 3, pp. 1760–1766). Oxford, England: Pergamon Press.

Alkin, M., & House, E. (1992). Evaluation of programs. In M. Alkin (Ed.), *Encyclopedia of educational research.* New York, NY: Macmillan.

Bamberger, M., Mabry, L., & Rugh, J. (2011). *Real World evaluation: Working under budget, time, data, and political constraints* (2nd ed.). Thousand Oaks, CA: Sage.

Chen, H. (1990). *Theory-driven evaluation.* Newbury Park, CA: Sage.

Cousins, J., & Earl, L. (1992). The case for participatory evaluation. *Educational Evaluation and Policy Analysis, 14*(4), 397–418.

Fitz-Gibbon, C., & Morris, L. (1975). Theory-based evaluation. *Evaluation Comment: The Journal of Educational Evaluation, 5*(1), 1–4.

Fitzpatrick, J. L., Sanders, J. R., & Worthen, B. R. (2011). *Program evaluation: Alternative approaches and practical guidelines.* Upper Saddle River, NJ: Prentice Hall.

Glass, G., & Ellett, F., Jr. (1980). Evaluation research. *Annual Review Psychology, 31,* 211–228.

Henry, G., & Mark, M. (2003). Toward an agenda for research on evaluation. *New Directions for Evaluation, 97,* 69–80.

House, E. (1977). *The logic of evaluative argument.* Los Angeles, CA: Center for the Study of Evaluation.

House, E. (1978). Assumptions underlying evaluation models. *Educational Researcher, 8,* 4–12.

O'Sullivan, R. G. (2004). *Practicing evaluation: A collaborative approach.* Thousand Oaks, CA: Sage.

Perelman, C., & Olbrechts-Tyteca, L. (1969). *The new rhetoric: A treatise on argumentation.* Notre Dame, IN: University of Notre Dame Press.

Popham, W. (1975). *Educational evaluation.* Englewood Cliffs, NJ: Prentice Hall.

Posevac, E. J., & Carey, R. G. (2007). *Program evaluation: Methods and case studies*. Upper Saddle River, NJ: Prentice Hall.

Rodriguez-Campos, L. (2005). *Collaborative evaluations: A step-by-step model for the evaluator*. Tamarac, FL: Llumina Press.

Scriven, M. (1967). The methodology of evaluation. In R. W. Tyler, R. M. Gagne, & M. Scriven (Eds.), *Perspectives of curriculum evaluation* (Vol. 1, pp. 39–83) (AERA Monograph Series on Curriculum Evaluation). Chicago, IL: Rand McNally.

Shadish, W., Cook, T., & Leviton, L. (1991). *Foundations of program evaluation: Theories of practice*. Newbury Park, CA: Sage.

Stake, R. (1975). *Program evaluation, particularly responsive evaluation* (Occasional Paper No. 5). Kalamazoo: Western Michigan University Evaluation Center.

Tyler, R. W. (1942). General statement on evaluation. *Journal of Educational Research, 35*, 492–501.

Weizenbaum, R. (1976). *Computer power and human reason*. San Francisco, CA: W. A. Freeman.

Williams, J. (1988). A numerically developed taxonomy of evaluation theory and practice. *Evaluation Review, 13*(1), 18–31.

Worthen, B., & Sanders, J. (1973). *Educational evaluation: Theory and practice*. Worthington, OH: Charles A. Jones.

❧ 2 ❦

AN EVALUATION THEORY TREE

Christina A. Christie and Marvin C. Alkin

As indicated in Chapter 1, we use the metaphor of a tree to describe the purposes and development of evaluation theory. This approach very concretely and visually depicts the foundations (i.e., the "roots") of evaluation from which the field of evaluation emerged, as well as the different branches of work that have grown from these foundations. Furthermore, it provides an instructive way of grouping various scholars whose work has developed from and clustered around these foundational ideas. We have depicted these authors as the branches and leaves on the tree (see Figure 2.1).

The three "roots" of the evaluation theory tree—social accountability, systematic social inquiry, and epistemology—serve as a foundation for evaluation work; each has served as an important impetus for evaluation work, and therefore, each has supported the development of the field in different ways. Social accountability, for example, presents an important motivation for evaluation, especially for programs funded by government entities. We conceive of social accountability not as a limiting activity but, rather, as a way to improve programs and society. The second root—systematic social inquiry—emanates from a concern for employing a methodical and justifiable set of procedures for determining accountability. Whereas accountability provides a rationale for evaluation, it is primarily from social inquiry that evaluation models have been derived. And finally, the third foundational root, epistemology, is the area of philosophy that deals with the nature and validity (or limitations) of knowledge. Key evaluation concerns that are based in epistemological arguments include the legitimacy of value claims, the nature of universal claims, and the view that truth (or fact) is what we make it to be. These three roots, each of which is described in greater detail below, provide the basis or rationale on which the evaluation theory tree has grown.

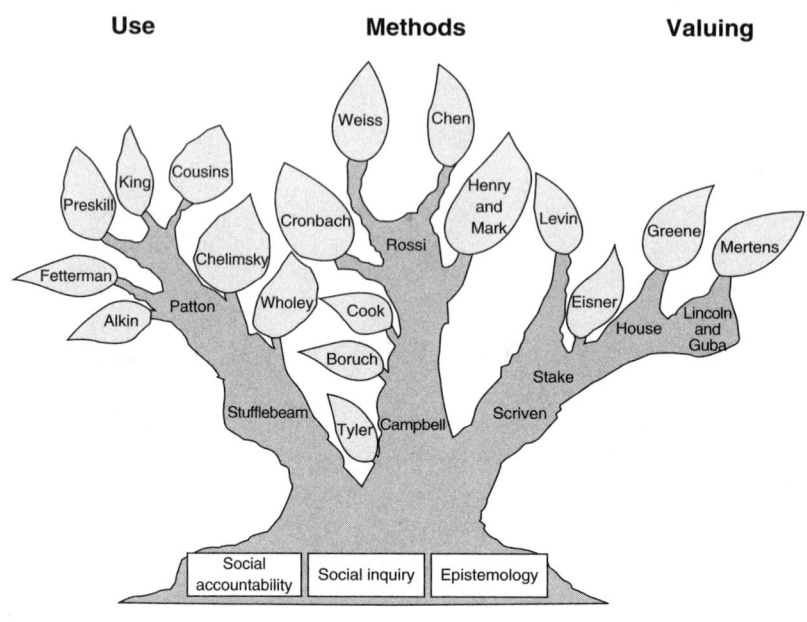

Figure 2.1 Evaluation Theory Tree

The central branch of the evaluation tree grows from the social inquiry root. This is the branch of the tree in which evaluation is primarily guided by research methodology. Theorists on this branch are typically concerned with obtaining the most rigorous knowledge possible given the contextual constraints, in support of "knowledge construction," as described by Shadish, Cook, and Leviton (1991). Although we refer to this as the methods branch, we recognize that it is more accurate to describe these approaches as emphasizing research *methodology*, specifically the techniques used in the conduct of evaluation studies, rather than just the methods used to conduct such studies. However, because we called this the methods branch in the first version of the tree, we have chosen to continue with this label.

To the right of the methods branch is what we call the *valuing* branch. Initially, driven by the work of Michael Scriven (1967) and Robert Stake (1967, 1975), this work firmly establishes the vital role of valuing in evaluation. Theorists on this branch maintain that placing value on the subject of the evaluation, the evaluand, is essential to the process. This branch is split in two—objectivist and subjectivist—which distinguishes the two fundamental perspectives informing the valuing process. More precisely, subjectivists argue that value judgments should be based on "publicly observable" facts. Because human action is governed by subjective factors, a unique characteristic of human behavior is its "subjective meaningfulness," and any science that "ignores meaning and purpose is not social science" (Diesing, 1966, p. 124). The objectivist side of the branch, on the other hand, is closest to the methods branch, because objectivist thinking is compatible with the postpositivist philosophical ideas that by and large inform methods theorists' work.

The third branch is *use*, which, with the pioneering work of Daniel Stufflebeam (initially with Egon Guba) and Joseph Wholey, originally focused on an orientation toward evaluation and decision making. In essence, work done by these theorists expresses an explicit concern for the ways in which evaluation information will be used and focuses specifically on those who will use the information.

The three tree branches are not meant to be viewed as independent from one another but rather have been drawn to reflect a relational quality between them. Thus, if the tree were in a three-dimensional space, the far right of the valuing branch would relate to (or touch) the far left side of the use branch. This is important to note because theorists are positioned on each branch in a way that reflects not only their primary emphasis but also the secondary emphases of their particular approaches. Thus, the relational nature of the three branches helps further depict theorists' approaches.

The three branches of the evaluation tree are related more specifically in the following ways. To the immediate right of the methods (center) branch is the objectivist arm of the valuing branch. Thus, the work of those theorists who are placed on the right side of the methods branch, leaning toward the valuing branch, reflects a secondary importance placed on valuing. Theorists on the left side of the valuing branch, closest to the methods branch, are primarily objectivist valuing theorists, with a secondary concern for methods. For example, Levin, as a cost analyses theorist, is placed on the left side of the valuing branch to reflect the importance of methodology in his approach.

Moving to the far right side of the tree—the subjectivist arm of the valuing branch—we find theorists who reflect the relationship between valuing and use. Theorists placed here are more concerned with individual stakeholders' actionable use of findings than are those placed on the left arm of the valuing branch. Correspondingly (again imagining the tree in three-dimensional space), the far left of the use branch reflects theorists whose primary concern is use but who have a secondary concern for valuing—in other words, a secondary concern for social justice and empowerment. The right side of the use branch reflects the relationship between use and methods. Thus, theorists on the right side of the use branch have a secondary emphasis on rigorous methods, while those on the left side of the methods branch place a greater emphasis on use than others who fall elsewhere on this branch.

The evaluation theory tree is a visual depiction of key theorists' contributions to evaluation theory. It describes how these ideas have helped develop and influence the larger body of evaluation theory literature. Each theorist on the tree has developed a theoretical approach in essential ways; however, the theory tree is not intended to depict the evaluation approach (e.g., theory-driven evaluation, participatory evaluation) in the broader context of the evaluation theory literature. Therefore, we populated the tree with the theorists who are most commonly associated with or who have made the initial and most notable and substantial contributions to each of the particular approaches represented. For example, Rossi and Weiss have made important fundamental contributions to the theory-driven evaluation approach. It was Chen, however, who synthesized and advanced these ideas in substantial ways in the first text focused exclusively on the approach, *Theory-Driven Evaluation* (1990). Thus, we chose to place Chen on the theory tree for his work in this area.

We will start with a discussion of social accountability, social inquiry, and epistemology—the foundational roots of our theory tree—and then discuss each of the major branches of the tree.

FOUNDATIONAL ROOTS

Social Accountability

Many theorists acknowledge the important role that accountability plays in evaluation. Mark, Henry, and Julnes (2000), for example, cite it as one of the four purposes of evaluation. At its most basic, accountability refers to the process of "giving an account" or being accounted for or answerable. Wagner (1989) indicates that there are several dimensions to accountability, including "reporting," in which only description is provided, and a "justifying analysis" or explanation. But accountability in its broadest sense may be more. In instances where a justifying analysis recognizes deficiencies, for example, true accountability requires "answerability"—that is, those responsible must be held accountable. This phase of accountability is not reflected in evaluation; evaluation simply provides the information for "being answerable."

Alkin (1972a) defines three types of accountability: (1) goal accountability, (2) process accountability, and (3) outcome accountability. Goal accountability, typically the responsibility of governing boards and upper levels of management, examines whether reasonable and appropriate goals have been established. Process accountability reflects whether reasonable and appropriate procedures for accomplishing those goals have been established and implemented, and outcome accountability refers to the extent to which established goals have been achieved. Typically, management and program operators bear responsibility for both process and outcome accountability. All three of these accountability types are reflected in the evaluation literature. Concern for the evaluator's role in valuing goals is evident in Michael Scriven's work; program accountability is prominent in the "process" section of Daniel Stufflebeam's CIPP (an acronym for four types of evaluation: *c*ontext, *i*nput, *p*rocess, and *p*roduct) model; and outcome accountability is a major focus of most evaluation efforts.

Today, most evaluations have a strong focus on goal accountability, with an eye toward the improvement of institutional performance. The results of these evaluations are often used in policy making or other governmental decision making. The tradition of process accountability, while less visible in today's evaluation writing, nonetheless provides important roots for evaluation. For example, the European tradition of school inspectors (now largely outdated) has been depicted in countless movies. The dreaded visits from the school inspector were designed to ensure that teachers were engaged in the prescribed lessons at the prescribed times. A more contemporary example of process accountability is the system of school accreditation employed in secondary schools, private schools, universities, and professions. In these instances, an evaluation team with presumed expertise, frequently guided by established process standards, visits a site to observe, account, and make a report. The result is a judgment about whether institutions are accountable and should be accredited.

The evaluation unit of the U.S. Government Accountability Office (GAO) typifies how accountability is often viewed in contemporary North American evaluation practice. The GAO is independent, nonpartisan, and often described as the "congressional watchdog" because it investigates how the federal government spends tax dollars. The GAO's mission is to "examine the use of public funds, evaluate federal programs and activities, and provide analyses, options, recommendations, and other assistance to help the Congress make effective oversight, policy, and funding decisions through financial audits and program reviews" (see www.gao.gov). It is important to note that this notion of accountability implies the provision of an account to an individual or group in a position of formal authority. Thus, the GAO's activities are designed to ensure the executive branch's accountability to the Congress and the federal government's accountability to all Americans.

Social accountability, then, situates and legitimizes evaluation as a fundamental process for generating systematic information for decision making. This can occur within the configuration of government-sponsored programs and policies or can be more localized and occur at the intervention or program level.

Social Inquiry

Social inquiry, in its broadest sense, can be characterized as the systemic study of the behavior of groups of individuals in various social settings by a variety of methods. It begins with the recognition that human action has a unique social dimension rather than simply a natural or psychological dimension. The central overriding question is "Why do people in social groups act as they do?"

In the Western world, inquiry along these lines has its origins in 17th- and 18th-century figures such as Hobbes, Montesquieu, and Rousseau. While these theorists systematically studied and commented on social groups, their descriptions and theories were a product more of contemplation than of rigorous empirical investigations. It wasn't until the mid- and late 19th century, as demonstrated in the works of Karl Marx, Emile Durkheim, and Max Weber, for instance, that society and social groups began to be studied empirically through the collection and analysis of empirical data on social groups.

A perennial question in social inquiry is which methods are appropriate for the study of society, social groups, and social life and, more specifically, whether the methodologies of the physical sciences, broadly defined, are applicable to social phenomena. The classical social theorists Marx (1932) and Durkheim (1966), for example, made extensive use of statistics, among other data, to form particular judgments regarding social life. The discipline of psychology introduced the experimental method, where the central overriding question is whether a treatment is effective in bringing about the desired effects. Discussions regarding the feasibility and desirability of this methodology for the study of the social world continue to this day, giving rise to heated debates and never-ending accusations of positivism. These debates are related to and reflective of the more general question of the applicability of the methods of the sciences to the social sciences.

Alternatively, the discipline of anthropology has given rise to ethnographies and, more broadly, qualitative studies of the social world. The distinction between these methods and the ones just mentioned above is sometimes couched in terms of the distinction between explanation and prediction, on the one hand, and interpretation and understanding, on the other. Clifford Geertz's classical essay "Thick Description: Toward an Interpretive Theory of Culture" in *The Interpretation of Cultures* (1973) epitomizes the latter approach and, in part, has come to define interpretive social science, where the emphasis is placed not on prediction but on meaning.

Philosophers continue to disagree about what constitutes the methods of the sciences and their potential applicability to the study of social life (e.g., as described in Tashakkori & Teddlie, 1998). Cutting across social science disciplines are broad philosophical and methodological questions that continue to be debated in contemporary social inquiry. Important questions include the following: What is the relationship between theory and observation? Should social scientists have a moral stance toward the individuals and groups that they study? Is this stance appropriate, and would it compromise the researchers' objectivity? These and other questions form part of the theory and practice of social inquiry.

Each of these social inquiry influences is readily seen in the evaluation theories discussed in this section. The influence of experimental psychology and quantitative sociological disciplines is readily noted in the methods branch. Constructs commonly associated with anthropology, such as "thick description," are evidenced in the work of Stake, for example, and attention to concerns raised within the philosophy of science has clearly influenced Scriven's thinking about evaluation as a practice and as a discipline.

Epistemology

The vast body of philosophical literature includes discussions of paradigms. A paradigm is

> a worldview or perspective that, in the case of research and evaluation, includes conceptions of methodology, purposes, assumptions, and values . . . that typically consists of an ontology (the nature of reality), an epistemology (what is knowable and who can know it), and a methodology (how one can obtain knowledge). (Mathison, 2005, p. 289)

With these philosophical underpinnings in mind, we include in the theory tree a third root, epistemology, to address arguments on the nature of knowledge.

Those in evaluation who have historically and are currently engaged in epistemological discussions typically draw on one of three broad areas of thinking: (1) postpositivism, (2) constructivism (and related thinking), or (3) pragmatism. Thus, the basic axioms of these paradigms offer a broader framework for understanding the theoretical influences on evaluation theorists'

Note: Portions of this section of this chapter are reprinted from *What Counts as Credible Evidence in Applied Research and Evaluation Practice?* by Stewart I. Donaldson, Christina A. Christie, and Melvin M. Mark © 2009 by SAGE Publications, Inc.

work. Importantly, some evaluation perspectives are shaped more exactly by a philosophical theory, while in others, only a theory's undercurrent can be detected. Epistemology serves as an important influence on evaluation theory more generally, albeit to varying degrees.

Views of science shifted during the 20th century away from positivism toward postpositivism. Where positivists believe that the goal of science is to uncover the truth, postpositivists believe its goal is to attempt to measure truth, even though that goal cannot be attained because all observation is fallible and has error. Thus, a full understanding of truth can be approached but never reached. This type of realism is referred to as "critical realism." The ideal of "approaching" truth extends to views on causality as well, as it is believed that causation is observable and that over time predictors can be established; however, some degree of doubt associated with the conclusion will always exist. Values and biases are noted and accounted for, yet the belief is that they can be controlled within the context of scientific inquiry. This thinking is clearly evident in Campbell's work as well as the work of others on the *methods* branch (Christie & Fleischer, 2009).

Constructivism is one element of intrepretivism. Constructivists agree that there is no one reality, rather that several realities emerge from one's subjective belief system. Hence, new knowledge and discovery can only be understood through a person's unique and particular experiences, beliefs, and understandings of the world. These multiple realities are believed to be subjective and will vary based on the "knower." In the inquiry process, the "knower" and the "known" are interrelated, and to determine what is "known," the knower constructs a reality that is based on and grounded in context and experience. This differs from positivist epistemology, which purports that the knower and the known can be independent. For constructivists, inquiry is considered value-bound, not value-free, and therefore, bias should be acknowledged rather than attempting to position the inquiry process so as to control it. Inductive logic drives the inquiry process, which means that particular instances are used to infer broader, more general principles. Local relevance, then, outweighs and is of much greater priority than generalizability. Cause and effect are thought to be impossible to distinguish because relationships are interdependent, and so simultaneously, all things have influence on all things. And while relativism is a distinct school of thought, notions of truth and inquiry are similar to those put forth by constructivists. Specifically, relativist theorists argue that truth is relative to one's own frame of reference. Hence, a person's cultural and historical experiences influence how she or he perceives and understands the world. Thus, there are no absolute truths, only relative truths. Notions drawn from constructivist and relativist philosophy inform some of the ideas presented on the *valuing* branch of the theory tree, such as those of Stake, Guba, and Lincoln.

Pragmatists embrace objectivity and subjectivity as two positions on a continuum and argue that deductive and inductive logic should be used in concert. Pragmatists do, however, move away from embracing equally the axioms of the postpositivist and constructivist paradigms. For example, pragmatists are more similar to postpositivists with regard to notions about external reality, with the understanding that there is no absolute "truth" concerning reality. More in line with constructivist thought, however, pragmatists argue that there are multiple explanations of reality and that at any given time there is one explanation that makes the most sense. In other words, at one point in time, a single explanation of reality may be considered "truer" than another. Furthermore, pragmatists, like postpositivists, believe that causes may be linked to effects. However, they temper this thinking with the caveat that absolute certainty of causation is impossible. Pragmatists are similar to constructivists in that they do not believe inquiry is value-free; rather, they consider their values important to the inquiry process. The pragmatist paradigm is given attention here, as it seems to influence the thinking of those on the *use* branch, particularly those who have an interest in promoting instrumental use of evaluation findings, such as Patton.

TREE BRANCHES

Methods

In the beginning, there was research. And positivist and postpositivist research methodologies dominated the conduct of studies. While most evaluation theorists have methodological concerns and view applied research as the genesis of program evaluation, some theorists have been steadfast in emphasizing that orientation. In the social sciences, an emphasis on applied research depends on well-designed experimental studies and other controls. Fundamental to these theories is the early work of Donald Campbell (1957) and, in particular, the better-known Campbell and Stanley (1966) volume, which defines the conditions for appropriate experimental and quasi-experimental designs. With the exception of Tyler, the work of theorists on this branch is either grounded in or expands on this work.

Donald Campbell

Shadish and colleagues (1991) call Donald Campbell the "Methodologist of the Experimenting Society." And indeed he is. Campbell is best known for his pathbreaking work on the elimination of bias in the conduct of research in field settings. Most notable from an evaluation perspective are his papers on experimental and quasi-experimental designs for research (Campbell, 1957; Campbell & Stanley, 1966). The focus on experimental designs (and the more practical quasi-experimental designs) is an attempt to "rule out many threats precluding causal inference" (Shadish et al., 1991, p. 122).

There were few papers published during the 20th century that had as great an impact on social science research as Campbell and Stanley's *Experimental and Quasi-Experimental Designs for Research* (1966). Three major areas of social science research design are advanced in this paper. First, the authors explain the conditions necessary to conduct a true experimental study where randomization is the hallmark. Second, two key notions relevant to this are articulated and explained. They call the degree to which an experiment is properly controlled *internal validity* and refer to the degree of applicability of the results of an experiment as *external validity*. Third, they recognize that experiments are not perfect and that they should not, and cannot, be used in a great many situations. Thus, as an alternative to the true experiment, they describe, in great detail, quasi-experimental designs.

Until their paper was published, in the name of "good science," the social sciences had used the scientific methods found in the physical sciences. In fact, experimental designs are still often touted as the most rigorous of all research designs or as the "gold standard" against which all other designs are judged. Recognized as a striking shift in thinking about social science research, Campbell and Stanley's paper acknowledges the shortcomings of experiments; in many contexts, experiments are not achievable or desirable. As an alternative to the true experiment, they describe a lengthy set of what they call "quasi-experimental designs." Quasi-experimental designs were developed to deal with the messy world of field research, where it is not always practical, ethical, or even possible to randomly assign persons to experimental and control groups. Generally speaking, quasi-experimental designs include some type of intervention or treatment and provide a comparison, but they lack the degree of control found in true experiments. Just as randomization is the key to true experiments, lack of randomization is the defining characteristic of quasi-experiments.

The ideas put forth in Campbell and Stanley's manuscript are now the foundation of almost all social science research methods courses. Perhaps even more remarkable was this paper's impact on the promotion of new ideas related to research design. It could be argued that the introduction of and favorable response to quasi-experimental designs helped give rise to a climate that was apparently more accepting of alternative thinking about social science research.

Campbell's work was directed at social science researchers, and it was not until Suchman (1967) saw the relevance of it to evaluation that his name became prominently identified with that field. It is because Campbell's work on quasi-experimental design precedes Suchman's application of it to evaluation that we choose to discuss Campbell prior to Suchman. It should be noted that Campbell (1975a, 1975b) has also written papers indicating the potential appropriateness of qualitative methods as a complement to quantitative experimental methods. Qualitative methods are helpful for evaluation areas such as implementation, identification, and interpretation of side effects. Despite these forays into broadening his methodological perspectives beyond experimental approaches,[1] Campbell is primarily an experimentalist. His views, along with those of his students, colleagues, and coauthors, have shaped the way evaluation has been conducted, particularly by those evaluators whom we classify on the methods branch of the evaluation tree. Donald Campbell remains the heart and soul of this branch because of how he directly influenced other theorists with his work on experiments, quasi-experiments, and validity, as well as the way in which his views provided a basis for counterpoint, particularly with respect to Lee Cronbach's work.

Edward Suchman

We have not included Edward Suchman on this version of the tree. However, a brief discussion of his work will be presented here because we recognize the important influence of his writing on evaluation—particularly in positioning Campbell's work prominently in the evaluation discourse. Suchman promoted Campbell's work as the most effective approach for conducting evaluation studies to measure program impact. Suchman's book, *Evaluative Research*

(1967), was perhaps the first full-scale description of the application of research methods to evaluation. The title demonstrates his view of evaluation as a form of research. In citing the need for experimental (and quasi-experimental) design, Suchman (1967) highlights the earlier work by Campbell (1957) and the subsequent publication of Campbell and Stanley (1966).

Suchman (1967) distinguishes between evaluation as a commonsense usage, referring to the "social process of making judgments of worth" (p. 7), and evaluative research that uses scientific research methods and techniques. He affirms the appropriate use of the word *evaluative* as an adjective specifying the type of research being done. He notes, for example, in reviewing early "evaluation guides" put out by various government agencies, that their major deficiency is the absence of experimental design. Indeed, Suchman strongly adheres to the importance of conducting evaluative research in scientific ways. To reflect this emphasis, he states that the evaluator must often ask that procedures be altered to secure some form of control or comparative group.

The reason Suchman is not defined solely as a researcher applying his work to field situations is his recognition of the administrative context. He comments that the evaluative researcher, in addition to recognizing scientific criteria, must also acknowledge administrative criteria for determining the worthwhileness of doing the study. This had influence on and helped set the tone for many others on the methods branch (e.g., Rossi, Weiss, Chen, and Cronbach). But evaluative research is generally applied or administrative research, the primary objective of which is to determine the extent to which a given program or procedure is achieving some desired result. The "success" of an evaluation project will thus largely depend on its usefulness to the administrator in improving services (Suchman, 1967, p. 21).

It should be noted that Suchman recognizes the role of judgment in evaluation, noting that values and assumptions affect the formulation of goals for evaluative research. However, his extensive discussion of the interlocking of evaluation and administrative roles in program planning and operation places judgment more heavily in the administrative domain—particularly as a second recycling phase following the assessment of outcomes. Thus, while Suchman addresses valuing, his main emphasis is on methods.

Clearly Suchman's work had a strong influence on the subsequent writings of many who followed, particularly Peter Rossi. There are many examples of his influences, but one in particular is Suchman's identification of five categories of evaluation: (1) effort (the quantity and quality of activity that takes place), (2) performance (effect criteria that measure the results of effort), (3) adequacy of performance (the degree to which performance is adequate for the total amount of need), (4) efficiency (examination of alternative paths or methods in terms of human and monetary costs), and (5) process (how and why a program works or does not work). These multiple emphases also seem evident in Rossi's work.

Robert Boruch

Robert Boruch's philosophy of evaluation is most similar to the work of Donald Campbell in its consideration of the randomized field experiment as the ideal evaluation approach.

Randomized field experiments, however, are distinct from the quasi-experiments put forth by Campbell and Stanley in their seminal piece, *Experimental and Quasi-Experimental Designs for Research* (1966). Boruch (1997) elucidates the distinction between the study designs:

> Randomized field tests are also different from *quasi-experiments*. The latter research designs have the object of estimating the relative effectiveness of different treatments that have a common aim, just as randomized experiments do, but they depend on methods other than randomization to rule out the competing explanations for the treatment differences that may be uncovered. Quasi-experiments and related observational studies then attempt to approximate the results of a randomized field test. (p. 4)

For Boruch, evaluation is likened to conventional scientific research. It involves the systematic application of rigorous randomized research designs for measuring the extent of a social problem and assessing the implementation, relative efficacy, and cost-effectiveness ratio of social intervention programs (Boruch, Synder, & DeMoya, 2000). Boruch is steadfast in viewing the randomized field experiment as the most effective way of obtaining the least equivocal estimate of a social program's effects (Boruch et al., 2000).

Boruch, McSweeney, and Soderstrom (1978) explain the randomized experiment as an approach that randomly assigns individuals, or clusters of individuals, to one of two treatment groups. This procedure makes certain that at the outset, in the absence of program-induced differences, groups will be statistically equivalent, thereby maximizing the internal validity of an evaluation. The random assignment approach also avoids the interpretive problems that affect alternative evaluation designs by ensuring a fair comparison between groups (Boruch et al., 2000), thus making sure a legitimate statement can be made about the role of chance in the results.

Boruch (1997) claims that any program, be it social, educational, or welfare, should be studied in a systematic manner, employing randomized controlled experimental methods to gather valid and reliable evidence. It is his commitment to the randomized controlled field experiment[2] that defines the Boruch perspective on evaluation. The experimental design approach can "introduce social change in a way that allows one to effectively discern the net effect of the change on important social outcomes" (Berk, Boruch, Chambers, Rossi, & Witte, 1985).

Berk and colleagues (1985) assert that randomized field experimentation is particularly illuminating when the goal is investigating causal inference and making generalizations to other subjects and settings. They contend that when causal inference is the dominant concern, statisticians widely advocate for experiments that randomly assign subjects to various treatments because random assignment ensures that experimental and control groups are, on average, equivalent before the treatments are introduced. They maintain that given that social policy experimentation relies on drawing samples from a known population and then randomly assigning subjects to treatments, sound generalizations will follow (Berk et al., 1985).

More recently, Mosteller and Boruch (2002) edited *Evidence Matters: Randomized Trials in Education Research*, arguing for the increased implementation of randomized trials in educational research to identify effective educational interventions. This volume was published during the same time that the National Research Council (Shavelson & Towne, 2002) released *Scientific Research in Education*, which also explicitly called for an increase in randomized controlled trials (RCTs) in educational research (noting that the shift toward more evidence-based programming officially began in 1993 with the Government Performance and Results Act, GPRA). These two publications have been cited as offering key arguments for RCTs in educational research and have been noted for shaping the ways in which funding for educational research has been awarded under the No Child Left Behind legislation.

We have placed Boruch on the methods branch of the theory tree as a direct continuation of the Campbell experimentation influence. This is in contrast to other disciples of Campbell (e.g., Thomas Cook) who have advocated more strongly for quasi-experimentation or who have sought to define evaluation more broadly.

Thomas Cook

The randomized field experiment is seen as the most scientific design available for answering evaluation questions. However, as Cook points out (and as noted previously), this design can be impossible to implement in social and educational program evaluation studies because of contextual factors that are beyond the control of the evaluator. Campbell and Stanley's classic *Experimental and Quasi-Experimental Designs for Research* (1966) delineates an alternative. Quasi-experimental designs are applicable to evaluation because they address the difficulties of experimental control inherent in field research, specifically random assignment. Generally, quasi-experiments involve the administration of pre- and posttests and compare groups, but they do not involve randomization.

During the 1970s, Cook and Campbell extended the work of Campbell and Stanley. They contributed new quasi-experimental designs and also called attention to some less recognized threats to internal validity (e.g., resentful demoralization). However, during the mid-1970s, Campbell returned to his initial position supporting the use of the classic experimental design. In fact, he denounced the use of quasi-experimental designs and went so far as to state that perhaps he had committed an injustice by suggesting that quasi-experimental designs were a viable alternative to classic randomized design. Cook, however, remained a proponent of quasi-experiential designs and continued to focus on their use. Cook was influential in developing the field of study related to quasi-experimental designs.

Cook has expanded on the ideas he put forward with Campbell in several areas. With his interest in methodology, evaluation research, and social reform, Cook is concerned with the contextual factors of an evaluation and the ways these factors can affect an evaluation research study. Over the years, he has written extensively on sampling, addressing the issues of and alternatives to random selection, methods, the evaluation context, and stakeholder involvement in evaluation studies—all matters that seldom demand attention when implementing the classic experiment. Cook focuses on the importance of using a number of different designs and methods to properly conduct an evaluation. He asserts that it is imperative for evaluators to choose methods that are appropriate to the particular evaluation being conducted and that they take into consideration the context of each evaluation rather than using the same set of methods and designs for all evaluations—a direct attack on experimental design.

Fairly early on, Cook, unlike other methods-driven theorists of the time, also recognized the importance of involving stakeholders when determining evaluation questions, to gather useful information. He explains that a primary problem with evaluations, as he has experienced them, is that the evaluators do not consult decision makers or any other interested parties when forming the research questions that will be addressed. This results in general program goals that are either "operationally vague or of limited importance to many potential users" (Cook & Gruder, 1978, p. 15). Consequently, he suggests that stakeholders work together with evaluators to decide what an evaluation should examine.

Nonetheless, while Cook expresses concern for identifying users and their interests, he does this within the context of a primary interest in selecting field-relevant methods that closely resemble the classic experiment. Thus, we place Cook on the methods branch of the tree as someone whose work closely follows Campbell, emphasizing quasi-experimental methods. He is not represented by a chapter in this volume. However, the chapter from the first edition is available online at www.sagepub.com/alkin2e.

Lee J. Cronbach

Lee J. Cronbach was one of the methodological giants of our field. His contributions include Cronbach's coefficient alpha, generalizability theory, and notions about construct validity. Thus, his strong evaluation roots in methodology and social science research led us to place him on the methods branch of the theory tree. Yet there are elements in his work that reflect a broader view than the Campbell-like social science research mode. To begin with, Cronbach was a student of Ralph Tyler, which lends his work a kind of field orientation not present in the work of many social science researchers. Furthermore, his association with more policy research–oriented Stanford University colleagues, notably in his book *Toward Reform of Program Evaluation* (Cronbach & Associates, 1980), helped establish his concern for evaluation's use in decision making.

Following on the work of Weiss, Cronbach rejects the simplistic model that assumes a single decision maker and "go/no-go" decisions. Instead, he views evaluation as an integral part of policy research focused on "policy-shaping communities" and necessitating potential political accommodation. Thus, his work is oriented more toward evaluation utilization for enlightenment purposes than toward a concern for immediate instrumental use. He does, however, affirm the evaluator's active role in providing data to local decision makers for instrumental use in accordance with contractual obligations.

To define the manner in which evaluators might most productively enhance enlightenment use, Cronbach (1982) coins a set of symbols to define the domains of evaluation. These domains consist of *units* (populations), *treatments*, *observations* (outcomes), and *settings*. The sample examined by the evaluator is referred to by the acronym "utos," and it represents the larger population from which sampling took place, which is referred to as "UTOS." Cronbach maintains that the most important area of concern for evaluation is external validity, which he refers to as the plausibility of the conclusions to UTOS that is manifestly different from the population under study. He refers to this manifestly different population as "*UTOS" (pronounced "star-UTOS").

In the concern for evaluations contributing to enlightened discussion, Cronbach focuses on what he refers to as "bandwidth," by which he means that it is more important for the evaluation to focus on a broad range of relevant issues than to achieve absolute fidelity (accuracy) on a small number of issues. Cronbach's concern about generalizing to *UTOS leads him to reject Campbell and Stanley's emphasis on experimental design and Scriven's focus on comparison programs. He proposes that generalization to *UTOS can be attained by extrapolating through causal explanation, using either causal modeling or the "thick description" of qualitative methods. Furthermore, it is sometimes beneficial to examine subpopulations (sub-UTOS). Thus, focusing on the subset of data for a particular group might enable generalization to other domains. Furthermore, he seeks to capitalize on naturally occurring variability within the sample as well as the consequences of different degrees of exposure to treatments. This work is an extension of earlier research on aptitude–treatment interactions conducted jointly with Richard Snow (Cronbach & Snow, 1977).

Cronbach displays sensitivity to the values of the policy-shaping community and seeks to incorporate their views on the evaluation questions most worth asking. This is done systematically with an eye to what will contribute most to generalization: issues receiving attention from the policy-shaping community, issues relevant in swaying important (or uncommitted) groups, issues having the greatest uncertainty, and issues that would best clarify why a program works. Shadish et al. (1991) make the following keen distinction between Cronbach and several other major theorists: "[Cronbach views] evaluators [as] educators rather than [as] the philosopher-kings of Scriven, the guardians of truth of Campbell or the servants of management of Wholey" (p. 340).

As such, Cronbach does not aspire to the instrumental use of evaluation as Wholey and others on the decision-making/use branch do. And as we have pointed out, he does not adhere to the strict experimental controls that Campbell advocates. Likewise, he does not call on the evaluator to impose his or her own value system on the program or to reach summary judgments about programs. Rather, he sees the evaluator's role as providing "readers" with information that they may take into account when forming their own judgments.

We have placed Cronbach on the methods branch of the evaluation tree but in a position that is the direction of the use branch. This placement in part reflects the influence of Weiss on his ideas with respect to enlightenment use directed toward policy-shaping communities.

Peter Rossi

Peter Rossi was well-known for his highly popular textbook on evaluation. His first edition depicted and relied most heavily on design considerations from Campbell and Stanley (1966), as reflected in Suchman's influential evaluation book, which focused on evaluation as research. In fact, the title of Rossi's first edition was *Evaluation: A Systematic Approach* (Rossi, Freeman,

& Wright, 1979). Now in its sixth edition (with different coauthors), it is still a very popular and influential text. Over time, however, because of the influences of other evaluation theorists, the text now includes discussions of qualitative data collection, evaluation utilization, the role of stakeholders, and so on. It is interesting to note the ways in which other perspectives and the changing nature of the field modify views.

Rossi's earlier writings stressed the use of the experimental design. However, to describe him as exclusively an experimentalist would be erroneous. He contributed significantly to the conceptualizations of theory-driven evaluation and of comprehensive evaluation, which he describes as "the systematic application of social research procedures in assessing conceptualization and design, implementation, and utility of social intervention programs" (Rossi & Freeman, 1985, p. 19). However, as is evident from this quote, while he has moved away from considering the experimental model as the sine qua non of evaluation, he still clearly views evaluation as social research.

Rossi's departure from the randomized experiment was initiated in part by his broadening vision of evaluation. Concerning himself with issues such as internal and external validity, implementation, and use, his ideas eventually evolved to a place that some say was so comprehensive that the approach he suggested was virtually impossible to implement. Rossi's response to this criticism led him to develop "tailored evaluations" that assisted in refining the evaluation focus. In this work, Rossi suggests that methods be tailored to the stage of the program, that is, "fitting evaluations to programs" (Rossi & Freeman, 1985, p. 102). For example, if commissioned to conduct an evaluation of a program that is well under way, the evaluation would be designed to focus on current work rather than on the development of the program. That is not to say that program development would not be addressed by the evaluation; rather, it would receive less attention than if the commencement of the evaluation were concurrent with the start of the program.

Rossi, along with Weiss and Chen, provided some of the foundational thinking about theory-driven evaluation. This approach, which is discussed in depth later in this chapter in relationship to Chen, can be seen as a particular type of comprehensive evaluation. Briefly, theory-driven evaluation involves the construction of a detailed program theory, which is then used to guide the evaluation. Rossi maintains that this approach helps reconcile the two main types of validity—internal and external. Since, for a variety of reasons, it is difficult to design studies that emphasize both, many theorists believe that one must be traded for the other. Nevertheless, both are important. Rossi's earlier work focusing on the use of the experimental design was obviously concerned more with internal than with external validity. However, he began to question whether internal validity should have priority. Rossi asserted that theory-driven evaluation is to a certain extent a fusion of Campbell's and Cronbach's approaches. This fusion allows the evaluator to address internal validity through a specified program model and implicit external validity through an investigation of the ways in which the program is similar to and different from the future program to which the evaluation is to be generalized.

Shadish et al. (1991) say that Rossi presents a multifaceted, broad-based point of view to appeal to a wide audience. In our view, however, Rossi has demonstrated a dominant predilection for the purity of experimental and quasi-experimental methods. Thus, we believe that it is more accurate to say that the recent edition of Rossi's text (Rossi, Lipsey, & Freeman, 2004) reflects a concern for demonstrating great breadth and for the depiction of evaluation possibilities to capture the interests of broader audiences.

Carol Weiss

Carol Weiss has made many important contributions to evaluation and has influenced our thinking about what evaluation can do. Much of her thinking was informed by the research she conducted on evaluation use in the context of political decision making. Through her empirical work, Weiss expands on or defines many of our key concepts and terms related to evaluation use, perhaps most notably the following: conceptual use, or use for understanding (Weiss, 1979, 1980); enlightenment use, or more subtle and indirect use that occurs in the longer term (Weiss, 1980); and, more recently, imposed use, such as a requirement by federal funding agencies that recipients use the grant to run only programs that have reported scientific evidence of success (Weiss, Murphy-Graham, & Birkeland, 2005; Weiss, Murphy-Graham, Petrosino, & Gandhi, 2008). Based on her empirical work, Weiss argues for more evidence-based policy making and concludes that the most effective kinds of evaluations are those that withstand the test of time—that is, are generalizable and therefore use the most rigorous methods possible. Thus, Weiss's empirical work, which examines evaluation use, informs her prescriptive theoretical work where she argues for the use of research methods to inform evidence-based policy making.

Weiss's early evaluation work was influenced by research methodologists, political theorists, and expositors of democratic thought (e.g., Rousseau, the *Federalist Papers*). Weiss's firm commitment to evaluation as being akin to carefully conducted research is documented in many of her writings. In fact, her first evaluation text, *Evaluation Research*, was intended to be a supplementary text for research methods courses. Shadish et al. (1991) point out that Weiss's early writings focus almost exclusively on "traditional experimental methods in evaluation" (p. 183). She later expresses a similar position: "Evaluation is a kind of policy study, and the boundaries are very blurred . . . I think we have a responsibility to do very sound, thorough systematic inquiries" (Weiss, cited in Alkin, 1990, p. 90).

Throughout her writings, Weiss demonstrates an appreciation for evaluation as a political activity. Her notion of evaluation extends to how study findings affect and are affected by the political context. Weiss (1991) is particularly pointed in recognizing that the process of conducting an evaluation affects a political situation in which there are vested interests, negotiations, constituents, critics, and so on:

> Politics intrudes on program evaluation in three ways: (1) programs are created and maintained by political forces; (2) higher echelons of government, which make decisions about programs, are embedded in politics; and (3) the very act of evaluation has political connotations. (p. 213)

Weiss recognizes the complexity of this political context. Thus, she has been adamant in noting that evaluation results are not necessarily (or generally) heeded in isolation of other input or at the time of evaluation reporting. She is known for, among many other contributions, introducing the term *decision accretion* into the evaluation lexicon. By this, she means that decisions are the result of "the build-up of small choices, the closing of small options and the gradual narrowing of available alternatives" (Weiss, 1976, p. 226).

Given the belief that decisions accrete, Weiss has studied policy research to determine the characteristics of evaluative research work that have longevity—that is, those that would be considered credible during an accretion process. She concludes that research quality is of greatest importance "not only because of adherents to the norms of science, but perhaps more importantly because it increases the power of research as ammunition in intra-organizational argument" (Weiss, 1980, p. 256). It is this type of "careful and sound research" (Weiss, 1981, p. 400) that, she continues to argue, is the most important kind of evidence an evaluation can offer policymakers. Because Weiss places limits on the likelihood of instrumental use and instead views evaluation's greatest contribution as conceptual or enlightenment, she does not fit within the use branch. As Shadish et al. (1991) note about Weiss, "When forced to choose between traditional scientific rigor versus other goals such as use, she seems to lean in the former direction" (p. 208).

Huey T. Chen

Huey Chen is most influential in developing the concept and practice of theory-driven evaluation (Chen, 1990, 2005). He has frequently coauthored articles with Peter Rossi and, in addition, has authored a book and articles on the topic. Chen acknowledges the attractiveness of controlled experiments in estimating net effects through randomization, but when no effect is shown in a controlled experiment, Chen (2005) points out that there is no indication as to whether failure is due to, for example, poorly constructed causal linkages, insufficient levels of treatment, or poor implementation. Chen proposes a solution to this dilemma:

> We have argued for a paradigm that accepts experiments and quasi-experiments as dominant research designs, but that emphasizes that these devices should be used in conjunction with a priori knowledge and theory to build models of the treatment process and implementation system to produce evaluations that are more efficient and that yield more information about how to achieve desired effects. (Chen & Rossi, 1983, p. 300)

Chen recognizes the dominance of the experimental paradigm but strongly believes that it must be supplemented by the development of theoretical models of social interventions: "An unfortunate consequence of this lack of attention to theory is that the outcomes of evaluation research often provide narrow and sometimes distorted understandings of programs" (Chen & Rossi, 1983, p. 284).

Chen is concerned with identifying secondary effects and unintended consequences. This is similar to Scriven.[3] Chen, however, relies on social science theory for the identification of potential areas for investigation. In pursuing theory-driven evaluation, Chen acknowledges the potential effects of a program as related to its official goals, but he also sees the necessity for using social science knowledge and theory related to the subject matter in question to identify effects that go beyond those goals. The theories that he seeks to construct are not global or grand but "plausible and defensible models of how programs can be expected to work" (Chen & Rossi, 1983, p. 285).

Chen acknowledges the validity questions raised in following Campbell's and Cronbach's approaches but believes that they can be resolved: "We are not convinced that the trade-off problem between internal and external validity, which is so sharply portrayed by Campbell, Cronbach, or others, that dealing with one type of validity must seriously sacrifice the other types of validity" (Chen & Rossi, 1987, p. 97). He believes that theory-driven evaluation enhances the possibility of achieving each type of validity and that this can be accomplished through randomized experiments and simultaneous study of causation within the context of constructed theories (usually through structural equation modeling). In conducting evaluations, Chen places his focus not only on the use of social science knowledge but also on traditional research methods. Chen's place on the evaluation tree is on the methods branch, because his work is rooted in the methodological traditions of social science.

Gary Henry and Melvin Mark (With George Julnes)

In the first edition of the *Roots* book, in discussing any decision to include the work of Melvin Mark and Gary Henry, we wrote,

> These authors view social betterment as the ultimate objective of evaluation and present a point of view grounded in what they refer to as a "common sense realist philosophy." . . . The very diversified nature of this perspective, while a great strength in presenting an understanding of evaluation, precludes its inclusion on the tree. (Alkin & Christie, 2004, pp. 58–59)

Our views in determining exclusion were based heavily on the Mark et al. (2000) book. However, in reflecting further on the writings of these authors, we were struck by the views presented in the "realist evaluation" monograph in *New Directions for Evaluation* (Henry, Julnes, & Mark, 1998) and decided to include them in this chapter.

Emergent realist evaluation (ERE) is described by the authors as a comprehensive new evaluation model that offers reconceptualized notions of use, methods, and valuing. Mark and Henry's collaboration with George Julnes developed into "a new theory that captures the sense-making contributions from post-positivism and the sensitivity to values from constructivist traditions" (Henry et al., 1998, p. 1). Recognizing the power of evaluation within democracies, the authors argue that "social betterment, rather than the more popular and pervasive goal of utilization, should motivate evaluation" (Mark, Henry, & Julnes, 1998, p. 19).

ERE is an evaluation methodology that (a) gives priority to the study of generative mechanisms, (b) is attentive to multiple levels of analysis, and (c) is mixed methods appropriate. Because ERE focuses on understanding the underlying mechanisms of programs, Mark and Henry are concerned primarily with addressing the research questions that identify which mechanisms are operating and which are not (Mark et al., 1998). This is done in an effort to identify casual linkages and to enhance the generalizable knowledge base of a particular set of programs or program theories.

Mark and Henry argue that an evaluation should examine program effects that are of most interest to the public and other relevant stakeholders, so evaluators must determine stakeholders' values when investigating possible mechanisms. Henry (1996) argues that understanding the values of the various stakeholder groups, including areas of consensus and conflict, helps promote democratic policy. ERE offers three methods for investigating stakeholder values: The first involves surveying and sampling possible stakeholders, the second utilizes qualitative methods such as interviews and/or focus groups to determine their needs and concerns, and the third involves analyzing the context of the evaluation from a broad philosophical perspective, focusing on issues such as equity, equality, and freedom. These value investigations should then be communicated to the multiple audiences of the evaluation (Mark et al., 1998).

The ERE evaluator also engages in a process of either *competitive elaboration* or *principled discovery*. Competitive elaboration involves ruling out alternative explanations for study findings, which includes exploring alternative program theories and threats to validity (Mark et al., 1998). This requires a preexisting body of knowledge of possible program mechanisms and, ideally, a study design that experimentally tests each relevant mechanism to identify those with the greatest or least impact. This approach lends itself to quantitative methods of inquiry (e.g., fully randomized experiments and quasi-experiments). Principled discovery is used when programs are evaluated before practitioners are able to develop experientially tested theories (Mark et al., 1998). Approaches to discovering program mechanisms include exploratory data analysis, graphical methods (Henry, 1995), and regression analysis.

More recently, Mark and Henry have extended their theoretical work into the area of evaluation influence (Henry & Mark, 2003; Mark & Henry, 2004). Evaluation influence is defined as "the capacity or power of persons or things to produce effects on others by intangible or direct means" (Kirkhart, 2000, p. 7). Henry and Mark (2003) have described a theory of evaluation influence that depicts three levels—individual, interpersonal, and collective—at which influence can occur. Each level is further explained by identifying specific mechanisms, measurable outcomes, and forms of influence. To our minds, this work expands their ERE work by offering further description of the use dimension of evaluation practice within the ERE approach.

Because of their emphasis on the use of social science methods in an effort to promote social betterment, we place Mark and Henry on the methods branch of the tree, in a location following Tom Cook, leaning toward the valuing branch.

Ralph Tyler

We view Ralph Tyler's work on The Eight-Year Study as one of the major starting points for modern program evaluation (if one can accept the 1940s as modern). As noted in the introductory chapter of this book, Tyler's work was far-reaching, affecting the work of many future evaluation theorists. Indeed, Madaus and Stufflebeam (1989) credit Tyler for "ideas such as the taxonomic classification of learning outcomes, the need to validate indirect measures against direct indicators of the trait of interest . . . the concept of formative evaluation, content mastery, decision-oriented evaluation, criterion-referenced and objectives-referenced tests" (p. xiii).

Furthermore, Tyler avows that the curricula to be evaluated are based on hypotheses that are the best judgments of program staff regarding the most effective set of procedures for attaining program outcomes. The purpose of evaluation is to validate the program's hypotheses.

Although he provided a foundation for many theoretical ideas, Tyler's main focus is on the specification of objectives and measurement of outcomes. He rejects the applicability of norm-referenced tests for program evaluation. He argues that discarding items that were answered correctly by too many or too few respondents does not provide the necessary information about what students are learning. Tyler's point of view has come to be known as *objectives-oriented* (or *objectives-referenced*) evaluation. The approach focuses on (a) formulating a statement of educational objectives, (b) classifying these objectives into major types, (c) defining and refining each of these types of objectives in terms of behavior, (d) identifying situations in which students can be expected to display these types of behavior, (e) selecting and trying promising methods for obtaining evidence regarding each type of objective, (f) selecting on the basis of preliminary trials the more promising appraisal methods for further development and improvement, and (g) devising means for interpreting and using the results (Tyler, 1942, pp. 498–500). Madaus and Stufflebeam (1989) claim that Tyler coined the term *educational evaluation* in the 1930s to describe his procedures—the comparison of (well-stated) intended outcomes (called objectives) with (well-measured) actual outcomes.

A number of later theoretical works rest heavily on Tyler's views of evaluation, emphasizing particularly the methodology of objectives-based measurement. Metfessel and Michael's (1967) work follows Tyler's evaluation step progression but pays greater heed to expanding the range of alternative instruments. Hammond (1973) includes Tyler's views as a behavioral objectives dimension that is part of a model that also includes a more precise definition of instruction and the institution. Popham (1973, 1975) follows the Tyler model and focuses primarily on the championing of "behavioral objective specification." Early work by Popham (1973) called for a narrow scope for individual educational objectives, resulting in a massive number of objectives required to conduct an evaluation and subsequent system overload. In his later evaluation textbook, Popham (1988) recognized this problem and called for a focus on a manageable number of broad-scope objectives and the use of the taxonomies of educational objectives only as "gross heuristics."

Objectives-oriented evaluation has had a strong continuing influence on education for many decades. As a part of the expansion of Tyler's work, Bloom, Englehart, Furst, Hill, and Krathwohl (1956) developed a taxonomy of educational objectives for the cognitive domain, and Krathwohl, Bloom, and Masia (1964) developed one for the affective domain. These efforts encouraged users to invest a great deal of time and effort into objective specification.

We had previously noted the broad impact of Ralph Tyler's work in the 1940s on many evaluation theory views and placed him on the methods branch because we believe that his attention to educational measurement as the essence of evaluation is the most prominent feature of his work. A change from the version of the tree published in the first edition of *Roots* is that Ralph Tyler has now been repositioned to a subbranch. This reflects our revised view that while his theoretical point of view is, in fact, heavily methods related (objectives-based evaluation), he is not a theoretical predecessor of those further up on the branch. His original positioning was intended to reflect his influence on the field of educational evaluation—which was very significant—but on further reflection, we concluded that his overall influence on the methods branch specifically was less than his original position suggested. Thus, we placed him on a subbranch near the base of the methods branch.

Valuing

Out of the root of epistemology has grown a branch of evaluators who focus on concerns related to valuing in the evaluation process. Of particular importance is the fact/value distinction delineated by the 18th-century Scottish philosopher David Hume. To some extent, the issue of what is "fact" has been addressed and amplified using a strict distinction between fact and value in the second root, social inquiry. The variance from this view of "fact" is important in itself as a root. Important issues raised when considering valuing in evaluation include the legitimacy of value claims (as ably described by House & Howe, 1999), the nature of universal (justifiable) claims, and the constructivist view that truth (or fact) is guided by "the meanings that people construct in particular times and places" (Greene, 2009, p. 159).

To better reflect the philosophical theories informing evaluation theorists on this branch, we have split the branch in two, naming the left arm of the branch stretching toward the methods branch as "objectivist influenced" and the right arm, "subjectivist influenced." Again, we underscore the use of the word *influence* here when describing the newly reshaped valuing branch. At the base, prior to the split, are Michael Scriven (1967, 1972a) and Robert Stake (1967, 1974), both of whom significantly influenced the field in terms of its conceptual underpinnings and procedures.

It is Scriven who proclaims that evaluation is not evaluation without valuing. He argues that it is the work of the evaluator to make a value judgment about the object that is being evaluated and that this value judgment should be based on observable data about the quality and effectiveness of the evaluand under study. Scriven's philosophical training in logic, which helps inform his argument for a systematic, objective approach to valuing and evaluation, has importantly influenced his thinking.

This branch also includes the work of those who reject the notion that we should strive for an objectivist judgment about the merit or worth of the evaluand. Rather, they espouse the philosophy of relativism or subjectivism—that is, the claim that human activity is not like that in the physical world but, rather, reality is an ongoing, dynamic process and a truth is always relative to some particular frame of reference. This is quite different from the type of valuing that concerns Scriven. Stake's (1967) article "The Countenance of Educational Evaluation" offers hints of subjectivist thinking, but not until his paper on responsive evaluation (Stake, 1974) does he explicitly reject "preordinate evaluation" (evaluation conducted in the spirit of obtaining objective information). There, he argues for a responsive approach using case studies as a means of capturing the issues, personal relationships, and complexity of the evaluand and for judging the value of the evaluand under study. His early subjectivist conceptualization of and approach to evaluation has served as an important influence in the thinking of others who argue for attention to complexity, dialogue, and meaning in evaluations and use this as a basis for informing value claims in evaluation studies.

Michael Scriven

Scriven's major contribution is the way in which he adamantly defines the role of the evaluator in making value judgments. Shadish et al. (1991) note that Scriven was "the first and only major evaluation theorist to have an explicit and general theory of valuing" (p. 94). Scriven (1986) is unequivocal in his position that society requires valuing and it is the role of the evaluator to do that job. In fact, he maintains that there is a science of valuing and *that* is evaluation: "Bad is bad and good is good and it is the job of evaluators to decide which is which" (p. 19). Scriven (1983) notes that the greatest failure of the evaluator is in simply providing information to decision makers and "passing the buck [for final judgment] to the non-professional" (p. 248).

The evaluator, in valuing, must fulfill his or her role in serving the "public interest" (Scriven, 1976, p. 220). By public interest, Scriven does not simply refer to clients, users, or stakeholders but to all potential consumers. Indeed, he views the evaluator's role in valuing as similar to producing a study for *Consumer Reports*, in which the evaluator determines the appropriate criteria by which judgments are to be made and then presents these judgments for all to see. As in *Consumer Reports*, there is the necessity for identifying "critical competitors," or competing alternatives. Comparisons are key in making value judgments, and the evaluator has the responsibility for identifying the appropriate alternatives. Just as *Consumer Reports* would identify "midsize cars" to be evaluated, so, too, would the evaluator seek out similar entities for evaluation.

Scriven adamantly states that it is not necessary to explain why a program or product works in order to determine its value. Nevertheless, he introduces an alternative to experimental and quasi-experimental design called the "modus operandi" (MO) method (Scriven, 1991, p. 234), which is analogous to procedures used to profile criminal behavior:

> The MO of a particular cause is an associated configuration of events, processes, or properties, usually in time sequence, which can often be described as the *characteristic causal chain* (or certain distinctive features of this chain) connecting the cause with the effect. (Scriven, 1974, p. 71)

In a manner similar to that which Scriven uses to grade critical competitors, the MO method requires that the evaluator first develop a thorough list of potential causes and then narrow it down in two steps. In the first step, the evaluator determines which potential causes were present prior to the effect. In the second step, the evaluator can determine which complete MO fits the chain of events and thus determine the true cause. To ensure accuracy and bias control, the evaluator looks for instances of "co-causation and over determination" and calls in a "goal-free or social process expert consultant to seek undesirable effects" (Scriven, 1974, p. 76). Scriven believes that, ultimately, the evaluator is able to deliver a picture of the causal connections and effects that eliminate causal competitors without introducing evaluator bias.

Scriven (1972b) advocates for "goal-free evaluation," in which the evaluator assumes responsibility for determining which program outcomes to examine, rejecting the objectives of the program as a starting point. He maintains that by doing so, the evaluator is better able to identify the real accomplishments (and nonaccomplishments) of the program. An essential element of Scriven's valuing is the determination of a single value judgment of the program's worth ("good" or "bad"). In requiring the synthesis of multiple-outcome judgments into a single value statement, Scriven is alone among evaluation theorists.

In both goal-free evaluation and the synthesis stage, Scriven justifies his point of view by relying on the extent to which the program is able to meet "needs." Needs are the presumed cost to society and to individuals and are determined through a needs assessment. Shadish et al. (1991) maintain that Scriven's conception of valuing depends on his definition of needs and note that his "conception of needs implies a prescriptive theory of valuing and that he disparages descriptive statements about what people think about the program" (p. 95). Moreover, they maintain that his needs assessment is not independent of the views of the evaluator and that failing to directly reflect the views of stakeholders inhibits the potential use of evaluation findings in policy making. Scriven is apparently unconcerned by this, maintaining that determining the "truth" is sufficient. Scriven's unique training in philosophy, mathematics, and mathematical logic provides him with the assurance that he can make sound, unbiased judgments.

Extending his supposition for evaluation as the science of valuing, Scriven (1991, 2001, 2003) reasons that evaluation is a transdiscipline, that is, a discipline that possesses its own unique knowledge base while serving other disciplines as a tool. He maintains that, like logic and statistics, evaluation is a major transdiscipline because all disciplines rely on the evaluation process to judge the value of the entities within their own purview, as evidenced by the peer review publication process. This view of evaluation has given rise to Scriven describing evaluation as an "alpha discipline."

Scriven's thinking pushed the field to consider valuing as a central feature of evaluation more so than anyone else. He has been positioned on the valuing branch at the base of the objectivist influence arm to reflect this perspective.

Henry Levin

Cost analyses are a critical domain of evaluation work because they offer information to address what some consider to be the ultimate evaluation question: What is the overall value of the program? Cost analyses are economics-based strategies for determining the value of a program or policy. Henry Levin is a leading and noteworthy educational policy researcher and evaluator who for several decades has focused on developing, promoting, and using cost analyses as a means for drawing evaluative conclusions about programs. Levin's position on the valuing branch in the direction of the methods branch reflects the primary object of cost analyses as a method for informing object value judgments about a program using a specific methodological approach.

Levin (2005; Levin & McEwan, 2001) offers evaluators an array of economics-based strategies for determining program costs prior to and during implementation. In a program's planning stages, cost analysis strategies can be used to project what a program might cost and whether it is fiscally possible to implement. Likewise, a cost analysis procedure might be used to keep track of the costs of an ongoing program. Cost-effectiveness procedures are used to determine which program out of many achieves a target outcome most frugally (cost-effectiveness) or which program of many with equal costs produces the greatest outcome (also cost-effectiveness). Furthermore, a program's cost may be examined relative to its monetary impact (or benefits) on clients or society (cost–benefit analysis). An essential part of preparing to undertake a cost study involves thinking about how "costs" are defined, what costs are important, and how best to assess them. Because costs can be calculated and evaluated differently across strategies, it is important for evaluators and stakeholders to clarify what they need from a cost strategy and to understand how each works.

Robert Stake

Early in the field's development, Stake authored three manuscripts—"The Countenance of Educational Evaluation" (Stake, 1967), *Program Evaluation, Particularly Responsive Evaluation* (Stake, 1974), and *Case Studies in Science Education* (Stake & Easley, 1979)—that served as the primary foundation for his later work. As House (2001b) points out, the essential components of Stake's responsive evaluation are the beliefs that (a) there is no true value to anything (i.e., knowledge is context bound), (b) stakeholder perspectives are integral elements in evaluations, and (c) case studies are the best method for representing the beliefs and values of stakeholders and of reporting evaluation results.

Stake has been a strong advocate of producing "thick description," maintaining that a case study approach is necessary for context and activity description but might, for some audiences, be a poor way to judge quality. In Abma and Stake's (2001) words, "I think of the judgmental act as part of the descriptive, part of the observational act" (p. 10). In other words, he maintains that seeing and judging the evaluand regularly are part of the same act and that the task of evaluation is as much a matter of refining early perceptions of quality as of building a body of evidence to determine the level of quality.

Stake maintains the subjectivist position that there are multiple realities and that stakeholder perspectives need to be represented within the evaluation. This is not to be confused with the belief that stakeholders should participate in the evaluation in the same way that participatory theorists endorse such actions; Stake is opposed to stakeholder participation in many evaluation activities and processes and instead asserts that evaluation is the job of the evaluator (Alkin, Hofstetter, & Ai, 1998, p. 98). As House (2001a) notes in discussing Stake, "What goes into the report and what the evaluator responds to is at the discretion of the evaluator" (p. 26). Stake's view on how evaluators draw conclusions is that "ultimately the evaluator decides, which must mean that judgment is dependent on the evaluator's values and personality" (House, 2001a, p. 28). However, judgment does not depend on this alone. Stake (2000) notes that it is the evaluator's job "to hear the [participants'] pleas, to deliberate, sometimes to negotiate, but regularly, non-democratically, to decide what [the participants'] interests are" (p. 104). Stake (1975) cautions that "whatever consensus in values there is [among participants] . . . should be discovered. The evaluator should not create a consensus that does not exist" (pp. 25–26). Furthermore, he notes, "The reader, the client, the people outside need to be in a position to make their own judgments using grounds they have already, plus the new data" (Abma & Stake, 2001, p. 10).

Stake, like Campbell, Cronbach, and Scriven, is one of the evaluation field's pioneers, and his work has influenced all aspects of evaluation theory. Stake's attention to the notion of stakeholder participation in his responsive evaluation and the visibility that he accords these ideas has had a strong influence on theorists on the use branch of the evaluation theory tree. Stake differs from use theorists, however, in that he neither describes the motivation for including stakeholders in the evaluation as an effort to promote use nor pays particular attention to decision makers or how evaluation findings might be used. In placing Stake on the valuing branch, there is an easy transition to Ernest House, who embraces the stakeholder notion but adds the perspective of giving voice to the underrepresented. Moreover, the subjectivist thinking underpinning Stake's views on the role of the evaluator in providing the basis for alternative values to be expressed rings deeply in the work of Guba and Lincoln, which is centered on the constructivist philosophy. Thus, we place Stake on the valuing branch, acknowledging his substantial contribution to theorists across the tree.

Elliott Eisner

Eisner first presented his views on what he called "educational connoisseurship" in an issue of the *Journal of Aesthetic Education* (1976) and subsequently expanded on those views (Eisner, 1985, 1991a, 1991b, 1998) in several important ways. His evaluative viewpoint is a direct response to his negative perceptions of more traditional approaches to evaluation, where the focus is on educational outcomes, whether measured by standardized tests using the principles of psychological testing or by criterion-referenced testing procedures. Eisner's (1976) rejection of "technological scientism" includes a rejection of the extensive use of research models employing experimental and quasi-experimental designs, which depend heavily (if not exclusively) on quantitative methods. Eisner notes that "things that matter" cannot be measured quantitatively. He argues that while quantitative techniques can provide some useful information, "evaluation requires a sophisticated, interpretive map not only to separate what is trivial from what is significant, but also to understand the meaning of what is known" (Eisner, 1994, p. 193).

Drawing heavily from his prior experience as both curriculum expert and artist, Eisner uses the role of critics in the arts as an analogy for an alternative conception of evaluation. Central to his evaluation theoretic views are the twin notions of connoisseurship and criticism. To be a connoisseur is to have knowledge about what one sees, to have the ability to differentiate subtleties, and to be aware of and understand the experience. Eisner (1991b) notes that "a connoisseur is someone who has worked at the business of learning how to see, to hear, to read the image or text and who, as a result, can experience more of the work's qualities than most of us" (p. 174).

Criticism, in Eisner's view, is making the experience public through some form of representation. Eisner describes three aspects of criticism. First, there is critical description, in which the evaluator draws on his or her senses to describe events, reactions, interactions, and everything else that is seen. By doing this, the evaluator portrays a picture of the program situation, frequently imagining himself or herself as a participant and drawing on the senses to describe the feeling in the participant's terms. The second dimension of criticism is expectation, in which the evaluator tries to understand or make sense of what was seen. The evaluator asks, "What is the meaning of this?" and "What message are the participants getting?" In responding to these questions, the evaluator must draw on his or her own experience to understand the minds of participants. Eisner emphasizes the importance of necessary background knowledge, since good critics cannot interpret or evaluate what they have not experienced themselves. The critic must ask, "What is the value of what is happening?" Eisner (1991b) notes that valuing is a critical element in the process:

> The essence of perception is its selectivity; the connoisseur is as unlikely to describe everything in sight as a gourmet chef is to use everything in his pantry. The selective process is influenced by the value one brings to the classroom. What the observer cares about, she is likely to look for . . . Making value judgments about the educational import of what has been seen and rendered is one of the critical features of educational criticism. (p. 176)

Like Scriven, Eisner considers the valuing role important and includes not only making final judgments about data (or observations) but also making judgments about what questions to ask and where to focus the evaluation study. Eisner recognizes that goals, possible outcomes, and observations are limitless. Eisner and Scriven each place the determination of what is important to look at in the hands of the evaluator, yet Scriven's evaluator draws his or her expertise from philosophy, logic, mathematics, and scientific methods, while Eisner's (1991a) evaluator draws from the subjectivist notions of connoisseurship and experience or "the enlightened eye." Eisner is also similar to Scriven in that he posits that the evaluator is the expert and thus determines the final value of a program. He differs from Scriven, however, in that he believes that the evaluator has the authority to judge a program's merit because of expert understanding of the subject area (e.g., education or public health) rather than because of expertise as an evaluator. Eisner's data collection methods are also subjectivist in nature. He advocates the use of intense observation, which includes both quantitative and qualitative measures, while emphasizing the use of qualitative work in evaluation. Because subjectivist thinking informs Eisner's ideas and because he argues for the evaluator to make the judgment of value in the evaluation process, we positioned Eisner on the right limb, toward the objectivist influence side of the valuing branch.

Ernest House

Ernest House recognizes that evaluation serves the purpose of providing information to decision makers so that they can determine the legitimate allocation of vital resources. He denounces as inadequate the utilitarian framework that underlies key theories of evaluation (primarily those of writers we classify on the methods branch and the early theories of those we classify on the use branch). House (1991) notes, "Utilitarianism is a moral theory which holds that policies are morally right when they promote the greatest sum total of good or happiness from among the alternatives" (p. 235). In the pursuit of social justice, he argues that attempts at being responsive to stakeholders are superior to prior evaluation conceptions. He also deplores the lack of value neutrality in stakeholder approaches, which he says results from the general lack of full inclusion of the represented interests of the poor and powerless in stakeholder groups (pp. 239–240).

House comes to these views by drawing on Rawls's (1971) justice theory. House (1991, 1993) argues that evaluation is never value-neutral and should tilt in the direction of social justice by specifically addressing the needs and interests of the powerless. House's evaluator is thus faced with the task of understanding the needs and positions of various stakeholder groups, especially the powerless, and of balancing this information with his or her perception of social justice. In doing this balancing, the evaluator shapes the kind of information collected as well as its analysis. In essence, evaluators cast themselves in the role of spokespeople or representatives of the poor and powerless.

It is important to note that for House, the role of evaluator is not to define value in terms of good or bad, as Scriven does, but in terms of truth, beauty, and justice. In this sense, the value judgments accorded to the least advantaged should receive the utmost importance. Thus, both Scriven and House place the valuing component in a position of eminence, but they do so with substantially different emphases.

It is informative to examine what House refers to as "ethical fallacies" in evaluation: *clientism* (taking the client's interest as the ultimate consideration), *contractualism* (adhering inflexibly to the contract), *managerialism* (placing the interest of the managers above all else), *methodologicalism* (believing that proper methodology solves all ethical problems), *pluralism/elitism* (including only the powerful stakeholders' interests in the evaluation), and *relativism* (taking all viewpoints as having equal merit). By referring to these as ethical fallacies, House disassociates himself from the views that are consistent with each. For example, the first three of these can easily be thought of as associated with the use branch of the theory tree (particularly the early part of the branch). Methodologicalism is clearly associated with the methods branch, and pluralism/elitism and relativism are associated with various stakeholder approaches.

A bit later in his career, House began writing with Kenneth Howe, and it is in this writing that we find some of House's most prescriptive thinking on how evaluation should be conducted. House believes that "evaluators should accept authority but not power" (House & Howe, 1999, p. 102). An evaluator who caters to those with power perpetuates inequality, which is why inclusion is the first criterion of "deliberative democratic evaluation." Inclusion wards off stakeholder bias and invites stakeholders with and without power to participate in the evaluation. Dialogue, the next criterion, is necessary to ensure that stakeholder contributions are well thought out and can be honestly weighed along with all other stakeholder contributions to the evaluation. Deliberation, the final criterion for deliberative democratic evaluation, is the weighing of each contribution to generate an accurate conclusion. House and Howe's approach is value-engaged. Fact and value are not mutually exclusive. They exist on a continuum where a middle ground exists between "brute fact" and "bare values" (House & Howe, 1999, p. 6). The deliberative democratic evaluation process is described as follows: "We can imagine moving along the value–fact continuum from statements of preferences and values collected through initial dialogue, through deliberations based on democratic principles, to evaluative statements of fact" (House & Howe, 1999, p. 100).

House is often cited as the theorist who first acknowledged the ways in which evaluation affects power and social structures and described how it can be used to either shift or maintain existing repressive structures. He reminds us that evaluation is used to determine "who gets what" and that without explicit concern for those from underrepresented groups, evaluation is not meeting its primary purpose, namely, to promote social justice. House's emphatic concern with values and judgment in his theoretical views firmly establishes his place on the valuing branch of the evaluation tree.

Jennifer C. Greene

Greene argues that evaluation should be used to determine value, specifically by developing a consensus around a set of criteria used to determine the value of a program. Greene (2005) describes what she calls a value-engaged approach to evaluation, which incorporates elements of responsive evaluation (Stake, 1975, 2005) along with principles from democratic evaluation (House & Howe, 1999). Her approach uses three criteria of deliberative democratic evaluation: inclusion, dialogue, and deliberation. She stresses stakeholder involvement, however, which closely resembles participatory evaluation approaches. She also explicitly emphasizes the use of mixed methods designs and fieldwork within her evaluations. Greene's (2005) approach to evaluation emphasizes responsiveness to the particularities of the context, inclusion of and engagement with multiple stakeholder perspectives and experiences, and attention to the social and relational dimensions of evaluation practice. Her approach is responsive in that the evaluation design is developed in response to the program context. It is democratic in that it places great importance on considering the perspectives and values of all legitimate stakeholders, especially stakeholders who are typically alienated from evaluation processes. Greene (2000) argues that evaluations can be "used to surface and legitimate differing views and values and move [stakeholder] towards shared understanding of the values of educational outcomes" (p. 16).

Greene offers three "justifications" for including stakeholder views when conducting evaluations: pragmatic, emancipatory, and deliberative. The *pragmatic* justification argues for stakeholder inclusion because it increases the chance of evaluation utilization and organizational learning. The *emancipatory* justification focuses on the importance of acknowledging the skills and contributions of stakeholders and empowering them to be their own social change agents. The *deliberative* justification argues that evaluation should serve to ensure that program or policy conversations include all relevant interests and are "based on the democratic principles of fairness and equity and on democratic discourse that is dialogic and deliberative" (Greene, 2000, p. 14). Implementation of these principles is intended to "extend impartiality by including relevant interests, values, and views so that conclusions can be unbiased in value as well as factual aspects" (House & Howe, 2000).

Greene is explicit about the extent to which Stake and House have influenced her work. The impact of their work on her own ideas is evident throughout her writings. Placing Greene on the valuing branch after House offers a visual depiction of the relationship between her ideas and those of key theorists before her.

Egon Guba and Yvonna Lincoln

Guba and Lincoln, unlike others on the valuing branch, who view the evaluator as the "valuer," view stakeholders as the primary individuals involved in placing value. This viewpoint rests on the belief that instead of just one reality, there are multiple realities, based on the perceptions and interpretations of the individuals involved in the program to be evaluated. Thus, Guba and Lincoln believe that the role of the evaluator is to facilitate negotiations between individuals reflecting these multiple realities.

Guba and Lincoln's (1989) *Fourth Generation Evaluation* is based on a constructivist paradigm—that is, in place of the existence of a single reality, individuals "construct" their perceptions of reality. The role of the constructivist investigator is to tease out these constructions and "to bring them into conjunction . . . with one another and with whatever information . . . can be brought to bear on the issues involved" (p. 142). More specifically, evaluators are "orchestrators of a negotiation process that aims to culminate in consensus on better informed and more sophisticated constructions" (p. 110).

Guba and Lincoln (1989) claim that *Fourth Generation Evaluation* is "a marriage of responsive focusing—using the claims, concerns and issues of stakeholders as the organizing elements—and constructivist methodology aiming to develop judgmental consensus among stakeholders who earlier held different, perhaps conflicting, emic constructions" (p. 184). Thus, they use maximum-variation sampling to identify the broadest scope of stakeholders, who are interviewed sequentially, in order to place on the table the great variety of individual constructions. These are part of what they refer to as "the hermeneutic circle," which defines a continuous interplay of data collection and analysis. Ideally, out of this process, a joint construction will begin to emerge. Additional roles for the evaluator include "testing and enlarging within-group constructions by introducing new or additional information," "sorting out resolved CC & I [claims, concerns, and issues]," "prioritizing unresolved CC & I," "collecting information bearing on unresolved CC & I," "preparing an agenda for negotiation," "carrying out a negotiation," and "reporting via the case study—the joint construction as product" (p. 185).

Apart from the emphasis on bringing together constructions to facilitate valuing by stakeholders, there are numerous places in the process where the evaluator himself or herself engages in valuing. Indeed, according to these theorists, "'facts' and 'values' are interdependent. 'Facts' have no meaning except within some value framework; they are value-laden. There can be no separate observational and valuational languages" (Guba & Lincoln, 1989, p. 105).

A number of comments in Guba and Lincoln (1989) seem to validate the point that fourth-generation evaluators do play at least a moderate personal role in valuing. Note the following:

> As the several constructions begin to take shape, however, certain elements will seem to be more salient than others (and will probably first appear this way to the inquirer). (p. 153)
>
> The human is the instrument of choice for the constructivist for only a human can enter a context without prior programming, but . . . after a short period begin to discern what *is* salient (in the emic view of the respondents). (p. 175)
>
> The inquirer's own etic (outsider) construction may be introduced for critique . . . so long as all respondents have the opportunity to criticize the inquirer's formulations as they must do with their own. (p. 154)

Thus, it is clear that Lincoln and Guba's views fit nicely on the valuing branch of the evaluation theory tree. It is particularly interesting to observe among the various theorists on this branch the great diversity in the manner in which valuing takes place, yet all share a primary concern for valuing, either by the evaluator or through the evaluator, acting in a role designed to facilitate the valuing by others.

Donna Mertens

Donna Mertens's (1999, 2009) inclusive approach could be considered a direct descendant of Guba/Lincoln and House, but it is unique in its emphasis on diversity and the inclusion of diverse groups. Mertens is best known for her inclusive/transformative model of evaluation. She emphasizes the transformative paradigm, which is made up of four philosophical assumptions that include the nature of reality, knowledge, and inquiry. Her primary focus is on the fourth assumption, however: the ethics that specifically relate to social justice and human rights.

In Mertens's (2009) model, the evaluator's primary role is to include marginalized groups, not to act as decision maker. Although the evaluator advocates for the inclusion of marginalized groups, he or she does not advocate *for* the marginalized groups. Mertens maintains that evaluators working within an inclusive framework should ask themselves the following questions at the planning stages of the evaluation:

- Are we including people from both genders and with diverse abilities, ages, classes, cultures, ethnicities, families, incomes, languages, locations, races, and sexualities?
- What barriers are we erecting to exclude a diversity of people?
- Have we chosen the appropriate data collection strategies for diverse groups, including providing for preferred modes of communication?

The aim of inclusion is to ensure that the evaluation is conducted within the context of the program's entirety in a way that discourages bias—not to advocate for one group over another. A primary goal of inclusive/transformative evaluation is to challenge the status quo in a quest to transform society. Mertens agrees with and quotes Chelimsky, who argues that challenging the status quo is "our most important task and the best justification for our work" (quoted in Mertens, 1999, p. 2). In this paradigm, evaluations are a tool to confront social inequality and to promote equality.

Use

The use branch began its growth with what are often referred to as "decision-oriented theories." Decision-oriented theorists felt that it was critical to conduct evaluations that were designed specifically to assist key program stakeholders in program decision making. Such stakeholders are most often those that commission the evaluation. Stufflebeam's CIPP model (described below) is one of the most well-known of these theories. Subsequently, based on empirical knowledge about the conditions under which evaluation use takes place, utilization theorists built on the notions that had been put forth earlier by decision-oriented theories. The resulting class of theories is concerned with designing evaluations that are intended not only to inform decision making but also to ensure that evaluation results have an impact on decision making, organizational change, and conceptual understandings of the program. This concern for the use of an evaluation focuses primarily on the program at hand—*this* program at *this* time.

With recent extensions of the use concept in the literature to include "evaluation influence," it is important to concisely clarify what we mean by use as it relates to this branch of the theory tree. Evaluation influence refers to the capacity of evaluation processes, products, or findings to indirectly produce a change in understanding or knowledge either at the evaluation site at a future time or at other sites (Alkin & Taut, 2003; Christie, 2007; Kirkhart, 2000; Mark & Henry, 2004). Rather than drawing from this broad definition of use, the use branch as we envision it depicts the work of theorists concerned with direct program site use (in action or understanding) that results from a particular evaluation study. Accordingly, the theorists presented on the use branch aim to promote the kind of actionable use that is within the purview of the evaluator.

Daniel Stufflebeam

Daniel Stufflebeam, along with Guba, initially developed the CIPP model as an approach to evaluation focused on the decision-making process. As mentioned earlier, CIPP is an acronym for four types of evaluation: *c*ontext, *i*nput, *p*rocess, and *p*roduct. *Context evaluation* involves identifying needs to decide on program objectives. *Input evaluation* leads to decisions about strategies and designs. *Process evaluation* consists of identifying shortcomings in a current program to refine implementation. And *product evaluation* measures outcomes for decisions regarding the continuation or refocus of the program.

Stufflebeam describes the CIPP model of evaluation as a cyclical process. The key strategy is to work with a carefully designed evaluation while maintaining flexibility. According to Stufflebeam (1983), evaluators must view design as a process, not a product. Evaluations should provide a continual information stream to decision makers to ensure that programs continually improve their services. To improve services, evaluations should aid decision makers in allocating resources to programs that best serve clients.

Stufflebeam (2000) often keys his evaluations to *The Program Evaluation Standards* (Joint Committee on Standards for Educational Evaluation, 1994). This book describes the professional standards by which evaluators should conduct their work, pointing to four domains of practice: utility, feasibility, propriety, and accuracy. *Utility* standards ensure that an evaluation will serve the information needs of intended users; *feasibility* standards ensure that an evaluation will be realistic, prudent, diplomatic, and frugal; *propriety* standards ensure that an evaluation will be conducted legally, ethically, and with due respect for the welfare of those involved in the evaluation as well as of those affected by its results; and *accuracy* standards ensure that an evaluation will reveal and convey technically adequate information about the features that determine the worth or merit of the program being evaluated. Moreover, citing the feasibility standard of formal contracts, Stufflebeam (2000) advises evaluators and clients to reach formal written agreements that detail "what is to be done, how, by whom, and when so that these parties are obligated to adhere to all conditions of the agreement or formally to renegotiate it" (p. 311).

Using Stufflebeam's (2003) approach, an evaluator engages a "representative stakeholder panel to help define the evaluation questions, shape evaluation plans, review draft reports and disseminate the findings" (p. 57). The stakeholder panel is the primary group with whom the evaluator interfaces regularly, and the success of the evaluation can hinge on these regular interactions because it is believed that without them, the evaluation approach will fail. The evaluator keeps the panel abreast of the formative information produced, so that decisions about both the program and the evaluation can be made. Evaluations produce a comprehensive assessment of merit and program worth.

In sum, Stufflebeam's (2001) evaluation approach engages stakeholders (usually in decision-making positions) in focusing the evaluation and in making sure that it addresses their most important questions; provides timely, relevant information to assist decision making; and produces an accountability record. Both formative and summative information become available to a panel of stakeholders that promotes the use of the evaluation findings. By including multiple stakeholder perspectives, Stufflebeam increases the possibility that relevant value perspectives are represented, thus fostering a comprehensive evaluation of program value. With this as his evaluation focus, Stufflebeam is positioned as the first name on the use branch of the theory tree.

Joseph Wholey

From Joseph Wholey's academic training and exposure to large-scale program evaluations, one might anticipate his placement on the methods branch. Indeed, Wholey's early writing depicts a theoretical view consistent with that of the methods-oriented Suchman. However, his long-standing participation in federal government programs has made him sensitive to the needs of program managers, and in many respects, Wholey's focus on managers and policymakers (he is less concerned about other stakeholders) is similar to Stufflebeam's attention to decision makers. Much of Wholey's writings (e.g., Wholey, 1983; Wholey, Hatry, & Newcomer, 2010) have as a central focus the use of evaluation for the improvement of management. Wholey (1983) recognizes and attends in great detail to the complexity of managing an organization and views evaluation as an important process to "stimulate effective management." Consequently, we have placed Wholey on the use branch.

In viewing an organization and its constraints, Wholey recognizes that obtaining evaluation information is costly. Thus, he proposes a four-stage procedure for the "sequential purchase of information." The first of these, *evaluability assessment*, concerns itself with making an initial assessment (or pre-assessment) of the feasibility of conducting an evaluation with respect to the organization and issues to be examined. This stage of the assessment also considers the extent to which evaluation results are likely to be useful for program managers in effecting improved program performance.

The other three stages in the "sequential purchase of information" strategy are (1) *rapid-feedback evaluation*, which focuses primarily on extant and easily collected information; (2) *performance* (or outcome) *monitoring*, which measures program performance, usually in comparison with prior or expected performance; and (3) *intensive evaluation*, which uses comparison or control groups to better estimate the effectiveness of program activities in causing observed results. Wholey is firmly connected to the potential management benefits (particularly the short-term, instrumental utilization) of his evaluation work, placing him naturally on the use branch of the tree.

Eleanor Chelimsky

"Telling the truth to people who may not want to hear it is, after all, the chief purpose of evaluation" (Chelimsky, 1995). Chelimsky is best known for establishing and directing the evaluation unit of the General Accountability Office (GAO), the largest independent internal evaluation unit in existence (U.S. GAO, www.gao.gov). In this role, Chelimsky has developed a unique perspective on evaluation utilization, motivated by the need to inform each of the three branches of the U.S. government as well as by a recognition of the need for public accountability. Chelimsky (2006) maintains that the evaluation of public policies, programs, and practices is fundamental to a democratic government for four reasons:

> (1) to support congressional oversight; (2) to build a stronger knowledge base for policy making; (3) to help agencies develop improved capabilities for policy and program planning, implementation, and analysis of results, as well as learning-oriented direction in their practice; (4) to strengthen public information about government activities through dissemination of evaluation findings. (p. 33)

In essence, Chelimsky is saying that evaluation should generate information for conceptual and enlightenment use, for organizational change and development, and for formative program improvements (i.e., actionable, instrumental use). While her work does not focus on individual primary users—but rather on larger user groups such as congressional subcommittees, members of particular government agencies, or the general public—Chelimsky pays less attention to the involvement of particular stakeholders in the evaluation process. Instead, she describes strategies for presenting information, so that it is likely to be consumed by members of her target audience(s).

Because of the political nature of Chelimsky's work, she argues for the most rigorous evaluation study possible, given the restraints placed on the evaluation. She maintains that excellence in procedure and practice can never be compromised in an evaluation and that accuracy and credibility are necessary conditions for evaluation use to occur in political environments. To attain that excellence, under her direction, GAO has devised a wide variety of methods to suit different question types (Chelimsky, 1997), and this flexibility of methodology is a major reason for her inclusion on the use branch.

Marvin Alkin

In early years, Alkin was identified as focused on evaluation and decision-making concerns. Alkin's early model (1972b) had many similarities to Stufflebeam's CIPP model, though the primary distinction was Alkin's recognition that *process* and *product* have both summative and formative dimensions. Thus, one could look at process summatively (through program documentation) or at product formatively (through outcomes). The Center for the Study of Evaluation (CSE) model was used as the basis for the CSE Evaluation Kit, which sold almost 15,000 copies.

More recent writings place Alkin's (1991) views as "user-oriented," as he prefers to call it; to enhance the possibility of use, the focus is on the identified potential user(s) and evaluator interactions with them. This extension of the use branch concerns itself with theorists who are not primarily focused on decision makers' needs but on emphasizing procedures that would enhance the use of evaluation to a broader spectrum of identified stakeholders. Major research on evaluation utilization influenced this extension of the evaluation use branch.[4] The view based on this research is that it is not sufficient to think of evaluation as related solely to decision makers; rather, it is necessary to think about the evaluator's obligation to help ensure that utilization takes place. Hence, the evaluator should be proactive and not satisfied with an evaluation that might simply be put on the shelf.

Another distinctive element of Alkin's approach is the strong emphasis on a thorough examination of program context as a guide for conducting the evaluation. Furthermore, Alkin has a distinct view on the role of the evaluator in valuing. He strongly rejects the dominant role of evaluators as valuing agents. Instead, he prefers to work with primary users at the outset of the evaluation process to establish value systems for judging potential outcome data. In interactive sessions, he presents a variety of simulated potential outcomes and seeks judgments (values) on the implications of each. This predetermined system forms the basis for judging evaluation findings. Alkin acknowledges that there are conditions under which it is not tenable to engage intended primary users in this prejudgment process, and under such circumstances, he prefers to present evaluation data as factually as possible without imposing value judgment, unless there are extreme cases that demand that valuing take place.

We have placed Alkin's evolved position on the use branch in close relationship to Patton's focus on evaluation utilization within program settings.

Michael Patton

The most prominent theoretical explication of the utilization (or use) extension was developed by Michael Patton (1978, 1986, 1997, 2008). At variance with earlier evaluation and decision-making theorists, Patton maintains that the evaluator must seek out individuals who are likely to be real users of the evaluation. Patton refers to them as "primary intended users." In Patton's *utilization-focused evaluation* (UFE), the first step is the identification of intended users, including primary intended users. The other four major phases of UFE are (1) the development of users' commitment to the intended focus of the evaluation and to evaluation utilization; (2) involvement in methods, design, and measurement; (3) user engagement—actively and directly interpreting findings and making judgments; and (4) making decisions about further dissemination.

The essence of UFE derives from evaluation utilization research that has demonstrated that a primary element in obtaining use is the "personal factor" (Patton et al., 1977). In other words, the likelihood of an evaluation being utilized is greatly enhanced by the identification of people who have a stake in the evaluation and who personally care about the findings it generates—thus, the strong focus on identifying primary intended users. Likewise, there is the need for a commitment to utilization. The evaluator should be actively involved in developing intended users' commitment to potential utilization, which is enhanced by engaging intended users actively and directly in all stages of the evaluation, fostering "buy-in."

To enhance the relevance of the evaluation, and thus its use, Patton (2002) urges that the evaluator be "active—reactive—interactive—adaptive." Evaluators need to be active in identifying intended users and focusing questions, reactive in continuing to learn about the evaluative situation, and adaptive "in altering the evaluation questions and designs in light of their increased understanding of the situation and changing conditions" (p. 432). Interaction is an essential part of each of these three activities. This utilization focus differs from the evaluation and decision-making thrust not only in its concern for identifying intended users but also in its willingness to be flexible in modifying prespecified evaluation questions and issues to better serve user needs.

In recent years, Patton has broadened the scope of his theoretical views on evaluation to incorporate other dimensions. He has identified that use might take place as a consequence of "the evaluation process—process use—and not just from evaluation findings" (Patton, 1997, p. 103). Another addition to Patton's evaluation menu is the introduction of the term *developmental evaluation* (Patton, 2010). In this activity, the evaluator becomes part of a program's design team or management team. He or she is not separate from the team but rather fully participates in decisions and in facilitating discussion about how to evaluate. In essence, the evaluator is helping develop the intervention, and as a result, we believe that he or she takes on a management-consulting role.

David Fetterman

David Fetterman (1996, 2001) is the author of books on *empowerment evaluation*, which he describes as a process that encourages self-determination among recipients of the program evaluation, often including "training, facilitation, advocacy, illumination and liberation." The goal of empowerment evaluation is to foster self-determination rather than dependency, to the point where program participants—including clients—essentially conduct their own evaluations. The outside evaluator often serves as a coach or additional facilitator, providing clients with the knowledge and tools for continuous self-assessment and accountability. Fetterman argues that training participants to evaluate their own programs and coaching them through the design of their evaluations is an effective form of empowerment.

Fetterman (1994) describes two general forms of empowerment evaluation that are only subtly different. The main distinction between the two is the extent to which the evaluator participates in the evaluation process. In the first case, evaluators teach program participants to conduct their own program evaluations, training program staff to conduct evaluation studies, thus making them more self-sufficient. In this case, the primary work of the evaluator is to build evaluation capacity. In the second case, the evaluator serves as a coach to facilitate others to conduct their own evaluations. Using this approach, evaluators allow participants to shape the direction of their evaluations, suggest ideal solutions to their problems, and then take an active role in making social change. Fetterman sees all empowerment evaluators as having the potential to serve as "illuminating and liberating facilitators, assisting program participants, freeing themselves from traditional roles and expectations" (p. 306).

For Fetterman (1998), the end point of evaluation is not the assessment of the program's worth. In his view, value and worth are not static, and he therefore sees evaluation as an ongoing process: "Through the internalization and institutionalization of self-evaluation processes and practices, a dynamic and responsive approach to evaluation can be developed to accommodate shifts in populations, goals, value assessments and external forces" (p. 382).

Although participatory and empowerment evaluation employ similar practices, their goals are different, and to consider them synonymous would be a fundamental misunderstanding of the theories. In practice, the conception of stakeholder involvement that underlies both participatory and empowerment evaluation looks very similar; that is, stakeholders decide on and assist in conducting all aspects of the evaluation, including design, implementation, analysis, and interpretation. But in practical participatory evaluation, the goal of the participatory process is increased utilization through these activities. This differs from empowerment evaluation, which promotes self-evaluation as a means of empowering those related to the evaluation in a political or emancipatory fashion.

J. Bradley Cousins

The evaluation use limb continues to grow and has gained additional adherents who have made their own enhancements of earlier utilization ideas. Cousins's *participatory evaluation* (Cousins & Earl, 1992; Cousins & Whitmore, 1998) is a further extension of this branch. Cousins's presumption is that if we care about utilization, then the way to achieve it is through buy-in. And the way to achieve buy-in is to have program personnel participating in the evaluation.

Cousins's ideas flow from the concern for evaluation utilization expressed in the work of Patton and others. As such, his work continues to reflect the importance of the personal factor in evaluation and the need for participation to heighten the possibility of utilization. However, he extends the notion of intended primary users, arguing for the importance of organizing groups of intended users. Furthermore, his evaluations are designed for structured, continued, and active participation of these users, as opposed to Patton's user participation, which could take on a variety of different forms. Implicit in Cousins's approach is the understanding that utilization takes place within the context of an organization and is best accomplished as a part of organizational development. Cousins calls this "practical participatory evaluation" (Cousins & Earl, 1995).

Cousins, together with Earl, defines practical participatory evaluation as "applied social research that involves trained evaluation personnel *and* practice-based decision makers working in partnership" (Cousins & Earl, 1995, p. 8). In other words, primary users and evaluators are explicitly recognized as collaborators in the evaluation process. This approach is grounded in a framework that adopts strategies intended to enhance the learning capacity of organizations. Consequently, it is best suited for evaluation projects that "seek to understand programs with the expressed intention of informing and improving their implementation" (Cousins & Earl, 1995). More recently, Cousins has extended his research to gain greater understanding of evaluation as an organizational learning system (Cousins, Goh, & Clark, 2005).

Cousins maintains that the desire for and commitment to program improvement attracts primary users to the evaluation process, that the partnership within the organization engages them, and that this in turn increases utilization. Responsibilities are shared equally between organization staff and the evaluator. The evaluator trains and supervises agency personnel in technical evaluation skills, so that eventually they can coordinate new evaluation efforts. Thus, practitioners learn on the job, and in time, the evaluator becomes a consultant responsible only for technical activities such as instrument design, data analysis, and technical reporting.

Because of these emphases related to utilization, we have placed Cousins on the use branch of the tree. However, as we have also noted in other research (Christie, 2003), Cousins emphasizes the use of rigorous methods during the participatory process, with the ultimate goal of increased utilization. This may be explained by his earlier training in experimental psychology. To reflect his receptiveness to the ideas reflected in methods theorists' work, Cousins's placement extends toward the methods branch.

Hallie Preskill

The work of Hallie Preskill continues the use branch with a focus on organizational learning and development. She contends that substantial evaluation utilization can occur during the evaluation process and that this can be a valuable tool for transformative learning. Influences on her work include Patton's utilization-focused approach (particularly process use) and Cousins's participatory evaluation model. As such, Preskill and her occasional coauthor Rosalie Torres are concerned with tailoring evaluations to fit the needs of primary users and with getting buy-in from program personnel participating in the evaluation.

Preskill's theory is concerned with creating transformational learning within an organization through the evaluation process. *Transformational learning*, according to Preskill and Torres (2000), refers to a process where individuals, teams, and even organizations identify, examine, and understand the information needed to meet their goals. They maintain that to aid transformational learning, when an evaluator approaches an organization, he or she should (a) use a clinical approach, (b) span traditional boundaries between evaluator and program staff, and (c) diagnose the organizational capacity for learning.

Preskill advocates providing organizations with more than technical expertise (e.g., methods design and data analysis) to conduct an evaluation. Taking a clinical approach to evaluation allows for greater focus on the current needs, contextual settings, and historical surroundings of an organization. The approach "is inherently responsive to the needs of an organization and its members" (Preskill & Torres, 2000, p. 31) and allows for reflection and the creation of dialogue, which in turn facilitates transformational learning. Furthermore, she maintains that an evaluator should span the traditional boundaries between evaluator and program staff, becoming a facilitator to help guide the learning process that occurs during an evaluation. This process can be used to increase understanding of how the evaluation findings are arrived at, how they can be implemented, and what still needs to be done. The ultimate goal of this process is to create a seamless blend of program work, research, evaluation, and organizational development. Finally, an evaluator needs the ability to diagnose an organization's capacity for learning (Preskill & Torres, 1998), because this offers a contextual setting to frame evaluation findings and to set realistic goals and expectations for evaluation use. Preskill contends that organizational learning can occur when results from the diagnosis are shared, because this provides an opportunity for reflection, transformational learning, and, ultimately, utilization.

More recently, Preskill has been writing about and using appreciative inquiry (AI) techniques in evaluation. AI is a process that builds on past successes (and peak experiences) in an effort to design and implement future actions. The philosophy underlying AI is that deficit-based approaches to organizational change are not necessarily the most effective or efficient. That is, when evaluators look for problems, more problems are found, and when deficit-based language is used, stakeholders often feel hopeless, powerless, and generally more exhausted. Proponents of AI have found that by reflecting on what has worked well, by remembering topics of study that created excitement and energy, and by using affirmative and strengths-based language, participants' creativity, passion, and excitement about the future are increased.

Preskill (2004) takes the philosophy and principles put forth by organizational change AI theorists and applies them to the evaluation context, maintaining that they increase the use of the evaluation processes and findings. Given her commitment to organizational change through evaluation, and the role that use has in facilitating the learning process associated with organizational change, Preskill has been placed on the use branch.

Jean King

Jean King further extends the use branch with her focus on the development of participatory evaluation models. Influences on her work include various participatory, user-focused, and capacity-building approaches. King prefers working long term with organizations to develop joint understandings and, over time, creating structures that will continue to build evaluation capacity (Volkov & King, 2007). This extended engagement has been a primary focus of much of her work.

However, King recognizes that many evaluations will be more short term in nature. Thus, she recently developed a procedure, called *interactive evaluation practice* (IEP), for fostering participation and obtaining use. She defines IEP as "the intentional act of engaging people in making decisions, taking action, and reflecting while conducting an evaluation study" (King &

Stevahn, 2007). In this procedure, King defines evaluation as "a process of systematic inquiry designed to provide sound information about the characteristics, activities, or outcomes of a program or policy for a valued purpose" (King & Stevahn, 2007). To enhance the possibility of use, King is concerned with creating a participatory environment throughout the evaluation process. This environment must include, among other things, shared meaning of experiences among participants and a great degree of interpersonal and organizational trust.

King advocates for efforts toward engagement in communication and discussion to create shared meaning among participants. She is concerned about identifying and fostering leaders during the evaluation process, contending that leaders are needed to "attract or recruit people to the evaluation process, who are eager to learn and facilitate the process . . . and who are willing to stay the course when things go wrong" (King, 1998, p. 64). King also focuses on trust building as one of the fundamental requirements for a successful participatory evaluation, urging evaluators to pay close attention to the interpersonal dynamics that occur (King & Stevahn, 2007). She indicates that without effective interpersonal interaction, there is a possibility that the success of the evaluation enterprise is at risk.

King describes the evaluator's role as part leader, part manager, and part wise counselor. The evaluator is aided in these roles by acting as a reflective practitioner, which "is especially important at key transition points in the study." The roles suggested by King acknowledge the importance of the interpersonal factor when conducting evaluations.

A FINAL NOTE

We faced two main challenges in writing this chapter. First, in sorting out the views and positions of theorists, we needed to make specific placements on particular branches of the tree. Second, we needed to determine which theorists to include on the tree.

Let us consider the first of these issues. The theory tree is posited on the view that ultimately one or another of the three dimensions, depicted as branches, is of the highest priority for each theorist. We offer a concrete example to demonstrate the way we made decisions and the difficulty we faced in making these judgments. When writing the first version of the tree, one of our students, as part of a class assignment, contacted David Fetterman to inquire about the influences on his evaluation theoretic positions. He cited three: (1) anthropological/ethnographic (Spindler and Pelto being the two most prominent), (2) social justice (House being the most prominent), and (3) evaluation utilization (Patton and Alkin being the two most prominent). Now, where should we place him?

An emphasis on educational anthropology/ethnography could possibly center him on methods, albeit an alternative view of methods from those who dominate the methods branch. Such a focal point would mean that to Fetterman the most important element of evaluation would be the use of ethnographic methods. And although he has a strong preference for using qualitative methods in evaluation, he certainly does not limit his work to the use of such methods. An emphasis on social justice would imply that the purpose of an evaluation is to place a value on the outcome of the evaluation that in some way supports social justice ideals. For Fetterman, social justice is served through the elimination of reliance on others to engage in activities that lead to program improvement; it does not mean judging a program based on whether or not it meets the criteria derived from a specific set of socially just ideals. And finally, an emphasis on utilization implies that the main concern is that utilization of evaluation findings occurs. In the case of Fetterman, the utilization is process use, namely, the process of conducting the evaluation leads to empowerment.

It may be that Fetterman was led to evaluation through his work in educational anthropology and ethnography (see Fetterman, 1984, 1988; Fetterman & Pitman, 1986). In his earliest writings, Fetterman identifies participant observation as a key element of ethnographic educational evaluation and stresses the importance of using a cultural perspective to interpret and analyze data. He advocates strongly for data interpretation through the eyes of those involved in the evaluation rather than through the eyes of the researcher. Yet despite these anthropological roots, he later began to think of the principal focus of an evaluation in another way; that is, ethnography became the primary methodology for the conduct of evaluations that had other primary motivations.

Another question arises in analyzing Fetterman's work: Is the primary focus valuing outcomes in a way that achieves social justice, which would place him on the valuing branch? Or, alternatively, is the primary focus for Fetterman related to the use, specifically the process use, of evaluation? We believe that, as Fetterman describes it, the act of empowering focuses on the process of engaging in evaluation; that is, by training individuals to engage in evaluation activities, they become empowered. In the language of evaluation utilization, empowerment evaluation involves instrumental process use. Thus, while noting a deep concern for social justice and a strong preference for (and early evaluation roots in) anthropological/ethnographic methods, we were led to place Fetterman on the utilization branch. The determination of a theorist's placement on a branch of the evaluation theory tree was not always this difficult, but it always required similarly careful consideration and analysis of trade-offs.

The second issue, concerning which evaluation theories to include on the tree, also offered particular challenges. These have been addressed to a certain extent earlier in Chapter 1, where we designated distinctions between evaluation methodologists, evaluation analysts, evaluation interpreters/teachers, and evaluation theorists. A further limitation on theory selection is our focus on general evaluation theorists, as opposed to those who specifically focus on evaluation in a particular field (e.g., education, social welfare, or public health). Consequently, evaluation works authored by theorists such as Steckler and Linnan (2002) or Astin (1991) have not been included.

It is also important to note that this book represents the theoretical perspectives of those residing and working in North America. Certainly, there are broad theoretical views from other parts of the world, written in English or in other languages and not translated into English. While it is not included in this chapter, the work of theorists in Europe and Australasia is discussed in later chapters, and some of what is presented there is incorporated into an expanded theory tree described in the last chapter.

With our more restrictive focus on North American theorists, we also deleted Barry MacDonald and John Owen from this version of the tree because both reside outside North America (Great Britain and Australia, respectively) and their writings relate to work in these countries. We also removed Eisner from the tree, but we did choose to include a description of his work in this chapter. This is because a primary argument of Eisner's is centered on the importance of evaluators having domain-specific knowledge and expertise—and an argument around this issue still exists today. Nevertheless, his connoisseurship approach as a prescriptive evaluation approach is less relevant. Finally, while the ideas of Thomas Owen, Robert Wolf, and Malcolm Provus were innovative at the time, there is little evidence to suggest that their theoretical work has persisted in influencing the field today, and so we also removed these theorists from the current version of the tree.

NOTES

1. This additional dimension of his work is reflected, in part, in his work with Cook (Cook & Campbell, 1976, 1979, 1986).

2. In the Berk et al. (1985) manuscript, the randomized field experiment approach is referred to as "social policy experimentation."

3. Scriven is discussed later in this chapter.

4. Weiss did some of the early writing on evaluation utilization (e.g., Weiss, 1972). Subsequent research was conducted by Alkin, Kosecoff, Fitz-Gibbon, and Seligman (1974), Patton (1978), Alkin, Daillak, and White (1979), King and Pechman (1982), Braskamp, Brown, and Newman (1982), and others.

REFERENCES

Abma, T., & Stake, R. (2001). Stake's responsive evaluation: Core ideas and evolution. In J. Greene & T. Abma (Eds.), *Responsive evaluation: Vol. 92. New directions for evaluation* (pp. 7–22). San Francisco, CA: Jossey-Bass.

Alkin, M. (1972a). Accountability defined. *Evaluation Comment: The Journal of Educational Evaluation, 3,* 1–5.

Alkin, M. (1972b). Evaluation theory development. In C. Weiss (Ed.), *Evaluation action programs* (pp. 105–117). Boston, MA: Allyn & Bacon.

Alkin, M. (1990). *Debates on evaluation.* Newbury Park, CA: Sage.

Alkin, M. (1991). Evaluation theory development. In M. W. McLaughlin & D. C. Phillips (Eds.), *Evaluation and education: At quarter-century* (90th yearbook of the National Society for the Study of Education, Part II; pp. 91–112). Chicago, IL: University of Chicago Press.

Alkin, M., & Christie, C. A. (2004). An evaluation theory tree. In M. C. Alkin (Ed.), *Evaluation roots* (pp. 12–66). Thousand Oaks, CA: Sage.

Alkin, M., Daillak, R., & White, P. (1979). *Using evaluations: Does evaluation make a difference?* (Sage Library of Social Research, Vol. 76). Beverly Hills, CA: Sage.

Alkin, M., Hofstetter, C., & Ai, X. (1998). Stakeholder involvement in evaluation. In A. Reynolds & H. Walberg (Eds.), *Evaluation for educational productivity.* Greenwich, CT: JAI Press.

Alkin, M., Kosecoff, J., Fitz-Gibbon, C., & Seligman, R. (1974). *Evaluation and decision-making: The Title VII experience.* Los Angeles, CA: Center for the Study of Evaluation.

Alkin, M., & Taut, S. (2003). Unbundling evaluation use. *Studies in Educational Evaluation, 29*, 1–12.

Astin, A. (1991). *Assessment for excellence: The philosophy and practice of assessment and evaluation in higher education.* New York, NY: Macmillan.

Berk, R., Boruch, R., Chambers, O., Rossi, P., & Witte, O. (1985). Social policy experimentation: A position paper. *Evaluation Review, 9*(4), 387–429.

Bloom, B., Englehart, D., Furst, E., Hill, W., & Krathwohl, D. (1956). *Taxonomy of educational objectives: Book I. The cognitive domain.* New York, NY: David McKay.

Boruch, R. (1997). *Randomized experiments for planning and evaluation.* Thousand Oaks, CA: Sage.

Boruch, R., McSweeney, A., & Soderstrom, E. (1978). Randomized field experiments for program planning, development and evaluation. *Evaluation Quarterly, 2*(4), 655–695.

Boruch, R., Synder, B., & DeMoya, D. (2000). The importance of randomized field trials. *Crime & Delinquency, 46*(2), 156–180.

Braskamp, L., Brown, R., & Newman, D. (1982). Studying evaluation utilization through simulations. *Evaluation Review, 6*(1), 114–126.

Campbell, D. (1957). Factors relevant to the validity of experiments in social settings. *Psychological Bulletin, 54*, 297–312.

Campbell, D. (1975a). Assessing the impact of planned social change. In G. M. Lyons (Ed.), *Social research and public policies* (pp. 3–45). Hanover, NH: Dartmouth College, Public Affairs Center.

Campbell, D. (1975b). "Degrees of freedom" and the case study. *Comparative Political Studies, 8*, 1178–1193.

Campbell, D., & Stanley, J. (1966). *Experimental and quasi-experimental designs for research.* Chicago, IL: Rand McNally.

Chelimsky, E. (1995). The political environment of evaluation and what it means for the development of the field. *Evaluation Practice, 16*(3), 215–225.

Chelimsky, E. (1997). The coming transformations in evaluation. In E. Chelimsky & W. R. Shadish (Eds.), *Evaluation for the 21st century: A handbook* (pp. 1–26). Thousand Oaks, CA: Sage.

Chelimsky, E. (2006). The purposes of evaluation in a democratic society. In I. F. Shaw, J. C. Greene, & M. M. Mark (Eds.), *The SAGE handbook of evaluation* (pp. 33–55). Thousand Oaks, CA: Sage.

Chen, H. (1990). *Theory-driven evaluation: A comprehensive perspective.* Newbury Park, CA: Sage.

Chen, H. (2005). *Practical program evaluation.* Thousand Oaks, CA: Sage.

Chen, H., & Rossi, P. (1983). Evaluating with sense: The theory-driven approach. *Evaluation Review, 7*, 283–302.

Chen, H., & Rossi, P. (1987). The theory-driven approach to validity. *Evaluation and Program Planning, 10*, 95–103.

Christie, C. A. (2003). What guides evaluation? A study of how evaluation practice maps onto evaluation theory. In C. A. Christie (Ed.), *The practice-theory relationship in evaluation: Vol. 97. New directions for evaluation* (pp. 7–35). San Francisco, CA: Jossey-Bass.

Christie, C. A. (2007). Reported influence of evaluation data on decision-makers' actions: An empirical examination. *American Journal of Evaluation, 28*(3), 8–25.

Christie, C. A., & Fleischer, D. N. (2009). Social inquiry paradigms as a frame for the debate on credible evidence. In S. I. Donaldson, C. A. Christie, & M. M. Mark (Eds.), *What counts as credible evidence in applied research and evaluation practice?* (pp. 19–30). Thousand Oaks, CA: Sage.

Cook, T., & Campbell, D. (1976). The design and conduct of quasi-experiments and true experiments in field settings. In M. D. Dunnette (Ed.), *Handbook of industrial and organizational psychology* (pp. 223–326). Chicago, IL: Rand McNally.

Cook, T., & Campbell, D. (1979). *Quasi-experimentation: Design and analysis issues for field settings.* Chicago, IL: Rand McNally.

Cook, T., & Campbell, D. (1986). The causal assumptions of quasi-experimental practice. *Synthese, 68,* 141–180.

Cook, T., & Gruder, C. (1978). Metaevaluation research. *Evaluation Quarterly, 2,* 5–51.

Cousins, J., & Earl, L. (1992). The case for participatory evaluation. *Educational Evaluation and Policy Analysis, 14*(4), 397–418.

Cousins, J., & Earl, L. (Eds.). (1995). *Participatory evaluation in education: Studies in evaluation use and organizational learning.* London, England: Falmer Press.

Cousins, J. B., Goh, S., & Clark, S. (2005). Data use leads to data valuing: Evaluative inquiry for school decision making. *Leadership and Policy in Schools, 4,* 155–176.

Cousins, J. B., & Whitmore, E. (1998). Framing participatory evaluation. In E. Whitmore (Ed.), *Understanding and practicing participatory evaluation: Vol. 80. New directions for evaluation* (pp. 5–23). San Francisco, CA: Jossey-Bass.

Cronbach, L. (1982). *Designing evaluations of educational and social programs.* San Francisco, CA: Jossey-Bass.

Cronbach, L., & Associates. (1980). *Toward reform of program evaluation: Aims, methods, and institutional arrangements.* San Francisco, CA: Jossey-Bass.

Cronbach, L., & Snow, R. (1977). *Aptitudes and instructional methods: A handbook for research on interactions.* New York, NY: Irvington.

Diesing, P. (1966). Objectivism vs. subjectivism in the social sciences. *Philosophy of Science, 33*(1–2), 124–133.

Durkheim, E. (1966). *The rules of sociological method* (8th ed.; G. C. Catlin, Ed.; S. A. Sulovay & J. H. Mueller, Trans.). New York, NY: Free Press.

Eisner, E. (1976). Educational connoisseurship and criticism: Their form and function in educational evaluation. *Journal of Aesthetic Evaluation or Education, 10,* 135–150.

Eisner, E. (1985). *The art of educational evaluation: A personal view.* Philadelphia, PA: Falmer Press.

Eisner, E. (1991a). *The enlightened eye.* New York, NY: Macmillan.

Eisner, E. (1991b). Taking a second look: Educational connoisseurship revisited. In M. W. McLaughlin & D. C. Phillips (Eds.), *Evaluation and education: At quarter-century* (90th yearbook of the National Society for the Study of Education, Part II; pp. 169–187). Chicago, IL: University of Chicago Press.

Eisner, E. (1994). *The educational imagination: On the design and evaluation of educational programs* (3rd ed.). New York, NY: Macmillan.

Eisner, E. (1998). *The enlightened eye: Qualitative inquiry and the enhancement of educational practice.* Upper Saddle River, NJ: Merrill.

Fetterman, D. (1984). Ethnography in educational research: The dynamics of diffusion. In D. M. Fetterman (Ed.), *Ethnography in educational evaluation* (pp. 21–35). Beverly Hills, CA: Sage.

Fetterman, D. (1988). A national ethnographic evaluation: An executive summary of the ethnographic component of the Career Intern Program Study. In D. M. Fetterman (Ed.), *Qualitative approaches to evaluation in education: The silent scientific revolution* (pp. 262–273). New York, NY: Praeger.

Fetterman, D. (1994). Steps of empowerment education: From California to Cape Town. *Evaluation and Program Planning, 17*(3), 305–313.

Fetterman, D. (1996). Empowerment evaluation: An introduction to theory and practice. In D. M. Fetterman, S. J. Kaftarian, & A. Wandersman (Eds.), *Empowerment evaluation: Knowledge and tools for self-assessment and accountability* (pp. 3–48). Thousand Oaks, CA: Sage.

Fetterman, D. (1998). Empowerment evaluation and accreditation in higher education. In E. Chelimsky & W. Shadish (Eds.), *Evaluation for the 21st century: A handbook* (pp. 381–395). Thousand Oaks, CA: Sage.

Fetterman, D. (2001). *Foundations of empowerment evaluation.* Thousand Oaks, CA: Sage.

Fetterman, D., & Pitman, M. (Eds.). (1986). *Educational evaluation: Ethnography in theory, practice, and politics.* Beverly Hills, CA: Sage.

Geertz, C. (1973). *The interpretation of cultures*. New York, NY: Basic Books.

Greene, J. C. (2000). Challenges in practicing deliberative democratic evaluation. In K. E. Ryan & L. DeStefano (Eds.), *Evaluation as a democratic process: Promoting inclusion, dialogue, and deliberation: Vol. 85. New directions for evaluation* (pp. 13–26). San Francisco, CA: Jossey-Bass.

Greene, J. C. (2005). Evaluators as the stewards of the public good. In S. Hood, R. Hopson, & H. Frierson (Eds.), *The role of culture and cultural context: A mandate for inclusion, the discovery of truth, and understanding in evaluative theory and practice* (pp. 7–20). Greenwich, CT: Information Age.

Greene, J. C. (2009). Evidence as "proof" and evidence as "inkling." In S. I. Donaldson, C. A. Christie, & M. M. Mark (Eds.), *What counts as credible evidence in applied research and evaluation practice?* (pp. 153–167). Thousand Oaks, CA: Sage.

Guba, E., & Lincoln, Y. (1989). *Fourth generation evaluation*. Newbury Park, CA: Sage.

Hammond, R. (1973). Evaluation at the local level. In B. R. Worthen & J. R. Sanders (Eds.), *Educational evaluation: Theory and practice*. Belmont, CA: Wadsworth.

Henry, G. (1995). *Graphing data: Techniques for display analysis*. Thousand Oaks, CA: Sage.

Henry, G. (1996). Does the public have a role in evaluation? Surveys and democratic discourse. In M. T. Braverman & J. K. Slater (Eds.), *Advances in survey research: Vol. 70. New directions for evaluation* (pp. 3–15). San Francisco, CA: Jossey-Bass.

Henry, G., Julnes, G., & Mark, M. (Eds.). (1998). *Realist evaluation: An emerging theory in support of practice: Vol. 78. New directions for evaluation*. San Francisco, CA: Jossey-Bass.

Henry, G. T., & Mark, M. M. (2003). Beyond use: Understanding evaluation's influence on attitudes and actions. *American Journal of Evaluation, 24*, 294–314.

House, E. (1991). Evaluation and social justice: Where are we? In M. W. McLaughlin & D. C. Phillips (Eds.), *Evaluation and education: At quarter century* (90th yearbook of the National Society for the Study of Education, Part II; pp. 233–247). Chicago, IL: University of Chicago Press.

House, E. (1993). *Professional evaluation: Social impact and political consequences*. Newbury Park, CA: Sage.

House, E. (2001a). Responsive evaluation (and its influence on deliberative democratic evaluation). In J. C. Greene & T. A. Abma (Eds.), *Co-constructing a contextually responsive evaluation framework: Vol. 92. New directions for evaluation* (pp. 23–30). San Francisco, CA: Jossey-Bass.

House, E. (2001b). Unfinished business: Causes and values. *American Journal of Evaluation, 22*, 309–315.

House, E. R., & Howe, K. R. (1999). *Values in evaluation and social research*. Thousand Oaks, CA: Sage.

House, E. R., & Howe, K. R. (2000). Deliberative democratic evaluation. In K. E. Ryan & L. DeStefano (Eds.), *Evaluation as a democratic process: Promoting inclusion, dialogue, and deliberation: Vol. 85. New directions for evaluation* (pp. 3–12). San Francisco, CA: Jossey-Bass.

Joint Committee on Standards for Educational Evaluation. (1994). *The program evaluation standards: How to assess evaluations of educational programs* (2nd ed.). Thousand Oaks, CA: Sage.

King, J. A. (1998, Winter). Making sense of participatory evaluation on practice. In E. Whitmore (Ed.), *Understanding and practicing participatory evaluation: Vol. 80. New directions for evaluation* (pp. 57–67). San Francisco, CA: Jossey-Bass.

King, J. A., & Pechman, E. (1982). *Improving evaluation use in local schools*. Washington, DC: National Institute of Education.

King, J. A., & Stevahn, L. (2007). *Interactive evaluation in practice: Managing the interpersonal dynamics of program evaluation*. Thousand Oaks, CA: Sage.

Kirkhart, K. E. (2000). Reconceptualizing evaluation use: An integrated theory of influence. In V. J. Caracelli & H. Preskill (Eds.), *The expanding scope of evaluation use: Vol. 88.*

New directions for evaluation (pp. 5–23). San Francisco, CA: Jossey-Bass.

Krathwohl, D., Bloom, B., & Masia, B. (1964). *Taxonomy of educational objectives: Book 2. Affective domain.* New York, NY: David McKay.

Levin, H. M. (2005). Cost–benefit analysis. In S. Mathison (Ed.), *Encyclopedia of evaluation* (pp. 86–90). Thousand Oaks, CA: Sage.

Levin, H. M., & McEwan, P. J. (2001). *Cost-effectiveness analysis: Methods and applications* (2nd ed.). Thousand Oaks, CA: Sage.

Madaus, G., & Stufflebeam, D. (1989). *Educational evaluation: Classic works of Ralph W. Tyler.* Boston, MA: Kluwer.

Mark, M. M., & Henry, G. T. (2004). The mechanisms and outcomes of evaluation influence. *Evaluation, 10*(1), 35–57.

Mark, M., Henry, G., & Julnes, G. (1998). A realist theory of evaluation practice. In G. Henry, G. Julnes, & M. M. Mark (Eds.), *Realist evaluation: An emerging theory in support of practice: Vol. 78. New directions for evaluation* (pp. 3–32). San Francisco, CA: Jossey-Bass.

Mark, M., Henry, G., & Julnes, G. (2000). *Evaluation: An integrated framework for understanding, guiding, and improving public and nonprofit policies and programs.* San Francisco, CA: Jossey-Bass.

Marx, K. (1932). *Capital: A critique of political economy* (F. Engels, Ed.; S. Moore & E. Aveling, Trans.; Vol. 1). Chicago, IL: Charles H. Kerr. (Revised and amplified according to the fourth German edition by Ernest Untermann)

Mathison, S. (Ed.). (2005). *Encyclopedia of evaluation.* Thousand Oaks, CA: Sage.

Mertens, D. M. (1999). Inclusive evaluation: Implications of transformative theory for evaluation. *American Journal of Evaluation, 20,* 1–14.

Mertens, D. M. (2009). *Transformative research and evaluation.* New York, NY: Guilford Press.

Metfessel, N., & Michael, W. (1967). A paradigm involving multiple criterion measures for the evaluation of the effectiveness of school programs. *Educational and Psychological Measurement, 27,* 931–943.

Mosteller, F., & Boruch, R. (Eds.). (2002). *Evidence matters: Randomized trials in education research.* Washington, DC: Brookings Institution Press.

Patton, M. Q. (1978). *Utilization-focused evaluation.* Beverly Hills, CA: Sage.

Patton, M. Q. (1986). *Utilization-focused evaluation* (2nd ed.). Beverly Hills, CA: Sage.

Patton, M. Q. (1997). *Utilization-focused evaluation: The new century text* (3rd ed.). Thousand Oaks, CA: Sage.

Patton, M. Q. (2002). Utilization-focused evaluation. In D. L. Stufflebeam, G. F. Madaus, & T. Kellaghan (Eds.), *Evaluation Models: Vol. 49. Evaluation in education and human services* (pp. 425–438). Boston, MA: Kluwer Academic.

Patton, M. Q. (2008). Advocacy impact evaluation. *Journal of Multidisciplinary Evaluation, 5*(9), 1–10.

Patton, M. Q. (2010). *Developmental evaluation: Applying complexity concepts to enhance innovation and use.* New York, NY: Guilford Press.

Patton, M. Q., Grimes, P., Guthrie, K., Brennan, N., French, B., & Blyth, D. (1977). In search of impact. In C. H. Weiss (Ed.), *Using social research in public policy making* (pp. 141–164). Lexington, MA: Lexington Books.

Popham, W. (1973). *Evaluating instruction.* Englewood Cliffs, NJ: Prentice Hall.

Popham, W. (1975). *Educational evaluation.* Englewood Cliffs, NJ: Prentice Hall.

Popham, W. (1988). *Educational evaluation* (2nd ed.). Englewood Cliffs, NJ: Prentice Hall.

Preskill, H. (2004). The transformational power of evaluation: Passion, purpose, and practice. In M. C. Alkin (Ed.), *Evaluation roots: Tracing theorists' views and influences* (pp. 343–355). Thousand Oaks, CA: Sage.

Preskill, H., & Torres, R. T. (1998, November 4–7). *Evaluative inquiry as transformative learning.* Paper presented at the American Evaluation Association Annual Conference, Chicago, IL.

Preskill, H., & Torres, R. T. (2000). The learning dimension of evaluation use. In V. J. Caracelli & H. Preskill (Eds.), *The expanding scope of* evaluation use: Vol. 88. New directions for evaluation (pp. 25–37). San Francisco, CA: Jossey-Bass.

Rawls, J. (1971). *A theory of justice*. Cambridge, MA: Harvard University Press.

Rossi, P., & Freeman, H. (1985). *Evaluation: A systematic approach* (3rd ed.). Beverly Hills, CA: Sage.

Rossi, P., Freeman, H., & Wright, S. (1979). *Evaluation: A systematic approach*. Beverly Hills, CA: Sage.

Rossi, P., Lipsey, M., & Freeman, H. (2004). *Evaluation: A systematic approach* (7th ed.). Thousand Oaks, CA: Sage.

Scriven, M. (1967). The methodology of evaluation. In R. E. Stake (Ed.), *Curriculum evaluation* (American Educational Research Association Monograph Series on Evaluation No. 1). Chicago, IL: Rand McNally.

Scriven, M. (1972a). The methodology of evaluation. In C. H. Weiss (Ed.), *Evaluating action programs: Readings in social action and education*. Boston, MA: Allyn & Bacon.

Scriven, M. (1972b). Pros and cons about goal-free evaluation. *Evaluation Comment: The Journal of Educational Evaluation, 3*(4), 1–7.

Scriven, M. (1974). Evaluation perspectives and procedures. In J. W. Popham (Ed.), *Evaluation in education: Current application* (pp. 3–93). Berkeley, CA: McCutcheon.

Scriven, M. (1976). Evaluation bias and its control. In G. V. Glass (Ed.), *Evaluation studies review annual* (Vol. 1). Beverly Hills, CA: Sage.

Scriven, M. (1983). Evaluation ideologies. In G. F. Madaus, M. Scriven, & D. L. Stufflebeam (Eds.), *Evaluation models: Viewpoints on educational and human services evaluation* (pp. 229–260). Boston, MA: Kluwer-Nijhoff.

Scriven, M. (1986). New frontiers of evaluation. *Evaluation Practice, 7,* 7–44.

Scriven, M. (1991). *Evaluation thesaurus* (4th ed.). Newbury Park, CA: Sage.

Scriven, M. (2001). Evaluation: Future tense. *American Journal of Evaluation, 22*(3), 301–307.

Scriven, M. (2003). Evaluation theory and metatheory. In T. Kellaghan, D. L. Stufflebeam, & L. A. Wingate (Eds.), *International handbook of educational evaluation: Part one* (pp. 15–31). Dordrecht, Netherlands: Kluwer Academics.

Shadish, W., Cook, T., & Leviton, L. (1991). *Foundations of program evaluation: Theories of practice*. Newbury Park, CA: Sage.

Shavelson, R. J., & Towne, L. (Eds.). (2002). *Scientific research in education* (National Research Council, Committee on Scientific Principles for Educational Research). Washington, DC: National Academy Press.

Stake, R. (1967). The countenance of educational evaluation. *Teachers College Record, 68,* 523–540.

Stake, R. (2000). A modest commitment to the promotion of democracy. In K. E. Ryan & L. DeStefano (Eds.), *Evaluation as a democratic process: Promoting inclusion, dialogue, and deliberation: Vol. 85. New directions for evaluation* (pp. 97–107). San Francisco, CA: Jossey-Bass.

Stake, R. (2001). A problematic heading. *American Journal of Evaluation, 22,* 349–354.

Stake, R. (2005). Qualitative case studies. In N. K. Denzin & Y. S. Lincoln (Eds.), *The SAGE handbook of qualitative research* (3rd ed., pp. 433–466). Thousand Oaks, CA: Sage.

Stake, R., & Easley, J. (Eds.). (1979). *Case studies in science education*. Urbana: University of Illinois, Center for Instructional Research and Curriculum Evaluation.

Stake, R. E. (1974). Program evaluation, particularly responsive evaluation. In *New trends in evaluation* (Report No. 35, pp. 1–20). Gothenburg, Sweden: University of Gothenburg, Institute of Education.

Stake, R. E. (1975). *Program evaluation, particularly responsive evaluation* (Occasional Paper No. 5). Kalamazoo: Western Michigan University Evaluation Center.

Steckler, A., & Linnan, L. (2002). *Process evaluation for public health interventions and research*. San Francisco, CA: Jossey-Bass.

Stufflebeam, D. (1983). The CIPP model for program evaluation. In G. F. Madaus, M. S. Scriven, & D. L. Stufflebeam (Eds.), *Evaluation models: Viewpoints on educational and human services evaluation* (pp. 117–141). Boston, MA: Kluwer-Nijhoff.

Stufflebeam, D. (2000). Lessons in contracting for evaluations. *American Journal of Evaluation, 21,* 293–314.

Stufflebeam, D. (2001). Interdisciplinary Ph.D. programming in evaluation. *American Journal of Evaluation, 22,* 445–455.

Stufflebeam, D. (2003, October). *The CIPP model for evaluation.* Paper presented at the annual conference of the Oregon Program Evaluators Network, Portland, OR. Retrieved from http://www.wmich.edu/evalctr/pubs/CIPP-ModelOregon10-03.pdf

Suchman, E. (1967). *Evaluative research: Principles and practice in public service and social action programs.* New York, NY: Russell Sage.

Tashakkori, A., & Teddlie, C. (1998). *Mixed methodology: Combining qualitative and quantitative approaches.* Thousand Oaks, CA: Sage.

Tyler, R. W. (1942). General statement on evaluation. *Journal of Educational Research, 35,* 492–501.

Volkov, B. B., & King, J. A. (2007). *A checklist for building organizational evaluation capacity.* Retrieved from http://www.wmich.edu/evalctr//archive_checklists/ecb.pdf

Wagner, R. B. (1989). *Accountability in education: A philosophical inquiry.* New York, NY: Routledge.

Weiss, C. H. (Ed.). (1972). *Evaluating action programs: Readings in social action and education.* Boston, MA: Allyn & Bacon.

Weiss, C. H. (1976). Using research in the policy process: Potential and constraints. *Policy Studies Journal, 4,* 224–228.

Weiss, C. H. (1979). The many meanings of research utilization. *Public Administration Review, 39*(5), 426–431.

Weiss, C. H. (1981). Doing research or doing policy [Review of *Toward Reform of Program Evaluation*]. *Evaluation and Program Planning, 4,* 397–402.

Weiss, C. H. (1991). Evaluation research in the political context: Sixteen years and four administrations later. In M. W. McLaughlin & D. C. Phillips (Eds.), *Evaluation and education: At quarter century* (90th yearbook of the National Society for the Study of Education, Part II; pp. 211–231). Chicago, IL: University of Chicago Press.

Weiss, C. H. (with Bucuvalas, M.). (1980). *Social science research and decision-making.* New York, NY: Columbia University Press.

Weiss, C. H., Murphy-Graham, E., & Birkeland, S. (2005). An alternate route to policy influence: How evaluations affect D.A.R.E. *American Journal of Evaluation, 26,* 12–30.

Weiss, C. H., Murphy-Graham, E., Petrosino, A., & Gandhi, A. (2008). The fairy godmother—and her warts: Making the dream of evidence-based policy come true. *American Journal of Evaluation, 29,* 29–47.

Wholey, J. (1983). *Evaluation and effective public management.* Boston, MA: Little, Brown.

Wholey, J. S., Hatry, H. P., & Newcomer, K. (Eds.). (2010). *Handbook of practical program evaluation.* San Francisco, CA: Jossey-Bass.

PART II

METHODS

3

DONALD CAMPBELL

The Accidental Evaluator

William R. Shadish and Jason K. Luellen

CAMPBELL'S EVALUATION POINT OF VIEW

Donald T. Campbell passed away in 1996, but given his central importance to the field of evaluation, representing him in this book seems almost essential, so we have been asked to write this chapter about him in his place. Though we have more than passing familiarity with Campbell and his ideas (Shadish, Cook, & Campbell, 2002; Shadish, Cook, & Leviton, 1991), our reconstruction in this chapter may be as debatable as it is accurate, especially on personal matters in the last section, so we encourage additions and corrections to what we write below.

Campbell took on many roles throughout his 40-year intellectual career: social psychologist, social science methodologist, philosopher of science, sociologist of science, and evaluator. Yet underlying all this apparent diversity, the central theme of Campbell's work was describing, explaining, and improving how humans, including scientists, learn about the real world; and he was particularly interested in understanding and controlling both substantive and methodological biases. His substantive work is less well-known among evaluators, but it included bias in visual illusions, lines of communication, and especially social attitudes (Campbell, 1981).

Most evaluators are more familiar with Campbell's work on methods, with factors that bias the collection, analysis, and interpretation of social data. Most prominently, he proposed a validity typology (Campbell, 1957; Campbell & Stanley, 1963) that introduced the concepts of internal validity and external validity, outlined experimental and quasi-experimental research designs, and advocated ruling out threats to internal validity, such as selection, history, and maturation, using experimental methods. He preferred the use of random assignment to treatments, but he encouraged the use of quasi-experiments when that was all the situation allowed. The quasi-experimental design options offered by Campbell and Stanley (1963) empowered practicing researchers to test causal hypotheses in less-than-ideal field settings. Campbell's validity typology evolved over the years (Cook & Campbell, 1979; Shadish et al., 2002), and the language he introduced persists to this day.

The profession of evaluation came to know Campbell through this methodological work: "Suchman's 1967 founding book on evaluative research cited my 'experimental and quasi-experimental designs' as the appropriate methodological mode, I thus became overnight both a senior program evaluator by fiat" (Campbell, 1984b, p. 13). Thus, Campbell's induction to the profession of evaluation was as much by accident as by his own design. Nevertheless, Campbell and Stanley (1963) has been rated among the most influential evaluation works (Shadish & Epstein, 1987). Campbell wrote several other influential papers linked to evaluation, including "Reforms as Experiments" (1969), "Methods for the Experimenting Society" (1971), and "Qualitative Knowing in Action Research" (1978). His "Experimenting Society," an early intellectual vision of the role of evaluation in society, proposed a society committed to identifying effective reforms suitable for broad implementation. His writing on evaluation so centered on hypotheses about cause and effect that he came to represent the experimental approach to evaluation. Campbell never said that all evaluation should be solely concerned with causal questions and experimental methods, but he clearly viewed other methods as subordinate to experimentally based knowledge.

In much of the field of evaluation, however, Campbell's writings about methods are viewed in isolation, with little awareness of the key conceptual background in his work that led him to his experimental preference. That background is best exhibited by his writings on *evolutionary epistemology* (Campbell, 1974, 1977), a term that he introduced. Evolutionary epistemology extends the Darwinian notion of biological evolution to cognitive mechanisms and ideas. Thus, the acquisition of knowledge was viewed as a process of generating and testing falsifiable hypotheses, and retaining those that solved the problems at issue. Experimental methods were the key to evaluating those solutions. His work on evolutionary epistemology spanned 40 years, bringing him into personal acquaintance with Karl Popper, Michael Polanyi, W.V. Quine, and Konrad Lorenz. The work is summarized in his William James Lectures at Harvard, which long lay unpublished because Quine (who was rarely enthusiastic about any work) liked but did not love the work, so Campbell kept revising.

His interest in the evolution of ideas led him beyond philosophy to the history and sociology of science, discovering some sources of validity and invalidity that lie in the social organization of science rather than in the mechanics of research design. He adopted Popper's stance that knowledge is facilitated through criticism, calling for a "disputatious community of scholars" (Campbell, 1984a, p. 44) whose intellectual debates would help evaluation to flourish, creating a field that takes from science its open system of criticism and support, and expose more biases. He preferred the simultaneous funding of multiple evaluations of a program from different perspectives.

Yet through all this, Campbell rejected the "anything goes" philosophy prominent in scholars, from philosophers such as Feyerabend to some qualitative sociologists, and he rejected the antiscience, antiquantitative turn that came to dominate some areas of scholarship. After all, in biological evolution, variations are evaluated by their survival value, and Campbell believed the same should be true in knowledge construction. By all means, he said, diversify and debate the nature of the critical standards to be applied in this process, but be critical. Though his advocacy of experimental methods led him to be branded a logical positivist among evaluators who did not know his corpus of works, it is clear he rejected that philosophy of science in favor of evolutionary epistemology, a weak relativist sociology of knowledge, and an appreciation for cultural relativism.

In the end, however, Campbell's experimental approach to evaluation became just one small part of the field. Critics challenged his Experimenting Society, particularly the notion that experimental methods were preferred for evaluation. They argued that experimental methods were insufficient to address social problems in a world where policy practice is entangled with politics, economy, and social pressures; questioned the importance of noncausal questions and nonexperimental methods; complained that experimentally based knowledge was not fully implemented in solving social problems; and pointed out limitations of experimental methods. Eventually, the field of evaluation rejected Campbell's Experimenting Society as too narrow and Utopian, preferring a broader vision of the role of evaluation. Even so, because bias remains a central problem for evaluation, the solutions Campbell offered will be his greatest legacy.

Christie and Alkin's theory tree incorporates a large array of diverse evaluation thinking in one fell swoop. As such, it could be a useful orienting device to general thinking in evaluation, especially for the novice who is just learning about the field. Christie and Alkin place Campbell on the methods branch of their theory tree, referring to him as a "methodologist who has influenced evaluation." This is an apt characterization given that Campbell's early methodological writings on experimental and quasi-experimental designs were appropriated by Suchman to be a paradigm for evaluation, despite the fact that Campbell did not originally have that intention. Though Campbell did discuss such matters as use and valuing, those discussions were secondary to his thinking on knowledge construction.

In the system we used in Shadish et al. (1991), methodology was part of the larger topic of knowledge construction that included epistemology and ontology. These topics are not specifically addressed in the theory tree. The loss is not trivial, for Campbell's advocacy of experimental methods cannot adequately be understood apart from his evolutionary epistemology and his sociology of knowledge construction. Those works address issues that are mostly ignored by other theorists on the methods branch.

Further, Shadish et. al. (1991) comment on a theory of the evaluand—for example, of social programs in the case of program evaluation or of products in the case of product evaluation—that helps the evaluator to understand how change occurs in the evaluand (Shadish et al., 1991). Such a theory is central to Campbell's work in the form of his Experimenting Society. Even though the Experimenting Society was too Utopian for evaluation, evaluation theory needs to have a place to discuss and compare it with parallel theories that are implicit or explicit in other evaluation theories.

PERSONAL INFLUENCES ON CAMPBELL'S CAREER

Reconstructing personal influences on the intellectual career of another is a difficult and dangerous task, particularly when that person is no longer living to offer rebuttal. So, in preparing this section, we relied on Campbell's autobiographical commentary (Campbell, 1981) and on personal observations passed on to us by those who knew him at Northwestern University.

Reading about Campbell is inspirational to any young researcher worried about projects that are rejected, failed, unfinished, unpublished, or mistaken in retrospect. He was age 33 before his first publication. He published in unrefereed journals. Among his most highly cited works were his unpublished William James Lectures at Harvard on evolutionary epistemology and his also unpublished "Qualitative Knowing in Action Research." (He eventually did publish them in an edited book toward the end of his career.) He worked on a diverse array of research topics, which included Yurok tribal myths as projective test protocols, emotional judgments using Olive Oyl cartoons from the "Popeye" series in *The New Yorker*, social attitudes toward various ethnic groups (his dissertation), morale among submarine crews after World War II, and the relationship between hair length and hardheadedness.

Campbell tells us little about personal influences on his work before graduate school, save for passing comments on how his fundamentalist religious upbringing affected his work on human moral behavior, and on how his family encouraged children to discuss matters of intellect at home. We can infer some other influences through knowledge of Campbell's work, for example, the influence of Tolman on Campbell's understanding of academic leadership and his graduate exposure to Kurt Lewin's action research seminar. However, many sources suggest that a crucial influence on Campbell was his time on the faculty at University of Chicago, his second position after a brief stint at Ohio State University. He experienced the atmosphere at Chicago as repressive, with many young professors hired to compete for few tenured positions and where faculty were afraid to share or publish ideas lest they be found to be less than intellectual giants. After a few years, he left Chicago for Northwestern after being told of the low likelihood he would ever be tenured there. His Chicago experience led him to foster the opposite atmosphere at North-western, where people could speak their minds without fear of ridicule and could generate diverse ideas that might often be dead ends; where the intellectual culture was more important than the individual persons; and where the best work came from theory groups working together more than from individuals competing with each other. The weekly "Social Psychology Sack Lunch" epitomized this atmosphere, aiming to generate ideas that might lead to novel methods, many of which did not succeed as well as hoped (e.g., cross-lagged panel design) but some of which bore fruit (e.g., regression discontinuity).

His Chicago experience also led him to be generous and gentle with young scholars (though he speaks of giving priority to student coauthors even at Ohio State), both graduate students and young professors, encouraging them to disagree with him and focusing on the positives in their work more than on the negatives. This extended beyond the intellectual to the social relationships. He would frequently take young scholars out and pay for their meals. Campbell was loved for this supportive style, generating great loyalty to him as person and scholar.

One can see, then, that Campbell put his evolutionary epistemology into practice in his academic and social career. He was an intellectual Darwinist of the kind who believed in generating and spreading a very large number of ideas (akin to blind variations) in hopes that some of them would solve problems and be incorporated into the accepted canon. From his early diverse undergraduate coursework in genetics, anthropology, and sociology, he constantly exposed himself to a wide array of ideas from many different disciplines. For every successful work like Campbell and Stanley (1963) or Campbell and Fiske (1959), he produced many research projects that received little or no attention and that often were never published. He did his best to create an environment at Northwestern that encouraged such intellectual diversity, whether it be the Social Psychology Sack Lunch; interdisciplinary research groups that included philosophers, qualitative sociologists, and policy researchers as well as psychologists; or his mentoring of experimental psychology graduate students who were encouraged to take coursework in art, philosophy, and religion. In doing this, he left a legacy of intellectual creativity larger than himself, one that spread over fields as diverse as evaluation, philosophy, sociology, and psychology. His ideas, like any successful genetic variation, survive because we need them.

REFERENCES

Campbell, D. T. (1957). Factors relevant to the validity of experiments in social settings. *Psychological Bulletin, 54,* 297–312.

Campbell, D. T. (1969). Reforms as experiments. *American Psychologist, 24,* 409–429.

Campbell, D. T. (1971). *Methods for the experimenting society.* Paper presented to the Eastern Psychological Association, New York City, and to the American Psychological Association, Washington, DC.

Campbell, D. T. (1974). Evolutionary epistemology. In P. A. Schilpp (Ed.), *The philosophy of Karl Popper.* La Salle, IL: Open Court Publishing.

Campbell, D. T. (1977). *Descriptive epistemology: Psychological, sociological, and evolutionary.* William James Lectures, Harvard University.

Campbell, D. T. (1978). Qualitative knowing in action research. In M. Brenner, P. Marsh, & M. Brenner (Eds.), *The social context of methods* (pp. 184–209). London: Croom Helm.

Campbell, D. T. (1981). Comment: Another perspective on a scholarly career. In M. B. Brewer & B. E. Collins (Eds.), *Scientific inquiry and the social sciences* (pp. 453–501). San Francisco: Jossey-Bass.

Campbell, D. T. (1984a). Can we be scientific in applied science? In R. F. Connor, D. G. Altman, & C. Jackson (Eds.), *Evaluation studies review annual* (Vol. 9, pp. 26–48). Newbury Park, CA: Sage.

Campbell, D. T. (1984b). Hospital and *landsting* as continuously monitoring social polygrams: Advocacy and warning. In B. Cronholm & L. von Knorring (Eds.), *Evaluations of mental health service programs* (pp. 13–39). Stockholm: Forskningsraadet Mediciniska.

Campbell, D. T., & Fiske, D. W. (1959). Convergent and discriminant validation by the multitrait-multimethod matrix. *Psychological Bulletin, 56,* 81–105.

Campbell, D. T., & Stanley, J. C. (1963). Experimental and quasi-experimental designs for research on teaching. In N. L. Gage (Ed.), *Handbook of research on teaching* (pp. 171–246). Chicago: Rand McNally.

Cook, T. D., & Campbell, D. T. (1979). *Quasi-experimentation: Design and analysis issues for field settings.* Chicago: Rand-McNally.

Shadish, W. R., Cook, T. D., & Campbell, D. T. (2002). *Experimental and quasi-experimental designs for generalized causal inference.* Boston: Houghton Mifflin.

Shadish, W. R., Cook, T. D., & Leviton, L. C. (1991). *Foundations of program evaluation: Theories of practice.* Newbury Park, CA: Sage.

Shadish, W. R., & Epstein, R. (1987). Patterns of program evaluation practice among members of Evaluation Research Society and Evaluation Network. *Evaluation Review, 11,* 555–590.

4

ROOTS, CAHOOTS, AND COUNSEL

Robert F. Boruch

Working in the evaluation sector has been a privilege. It has been profitable in ways that have nothing to do with money. In any case, I've never been paid well enough to work with people I don't trust. This essay acknowledges only senior colleagues who account for some of my intellectual roots, in accordance with comrade Marvin Alkin's theme for this edited volume.

Regrettably, some of the colleagues recognized here are dead. Contemporary peers, younger colleagues, and family members and friends, from whom it has also been pleasing to learn, are not identified. Their recognition will come later, provided that I stay above ground long enough. As a good evaluator, I take the timeline into account. For those with little time to read, or those with restricted attention spans, the lessons laid out below are put succinctly and in italics.

THEORY AND EXPERIMENTS: ENGINEERING

Engineering education during the 1960s put little explicit value on theory. As a student at Stevens Institute of Technology, I and others in this industrious community aimed to build a structure that could stand up in a hostile environment: a bridge that would carry loads safely, a deck cannon that would not explode and kill its users, a sheet of plastic that would be uniform in quality and perform well for consumers.

Theories were nonetheless implicit in the equations that engineers used to design and test the equipment and processes of production. Those equations took time to understand. But the equations, and the theories, were imperfect, even wrong, at times.

For instance, I depended on equations published in well-regarded textbooks in mechanical engineering to design the heated extrusion barrels (cannon-like devices) that were used to produce plastic products. The barrels failed at times. I learned later that the equations on which I had depended, dignified by their presence in textbooks, were developed during World War II for the design of a naval deck cannon and that those cannons also failed at times. This was a secret of the war. So was the failure of the equations. For a contemporary example of a similar kind of learning, see Chang's article (2003) on the crater equations used to estimate the effect of low-mass, high-velocity debris hitting the ill-fated Columbia shuttle. The equations or their application were wrong, with catastrophic consequences when the shuttle reentered the atmosphere.

The more general understanding, then as now, is that mathematical models can be wrong, as well as right, and are often ambiguous in both respects, in engineering, econometrics, or any of the quantitative social sciences, including parts of evaluation research. Evidence from well-run experiments and other sources can trump the theoretical models and should do so.

STATISTICS, MODELING, AND THEORY: GRADUATE EDUCATION

As a young man, and in very small measure, I emulated Mark Twain. He declared that he would not shoot a man he had not been introduced to. Nor did he trust politicians who put younger people in the line of fire.

Consequently, I did not join the military during the Vietnam War. Having become interested in the behavioral sciences while at engineering school, I applied for PhD-level studies at a few universities. Once admitted to Iowa State University's (ISU) psychology department, I was deferred from the military draft. Deferments in the 1960s were justifiable in some respects and dreadfully unfair in others.

ISU had, in the 1960s, an ambitious psychology department, an excellent statistics department, and a very good metallurgical engineering department. I chose to study at ISU, figuring that if I flopped in psychology, I could always get back into metallurgical studies there, or I could even get back to Stevens Institute, where I'd been offered an MS fellowship in metallurgy. Also, ISU provided a research assistantship supported initially by a post-Sputnik federal grant under the National Defense and Education Act and later by fellowships from IBM and contracts from the U.S. Air Force (USAF) and other benefactors. May they be blessed. Being able to put food on the table seemed sensible for someone from a low-income family.

As a graduate student, statistical theory and applications came as revelations—beautiful in ideas, symbols, and visual portrayal. A probability distribution function, Poisson, Student's t, and so on could accurately characterize some realities in ways that were important in a scientific context. *More pertinent here, the idea of a statistical model as a rudimentary representation of how one dependent variable might be correlated with or even caused by another variable and in which one could also account for random error—a packet of ignorance about all other causes or correlates—was elegant. Though also simplistic, it was a mighty attractive and sturdy basis for impact evaluations and for correlation studies.*

The dissertation research involved fitting statistical latent trait models to multitrait, multimethod correlation matrices using restricted maximum likelihood factor analysis. This work, under the direction of Leroy Wolins, applied the models to empirical data and employed the theoretical ideas generated by Donald T. Campbell at Northwestern University and Donald Fiske at the University of Chicago. The aim was to understand the structure underlying the relationships among different ways to measure different traits—that is, statistically modeling the relationships among traits such as leadership ability, talent, and productivity, based on separate ratings made on each individual by subordinates, superiors, and peers.

I can no longer understand some of my dissertation's technical ingredients or those of the publications that resulted from it, in *Educational and Psychological Measurement, Multivariate Behavioral Research*, and elsewhere. Nor can I properly remember the contents of a paper presented at the University of Chicago, with an audience of $N = 4$, which concatenated models underlying analysis of variance with fewer constraints with models underlying factor analysis with explicit constraints (e.g., parameters specified as zero). The ideas were pretty advanced for their time, but they are now out of date. *For evaluators, new learning must at times displace the old. But keeping the history of ideas in mind is also very important.* More about this anon.

My PhD dissertation hearing was a purgatory. This was partly on account of being hung over from premature celebration and partly on account of zealous questioning during the hearing by Oscar Kempthorne, a member of my dissertation committee. It was one of the longest dissertation committee meetings on record for ISU's psychology department. *Lesson: The able evaluator needs to ensure complete sobriety in advance of meetings that involve serious interrogation even if the work product under examination is good.*

The kinds of statistical models that I used in earlier times have been elevated to a higher status and greater complexity in various disciplines. I worked my way through early versions of latent trait theory, structural modeling, and path analysis and published some decent papers in the process. *Statistical models of passive observational data help build plausible scientific story lines, as indeed they are supposed to.* Other scholars, of more talent, persistence, or aggressive temperament, especially in economics, can get Nobel prizes for such things nowadays.

An interest in learning about fair comparisons, and in making inferences in a less equivocal way than the theoretical modeling of observational data permitted, drove me to randomized controlled trials. *Results of randomized trials, when the trials are properly designed and run, produce unbiased estimates of the relative difference in the effects of two or more interventions. That the interventions are assigned randomly to individuals or entities ensures a fair comparison without heroic assumptions. Moreover, randomization tests required no complex models, just some understanding of distribution theory based on the random assignment.* Heady stuff.

ISU's statistics faculty, especially Oscar Kempthorne, a protégé and colleague of Sir Ronald Fisher, deserve high credit for mentorship about the idea of randomized controlled trials and randomization tests. In his writing at least, Kempy explained matters better than R. A. Fisher did. I and other students at the time cared little for the epistemological aspects of the topic that concern writers nowadays. *It was fairness in a comparison and a statistical statement about one's confidence that counted, and still counts, in the evidence-based policy sector.*

Despite his international stature, Kempthorne was a bit of an anomaly. Possessing only a master's degree, he took a mischievous delight in telling students that he might be an embarrassment to academia. *Lesson: Never depend only on academic credentials in universities to judge the worth of the work.* Despite Kempthorne's example, I got my PhD.

Under a USAF contract for research at ISU, my job was troubleshooting the use of UNIVAC computers for base supply systems at half a dozen USAF sites. If the wing fell off your airplane and you deserved a replacement, I was the civilian who assisted the real USAF people in trying to make the computers work properly and to re-sort the 100-odd 80-column IBM cards that had fallen to the floor, so as to get the more or less correct wing onto your flying machine. *To err is human, but it takes a computer to really screw things up*, as others have declared. A major and a senior master sergeant were valuable mentors. The major's advice was "never trust anybody above the rank of major," and the sergeant's advice was "never trust anybody above the rank of senior master sergeant." *Another lesson in distrusting credentials—facetious but important in many contexts.*

POSTGRADUATE ROOTS

Having spent much time watching the Iowa corn grow, I was eager to get to a big city. I turned down a nice opportunity to work with Harry Harman, of factor analysis fame, at Educational Testing Service in Princeton, which is a fine organization. Harman, an indirect mentor on account of my use of his book, was a peach. Princeton, however, was too precious a village and contained far too few single women with any interest in me.

In 1968, I opted for a position as research associate at the American Council on Education (ACE) in Washington, D.C. The ACE's Office of Research had developed annual surveys, under Sandy Astin's leadership, on incoming college freshmen in the United States and also engaged in research on campus protests during the Vietnam War years. I focused on programming (FORTRAN II and IV) statistical analyses of the survey results and published with other colleagues in *Sociology of Education, Education Record, Journal of Chemical Education*, and elsewhere. In those days, there was no SAS, R, or Stata. But I did have the benefit of an editor, paid by ACE, whom I exploited shamelessly to revise the ways I had learned to write (or not write) in engineering school and graduate school. *Good editors are valuable training wheels.*

The research on protests against the Vietnam War led me to the streets. It was challenging to find people on college campuses who were willing to talk under volatile conditions, as opposed to merely analyzing the data from their questionnaires. Nobody taught me how to do the fieldwork right, though the USAF experience helped. *More important, as a consequence of the street work, I developed a serious empathy with and admiration for anthropologists, ethnographers, and others who do it. Properly connecting statistical surveys or experiments with good qualitative, process-oriented investigation at the street level is important but still very hard to do.* My 1997 forecast, published in *Evaluation Practice*, that the connections would be developed well, is one that has not fully panned out as of this writing. Other forecasts, especially about the increased use of cluster randomized trials, did. Being unduly proud of this prognostication, I presented the results at a joint National Academy of Education/ National Academy of Sciences (NAS) meeting in 2010.

As important was the challenge of ensuring the privacy of individuals and the confidentiality of the research records on the respondents in this kind of social research. Wariness of interviewers, at the time, was justified. It is warranted nowadays in countries in which asking certain questions in a survey is risky and answering them is riskier. My thinking and research on statistical, procedural, and legal approaches to meeting the challenge in this study and later ones were published in *American Psychologist, Sociological Methods & Research, Evaluation Review, Policy Science, American Sociologist*, the reports of NAS committees, and elsewhere. Driven by the idea of concatenating statistical research, ethics, and privacy law, I took time to direct a sample survey of institutions (banks, colleges, insurance companies, etc.) to learn about their privacy practices. This survey was part of a project run under the auspices of the NAS. And so I became a civil servant in the academy's ambit. *Most important, the survey provided an opportunity to design and help execute probability sample surveys of institutions at a time when institutional surveys were a youthful enterprise. A thorough understanding of the target populations and population/sample frames, persistence in inquiry, incentives, and skills in posing questions, then as now, all count heavily in producing dependable results.*

Becoming dissatisfied with my prospects at ACE, I looked around for options. One opportunity emerged through Don Campbell's referral to the Social Science Research Council's president Henry Riecken. Riecken had initiated tantalizing research agendas in Washington, D.C., on the incipient "social indicators" movement, which his successor, Eleanor Sheldon, built on, as did the National Science Foundation and other government agencies. This and work on experiments are what would now be called evidence-based policy research. Under his brave leadership, Riecken formed an interdisciplinary Committee on Social Experimentation, whose members included Riecken, Donald Campbell, Nate Caplan (social psychology and delinquency), Tom Glennan (federal education policy and economics), Walt Williams (economics), Al Rees (economics), and John Pratt (statistics). The consultants were eminent—Edgar Borgotta, Peter Rossi, Carol Weiss, Rob Hollister, and Harold Watts, among others. The results were published in Riecken et al. (1974), Boruch and Riecken (1975), and a variety of journals such as the *Evaluation Review, Public Administration, American Statistician*, and *Education Researcher*. The people involved helped one another understand the why and how of randomized field trials in the context of social policy. They exemplified collegiality and collaboration. *Lesson: In social research generally and in controlled randomized trials in particular, the ethics issues, the political and institutional challenges, and the managerial demands of high-quality trials get well beyond statistical models and measurement. These demands, then and now, transcend the conventional academic disciplines.* As Einstein put the matter somewhere, the remarkable contributions to the sciences lie at the interstices of the existing disciplines.

The prospect of connecting the ostensibly different intellectual worlds was a joy. Part of the virtue of the Social Science Research Council committee's effort then lay in bringing ideas about randomized trials out of the psychological and medical laboratories and out of the agricultural fields and into policy and public administration. The randomized allocation in the interest of fair comparison can be done in any social context, though sometimes with difficulty. *Learning to speak the tribal languages that characterize the different academic disciplines and policy sectors, to understand the common ideas about evidence despite vernacular differences, and to collaborate in interdisciplinary work is essential and also a grand privilege.*

TRANSCENDING THE ACADEMIC DISCIPLINES, BUREAUCRATIC BOUNDARIES, AND GEOPOLITICAL JURISDICTIONS

After the tours of duty with ACE and NAS, I got a backdoor academic appointment as a research associate at Northwestern University on one of Don Campbell's National Science Foundation grants. Campbell's behavior taught me to understand and appreciate the virtues of the young and industrious colleagues and later to hire them, work with them, and admire their efforts often. I walked through Northwestern's front door when an assistant professorship position opened in the Psychology Department. It was easy in some respects to learn from Campbell, a polymath, about how to think about evaluation questions and methods appropriate for addressing the questions. Fine senior colleagues at Northwestern in psychology—Ken Howard, Benton Underwood, and Lee Sechrest—and in statistics and mathematics—Myer Dwass and Jerry Sacks, for instance—were creative, smart, and generous in sharing ideas. Moreover, all of them worked in different academic vineyards. These were kindred spirits. I decided, more or less, to apply (or misapply) myself in different academic disciplines too.

During the 1970s, for instance, manpower economics involved robust controversies over whether manpower training programs worked and especially whether the evidence regarding their effectiveness was dependable. The *YEDPA Years* was a milestone. Produced by an NAS committee, under Robinson Hollister's chairmanship, the report helped foster better evaluations of the effectiveness of manpower-training programs, especially the design and execution of randomized trials. As a member of the committee, *it was pleasing to be educated about concerns in this branch of economics simply because I was so ignorant.* It also opened up the opportunity to contribute as an advisor to other efforts, including commenting on the drafts of the Seattle and Denver Income Maintenance Experiments; advising on the remarkable field experiments on job training for minority, female, single parents sponsored by the Rockefeller Foundation and later providing counsel at the Rockefeller's Jobs Plus trials; and doing occasional stints for the World Bank.

One of the World Bank encounters led to another lesson on when not to do a randomized trial. It is implicit in a World Bank colleague's question following a panel on which I was a commentator for excellent papers on the topic of randomized experiments: "Why don't you economists make better predictions about what would happen in the absence of the program being evaluated? Like astronomers," *he said. The lesson is implicit in the Boruch response, which is also a question:* "How many randomized, naked, and defenseless control group pigs does one need, and why, to make a causal inference about the effectiveness of Kevlar for bulletproof vests for the police?" *The succinct answer is none, provided one is willing to make some assumptions, about ballistic trajectories and counterfactuals, for instance.* My reasons and assumptions are published as essays or commentaries in papers in volumes issued by the World Bank, Brookings Institution, and others.

During my graduate studies at ISU, sociology was "rural" and had an excellent reputation. It was also theoretical. As a city-bred engineer, I did not properly recognize the value of rurality or theory. I thought of the sociological tracts as throat-clearing essays, for example, and not worthy of serious consideration. During the 1980s, two eminent sociologists who were prescient in their taste for good evidence in the public sector, Peter Rossi and Al Reiss, taught me otherwise. I learned to be more critical, though not as critical as Pete was, about stupidity in government and in academia and the weakness of evaluation research in the social services and corrections sectors, about courage (both men had a lot of the stuff), and about wit (ditto). Each was a *rara avis*.

Having grown up in urban New Jersey, I had developed no early interest in criminological research. Cities like Bayonne, Jersey City, Newark, and others were afflicted with banal sorts of crimes committed by cops, judges, senators, city council members, and ordinary citizens. Neighborhood conversations focused on bribes, corruption, and "five-finger discounts"—that is, the stuff that "fell off the truck." *Despite having found no incentive to work this vineyard, I learned to discount the venality, or at least to suppress disgust, from my betters. And I learned to learn where the interesting scientific questions were in criminology and about the evaluation issues that the questions engender.* Organizations such as the Center for Evidence Based Crime Policy at George Mason University and the Jerry Lee symposiums at University of Maryland, led by younger and very smart colleagues, have been remarkably productive vehicles for this sort of learning (see http://gunston.gmu.edu.cebcp).

Among other things, Reiss taught me by example to get into the field again, teaching me how to ride around with cops on patrol, so as to learn beyond my naïveté, and to keep my cop colleagues well fed and amused during patrols. *To reiterate an earlier lesson, this is part of the normal skill set in anthropology or ethnography and should also be exploited by quantitative evaluators.* The project was the Spouse Assault Replication Program (SARP), a multisite randomized controlled trial on police handling of misdemeanor domestic violence. Reiss was an intellectual root. I also learned about the idea of replications in SARP. *The idea of replication is fundamental and good on scientific policy grounds but mushy on operational grounds.* Parts of the resulting work were published, again with others, in *New Directions for Program Evaluation*, and follow-up work on the methodological aspects of such trials has been published in *Evaluation Review*, *Prevention Science*, *Journal of Experimental Criminology*, and *Crime & Delinquency*, among others.

I bought two bulletproof vests during that SARP tour of duty. Evaluation studies done by others had found that the effectiveness of body armor decayed with the fabric's aging. Contingency planning in the street is as it is when conducting randomized controlled field trials. *In particular, designing trials in at least two stages so that the lessons learned in the first stage (with a first cohort, say) can be used to improve the second stage, figuring that the outcome data in the first would be far from perfect given the unknowns of the field, the mistakes and mishaps that occur, and the need to rectify them in the second stage.*

In the late 1970s, U.S. Congresswoman Elizabeth Holtzman's legislative initiative demanded a review of evaluations of education programs. This took some people by surprise. She declared that the quality of evaluations run by the U.S. Department of Education (USDE) were not up to a good standard and, moreover, that the USDE evaluations of education programs might be useless. To her credit, Holtzman got money put into the relevant legislation so as to support independent reviews of the department's evaluation work. *Both money and independence continue to be important in credible evaluations.* "Independence" is always relative, of course, and trust in the funder's willingness not to interfere with work that is supposed to be independent is crucial.

Peter Rossi was invited first to do the congressionally mandated review but did not have the time to do it. He referred the USDE to me. Having a cadre of bright, eager, and very smart post-doctoral and doctoral fellows at Northwestern, I jumped at the opportunity. I was more agile then. We produced a numbingly detailed report, and lots of good publications in peer-reviewed journals such as *Educational Researcher, American Statistician, Educational Evaluation and Policy Analysis, Journal of Policy Analysis and Management,* and others. The products of the report to the Congress were largely ignored when the federal administration changed. This was with the exceptions of the U.S. Government Accountability Office (GAO, called the General Accounting Office at the time) and kindred federal government and academic souls with long memories and an interest in better evidence. The sturdy indifference with which our reports were greeted by Congress, if not academia, refreshed my interest in the topic of utilization of research.

And the latter led to some lessons. *Exploit an interrogatory approach to understanding the phenomenon of information use, a phenomenon that includes manipulable factors that can be put into a conditional probability framework. Does the potential user know about the information? If so, does the potential user understand it? If so, does the potential user have the capacity (power, clout, authority) to use the information? If so, is the potential user willing to use it—that is, what are the incentives for use?* This may be construed as an elementary theory of utilization despite its catechized character. It accords with the theoretical and empirical work done by Alkin, Weiss, and others. It lends itself to elementary applications of conditional probability—with shades of Reverend Bayes (the English clergyman who set out his theory of probability in 1764).

Pete Rossi subsequently agreed to chair an NAS committee on the topic that was initiated by Mike (Marshall) Smith, who was then at the USDE. Rossi's NAS committee ran parallel to the Northwestern effort. The members of the NAS committee, on which I also served, were august and able—Marvin Alkin, Nate Caplan, Robert Yin, and others. My junior colleagues at Northwestern agreed that doing work parallel to this NAS group was a challenge. In effect, they said that they could do better than the old dogs, including me, on such a committee. Junior colleagues exceeded expectations. *I learned again to admire hungry, young, and trustworthy evaluators regardless of their pedigree and to expect them to do well relative to experienced people provided they had the right training, stamina, and willingness to learn and to broach new ideas.*

For some evaluators, transcending geopolitical boundaries is an enticing challenge. Standards of evidence and dependability of the evidence will vary, for instance, depending on the stage of development of the country, of the agencies involved in deploying programs, or of the science underlying the program's design. In the international sector, I served as an advisor during the 1970s, with Lee Sechrest and Don Campbell, in the randomized trials on education and cultural enrichment programs for children from the barrios in Cali (Colombia) and in the

Nicaraguan trials on radio-based mathematics education and on sundry other tasks. I served only as statistical advisor, and to my regret, I did not also get into the streets. *Nonetheless, the lessons that some standards of evidence are transcendent (notably, randomized trials) and that the study design must be tailored to the setting (e.g., randomization of entities or neighborhoods rather than people) were important then as now.*

In 1998, an opportunity to do something innovative and useful and to develop other international roots emerged. Iain Chalmers came from the United Kingdom to the United States to discuss the possibility of creating a new organization that would capitalize on the Cochrane Collaboration in health care, one that might focus on the social sector. Cochrane had been successful over the preceding decade or so and continues to generate high-quality systematic reviews of evidence on the effectiveness of programs in the health care sector (see http://cochrane.org). The MDs involved in Cochrane were wary, however, of bringing social science folks into the fold. Chalmers and some of his colleagues decided that a parallel organization in the social sector might be good.

After talking with Chalmers, I called up some of the owls in my tree to figure out what to do. Peter Rossi, Henry Riecken, and Fred Mosteller were among them. Deciding to contribute on the basis of their counsel, I then indulged in meetings during a freezing winter month through Oslo, Helsinki, Copenhagen, and Stockholm to assay those countries' interest in systematic reviews of dependable evidence on the effectiveness of social, educational, and crime-related programs. This forced march was with Haluk Soydan (Sweden, now at the University of Southern California), who led the Scandinavian charge, Geraldine MacDonald (United Kingdom), and Dorothy de Moya (United States). Following this and the later reconnaissance at the University of London's then new School of Public Policy, we and others established the international Campbell Collaboration at an inaugural meeting at the University of Pennsylvania in 2000. It was named in honor of Donald T. Campbell at Chalmers' suggestion. As of this writing, the Campbell Collaboration is productive under others' leadership, notably Arild Bjorndahl in Norway and Mark Lipsey in the United States (see the site at www.campbellcollaboration.org).

Having been knighted in the United Kingdom for his work on the Cochrane Collaboration, Chalmers is now Sir Iain. I regret that I have not yet seen his sword as evidence of his elevation. I count the man as an intellectual root on account of his counsel on developing an international organization dedicated to the often unpopular and dangerous idea of dependable reviews of evidence. The Campbell experience taught me something that some statesmen and stateswomen have learned. *Remarkable ideas can attract and engage colleagues, whether paid or not, in productive collaborative enterprise. If the idea is good, the effort can get beyond conventional science and government. In the jargon of my marketing research colleagues at the Wharton School, the idea "has legs."* Since I was a cofounder of the Evaluation Research Society (predecessor to the American Evaluation Association) and having helped in the creation of the Society for Research on Educational Effectiveness, the lesson seems to hold up well in different areas.

A remarkable consequence of the Campbell Collaboration's formation was, I believe, the creation of the USDE's What Works Clearinghouse (WWC). Arranged under the leadership of Grover (Russ) Whitehurst, the first director of the Institute for Education Sciences, the WWC's mission had clear origins in the Campbell Collaboration. It has become a potent vehicle for producing systematic reviews of dependable evidence on the effectiveness of education programs and packages. As in the

Campbell and Cochrane Collaborations, randomized controlled trials were put at high priority when the question is "What works?" *The WWC illustrates how good government can at times exploit big ideas and institutionalize them.* I should have learned this earlier from senior colleagues who contributed mightily to good government, such as Bill Morrill.

I was appointed principle investigator for the first five years of the WWC contract from the Institute for Education Sciences. It took only a couple of years to discover that the "principle investigator" denomination meant little, and might even have been dysfunctional, given the complexity of determining where and when the evidence is adequate or paltry in the very large and diversified arena called education. *This was another lesson in distrusting titles, even my own, and in the need to collaborate without pretense in actualizing a remarkable initiative in a very complex scientific and institutional environment.*

The leadership and senior staff of government agencies can, at times, be a very good source of ideas, voyeuristic understanding, and counsel for the evaluator who is willing to learn. For instance, the U.S. GAO from the 1970s through the 1990s constituted a kind of invisible college in the evaluation sector. Comptroller General Elmer Staats created a Program Evaluation and Methodology Division (PEMD), which continued until near the end of Comptroller General Chuck Bowsher's term. PEMD elevated the GAO and congressional understanding of evidence in all social sectors and produced reports based on that evidence that still constitute good case studies in graduate schools. PEMD helped attract a stable of talent to the GAO under Eleanor Chelimsky's leadership. She fired me from her advisory committee, or maybe I was "relieved of my duties," along with a couple of others, for reasons that were good by her lights and okay by ours.

Good evaluators should expect to be fired and should not keep grudges. They certainly should not expect to be taken out to dinner once they have given honest advice or when the evaluation is done, unless the evaluation declares that the program is successful, which is not a common event. It was also a real privilege to serve the GAO from 1976 to 1996 as a member of the Comptroller General's Research and Education Advisory Panel under Elmer Staats and Charles (Chuck) Bowsher, which was later disbanded by Comptroller General David Walker. *Lesson: In the United States at least, organizations such as the GAO have remarkable access to information from any other government agency in the United States and have direct access to the congressional staff people who pose evaluation questions. The GAO has helped frame evaluation questions properly, and young evaluators, and I, can learn from this. Nonetheless, the GAO is not omnipotent with respect to access to information. Stonewalling by intelligence agencies in the United States is not unknown.*

At times, committees and workshops of the NAS have been fine opportunities to learn and develop roots. I have been pleased to serve on committees or to contribute to workshops for about 30 of these things in one way or another. For instance, during the deliberations of the committee on the Concorde's noise level, we learned how the Federal Aviation Administration (at the time) did surveys that made a fashionable airplane's noise level appear deceptively low. The agency did acoustic sound tracks in winter, when people close their windows unlike in summer. Fred Mosteller, a member of the committee, and Angus Campbell, its chair, were a delight in teaching some of us how to ask questions and how to reserve judgment until the evidence is in. That airplane was noisy.

The NAS Committee on Youth Employment Programs, discussed earlier, helped reshape research on employment and training programs in the United States. The NAS Committee on AIDS Prevention included people senior to me and from whom I learned—namely, Harry Hatry, Lincoln Moses, and Robyn Dawes. Another committee report superseded my original report on evaluating AIDS prevention programs when some members of the academy, the economic modeling mob, discovered my report's emphasis on controlled randomized trials and demanded equal time. In the NAS Committee on Scientific Principles in Education Research, chaired by Richard Shavelson, two of its members, Eric Hanushek and Jack Fletcher, were particularly eloquent and effective in arguing for randomized trials.

At the USDE, Alan Ginsburg, a remarkably able and thoughtful senior executive service colleague, developed an evaluation review panel (ERP), a kitchen cabinet that had no official standing in the context of the federal government. Its members were nominated by professional organizations, but it could not be counted as a government committee operating under the Federal Advisory Committee Act. I joined up. Ginsburg's ERP was a good idea for its time. It included able people who were streetwise at the state and local levels and in the science policy sector. The ERP survived at least three or four political administrations, a mark of success in unstable evidential environments, to do incremental good.

The National Academy committees, the USDE, the GAO, panels and others in the federal ambit, professional organizations such as Campbell Collaboration, and so on, are opportunities for learning in adult seminars. The committees and panels have a mission. Figuring out how to support the mission in the sense of finding or generating high-quality evidence that may run contrary to colleagues' views at times is a real challenge for evaluators. Don't always expect to get paid well.

FOUNDATIONS

I've mentioned engagements earlier with the Rockefeller Foundation in the advancement of methodological and policy-related research in social services and jobs. I would be remiss if I did not acknowledge the Robert Wood Johnson Foundation for partial support of a fellowship program in the context of the Campbell Collaboration. *Each illustrates in small ways the fact that private foundations can support research and development work that is substantial, and at best in advance of what the government can sometimes do, and moreover can pay for generating dependable evidence on whether the target programs are effective or not in randomized trials.*

Partly on account of Henry Riecken, I got elected to the board of trustees of the William T. Grant Foundation. It was a delightful privilege. The CEO as of this writing, Bob Granger, wears his head above his shoulders. He has done a lot to ensure that a small research-oriented foundation influences and assists in the matter of generating better evidence in a much larger context. Recall the earlier remarks on credentials in academia and the military, where some distrust is warranted. *Here, the point is that foundations of modest size can be exceedingly productive in regard to fostering good evidence and good ideas.*

EVALUATION FIRMS

We, in universities, are paid to generate ideas, figure out what evidence bears on the ideas, and to teach. With some remarkable exceptions, we are not good at contract work, including delivering specified products on time. As Don Campbell was fond of declaring, "Science is timeless." *Indeed, a certain inattentiveness to time is arguably essential for generating and germinating ostensibly good ideas. Even more time is often required to figure out what's wrong with them. Those of us in universities have the luxury to take the time, at times. Others do not.*

Partly as a consequence, I have thumped on my drum for the development of organizations such as the American Institutes for Research (on whose board of directors I serve), Mathematica Policy Research, and Manpower Development Research Corporation since the 1970s, and I have thumped for new and smaller firms such as Analytica, and others that attempt to produce good evaluations in a timely way for use by local, state, federal, or multinational clients. Such organizations have a capacity to capitalize well on talent so as to ensure that the evaluation evidence gets produced and used. They do so while maintaining integrity in this. And they make a living at the same time. This is not easy.

Such organizations, small or large, are critical in field studies that demand managerial expertise in the interest of generating good evidence so as to inform public policy and doing the fieldwork that must meet the ethical, political, and institutional challenges that evaluations engender. Similar organizations are likely to be formed in Asia and the Middle East and eventually in the countries of Africa. University people who are attentive to time and who have good ideas are entrenched at times in the contracts that the firms get. That is excellent so long as the professors are not merely decorative. The intersecting box of basic and applied sciences in Pasteur's Quadrant can be filled in nicely this way.

PUBLICATIONS

Readers who have not yet done so will note that there is, with small exception, no self-citation or a listing of particular articles here or at the end of this chapter. This absence is not a conceit. It is merely a reflection of my unwillingness to afflict the reader with a list that would glaze the eyeballs like a Sung vase. My identifying the journals here that have published my work is to emphasize the fact that good ideas about research methods and strategy are welcome in many different disciplines and peer-reviewed publications. Some readers might politely label the multiplicity of journals, and the fact that some are of high impact and some of low impact, as migratory scholarship. Others may view it as a mongrelized approach to evaluation. In some respects, both characterizations are apt.

Don Campbell's perspective was that one must publish good ideas that have been vetted well somewhere. One need worry less about the prestige and circulation of the journal or book than about the quality of the report. In olden days, one could always paper the landscape with reproductions of the published work. Now, electronic reproductions are inescapable.

Campbell said little to me about publication in edited volumes, such as this one, or the production of books and reports for government. Others, such as Rossi, Reiss, and Mosteller, were more encouraging and persistent, and exemplary on this account. Indeed, Mosteller was one of the most careful readers of draft manuscripts in the Western world. He was getting on in years but gently tenacious and alarmingly thorough when we collaborated on *Evidence Matters*. To get to the larger point, books are important in evaluation and other scientific sectors. This is regardless of the fact that Googlers will have to catch up or be able to retrieve despite the massively energetic search engines that value blogs over books.

THERE IS NO CLOSING . . . YET

There is no real closing to this chapter.

Instead of allowing it to fizzle out, let me give you, dear readers, some brief declarations made by my senior colleagues. I have put the declarations in quotes below, though they ought to be dignified by italics. All are based on personal communication. Each declaration can be construed as an aphorism, embodying counsel about how to do better.

W. Edwards Deming, of statistical quality control fame, said, to a talkative Boruch, over breakfast at the Cosmos Club in the 1970s, "Shut up and listen." I did. Listening carefully is good preparation for posing hard questions gently but succinctly. *Evaluations are often complex, and interrogating the principals is both a privilege and an essential part of learning whether the results and claims can be justified.*

Fred Mosteller, after our having listened to a high-toned academic colleague who discussed the epistemology of causal inference, whispered to Boruch, "I can't understand what he said." Fred was being polite. *Jargon is a functional shorthand within each discipline. It is dysfunctional when the effort or idea transcends academic disciplines.* "Fair comparison" is clearer to many than phrases such as "statistically unbiased estimate," "wrong statistical model" is more informative to many than "misspecification," and so on.

Pete Rossi's iron law for evaluation-to-evaluation researchers was *"The better the study is designed, the more likely it is that you will find no effect of the program being evaluated."* Later, in an e-mail, before he died, Pete said to Bob, "My body parts are fighting with one another to see which one is going to kill me first, and I am next in line." Bob should have responded, "Pete, find the last place in the line and go there." But he was too late. Pete would have enjoyed this mordant counsel.

Don Campbell broached splendid ideas to the evaluation research community in his "Honestly Experimental Society." Don never used the phrase "honestly experimental" with me in private conversations, despite his deserved fame for its use in his *American Psychologist* article. Campbell got some of the idea from Walter Lippmann. But Don was a far better scientist than Lippmann. At its best, for instance, the honest experiment entails making original data available for secondary analysis by independent researchers so as to confirm original analyses, test new hypotheses, and identify vulnerabilities in the design and execution of studies and options for reducing the vulnerabilities. This is a small part of the movement toward publication of proposals, interim reports, and open-access, peer-reviewed journal articles and government reports, and making microrecords accessible for reanalysis.

Lincoln Moses said to Boruch sometime in the 1980s, "Do the statistical power analysis. Then, get as many as you can." This is still good advice regardless of the remarkable advances in the theory of and software for statistical power analysis for cluster/group/place randomized trials with continuous or binary outcome variables at multiple levels of a system. Another piece of advice from Lincoln Moses was that "the best way to handle missing data is not to have any." This is still fine counsel despite the excellent contributions by Don Rubin, Rod Little, Paul Allison, and others to the statistical methods for imputing missing data and handling missingness in data analyses. *More to the point, controlled trials can be construed as parallel surveys in which measurement and attention to nonresponse across the arms of the trial are especially critical in making fair comparisons.*

Oscar Kempthorne said, "Analyze them as you have randomized them." *Falling nowadays under the rubric of intent-to-treat analysis (ITT), the advice still holds value for unbiased estimates of effects and of variance and for proper statistical tests and indicators of one's confidence in studies that involve entities (villages, police hot spots, schools) as the units of randomization.* That is, response at the entity level is what is critical, not the number of units below the level of randomization. This is regardless of the advances in hierarchical modeling and the experimental designs developed by ingenious colleagues such as Steve Raudenbush, Larry Hedges, and others.

Lee Sechrest, declaiming the importance of measurement in the psychological/educational social sciences, asked, "Would you want to fly without a good altimeter?" The challenges in the social sciences are at least as great as those in the physical sciences—arguably greater. Subatomic particles require no informed consent, susceptibility to response burden is not an issue, and propensity to mislead, forget, or dissemble is not in their skill set. *Developing cheap, continuous, and dependable measurements that entail no unusual burden or constraint or intrusion on people is a noble and challenging scientific aspiration.*

The title of Carol Weiss's essay in Mosteller-Boruch's *Evidence Matters* is "What to Do Before the Randomizer Comes." A subtitle could have been "And Even if the Randomizer Does Arrive." Either way, a theory or logic model for how the interventions in the arms of the trial are supposed to work counts. *We in the evaluation sector ought to enhance our ability to design controlled trials so as to construct interesting and good questions beyond estimates of effect and to give speculative answers to them in a reasonable theoretical framework. Anticipating failure of the intervention that is tested is a good thing to do. Lots of things don't work as well as we would have liked, and we should learn better from the failures.*

Finally, let me quote, more or less, from a man who I've never met but who can be counted as a root at a distance—Kurt Vonnegut. In one of his autobiographical essays, Vonnegut reported on what his father said to the young Kurt, "Always hang around with people who are smarter than you are." And his father added with a note of regret in his voice, "For you, that should be easy." Mothers don't like this quote, in my experience, but fathers understand it. And one senior colleague at the University of Pennsylvania, Ed Boe, reminded me to understand that integrity is as important as the smarts. The point is that one should seek out people from whom one can learn. There are lots of them regardless of what is construed as "smart" or not. And then, of course, you have to get beyond smarts, have integrity, and do something.

Being able to do evaluation research is a hunting license. Good luck to readers on the hunt for ideas, dependable evidence, and ways to do some good.

BIBLIOGRAPHY

Betsey, C. L., Hollister, R. G., & Papageorgiou, M. (Eds.). (1985). *Youth employment and training programs: The YEDPA years*. Washington, DC: National Academy Press.

Bootzin, R. R., & McKnight, P. E. (Eds.). (2006). *Strengthening research methodology: Psychological measurement and evaluation (in honor of Lee Secrest)*. Washington, DC: American Psychological Association Books.

Boruch, R. F. (1984). Ideas about social research, evaluation, and statistics in medieval Arabic literature: Ibn Khaldun and al-Biruni. *Evaluation Review, 8*(6), 823–842.

Boruch, R. F. (1997). *Randomized experiments for planning and evaluation: A practical guide*. Thousand Oaks, CA: Sage.

Chang, K. (2003, June 8). Questions raised on equation NASA used on shuttle peril. *The New York Times*, p. 38.

Evans, I., Thornton, H., Chalmers, I., & Glasziou, P. (2011). *Testing treatments: Better research for better healthcare* (2nd ed.). London, England: Pinter & Martin. Retrieved from http://testingtreatments.org

Kempthorne, O. (1952, 1967, 1973, 1975, 1979, 1983). *The design and analysis of experiments*. New York, NY: Wiley (1952, 1967 editions), Malabar, FL: Robert E. Krieger (remaining editions).

Moses, L., & Mosteller, F. (Eds.). (1983). *William Cochrane's planning and analysis of observational studies*. New York, NY: Wiley.

Mosteller, F., & Boruch, R. F. (2002). *Evidence matters: Randomized trials in education research*. Washington, DC: Brookings Institution.

Overman, E. S. (Ed.). (1988). *Methodology and epistemology for social science: Selected papers by Donald T. Campbell*. Chicago, IL: University of Chicago Press.

Reiss, A. J. (2006). *In memoriam: Albert J. Reiss, 1922–2006*. Retrieved from www.crim.upenn.edu/history/memoriam/reiss.html

Riecken, H. W., Boruch, R. F., Campbell, D. T., Caplan, N., Glennan, T. K., Pratt, J. W., . . . Williams, W. (1974). *Randomized experiments for planning and evaluation*. New York, NY: Academic Press.

Wolins, L. (1962). Responsibility for raw data. *American Psychologist, 17,* 657–658.

5

CAUSAL GENERALIZATION

How Campbell and Cronbach Influenced My Theoretical Thinking on This Topic

Thomas D. Cook

This chapter is about the intellectual influences on me when, in the late 1980s, I began to develop a theory of causal generalization that might justify practical ways of extending external validity without prejudicing internal validity. The fruits of this work are evident in four overlapping papers (Cook, 1990, 1991, 1993, 2000) and in the book by Shadish, Cook, and Campbell (2002). Indeed, the book's very title—*Experimental and Quasi-Experimental Designs for Generalized Causal Inference*—is meant to signal the new importance of external validity. The book's chapter structure reflects this. . . . The book still contains more on internal than external validity. But the emphasis is less disproportionate than in its predecessors.

In the late 1980s and early 1990s, I was trying to understand why Donald Campbell and Lee Cronbach differed so much in their preferred goals and methods for evaluation. I wrote the chapters on each of them that appeared in the evaluation theory book by Shadish, Cook, and Leviton (1991), analyzing each person's work relative to a set of explicit criteria about what makes a good theory of evaluation. Implicit throughout these two chapters—and explicit at many points—is an analysis of how Cronbach and Campbell differ. Perhaps the most striking differences is that Cronbach's 1980 and 1982 books placed external validity (as he understood it) at the forefront of his Pantheon of evaluation Gods, while he relegated internal validity (again as

---

Source: Excerpted from Cook, T. D. (2004). Causal Generalization: How Campbell and Cronbach influenced my theoretical thinking on this topic, including in Shadish, Cook, and Campbell. In M. C. Alkin (Ed.), *Evaluation roots*. Thousand Oaks, CA: Sage Publications.

he understood it) to a minor role. This reversed Campbell's explicit priority ordering and challenged him and his collaborators to make external validity more important. My 1993 paper is one response to that challenge, and this chapter illustrates how that response developed and how, with some minor modifications, it was incorporated into Shadish et al. (2002).

AN ALTERNATIVE THEORY OF THE GENERALIZATION OF CAUSAL RELATIONSHIPS

The Four Interconnected Domains

According to Campbell (1957), every test of a causal connection entails generalization in at least four domains—about the cause, the effect, the population, and the setting. In some writings, he adds a fifth domain, time.

Many causal statements are expressed as universals (e.g., "out-group threat causes in-group cohesion"). Universals specify a cause-and-effect relationship but not the populations of persons, settings, or times over which it is thought to hold. They therefore seem at odds with Campbell's assertion that four domains are involved in any causal generalization. However, there is no real discrepancy. Universal causal propositions assume that a relationship holds in all populations and settings and at all times, as well as across all ways of operationally representing the cause and effect. So, all the domains are included in the inference; they are just not mentioned. Nor are the many individual instances listed that could have been enumerated within each of the person, setting, cause, effect, or time domains.

Contingent causal propositions acknowledge the conditional nature of most causal knowledge. They specify the unique person, setting, cause, or effect domains in which a causal relationship holds, thus identifying causal boundaries, the limits of generalization. Historical knowledge of how the Moors drifted away from the defense of Grenada in 1492 or how some Central Asian cities capitulated before Genghis Khan questions the generality of the claim that "out-group threat causes in-group cohesion." Such counterinstances protect us against overgeneralizing and help identify some of the specific causal boundary conditions. They also prompt us to explain why an effect holds under some conditions but not others. For instance, the inhabitants who remained in Grenada to face the Catholic Spanish troops knew that many of their fellow citizens had already deserted; and the Central Asian residents knew that Genghis Khan's troops routinely killed every single person if a city did not surrender immediately. So, does out-group threat increase in-group cohesion only when the in-group is not initially demoralized?

Cronbach and Campbell agree about the need to specify targets of generalization, and each of them invokes the same four. Cronbach even invents a notational system to represent each of them. In this system, "u" refers to units of assignment (usually persons), "t" refers to treatments, "o" to observations (including outcomes), and "s" to settings. My 1993 paper borrowed this same "utos" notational system to index the four targets of generalization implicated in any causal statement.

The Generalization Tasks

1. Generalizing to UTOS

Cronbach postulates two separate generalization tasks, and my paper followed him in this. The first involves generalizing from specific lower-order samples, instances, cases, and exemplars (terms we use interchangeably) to populations, constructs, classes, and categories (which we also use interchangeably). Cronbach uses lowercase utos to designate this operational level, the level at which social scientists actually work in selecting samples, choosing measures, and conducting analyses. Uppercase UTOS refers to the more conceptual realm about which general conclusions are to be drawn. In planning research, target populations and constructs are specified at the UTOS level, and attempts are made to select utos-level cases and samples that represent these targets—essentially a deductive process. But, however selected, disputes are still common about what a given u, t, o, or s actually represents, with some commentators analyzing the utos level and concluding that the achieved UTOS is not the intended one. So, correspondence rules are needed to justify what elements of UTOS a given utos represents.

Formal sampling theory provides the best-known algorithm for moving between the utos and UTOS levels. The theory's primacy is widely acknowledged in survey research where practical procedures now specify how to draw samples that justify generalizing to populations of people and settings within known limits of sampling error. Formal sampling theory, and the research practices that have developed around its implementation, constitute the best way of generalizing from u to U and from s to S.

But generalization is also required from an outcome measure to an effect (o to O) and from a manipulation or measure to a cause (t to T). For these two purposes, the best-known algorithms do not depend on random selection. Instead, they are based on psychometric theories whose starting point is the theoretical explication of a category (T or O) followed by the purposive selection of instances that seem to belong in that category (t or o). Theorists rarely disagree totally about the attributes of a given T or O—otherwise, there could be no shared language. The attributes most widely agreed upon are called "prototypical" (Lakoff, 1985) and are central for drawing conclusions about the constructs that specific manipulations and measures represent. Indeed, the process of moving from operational definitions to abstract constructs can be paraphrased as follows: "To what extent does a specific t or o match the prototypical attributes of T and O as the focal community of researchers has explicated these attributes?"

Missing in this formulation is an omnibus mechanism like random selection that guarantees a formal probabilistic correspondence between the sample and population on all measured and unmeasured attributes. Substituted for this is a form of matching, and then only on the prototypical attributes of a construct. This creates an asymmetry. The preferred methods for generalizing to U and S are based on random selection, while the preferred methods for generalizing to T and O are based on theory-informed, purposive selection. . .

These different models of generalization seem to coexist comfortably within the same research project. For instance, many survey researchers insist on random samples as the sine qua non for generalizing to human populations. But when they select questionnaire items to go into their surveys, they routinely use purposive selection, even though their aim is to justify generalization. It is true that persons and settings are usually more ostensive than abstract cause-and-effect constructs, and so it is easier to enumerate people and settings for sample selection. But enumeration of all conceivable manipulations and measures is also possible. Yet social scientists rarely do it...

2. Generalizing to *UTOS

Cronbach's second generalization task is about extrapolating beyond the sampled UTOS. He wants to generalize to people, causes, effects, settings, and times that are manifestly different from those that were actually studied. He asks: How can data at the utos level be used to draw inferences about populations and constructs that do not even look like the available data? They might share some attributes; but, by definition for extrapolation, they cannot share all of them. Cronbach designates nonrepresented targets of inference as entities at the *UTOS level (spoken as "star-UTOS"). My 1993 paper followed him in this notation and in the idea of generalization needing to encompass concerns about both representation and extrapolation.

According to Cronbach, we need to invoke *UTOS because the conditions under which a causal hypothesis is tested are never isomorphic with how the same causal knowledge is likely to be applied... And since policy use is Cronbach's ultimate evaluation goal, extrapolation beyond the conditions of testing is a more useful form of causal generalization for him than is representing a prespecified UTOS.

However, his judgment raises a great practical problem. Forecasting studies aside, social science practice evolved to represent more than to extrapolate. So, how can studies be designed to learn about populations, causes, effects, and settings that are manifestly different from those incorporated into the research specifics from which generalization is to be made? That is the pragmatic puzzle raised by Cronbach's second formulation of external validity.

3. External Validity as Robust Replication

Both of Cronbach's understandings of external validity seem different from Campbell's. For Campbell, external validity has to do with how broadly a causal connection is empirically replicated across persons, settings, times, and ways of operationalizing the cause and effect. It even has to do with generalizing a single treatment's impact across different outcomes and with generalizing the impact of multiple treatments on the same outcome. Central to Campbell's perspective is a reliable description of how consistently a causal relationship is replicated, not what the relationship represents or how far it can be extrapolated.

Yet Campbell and Cronbach are not that far apart. To probe whether a cause-effect relationship replicates, Campbell has to presuppose that each of the samples he analyzes for this purpose represents the populations whose names he attaches to the samples. So, his view of external validity subsumes UTOS, treats it as a matter of course. As to extrapolation, one can argue by induction that a causal relationship that stubbornly replicates across many U's, S's, O's, and even

T's is especially likely to replicate in as yet unexamined contexts (that is, in *UTOS). Thus, Campbell's multiple-UTOS formulation is related to Cronbach's extrapolation. But even so, they are not identical. Campbell prioritizes on the demonstrated empirical robustness of a causal connection across possible moderator variables, while Cronbach's emphasizes what the sampling particulars represent and whether they justify extrapolation.

In my 1993 paper, I acknowledged the four domains involved in causal generalization and the two causal generalization tasks of Cronbach plus the related one of Campbell, thus treating causal generalization as a concept requiring multiple framings—not as a unitary concept. I also chose to use Cronbach's utos notational system as a convenient shorthand for discussing the objects and types of generalization. I further emphasized that many social science projects use two apparently contradictory theories of generalization without apparent discomfort. . . Examining these two approaches led me to the observations below.

The Limited Reach of Formal Sampling Theory

In statistics, generalization is equated with formal sampling theory. Its central postulate is that random selection makes a sample representative of the population from which it is chosen, at least within known limits of sampling error. Thanks to this feature, fields such as survey research and demography now flourish, routinely describing human populations and even aggregates of individuals such as neighborhoods, cities, schools, or work sites.

As elegant and as useful as this theory is, the 1993 paper notes how restricted it is when the goal is to generalize causal relationships, as opposed to describing populations. Experiments provide the best test of causal hypotheses. It is sometimes possible to sample people and settings at random and then to conduct experiments within the samples so selected. However, intervention studies with random selection followed by random assignment are very rare. Mostly, this is because some individuals or organizations will refuse to participate in an experiment if they have to receive whichever treatment chance assigns them, including the no-treatment control status. (The same is basically true with quasi-experiments.) So, when generalizing to U and S, practicality often limits the range of application of sampling theory . . .

Random sampling is even less relevant to the other domains involved in causal generalization. Within a single experiment, it is impossible to have much variation in historical time period. Even with shorter time frames, by the time a study's results are written up, they are bound to be partially anachronistic comments on a causal relationship from the past rather than truth-filled insights into the future. Also, random sampling is never used to select the items or manipulations constituting the cause or the measures of an effect. So, it is irrelevant to generalizing to the cause-and-effect constructs. Moreover, random sampling is about the relationship between utos and UTOS and has no obvious connections to generalizing to any part of *UTOS. So, as theoretically elegant as random sampling indubitably is, its role in generalizing causal statements from experiments is limited. It applies to U and S, but not routinely so. It does not apply to T and O. It does not apply to *UTOS. And it is irrelevant to historical variation.

However, random selection is routinely used in surveys of individuals and households, and the data collected from these surveys are sometimes used to test causal hypotheses. When the survey work is longitudinal, a variable measured at an early wave is often designated as the possible cause, and a variable measured later as the possible effect. The earlier-wave outcome and other measures from that time are then frequently used as selection controls, and the residual relationship between the early cause and the later outcome is treated as causal . . . The survey context renders random selection feasible for generalizing to U and sometimes S, but it fails to support strong causal inference within the sampled U and S; it does not involve strong generalization from t to T; and it is largely irrelevant for generalizing to *UTOS.

My 1993 paper argued that random selection should be used wherever possible. No alternative is as good (see Cook, 2002a). However, the gain in generalization is limited if it comes at the price of less clear causal inference, as in the survey research context. Experiments provide clearer causal findings, but random selection has even less relevance in this context than the survey. Anyway, random selection is irrelevant for generalizing to T and O and to *UTOS. So, successful causal generalization cannot depend on formal sampling theory alone, despite its real success in describing populations.

Construct Validity: An Alternative Model for Causal Generalization

Social scientists routinely use theories of construct validity to justify claims about what the specific measures and manipulations they use represent as cause-and-effect constructs. So, I asked whether the principles involved in validating constructs are also relevant to validating inferences about populations of people and settings.

If the answer is in the affirmative, this only raises a second issue. Are principles derived from construct validity also germane to Cronbach's conception of external validity as extrapolation and to Campbell's conception of external validity as robust replication? Any viable theory of causal generalization also has to identify which specific construct validity methods are feasible in social science practice and also serve to extend causal generalization in its multiple meanings. And these methods then have to be justified epistemologically.

Positivists want nothing to do with construct validity. They believe that no conceptual meanings should be attached to measures, and so they feel no need to generalize from o to O. But modern theories of construct validity reject this position and agree that a limited set of prototypical attributes has a special role to play in generalizing from t to T and from o to O because these attributes "define" what a construct means. They also give rise to the idea of "proximal similarity," assessing the extent to which the prototypical attributes of a person, setting, cause, or effect category are matched by the sampled particulars in an actual research project . . . Every construct validation exercise requires explicating the components of the construct to be represented and then selecting instances that manifestly embody these components. To construct the utos level at which they work, nearly all social scientists choose manipulations and measures in this theory-informed and purposive way.

Unfortunately, many of them do nothing more to justify what their selected research procedures "mean" at the UTOS level. However, theories of construct validity demand more than proximal similarity alone to justify that a given instance represents a specific category. Proximal similarity can be only one principle of construct validation because in privileging verification over falsification, it fails to rule out alternative interpretations of what a given measure might represent. . . . Campbell's theory of construct validity is explicitly falsificationist and specifies other principles useful for generating better inferences about construct validity. My 1993 paper relied heavily on his work for explicating construct validity, though it will soon be apparent that Cronbach's theory of construct validity was needed to supplement Campbell's.

In addition to proximal similarity, Campbell's theory emphasizes controlling for theoretical irrelevancies that might be associated with a measure or manipulation and related to an outcome. For instance, a measure might be collected face-to-face, versus by mailed questionnaire, versus by observation, but the mode of data collection is not part of the construct description. Another example is when a single domain is sampled though a construct is multidimensional: For example, a purported measure of general prejudice contains items only on racial prejudice, overlooking religious or intellectual prejudice. Since it is impossible to design operational definitions devoid of all irrelevancies, what should we do about them?

Campbell's answer is that we should deliberately sample so as to create a "heterogeneity of irrelevancies." This entails building into the research as many sources of irrelevant variation as possible. Thus, one might measure a given outcome in several different modes or take pains to represent the multiple life domains in which prejudice can occur. One can then probe the data to ascertain whether the causal relationship of interest holds despite the various ways of manipulating or measuring the construct. Or if the sampling design and statistical analysis permit separate breakdowns, we can seek to learn about the unique effects of specific irrelevancies—a core task in Cronbach's generalizability theory, for example (Cronbach, Gleser, Nanda, & Rajaratnam, 1972). The point is to imbue operational representations of a cause or effect with multiple sources of irrelevancy so that the various t's and o's are not confounded with a single irrelevancy.

Another component of Campbell's theory of construct validity is discriminant validity (Campbell & Fiske, 1959). This entails explicating and measuring cognate constructs that share attributes with the target construct but are conceptually distinct from it . . . Once these cognate constructs have been conceptualized, the analyst's task is then to measure each of them and to identify with which of them the causal relationship varies . . . The principle of discriminant validity reminds us that substantive theory is central to construct validation, partly because it suggests the specific cognate constructs that need to be examined.

Causal explanation is a fourth principle of construct validation, and Cronbach emphasizes it even more than Campbell (Cronbach, 1989; Cronbach & Meehl, 1955). For Cronbach, every cause or effect is embedded within a theory-based nomological net that promotes its unique naming. This net is made up of many different kinds of theoretical postulates about the antecedents, components, and processes associated with a given entity. Thus, causal explanation requires (a) probing the antecedents of the cause, (b) identifying antecedents of the effect other than the cause, and (c) decomposing both the cause and effect so as to learn which of their components are implicated in the more macrocausal connection under examination. Perhaps most important, though, is (d) testing theories of the micromediating processes through which the cause influences the effect.

Once the true theory of micromediation is known, Cronbach assumes that it will be possible to set the micromediating process in motion many different ways (and not just via the manipulated cause) and with many different populations and in many different settings from those already studied. From this perspective, promoting causal generalization requires an explicit substantive theory of the cause, of the effect, and of the reasons for a relationship between the two, plus empirical tests of the interpretations offered. These tests will identify what the causal concepts are and how they are related, identifying the boundary conditions affecting a causal relationship's size while also suggesting alternative ways of setting the causal process in motion. This makes causal explanation central for extrapolating experimental results to as yet unstudied causes, populations, and settings, thus speaking to Cronbach's second understanding of external validity.

A final principle of construct validation involves interpolation and extrapolation.... In experiments in particular, very few levels of the independent variable are manipulated. Needed is parameterization, sampling more levels on the independent variable to learn the functional form of the relationship... within the range actually studied. Extrapolation is about making causal inferences at ... levels above or below the sampled range. This entails an inductive leap whose eventual credibility depends on the certainty of extant knowledge about the functional form of the cause-effect relationship and also on the need for a shorter rather than longer extrapolation from the ends of the range actually sampled.

My 1993 paper identified five prototypical components of construct validation: proximal similarity, heterogeneity of irrelevancies, discriminant validity, causal explanation, and interpolation/extrapolation. The paper pointed out how these procedures do a reasonable job of generalizing from o to O and from t to T, certainly a better job than resorting to proximal similarity alone, which is basically just a matching technique. Fortunately, the other principles we outline require empirically falsifying alternative interpretations about what a measure or manipulation might mean. Once I had explicated construct validity through others' work, the next task was to ask the question below.

Do Principles of Construct Validation Also Apply to Persons and Settings?

The principles of construct validation listed above are not novel, though their mix might be slightly so. However, it is novel to ask how these principles apply to generalizing about people and settings. Can they "substitute" for random sampling in the many circumstances where such sampling is not possible?

To understand why the answer is a qualified "yes," imagine asking whether a causal relationship holds among men in general. The proximal similarity criterion is easy to meet here. Self-report or observation can place almost all humans into the relevant male and female categories with a high degree of validity. But if all the men in the studied sample come from Baltimore and are recruited in an employment agency, the sample is then homogeneous in these two attributes and in all factors correlated with them. For most purposes, Baltimore and employment agencies are conceptual irrelevancies, and to reduce this threat requires adding samples of men from other cities and social classes. Men also belong in the higher-order class of "human being." To demonstrate that a causal relationship is unique to men requires showing that it does not hold with women, a matter of discriminant validity that sharpens the generality of any obtained causal inference. Imagine, further, that exploration of causal explanatory processes shows that the causal relationship holds only with men over 30 or when men behaviorally engage themselves in job training, thus allowing an even more accurate specification of the causally affected group. (Note also how interpolation by age is involved in this hypothetical example.)

Now, imagine a more abstract case. Does the same causal relationship hold with depressives? We can conduct a causal study with a sample whose scores reach clinical levels on a broadly known depression test. By the proximal similarity criterion, we would then know we were working with depressives. But if they were all or mostly female, or elderly, or living alone, then gender, age, and household composition would be confounded with depression and might potentially undermine an interpretation in terms of depression. To make these irrelevancies heterogeneous requires expanding the sampling design to include depressives who vary by gender, age, and household composition. It is also important to make sure that the causal results are not artifacts of different concepts whose attributes partially overlap with those of depression, anxiety for instance. Thus, measures of anxiety are needed to probe whether the causal relationship under test is found with depressives but not with those who are anxious. When we turn to causal explanation, there are presumably theories of why a given intervention should affect depressives. If the postulated causal pathways involve steps unique to depressives because of suppositions about the nature of their illness, then empirically corroborating this pathway further strengthens the interpretation that the intervention is effective with depressives. And when we finally turn to interpolation, we ask how the causal relationship varies along the distribution of depression scores.

All this points to the utility of a construct validation framework for obtaining not just more secure generalizations about a cause and effect but also better generalizations about the kinds of people and settings involved in a causal relationship. A falsificationist epistemology is involved that complements the verificationism that pertains when proximal similarity alone is used for selecting measures and manipulations. Generalizing to types of persons and settings is a theoretical exercise that speaks to decisions about sampling, measurement, and substantive theory. It goes far beyond selecting instances because they manifestly belong within the classes of persons, settings, causes, and effects to which generalization is sought. Mere category membership is not enough in this alternative theory, which depends more on substantive theory and purposively selected samples and measures that are designed to rule out alternative interpretations of what a sample or measure represents. However, the foregoing discussion speaks to improving our knowledge of the UTOS that a given utos represents. But what about *UTOS and empirical robustness as additional external validity criteria?

Do These Principles of Construct Validity Apply to All Ways of Framing External Validity?

Taking construct validity seriously leads to designing studies whose sampling and measurement frameworks are broad enough to test whether a causal relationship is robust across various sources of irrelevancy and also across various cognate cause-and-effect concepts. Empirical replication implies a robust finding, while failure to replicate points to some of the conditions influencing effect size. To pin down meaning also demands falsifying alternative interpretations of who the persons and what the settings are in a study, and to this end, it is also useful to test a cause-effect relationship across the various subgroups in a study, statistical power permitting. Cronbach calls these sub-utos tests, and they are related to Campbell's notion of external validity as empirically demonstrated robust causal generalization.

However, in a single study, it is impossible to calculate independent effect sizes for all or even most of the major sources of variation in people, settings, effects, and ways of conceptualizing the cause or effect. The situation improves as the number of relevant studies grows, since this growth enlarges the number of UTOS domains across which robustness can be probed. A theory of causal generalization based on the construct validity literature requires extensive sampling to facilitate probes of causal robustness across persons, settings, causes, and effects. This sampling frame then facilitates learning some of the conditions under which a cause and effect are related. And when the relationship is demonstrably robust across many U, T, O, and S categories, this encourages the inferential claim that it is a reasonable bet to hold with as yet unexamined categories—thus reducing the *UTOS problem.

Once one accepts that interpretations are validated and not constructs themselves, it is evident that construct validation depends on substantive theory. If one knows which dimensions of the cause and effect are most involved in a causal relationship and which mediating processes generate the effect, then one can also ask some highly pertinent questions: Are these specific components and processes present in novel contexts? Can they be brought together by human design to set in motion the causal processes that generate the valued change? To what extent can components be substituted and still set this process in motion? Policy agents have more flexibility if an effective generative mechanism can be activated multiple ways and not just how it was first set in motion.

These thoughts about the transfer potential of explanatory knowledge are central to Cronbach's framing of causal generalization as extrapolation. He stresses that causal explanation is the Holy Grail of Science because it identifies causal mechanisms that can be transferred across a variety of different settings, persons, and causal agents. The mechanisms he describes function at a more microlevel than do experimental manipulations and are more proximal to the outcome, making them especially dependable as causal agents. In educational research, engaged time-on-task is such a generative mechanism and can be activated many different ways: as longer school days or years, more enthusiastic teachers, more personally relevant school materials, and so on. The crucial assumption is that so long as the generative mechanism is activated, the causal relationship will hold with all kinds of students, in all kinds of settings, and at all times. It should even work with different ways of instantiating academic engagement and with different curriculum topics and hence different outcomes. In promoting more exact causal knowledge of components and processes, construct validation promotes generalization to unstudied populations and settings—thus to *UTOS via a second mechanism over and above robust replication across a broad range of UTOSs. But some leap of faith is inevitably involved in all extrapolation to *UTOS. The size of the leap is less when a causal relationship has been well specified theoretically, when it is demonstrably cross-situational in its already established effects, and when the major factors that set a causal generative process in motion are clearly known.

Generic Methods for Extending External Validity Understood as Generalizing to UTOS

Preferred practice in the social sciences emphasizes being initially very explicit about the specific UTOS a research study is supposed to represent. This requires clearly delimiting the cause (T) and effect (O), as well as the set of populations (Us) and situations (Ss) in which the causal relationship should hold. Next, researchers should randomly select a sample of instances from within U and S so as to guarantee that the u and s with which they actually work formally represent these targets. This random selection should then be followed by randomly assigning units either to a comparison group or to experiencing what is usually a single purposively selected instance of T, hopefully one that meets explicit construct validity standards. Also required is measuring one or more purposively selected instances of O, provided they also meet such standards.

As my 1993 paper points out, this practice is much more honored in the breach than the observance. Indeed, Shadish et al. found only six studies meeting these exalted standards, and among these, some involved random selection from only locally meaningful populations. This almost universal design shortfall occurs because many experiments can be done only with those who are ready to volunteer for whatever experimental treatment they might be assigned. Yet such volunteering is rarely part of the definition of U. Nor will all of the schools or work sites that are approached be willing to take part in a randomized experiment, again limiting generalization. Furthermore, logistical realities preclude deliberately varying a number of different versions of an intervention so as to ensure variation in theoretical irrelevancies. And it is practically impossible to have much variation across historical time periods.

So, experimental practice has drifted toward purposive selection of u, t, o, and s, not to speak of time. Such selection cannot ensure that samples and populations are similar in the long run on both observed *and* unobserved variables. So, a more complex argument about correspondence has to be constructed, and I sought to develop one based on the construct validation principles mentioned earlier. My 1993 paper was titled: "A Quasi-Sampling Theory of the Generalization of Causal Relationships" to highlight that the sampling methods used in causal generalization are suboptimal if they do not involve random selection, just as experimental methods are suboptimal if they do not use random assignment. So, theory, data collection, and statistical analysis are going to be needed to falsify the many alternatives that usually remain because random selection could not be used in selecting samples of persons, settings, measures, and manipulations. "Quasi-sampling" highlights the notion that formal and purposive sampling methods are related to each other within external validity, much like experiments, and quasi-experiments are related to each other within internal validity.

In selecting instances of t and o, researchers are used to explicating the relevant theory and choosing proximally similar measures, even assessing the outcome using multiple items and multiple modes so as to vary some of the more salient sources of conceptual irrelevancy. Increasingly common is measuring treatment implementation in hopes of identifying those treatment components that are most and least causally efficacious and explicating and measuring the theoretical process through which the cause should have an impact on the effect. Black-box causal studies find little favor today (Cook, 2002b). Such sampling and measurement frameworks help data analysts elucidate what caused what and also generate greater causal specificity when compared with reliance on the construct labels that motivated the original treatment and outcome choices.

Less often explicated is how to choose instances of u and s when random selection is not possible. I argued that the same principles apply in these domains as in selecting measures and manipulations. However, practical issues loom more serious with u and s than with t and o. While all instances should be chosen to be proximally similar, heterogeneity of irrelevancies requires multiple subsamples. Discriminant validity requires sampling at least one contrast population. Causal explanation requires measures of processes that might account for why a given cause should affect a certain population. Interpolation requires sampling many levels within the population of interest, and extrapolation requires sampling from the extremes of relevant distributions. Taken together, the sampling burden is tremendous and has obvious implications for budgets, logistics, and statistical power. When generalizing to populations of persons and settings, it is tricky to sample several populations and subpopulations, different measures, and different levels within these measures. The whole thing has to be done selectively, targeted at where the sampling variation will make most difference to clear inference about the generality of a causal connection. As useful as a construct validity approach to generalization is, it is not perfect either theoretically or practically. It is no wonder that causal generalization is an inchoate, underexplored area in the theory of method.

Practical Methods to Extend Causal Generalization

Campbell (1975) maintained that causal generalization in the bench sciences is simple. When a finding is announced, it is quickly replicated in an independent laboratory. If the replication is successful, the phenomenon is then treated as general until proven otherwise. If it does not replicate, then, if it is important enough, theoretical hypotheses are specified about the conditions under which the treatment works, and these explanatory hypotheses are then tested in the next study in a planned program of research. As Campbell noted, this practice is easier in fields with a tradition of fast and frequent replication, as in the bench sciences. Unfortunately, replication is slower in the social sciences. It is also less frequent, both because it is not valued for its own sake and also because it does not routinely take place as part of the round of studies set off by an earlier discovery. We might also add that social phenomena are probably more variable by population, by setting, and by time than are the phenomena studied in the lab. So, the natural science model is not a great help, and my 1993 paper rejected it.

Instead, social scientists have struggled toward two sets of practices to improve causal generalization, the one set within individual, single empirical studies and the other across such studies—thus, as a literature review. My paper concentrated on these two sets of practices and sought to examine a justification for them through the principles of causal generalization derived from construct validity.

1. Within-Study Improvements

Cook and Campbell (1979) noted that in the planning process, researchers sometimes list targets of generalization other than the cause and effect. This practice outlines the UTOS to which generalization is to be made, though multiple U's and S's can be included. Once this is done, Cook and Campbell counsel sampling modal instances where this is possible. That is, if we want to generalize to African Americans living in the United States, we first profile this national population using extant data—usually demographic—and then choose a study sample that matches this profile in terms of income, education, city/suburban, location, and so on. This procedure ensures that any causal relationship discovered in the research applies to the most frequently occurring subpopulation within the class to which generalization is sought. It is quite different from doing the research with a convenience sample of persons who happen to belong in the target class but may be quite atypical of African Americans in general.

Even so, external validity is promoted when resources permit sampling additional subpopulations that vary in any irrelevant attributes that might be associated with the modal sample. This speaks to sampling for heterogeneity, if possible sampling the ranges within which African Americans can be found, whether these ranges be socioeconomic, regional, or urban/suburban/rural. (The best sources of heterogeneity to sample on are those that theory suggests will interact with the treatment under analysis, thus creating the greatest chance of identifying the specific boundary conditions that limit a causal relationship.)

Sometimes, the population cannot be specified in the multivariate terms profiling requires. Sometimes, also, logistical resources preclude sampling to match to a manifest central tendency. Then, sampling occurs to obtain instances belonging in the referent class, however atypical they may be. But statistical power permitting, it is still possible to do internal analyses to examine whether the treatment statistically interacts with respondent or setting characteristics to probe the robustness of results and to identify boundary conditionals. In a similar vein, treatment and control group slopes can be examined across the sampled range of some variables—say, age—to identify any causal thresholds that limit the application of a causal connection. This is interpolation at work.

But when all is said and done, sampling variation is difficult to achieve in single studies unless they have large budgets. So, greater reliance has to be placed on causal explanation, on understanding why and how a treatment made a difference. This is to examine whether this process could be instantiated different ways and to examine what light the causal process throws on the kinds of people and settings where the causal relationship is most and least likely to be replicated. My 1993 paper mentioned the role that qualitative data collection can play in this explanatory process, a feature that Cronbach especially highlighted. However, my discussion placed more emphasis on the role that carefully interpreted forms of path analysis can also play. Both strategies require careful and extensive data collection and reject the idea of black-box experiments. They also require careful analysis to deal with the errors in variables and the causal specification problems that are endemic to causal modeling, whether qualitative or quantitative. Nonetheless, the paper advocated carrying out such explanatory work in necessarily exploratory fashion. Cronbach was clearly the dominant force in this part of the paper. Campbell's deep suspicions about measurement error and specification biases did not make him a fan of causal modeling.

2. Between-Study Improvements

Literature reviews have a base in multiple studies, and so have the potential to include a greater range of persons, settings, times, ways of operationalizing the cause and effect, and even different outcomes and variants of the cause. So, the potential of literature reviews for promoting causal generalization is great.

Neither Campbell nor Cronbach wrote much about meta-analysis, the form of literature review on which my 1993 paper concentrated. It sought to show that meta-analysis achieves its benefits for causal generalization, not through random sampling, but through the construct validity principles outlined above. There can be no strong assumption that meta-analysis is based on the population of all possible studies or even a formally representative sample of them, however great the efforts put into finding unpublished studies.

Instead, I made the case that meta-analysis promotes causal generalization through (a) the greater opportunity it affords to represent the prototypical elements of any population, treatment, outcome, or situation across all the samples and instances achieved; (b) the greater variation it achieves in the sources of irrelevant heterogeneity; and (c) the greater chance it creates for discriminant validity, interpolation between levels, and casting light on how and why a causal connection holds.

All this applies to generalization to some highly specific UTOS. But it also can pertain across a broader array of human populations, causal constructs, outcomes, settings, and times than any single study can realistically achieve. By subgroup breakdowns (or the equivalent thereof within a multiple-regression framework), meta-analysis creates the potential to identify more boundary conditionals influencing effect sizes. It also provides a better test of the robustness of a causal relationship across a larger number of intended targets of generalization as well as across a greater range of sources of irrelevant variance, not to speak of relevant concepts for discriminant validity purposes. Since different levels of an independent variable might be sampled across studies, a greater chance also emerges of being able to interpolate and extrapolate in the parametric sense. Causal explanation has been partially promoted in the meta-analytic context by analysis of the conditions under which an effect appears. But meta-analysts have been less successful in identifying micromediating generative processes, in part because of fashion shifts in preferred explanatory variables, in part due to a predilection for black-box studies, and in part due to investigators measuring only the processes they personally prefer. So, meta-analysis has gone far in probing the empirical robustness of causal results, but this has not been because of random sampling.

As to research synthesis and *UTOS, some planned programs of research systematically explore the explanations that might account for some stable causal connection. There may be many different investigators in this planned research program, not all with the same theoretical beliefs. But their joint work on the topic promises to identify generative mechanisms. Another path to *UTOS is via extrapolation from robust findings, and here the clue is the heterogeneity and range of the samples across which a causal effect is found. The greater such sources of sampling are, the greater is the inductive confidence that a similar result will be obtained in as yet unexamined instances. The final path to *UTOS is by establishing the contingencies that condition a cause-effect relationship. If one securely knows what they are, and if one can measure in as yet unexamined contexts to see whether these conditions are met there, then one can get a better handle on knowing whether the effects will be found in the novel setting. So, meta-analysis constitutes an important path to better *UTOS extrapolations as well as to more secure and more numerous UTOS representations.

. . .

CONCLUSION

The purpose of this paper has been to illustrate how a struggle to understand differences between Cronbach and Campbell led me to borrow selectively from each of them to construct a theory of causal generalization. This theory was laid out in obscurely published papers in 1990, 1991, 1993, and 2000 and was then edited and elaborated in Shadish et al. (2002). My theory emphasizes three understandings of causal generalization, and the methods it suggests lean heavily on substantive theory and purposive selection instead of random selection. It acknowledges the superiority of the latter and advocates its use wherever possible. But it questions how often random sampling can be used when the object to be generalized is a causal statement, and it also questions whether, in the relatively rare cases where such sampling is used, it can successfully deal with all the topics that a broad theory of causal generalization should struggle with. Science moves slowly. Cronbach threw down his gauntlet to the Campbell tradition in the very early 1980s. A response took 10 years to make. And the elaboration and dissemination of this response took another 10 years. Intellectual titans struggle, while pygmies eventually respond.

REFERENCES

Campbell, D. T. (1957). Factors relevant to the validity of experiments in social settings. *Psychological Bulletin, 54,* 297-312.

Campbell, D. T. (1975). Prospective: Artifact and control. In R. Rosenthal & R. L. Rosnow (Eds.), *Artifact in behavioral research* (pp. 351-382). New York: Academic Press.

Campbell, D. T., & Fiske, D. W. (1959). Convergent and discriminant validation by the mulitrait-multimethod matrix. *Psychological Bulletin, 56,* 81-105.

Cook, T. D. (1990). The generalization of causal connections: Multiple theories in search of clear practice. In L. Sechrest, E. Perrin, &

J. Bunker (Eds.), *Research methodology: Strengthening causal interpretations of nonexperimental data* (DHHS Publication No. PHS 90-3454, pp. 9-31). Rockville, MD: Department of Health and Human Services.

Cook, T. D. (1991). Clarifying the warrant for generalized causal inferences in quasi-experimentation. In M. W. McLaughlin & D. C. Phillips (Eds.), *Evaluation and education: At quarter-century* (90th yearbook of the National Society for the Study of Education, Part II) (pp. 115-144). Chicago: University of Chicago Press.

Cook, T. D. (1993). A quasi-sampling theory of the generalization of causal relationships. *New Directions for Evaluation, 57,* 39-82.

Cook, T. D. (2000). Towards a practical theory of external validity. In L. Bickman (Ed.), *Contributions to research design: Donald Campbell's legacy* (Vol. 1). Thousand Oaks, CA: Sage.

Cook, T. D. (2002a). Generalization in the social sciences. In N. Smelser & P. Baltes (Eds.), *Encyclopedia of the social and behavioral sciences.* Oxford: Elsevier.

Cook, T. D. (2002b). Randomized experiments in educational policy research: A critical examination of the reasons the educational evaluation community has offered for not doing them. *Educational Evaluation and Policy Analysis, 24*(3), 175-199.

Cook, T. D., & Campbell, D. T. (1979). *Quasi-experimentation: Design and analysis issues for field settings.* Chicago: Rand McNally.

Cronbach, L. J. (1982). *Designing evaluations of educational and social programs.* San Francisco: Jossey-Bass.

Cronbach, L. J. (1989). Construct validation after thirty years. In R. L. Linn (Ed.), *Intelligence: Measurement, theory and public policy* (pp. 147-171). Urbana: University of Illinois Press.

Cronbach, L. J., Ambron, S. R., Dornbusch, S. M., Hess, R. D., Hornik, R. C., Phillips, D. C., et al. (1980). *Toward reform of program evaluation.* San Francisco: Jossey-Bass.

Cronbach, L. J., Gleser, G. C., Nanda, H., & Rajaratnam, N. (1972). *The dependability of behavioral measurements: Theory of generalizability for scores and profiles.* New York: Wiley.

Cronbach, L. J., & Meehl, P. E. (1955). Construct validity in psychological tests. *Psychological Bulletin, 52,* 281-302.

Lakoff, G. (1985). *Women, fire, and dangerous things.* Chicago: University of Chicago Press.

Shadish, W., Cook, T. D., & Campbell, D. T. (2002). *Experimental and quasi-experimental designs for generalized causal inference.* Boston: Houghton Mifflin.

Shadish, W. R., Cook, T. D., & Leviton, L. C. (1991). *Foundations of program evaluation: Theories of practice.* Newbury Park, CA: Sage.

⚜ 6 ⚜

THE EDUCATIVE EVALUATOR

An Interpretation of Lee J. Cronbach's Vision of Evaluation

Jennifer C. Greene

———•◦•———

Lee J. Cronbach was a brilliant, visionary thinker whose extraordinary career spanned multiple decades and disciplines. Cronbach invented original methodological theorems of lasting value and made significant contributions to real-world challenges of measurement and evaluation that are still vitally relevant today. Every time I teach a course in evaluation theory, I reread parts of Cronbach's classic works in evaluation (especially, Cronbach, 1982; Cronbach & Associates, 1980). And with every rereading, I gain additional insights into Cronbach's profoundly educative vision of evaluation—insights that are importantly applicable to my own thinking about evaluation and to my own evaluation practice. Cronbach's legacy in our field is huge and enduring.

Like Alkin and Christie in the present volume, I have always had great difficulty placing Lee Cronbach's ideas about evaluation into any given typology or categorization of evaluation theories, approaches, or traditions. I generally sort evaluation approaches by whose interests are being served and thereby by whose and which values are being promoted (see Greene, 2000). Different methodologies fairly neatly accompany my four main clusters of evaluation approaches, namely, those serving (1) the efficiency interests of policy-makers, (2) the accountability and ameliorative interests of on-site program managers, (3) the understanding and

---

Author's note: My sincere thanks to Lizanne DeStefano and Marvin Alkin for their thoughtful and critical comments on an earlier version of this paper.

development interests of direct service staff and affiliates, and (4) the democratic and social change interests of program beneficiaries and their allies. But my typology is not fundamentally about method. And I don't think Cronbach's contributions to the evaluation community are fundamentally about method, either. Perhaps his theory was launched from his lifelong expertise and interest in method. But Cronbach's vision of evaluation has more to do with positioning evaluation to importantly inform broad, extensive discourse about enduring social problems, and thereby to advance societal betterment, than with championing a particular methodology or even methodological rigor per se as evaluation's most prized quality. Moreover, with his expansive concept of the policy-shaping community (PSC) as the appropriate audience for evaluation—an audience that includes policymakers, civil servants, interested citizens, advocacy groups, and the media, among others—Cronbach's theory defies simple categorization by whose interests are served. In my typology, therefore, Cronbach's ideas about evaluation jump off the two-dimensional page into complex, multidimensional interweavings of method, program complexity, valued interests, and standpoint.

My discussion of Cronbach's ideas about evaluation is organized around these four interrelated core issues: method in evaluation, understanding of programs in context, evaluation's educative interests, and the political location of evaluation in society. I will include relevant roots of these ideas, as available. And I will endeavor to frequently remind the reader that what follows is my interpretation of the ideas of this great mind. I am deeply humbled by the challenge of this task.

ON METHOD IN LEE J. CRONBACH'S THEORY OF EVALUATION

> Merit lies not in form of inquiry, but in relevance of information. The context of command or accommodation, the stage of program maturity, and the closeness of the evaluator to the probable users should all affect the style of an evaluation.
>
> Much that is written on evaluation recommends some one "scientifically rigorous" plan. Evaluations should, however, take many forms, and less rigorous approaches have value in many circumstances. (Cronbach & Associates, 1980, p. 7)

These are two of the infamous 95 theses figuratively nailed to the wall by Cronbach and his Stanford University colleagues in their bold call for reform of program evaluation. They reflect both constancy and evolution in Cronbach's methodological thinking over time, as well as, more importantly his robust appreciation for the complex challenges of field applications of social science such as program evaluation.

Cronbach began his career in psychological and educational tests and measurement, an interest he maintained throughout his lifelong work. "My most sustained line of investigation, with publications extending over more than 40 years, has had to do with methods for appraising the accuracy of psychological or educational measurements and of inferences from them" (Cronbach, 1991, p. 385, as cited in Kupermintz, n.d., p. 2). This line of investigation included numerous seminal works, including the invention of the Cronbach alpha

(Cronbach, 1951), an inspired treatise on construct validity (Cronbach & Meehl, 1955), and the ingenious development of generalizability theory (Cronbach, Gleser, Nanda, & Rajaratnam, 1972). As these works clearly indicate, Cronbach's measurement commitment was indeed to enhancing the accuracy, quality, and defensibility of our measurement *inferences,* to enhancing our confidence that we are measuring, for instance, algebraic problem solving and not recall of standard algorithms. Generalizability theory, for example, is an explication of various sources of previously undifferentiated error, which prominently feature psychological and environmental testing conditions, such as surface features of test design and differences in testing settings across occasions. For Cronbach, that is, these kinds of contextual factors constituted significant influences on the test-taking experience that must be accounted for and understood in assessing inference quality. This attention to testing context parallels Cronbach's deliberate consideration of program context in his ideas about high quality and defensible inferences in program evaluation. Similarly, Cronbach's sustained interest in construct validation as the most important facet of inference quality is mirrored in his evaluative emphasis on the importance of substantive program understanding. These ideas are discussed in the next section.

But first, back to method, Cronbach was unquestionably a brilliant methodologist whose life work is a testament to the power of good and thoughtful method. Yet, for Cronbach, good method was always *in the service of* defensible inferences, solid conceptual understanding, and actionable substantive insights. Cronbach's theory of evaluation does not champion a particular methodology. Rooted in his highly influential work in the "two disciplines" of psychology (Cronbach, 1957, 1975), Cronbach's advice to evaluators is "to not declare allegiance to either a quantitative-scientific-summative methodology or a qualitative-naturalistic-descriptive methodology" and "to launch a small fleet of studies [rather] than to put all [the evaluation] resources into a single approach" (Cronbach & Associates, 1980, p. 7). Related to this stance of methodological pluralism, but perhaps more fundamentally, Cronbach's evaluation theory does not advance a particular evaluation question (as in a causal question about treatment effectiveness) or a specific audience, as noted previously. So, evaluation for Cronbach is not about using a particular methodology to answer a particular kind of question of importance to a particular privileged audience. Rather, Cronbach envisioned evaluation as an educative enterprise, centered on better understanding society's enduring social problems and the ways in which the specific policy and program being evaluated are meaningfully addressing one such problem.

LEE J. CRONBACH'S COMMITMENT TO CONTEXTUALIZED PROGRAM UNDERSTANDING

Cronbach's commitment to a deep and comprehensive understanding of the intricacies and interstices of the program being evaluated *as embedded within* its complex and dynamic context arose, I believe, from his midcareer work in interactionism.[1] This work, which

Cronbach conducted with his colleague Dick Snow, sought to identify not the single educational intervention that worked the best on the average, but rather the various educational treatments that worked best for different learners with different constellations of aptitudes. Recognizing and honoring the complexity of meaningful human action, Cronbach and Snow rejected the relevance of main effects or even first-order interactions for explaining such action in favor of complex, higher-order aptitude-treatment interactions (ATIs) (Cronbach & Snow, 1977).

> [And] a three-year project turned into a ten-year search in the literature, laboratory, and field for the elusive aptitude-treatment holy grail(s). Little that was consistent could be defended with the empirical base Cronbach and Snow were working from, save for the conclusion that students with higher general cognitive ability typically profit from a learning environment that offers them autonomy, responsibility, and control. But the quest [itself] nevertheless led to profound insights about the scope of the challenge and the needed reform in thinking and methodology.... It became clear that a rigid scientific ideal of a network of general propositions, grounded in a strong empirical set of quantifiable observations across many contexts, would fall short. (Kupermintz, n.d., p. 13)

That is, the failure of the ATI framework to generate significant and consistent interaction effects of teaching on learning led Cronbach to reject the search for generalizable propositions as the primary aim of science and to turn instead to comprehensive understandings of the complexities of human interaction in contexts that are themselves unique, dynamic, and changing. Cronbach thus came to believe that both context and time matter in our understanding of the social or human world. What might be "true" in one context—say, for example, the success of a drill-and-practice approach for learning math facts—may not be "true" in a different context. Even two classrooms in the same school serving much the same kinds of children are inevitably different in important and unique ways. Moreover, said Cronbach, in one simple and oft-quoted declaration, "Generalizations decay!" What may have been "true" in 1993 is not likely to stay "true" in 2003, and certainly not in 2023. Routines, norms, behaviors, and indeed cultures evolve and change over time; thus, often, so does the warrant for a given scientific understanding or statement of "fact." The failure of the ATI adventure, in short, led Cronbach to rethink the priorities and fundamental purposes of applied social science:

> Instead of making generalization [and nomothetic theoretical networks] the ruling consideration in our research, I suggest that we reverse our priorities [and focus instead on rich contextual understanding]. An observer collecting data in one particular situation is in a position to appraise a practice or proposition in that setting, observing effects in context. In trying to describe and account for what happened, he[2] will give attention to whatever variables were controlled, but he will give equally careful attention to uncontrolled conditions, to personal characteristics, and to events that occurred during treatment and measurement. As he goes from situation to situation, his first task is to describe and interpret the effect anew in each locale, perhaps taking into account factors unique to that locale of series of events. (Cronbach, 1975, pp. 124–125)

In this restatement of the purposes and character of applied social science, Cronbach first highlighted the importance of attending to multiple features, both controlled and uncontrolled, of the educational or social practice-in-context being studied. Second, he underscored the importance of going from "situation to situation" and refining our understanding as we go, as well as extrapolating what is learned in one setting to others.

In evaluation, these ideas are well captured in Cronbach's evaluation design concept of UTOS (Cronbach, 1982), a systematic framework of units (populations, sites); treatments; observations (data collected, notably on outcomes); and settings for the design and use of evaluation studies. By intention, it provides a structure for systematically planning a given evaluation study to extend the results of that study to future program settings, as in evaluating a demonstration program for possible wider dissemination. Beyond this somewhat limited intention, the UTOS framework offers a comprehensive way of thinking about what is important for evaluators to understand, *and* it represents a structure within which such understandings can be aggregated and continually refined across settings. Cronbach's primary emphasis in this framework for evaluation was thus on the quality and defensibility of inferences to other contexts, on external validity rather than internal validity. Cronbach was committed to situating evaluation as serving to enhance our understanding of the character of enduring social problems and how we can best address them in this context and the next and the next, rather than to strong inferences about the causal effects of a particular intervention in a given set of sites. Here, Cronbach's views were in sharp disagreement with those of Donald Campbell, leading to a superb exchange in the literature on the relative merits of external versus internal validity (Mark, 1986; see also Campbell & Stanley, 1966; Cronbach, 1982).

In some important ways, Lee Cronbach crafted a kind of "program champion" role for evaluators. He believed that the thoughtful development and implementation of worthy social and educational programs was a far more difficult task than the evaluation of such programs. Evaluation, therefore, should most importantly serve to help identify promising and effective programs or program components, activities, materials, and combinations thereof, through the comprehensive, in-depth, and contextualized assessment of program implementation and impact. Evaluation should be conducted *in the service of* stronger social programming. Moreover, in support of this mission, evaluators should be basically sympathetic toward the program they are evaluating—on the lookout for such promise and potential and, in this way, program champions.

In short, Cronbach argued against using evaluation simply to answer the question, "Did this program cause the desired outcomes in participants?" both because that question is very difficult to answer in the diverse settings of the real world and because the question misses the point. The point being that because the program will look somewhat different in each context, evaluation should endeavor to understand in rich detail the challenges *and* the potentialities of a given social or educational intervention in this context and in that one and in that one over there, toward important insights into how to best address our persistent social problems. Again from the 95 theses, "Program evaluation is a process by which society learns about itself" (Cronbach & Associates, 1980, p. 2).

THE EVALUATOR AS EDUCATOR:
LEE J. CRONBACH'S ENDURING LEGACY

Envisioning evaluation as fundamentally educative, positioning evaluation in society as an educational endeavor, thinking of evaluators as educators, these are Lee J. Cronbach's most significant and profound contributions to the theory and practice of evaluation. Once again, from the 95 theses (Cronbach & Associates, 1980):

> The evaluator is an educator; his success is to be judged by what others learn. (p. 11)
>
> Program evaluation should contribute to enlightened discussion of alternative plans for social action. (p. 2)

As noted previously, Cronbach was not primarily interested in advancing a particular methodology for evaluation. Rather, he adopted a stance of methodological eclecticism for evaluation *in the service of* generating comprehensive understandings of program challenge and promise in varied contexts. These understandings, as framed and structured by his systematic UTOS program theory, could importantly illuminate key features of the contexts that matter for this particular social or educational program and key features of the program that appear to be effective, or promising, or perhaps miss the mark. Then, we could accumulate such understandings across multiple evaluation studies: Recall that Cronbach rejected the single grand evaluative study (especially experimental ones) in favor of "launching a fleet" of smaller studies. With thoughtful review and open discussion and critique of these accumulated understandings, argued Cronbach, society could develop important insights into the character of our most enduring and challenging social and educational problems *and* into the kinds of interventions that offer hope and promise of providing some effective responses to these problems. Program evaluation thereby contributes to enlightened discussion of alternative plans for social action, and program evaluation becomes a process by which society learns about itself.

Another critical facet of Cronbach's educative vision for evaluation was his promotion of evaluation's role in providing constructive feedback in real time for program implementers and clients. Cronbach was the first to advance this "formative" role for evaluation, in marked contrast to evaluation's dominant "summative" role at that time (Cronbach, 1963, 1964; Scriven, 1967). Cronbach viewed summative evaluation as too often limited to those aspects of the program that could be experimentally manipulated or quantitatively measured with standardized instruments, leaving other equally important aspects unattended or, even worse, concealed from the light of public debate. Beyond these methodological concerns, Cronbach also asserted his educative vision for evaluation in his argument for formative evaluation. The evaluator as educator, stated Cronbach, is not a distant, ostensibly impartial observer and judge, but rather an engaged actor in the setting, learning alongside program stakeholders about the highs and lows of the program and sharing insights along the way that program staff could use for ongoing program improvement, "even if such real-time adjustments spoiled the scientific elegance of the study" (Kupermintz, n.d., p. 17). Scores of evaluators have been inspired by Cronbach's abiding commitment to evaluation as education, a commitment that should always trump the technical requirements of scientific method.

EVALUATION AS EDUCATION IN THE SERVICE OF A MORE DEMOCRATIC SOCIETY

Finally, the political dimensions of Cronbach's thinking about evaluation must be acknowledged.[3] Along with Carol Weiss, Cronbach is credited for drawing attention to the inevitable political inherency of evaluation and to the ways in which politics influences all aspects of evaluation, from the very decision to evaluate to the uses made of the evaluation results.

> A theory of evaluation must be as much a theory of political interaction as it is a theory of how to determine facts. (Cronbach & Associates, 1980, p. 3)

> Evaluations are to be judged by the extent to which they help the political community achieve its ends. The logic of science must come to terms with the logic of politics. (Cronbach, 1982, p. ix)

Beyond these general pronouncements, Cronbach offered particular standpoints on just who constitutes the "political community" and just what this community should do with evaluation results. I interpret these standpoints as underscoring the *public value* of evaluation through encouraging open, critical conversation among multiple, diverse evaluation stakeholders about the meaning and implications of evaluation findings. And in my view, open and inclusive conversation about important public issues is a key element of a working democracy. So, although I do not think that Cronbach intended to explicitly position evaluation as a democratizing practice in and of itself, I do perceive some of the seeds of the contemporary interest in democratizing approaches to evaluation in some of Lee J. Cronbach's ideas. I share two of these ideas herein.

First, Cronbach (1982) believed that "evaluation can rarely play its proper role . . . which is to assist participants in the political process to resolve conflicts intelligently . . . by letting a single decision maker or a single center of power set the questions for its attention" (p. 8). In place of a single decision maker, Cronbach defined and positioned a broad PSC as the important audience for evaluation. The PSC comprises (a) public servants, that is, policy and program decision makers and implementers; (b) interested citizens and special interest/advocacy groups (which could readily include program participants and their allies); and (c) "illuminators," notably "reporters and commentators, academic social scientists and philosophers, gadflies such as . . . Ralph Nader, and some novelists and dramatists" (Cronbach & Associates, 1980, p. 103). The PSC should also include the administrators and direct service staff of the program being evaluated.

> All those persons whose voices may be raised during the political discussion and all those who will shape the program as it operates are part of the evaluator's target audience. Ideally, he will reach even further, to normally silent citizens whose voices *should* be raised. (Cronbach, 1982, p. 11)

This is a broad inclusive statement of who are legitimate audiences for evaluation. It acknowledges the legitimacy of multiple perspectives on the evaluation issues at hand. It embraces those usually excluded from important conversations, while not silencing those usually in control. And it seeks to mitigate these dynamics of power and privilege by encouraging open and public conversations about the issues at hand.

Second, that is, Cronbach encouraged the PSC to not just passively receive evaluation results, but to actively engage in discussing and critiquing them. "There is need for exchanges [about evaluation results] more energetic than the typical academic discussion and more responsible than debate among partisans" (Cronbach & Associates, 1980, 95 theses, p. 10). In this context, Cronbach and Associates (1980) proposed the mechanism of the social problem study group as one forum for such responsible, nonpartisan exchanges. Such groups would comprise specialists outside the political arena. While clearly not as inclusive or dialogic as many contemporary approaches to democratic evaluation (see House & Howe, 1999), I believe that Cronbach was endeavoring to position evaluation as public enterprise, a vehicle for enhanced societal understanding, an opportunity for public discourse about important public issues, much like John Willinsky's promotion of educational research as "an intelligible source of public edification and political deliberation" (Willinsky, 2001). In Cronbach's vision, evaluation practice would offer an opportunity for ongoing reflection and learning,[4] and evaluation results would inform ongoing public discourse about important public issues, a discourse actively engaged by participants from multiple corners of the PSC.

AND SO . . .

Influence comes from engagement, not detachment.

—Cronbach & Associates, 1980, p. 53

Cronbach sought an engaged, influential role for evaluation. And so he framed evaluation as a fundamentally educative endeavor. For meaningful education is at root inspirational and revolutionary. And that is influence.

NOTES

1. It was during this period, the first half of the 1970s, that I studied at Stanford and had many engagements with Lee Cronbach. I also conducted a dissertation that contributed to the aptitude-treatment interaction (ATI) discourse at the time.

2. In Cronbach's writing, all evaluators were male, and all evaluation stakeholders were female.

3. This is undoubtedly the most-interpreted part of this paper, or the part of the paper in which I speak almost as loudly as Cronbach. As a former student in Cronbach's evaluation and measurement classes and a present proponent of democratizing approaches to evaluation, I see these connections clearly. But, I acknowledge that *my* standpoint may well be unique.

4. "Teaching begins when the evaluator first sits down with members of the policy-shaping community to elicit their questions. It continues during every contact the evaluator has with program participants or others in his audience" (Cronbach, 1982, p. 9).

REFERENCES

Campbell, D. T., & Stanley, J. C. (1966). *Experimental and quasi-experimental designs for research.* Chicago: Rand McNally.

Cronbach, L. J. (1951). Coefficient alpha and the internal structure of tests. *Psychometrika, 16,* 297–334.

Cronbach, L. J. (1957). The two disciplines of scientific psychology. *American Psychologist, 12,* 671–684.

Cronbach, L. J. (1963). Course improvement through evaluation. *Teachers College Record, 64,* 672–683.

Cronbach, L. J. (1964). Evaluation for course improvement. In R. W. Heath (Ed.), *New curricula* (pp. 231–248). New York: Harper & Row.

Cronbach, L. J. (1975). Beyond the two disciplines of scientific psychology. *American Psychologist, 30,* 116–127.

Cronbach, L. J. (1982). *Designing evaluations of educational and social programs.* San Francisco: Jossey-Bass.

Cronbach, L. J., & Associates (1980). *Toward reform of program evaluation.* San Francisco: Jossey-Bass.

Cronbach, L. J., Gleser, G. C., Nanda, H., & Rajaratnam, N. (1972). *The dependability of behavioral measurements.* New York: Wiley.

Cronbach, L. J., & Meehl, P. E. (1955). Construct validity in psychology tests. *Psychological Bulletin, 52,* 281–302.

Cronbach, L. J., & Snow, R. E. (1977). *Aptitudes and instructional methods: A handbook for research on aptitude-treatment interactions.* New York: Irvington.

Greene, J. C. (2000). Understanding social programs through evaluation. In N. K. Denzin & Y. S. Lincoln (Eds.), *Handbook of qualitative research* (2nd ed., pp. 981–999). Thousand Oaks, CA: Sage.

House, E. R., & Howe, K. R. (1999). *Values in evaluation and social research.* Thousand Oaks, CA: Sage.

Kupermintz, H. (n.d.). *The Tao of Lee: Lee J. Cronbach's contributions to educational psychology.* Unpublished paper, University of Colorado, Boulder.

Mark, M. M. (1986). Validity typologies and the logic and practice of quasi-experimentation. *New Directions for Evaluation, 31,* 47–66.

Scriven, M. (1967). The methodology of evaluation. In R. W. Tyler, R. M. Gagne, & M. Scriven (Eds.), *Perspectives of curriculum evaluation* (pp. 39–83). Chicago: Rand McNally.

Willinsky, J. (2001). The Strategic Education Research Program and the public value of research. *Educational Researcher, 30*(1), 5–14.

7

MY VIEWS OF EVALUATION AND THEIR ORIGINS

Peter H. Rossi

ORIGINS AND INFLUENCES

Born in New York City in 1921, I grew up in a bilingual, working-class family; my parents migrated in 1910 from Italy. We lived in neighborhoods dominated by recent Italian immigrants but also with Germans, Irish, and a few blacks. My public schooling began just as the Great Depression started. Although my family was not among the worst off, all around us were many families suffering from grinding poverty resulting from long-term unemployment of workers in those families. Working-class children growing up in those years faced a bleak future of poverty and severely restricted opportunities. These conditions made a deep impression on me, and I drifted toward the political left in high school.

I was fortunate in being one of the few in my neighborhood who was able to go to college, a step made possible by the no-tuition policies of New York's municipal colleges. I became an undergraduate in the late 1930s at the College of the City of New York. By that time, my political views were at the extreme left. I was a Trotskyist deeply concerned with issues of poverty, inequality, and oppression and convinced that change for the better could come only through a socialist revolution. My concerns for social justice persist to this day, although I abandoned the far left when it became clear to me in the late 30s that socialist regimes, such as in the U.S.S.R., were the inevitable outcomes of Bolshevik Leninism, viciously totalitarian and cesspools of injustice. A confirmed liberal and advocate for a welfare state, my subsequent lifelong political views are surely one important motivation for my pursuit of evaluation research as a career.

Source: Excerpted from Rossi, P. H. (2004). My views of evaluation and their origins. In M. C. Alkin (Ed.), *Evaluation roots*. Thousand Oaks, CA: Sage Publications.

My undergraduate major was in sociology, chosen because I thought it would lead to a safe civil service job as a social worker, where I would have opportunities to do some good. Although I enjoyed the social work courses I took, much more intriguing were the required research methods and statistics courses, leading me to consider becoming a social researcher. Of course, I had only the fuzziest ideas about what social researchers did, and I did not know how to become one, except that I needed graduate training.

World War II intervened, and I was drafted into the armed forces in 1942. I spent more than 3 years as an enlisted man in the Army, serving in France and Germany. When I was discharged in 1945, the educational entitlement provisions of the G.I. Bill provided me with 4 years' tuition and a small stipend, which enabled me to enroll in Columbia University's graduate sociology department. There, I had the extraordinary luck to become a research assistant in Columbia's Bureau of Applied Social Research, headed by Paul F. Lazarsfeld, who also became my primary mentor and my dissertation advisor. I worked on several studies as an apprentice learning survey design and analysis, ending up as the principal investigator (PI) on a study of residential mobility, later published as *Why Families Move* (Rossi, 1956). Lazarsfeld was an inspiring teacher, especially one-on-one. The main lesson I learned from him is that the primary problem in all empirical social research is how best to make convincing causal analyses. Lazarsfeld also thought that randomized experiments in principle generated the most plausible causal analyses but that experiments were not practical for social research. His primary approach was to use designs that we would call "quasi-experiments"—mainly sample surveys—relying on cross-tabs to impose statistical controls. In particular, he had great hopes that panel studies involving repeated measurements would become the primary design used in the best of social research. My residential mobility study followed his advice in being a two-wave panel study relating household composition changes to subsequent residential moves.

Working under Lazarsfeld also gave me an appreciation for applied social research. Although much of the applied work at the bureau centered around exploring the effects of mass media, the prize studies were those concerned with policy issues such as voting behavior, the correlates of totalitarian attitudes, and the effects of housing design on the social relations of residents.

After receiving the PhD in 1951, my first appointment was in Harvard's Department of Social Relations. My interests in applied research were not in tune with the department's central concern with the development of social relations theory, so when the University of Chicago offered me a position in 1955, I jumped at the chance to move to a more congenial environment.

At Chicago, I was attracted to work within the National Opinion Research Center (NORC), affiliated with the university. I became the director of NORC in 1960. At NORC, I was able to participate with great enthusiasm in the burgeoning of applied social research that got under way initially under the Kennedy administration and continued under the Johnson administration. Much of the research undertaken at NORC was funded by grants from and contracts with federal agencies and by grants from major private foundations. These were mainly public policy studies evaluating the effectiveness of programs such as federal science and engineering fellowships and community action programs, all related to ongoing federal programs. We also undertook evaluation studies with funding from private foundations, notably a study of the effects of attending

Catholic schools on the occupational and income attainments of adult Catholics. NORC also undertook needs assessment studies such as the first national survey of criminal victimization and a national survey of participation in adult educational programs.

For the most of the NORC period, I did not identify my research activities as evaluation. Indeed, at the time, evaluation was just beginning to emerge as a professional field. Sometime in the middle 1960s, Fred Mosteller asked me to give a paper at the American Statistical Association meetings on the evaluation strategies we were following at NORC. My first impulse was to turn Fred down and claim that we were not conducting evaluations, but after some thought, I began to understand that Mosteller was right; much of the NORC research was really one form or another of evaluation. Around the same time, I read an early draft of Don Campbell's 1963 classic paper (with Julian Stanley). Campbell's paper was especially important in giving me a framework that led me to more completely understand the limitations in the kind of quasi-experimental designs we were using and led me to develop a deep appreciation of the value of randomized experimental designs. In the late 1960s, I became familiar with the New Jersey-Pennsylvania Income Maintenance Experiment being conducted by Mathematica and the University of Wisconsin, a dramatic, convincing demonstration that large-scale field experiments could be carried out successfully.

Donald Campbell wielded probably the most important influence on my thinking about evaluation. Other important figures include Paul Lazarsfeld, Fred Mosteller, Lee Cronbach, William Cochran, and later, Richard Berk, Howard Freeman, Tom Cook, and Robert Boruch.

As NORC grew larger, I found myself becoming more an administrator and salesman than a hands-on researcher. In addition, I was not a top-notch administrator. I was good at getting grants and contracts, but I never developed the administrative skills that would assure that research projects were finished on time and within budget.

Seeking to return to research, I left Chicago in 1967 to join the Department of Social Relations at Johns Hopkins as department chair. While there, I conducted policy-related studies for the Kerner Commission. I was also invited to join a small group sponsored by the Russell Sage Foundation concerned with "evaluating evaluations." Members of our group included Howard Freeman, Thomas Cook, Richard Snow, and Henry Levin. My assignment was to write a critique of the New Jersey-Pennsylvania Income Maintenance Experiment (Rossi & Lyall, 1974). Meeting about twice a year to discuss progress on our evaluations of evaluations, our sessions were exciting and challenging experiences. I began to get more and more involved in evaluation issues.

In 1974, I moved to the University of Massachusetts at Amherst as the Stuart A. Rice Professor of Sociology, from which I retired in 1992. My quarter century at U-Mass was consumed largely with applied research, almost a score of monographs, some 150 articles, and five editions of *Evaluation: A Systematic Approach*. Since retirement, I have continued my work. My last monograph, on federal food programs, was *Feeding the Poor* (1999), and the seventh edition of *Evaluation* will appear in fall 2003.

Looking back over my intellectual development, I started out identifying myself as a social researcher concerned largely with applied work. However, by 1970, my primary professional self-identification changed, and I began to consider myself primarily as an evaluation researcher. That change was more terminological than substantive. There is substantial continuity in my work over my entire career. If anything, the change meant that I was more attentive to evaluation as a field and to evaluators as the audience for my work.

I also thought of myself less as a sociologist and more as a social scientist, using the theories, methods, and knowledge of all the social sciences and statistics when relevant to the empirical studies in which I was engaged.

Although I have been called an "evaluation theorist," I do not consider myself to be one. Rather, my self-image is that I am first of all a working evaluation researcher. I believe that the reason I am considered as a theorist is that I am the senior author of one of the major evaluation textbooks, *Evaluation: A Systematic Approach*. Indeed, my coauthors, the late Howard Freeman and now Mark Lipsey, have contributed as much as I did to each of the seven editions of the book and, in fairness, ought also to be considered theorists on account of their contributions.

Until 1978, I am sure I would have turned down any suggestion that I write a textbook on evaluation. In that year, Howard Freeman and I were separately asked to write papers on evaluation in the United States for a conference sponsored by the State Department. Our papers were almost identical in content. After listening to our papers, an Organization for Economic Cooperation and Development (OECD) staff member took the two of us to lunch and proposed that we write a small monograph on evaluation that OECD could distribute to its evaluators who worked in developing countries. Howard and I agreed to take on the project. It turned out that we enjoyed working with each other so much that we decided to expand the resulting monograph into a textbook for the U.S. market. When we finished the textbook in 1979, we went on turning out edition after edition over 15 years, mainly to continue our enjoyable collaboration. That is why the textbook has persisted in print for 20 years. Indeed, when Freeman died prematurely in 1993, I decided to let the fifth edition be the last. I changed my mind later when my editor at Sage arranged a meeting with Mark Lipsey and I found another congenial collaborator.

As most academics know, successful textbooks are those that are ecumenical in coverage and evenhanded in expounding alternative professional viewpoints. My coauthors and I have tried to write a successful textbook that is useful and informative to beginning students of evaluation and, importantly, attractive to their instructors. Consequently, the textbook does not expound a single coherent view of evaluation, nor does it represent only my own (or my coauthors') view of the field. Nor do I consider it to be among the best of my work; that high position is occupied by the monographs and articles based on the empirical research I have conducted. Indeed, *Down and Out in America* (1989), essentially a social epidemiological study of the Chicago homeless in the mid-1980s, is the work of which I am most proud.

WHAT IS EVALUATION?

My own view of evaluation research is that it is *applied* social research. It consists essentially in the application of the repertory of social research methods to provide credible information that can aid in the formation of public policy, in the design of programs, and in the assessment of the effectiveness and efficiency of social policies and social programs.[1] There are several critical components of this view of evaluation:

1. Evaluation is social research applied to answering policy-oriented questions. As such, an important criterion for judging evaluations is the extent to which they successfully apply the canons of social research.

2. The primary aim of evaluation is to aid stakeholders in their decision making on policies and programs. This implies that evaluation findings are to be made available to stakeholders but may or may not be critically influential in decision making. Evaluators should try to be useful within the limits of professional ability and ethics, but being useful is not a primary goal. "Getting it right" is more important than "getting along."

3. Evaluation involves making judgments. The several major activities of evaluation each have judgments as part of their findings.

    a. Needs assessments: Does a program correctly conceptualize the social problem it addresses?
    b. Program "theory": Is the alleged "theory" of a program consistent with existing social science knowledge and theory and internally consistent?
    c. Implementation: Has a program been implemented with fidelity and at the level of intensity needed?
    d. Impact: Is a program effective in the sense that desired outcomes are statistically and substantively greater for program participants than had they not participated in the program?
    e. Efficiency: Do the benefits of the effects produced by an effective program justify the costs of the program to society and participants?

Note that there are several activities often called evaluation that are not covered by this view. I do not consider designing programs and providing advice on how to manage programs to be evaluation activities. Such activities might involve the application of knowledge derived from social research, but I do not consider them to be social research. I do not deny that designing and managing programs are important activities calling for high levels of skill; however, they are not social research.

Social policy is made in a democratic society through democratic political processes. Evaluation research contributes to the formation and changes in social policy through providing information to decision makers consisting of judgments in each of the five aspects of programs listed above. The best an evaluator can hope for is that the findings of evaluations are paid attention in decision making about the programs involved. In democratic decision making, many factors are involved, including evaluation findings. Indeed, I would not have it any other way!

My view of evaluation is not specifically tied to any one social science discipline. Indeed, important evaluations have been undertaken by psychologists, sociologists, economists, political scientists, anthropologists, statisticians, and researchers from the professions of education, public health, and public administration. In my own work, I have borrowed theory, concepts, and methods from many fields, and I urged my students to cross disciplinary boundaries in coursework and in seeking advice.

Of course, there are many tools in the social research repertory. Given some specific evaluation issue, some tools are to be preferred over others. The preference hierarchy is formed by the likelihood that the findings produced will be found credible by formal or informal peer review of evaluators. Unfortunately, the better research designs are usually the most expensive, time-consuming, and sometimes unethical. Recognizing that fiscal, ethical, and time constraints are always present, Freeman and I proposed the "good enough rule," namely that the evaluator faced with a specific program to evaluate should choose the best evaluation design possible that could be accomplished under the constraints involved. In some circumstances, the constraints are so heavy that the only design possible is very far from the top of the goodness hierarchy of designs, in which case the evaluator should simply refuse to undertake the evaluation. In other instances, it may not be possible to conduct an ethical evaluation, and an evaluator must refuse to undertake it. Freeman and I have never been completely enthusiastic about the "good enough rule" because the goodness hierarchy of evaluation designs has never been authoritatively defined, nor is it likely that firm consensus will arise over any proposed hierarchy. Consequently, the "good enough" rule currently provides ample room for excuses for sloppiness in evaluation. My hope is that stronger consensus about the goodness hierarchy of research designs will eventually remove at least some of the ambiguities encountered in applying the "good enough" rule.

Of all the evaluation tasks, impact assessment is the most challenging technically. Whenever an opportunity in my career arose to design and conduct an impact assessment, I enjoyed that evaluation task more than any of the other evaluation tasks. The chief obstacle to estimating impact is the always-present possibility that changes appearing to result from a program may have actually occurred absent the program. The evaluation design that has the best chance of detecting program-specific impact is the controlled randomized experiment. I regret that I was able to be only a PI on one randomized experiment, but that experience was the most satisfying among all the evaluations I have conducted.

Although I am ideologically committed to advocating for social change that will reduce inequality and improve social conditions for all in this country and all over the world—especially for the lowest socioeconomic layers—I believe that the proper path to those goals is through democratic political processes. Evaluation is not and should not be used as an instrument for social change; that is the central task of political processes. Evaluation's contribution in this respect is to add to our body of knowledge about social processes and particularly to improving communal efforts (programs) used to better social conditions. Evaluation is a servant to incremental social change.

In the long run, the most important contribution that evaluation research can make toward improving our society will stem from the accumulation of knowledge about which attempts to ameliorate adverse social conditions work and which do not. This vision is a variant on Campbell's "Experimenting Society," in which we try to design effective programs, sometimes fail, and sometimes succeed. The function of evaluation research is to distinguish between failure and success. I believe that our successes will lead to an increasingly better society.

NOTE

1. Mainly for convenience, I restrict the term *evaluation* to the evaluation of social programs. There are other activities that are quite similar, such as medical clinical trials and quality control in manufacturing, but have special features with which it would be too difficult to deal here.

REFERENCES

Alkin, M. C., (2004). *Evaluation roots: tracing theorists' views and influences.* Thousand Oaks, CA: Sage.

Campbell, D. T., & Stanley, J. C. (1963). Experimental and quasi-experimental designs for research on teaching. In N. L. Gage (Ed.), *Handbook of research on teaching* (pp. 171–246). Chicago: Rand McNally.

Rossi, P. H. (1989). *Down and out in America.* Chicago: University of Chicago Press.

Rossi, P. H., (1999). *Feeding the poor: Assessing federal food programs.* Washington, DC: American Enterprise Institute.

Rossi, P. H. (1956). *Why families move.* Glencoe, IL: Free Press.

Rossi, P. H., Lipsey, M., & Freeman, H. (2004). *Evaluation: A systematic approach* (7th ed.). Thousand Oaks, CA: Sage.

Rossi, P. H., & Lyall, C. (1974). *Reforming public welfare.* New York: Russell Sage.

8

THE ROOTS AND GROWTH OF THEORY-DRIVEN EVALUATION

An Integrated Perspective for Assessing Viability, Effectuality, and Transferability

Huey T. Chen

An impressive amount of literature on theory-driven evaluation has been published in the past few decades. The literature devoted to this topic includes four volumes of *New Directions for Evaluation* (Bickman, 1987, 1990; Rogers, Hasci, Petrosino, & Huebner, 2000; Wholey, 1987), several books (Chen, 1990, 2005; Chen & Rossi, 1992; Connell, Kubisch, Schorr, & Weiss, 1995; Donaldson, 2007; Fulbright-Anderson, Kubisch, & Connell, 1998; Pawson & Tilly, 1997), and numerous articles published in various journals (see recent reviews by Coryn, Noakes, Westine, & Schoter, 2011; Hansen & Vedung, 2010). Furthermore, major evaluation textbooks (Patton, 1997; Posavac & Carey, 2007; Rossi, Lipsey, & Freeman, 2004; Weiss, 1998) have a chapter(s) introducing the concepts, methodology, and usefulness of theory-driven evaluation. The purpose of this chapter is to discuss the roots, conceptual framework, applications, and new developments of theory-driven evaluation for facilitating further advancement.

ROOTS

Theory-driven evaluation has been developed under the premise of providing evaluative evidence of a program that has scientific credibility and practical worth for serving stakeholders'

Author's Note: The author greatly appreciates Lisa Liberman, Amanda Birnbaum, Jennifer Urban, Tamara Lucas, and Marvin Alkin for their valuable comments on an earlier work.

evaluation needs. Scientific credibility reflects the extent to which an evaluation meets the standards of scientific principles and provides trustworthy evidence. Practical worth refers to the extent to which an evaluation provides information that is relevant to stakeholders' practice and useful for improving their services. Theory-driven evaluation has benefited from the work of early masters in addressing these issues. For example, Campbell and associates' work (Campbell & Stanley, 1963; Cook & Campbell, 1979; Shadish, Cook, & Campbell, 2002) on the validity typology and experimental and quasi-experimental methods for enhancing rigor (internal validity) has been useful for theory-driven evaluation to address scientific credibility. Similarly, Cronbach's (1982) work on external validity is beneficial for theory-driven evaluation to address utility issues. Cronbach persuasively argued that external validity (generalizability) is vital for evaluation and that evaluation should facilitate stakeholders' search for appropriate actions to take in addressing problems and improving programs.

While Campbell prioritized internal validity and Cronbach prioritized external validity, theory-driven evaluation views both types of validity as essential; both need to be systematically addressed in evaluation for producing useful results. This kind of balancing view can be traced back to William S. Gosset's agricultural research seven decades ago (Student, 1936a, 1936b). Gosset indicated that randomized experiments are not de facto the most appropriate design. Instead, he favored designs that can keep the standard error as low as possible, that have research procedures similar to farmers' actual platting practices, and that encompass direct implications for farmers to improve their work. In my view, Gosset's arguments are as fresh and inspiring as ever.

This integrated approach for solving practical and scientific challenges in an evaluation has further benefited from the work of Peter Rossi (Rossi et al., 2004), my mentor in graduate school and coauthor of earlier theory-driven evaluation articles (Chen & Rossi, 1980, 1992). He suggested that evaluation ideas and thoughts are empty words unless they have empirical and utilizable implications; his views have had a strong and persistent influence on my work. These masters' works provide a solid ground on which to develop theory-driven evaluation.

CONCEPTUAL FRAMEWORK OF PROGRAM THEORY

Theory-driven evaluation argues that if an evaluation mainly assesses the relationship between an intervention and its outcomes (an approach commonly called black box evaluation), it has limited usefulness for stakeholders because the evaluation provides no information about the context of the effectuality and few clues on the strengths and weaknesses of a program and how to improve it (Chen, 1990). For overcoming these limitations, theory-driven evaluation uses program theory as a conceptual framework for expanding the scope of an evaluation. Program theory is a systematic configuration of stakeholders' prescriptive and descriptive assumptions underlying programs, whether explicit or implicit (Chen, 1990, 2005). Descriptive assumptions, called a change model, deal with what causal processes are expected to happen to attain program goals. Prescriptive assumptions, called an action model, deal with what actions must be taken in a program to produce desirable changes. With the action model and change model, theory-driven evaluation incorporates causal mechanisms and contextual factors into evaluation processes for enhancing the utility of an evaluation.

Change Model

A change model describes the causal process generated by the program. It consists of the following three elements:

1. *Goals and outcomes:* Goals reflect the desire to fulfill unmet needs, as with poor health, inadequate education, or poverty. Outcomes are the concrete, measurable aspects of these goals.

2. *Determinants:* To reach goals, programs require a focus, which will clarify the causal chain their design should follow. More specifically, each program must identify a leverage or mechanism on which it can develop a treatment or intervention to meet a need. That leverage or mechanism is variously called the determinant, mediator, or intervening variable.

3. *Intervention or treatment:* Intervention or treatment comprises any activity(ies) in a program that aim directly at changing a determinant. It is, in other words, the agent(s) of change within the program.

The change model has been extensively discussed in the theory-driven evaluation literature (Donaldson, 2007; Fulbright-Anderson et al., 1998; Weiss, 1998).

Action Model

An action model is a systematic plan for arranging staff, resources, settings, and support organizations to reach a target group and deliver intervention services. It consists of the following elements.

1. *Implementing organization—to assess, enhance, and ensure its capabilities:* A program relies on an organization to allocate resources, to coordinate activities, and to recruit, train, and supervise implementers and other staff. How well a program is implemented may be related to how well this organization is structured. Initially, it is important to ensure that the implementing organization has the capacity to implement the program.

2. *Program implementers—to recruit, train, and maintain both competency and commitment:* Program implementers are the people responsible for delivering services to clients: counselors, case managers, outreach workers, school teachers, health experts, and social workers. The implementers' qualifications and competency, commitment, enthusiasm, and other attributes can directly affect the quality of service delivery.

3. *Peer organizations/community partners—to establish collaborations:* Programs often may benefit from, or even require, cooperation or collaboration between their implementing organizations and other organizations. If linkage or partnership with these useful groups is not properly established, implementation of such programs may be hindered.

4. *Intervention and service delivery protocols to assure their availability:* Intervention protocol is a curriculum or prospectus stating the exact nature, content, and activities of an intervention—in other words, the details of its orienting perspective and its operating procedures. Service delivery protocol, in contrast, refers to the particular steps to be taken to deliver the intervention in the field.

5. *Ecological context—to seek its support:* Some programs have a special need for *contextual support*, meaning the involvement of a supportive environment in the program's work. Both *microlevel contextual support* and *macrolevel contextual support* can be crucial to a program's success. Microlevel contextual support comprises the social, psychological, and material supports clients need to allow their continued participation in intervention programs. In addition to microlevel contextual support, program designers should consider the macrolevel context of a program, that is, community norms, cultures, and political and economic processes. These, too, have the ability to facilitate or hinder a program's success.

6. *Target group—to identify, recruit, screen, and serve:* In the target group element, crucial assumptions at work include the presence of validly established eligibility criteria, the feasibility of reaching and effectively serving a target group, and the willingness of potential clients to become committed to, cooperate with, or at least be agreeable to joining the program.

The relationships among the components are illustrated in Figure 8.1.

Figure 8.1 indicates that the action model must be implemented appropriately to activate the "transformation" process in the change model. For a program to be effective, its action model must be sound and its change model plausible; its implementation is then also likely to be doing well. Figure 8.1 also illustrates evaluation feedback, as represented by the dotted arrows. Information from implementation can be used to improve the planning or the development of the action model. Similarly, information from the change model can be used to improve the implementation process and the action model. This conceptual framework of program theory should be useful to evaluators charged with designing an evaluation that produces accurate information about the dynamics leading to program success or program failure.

PROGRAM THEORY, THEORY-DRIVEN EVALUATION, AND THEIR USEFULNESS

The conceptual framework of program theory provides a comprehensive way to design and conduct different types of theory-driven evaluations depending on stakeholders' evaluation

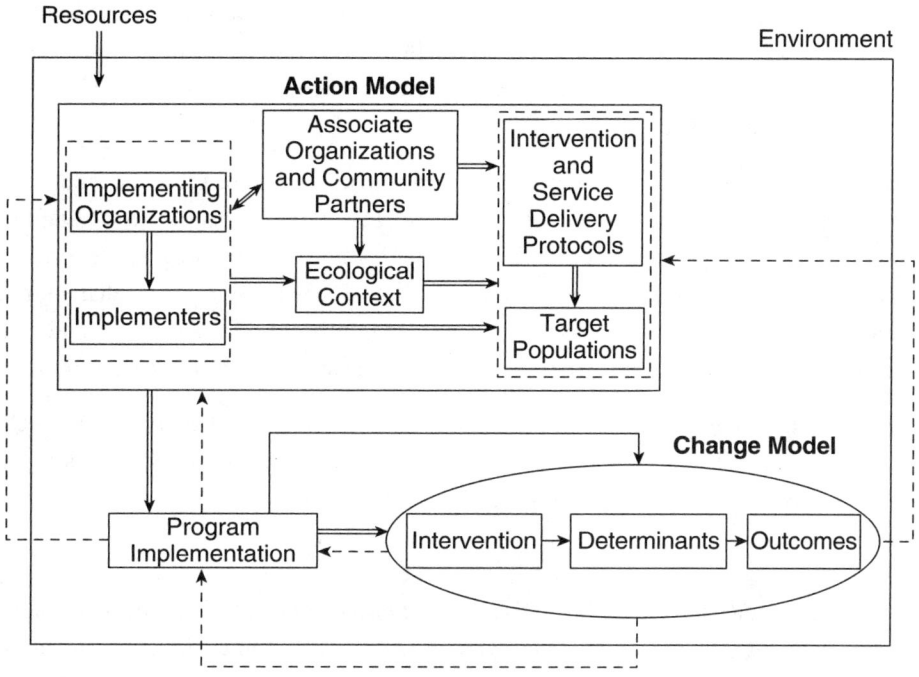

Figure 8.1 Conceptual Framework of Program Theory

interests and needs. Readers are referred to Chen (1990, 2005) for detailed information on the following applications of theory-driven evaluation: facilitating stakeholders to clarify a program theory underlying a program, using program theory to facilitate stakeholders to develop a sound intervention program, using an action model to design a systematic process evaluation, using a change model to design a theory-driven outcome evaluation, and integrating an action model and change model for a comprehensive evaluation.

Advantages of theory-driven evaluation include the following:

1. *Delineation of a strategy to consider stakeholders' views and interests:* An evaluation suffers without adequate input from stakeholders. The challenges, however, are how to understand stakeholders' views and how to integrate their interests in evaluation. The conceptual framework of program theory provides an effective tool for evaluators to communicate major evaluation issues to stakeholders and to design an evaluation that incorporates their interests.

2. *Holistic assessment:* The conceptual framework of program theory allows a holistic approach to assessing the merits of a program. Theory-driven evaluation can explain how and why a program achieves particular results by illustrating its means of implementation as well as underlying mechanisms of influence. The conceptual framework of program theory addresses issues in both the action model and the change model, so it helps evaluators achieve a balanced view from which to assess the worth of a program.

3. *Comprehensiveness of information needed to improve programs:* A theory-driven evaluation that examines how a program's structure, implementation procedure, and causal mechanisms actually work in the field will provide useful information to stakeholders for program improvements.

4. *Balance of scientific and practical concerns:* Researchers are greatly concerned about the scientific rigor of an evaluation, while stakeholders desire an evaluation that addresses service issues. Since the conceptual framework of program theory uses an action model to address service issues and tackle issues of rigor in the change model, it has potential for greater dialogue and collaboration between academic and practical communities and for narrowing the gap between scientific and service communities.

5. *Further advancement of evaluation theory and methodology:* Theory-driven evaluation has been applied in addressing scientific and service issues for a few decades. The lessons learned from the applications can be applied to further advance evaluation theory and methodology.

The first four topics have been well discussed in the literature. The rest of this chapter will focus on topics by introducing recent developments of theory-driven evaluation in areas such as the integrative validity model and bottom-up evaluation approach.

INTEGRATIVE VALIDITY MODEL

Stakeholders are clients and users of evaluation results; evaluators must understand and address their views and needs in evaluation. Theory-driven evaluation recognizes that stakeholders have a great interest in knowing whether an intervention program accomplishes two functions: (1) goal attainment and (2) system integration. Goal attainment means that an intervention can activate causal mechanisms for attaining its prescribed goals in the real world as illustrated in the change model. System integration refers to an intervention that is compatible or even synergistic with other components in a system. These components include organizational missions and capacity, service delivery routine, implementers' capability, relationships with partners, clients' acceptance, and community norms as illustrated in the action model. Stakeholders value goal attainment, but they are equally or even more interested in system integration. Stakeholders are responsible for organizing and delivering services. An intervention that is difficult to integrate into a real-world system has little value to them. Note also that although goal attainment and system integration are related outcomes attributable to an intervention, they do not necessarily go hand in hand. An efficacious or effective intervention does not mean that it is suitable for a community-based organization to implement it or vice versa (Chen, 2010; Chen & Garbe, 2011).

Stakeholders are keen on evaluative evidence in system integration and goal attainment, but this interest has often not been satisfactorily met in evaluations. Traditionally, evaluators have conceptualized outcome evaluation under the scope of goal attainment (Suchman, 1967) and have been advised to apply the Campbellian validity typology (Campbell & Stanley, 1963; Cook & Campbell, 1979; Shadish et al., 2002) for assessing the outcomes of an intervention. This application has created mixed results (Chen, Donaldson, & Mark, 2011b). On the one hand, when designing a rigorous outcome evaluation, we greatly benefit from the principles and methods highlighted by the Campbellian typology. The typology enhances our ability to present or defend the evidence provided from an outcome evaluation. On the other hand, stakeholders tend to view the evaluation results as often insufficient in meeting their needs and expectations, especially in addressing service issues. To overcome the problem, we must recognize that the Campbellian validity typology was developed for experimental research rather than for evaluation purposes (Chen, 2010). Not surprisingly, there are limits to how far the typology can help advance evaluation. Perhaps the ongoing and heated debates and controversies on the Campbellian validity typology in the context of program evaluation (Chen, Donaldson, & Mark, 2011a; Donaldson, Christie, & Mark, 2008) may indicate that the typology's contribution to evaluation may have reached the limit at the current stage of evaluation. Since it is neither the scope nor the intention of the Campbellian validity typology to be used for the purpose of designing well-balanced evaluations for addressing stakeholders' evaluation needs, it is up to evaluators to develop a more comprehensive perspective for satisfactorily addressing both goal attainment and system integration issues.

Theory-driven evaluation proposes an integrative validity model (Chen, 2010; Chen & Garbe, 2011) to take on this challenge. Building on Campbell and Stanley's (1963) distinction of internal and external validity, the integrative validity model proposes three types of validity for evaluation: (1) viable, (2) effectual, and (3) transferable.

The integrative validity model proposes viable validity to address stakeholders' interest in system integration. *Viable validity* is the extent to which an intervention is successful in the real world. Here, viable validity refers to stakeholders' views and experiences regarding whether an intervention program is practical, affordable, suitable, evaluable, and helpful in the real world. More specifically, viable validity means that ordinary practitioners—rather than research staff—can implement an intervention program adequately and that the intervention program is suitable for coordination or management by a service delivery organization such as a community clinic or a community-based organization. An additional inquiry is whether decision makers think that the intervention program is affordable and can (a) recruit ordinary clients without paying them to participate, (b) have a clear rationale for its structure and linkages connecting an intervention to expected outcomes, and (c) be regarded by ordinary clients and other stakeholders as helpful in alleviating clients' problems or in enhancing their well-being as defined by the program's real-world situations. In this context, *helpful* means whether stakeholders can notice or experience progress in alleviating or resolving a problem.

In the real world, stakeholders such as supervisors and practitioners manage and provide day-to-day services to clients. Thus, viability issues are vital to them. Viability alone might not guarantee an intervention's efficacy or effectiveness, but in real-world settings, viability is essential for an intervention's overall success. That is, regardless of the intervention's efficacy or effectiveness, unless that intervention is practical, suitable to community organizations' capacity for implementation, and acceptable to clients and implementers, it has little chance of survival in a community.

The integrative validity model also contributes to identifying viability evaluation—a new evaluation type that can assess the extent to which an intervention program is viable in the real world (Chen, 2010). Viability evaluation requires mixed (qualitative and quantitative) methods. On the one hand, evaluation relies on quantitative methods to collect data with which it can monitor progress on recruitment, retention, and outcome. On the other hand, evaluation requires an in-depth understanding of stakeholders' views on, and their experience with, the specific intervention program.

The integrative validity model proposes effectual validity to address goal attainment issues. *Effectual validity* is the extent to which an evaluation provides credible evidence that an intervention causally affects specified outcomes. This validity is similar to the concept of internal validity proposed by Campbell and Stanley (1963). Effectual validity commonly covers two types of evidence: (1) efficacy and (2) effectiveness. Efficacy is effectual evidence provided in an ideal and controlled setting, such as the use of randomized controlled trials (RCTs). Effectiveness refers to evidence provided in a real-world setting. Effectiveness is usually assessed by using quasi-experimental methods.

The third component of the integrative validity model is *transferable validity*. The concept is a revision of the Campbellian validity typology's external validity. Since the Campbellian typology was developed for research purposes, external validity is conceptualized as an endless quest for confirmation of an intervention's universal worth—impossible for any evaluation to achieve (Chen, 2010). The integrative validity model proposes a reconceptualization of external validity as transferable validity from a stakeholders' perspective for use in evaluation. Qualitative evaluators (Guba & Lincoln, 1989) prefer to use the term *transferability* rather than external validity to emphasize that generalizability can be enhanced by qualitative methods such as thick description. This chapter uses transferability to represent issues related to generalizability but stresses that transferability can be enhanced by qualitative and/or quantitative methods. Transferable validity for program evaluation is defined according to such concerns. Thus, the integrative validity model defines transferable validity as the extent to which evaluation findings of viability and effectuality can be transferred from a research setting to a real-world setting or from one real-world setting to another targeted setting. This definition stresses that transferability for program evaluation has a boundary—the real world.

Evaluation approaches with strong effectual validity tend to be low in transferable validity. For example, efficacy evaluation provides the most rigorous evidence on effectual validity, but it maximizes effectual validity at the expense of transferable validity. For example, efficacy evaluation applies RCTs to rigorously assess an intervention's effect. Manipulation and control used in maximizing effectual validity greatly reduce evaluation results' transferable validity to the real world. For example, to maximize effectual validity, RCTs usually use highly qualified and enthusiastic counselors as well as homogeneous and motivated clients who hardly resemble real-world operations. Stakeholders may regard evidence provided in efficacy evaluation to be irrelevant to what they are doing.

Effectiveness evaluation is not as rigorous as efficacy evaluation in terms of providing effectual evidence, but it is superior to efficacy evaluation for addressing transferable validity issues. Effectiveness evaluation estimates intervention effects in ordinary patients in real-world, clinical practice environments. To reflect the real world, recruitment and eligibility criteria are representative of the targeted populations. Intervention delivery and patient adherence are less tightly monitored and controlled than in efficacy evaluations. The central idea is that to enhance transferability, effectiveness studies must resemble real-world environments. Effectiveness evaluation usually applies non-RCT methods. Through sacrificing some level of effectual validity, effectiveness evaluation enhances transferable validity.

Furthermore, it is important to stress that transferable validity can mean either transferability of effectuality or transferability of viability. Transferability of effectuality has been the focus of the literature discussing external validity or generalizability. Transferability of viability, however, is an emerging concept that asks the question "To what extent can evaluation findings of an intervention's viability be transferred from one real-world setting to another targeted setting"? The distinction is important: An intervention's *effectuality* might transfer to another setting, but this does not guarantee that an intervention's *viability* will similarly be transferable.

Furthermore, theory-driven evaluation argues that an evaluation's transferable validity can be further enhanced by incorporating contextual factors and causal mechanisms as described in the action change framework in the assessment (Chen, 1990, 2005). For facilitating the application, theory-driven evaluation proposes the concepts of exhibited or targeted generalization for addressing transferability issues (Chen, 2010). Exhibited generalization of an evaluation itself provides information on the contextual factors and causal mechanisms relevant to an intervention's viability and effectuality. Potential users can adapt the information on the viability and effectuality of the intervention together with the contextual factors and causal mechanisms. Users can thereby assess its generalization potential with regard to their own populations and settings and decide whether the evaluation results in viability and effectuality are transferable to their communities. Exhibited generalization can be addressed through the "action model/change model" framework in the theory-driven approach (Chen, 1990, 2005), as previously discussed. Stakeholders sometimes have a particular real-world target population or setting to which they want to transfer the evaluation results. This is targeted generalization—that is, the extent to which evaluation results can be transferred to a specific population and real-world setting. Targeted generalization is achieved through methods such as sampling (Shadish et al., 2002), Cronbach's (1982) UTOS (population, treatment, observation, and setting) approach, or the dimension test (Chen, 1990). Thus, through exhibited or targeted generalization, transferable validity adds a workable evaluation concept to program evaluation.

TOP-DOWN VERSUS BOTTOM-UP APPROACHES FOR ADVANCING VALIDITY

It is desirable for an evaluation to provide evidence of effectual validity, viable validity, and transferable validity in assessing an intervention. As discussed previously, these types of validity do not go hand in hand; it is extremely difficult to simultaneously maximize all three types of validity in an evaluation. Two approaches have been proposed to sequentially deal with them: (1) top-down and (2) bottom-up (Chen, 2010; Chen & Garbe, 2011). The traditional top-down approach is a series of evaluations, beginning with maximizing effectual validity by efficacy evaluations and then moving on to effectiveness evaluations aimed at strengthening transferable validity. This strategy has been intensively and successfully used in biomedical research. Many scientists and evaluators traditionally regard such a top-down approach as the gold standard of scientific evaluation. However, the application of this approach to evaluate health promotion or social betterment programs is found to be not as fruitful as expected. Recently, evaluators and researchers have increasingly recognized that the application of this approach results in a huge gap between intervention research and real-world practice (Chinman et al., 2008; Green & Glasgow, 2006).

Theory-driven evaluation proposes the bottom-up approach (Chen, 2010; Chen & Garbe, 2011) as an alternative to sequentially address validity issues. Since stakeholders regard viable validity as of prime importance at the initial stage of a program, the bottom-up approach proposes that the evaluation sequence begin with a viability evaluation. If this real-world intervention is in fact viable, a subsequent effectiveness evaluation would provide sufficient objective evidence of the intervention's effectiveness in the stakeholder's real world. If necessary, the effectiveness evaluation could also address issues of whether such effectiveness is generalizable to other real-world settings. After the intervention is deemed viable, effective, and generalizable in real-world evaluations, an efficacy evaluation using methods such as RCTs will rigorously assess the causal relationship between intervention and outcome. The differences between the top-down approach and the bottom-up approach are illustrated in Figure 8.2.

The bottom-up approach has a number of advantages over the top-down approach in evaluating health promotion/social betterment programs.

It ensures an intervention's usefulness to stakeholders and avoids wasting money. The traditional top-down approach usually begins with an expensive and time-consuming efficacy evaluation to assess an innovative intervention. After millions of dollars are spent on an efficacy evaluation, it might be found that the efficacious intervention is very difficult to implement in the real world, is not of interest to stakeholders, or may not be real-world effective. This kind of approach tends to waste money.

In contrast, the bottom-up approach starts from a viability evaluation. It first assesses the viability of an intervention as proposed by researchers or stakeholders. Because interventions with low viability are screened out in the beginning, this approach could save funding agencies considerable money and resources. The bottom-up approach encourages funding agencies to fund many viability evaluations and to select highly viable interventions for further rigorous studies.

It provides an opportunity to revise and improve an intervention in the real world before its finalization. One top-down approach limitation is finalizing the intervention protocol or package before or during efficacy evaluation—the protocol is not supposed to change after the evaluation. And when an intervention protocol is finalized at such an early stage, it prevents the intervention from gaining feedback from the real-world implementation or stakeholders' inputs for improvement. This approach seriously restricts an intervention's generalizability to the real world.

Chapter 8. The Roots and Growth of Theory-Driven Evaluation

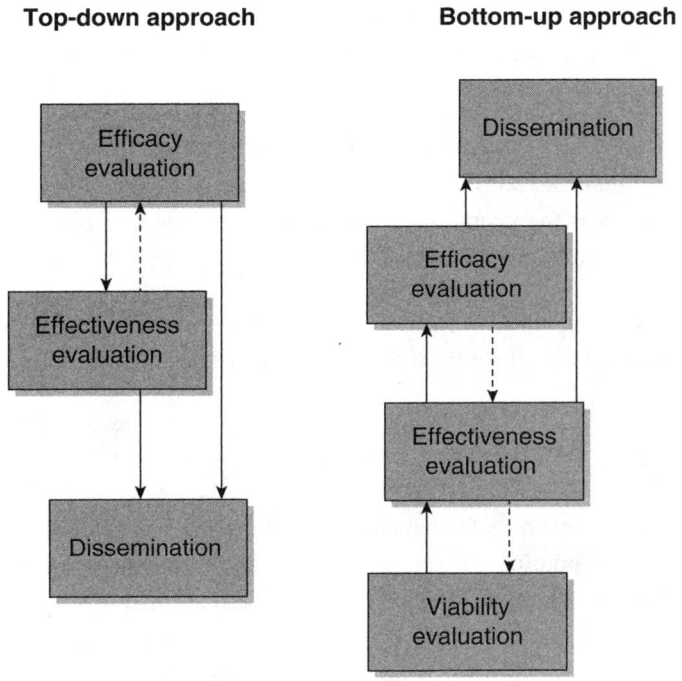

Figure 8.2 Top-Down Approach Versus Bottom-Up Approach

In contrast, the bottom-up approach affords an opportunity to improve an intervention during the viability evaluation. Intervention protocols refined from stakeholder inputs and implementation experience increase their real-world relevancy and contribution.

It provides an alternative perspective for funding. In theory, funding agencies are interested in both scientific and viability issues. They want to see their funded projects being successful in communities or having the capability of solving real-world problems. In practice, however, many agencies tend to heavily emphasize scientific factors such as RCTs or other randomized experiments as a qualification criterion for a grant application (Donaldson et al., 2008; Huffman & Lawrenz, 2006) while paying insufficient attention to viability issues. As discussed previously, if funding policy excessively stresses internal validity issues, it could waste money on projects that might be rigorous and innovative but that have little practical value. The bottom-up approach provides an alternative perspective for funding agencies to address scientific and viability issues in the funding process. This perspective suggests three levels of funding:

1. *Funding for viability evaluation:* This funding level provides funds for assessing the viability of existing or innovative interventions. It will formally recognize a stakeholder's contribution in developing real-world programs. Researchers can also submit their innovative interventions for viability testing. In doing so, however, they will have to collaborate with stakeholders in addressing practical issues.

2. *Funding for effectiveness evaluation:* The second level of funding is an effectiveness evaluation for viable and popular interventions. Ideally, these evaluations should address both effectual and transferable validity issues.

3. *Funding for efficacy evaluation:* The third level of funding is efficacy evaluation for those interventions proven viable, effective, and transferable in the real world. Efficacy evaluation provides the strongest evidence of an intervention's precise effect, with practical value as an added benefit.

These three levels of funding will promote collaborations between stakeholders and researchers and ensure that evaluation results meet both scientific and practical demands.

CONCURRENT VALIDITY APPROACHES

Under the conceptual framework of the integrative validity model, concurrent validity approaches contemplate dealing with multiple validity issues in a single evaluation. A concurrent approach has important implications for program evaluation. Outcome evaluation is often time-consuming. For example, the turnaround time for an efficacy or effectiveness evaluation of a program could easily be a few years. A long turnaround time plus the related expenses are major reasons why stakeholders ask for only one outcome evaluation as opposed to multiple outcome evaluations, as discussed in the top-down or bottom-up approaches for a new or existing program.

In conducting a concurrent evaluation, evaluators face a challenging question: What type of evaluation is preferable for addressing validity issues? General guidance for concurrent approaches follows.

Maximizing Effectual Validity. When stakeholders need strong, objective proof of a causal relationship between an intervention and its outcomes, when they are willing to provide abundant financial resources to support the evaluation, and when they are willing to accept a relatively long timeline for conducting the evaluation, effectual validity is a priority. Evaluators will use the Campbellian validity typology, and when they do, RCT is the gold standard.

Maximizing Viable Validity. If stakeholders have a program with multiple components that are challenging to implement in a community and if they need evaluative information to ensure the survival of the program, viable validity should be a priority. If stakeholders need information about whether a program is practical or helpful in the real world or whether real-world organizations, implementers, and clients favor the program, an appropriate choice would be to maximize viable validity. Evaluators could apply a viability evaluation for this purpose. Mixed (qualitative and quantitative) methods (Greene & Caracelli, 1997; Tashakkori & Teddlie, 2003) are particularly appropriate for viability evaluation.

Optimizing. If stakeholders prefer that an evaluation provide evidence of two or three types of validity (e.g., viable, effectual, and transferable), they must focus on finding an optimal solution for multiple validities in an evaluation (Chen, 1988, 1990; Chen & Rossi, 1983). A combination of effectiveness evaluation methodology with program theory is particularly useful for optimizing multiple validities (Chen, 1990, 2005).

THEORY-DRIVEN EVALUATION AS AN INTEGRATED PERSPECTIVE

Divergent and conflicting views as illustrated in the chapters of this book make evaluation interesting and offer a wealth of approaches. However, to become a matured, applied science, program evaluation must also comprise integration work. House (2002) and Shadish, Cook, and Leviton (1991) indicated that theory-driven evaluation has a potential for integrating different evaluation ideas and approaches. This chapter supports the argument by demonstrating its capability for addressing both scientific and practical issues. Furthermore, theory-driven evaluation's potential for reconciling conflicting views or further illuminating evaluation issues is discussed as follows.

Providing a Contingency Perspective on Methods

Theory-driven evaluation provides a contingency perspective that offers fresh insight into the role of RCTs and other methods that might be useful for qualitative and quantitative evaluators to narrow differences or identify common ground. Different methods are useful for different evaluation circumstances. For example, theory-driven evaluation recognizes the power of RCTs in maximizing effectual validity, but it is contrary to a wide application of RCTs in evaluation as proposed by the top-down approach. Instead, RCTs must be applied discreetly and only for those popular interventions already assessed by viability and effectiveness evaluations. Similarly, theory-driven evaluation recognizes the essential values of qualitative methods in addressing viable and transferable issues but argues that these methods alone are less powerful than experimental methods in ruling out rival hypotheses in addressing effectual issues. Because the contingency perspective emphasizes the strengths and limitations of different methods under different evaluation contexts, this view might be useful for reconciling differences between the qualitative and quantitative camps.

Providing a Balanced View on Credible Evidence

The integrative validity model posits that credible evidence of health promotion/social betterment programs includes a set of three related types of evidence: (1) viable validity, (2) effectual validity, and (3) transferable validity. Under this model, evidence on intervention effectuality is not a stand-alone or context-free concept. Rather, it should be viewed or discussed with reference to transferability and viability.

Viewing the evidence of intervention effectuality as a totality of evidence without reference to transferability, however, can be problematic. This is illustrated in the effectiveness of a health promotion/social betterment intervention being contingent on contextual factors such as the types of implementers, the implementing organizations, and clients (Chen, 1990, 2005). If the context of an intervention is changed, the effectuality of the intervention is also likely to change. For example, an innovative intervention is evaluated in a controlled setting. Clients are paid to ensure their participation and retention. Furthermore, intensively trained, highly paid, and highly motivated research staff implement the intervention to ensure its fidelity. In the controlled setting, the evaluation provides strong evidence of effectuality. Because, however, the current evidence-based approach counts as evidence of effectual validity only, it will classify the intervention as an evidence-based intervention.

But factor in transferable validity, and the credible evidence picture is altered. In the real world, clients are not paid for participation, and the intervention is typically implemented by a staff of community-based organizations rather than by research staff. Because of the drastic difference between the controlled setting and the real world, controlled-setting effectuality is not likely replicated. From the standpoint of stakeholders, controlled-setting effectuality may be an artificial effect, relevant or transferable only to that artificial situation. Accordingly, if the evidence-based intervention movements count only effectual validity as an evidentiary criterion, for real-world use, they might promote an intervention with strong but so-called artificial evidence of effectuality. A real-world situation is very different from an artificial situation in terms of factors such as participants, incentives, and implementers. Thus, the intervention will, in all likelihood, not work in the real world. An even worse scenario is that a funding agency may require community-based organizations to adopt the artificial, evidence-based intervention as a condition for receiving funds. In such a case, if the intervention does not work in the real world, community-based organizations may be forced to implement an ineffective intervention in their own communities.

Similarly, viability evidence should be factored in as a part of credible evidence. In the real world, an effective intervention in a controlled setting is not necessarily a viable intervention. And when stakeholders are not able or willing to implement a nonviable intervention—no matter how strong the evidence of effectiveness produced in controlled settings—the intervention is useless to them. Again, if the evidence-based intervention movement uses only internal validity as credible evidence, it may mistakenly promote interventions that have little chance of real-world survival. Pushing an effective intervention without evidence of real-world viability is not only a waste of valuable resources, it is also unscientific.

The integrative validity model may be useful for advocates of the evidence-based intervention movements to move from current narrow and rigid views of evidence to a well-balanced, credible-evidence model.

Recognize the Strengths and Limitations of Formal Theory/Stakeholder Theory–Based Interventions

In health promotion/social betterment programs, interventions are usually based on formal theories or stakeholder theories (Chen, 1990, 2005; Chen & Turner, in press). A formal theory–based intervention refers to an intervention that is formulated under the guidance of well-studied academic theory, while in stakeholder theory–based interventions, theories mainly come from stakeholders' ideas, observations, and experiences in working with clients and partners in a community. Formal theory–based interventions have rigorous evidence to show its effectuality; they are called evidence-based interventions. On the other hand, practitioners often apply stakeholder theory–based interventions because of their practicality.

A popular strategy for narrowing the gap is to encourage or persuade communities toward greater use of formal theory–based interventions as exemplified in the current evidence-based intervention movement (Donaldson et al., 2008). Stakeholders are offered incentives, such as funds, technical assistance, and capacity building, to enable them to adopt these interventions. This strategy is based on an assumption of the superiority of formal theory–based interventions or evidence-based interventions in addressing community problems. The assumption is questionable on several fronts. For example, currently the majority of evidence in formal theory–based interventions is efficacious evidence. Evidence is lacking whether these interventions are effective when they are organized, managed, and implemented by ordinary stakeholders and serve ordinary clients in a real-world situation. Furthermore, the assumption narrowly uses effectuality as the sole criterion for judging the merits of an intervention. The criterion hardly reflects stakeholders' views (Chen, 2010; Chen & Garbe, 2011).

Alternatively, the theory-driven evaluation perspective urges the use of a set of criteria of viability, effectuality, and transferability in examining the merits of formal theory–based versus stakeholder theory–based interventions in the real world. The new set of criteria provides a balanced view that formal theory–based interventions may have advantages in effectuality but stakeholder theory–based interventions may have merits in viability and transferability. The perspective recognizes the contributions made by stakeholders in solving community problems and argues that their knowledge, skills, experience, and wisdom should be systematically studied and included as an integral part of intervention science (Chen & Turner, in press). The perspective also respects the efforts and contributions made by formal theory–based interventions, but it does suggest that these interventions should address issues of viability and transferability at the beginning to ensure that the intervention has the support of stakeholders and a good chance of prospering or surviving in a community.

Synthesize Reductionism Versus Fluid Complexity's Program View

Different views on a program and how to solve a problem have a profound influence on evaluation. These issues are well illustrated by contrasting two program views: reductionism and fluid complexity. Reductionism postulates that a program is stable and can be analytically reduced to a few core elements for problem solving. For example, the focus of black-box evaluation is to assess whether a manipulation of the intervention can produce desirable outcomes. Other elements are subject to control for increasing precision in assessment. Reductionism coexists well with statistical models and has made significant contributions to quantitative evaluation. However, reductionism can oversimplify a program and provide an unsustainable solution.

As a contrast, fluid complexity argues that since a program is made of diverse and interactive elements and requires addressing environmental turbulence, it tends to constantly change. Problem solving requires a modification of groups of variables simultaneously and rapidly. For example, Christopher Columbus's expedition team had to not only constantly revise its plans to address ongoing external threats but also completely change its mission. After replacing the original mission of finding a route to India with the new mission of discovering a new world, the expedition was judged as an enormous success. Fluid complexity may be useful for program planning, but in its current form may present difficulties in applying the existing quantitative or qualitative methods to analyze such complex interactions. Furthermore, if a program is extremely complex and dynamic, it lacks an entity for meaningful evaluation. Consultants are more suitable than evaluators for offering opinions on how to address problems.

The theory-driven evaluation's program view represents a synthesis of reductionism and fluid complexity. It postulates that environment can create uncertainties and pressure a program to make changes, but a program can find proactive measures to reduce uncertainties and maintain some level of stability for performing its functions. Program theory indicates where proactive measures take place. For example, program managers and staff can build partnerships to buffer political pressure. Strategies such as building stronger action and change models, environmental scanning, or problem-solving networks as proposed by systems thinking (Urban, Osgood, & Mabry, 2011) are helpful in reducing uncertainties. By synthesizing reductionism and fluid complexity, theory-driven evaluation may have the benefits of both worlds. Theory-driven evaluation is more complicated than reductionism in program view, but its scope is analyzable within the existing quantitative and qualitative methods. Its view may be more applicable to a wider range of programs.

DISCUSSION

Program evaluation at its infancy had heavily borrowed methods and theories from matured sciences. These methodologies and theories have been applied and have been found to be useful. However, since these imports were not developed for evaluation, they may be limited as to how far they can help advance evaluation. To further advance program evaluation, in-born evaluation theories and methodologies dedicated for evaluation causes are needed to energize the field. Theory-driven evaluation as demonstrated in this chapter represents an endeavor in this direction.

REFERENCES

Bickman, L. (Ed.). (1987). *Using programtheory in evaluation.* San Francisco, CA: Jossey-Bass.

Bickman, L. (Ed.). (1990). *Advances in program theory.* San Francisco, CA: Jossey-Bass.

Cabrera, D., Colosi, L., & Lobdell, C. (2008). Systems thinking. *Evaluation and Program Planning, 31*(3), 299–310. doi:10.1016/j.evalprogplan.2007.12.001

Campbell, D. T., & Stanley, J. (1963). *Experimental and quasi-experimental designs for research.* Chicago, IL: Rand McNally.

Chen, H. T. (1988). Validity in evaluation research: A critical assessment of current issues. *Policy and Politics, 16*(1), 1–16.

Chen, H. T. (1990). *Theory-driven evaluations.* Newbury Park, CA: Sage.

Chen, H. T. (2005). *Practical program evaluation: Assessing and improving planning, implementation, and effectiveness.* Thousand Oaks, CA: Sage.

Chen, H. T. (2010). The bottom-up approach to integrative validity: A new perspective for program evaluation. *Evaluation and Program Planning, 33*(3), 205–214. doi:10.1016/j.evalprogplan.2009.10.002

Chen, H. T., Donaldson, S. L., & Mark, M. M. (Eds.). (2011a). *Advancing validity in outcome evaluation: Theory and practice: Vol. 130. New directions for evaluation.* San Francisco, CA: Jossey-Bass.

Chen, H. T., Donaldson, S. L., & Mark, M. M. (2011b). Validity frameworks for outcome evaluation. In H. T. Chen, S. L. Donaldson, & M. M. Mark (Eds.), *Advancing validity in outcome evaluation: Theory and practice: Vol. 130. New directions for evaluation* (pp. 5–16). San Francisco, CA: Jossey-Bass.

Chen, H. T., & Garbe, P. (2011). Assessing program outcomes from the bottom-up approach: An innovative perspective to outcome evaluation. In H. T. Chen, S. L. Donaldson, & M. M. Mark (Eds.), *Advancing validity in outcome evaluation: Theory and practice: Vol. 130. New directions for evaluation* (pp. 93–106). San Francisco, CA: Jossey-Bass.

Chen, H. T., & Rossi, P. H. (1980). The multi-goal, theory-driven approach to evaluation: A model linking basic and applied social science. *Social Forces, 59,* 106–122.

Chen, H. T., & Rossi, P. H. (1983). The theory-driven approach to validity. *Evaluation and Program Planning, 10,* 95–103.

Chen, H. T., & Rossi, P. H. (Eds.). (1992). *Using theory to improve program and policy evaluation.* Westwood, CT: Greenwood.

Chen, H. T., & Turner, N. (in press). Formal theory vs. stakeholder theory: New insights from a tobacco-focused prevention program evaluation. *American Journal of Evaluation.*

Chinman, M., Hunter, S. B., Ebener, P., Paddock, S. M., Stillman, L., Imm, P., & Wandersman, A. (2008). The getting to outcomes demonstration and evaluation: An illustration of the prevention support system. *American Journal of Community Psychology, 41*(3–4), 206-224. doi: 10.1007/s10464-008-9163-2

Connell, J. P., Kubisch, A. C., Schorr, L. B., & Weiss, C. H. (1995). *New approaches to evaluating community initiatives: Concepts, methods and contexts.* Washington, DC: Aspen Institute.

Cook, T. D., & Campbell, D. T. (1979). *Quasi-experimentation: Design and analysis issues for field settings.* Chicago, IL: Rand McNally.

Coryn, C. L. S., Noakes, L. A., Westine, C. D., & Schoter, D. (2011). A systemic review of theory-driven evaluation practice from 1990 to 2009. *American Journal of Evaluation, 32*(2), 199-266.

Cronbach, L. J. (1982). *Designing evaluations of educational and social programs.* San Francisco, CA: Jossey-Bass.

Donaldson, S. I. (2007). *Program theory-driven evaluation science: Strategies and applications.* New York, NY: Lawrence Erlbaum.

Donaldson, S. L., Christie, C. A., & Mark, M. M. (Eds.). (2008). *What counts as credible evidence in applied and evaluation practice?* Thousand Oaks, CA: Sage.

Fulbright-Anderson, K., Kubisch, A. C., & Connell, J. P. (Eds.). (1998). *New approaches to evaluating community initiatives: Vol. 2. Theory, measurement and analysis.* Washington, DC: Aspen Institute.

Green, L. W., & Glasgow, R. E. (2006). Evaluating the relevance, generalization, and applicability of research: Issues in external validation and translation methodology. *Evaluation and the Health Professions, 29*(1), 126-153.

Greene, J., & Caracelli, V. J. (Eds.). (1997). *Advances in mixed-method evaluation: The challenge and benefits of integrating diverse paradigm: Vol. 74. New directions for evaluation.* San Francisco, CA: Jossey-Bass.

Guba, E., & Lincoln, Y. (1989). *Fourth generation evaluation.* Newbury Park, CA: Sage.

Hansen, M. B., & Vedung, E. (2010). Theory-based stakeholder evaluation. *American Journal of Evaluation, 31*(3), 295-313. doi: 10.1177/1098214010366174

House, E. R. (2002). Unfinished business: Causes and values. *American Journal of Evaluation, 22*(3), 309–315.

Huffman, D., & Lawrenz, F. (Eds.). (2006). *Critical issues in STEM evaluation.* San Francisco, CA: Jossey-Bass.

Patton, M. Q. (1997). *Utilization-focused evaluation* (3rd ed.). Thousand Oaks, CA: Sage.

Pawson, R., & Tilly, N. (1997). *Realistic evaluation.* Thousand Oaks, CA: Sage.

Posavac, E. J., & Carey, R. G. (2007). *Program evaluation: Methods and case studies.* Upper Saddle River, NJ: Prentice Hall.

Rogers, P. J., Hasci, T. A., Petrosino, A., & Huebner, T. A. (Eds.). (2000). *Program theory in evaluation: Challenges and opportunities* (Vol. 87). San Francisco, CA: Jossey-Bass.

Rossi, P. H., Lipsey, M. W., & Freeman, H. E. (2004). *Evaluation: A systematic approach.* Thousand Oaks, CA: Sage.

Shadish, W. R., Cook, T. D., & Campbell, D. T. (2002). *Experimental and quasi-experimental designs for generalized causal inference.* Boston, MA: Houghton Mifflin.

Shadish, W. R., Cook, T. D., & Leviton, L. C. (1991). *Foundations of program evaluation.* Newbury Park, CA: Sage.

Student. (1936a). Co-operation in large-scale experiments. *Journal of the Royal Statistical Society Series B, 3,* 115–136.

Student. (1936b). The half-drill system agricultural experiments. *Nature, 138,* 971–972.

Suchman, E. (1967). *Evaluative research.* New York, NY: Russell Sage.

Tashakkori, A., & Teddlie, C. (Eds.). (2003). *Handbook of mixed methods in social and behavioral research.* Thousand Oaks, CA: Sage.

Urban, J. B., Osgood, N. D., & Mabry, P. L. (2011). Developmental system science: Exploring the application of systems science methods to developmental science questions. *Research in Human Development, 8*(1), 1–25.

Weiss, C. (1998). *Evaluation* (2nd ed.). Englewood Cliffs, NJ: Prentice Hall.

Wholey, J. S. (1987). Evaluability assessment: Developing program theory. In L. Bickman (Ed.), *Using program theory in evaluation* (Vol. 33, pp. 77–92). San Francisco, CA: Jossey-Bass.

9

ROOTING FOR EVALUATION

Digging Into Beliefs

Carol Hirschon Weiss

Marv Alkin and Tina Christie have undertaken to highlight the different strands of thinking among evaluators. It is a noble enterprise, and they are making a constructive contribution to the evaluation literature. I'd like to put in a word for the similarities among evaluators. I think that we share many basic beliefs about evaluation. Let me mention a few things that I believe and that I think the reader will find in many other chapters in this volume. I tend to think of my ideas as practical beliefs about how to do evaluations, with sensitivity to the context, demands, and constraints of the immediate situation.

My basic belief is that evaluation goes out into the world daily (with its bag of tools and its lunch) to work for the improvement of social programs and the people they serve. Evaluators are dedicated to using their knowledge for the benefit of society. I would imagine that everybody who is included in this volume shares the belief in evaluation as a guide to improvement.

But evaluation contains a variety of perspectives and an array of methods. Methodologically, evaluation can encompass simple techniques like talking to program staff about their problems and satisfactions. In professional practice, it is likely to be more rigorous in both its qualitative and its quantitative forms. Whatever methods are used, evaluation involves the collection of empirical evidence to form the basis of conclusions, and evaluators use disciplined and systematic procedures to collect and analyze the evidence.

In my work, I think about evaluation as a kind of applied research. I don't necessarily mean quantitative research; evaluation doesn't necessarily involve predetermined steps or fixed methods. Evaluation can be qualitative or quantitative, and often it is both. Evaluators can think of themselves as doing policy research, organizational research, psychosocial research, ethnographic research, or a study of many different breeds. There are three distinctive attributes of evaluation: (1) its task—to find out how interventions are functioning, what kinds of effects they are having, and how well they are satisfying the needs and desires of their several constituencies; (2) its situation—as part of the world of practice, evaluation should be responsive to the desires and wants of program constituents; and (3) its mission—to help improve the social, economic, and cultural condition of society. It benefits from insight and sensitivity to context as well as from methodological expertise.

We came through a period when evaluators engaged in verbal jousts about the relative value of qualitative and quantitative methods for acquiring data. What a relief that that dispute has simmered down. As a field, we now embrace what has come to be called "mixed methods." We have always used mixed methods. Even orthodox quantitative evaluators did informal interviewing when they developed questionnaires, so that they could understand what ideas their respondents were likely to have and how to word items that represented the range of possible answers. And ethnologists and other qualitative-style folk have been known to count. The important thing, it seems to me, is that evaluation involves systematic empirical work done with attention to method.

Sponsors usually invite us into the program arena because of our expertness in method, whether the method is qualitative or quantitative. They call for evaluation because they believe we know how to collect valid and useful information that is credible not only to them but also to the audiences they need to satisfy. Sometimes they call in a substantive expert, someone who has long years of experience and considerable knowledge about physical rehabilitation or teaching of third-grade math or whatever field the program deals with. Such experts can visit the program and render judgments without the benefit of much systematic data. They are trusted because of their credentials in the field of practice.

But for evaluators, the main touchstone is method. That is what we have to offer decision makers, and that is the basis for their invitation to us. Our quantitative and qualitative methods give us credibility in the eyes of others. Decision makers are besieged by advocates who promote a point of view about a program because they have interests at stake. The evaluator's interest is, or should be, to describe the situation as well and as truly as possible (understanding all the limitations to objectivity). Without that intent—and the scientific mind-set that enables the evaluator to pursue that intent—the evaluator is just another claimant seeking influence. Evaluation has become as prevalent as it is because it promises to provide unbiased and accurate information.

EVALUATION AS SEEKING OBJECTIVITY

I do not believe that evaluation studies are neutral or "objective." I have no illusions about evaluator neutrality. Even the most methodologically sophisticated and well-conducted studies have biases. All of us have beliefs and values, which inevitably influence the facet of the issue we see and how we address it, how we define the study, whose opinions carry weight, and so on.

But there is such a thing as more or less objectivity. Some evaluators come into a study committed for one reason or another to the welfare of the program they are going to study and pretty sure that the results will be positive. Or they may have a reason to want to show the program in a poor light. On the other hand, most evaluators are willing to be open to new information and suspend judgment. They put their professional evaluation obligations ahead of any predilections they may have. They will talk to a lot of people and frame study questions in ways best suited to satisfying the concerns of stakeholders, collect data to answer those questions carefully and systematically, and be open to surprises. In the quest for fair assessment, advantages accrue not only to methodological expertise but also to sensitive observation, insight, awareness of context, and understanding. Evaluators will be willing to explore all the directions that the findings open up. Inevitably, they won't attain complete objectivity, but we can try for it.

EVALUATION AS PROFESSIONAL PRACTICE

As evaluators, we can do the best that our knowledge, skills, and professionalism allow to represent the realities we see. My values lead me to say that, first, we should try to see that all viewpoints relevant to the questions being addressed are adequately represented in the evaluation. Second, if we have to make choices about whose perspectives to privilege, we should not automatically give priority to the sponsor's voice. Rather, we should try to ensure that the most deprived groups, usually the program recipients, have a strong chance to be heard.

Sponsors call for evaluation to meet many purposes, and they often want answers quickly. They have questions and face pressures *now*. But good evaluation takes time. Unless one is lucky enough to have an appropriate ready-made database or it relies solely on the opinions of the people on the spot, there is a lot of work to be done. Evaluators have to plan the design of the study and the methods of data collection, define what information is needed and how to collect it validly and responsively, and analyze the data with conscientious thoroughness. (Early on, they also should plan how to disseminate the information to the right audiences in ways that attract their attention.) I know the temptations to hurry up the study. But I believe that providing half-digested information, half of it wrong (when we don't know which half), is a disservice to programs, recipients, funders, and sponsors. The aim of evaluation is to provide sound information that people in authority can use to make things better for the often disadvantaged groups they serve. Giving them partial information may be as much a risk as a help. If by some chance, they take the results seriously and base big decisions on them, they may be rushing off in the wrong direction. The money then goes astray, and people's lives are not improved.

Critics may say, it's all very well to talk about the importance of valid results, but the issue is coming up for decision next month. Evaluation has to be ready by that time. Maybe so, but in my experience, decisions are often delayed, especially when they are controversial. Even when the decision point arrives, decision makers rarely apply the results immediately to the choice of solution. If the evaluation offers a critical perspective on current operations and suggests a set of new ideas, they will not absorb and act on them right away. They need time to think about alternative perspectives and new ways to cope with program shortcomings. Moreover, if a decision is important, it is not going to be settled once and for all next month. It will reappear, either on a regular cycle (e.g., the next year's budget) or when problems come up. There will be another opportunity for evaluation to influence events. Sound evaluation results for the next round of decisions may be more useful than flawed information right now.

It is important to take the time and use professional skills to reach conclusions that are likely to stand up to critical scrutiny. Often, an organization has factions within it, some of which will want to do something useful with the findings and some of which will oppose the move. When the evaluation results are offered as ammunition to support change, opponents are apt to probe the study, often calling in experts as witnesses to the study's shortcomings. The evaluation should be able to withstand such critical examination on its merits.

ACKNOWLEDGING THE LIMITS OF EVALUATION

I also believe that evaluators have a responsibility to point out the limitations of their work. With a limited budget and a straitened time schedule, we cannot do everything that we would like. Also, we are human, with the limitations that all human beings have. Overpromising seems to be an occupational hazard. Overpromising at the beginning may be understandable, because evaluators want to get the contract. But it can set up false expectations for definitive answers that we cannot give. It encourages sponsors to write specifications for future studies in pie-in-the-sky terms, on the assumption that the magic of evaluation will answer all questions and solve all problems. Perpetuating that kind of demand is not good for evaluation or evaluators.

Overpromising at the end of the study, not acknowledging the limits of the report, is not good either and, although understandable, perhaps less easy to forgive. It would be professional and ethical to say that our sample was limited to the people who happened to attend that day, that eight cases are not enough to use as a basis for firm conclusions, that outside conditions may have discouraged the respondents' candor, or that the results, although statistically significant, represent a very small practical gain. Such candor is probably good for business too.

EVALUATION AS ENMESHED IN POLITICS

Evaluation is not only a research activity but also a political activity, whether we like it or not. It is political in three different senses. First, we deal with programs that were brought into being through political processes. Program champions had to struggle against their opponents to get the organizations established or reformed and the particular programs and policies implemented. They may even now be embroiled in political argumentation. In fact, that controversy may be a reason for the evaluation. Thus, the entities that we study are creatures of a political process.

Second, the results of the evaluation will be fed into the decision-making process. Reports enter a political arena and can be used as ammunition for one point of view or another. Our reports are not usually journal articles in scholarly publications, at least in the near term. They go to people who have a say in how the program operates, and the reports may have consequences for the future of the program. The consequences may not be direct decisions to change or end them, but evaluations can influence the way stakeholders think about the program and give staff new ideas about things that need improvement. Evaluation reports can influence the climate of opinion around the program and can possibly set off a cascade of future events. Inasmuch as decision making about programs generally involves competition over the use of resources, political activity ensues. This is true whether the scene is the U.S. Congress, the Boy Scouts of America, or a local charter school.

Third, evaluation itself has a political stance. Our undertaking the study in the first place sends a message that we think the program is important enough to be worth our time and attention. It also suggests that the program has a reasonable chance of being successful or we would not bother. Evaluators are not interested in writing epitaphs. The possibility of success is a clear political message. Thus, evaluation gives an aura of legitimacy to the enterprise. At the same time, evaluation suggests that people think the program is problematic enough to *require* evaluation. Nobody evaluates programs that raise no doubts. An evaluation signals that there are questions about the program and its worth.

Furthermore, when we accept program goals as the standard against which to evaluate, we accept the desirability of meeting those goals. When we concentrate on the effects of only the variables that the intervention manipulates, we send an implicit message that other elements in the situation, such as the environments in which people live, are either unimportant or unchangeable. When we do the evaluation to answer the questions of program administrators and accept their terms of reference for the study, we ignore the concerns of other stakeholders, such as program recipients.

In these ways, evaluation tends to have an "establishment" orientation but with a reformist slant. Evaluation tends to accept the world as it is. We accept agency structures, official diagnoses of social problems, and the appropriateness of certain ways to address them. Evaluation tends to question only the limited set of interventions that the program introduces.

EVALUATION AND PROGRAM THEORY

Evaluations can do more than render judgments on a program in the style of "it works, or it doesn't work." The study can identify the particular aspects of behavior or performance that the participants did or did not achieve, such as continuity of employment or performance on long-division problems. But many evaluations cannot say much about *why* the program did or did not lead to the desired change. Why is it that programs designed to recruit college women into majors in the natural sciences have limited success? What is it about small class size that tends to improve the school performance of children? It would be good if we were able to give more explicit guidance. So another element in my approach to evaluation is basing some evaluations on the theory underlying the program. *Why* do people expect the program to work? *How* do they expect it to accomplish its ends? What do they expect to happen and through what sequence of microsteps? If they can set out the sequence of program actions and anticipated participant responses, the evaluation can then track the extent to which things go the way they expect—and where in the sequence they go awry or break down.

For example, if a program is expected to work by mobilizing community groups to work for improvement in traffic safety, we don't have to wait to find out whether safety improved. We can see whether the theory that a program can mobilize citizens' energies for a public purpose like traffic safety really holds up. How many residents join the community groups? How many attend meetings? Take on a task? Perform it? Long before we can find out whether they gained the attention of public authorities and influenced change in traffic safety procedures, we can see whether the underlying premise of citizen action works in this community.

This example suggests a feature of program theory, as I envision it, that may be different from other versions. A central focus of program theory involves not only the actions that the program takes but also the responses of participants. What do they do all along the way? In a training program, does the program hold training sessions in locations that are readily accessible to the intended recipients? Do the intended participants sign up? Do they attend regularly? Do the instructors attend regularly? Do the participants learn the material? And so on.

The program theory approach is particularly suitable to cases where randomized experiments are inappropriate. When schools insist on choosing their own constellations of programs or when museum trustees refuse to accept randomization of alternative forms of outreach, the absence of random assignment need not make us despair of reaching something approaching "causal" explanations. By following the microsteps of program action and participant response, we can almost "see" the causal chain working its way along, if not with the same clarity that randomization can bring. But theory-based evaluation has advantages that randomized trials do not. It helps to get at the *why* and *how* of program success or failure.

I also like to test several different theories of how the program is intended to work. Neither evaluators nor program staff usually have carefully thought-out theories of program action. We improvise and guess. Our theories, or logic models, are often ramshackle affairs. Does a program of raising teacher salaries to improve student learning actually work by motivating teachers to work harder, does it allow them to give up second jobs, does it improve their status among parents and students and thus motivate students to try harder, or do higher salaries attract better prepared people to teaching positions in the district? Provided it has enough resources, a theory-based evaluation can test out several of these hypotheses as it goes.

A long-term hope is that theory-based evaluations can go beyond the single case and contribute to the development of better programming theory. To do this, evaluators have to identify the nature of the intervention and the assumptions on which it is based. That is, they have to identify the operating *mechanisms* that the program takes for granted as the ways it is going to achieve success. Some programs, like the community safety program mentioned above, assume that organizing and mobilizing citizens will spur the desired changes. These programs seek to develop social capital that can be applied to many problem situations. Some programs use the mechanism of information giving. Information is the coin of the realm in diverse programs such as drug abuse prevention, patient education to adhere to medical regimens, job training, get-out-the-vote campaigns, and almost all formal education. Other programs are based on naming and shaming (Pawson, 2002). This is the strategy of programs such as sex offender registration, hospital ratings, public lists of companies that pollute, and publication of school test score averages. By publicizing the shortfalls and vices of these kinds of organizations, authorities expect to cause them to change their ways. Some programs work by providing something approaching "therapy," creating strong coherent groups that provide emotional comfort, support, and sanctions against inappropriate behavior. Once the underlying mechanisms are identified, it becomes possible for an evaluation to contribute to a larger body of knowledge about the *kinds* of interventions that work.

CUMULATION OF EVALUATION EVIDENCE

Everybody agrees that it would be sensible to aggregate the evidence from numerous evaluations of the same kind of program to reach judgments about appropriate avenues to pursue. But it is not always easy to make sense of a body of work that looks at discrete programs at different times under different conditions. Some versions of the program work well, some work with a limited subset of participants, some work in some locations and not in others, and some do not seem to work at all. Meta-analysis is a useful way to proceed. When meta-analysts reduce data on the effects of the programs to one or a few measures (e.g., effect size), they can aggregate the results and reach a summary judgment about "what works." Meta-analysis has the potential of drawing fairly clear conclusions from a mass of inconsistent evidence. But it has to be cautious about overpromising. The set of evaluations that are being combined may not represent the universe of programs that go by the same label. The studies may have weaknesses of their own, which is acceptable if the weaknesses vary all over the lot but dangerous if they are all of the same kind. Useful as it is, meta-analysis does not solve all problems.

In meta-analysis, it is also useful to disaggregate the results of the individual studies by the nature of the people who participated, the content of the program, and the circumstances under which it was run. (Not all evaluation reports provide this kind of data, and it would be useful if more of them did.) The meta-analyst can then calculate and compare the effectiveness of a particular kind of programming for specific kinds of participants and contexts.

EVALUATION USE

Utility is what evaluation is all about. Evaluation aims to help make things better. It accomplishes its betterment mission only if people pay attention. It is sensible for evaluators to aspire to influence decisions and to design their studies in such a way as to maximize their influence. I wish that policy and program people use evaluation results to improve the programs they fund, administer, and operate and that they do so promptly. But my work has shown that *direct* input into *immediate* decisions is not a hallmark of evaluations (or other social science research). Most studies that examine the consequences of evaluation find the same thing: that decision makers seldom use evaluation evidence as the basis of immediate decisions.

Evidence from evaluation can serve a variety of purposes. It can be used as a *warning*, as a signal that conditions are not improving as fast as program staff expected or that outside conditions are limiting the effectiveness of the actions the program is taking. It can become *ammunition* in struggles over direction. When the evaluation shows that a program is relatively ineffective, foes of the programs can wave copies of the evaluation to support their contention that something else should be done. When the evaluation shows relative success, its proponents can use the data to make their case. The evaluation supports and legitimates prior opinions. Occasionally, evaluation provides direct *evidence for action.* It may have comparative data that characterize some techniques or strategies as sufficiently superior to adopt across the program. It may have unforeseen findings that point to a particular weakness or hole in the program's operation. Decision makers can plug the findings into future steps.

Finally, evaluation can have a kind of use that occurs without slam-bang "utilization" of evaluation evidence. It is the longer-term percolation of ideas from evaluation into organizational discourse. I have called the phenomenon "enlightenment." Evaluations not infrequently change decision makers' perceptions about what is important, they cast doubt on some assumptions that had long been taken for granted, they evoke new ideas, and they alter priorities. One important reason why this kind of influence is so prevalent is that decisions are often not made in the clear-cut way that many of us believe. We envision a group of people sitting around a table, arguing, reviewing evidence, and finally coming up with a *decision.* When we go out and look, we find what James March and other organizational scholars have known for decades. Decisions are rarely made with that degree of order. Many times they just seem to happen. People in different places in the organization take small steps—answer a request, write a press release, hire a staff member with certain qualifications and not others—and they foreclose options. Over time, a pattern of action emerges, and the organization continues down the available path. A decision accretes. Because of the phenomenon of decision accretion, there is little opportunity for research to poke its nose into the proceedings.

Readers of my work sometimes get the impression that I *advocate* enlightenment as the proper mission of evaluation. That is not the case. I keep looking for ways to improve translation, dissemination, and long-term discussions with decision makers. But much of the time, enlightenment represents my understanding of what really happens. Even when I was an in-house evaluator, I had difficulty gaining the attention of local program staff. The federal grant that was supporting the program I had been evaluating expired. No more money was forthcoming from that source, so program staff were seeking other sources where funding was still available. Despite the cogency of the findings, they had no interest in the evaluation of an extinct program.

In other cases, in large-scale national and international evaluations, policymakers and agency administrators likewise had other things on their minds. Not the least were the demands of outside constituencies, the preferences of program staff, and the relative advantages of espousing one position or another in the complex world of political decision making.

From time to time, I have written about ways to gain a greater hearing for evaluation findings. In one large national study a generation ago, a research team at Columbia University studied elite policymakers across a wide range of sectors: industry, commerce and banking, Congress, federal departments, political parties, major media, and so on. We found that leaders in each sector were the most likely to get information from their own organizations, but the second most frequent source for each sector was the major media. So across the whole sample, the media were the most important source of data. It looked to me as though major newspapers, newsmagazines, and television news programs were critical avenues for getting across the messages from research and evaluation.

So I got a grant from the Russell Sage Foundation to do a study of how writers and broadcasters *hear* about research and how they *decide what to report* to the public. In a book that I wrote with Eleanor Singer on that study, I included some advice to researchers and evaluators on how to make a more effective case for their findings (Weiss & Singer, 1988). The advice included things such as getting acquainted with reporters on local TV stations and newspapers, listening to them and trying to understand what they are interested in, trying to hook your findings to a subject that is already in the news, being up-front about the limitations of the study, making use of the resources of your university's or organization's public affairs office, and in general cultivating relationships with reporters over the long term (Weiss & Singer, 1988, pp. 159–160).

Evaluators and communications experts are constantly seeking ways to make evaluation more central to decision-making processes. In a recent study, my colleagues and I came across a practice in operation in a federal agency that required applicants for program funds to show that research/evaluation supported the type of program they were proposing. Funding their applications was contingent at least in part on evaluative *evidence* regarding the merit of the program. We called this strategy "imposed use" (Weiss, Murphy-Graham, & Birkeland, 2005). Auspicious as "imposed use" sounds—and is—in the effort to improve the influence of evaluation, our studies found flaws in the way it operated. We titled our article "The Fairy Godmother—and Her Warts" (Weiss, Murphy-Graham, Petrosino, & Gandhi, 2008).

I wish I could provide a list of all-purpose tested techniques for ensuring attention to evaluation findings. I wish I could join the philosopher in the cartoon in Figure 9.1 in that blissful state "way past enlightenment." But so many factors get involved in program and policy decisions (political, organizational, economic, personal) that even with the best efforts the evaluator makes, it is hard to be sure what will happen. Evaluators have to do everything they can to be relevant and expert in stakeholder involvement during development of the evaluation, question definition, design, data collection, analysis, conclusion drawing, participatory processes for developing recommendations, presentation, dissemination, and interactive communication—and then hope for the best. I hope that my research on the uses of evaluation will alert evaluators to the complexity—and the possibilities—in the arena that their findings are entering.

"I am so past enlightenment."

Figure 9.1 I Am So Past Enlightenment

Source: "I Am So Past Enlightenment." The New Yorker Collection, www.cartoonbank.com. Artist: Kim Warp, June 13, 2005.

WHY I BELIEVE WHAT I BELIEVE ABOUT EVALUATION

Who Influenced My Ideas

For much of my career, I have studied the uses made of evaluation studies: how evaluation evidence reaches potential users, how much influence the studies have and for whom, and what happens as a result. One thing I learned early in this work is how hard it is for individuals to describe the influence that an evaluation or any other piece of research has had on their positions on an issue. The reason that they find it hard to describe is that they don't know themselves. They listen to a lot of people, they read, they are exposed to the professional and popular media, they attend meetings, and somehow at the other end, they have a point of view. But disentangling the separate influences is next to impossible.

When I try to answer the question about the authors and the body of ideas that influenced my development as an evaluator, I am similarly at sea. The true answer is that I don't know who or what influenced me the most. My parents obviously had a major influence. Their social and political conscience, their emphasis on social justice, was transmitted to me from my earliest days. My public school education in New York City schools was outstanding. In college, I received a fine liberal arts education, with an undergraduate and master's-level concentration in political science. I have firm commitments to the values of democratic government, while appreciating its limits and flaws. I could string a list of names here, Machiavelli, Hobbs, Rousseau, Mill, the *Federalist Papers*, and so on. My doctoral education was in sociology, which helped take the big ideas to the tangible world of communities and societies. I could string another long list of names here: Marx, Weber, Michels, Merton, and Bourdieu. Reading these thinkers must have had an influence, although it is hard to identify.

Three social scientists of the late 20th century have been obvious influences: James March, Charles Edward Lindblom, and Lee Cronbach. Lindblom is an economist/political scientist who helped me (and a generation) make sense of the uses of information in democratic politics. Jim March has been writing about organizations for more than 50 years, always with brilliance and insight. I have learned from him about the way organizations make decisions and the place of information. Lee Cronbach is probably closer to home for evaluators. His methodological work has had a broad influence, and his later work on evaluation and its uses is outstanding.

Because of Marv Alkin's prodding, I'll try to be more specific about the influences on my perspectives on evaluation. I have gone back to some of my early writings to see which authors I cite and which keep reappearing in my work. The pivotal influences probably came at the beginning. When I began my first study, in the mid-1960s, there were no courses in evaluation, no textbooks. I had already done evaluative surveys for youth service agencies but not a whole study. I had to teach myself how to proceed. I read everything I could find. Some people think that evaluation started with the "War on Poverty," but in the mid-1960s, I was able to find a lot of material. Edwin Powers and Helen Witmer had published an evaluation of the Cambridge–Somerville Youth Study in 1951. H. Ashley Weeks had written *Youthful Offenders at Highfields* in 1958. Elizabeth Herzog had written guidelines on evaluation (1959). Bob Dentler had evaluated three programs of the American Friends Service Committee (1959). Herb Hyman, Charles Wright, and Terry Hopkins had done an evaluation of Encampment for Citizenship (1962). Whenever the evaluators were at Columbia University, as many of them were, I went to talk to them. Unfortunately for me, Ed Suchman and Peter Rossi, whom I didn't know at the time, had finished their studies at the Columbia Sociology Department and hadn't yet published their work on evaluation. Ralph Tyler had done The Eight-Year Study of high schools in New York, but somehow I didn't come across it. I didn't know about any of these three potential mentors in that critical period.

By the end of the 1960s, a lot more groundbreaking work had been done. When I finished my 3-year evaluation of a Domestic Peace Corps program and became a consultant on evaluation for programs all over the country for the President's Committee on Juvenile Delinquency, I decided to write a textbook. I wanted to help people like those I had been consulting with, who were seeking advice on how to evaluate the social programs that the government had started funding in a large way. The book was *Evaluation Research* (1972b). Looking through the index, I see references to Alkin, Campbell, Cronbach, Freeman, Glass, Guba, Stufflebeam, Popham, Rossi, Scriven, Tyler (I'd obviously caught up with him), Wholey, and Worthen, among many others.

In 1972, I published a second book, an edited volume, *Evaluating Action Programs* (1972a). For that book, I selected already published articles that I thought were worth memorializing.

Among the authors were quite a few of those on Alkin's "theory tree": Stake, Suchman, Alkin, Wholey, Scriven, Campbell, Rossi, and Guba. I must certainly have absorbed ideas from these people. (Some of the other authors represented on the Alkin tree were too young to have done much publishing by 1972.)

Of the major evaluation theorists, Campbell was the one who probably influenced me the most. His and Julian Stanley's article on quasi-experimentation had been published in 1963 in a fat, expensive handbook on research on teaching. It was such a profoundly useful article that I splurged on a copy of the whole handbook. The article later came out as a stand-alone paperback (1966). While I was still a novice and writing *Evaluation Research*, Dr. Campbell called me. I'd never met him, but somehow he had heard that I was working on a manuscript about evaluation, and he invited me to Evanston to talk about it. When we met, he was extraordinarily informative, particularly about the perils of matched control groups, and very gracious.

Campbell's work on experimentation and quasi-experimentation had profound effects on the evaluation field. I have followed the evolution of the quasi-experimentation book through its versions by Cook and Campbell (1979) and Shadish, Cook, and Campbell (2002), and both Cook and Shadish have certainly influenced me. In fact, Will Shadish was kind enough to review the manuscript of my more recent evaluation book, *Evaluation* (Weiss, 1998), prior to publication. His comments helped improve the book and my thinking.

I am sure I owe a debt of gratitude to most of the other people in this book. I read the literature, I attend meetings and workshops, I teach students who ask searching questions, and I talk to people. Somewhere in my head, the ideas and opinions are no doubt absorbed. But like most people, I find it hard to say exactly how. Let me try. Rossi has been an all-purpose resource. I frequently test my ideas against his discussions in the successive revisions of his fine textbook. House has heightened my sense of the ethical dimensions of evaluation. Fetterman has added to my understanding of participatory evaluation. Patton and I trade ideas and verbal punches about usable evaluation knowledge. I published one of his early articles (Patton et al., 1977) in a book, *Using Social Research in Public Policy Making*. I like that article a lot, and I am glad to see that in his recent work, he has returned to recognition of the circuitous routes that evaluation can take to influencing policy.

I read and listen, but perhaps the major influences on my thought have been the evaluations I have done. Much of what I learned was from planning and conducting evaluation studies. In the words of William Whyte's (1984) book, it was "learning from the field," and in the words of Rossman and Rallis's book (1998), it was "learning in the field."

CONCLUSION

It is time to bring this discussion to a close. I admit that it is fun to talk about evaluation theory and to advocate undertaking more research *about* evaluation (Henry & Mark, 2003; King, 2003). These exercises can no doubt contribute to our knowledge and skills. But let the reader beware. All the chapters in this volume will take us only so far. Christie (2003b) wrote an article quoting

Chandler about his study of evaluators: "Evaluation theory did not overly influence the way most [evaluators] approached their [own] practice." Datta (2003) adds the charming note that when panels of eminent evaluation theorists were asked to extemporize what they would do in response to a specific evaluation problem, "there was little or no relation between what the theorist proposed and her or his theories as most understood them" (pp. 44–45). My own interpretation of these comments is that what the collection of wise old owls say in this book is important but contingent. Conditions in the turbulent program environment can sometimes prevent us from putting our best ideas into practice, and for other reasons we may sheer to the wind. Readers have to read critically and use their own good judgment.

A final note. Evaluation has become more prevalent around the world in recent years. It is not only funders of programs in developing countries who want to know the consequences of their interventions in order to hold local agencies accountable. It is also domestic policymakers and administrators who want to learn about which programs and procedures stand the best chance of improving the lot of their people. Furthermore, a growing number of local people are becoming expert evaluators and bringing their special sensitivities to the study of programs in their countries. It is a pleasure to see this volume open to a range of voices around the world.

REFERENCES

Alkin, M. C. (1972). Evaluation theory development. In C. H. Weiss (Ed.), *Evaluating action programs: Readings in social action and education* (pp. 105–117). Boston, MA: Allyn & Bacon.

Alkin, M. C. (1991). Evaluation theory development II. In M. McLaughlin & D. C. Phillips (Eds.), *Evaluation and education: At quarter-century* (90th yearbook of the National Society for the Study of Education, Part II; pp. 91–112). Chicago, IL: University of Chicago Press.

Birkeland, S., Weiss, C. H., & Murphy-Graham, E. (2005). Good reasons for ignoring good evaluation: The case of the Drug Abuse Resistance Education (D.A.R.E.) Program. *Evaluation and Program Planning, 28,* 247–256.

Campbell, D. T., & Stanley, J. C. (1966). *Experimental and quasi-experimental design for research.* Chicago, IL: Rand McNally.

Christie, C. A. (Ed.). (2003a). *New directions for evaluation: Vol. 97. The practice-theory relationship in evaluation.* San Francisco, CA: Jossey-Bass.

Christie, C. A. (2003b). What guides evaluation? A study of how evaluation practice maps onto evaluation theory. *New Directions for Evaluation, 97,* 7–35.

Cook, T. D., & Campbell, D. T. (1979). *Quasi-experimentation: Design and analysis issues for field settings.* Chicago, IL: Rand McNally.

Datta, L. E. (2003). Important questions, intriguing method, incomplete. *New Directions for Evaluation, 97,* 37–46.

Dentler, R. (1959). *The young volunteers: An evaluation of the American friends service committee.* Chicago, IL: National Opinion Research Center.

Henry, G. T., & Mark, M. M. (2003). Toward an agenda for research on evaluation. *New Directions for Evaluation, 97,* 69–80.

Herzog, E. (1959). *Some guidelines for evaluative research.* Washington, DC: U.S. Department of Health, Education, and Welfare.

Hyman, H. H., Wright, C. R., & Hopkins, T. K. (1962). *Applications of methods of evaluation: Four studies of the encampment for citizenship.* Los Angeles: University of California Press.

King, J. A. (2003). The challenge of studying evaluation theory. *New Directions for Evaluation, 97,* 57–67.

Patton, M. Q., Grimes, P. S., Guthrie, K. M., Brennan, N. J., French, B. D., & Blyth, D. A. (1977). In search of impact: An analysis of the utilization of federal health evaluation research. In C. H. Weiss (Ed.), *Using social research in public policy making* (pp. 141–163). Lexington, MA: D. C. Heath.

Pawson, R. (2002). Evidence and policy and naming and shaming. *Policy Studies, 23,* 211–230.

Powers, E., & Witmer, H. (1951). *An experiment in the prevention of juvenile delinquency: The Cambridge–Somerville youth study.* New York, NY: Columbia University Press.

Rossman, G. B., & Rallis, S. F. (1998). *Learning in the field: An introduction to qualitative research.* Thousand Oaks, CA: Sage.

Shadish, W. R., Cook, T. D., & Campbell, D. T. (2002). *Experimental and quasi-experimental designs for generalized causal inference.* Boston, MA: Houghton Mifflin.

Wagner, P., Weiss, C. H., Wittrock, B., & Wollmann, H. (Eds.). (1991). *Social sciences and modern states: National experiences and theoretical crossroads.* Cambridge, England: Cambridge University Press.

Weeks, H. A. (1958). *Youthful offenders at Highfields.* Ann Arbor: University of Michigan Press.

Weiss, C. H. (Ed.). (1972a). *Evaluating action programs: Readings in social action and education.* Boston, MA: Allyn & Bacon.

Weiss, C. H. (1972b). *Evaluation research: Methods of assessing program effectiveness.* Englewood Cliffs, NJ: Prentice Hall.

Weiss, C. H. (Ed.). (1977). *Using social research in public policy making.* Lexington, MA: D. C. Heath.

Weiss, C. H. (with Bucuvalas, M.). (1980). *Social science research and decision-making.* New York, NY: Columbia University Press.

Weiss, C. H. (Ed.). (1991). *Organizations for policy analysis: Helping government think.* Newbury Park, CA: Sage.

Weiss, C. H. (1998). *Evaluation: Methods for studying programs and policies.* Upper Saddle River, NJ: Prentice Hall.

Weiss, C. H., & Singer, E. (with Endreny, P.). (1988). *Reporting of social science in the national media.* New York, NY: Russell Sage.

Weiss, C. H., Murphy-Graham, E., & Birkeland, S. (2005). An alternate route to policy influence: How evaluations affect D.A.R.E. *American Journal of Evaluation, 26,* 12–30.

Weiss, C. H., Murphy-Graham, E., Petrosino, A., & Gandhi, A. G. (2008). The Fairy Godmother—and Her Warts: Making the dream of evidence-based policy come true. *American Journal of Evaluation, 29,* 29–47.

Whyte, W. (with Whyte, K. K.). (1984). *Learning from the field: A guide from experience.* Beverly Hills, CA: Sage.

10

MULTIPLE ROUTES

Evaluation, Assisted Sensemaking, and Pathways to Betterment

Melvin M. Mark and Gary T. Henry

It is a privilege and an honor to join the lineup of contributors to Marv Alkin's edited volume on evaluation roots. We were not included in the first edition, at least in part because our writing about evaluation was difficult to associate with a single branch of the Alkin and Christie evaluation theory tree. Referring to Mark, Henry, and Julnes (2000), Alkin (2004) wrote in the first chapter of the first edition, "The very diversified nature of this perspective, while a great strength in presenting an understanding of evaluation, precludes its presentation on the tree" (p. 59). We are pleased to join the second edition, comfortable with the location on the tree that Alkin and Christie have provided us and honored to be in the company of so many others whose work has provoked and influenced our own thinking. In this regard, we wish to recognize our intellectual debt both to those who stimulated our thinking about what we saw as problems in certain theories of evaluation and to those who inspired "I wish I had thought about that" moments. In the rest of the chapter, we lay out key aspects of the view of evaluation we have written about. We also summarize the history and motivation behind our work, including a brief recognition of a sample of key influences on it.

HISTORY, PART 1: ROOT BEERS

In a sense, the roots of our collaboration go back to a series of panels many years ago at annual meetings of the American Evaluation Association (AEA). For several years, Mark Lipsey and Mel Mark organized a set of panels at AEA. They solicited paper proposals from a group of colleagues, sorted these into sessions, and listed one person as discussant or chair to avoid the sessions being scheduled at the same time. Gary Henry took note of the overlap and fit between a smaller set of colleagues' presentations and started suggesting collaborations. The most persuasive of these arguments took place in the evening in the hotel lobby bar (hence "root beers"). A set of collaborations did result, some involving other partners (e.g., Henry & Rog, 1998; Julnes & Mark, 1998; Mark et al., 2000), but ours was the most durable and, we like to think, central of these collaborations. In that regard, we note that we are one of only two duos on the evaluation theory tree and the only duo not also married. In the pages that follow, we try to lay out the basic ideas and selected implications of the core aspects of our approach to evaluation. These include the notion of evaluation as assisted sensemaking, social betterment as the ultimate goal for evaluation, the multiple purposes of evaluation, alternative pathways to evaluation influence, and the need for contingent selection from alternative evaluation design choices. A key theme in our work is that there are multiple alternative routes (pun intended) whereby evaluation can make a positive difference and that the choices that highly skilled evaluators make about evaluation design and methods will vary across different situations. A related theme is that perhaps the central role for evaluation theory is to facilitate the ability of evaluators and others involved in evaluation planning (a) to be aware of a set of alternative evaluation questions, designs, and methods within a large toolkit of evaluation approaches and (b) to make thoughtful and defensible judgments in selecting from among the many options in the toolkit.

EVALUATION AS ASSISTED SENSEMAKING

Humans by nature strive to make sense of the world around them. Indeed, the sensemaking motivation is so strong that people often see patterns where none exist (Fiske & Taylor, 1991). In making sense of the world, people also make evaluative judgments, perhaps automatically (Albarracin, Johnson, & Zanna, 2005). As practicing evaluators know, but as evaluation theories sometimes seem to ignore, stakeholders do not hold off on making evaluative judgments until "the evaluator" arrives! However, the informal and everyday evaluations that stakeholders make are often inaccurate, as suggested by the extensive literature on psychological biases (e.g., Fiske & Taylor, 1991). For example, program staff members typically do not account for the methodologist's "counterfactual"; that is, they do not assess how well their clients would have done in the absence of the program (not to mention clients' rational self-selection into a program that could increase observed success). Moreover, staff members' personal investment in the program may stimulate biases, such as easier recall of successful cases.

In short, although humans naturally make evaluative judgments, these judgments are susceptible to limited information and potential biases. This observation motivates the idea of *evaluation as assisted sensemaking*[1] (Mark et al., 2000). The fundamental idea is that evaluation can contribute by extending, enhancing, and checking the natural sensemaking that people engage in about programs, policies, or other evaluands. Evaluators have at their disposal a set of tools (e.g., randomized experiments and case studies) as well as a set of general roadmaps to guide them (the evaluation theories, approaches, or models described in this book and elsewhere, e.g., Shadish, Cook, & Leviton, 1991), all of which can be deployed in service of facilitating the capacity of stakeholders to better understand and act in relation to the evaluated program or policy.

The notion of evaluation as assisted sensemaking, while perhaps not a stunning one to thoughtful members of the evaluation community, nevertheless has what we see as nontrivial implications. First, it locates evaluation practice squarely in a broader context of human judgment and action processes. It fits well with the idea of organizational decision making as complex and messy, and with information often competing with values and politics (Weiss, 1988). But it can also accommodate user-focused approaches in which the evaluator serves the information needs of specific, interested stakeholders to facilitate use (e.g., Patton, 1997). The organizational contexts in which sensemaking about programs takes place vary, so the demands on and approaches to evaluation should vary accordingly. Second, an evaluation, however technically proficient it may be, is of little value if the findings are not shared in ways that connect with the natural sensemaking processes of relevant parties. This has implications not only for the dissemination and presentation of evaluation findings but also for the potential array of evaluator roles related to evaluation influence—a topic to which we will return later. Third, the idea of evaluation as assisted sensemaking serves as a reminder that evaluation's tools are human-made aids that can help avoid the limits of everyday judgment, but they also have limits themselves. Eyeglasses are an invented technology that can reduce the limits of one's visual system, but they do not guarantee perfect sight.

We both came of age in a time of great excitement about the application of quantitative methods in the social sciences, and we both received training that contributed toward the idea of applying those methods for assisted sensemaking. We learned that with more attention to rigorous design, including quasi-experimental and experimental designs, came the promise of more accurate estimates of program impacts. We learned too how random sampling could produce accurate statistical pictures of a program's target population or coverage of intended beneficiaries. But we have viewed quantitative methods as *an* important set of tools in the toolkit, not the only set. Our view, shared with many others, is that the goal for assisted sensemaking in evaluation is to get the most accurate answer for the most pressing questions in a particular circumstance. But how do we propose to select the most pressing questions from all the interesting or at least possible ones?

SOCIAL BETTERMENT AS THE GUIDING STAR

Why does systematic evaluation exist? There are several ways of answering that question. One kind of response highlights the role of evaluation as assisting the natural, but all too frequently biased, sensemaking and evaluation in which stakeholders will engage. Another, complementary kind of response, highlights one or another position about the ultimate goal(s) of evaluation. For example, should the ultimate goal of evaluation, the guiding star and the key criterion for judging the success of evaluations (Miller & Campbell, 2006), be utilization, empowerment, or inclusion, to take a few examples represented elsewhere in this book? We hold instead that the ultimate guiding star for evaluation should be *social betterment*. Admittedly, social betterment is a fuzzy and distal concept—which is why clearer and more proximate evaluation purposes also need to be identified. Admittedly too, social betterment is a notion about which disagreement, sometimes serious, takes place—which is why we see evaluation as linked to a set of deliberative and decision-making processes, especially in the public sector of democratic societies. Also, we have suggested the use of systematic values inquiry in this process, often as a precursor to an evaluation. We use the term *values inquiry* to suggest that evaluators may need to use systematic research methods to understand better the values that should be infused into an evaluation. This would include getting a better understanding of which of the intended objectives for a program are most valued by various constituencies, as well as the unintended consequences or negative side effects that are feared by important constituencies. For example, Henry (2002) surveyed parents, teachers, program administrators, and the general public in an effort to understand each group's view of the most important outcomes that could result from a statewide pre-kindergarten program. The highest-priority outcomes were different for these groups, which required an array of outcomes to be measured for the evaluation.

The somewhat stilted term *social betterment*, which has nonetheless been widely adopted, was chosen very intentionally to convey several specifics. First, it is distinct from social progress, which has been taken to mean a steady, inevitable improvement of social conditions. Second, it is social, not individual, progress, which to us means something more than an increase in individual utility or individual consumption. Third, we define it as incorporating greater equality of access to the material, psychological, and other benefits of society, not simply a larger total amount of such benefits; thus the concept includes an explicit concern with social justice. Finally, it also allows us to recognize that societies are often better at achieving consensus about what they don't want (illiteracy) rather than what they do want (a functional definition of the minimum acceptable reading level). Social betterment provides evaluators with a *guiding star*, a term that summarizes our concern for the well-being of others and society as a whole and, we believe, establishes a clearer focus on our ultimate goals for evaluation and ourselves as evaluators.

While identifying social betterment as the ultimate purpose of evaluation may not seem especially revolutionary, we believe that explicit attention to it has some noteworthy implications. First, we do not take the direct and intended use of evaluation in decision making as a good criterion for judging the worth of the evaluation itself. Sometimes the impact of evaluation is indirect, delayed, and different from what an intended user might have specified. Nevertheless, such evaluation influence is important. Likewise, we suggest that evaluators and others involved in evaluation planning should not focus on maximizing the likelihood of intended use but should consider the risk–reward ratio of alternative approaches to evaluation. Imagine two alternative evaluations that might be conducted. Option A has a high likelihood of use, but if used would result in only marginal changes. Option B, in contrast, has a lower likelihood of use, but if influential could make a huge difference. Taking social betterment as the ultimate goal, those planning evaluations are invited to take thoughtful consideration of these options, often tilting toward B. A simple-minded emphasis on maximizing use sometimes can lead to less than optimal choices among evaluation options.

Second, in the public sector at least, the potential consumers of evaluation typically are legion and the decision-making processes diffuse. Evaluation planning, at least in the public sector, needs an approach that matches this reality. It should be more policy analytic, mindful of the potential environment for decision making and action rather than based on interactions with an identifiable intended user.

A third implication of explicitly identifying social betterment as the guiding star for evaluation relates to the choice of methods. Debates in evaluation and related fields have too often focused on a proposed priority for a given method, such as randomized controlled trials (RCTs), or conversely on the method's alleged frailties. Instead, the focus should be on when, why, and how alternative methods can facilitate evaluation's contribution to social betterment. Take as an example the idea of RCTs as a possible method choice. RCTs can have a relative advantage in generating unbiased estimates of the (relative) effect of a program. This is especially the case when the program is operating amid multiple other factors that might affect the outcome(s) of interest (also known as internal validity threats) and when small or modest effects are of interest. But information about the average effect of a substance abuse prevention program, say, is most relevant when a fork in the road is ahead—that is, when a decision will be made about which course of action, which program if any, to adopt or replace. Thus, from the social betterment perspective, the first question concerns whether the situation at hand is of this "fork in the road" variety (or some other circumstance where an RCT would be valuable). For instance, are potential actions expected such as the continuation of a newly funded program, which will occur when the Race to the Top grants to the states that were recently funded by the federal government reach an end? Alternatively, if no fork in the road is forthcoming but there are opportunities for evaluation to contribute to improvements in an ongoing program, an RCT or similar method of evaluating the overall program would likely not be a good choice. In addition, even if a fork in the road is anticipated, the question arises as to the relative contribution to betterment that an RCT would likely generate, in comparison with alternative methods such as various quasi-experiments, a case study, or even descriptive information from a program's set of performance indicators. As good evaluators know, and as the idea of social betterment clarifies, method choice is not primarily about methods but rather about the judged likelihood of a given method contributing to social betterment, relative to alternatives, in the anticipated decision-making and action context.

A fourth implication of locating social betterment as the ultimate, distal goal of evaluation is that it is necessary to identify intermediate, more proximal considerations to guide evaluation planning. There is more than one way in which evaluation can contribute to social betterment. Classic distinctions such as that between formative and summative evaluation imply as much. More generally, there are different ways in which evaluation can help. Accordingly, there is not a single predominant, specific purpose for evaluations. Rather, in our view, evaluators should be mindful of a range of immediate purposes for an evaluation that could serve the ultimate goal of social betterment.

MULTIPLE PURPOSES OF EVALUATION

Our theory or model of evaluation points to alternative evaluation *purposes* as more proximate guides to evaluation planning. In the 1990s, the distinction between formative and summative evaluation gave way to the idea of three general purposes of evaluation (at least, three purposes for evaluation findings, as opposed to evaluation process; Patton, 1997). Alternative but overlapping versions of the three purposes appeared. From Patton (1997), they were to judge merit or worth, to improve programs, and to generate knowledge. For Chelimsky (1997, 2006), the three purposes were (1) to support policy making and public accountability, (2) to facilitate program and organizational improvement, and (3) to contribute to knowledge development.

In Mark et al. (2000), we expanded the list of evaluation purposes to four: (1) overall assessment of merit and worth, when evaluation is intended to support bottom-line judgments; (2) program (and organizational) improvement, when evaluation is meant to point to changes in a program (or the organization providing it); (3) accountability and oversight, when evaluation is designed to provide information about a program's compliance with legislative or other mandates; and (4) knowledge development, when the goal is for evaluation to expand understanding, for example, of the nature of a social problem or the feasibility of implementing a new approach to its solution.

Recognition that there are alternative evaluation purposes, however, only takes you so far. More important is having a way to assess priorities, that is, to identify the conditions under which each of the four evaluation purposes should rise to the top in evaluation planning. Any list of factors involved in setting a priority among evaluation purposes will necessarily be incomplete. No model can capture adequately all of the nuances of every specific case, and considerations may change with historical shifts, such as when legislative agendas change with increased attention to budget deficits. Nevertheless, a set of general guides should be useful, and so we offered a set in Mark et al. (2000). For example, the previous discussion of whether a fork in the road is anticipated represents a major consideration of whether priority should be given to the purpose of assessing merit and worth. In contrast, when no fork in the road is anticipated, but limited formative evaluation has been conducted and/or multiple variants on program practices exist, priority might instead be placed on the purpose of program and organizational improvement. Oversight and compliance might receive higher priority when failure to follow mandates (e.g., client eligibility requirements or nature of services offered) is expected to harm program effectiveness or efficiency or, more simply, when this focus is demanded by those with oversight responsibilities. Knowledge development may take major priority when other contributions seem unlikely (e.g., if the evaluator comes to find that the evaluation actually is ritualistic) or when knowledge development can coexist with or even facilitate another purpose (e.g., when study of program moderators will enhance an assessment of merit and worth). A more detailed discussion of factors that should affect the prioritization of evaluation purposes is given in Mark et al. (2000), especially in Chapter 3.

In general, the central idea is to consider the anticipated range of potential decisions and actions in relation to the program. The goal is to identify which evaluation purpose is likely to optimize evaluation's contribution to social betterment. Of course, a degree of uncertainty is inherent in this process. But the alternative, we believe, is even less satisfactory. And at least some of the time, there are strong enough cues. For example, the initial funding for a program may be scheduled to run out in 3 years, as with Race to the Top (signaling a coming fork in the road). Or a program may be funded statewide via a voter referendum (signaling that the program will likely continue for the foreseeable future but may face challenges in statewide implementation).

With an evaluation purpose (or a sequence or combination of purposes) in mind, choosing a method can be done more sensibly. The evaluation purpose should lead to evaluation questions, and the questions should limit the range of viable methods. For example, the purpose of program improvement often suggests three questions: (1) Does program implementation vary? (2) Do program outcomes vary? (3) Are there variations in implementation that are systematically associated with variations in outcomes? In this case, comparative case studies and descriptive information from administrative and/or survey data seem to be likely method choices. This, in turn, leads to additional questions such as "How do we choose cases to maximize the ability to observe implementation variation?" or "How do we sample clients to provide the most accurate description of outcomes?" The questions are answered iteratively, injecting the issue of feasibility into the process whenever an answer is tentatively agreed on. Method choices, we believe, are best made in service of a deliberately chosen purpose that represents a pathway to social betterment, by addressing a series of questions that involve trade-offs between the ideal and the possible.

Mark et al. (2000) contains a more detailed discussion of method choice, in light of evaluation purpose. Rather than offer further details here, we will offer a partial summary of a subsequent portion of our "theory, model, or approach" to evaluation.

ALTERNATIVE PATHWAYS TO EVALUATION INFLUENCE

The literature has long differentiated between direct, conceptual, and symbolic use and, somewhat more recently, process use (Caracelli, 2000; Cousins & Leithwood, 1986). More recently, Kirkhart (2000) has been a leading voice in arguing that "evaluation influence," rather than "evaluation use," should be the focus. Influence includes those consequences of evaluation that are indirect, unintended, and distant from the evaluation itself, perhaps even without the relevant party's awareness of the influence. For example, a legislator's vote for a new program may be indirectly influenced by evaluation findings of the program's effectiveness in another state. The findings may have motivated the persuasive efforts of an aide, even though the legislator did not know the evaluation exists. We endorse a focus on evaluation influence, though we hasten to add that this does not imply an absence of concern about trying to bring about intended uses. We also encourage making explicit choices about what type of influence an evaluation should aim to achieve.

In a pair of articles (Henry & Mark, 2003; Mark & Henry, 2004) and an extension in an AEA address (Mark, 2006), we have attempted to identify different categories of consequences that evaluation may have, as well as various processes that might help lead to these consequences. The result is rather complicated, summarized in a 3 × 5 table, with 3 "levels of analysis" combined with 5 "types of consequences" and with several specific processes or consequences identified in each of the 15 cells of the 3 × 5 table. Here we try only to highlight a few of the bigger picture features of the evolving model of evaluation influence.

One feature of the model is that, for each type of evaluation consequence, it distinguishes between three "levels of analysis": (1) individual, (2) interpersonal, and (3) collective. The basic idea is that the consequences of evaluation sometimes involve a change within a particular person (individual), sometimes a change in the interaction between individuals (interpersonal), and sometimes a process at a more macro, organizational unit (collective). For example, consider instances in which evaluation findings suggest a behavioral change, that is, an action of the sort that could be classified under the older label of direct or instrumental use. As our model suggests, the desired behavioral change might be at any of the three levels. For example, in an educational evaluation, the behavioral change might involve (1) individual classroom teachers' instructional practices, (2) the initiation of certain collaborative practices across teachers (interpersonal), or (3) the collective-level implementation of a program-funding decision.

The distinction among these different levels of analysis is not trivial. As Henry and Mark (2003) suggest, the pathways that lead to individual or interpersonal change may be quite different from the pathways that lead to collective action (see also Weiss, 1998, pp. 264–265, on the distinction between the use of evaluation for policy and its use for practice). By getting beyond relatively gross categories such as "direct use," evaluators might do a better job of planning to increase the likelihood that evaluation contributes to action. Explicit recognition of the different levels of evaluation's influence can also help clarify debates and differences within the field. For example, we believe that advocates of RCTs and meta-analyses implicitly focus more on collective change, such as program-funding decisions, while evaluators interested in lived experience and practitioner judgment focus more on the individual (or perhaps interpersonal) level (cf. the debate between Lipsey, 2000a, 2000b, and Schwandt, 2000a, 2000b).

In addition to differentiating the three levels of analysis, Mark and Henry (2004) identify four categories of evaluation consequences. Two are familiar. *Behavioral processes*, according to Mark and Henry, refer to changes in actions. This category thus corresponds to instrumental use but is broader, including, for example, influence that the person is not aware of. *Cognitive and affective processes* refer to shifts in thoughts and feelings, such as attitude valence. This corresponds to conceptual use but, again, is broader. In contrast, two categories, general influence and motivational processes, are typically of interest not as the ultimate change that an evaluation might stimulate but as the initial or interim steps along a pathway to that change. *General influence processes*, according to Mark and Henry (2004), are not likely to be the intended end of an influence process but "are likely to set into motion some [other] change." For example, the individual-level process of *elaboration* refers to a person thinking more deeply about an issue—a process that extensive research shows can trigger long-lasting change in attitudes and perhaps behaviors. Similarly, Mark and Henry (2004) describe *motivational processes* as involving goals, aspirations, and responses to perceived rewards and punishments. Such motivational processes may play an important role in changing behavior, as when highly visible and recognizable orange bins lead homeowners to fear social disapproval if they do not participate in a curbside recycling program.

Recently, Mark (2006) proposed the addition of another category of evaluation consequences to the Mark and Henry (2004) framework. Mark (2006) tentatively labeled this new category as "relational consequences" because it includes efforts by evaluators to modify not behavior or attitude but aspects of ongoing relationships, structures, and organizational processes. The relational category includes, for example, potential consequences such as individuals' self-perception of their empowerment (Fetterman, 1996), the creation of a democratic forum for deliberation (House & Howe, 1999), and the facilitation of the learning organization (Preskill & Torres, 1998). In general, the evaluation theories (or models) that advocate for such relational consequences are more recent, relative to theories that focus on program-related action and understandings (Alkin, 2004). And they often tend to see evaluation not as narrowly concerned with the policy, program, or practice being evaluated; rather, these approaches often treat evaluation in part as a vehicle to use in trying to bring about other forms of change, such as empowerment or the creation of a learning organization. As a result, many of these approaches may be subject to the criticism "But is it evaluation?" from commentators who hold a more traditional definition of evaluation (e.g., Scriven, 1997). They are also subject to questions about whether in practice they achieve their stated relational goal; for example, Miller and Campbell (2006) ask whether evidence indicates that empowerment evaluation actually empowers people. However, these criticisms are not unlike ones that can be applied to traditional views about the intended consequences of evaluation, such as whether classic comparative evaluation designs actually are used in decision making. Although not established in the literature, the relational category or something like it seems useful, in part because it reminds us that there is a set of potential evaluation consequences that extends beyond the boundaries of the traditional direct and conceptual use.

We have only sketched the general structure of the influence process model from Henry and Mark (2003), Mark and Henry (2004), and Mark (2006). Admittedly, the model is complex. But that is because, we believe, the pathways by which evaluation becomes influential are varied and can be complex. In a sense, the model reflects our belief that evaluators gain by considering evaluations themselves as interventions and adopting something akin to program theories for evaluations. From this vantage, our influence model is like a catalog, a taxonomy and listing of a large array of processes and consequences, a subset of which might operate for a particular evaluation. Again, we believe that there are nontrivial implications.

First, the model invites evaluators to try to draw out the expected pathway by which an evaluation is expected to be influential. Our sense is that the traditional "end states" of instrumental and conceptual use do not capture the potentially long and complex path through which evaluation comes to have its influence. Consider a simplified example. A briefing about evaluation findings might trigger (a) a legislative aide in attendance to engage in elaboration of her or his thoughts about a program, (b) which, in turn, leads her or him to have a more positive attitude toward the program, (c) which then leads her or him to engage in interpersonal processes such as persuasion efforts directed at other legislative staff and her or his boss, (d) which might eventually contribute to the inclusion of language expanding program funding in an appropriations bill, leading to (e) collective-level policy change. The metaphor is of a set of dominoes, sitting upright on end, with the first consequence needing to fall and knock down the second, the second to knock down the third, and so on, to reach (or, if the sequence is interrupted without another line of dominoes in the background, to fail to reach) the end-state use, such as instrumental use in policy making. The reality is likely to be more complex, with multiple lines of dominoes.

Second, we believe that there is considerable promise for research and for practice if increased attention is given to this kind of "influence pathways." Thinking about influence pathways could be a useful guide to new kinds of research on evaluation influence and use. For example, case studies could trace the influence pathways from an evaluation. Experiments could examine the effects of arrangements designed to facilitate (or inhibit) a process of potential interest, such as elaboration. In terms of practice, if evaluators seriously consider possible influence pathways during evaluation planning, they might take steps to increase the likelihood that evaluation will matter.

Thinking about influence pathways could also sharpen our thinking about alternative evaluator roles in facilitating use and influence. In our view, there has been a kind of dichotomous thinking about the role of evaluators, either suggesting that the evaluator's primary responsibility is to facilitate use (e.g., Patton) or suggesting more of a hands-off role as provider of information (e.g., Campbell). Attention to alternative roles has perhaps been inhibited because there has not been a common vocabulary to identify the multiple steps in an influence pathway. And different potential roles do exist. For example, an evaluator working for an advocacy group or private foundation might stay involved all along the multiple series of steps in an influence pathway. An evaluator working for an independent government agency might be involved only for a few steps, perhaps relying on advocates, lobbyists, or other actors in the policy process to move beyond the initial steps. Evaluators at universities or research firms might operate in various ways, depending on their personal preferences, including an approach that calls for determined dissemination to others in the policy and practice communities related to the program but not taking responsibility for achieving the downstream portion of the influence pathway (Greenberg, Mandell, & Onstott, 2000).

EPISTEMOLOGICAL ROOTS

Alkin has asked us to address our epistemological roots. In Mark et al. (2000), we claimed allegiance to a form of realism. Our realism is not the "naïve realism" whereby people think that they have direct perception of the world but something closer to the "critical realism" of Campbell, assuming that one's access to the world is imperfect, mediated, and subject to bias. In part, we endorsed realism to distance our approach from what we see as antirealist claims in the rhetoric of some evaluation theorists. Among other realists, Bhaskar (e.g., 1975) reminds us that if we truly are to be fallibilists about knowledge claims, we need to be realists. A more relevant notion for evaluators might be that few successful evaluation-funding proposals begin with "There is no reality." At the same time, we recognize the importance of human constructions. These apply to evaluation planning, such as in the choice of values that inform evaluation design and measures, as well as to the perceptions and actions of program clients and others. Nevertheless, recognition of social construction does not, we think, imply that efforts to estimate program effectiveness are somehow wrong. Nor does it obviate notions such as bias in inference, construct and external validity, or gaming a testing system.

In retrospect, we wish there was no press for evaluators to lay claim to an epistemological position. Too often, these claims are associated with excess, at least in rhetoric if not in evaluation practice. Perhaps evaluation theorists need to follow the lead of most humans, including sensible evaluation practitioners, who in everyday life exhibit a combination of realism (e.g., stopping at a red light) and constructivism (e.g., recognizing that most traffic laws are arbitrary social constructions and people have differing views about risk taking). Moreover, most people realize that effective action does not require investing heavily in determining the relative priority of these or other philosophy of science positions.

INFLUENCES

For Mark, key influences related to evaluation certainly include Tom Cook, Donald Campbell, and others associated with the Northwestern University evaluation community in the 1970s (Oral History Project Team, 2003). Paul Wortman, Bob Boruch, Dave Cordray, Chip Reichardt, Will Shadish, Laura Leviton, Bill Trochim, and others constituted an impressive community interested in evaluation. As an undergraduate, Mark chose to apply to Northwestern's social psychology graduate program after being enamored with social research addressing important problems and conducted in real-world settings. Pivotal in this regard was the famous "Robbers' Cave" experiment conducted by Muzafer and Carolyn Sherif and their colleagues (Sherif, Harvey, White, Hood, & Sherif, 1961). Mark literally follows in their footsteps, as he lives in what had been Carolyn and Muzafer's house.

Doing our graduate studies in the late 1970s, we were caught up in the intellectual excitement of the day surrounding social science, methods development for the social sciences, evaluation, and other applied social research, which seemed like a challenging and rewarding application of the cutting-edge techniques. But the training we each received complemented the others' in many ways: Mark on experimental and quasi-experimental design and Henry on surveys and survey sampling; Mark in social psychology studying human motivation and behavior change efforts and Henry in political science particularly focusing on political participation and Dahl's theories about the role of information in complex modern democracies. We have overlapped substantially in our admiration for Carol Weiss's views on use and influence (e.g., Weiss, 1977, 1988); Ernie House's careful formulation of values and valuing (e.g., House, 2001; House & Howe, 1999); Campbell, Cook, and Donald Rubin's formulations of causal theories (e.g., Cook & Campbell, 1979; Rubin, 1974, 2008); as well as Campbell's and Hilary Putnam's take on the philosophy of science. We have been fortunate to have some of these folks as mentors and friends. Also, we have a group of colleagues and friends too numerous to mention who have collaborated, argued, mobilized, and agonized with us about many of the issues in evaluation.

CONCLUSION

Evaluation can be directed toward several alternative purposes. Evaluation can also be influential in various ways, with even more varied pathways to influence (or lack thereof). Indeed, most of the chapters in this book suggest one or other possible consequence of evaluation, along with recommendations about the best ways of getting there. This brings to mind the following question: Under what conditions should each potential consequence of evaluation take priority? Which calls forth two other questions: (1) By what process should one judge the relative priority of these alternatives? (2) And, given priority to a particular kind of evaluation consequence, how should one try to achieve it? Attempting to answer these questions is at the core of the work we have done, which has led Alkin and others to refer to some of our work under the label evaluation theory.

Allegiance to the idea of evaluation as assisted sensemaking implies a kind of modesty. Humans do not have access to what philosophers occasionally call the God's-eye view. Nor do evaluators have access to a God's-eye view of how evaluation should be done. Our own ideas about evaluation have evolved over time, and we anticipate that they will continue to evolve through processes akin to mutation, adaptation, and selection. We look forward to further influences by colleagues on and off the evaluation theory tree. And we heartily root for their efforts and for those of all who seek to contribute, in one way or another, to the endeavor of social betterment through evaluation.

NOTE

1. This phrase was the working title of our 2000 book, until the publisher said that its marketing people found this title "inert." Our apparently unpersuasive response was "Can you give us an example of an 'ert' title?"

REFERENCES

Albarracin, D., Johnson, B. T., & Zanna, M. P. (2005). *The handbook of attitudes*. New York, NY: Routledge.

Alkin, M. (Ed.). (2004). *Evaluation roots: Tracing theorists' views and influences*. Thousand Oaks, CA: Sage.

Bhaskar, R. A. (1975). *A realist theory of science*. London, England: Verso.

Caracelli, V. J. (2000). Evaluation use at the threshold of the twenty-first century. In V. Caracelli & H. Preskill (Eds.), *New directions for evaluation: Vol. 88. The expanding scope of evaluation use*. San Francisco, CA: Jossey-Bass.

Chelimsky, E. (1997). The coming transformation in evaluation. In E. Chelimsky & W. R. Shadish (Eds.), *Evaluation for the 2st century* (pp. 1–26). Thousand Oaks, CA: Sage.

Chelimsky, E. (2006). The purposes of evaluation in a democratic society. In I. F. Shaw, J. C. Greene, & M. M. Mark (Eds.), *The SAGE handbook of evaluation* (pp. 33–55). London, England: Sage.

Cook, T. D., & Campbell, D. T. (1979). *Quasi-experimentation: Design and analysis issues for field settings*. Chicago, IL: Rand McNally.

Cousins, J. B., & Leithwood, K. A. (1986). Current empirical research on evaluation utilization. *Review of Educational Research, 56*(3), 331–364.

Fetterman, D. M. (1996). *Foundations of empowerment evaluation*. Thousand Oaks, CA: Sage.

Fiske, S. T., & Taylor, S. E. (1991). *Social cognition* (2nd ed.). New York, NY: Longman.

Greenberg, D., Mandell, M., & Onstott, M. (2000). The dissemination and utilization of welfare-to-work experiments in state policymaking. *Journal of Policy Analysis and Management, 19*, 367–382.

Henry, G. T. (2002). Choosing criteria to judge program success: A values inquiry. *Evaluation, 8*(2), 182–204.

Henry, G. T., & Mark, M. M. (2003). Beyond use: Understanding evaluation's influence on attitudes and actions. *American Journal of Evaluation, 24*, 294–314.

Henry, G. T., & Rog, D. J. (1998). A realist theory and analysis of utilization. In G. Henry, G. Julnes, & M. M. Mark (Eds.), *New directions for evaluation: Vol. 78. Realist evaluation* (pp. 89–102). San Francisco, CA: Jossey-Bass.

House, E., & Howe, K. (1999). *Values in evaluation and social research.* Thousand Oaks, CA: Sage.

House, E. R. (2001). Unfinished business: Causes and values. *American Journal of Evaluation, 22,* 309–315.

Julnes, G. J., & Mark, M. M. (1998). Evaluation as sensemaking: Knowledge construction in a realist world. In G. Henry, G. W. Julnes, & M. M. Mark (Eds.), *Realist evaluation: An emerging theory in support of practice* (pp. 33–52). San Francisco, CA: Jossey-Bass.

Kirkhart, K. (2000). Reconceptualizing evaluation use: An integrated theory of influence. In V. Caracelli & H. Preskill (Eds.), *New directions for evaluation: Vol. 94. The expanding scope of evaluation use* (pp. 5–23). San Francisco, CA: Jossey-Bass.

Lipsey, M. W. (2000a). Meta-analysis and the learning curve in evaluation practice. *American Journal of Evaluation, 21,* 207–212.

Lipsey, M. W. (2000b). Method and rationality are not social diseases. *American Journal of Evaluation, 21,* 221–223.

Mark, M. M. (2006, November). *The consequences of evaluation: Theory, research, and practice* (Evaluation 2006). Presidential address at the annual meeting of the American Evaluation Association, Portland, ON.

Mark, M. M., & Henry, G. T. (2004). The mechanisms and outcomes of evaluation influence. *Evaluation, 10*(1), 35–57.

Mark, M. M., Henry, G. T., & Julnes, G. (2000). *Evaluation: An integrated framework for understanding, guiding, and improving policies and programs.* San Francisco, CA: Jossey-Bass.

Miller, R. L., & Campbell, R. (2006). Taking stock of empowerment evaluation: An empirical review. *American Journal of Evaluation, 27,* 296–319.

The Oral History Project Team (R. Miller, J. King, M. Mark, & S. Stockdill). (2003). The oral history of evaluation, Part I. Reflections on the chance to work with great people: An interview with William Shadish. *American Journal of Evaluation, 24,* 261–272.

Patton, M. Q. (1997). *Utilization-focused evaluation: The new century text.* Thousand Oaks, CA: Sage.

Preskill, H., & Torres, R. (1998). *Evaluative inquiry for organizational learning.* Thousand Oaks, CA: Sage.

Rubin, D. (1974). Estimating causal effects of treatments in randomized and nonrandomized studies. *Journal of Educational Psychology, 66*(5), 688–701.

Rubin, D. (2008). For objective causal inference, design trumps analysis. *The Annals of Applied Statistics, 2,* 808–840.

Schwandt, T. A. (2000a). Further diagnostic thoughts on what ails evaluation practice. *American Journal of Evaluation, 21,* 225–229.

Schwandt, T. A. (2000b). Meta-analysis and everyday life: The good, the bad, and the ugly. *American Journal of Evaluation, 21,* 213–219.

Scriven, M. S. (1997). Empowerment evaluation revisited. *Evaluation Practice, 18,* 165–175.

Shadish, W. R., Cook, T. D., & Leviton, L. C. (1991). *Foundations of program evaluation: Theories of practice.* Newbury Park, CA: Sage.

Sherif, M., Harvey, O. J., White, B. J., Hood, W. R., & Sherif, C. W. (1961). *Intergroup conflict and cooperation: The Robbers Cave experiment.* Norman: University of Oklahoma Book Exchange.

Weiss, C. H. (Ed.). (1977). *Using social research in public policy making.* Lexington, MA: Lexington Books.

Weiss, C. H. (1988). Evaluation for decisions: Is anybody there? Does anybody care? *Evaluation Practice, 9*(1), 5–20.

Weiss, C. H. (1998). Improving the use of evaluations: Whose job is it anyway? *Advances in Educational Productivity, 7,* 263–276.

11

RALPH W. TYLER'S CONTRIBUTION TO PROGRAM EVALUATION

George F. Madaus

Where does one begin to recount Ralph W. Tyler's immense contributions to the field of educational evaluation? For more than 60 years, Tyler was one of the most influential figures, nationally and internationally, in education in general and in testing and evaluation in particular. His groundbreaking work on achievement test construction from 1929 to 1938 at the Bureau of Educational Research and Service at Ohio State University; from 1938 to 1953 as University Examiner at the University of Chicago; and from 1943 to 1953 as Director, Examination Staff of the U.S. Armed Forces Institute became a basic component of the technology of testing. Furthermore, his contribution to the creation of the National Assessment of Educational Progress (NAEP) has led to new techniques and ways of thinking about testing, assessment, and accountability; his work on The Eight-Year Study (1934 to 1941) influenced the field of curriculum development and shaped the beginnings of program evaluation.

Arguably, Ralph's greatest legacy is his students and their students. As Lee Cronbach (1986), one of Tyler's students, put it so well, "While Ralph has made notable intellectual contributions, perhaps his main contribution has been in his development of people. He has been devoted to people; indeed his whole approach to evaluation was as a means of developing people" (p. 47).[1]

Given the scope of Ralph's many contributions, I will focus on the two central to this volume: the intersection of his contributions to testing and evaluation and the intersection of his work on curriculum and evaluation. But first, a little background on Tyler's own roots and influences is in order.[2]

Source: Excerpted from Madaus, G. F. (2004). Ralph W. Tyler's contribution to program evaluation. In M. C. Alkin (Ed.), *Evaluation roots.* Thousand Oaks, CA: Sage Publications.

ROOTS

Ralph Winfred Tyler was born in Chicago, on April 22, 1902. He graduated from Doane College in 1921 and taught high school in Pierre, South Dakota, from 1921 to 1922. He received his MA from the University of Nebraska in 1923, where he was a faculty member from 1922 to 1926, and his PhD from the University of Chicago in 1927. He was a faculty member at the University of North Carolina (1927–1929), Ohio State University (1929–1938), and the University of Chicago (1938–1953), where he was Chairman of the Department of Education from 1938 to 1948. From 1953 to 1967, he was the first Director of the Center for Advanced Studies in the Behavioral Sciences, which he helped found. (For details on his many other positions, honors, associations, and affiliations, see Madaus & Stufflebeam, 1989.)

As a graduate student, Tyler must have been familiar with, and influenced by, the early literature on testing and evaluation, such as White's (1888) work on using test results for decisions on grade-to-grade promotion; Rice's (1897) comparative evaluation of spelling instruction; the Starch and Elliot (1913) work on scoring essay exams; the Courtis (1916) and Ballou (1918) work on arithmetic testing; Thorndike (1918), Ayers (1918), and Judd's (1918) work on measurement; the development of the group intelligences tests for the army in World War I; the nascent commercial testing industry that began after the war; the various NSSE yearbooks dealing with curriculum and measurement (e.g., see the 15th, 1916; 17th, 1918; and 26th, 1927); and finally, G. Stanley Hall's work *The Content of Children's Minds* (see Hall, 1907, in which this paper was reproduced).[3]

Tyler's 1927 dissertation, under the direction of W.W. Charters, titled *Statistical Methods for Utilizing Personal Judgments to Evaluate Activities for Teacher-Training Curricula,* marks the beginning of his enduring interest in the development of reliable and valid techniques for use in both developing and evaluating curriculum. His dissertation work, influenced by the writings of Bobbitt and Charters on curriculum and Courtis and Bode on educational objectives, was in response to a demand "for clearly defined methods or techniques to be formulated, discarded, or validated to guide those who are engaged in curriculum construction" (Tyler, 1927, p. 8).

TESTING AND EVALUATION

Most of Tyler's evaluation ideas flow from his early work in the Bureau of Educational Research and Service at Ohio State. There, he assisted professors in evaluating their courses with the aim of improving instruction and, ultimately, student learning. As he worked with instructors at Ohio State, he used the word "evaluation" to refer to investigating what students were really learning, because as he recounted, "The term 'test' usually was interpreted as a collection of memory items" (interview with Nowakowski, 1989, p. 245).

These were seminal years in Tyler's career. Cronbach (1986) maintained that "virtually all of Tyler's ideas on evaluation were present in his writings of 1931" (p. 47). His *Constructing*

Achievement Tests (1934) grew out of this work at Ohio State and clearly served as the foundation for what emerged in *Appraising and Recording Student Progress* (1942) and *Basic Principles of Curriculum and Instruction* (1950).[4]

Tyler viewed test construction and curriculum development as a cooperative effort between teachers and test developers. He believed that ongoing course improvement required the continuous evaluation of student progress toward the realization of educational objectives. This approach foreshadowed by 30 years Scriven's distinction between formative and summative evaluation, and the systems of continuous monitoring of student achievement used by some school districts in the 1980s (Madaus & Stufflebeam, 1989).

Tyler began the process of test construction by giving the faculty nine types of educational objectives to consider: (1) recall important facts, principles, and technical terms; (2) understand technical terminology; (3) draw inferences from specific data and propose hypotheses; (4) plan an experiment to test a given hypothesis; (5) apply general principles to new situations; (6) make accurate observations; (7) develop skill in the use of essential tools; (8) express ideas effectively; and (9) state the sources that were most likely to give dependable information (Tyler, 1934). In these objectives, one can see the foundation of *The Taxonomy of Educational Objectives* (Bloom, 1956).

Tyler (1938) observed that most educational objectives stated in courses of study or by teachers were vague and not very useful. He argued that objectives must be stated in terms of student behavior to clarify and give them meaning. Tyler found that when teachers expressed their objectives in terms of changes in student behaviors, it helped them to modify the curriculum. Working closely with teachers to formulate behavioral objectives became a hallmark of The Eight-Year Study and a key element in *Basic Principles of Curriculum and Instruction.*

Tyler felt that instructional objectives were not the only basis on which to build a comprehensive evaluation, arguing that it was "important to find out many other things in order to understand what's going on in a program and to guide it" (Nowakowski, 1989, p. 252). However, he felt that to get started, it was important to find out whether teachers were accomplishing what they set out to do.

Nonetheless, Tyler's emphasis on behavioral objectives eventually became one of the most misunderstood aspects of his approach to curriculum evaluation. He commented that "I manufactured the term [behavioral objectives] originally, but not with the intent that it was going to be taken as little bits of things" (interview with Schubert & Schubert, 1986, p. 110). He told the Schuberts (1986) that when he was a graduate student at Nebraska, he read Thorndike's *Psychology of Arithmetic,* which had 3,000 objectives, and thought, "A teacher couldn't possibly keep all of these in mind" (p. 95). Suffice it to say that Tyler never saw the need for the behavioral specificity that Mager (1962) or Popham (1969) called for in their approach to defining objectives during the early years of the budding curriculum evaluation movement of the late 1950s and 1960s.[5]

Once the sought-after change in student behavior was rendered transparent in terms of what the student could do or produce, situations that allowed students to demonstrate those behaviors were developed. Tyler broke new ground with his insistence that achievement testing involve more than the use of paper-and-pencil exercises. He argued that many objectives demanded other methods, such as direct observation of children, appraisal of products they produced, and carefully planned interviews, questionnaires, and case studies. This catholic approach to achievement testing was lost after World War II—a victim to the efficiency of the burgeoning use of commercially available, standardized, machine-scored, multiple-choice achievement tests.[6] Tyler's forward-thinking attitude toward what we now call "assessment" did not seriously surface again until the "Authentic" or "Alternative" assessment movement in the 1990s.

Another underlying principle in Tyler's system of achievement testing was that before indirect indicators of student achievement are widely used, they be validated against the most direct measures possible. This piece of advice was largely ignored, in the service of efficiency, during the standardized testing boom that began in the 1950s. Related to this validation advice was Tyler's belief that different ways need to be employed when assessing a particular aspect of achievement, foreshadowing Campbell and Fiske's (1959) seminal rule that researchers always use at least two methods when studying social science phenomena.

Tyler also believed in and practiced what he called "cooperative test construction." That is, better tests could be built by the cooperative efforts of teachers, curriculum developers, and test technicians. Furthermore, he believed this approach was a useful device in teacher training. Tyler trusted the wisdom and hidden knowledge of classroom teachers about student learning. While, as noted above, he used a rudimentary taxonomy of objectives with teachers, he did not want them to become slaves to any taxonomy. He continually reminded teachers, "Don't look at some taxonomy to define your objectives. A taxonomy is what someone else states as the meaning of educational objectives. You're a teacher working with students. What have you found students learning that you think is important?" (Nowakowski, 1989, p. 252).

His efforts to build valid tests were bottom-up and local. He worked with classroom teachers on how to evaluate their students' learning and their own instruction. His focus was not commercial, state, or national, as is the case in today's accountability movement. Arguably, today's test-driven accountability movement is based in part on a strong mistrust of teacher judgments, a stance I believe would scandalize Tyler, so too, I believe, would the "one size fits all" tests used in state accountability programs.

CURRICULUM AND EVALUATION

Tyler brought his experiences in achievement test construction from Ohio State to The Eight-Year Study, undoubtedly the defining experience in Tyler's career. When asked in 1986 to talk about some of the prominent experiences that molded his thought on curriculum and evaluation, Tyler replied:

> If you consider that the contribution I have made which has influenced the largest number of people has been one of trying to look systematically at curriculum development, as expressed by that syllabus (Tyler, 1950) which I developed at the University of Chicago, then I would say that the experiences of working with the schools in The Eight-Year Study contributed most. (Schubert & Schubert, 1986, p. 92)

In the first year of The Eight-Year Study, schools rebelled over the use of tests developed by the Cooperative Test Services. The teachers argued that these off-the-shelf tests did not measure what they were trying to teach and therefore were not a fair measure to use to evaluate their work. To salvage the situation, Bode, who had an office close to Tyler's, recommended to the directing committee of The Eight-Year Study that they hire Tyler, "a young man in evaluation at Ohio State who bases evaluation on what the schools are trying to do. He works closely with them and doesn't simply take a test off the shelf" (quoted in Nowakowski, 1989, p. 251).

Tyler, using techniques honed at Ohio State, worked closely with the teachers in the Eight-Year schools to help them articulate what they were trying to bring about. He believed that the formulation of objectives was the teachers' job; classifying teacher objectives, the job of the evaluation staff; their refinement, the joint task of teachers and the evaluation staff; and the development of assessment tools to measure the teachers' objectives, the work of the evaluation staff (Madaus & Stufflebeam, 1989).

Tyler believed that a comprehensive program of evaluation of schools in The Eight-Year Study should serve a variety of purposes, including grading students; grouping students; guiding students; reporting to parents on their child's attainment; reinforcing teachers; reporting to school boards on the attainments of students, schools, and classrooms; validating the assumptions under which the institution operates; and providing feedback for public relations (Madaus & Stufflebeam, 1989).

He also maintained that when thinking about evaluation, schools need to keep in mind the following key ideas: (a) education seeks to change behavior of students in desirable ways; (b) these changes are the objectives of the school; (c) evaluation should assess the degree to which these objectives are realized; (d) human behavior is too complex to be measured by a single instrument along a single dimension; (e) evaluations must consider how patterns of behavior are organized; (f) paper-and-pencil tests are not sufficient to appraise all the objectives; (g) the ways schools measure outcomes determine what is taught, how it is taught, what is learned, and how it is learned; (h) the responsibility for evaluation belongs to the school's staff and clientele; and (i) evaluation is an ongoing, cyclical process that should lead to the refinement of the objectives, the learning experiences that foster their attainment, and the outcomes attained (Madaus & Stufflebeam, 1989).

Tyler recounts how in 1938, the curriculum staff of The Eight-Year Study complained that there was a rationale for evaluation but none for the curriculum and that the schools got more help from the evaluation staff than from the curriculum staff. At lunch one day, he said to his "right-hand" associate Hilda Taba, "Why, that's silly, of course there's a rationale for curriculum" (quoted in Nowakowski, 1989, p. 253). He then sketched out on a napkin a curriculum rationale that was inescapably shaped by his experiences in test construction and evaluation.

One can see these testing and evaluation influences at work in the four questions he posed in 1950 in *Basic Principles of Curriculum and Instruction: Syllabus for Education 30:*

> (1) What educational purposes should the school seek to attain? (2) What educational experiences can be provided that are likely to attain these purposes? (3) How can these educational experiences be effectively organized? and (4) How can we determine whether these purposes are being attained? (Tyler, 1950, pp. 1–2).

Tyler's views on curriculum and evaluation were abridged and depicted as the "Tyler triangle." Educational objectives were at the apex of the triangle, the learning experience and their organization were at the lower left angle, while the assessment of the outcomes was at the lower right angle of the triangle.

Concealed by the three uncomplicated angle descriptions, however, were some very important concepts. The behavioral objectives should emerge and be clarified through studies of the learner and of contemporary life. They should be written at the level of general principles, while the specific learning outcomes (the lower right angle of the triangle) rendered them unambiguous. Then, the proposed objectives should be screened through the school's philosophy of education, theories of learning and development, and input from subject matter specialists. The learning experiences should provide opportunities to practice the desired behaviors and be satisfying and feasible. Learning experiences should have vertical continuity, progressive sequence, and horizontal integration. They should vary the methods employed, and, finally, they must provide models of desired behaviors that the students can emulate. Finally, at the outcome angle of the triangle, there are two requirements: getting a record and summarizing and interpreting the evidence (Tyler, 1950).

Tyler's productive melding of testing, evaluation, and curriculum development was, unfortunately, ignored during the boom in program evaluation during the late 1950s and early 1960s. The passage of the National Defense Education Act of 1958 triggered a need to evaluate the many large-scale curriculum development projects in math and science funded by federal monies. The Elementary and Secondary Education Act of 1964 included specific evaluation requirements for Title 1 programs, which were aimed at providing compensatory education to disadvantaged children—including the use of standardized test data as the key element in the evaluation (Madaus & Stufflebeam, 2000).

Several things conspired to truncate Tyler's approach to curriculum evaluation. First, in Tyler's conceptualization, all sides of the triangle were bidirectional. Thus, for example, the educational experiences led to the outcomes, but the outcomes flowed back to inform the experiences. This bidirectionality fell by the wayside. Second, the educational objectives/outcome relationship became an obsession. Worse still, the screening/evaluation of objectives themselves tended to be ignored, and the outcomes were reduced to standardized paper-and-pencil tests that were not sensitive to instruction, thereby ignoring Tyler's views on testing and its relation to teaching and learning discussed above. Finally, the Tyler approach morphed into the caricature of the evaluator determining a program's objectives, selecting an off-the-shelf standardized test to measure those objectives, and administering it as a pre- and posttest to determine change brought about by instruction. The instruction and learning experiences—the curriculum itself—remained locked in a "black box."

CONCLUSION

Ralph Tyler's contributions to testing and to curriculum development and its evaluation were both a product and a victim of the times. His seminal work on testing and educational objectives coincided with the rise of behaviorism. His focus on the nexus between teachers and testing and his work during The Eight-Year Study, which focused on the aims of individual schools, emerged when federal and state obligations in education were minimal at best. *Basic Principles of Curriculum and Instruction* (Tyler, 1950) along with Bloom's (1956) *Taxonomy of Educational Objects for the Cognitive Domain* were on hand when the mandates for large-scale program evaluations had to be implemented. The adaptation of both works to the needs of the time changed the way people understood them over the ensuing four decades.

While political, cultural, and educational ethos that initiated and shaped Tyler's work will never return, it is time to reevaluate Tyler's contribution to all three branches of the evaluation theory tree, with its roots in accountability and control and social inquiry.

NOTES

1. On a personal note, one of Tyler's students, a professor at Boston College, John Walsh, gave me a copy of *Appraising and Recording Student Progress*. After reading it, I changed my major from School Administration to Educational Measurement. John also arranged a Post Doc for me at the University of Chicago, where I had the privilege of working with Ben Bloom and Tom Hastings, from the University of Illinois, both former students of Ralph's. When one considers Tyler's legacy, and if in addition to those who directly came under Tyler's orbit—Bloom, Cronbach, Furst, Goodlad, Havinghurst, Krawthwohl, Hastings, Raths, to mention but a few—you add those trained by them, and I might add those trained by Ralph's grand-students and great-grand-students, his impact on the fields of curriculum, testing, and evaluation has been immense.

2. For a more detailed treatment of Tyler's many other accomplishments based on his own writings, see Madaus and Stufflebeam (1989).

3. There is no doubt about some of these conjectures; see Schubert and Schubert (1986).

4. These concepts were further developed by Tyler; see Tyler (1935, 1938).

5. Tyler, in his interview with the Schuberts, characterized Mager's efforts as training objectives, not educational objectives.

6. The passage in 1958 of the National Defense Education Act marks testing's emergence as a tool in the national policy arena. By the late 1960s, standardized test results were widely used to evaluate curricula. The second technical development that made large-scale testing economically viable was Lindquist's invention of the high-speed scanning machine.

REFERENCES

Ayres, L. P. (1918). History and present status of educational measurements. In G. M. Whipple (Ed.), *The measurement of educational products* (17th yearbook of the National Society for the Study of Education, Part II) (pp. 9–15). Bloomington, IL: Public Schools Publishing Company.

Ballou, F. (1918). General organization of educational measurement work in city school systems. In G. M. Whipple (Ed.), *The measurement of educational products* (17th yearbook of the National Society for the Study of Education, Part II) (pp. 41–51). Bloomington, IL: Public Schools Publishing Company.

Bloom, B. S. (1956). *Taxonomy of educational objectives: The classification of educational goals, Handbook 1, Cognitive domain.* New York: McKay.

Bobbitt, J. F. (1918). *The curriculum.* Boston: Houghton Mifflin.

Campbell, D. T., & Fiske, D. W. (1959). Convergent and discriminate validation by the multitrait-multimethod matrix. *Psychological Bulletin 56,* 81–105.

Courtis, S. A. (1916). *Courtis standard research tests. Arithmetic: Test No. 2, Subtraction* (Series B, Form 1). Detroit, MI: Author.

Cronbach, L. (1986, Spring). Tyler's contribution to measurement and evaluation. [Special issue]. *Journal of Thought, 21,* 47–52.

Hall, G. S. (1907). *Aspects of child life and education.* Boston: Ginn & Co.

Judd, C. H. (1918). A look forward. In G. M. Whipple (Ed.), *The measurement of educational products* (17th yearbook of the National Society for the Study of Education, Part II) (pp. 152–160). Bloomington, IL: Public Schools Publishing Company.

Madaus, G. F., & Stufflebeam, D. (Eds.). (1989). *Educational evaluation: The classic works of Ralph W. Tyler.* Boston: Kluwer-Nijhoff.

Madaus, G. F., & Stufflebeam, D. (2000). Historical perspectives on evaluation. In D. Stufflebeam, G. F. Madaus, & T. Kellaghan (Eds.), *Evaluation models* (pp. 3–22). Boston: Kluwer.

Mager, R. F. (1962). *Preparing objectives for programmed instruction.* San Francisco: Fearon.

Nowakowski, J. R. (1989). An interview with Ralph Tyler, 1981. In G. F. Madaus & D. Stufflebeam (Eds.), *Educational evaluation: The classic works of Ralph W. Tyler* (pp. 241–272). Boston: Kluwer-Nijhoff.

Popham, W. J. (1969). Objectives and instruction. In W. J. Popham, E. Eisner, H. J. Sullivan, & L. L. Tyler (Eds.), *Instructional objectives* (pp. 32–52). Chicago: Rand McNally.

Rice, J. M. (1897). The futility of the spelling grind. *Forum, 23,* 163–172.

Schubert, W., & Schubert, A. L. (1986). A dialogue with Ralph W. Tyler: An interview conducted by William H. Schubert and Ann Lynn Schubert on October 12, 1980. *Journal of Thought 21*(1), 91–118.

Smith, E. R., & Tyler, R. W. (1942). *Appraising and recording student progress.* New York: Harper & Row.

Starch, D. (1916). *Educational measurements.* New York: Macmillan.

Starch, D., & Elliot, E. C. (1913). Reliability of grading work in mathematics. *School Review, 21,* 254–259.

Thorndike, E. L. (1918). The nature, purposes and general methods of measurements of educational products. In G. M. Whipple (Ed.), *The measurement of educational products* (17th yearbook of the National Society for the Study of Education, Part II) (pp. 16–24). Bloomington, IL: Public Schools Publishing Company.

Tyler, R. W. (1927). *Statistical methods for utilizing personal judgments to evaluate activities for teacher-training curricula.* Unpublished doctoral dissertation, University of Chicago.

Tyler, R. W. (1934). *Constructing achievement tests.* Columbus: Ohio State University.

Tyler, R. W. (1935). Elements of diagnosis. In G. M. Whipple (Ed.), *Educational diagnosis* (34th yearbook of the National Society for the Study of Education) (pp. 113–130). Chicago: University of Chicago Press.

Tyler, R. W. (1938). The specific techniques on investigation: Examining and testing acquired knowledge, skill and ability. In F. Freeman (Ed.), *The scientific movement in education* (37th yearbook of the National Society for the Study of Education, Part II) (pp. 341–356). Bloomington, IL: Public School Publishing Company.

Tyler, R. W. (1950). *Basic principles of curriculum and instruction.* Chicago: University of Chicago Press.

White, E. E. (1888). Examinations and promotions. *Education, 8,* 519–522.

PART III

VALUING

12

CONCEPTUAL REVOLUTIONS IN EVALUATION

Past, Present, and Future

Michael Scriven

This chapter presents a view of the overall situation in evaluation—as it was, is now, and might be in the future. As a one-sentence autobiographical note, the only such comment here, it happens that I now have produced about 100 publications on evaluation in the 44 years since I started off with an essay called "The Methodology of Evaluation,"[1] in which I introduced the concepts of formative and summative evaluation (and a few other ideas), so it seemed about time to try for an overview of what's happened and happening in the field. And, of course, to see if that overview leads to some suggestions as to how it could and should move in the next half-century or so. I'll begin by saying that I think our progress in developing the discipline—certainly my own—although substantial has been disappointingly slow. However, I think that our prospects for the future are enticing enough that we not only can and should but probably will accelerate impressively in the next few decades.

I propose here *three major revolutions* in our conception of evaluation that are needed to establish that future. The first one made the discipline of evaluation possible, but we have not yet completely accepted it; the other two are still ahead of us.

This chapter could be said to be a "state–of-the-art" review (of conceptualizations of evaluation), although for reasons of space it's a very condensed one, a mere touching on some highlights. In the usual sense of the phrase in quotes, it does not imply a judgment that evaluation is

---

Author's Note: Many thanks to Jane Davidson for some good suggestions for improving the first draft and to Jim Sanders for some good suggestions for improving the second version.

an art *rather than* a science. Certainly, there is much of an art in it, especially in its fieldwork components—interviewing is surely a great art. There is a good deal of science in it, too, but *evaluation*—as the term is defined in better dictionaries[2] and used by those who use it carefully—is not *just* a science any more than it is just an art or just a branch of literature. It is not just a science for the same reason that logic, mathematics, measurement, design, information theory, and communications are not just sciences: They are all transdisciplines, that is, disciplines in their own right that also serve not only the sciences but other disciplines in extremely important ways—sometimes to an extent that is characterized by saying that their contribution makes up a division or branch of a science (e.g., bio*statistics*, quantum *mechanics*, experimental *design*, *communications* technology). Since transdisciplines are not tied to the study of a specific subset of the world's phenomena like the sciences, calling them sciences is misleading.

In the case of evaluation, the nonscientific disciplines critically served by it include law, history, literature, technology, medical practice, education, architecture, craftwork, dance, athletics, gymnastics, and poker (yes, poker—don't forget that probability theory came from the card table, and don't try playing poker without evaluating your hand and your opponents). So it makes no sense to call it a science; at most, it can be said to be one element in science, like logic and mathematics. In particular, contrary to some texts, it is certainly not just applied social science: Evaluation, unlike any applied social science, is a crucial part of physics, chemistry, medicine, and mathematics.[3] Additionally, evaluation, like all the transdisciplines (and unlike applied social science), is also an autonomous discipline, and the study of just one of these transdisciplines, sometimes just its application to a single field of human activity, frequently takes up entire careers and fills many books, including the one for which this is written.

Most professional evaluators specialize in just one of the many branches of evaluation (e.g., program evaluation, product evaluation, personnel evaluation, performance evaluation, policy analysis) and, indeed, often only in the application of that branch to one area of human activity (e.g., education, health, business, technology, warfare, agriculture, real estate); it scarcely occurs to them that their discipline reaches across the whole domain of human knowledge and activity in an absolutely fundamental way. But the connection is there, and its presence is not a mere matter of semantic wordplay: The same logic of evaluation applies across all these fields with the same rigor and authority that it commands, or should command, in their own corner of the playing field. Their failure to have this overview is, of course, largely due to its virtual absence from almost all the teaching materials in evaluation, which is, in my view, an extremely serious deficiency in those materials.

Current thinking, even by evaluators, about the nature of evaluation is still extremely confused, and the results are extremely deleterious to its useful application. Misconceptions have cost our profession and our society dearly in many of the application areas of evaluation in two ways, which we can call Type A and Type B failures. Type A failures occur when *a misconception about, or misapplication of, evaluation causes worthless material to be treated as if it were good work*: for example, when our poor knowledge about the quality control system on which all sciences depend allows great slabs of faked or fallacious scientific results to be accepted—the most recent being the anesthesiology scandal. In the scientific field, the quality control system is the so-called peer review system, an indefensibly primitive version of which continues to be used because scientists are not taught to regard the evaluative infrastructure of their discipline with the respect and attention that civil engineers have been taught to have for checking the properties of the ground on top of which they spend their lives building structures like roads, bridges, and buildings. Recently, some very serious questions have been raised about the reliability and validity of both fingerprinting and DNA testing, and it turned out that they were indeed significantly less reliable than had been long and carelessly assumed. The situation in disciplines relying on peer review is analogous to finding that both of these are about as reliable as the opinion of a passerby at the courthouse. Those weaknesses turned up because there are 10,000 defense attorneys looking for them at any moment in time; with peer review, there has been virtually no one with the motivation of a defense attorney. There are only those who care about evaluation being done properly, and they are up against the forces of entrenched representatives of the disciplines who are very defensive about any suggestions of flawed foundations.

Perhaps, the most pervasive Type A failure within the current practice of evaluation is the provision of relevant purely empirical data as if these were the answer to an evaluative question. For example, suppose the question—explicitly stated or implicit—is the usual one as to whether a new initiative has been a worthwhile investment toward improving the mathematics education of a minority group, and the alleged evaluation investigates and provides evidence that the mathematics scores of that group on the required test have significantly improved. That's about a quarter of a decent answer and is a grossly incompetent evaluation.[4]

The second way in which we pay dearly for failing to treat evaluation with the care it deserves is where the Type B problems emerge—that is, where *a misconception about evaluation keeps us from doing much needed good work*. For example, we simply failed to address great needs in human affairs because of a misconception about evaluation—the view that evaluative concepts have no scientific basis (as the value-free doctrine maintained for most of the past century). This mistake meant that the social sciences failed, for many years, to pay serious attention to issues like poverty, corruption in government, or moral education because these were dismissed as areas defined in value-laden terms and hence not scientifically respectable. So whereas Type A mistakes about evaluation caused us to accept bad work as good, Type B mistakes caused us to spurn good work that we should have done. In many areas, such as international aid and disaster evaluation, mistakes of both kinds have combined to result in wastage of vast resources and failure to save vast numbers of people from avoidable disastrous consequences. Adding up the whole range of Type A and Type B mistakes forces us to the conclusion that the costs of slow progress in developing an understanding of—and the tools for properly using—serious evaluation are extremely high.

One more example of misunderstanding the nature of evaluation needs to be mentioned. It is still widely believed, even among professional evaluators, that the difference between evaluation and research is that *research* is aimed at the acquisition of new knowledge whereas *evaluation* is aimed at developing information for decision making. This view is seriously wrong—wrong in both directions—because research is often aimed at and is successful in aiding decisions (e.g., research to find oral AIDS drugs) and evaluation is often simply aimed at developing new knowledge (e.g., all historical evaluation of generals, presidents, and periods; magazine road tests of cars that cost more than a quarter million dollars). In fact, *there is no generic difference between research and evaluation*, since most professional program evaluation, for example, is a highly respectable kind of research. There *is* a difference between evaluative research and nonevaluative research, and it's simply the difference between the work required to develop conclusions that are not evaluative propositions[5] and those that are—that is, those that provide answers to questions about what's better or best or worth what it costs, and so on. Failure to get this clear leads to gaps in training (and competency lists), mistakes in funding, and, worst of all, mistakes in designing evaluations. That means we often don't get defensible answers to the questions we need answered about programs, products, policies, and so on, out of what are called evaluations, with consequent wastage of resources and failure to get problems solved that needed solving.

The applied disciplines—where many and perhaps most of the driving questions are evaluative—are still rife with myths, a sure sign of poor training. The mythical reliability of fingerprints and DNA testing have been mentioned, but there are many more. Nutritionists still peddle the doctrine that health requires drinking eight glasses of water a day: Only recently has the research been done that shows this to be simply a myth. Trainers still peddle the doctrine that you should do serious warm-ups before beginning serious exercise or competitive efforts: Only now has the research been done that shows this to be almost completely without a basis in fact. If we trained our scientists and other disciplinarians to treat evaluation as a fundamental investigatory discipline, we might significantly reduce the mythical element in what is proclaimed as scientific.

A key part of reaching that goal is attacking the myths about evaluation itself, including those that dominate behavior despite being denied at the conscious level, which is precisely the status of the first of the three great revolutions concerning the nature of evaluation that I'm going to discuss. Before we get to that, however, let's complete the preliminaries by defining a couple of the concepts we're using here.

1. What is meant here by *a revolution in thought about the nature of evaluation*, or about the nature of any other discipline, is roughly what Kuhn meant in the revised statement of his views in the second edition of his most famous book.[6] This kind of revolution is what he called a paradigm shift—a framework shift, which is typically a shift in what is taken to be a fundamental assumption in a field of study. This usually means a shift in what is taken as not requiring explanation or justification, that is, what is taken as the basic norm. The Copernican revolution is the standard case of such a revolutionary change from one norm to another; the Darwinian shift in explaining the origin of species was another.

2. What is meant here by *evaluation* is what the dictionaries and common language mean: the process of determining (or the act of declaring) something about the merit, worth, or significance of any entity. Professional evaluation, the kind we are mainly concerned with here, is simply evaluation done at a level of difficulty and defensibility that requires professional training to get valid results. Evaluation is not the same as "what evaluators do," although people often like to define it that way, since in practice evaluators do many other things besides just evaluation—they may seek to *explain* the behavior of evaluands rather than just evaluate them, they may *design or redesign* them, they may *advise* about them, they may do *survey research* about them, they may just *describe* them, and so on. Some of the people who describe themselves as evaluators in fact do little or no true evaluation—indeed, they may

even define evaluation without any reference to evaluative terms (a somewhat bizarre practice). For example, the current edition of the *Handbook of Practical Program Evaluation* defines evaluation as (roughly) the scientific study of programs. Now, merely determining and describing in detail the empirical characteristics of a program and its effects would qualify as a scientific study of that program, but it would not qualify as evaluating the program, because evaluation also involves *something more* than that, namely, the identification and validation of relevant standards for the merit/worth/significance of such phenomena—in the particular context of the particular evaluation—and the synthesis of those standards with the empirical facts about the evaluand to generate an evaluative conclusion. Also, the *Handbook* does not discuss how to do any of the "something more" activities (e.g., doing a needs assessment or validating value standards) and, hence, does not cover the essentials of practical program evaluation. Neither does the useful *Handbook of Applied Social Science*, which in fact includes no articles or even sections about evaluation, the discipline devoted to dealing with the hard questions in applied social science, the area the *Handbook* claims to cover. These illustrate what I mean about not *really* accepting the legitimacy of evaluation although thinking, and saying, that the value-free dogma is dead. In my terms here, this is why the first revolution (R1) is not complete.

R1—which evaluators have nearly all come to accept, at least verbally, as the basic assumption of our present framework of thought about evaluation—is the shift from treating evaluation as outside the domain of legitimate scholarly treatment, that is, as "scientifically untouchable," *to regarding it as scientifically legitimate*, that is, as respectable. I think a major reason why so many evaluators do not entirely accept this revolution (as is clear from their actions as illustrated above), although they may say and believe that they do, is that they are too smart to accept the usual argument given for supporting it. The usual argument is that scientists are clearly value driven in much that they do—for example, in their choice of fields to study or applications to develop—so science is clearly not value-free. But that argument is totally irrelevant to the value-free doctrine, which claims only that personal/social/political values have no legitimate place *within science*. The German sociologists, under Max Weber, who originated the value-free doctrine, were fully aware that values drive the approach to, and use of, science; they just wanted to keep them out of the core enterprise itself. Well, they were wrong, but not because of the argument just quoted: They were wrong because science has *internal* values and applying them, that is, evaluation, is a key part of the scientific method. I have called this component "intradisciplinary evaluation," and it is already leading to improvements in the conduct of science.[7] It is the theme of the second revolution (R2). Moreover, science can tackle many of the personal/social/political values in a scientific way, so even those cannot be excluded from legitimate science.

The bottom line of R1's consequences is that a competent program evaluator (or product evaluator, etc.) can show that, for example, a program for teaching reading is truly excellent or truly worthless *as a matter of scientific fact*. To have denied this was a colossal blunder based on the error of supposing that all value judgments are mere expressions of taste; and it diverted the efforts of applied social research away from the great needs of the very needy for most of a century. Many scientists realized that the reasons often given for abandoning the value-free doctrine were unsound, and so they continued to hew to it even if not speaking out to that effect.

In contrast with the acceptance status of R1, R2 still has *almost no explicit acceptance*, although it *is* implicitly conceded in everyone's professional behavior, and the third revolution (R3) is *completely contrary* to both the views *and* the practice of most academics, although acceptance of it is, I will argue, logically obligatory and both scientifically and socially desirable.

R2—which all scientific practice commits us to, although few scientists would accept it—is the shift from thinking of evaluation as merely a respectable discipline to recognizing it as the alpha discipline. We can lead into the discussion of R2 by mentioning some mini revolutions that served as precursors of it. One was the mini-revolutionary shift from the "geocentric" fallacy of thinking that evaluation was program evaluation—exhibited in the titles of textbooks and theories/models that announced their coverage as "evaluation" but with a content discussing only program evaluation—to the "heliocentric" approach, which takes the key focal element in evaluation to be *evaluation,* as the sun around which rotates a solar system of planets, including program evaluation, product evaluation, policy analysis, personnel evaluation, and so on. This shift paid off by helping us in program evaluation avoid mistakes of reinventing the wheel, mistakes one can avoid by learning from other subareas.[8]

A second mini-revolutionary precursor to the "geocentrism" of conceiving that evaluation is program evaluation occurred in the context of the 1960s, where the beginnings of formal professional evaluation emerged in the applied field of education and some textbooks were titled "educational evaluation," when the contents showed that by this they meant only the evaluation of students. The idea that educational evaluation might by definition include the evaluation of teachers, curricula, or schools simply did not register on the conscious mind of educators in those days. Their "evaluation frame of reference" was radically constrained in the same way in which scientific research on "human physiology" often used only male subjects.

A third and more important such precursor was the mini-revolutionary shift from the management-centric concept of evaluation as the investigation of whether a program had met its objectives to the consumer-centric view that it should be focused on whether it had met the needs of its impactees. This view of evaluation even turned up in some of the most positivistic social science texts, which might have been expected to deny the legitimacy of all evaluation. It bypassed the taboo because it did not require the evaluators to make any value judgments on their own: They just measured whether the manager's values had been attained. Abandoning the old view here led to many practical as well as theoretical/conceptual results of great importance, like the earlier shifts, including a reduction of exploitation of consumers and employees, but details of those are not my present topic.

The R2, on the account here, although analogous to these three lesser predecessors, reverses their focus, being a case where one of the subareas of evaluation is the star instead of being the villain. This revolution will eventually be more significant than its precursors, although it will probably meet even more resistance, since it will be seen as invading some of the turf of Big Science. It focuses on the subarea of evaluation that I referred to earlier as intradisciplinary evaluation—the evaluation that goes on within every discipline, of its methodological tools and their users. A discipline only deserves the name of discipline if its inferences and methods are valid, its data well established, and its theories testable or otherwise evaluable. (It's certainly not true, although often said, that its theories must be testable by generating verifiable *predictions*, since a great theory may simply be historical, as in cosmogony, or a brilliant conceptual simplification, as in relativity.[9]) Now, in the sciences and many humanities, the process of quality control boils down to peer review; but that process, as currently practiced, is fatally flawed. Of course, the peer review does do some good: Panels do pick up factual errors in the subject matter field, failures to consider competing explanations, and many other crucial matters. One major flaw lies in their accuracy or adequacy in evaluating overall significance (or importance, which may be, depending on the context, academic, practical, or social), especially—as Nobelers are prone to point out—when the evaluand or evaluee is an outlier, nonstandard, "out of the box." But the main problem is a simpler one.

Any trained evaluator, and most social scientists, faced with a claim of merit (in a manuscript, a journal, a candidate for a job, etc.) based on a group rating, as in peer review, will automatically want to know something about the interjudge consistency and any external evidence—such as interpanel consistency—that bears on the validity of such claims. She or he will not make the amateur's mistake of thinking that the good academic qualifications of the judges in the relevant subject matter area will ensure the validity of their evaluations. One might as well tell an expert in personnel test construction that the test you are using to select good accountants is valid because it was designed by a good accountant; she or he would just laugh and say that's a good start but a long way from the winners' circle. Similarly, the peer review panels will be expert at content checks, but the trained evaluator, and for that matter any applied psychologist, will want to know something about the reliability of such panels when more sophisticated judgments, such as overall merit for funding or publishing purposes, are required.

When we look for evidence of intrapanel or interpanel consistency or even test–retest reliability of panels, we find (a) only a tiny handful of studies across the whole span of science and other disciplines—the first sign of trouble—and (b) that these studies share the same finding of *extremely low* interpanel agreement—the sign of *big* trouble.[10] So the quality control system is seriously flawed; it even lacks reliability, and there are also serious, unanswered concerns about its validity, for which at least follow-up studies are required, which are virtually never done. Other kinds of studies on the same issue, especially in the field of medical journals, have uncovered similar evidence of pathetic quality control. The recent scandal in anesthesiology uncovered another type of flaw, since in that case, the highly successful deceiver had faked even the subjects' existence, not just the results—in many cases, there were often no (actual) studies at all, despite high rankings from the peer review panels. There are several commonsense and inexpensive ways by which we should have been guarding against that type of deception, not including the fundamental check of actual visits to the (alleged) labs, which would of course considerably increase the cost of evaluating research.

In short, the quality control system—which is the evaluation system—in the classical disciplines does not meet the minimum acceptable standards, which, it might plausibly be argued, require at least twice the current level of interpanel reliability. Since higher standards are readily achievable at feasible cost levels in the design of peer review procedures,[11] and since they are apparently not being implemented on any significant scale, the situation is not just imperfect but highly culpable. In other words, the practice of Big Science shows that it thinks it can get away with a really bad quality control system, despite thereby becoming a disgrace to basic scientific standards. The humanities are no better, but possibly less culpable, since the technical aspects of quality control do not fall in their bailiwick. Of course, much of the monetary and other resources wasted by poor evaluation come from our taxes or our payments for drugs and services, so there is an accountability issue here, which makes the continued failure to work on improving peer review a matter of unethical behavior. This is even more obvious if you consider that the opportunity costs of this failure in the areas funded by philanthropies as well as public monies means that it is costing potential but unfunded recipients their lives and health.

It is not being suggested here that peer review should be taken over by evaluators. Of course, they lack the relevant factual knowledge and "state-of-the-art" knowledge. But no one in the test construction field thinks that "test and measurement" specialists (i.e., evaluators from the "performance evaluation" subarea of evaluation) should take over all the work in constructing advanced mathematics tests; they just think, and can prove, that *leaving out all testing expertise* is a recipe for disaster. There are several important skills—and much knowledge—about test construction and validation that just aren't in the mathematician's repertoire. They include a considerable slice of the logic of evaluation plus all the subarea content about what works and what doesn't work. Similarly, there are evaluation skills and knowledge that are needed to set up a quality control system for knowledge or personnel development in a discipline. The practical solution is simple enough: Peer review committees need to have one member with real competence—meaning experience as well as specialized knowledge in intradisciplinary evaluation. (It's a plus, not a minus, that that person *not* be an expert in the subject matter field, because it avoids her or his involvement in the usual internecine wars.) But that's not quite enough; the others on the committee need to value the kind of validity that the evaluator on the committee is there to promote and the skills she or he has in protecting it, or else they'll simply outvote him or her. For it to work, this change will require a shift in the professional education of scientists rather like the shift that it took to get those in the psychological and medical fields to recognize the need for respecting rules governing the treatment of human subjects. And it should be a good deal more extensive than the shift it took to get blind reviewing into more or less general practice.

An alternative to having an evaluator on each panel would be to have a couple of them on a commission of disciplinary experts that would redefine the procedural rules for panel operation to achieve better standards of validity for their findings—for example, by requiring calibration and follow-up of raters and what Michael Quinn Patton calls developmental evaluation[12] of them and the whole procedure.

The moral of this discussion is that the discipline that determines the *general scientific legitimacy* of the sciences as practiced at any given time is the one with the expertise to identify and assist in the application of *the standards of quality that go beyond subject matter expertise.* That discipline is the specialism in intradisciplinary evaluation, which is of course a subarea of evaluation.[13] It follows that *evaluation is the alpha discipline:* It is the discipline that develops and validates the admissions requirements for membership in the club of the disciplines.

We could argue for this conclusion in another way. It's true that almost every scientist has a general idea of the concepts of validity and objectivity that have been broached so often in the conduct of the sciences. And they can see clearly enough that there is something wrong with the fundamental quality control mechanism of peer review when its failure to meet even the standard of reasonable reliability is pointed out. So we might argue that this vestigial knowledge—very loosely speaking, it's an extension of scientific method—is simply part of general scientific training, in the same way in which knowledge of basic statistics can now be said to be part of good scientific training in many scientific fields. Now, any scientist would agree that when a proposal involves fairly advanced statistics, evaluating it would require having at least one expert statistician on the review panel. Analogously, it makes sense to argue that since all reviewing involves a process of evaluation, a process that needs to be done with some sophistication, then, along with all the skills that a group of field experts brings to the task, an expert evaluator should be on every panel or at least on the design and monitoring team for the panels' procedures.

R3—which will complete a total reversal of the status of evaluation within about a century—involves a change in status from alpha discipline to paradigm discipline for (at least) the social sciences. Evaluation is the alpha discipline because its domain includes the methodology of the task of validation of any discipline's claim to legitimacy as a discipline: It is the master of credentials. But disciplinary credentials have two dimensions. First, the *quality* of the work must justify the claim to *disciplinarity:* That's the claim we have been discussing under the heading of R2. Second, the *coverage* must adequately deal with the subject matter claimed in the field's title: It must justify its claim to *territoriality*—that is, sociology must cover the field of human social behavior,[14] economics must cover the field of economic behavior, and so on. Since many of the most important questions about human social behavior are evaluative, this means that sociology and psychology, for example, should study and teach about answering those questions to justify their titles. But because R1 has not been complete, sociology and psychology, for example, have not in fact been treating personnel evaluation, or program evaluation, as mainstream components of their disciplines. These fields have a kind of fringe status, and the special methodology they require—the methodology of evaluation—has zero status. The latest edition of *The Handbook of Applied Social Research Methods* (Sage, 2008), as previously mentioned, contains essentially nothing about evaluation at all, let alone any guidance to the specific research methods required to handle evaluative questions about the quality—including the ethicality—of personnel or programs.[15] This omission is Achilles's second heel in the battle for the legitimacy of these disciplines—the first being the flaw in the basic legitimation methodology of peer review.

And this heel is just the most salient coverage flaw in the social sciences: The total omission problem is much larger. It just happened historically that the practical demand for evaluation of programs and personnel was so powerful that these subareas sprang up despite the taboo on evaluative inquiry and have boomed since the taboo faded away. There are many social entities besides programs about which important evaluative questions arise and that have not been addressed by mainstream sociology. Policies are one where a small renegade discipline—policy studies—has sprung up to deal with the demand. But ethnic, cultural, religious, and political groups are all of great evaluative interest, and they receive only sporadic attention from sociologists, who are still gun-shy about evaluative questions, instead of being just meticulous; and there are many more. What R3 does is simply to point to the well-developed evaluation subdisciplines that occupy a slice of social science territory and suggest that the sciences adopt their approach as a general model—a methodological paradigm—for applied social science.

There's one big caveat that must be stressed here: R3 comes third because it depends on R1 and R2 being more or less completed before it can work. At the moment, the methodology of program and personnel evaluations is still, up through the median case at least, well short of model status. Those areas need to get through the R1 and R2 stages in order to be paradigms; but they will, because they must, in order to weather attacks on their present casual or implicit procedures for dealing with the values they require.

So in the R3 phase, the social sciences will come to realize that they must each be seen as disciplines that have both a nonevaluative scope of work and an evaluative one, since they must otherwise abandon any claim to cover much of the area thought of as important applied science. For surely, applied psychology (or applied sociology, political science, economics, anthropology, or linguistics[16]) must, by the very definition of "applied science," deal with questions of the form "What's the *best* . . . ?" (e.g., What's the best way for the London County Council to counter bullying [or meth addiction, etc.] in their schools?), "Was some program *worth what it cost?*" (e.g., Is/was the Portuguese experiment in legalizing drugs under medical certification worth what it cost?), or "Was one method better than another?" (e.g., Is/was that approach *better* than the U.K. approach?)—and similarly for issues about significance and importance; and all of these questions require an evaluative answer, which they can get only by using the techniques developed in the logic of evaluation and exemplified in the best professional work in each of the subareas of applied evaluation, like program evaluation, personnel evaluation, and so on.

It would be absurdly crippling for the applied social sciences (ASS) to abandon the use of statistics in dealing with common questions, but it is equally limiting for applied social sciences to avoid the use of evaluation as part of their approach to applied social science, and if they continue in that course, they will simply become mummified figures in the academic museum, and evaluation itself will expand still further, beyond the many substantial subfields it has already taken over, to pick up the slack.

In the case of psychology, R3 means legitimating the somewhat uneasy relationship with personnel evaluation, organization evaluation, and leadership evaluation, which are currently part of what is sometimes called industrial/organizational (I/O) psychology and sometimes are free-floating specialties (e.g., consulting firms specializing in "HR" [human resources] issues). In sociology, much of program evaluation is—by the usual definition of sociology—a branch of applied sociology, but it's not treated as such by most sociologists, as one can see from the content of the anthologies[17] and, more important perhaps, the basic texts.[18] In political science, which should feature issues about the justification of forms of government, these are usually relegated to political philosophy. The scene in economics is in most ways even worse, but this requires a detailed discussion for which there is no space here.

The reorganization suggested in R3 is not a trivial one, because the added areas require an added section in the treatment of social science methodology, for which the leaders in the field are completely uneducated—the specter of their value-free education haunts them still. R3 therefore requires a major shift in the thinking of most of the leaders in the field, since the textbook authors come from that group, something that may be too late for them to manage. We must hope that their successors will be persuaded to do differently. Evaluation cannot be added to the social sciences like a new trick in statistics; it's a different way of thinking and not like the push for deconstruction that reformers have talked about for quite a while. That push is a way to expose past errors of commission, the making of unjustified assumptions. The evaluative approach begins by *deconstructing the questions* you are trying to answer, not the *answers* someone has given in the past; failing to do this is an error of omission because it sets you on the narrow road of the value-free fact finder instead of the broad road of the evaluative scientist. We need at least a narrow road—it provides us with the sidewalk and the bike lane and a single-lane slice of a real highway. But only the six-lane highway carries us quickly to our destination—the answers to the evaluative questions. Of course, you don't get a highway without doing more road building than a path requires, and learning how to do that is where the logic of evaluation comes in. So it must be taught as part of the methods courses in all social sciences.

What exactly does the logic of evaluation require? It's easiest to see the answer if you start by thinking back to an earlier mini revolution, the revolution that took us from the idea of program evaluation as measurement of goal achievement—the simple, value-free formula of the 1970s or so, often still cited as what evaluation does—to something like serious program evaluation. The extra road building for that change required the addition of the results from goal critique: (a) Are the goals really the optimal use of resources needed by this targeted population? (find or do a needs assessment to find out) (b) Are they a cultural good fit? (c) Are they legal and ethical? (d) What side effects occur? (e) To whom do any effects occur besides the intended recipients? (f) How do the intended *and* unintended effects fit the needs, cultural constraints, and ethical constraints of the total affected group? (g) Is the process of getting to the goals itself— that is, the intervention itself (including its evaluation)—consistent with needs/culture/ethics? (h) What are the true costs and to whom? (i) Given the costs, is the program cost-feasible for continued use (not just in the subsidized demonstration)? (j) Given the costs and the outcomes, both good and bad, is the program better than what was there already *and* the other alternatives that are readily available? (k) Is the program logistically exportable, repeatable, and sustainable under predictable or probable changes of personnel, politics, and environment?

That's (most of) what the mini revolution required,[19] and it's all part of the package that should now comprise professional program evaluation and that we're proposing as a paradigm for and, hence, as an essential import to serious applied social science in R3. But that's not all. In that list, there is mention of several types of value, including psychological needs and economic, cultural, and ethical requirements. Understanding the logic of evaluation involves understanding how to handle those, meaning how to (a) *identify* which of these and a dozen other types of value actually bear on this program in this context; (b) *validate* them in that context as relevant; (c) *weight* their relative importance; (d) *measure* their presence (quantitatively or qualitatively); and (e) *combine* them with the purely empirical findings about the program and its effects, process, and so on, to produce an answer to evaluative questions.[20]

So R3 is going to take a great deal of work as well as a great change in our conceptualization of the nature and role of evaluation, and the social sciences, and a recognition of the limited value of the social sciences without evaluation. It is clearly not going to be achieved without blood, sweat, and tears, so it's not just a conceptual revolution. And it's a revolution that has to come, because we have to get the social sciences into a form where it's part of their discipline to mentor and modify the building skills and materials they need to answer the really important practical questions within their subject matter field. Pure science will still exist, but even it, like theoretical physics and mathematics, will have to involve more serious evaluation of its infrastructure; applied social science will have to do more than that, since evaluation will be part of its main structure.

NOTES

1. Tyler, R. W., Gagne, R. W., & Scriven, M. (Eds.). (1967). *American Educational Research Association monograph series on curriculum evaluation: Vol. 1. Perspectives of curriculum evaluation* (pp. 39–83). Chicago, IL: Rand McNally (fifth printing, 1972; more easily located in various anthologies).

2. In this case, led by the Merriam-Webster third edition, not the Oxford family of dictionaries; see also the next footnote. Pulling together the rather heterogeneous definitions in six dictionaries and my own review of current language suggests that evaluation is the name of the process of determining, or the act of declaring, something about the merit, worth, or significance of an entity. I use the term *evaluand* to identify the entity evaluated (*evaluee* if it's a person).

3. The mistake here is like the one that has unfortunately found its way into dictionaries now, in defining technology as applied science (e.g., in the Oxford American). Technology is more than a million years old and science no more than 5,000 years old, so that definition is absurd. But of course it is true that technology now has many techniques and concepts from science in its toolbox, just as evaluation has many from applied social science. Yet, even recently, many of the notable inventions in technology still come from those with no scientific background at all, for example, the personal computer, the spreadsheet, the hyperlink (and all of Edison's 1,000 patents).

4. Some major missing components are the answers to the following: (a) How good is the test? (b) Was there any of the usual cheating on the scoring or in assisting students to answer? (c) What did the effort cost? (d) At that price, are there alternative approaches that would (probably) do as well for less? (e) Is this statistically significant result of any significant educational value? (f) What were the good or bad side effects? A good list of evaluation competencies would, in my view, benefit from requiring the respondent to identify examples of this kind of "missing link" errors, both of Type A and of Type B.

5. This kind of conclusion is often referred to as determining the relevant *facts*, as distinct from identifying the relevant *values*, but this is just another objectionable relic from positivist ideology. It's clearly just as much a fact about some homeless people that they are not well fed or not well dressed as it is that they have a shorter life expectancy than the average citizen; and it's simply a fact that Einstein was a brilliant physicist. So the "facts/values distinction" is a corrupt way of putting the evaluative/nonevaluative distinction; and even "empirical/evaluative" is not much better. Both are part of the attempt by the positivists to convey the idea that values are never objective but mere subjective preferences, or matters of taste.

6. In the first edition of *The Structure of Scientific Revolutions*, Kuhn appeared to support an extreme incommensurability doctrine that was clearly wrong. He retained the plausible view that there is some limited inability to communicate between supporters of a paradigm shift and those who reject it.

7. For example, Coryn, C. L. S., & Scriven, M. (2008). The logic of research evaluation. In C. L. S. Coryn & M. Scriven (Eds.), *Reforming the evaluation of research: Vol. 118. New directions for evaluation* (89–105). San Francisco, CA: Jossey-Bass.

8. For example, the simplest check on good product evaluation reveals that it does not depend on knowledge of what the designers intended to be the function of the product but only on what services it can provide to users (e.g., trucks make good campers, a use that early designers never thought of). This falsified the erstwhile common belief that evaluation is measuring goal achievement.

9. The special theory of relativity is a good example since, contrary to popular history of science, it was not verified by the eclipse observations—although that was the contemporary headline, they were miscalculated—and it had already been widely accepted on logical grounds.

10. The results so far have rarely exceeded a correlation of .3 between panels and never by much.

11. Ten examples are (1) calibration of panelists (training and testing them by using examples from the files chosen to illustrate typical errors), (2) selection based on calibration success, (3) increased pay to get higher-level raters, (4) follow-ups to identify poor and superior raters, (5) research on superior raters to improve selection and training, (6) better rewards for raters on their "professional contribution" score in faculty promotion and tenure review, (7) occasional use of two panels in parallel, (8) requiring raters to submit ratings before their first meeting, (9) phone or e-mail checks that the research was actually done at the sites referenced, and (10) required course in research quality control for all doctoral programs.

12. In my terminology, I think what's needed (and I think this is what his term means) is repeated formative evaluation coupled with carefully structured feedback to the evaluees *plus* regular formative and summative evaluation of the whole process, especially its effects.

13. While this is a relatively underdeveloped subarea, there are indeed some researchers with a major commitment to and expertise in it, even in sub-subareas of it: See, for example, the contributors to the special issue of *New Directions in Evaluation* on the evaluation of research proposals (cited in Footnote 7 above).

14. And perhaps also alien and animal social behavior and perhaps also social attitudes and experiences as well as behavior.

15. Ironically, the editors make an effort to be up-to-date by showing respect for *qualitative* methodology—they include a chapter on "mixed methods," that is, combining *qualitative* with quantitative methods—without having anything (that I could find) about *quality*.

16. The term *social science* is very inconsistently defined. Geography and history are often included in the category of social science, for example, by educational curriculum writers and legislators but usually not by social scientists in the disciplines named here or by philosophers of the social sciences, mainly, I think, because they are primarily idiographic rather than nomothetic. That is not a decisive consideration, in the present author's view (the same could be said of most of geology, some astronomy, and epidemiology), but we here keep the focus on the harder-core social sciences, principally because they all have stronger applied arms than the other two. Linguistics is also often excluded, but these reasons do not apply, and other cogent reasons for exclusion are hard to find. (Similar problems affect definitions of "behavioral science.")

17. For a current example, you can check the table of contents of the *Oxford Handbook of Analytical Sociology* (published March 11, 2011) without charge on Amazon.com.

18. The most recent sociology text listed in Amazon.com, Joan Ferrante's *Sociology: A Global Perspective* (2010), with more than 550 pages, has not a single indexed reference to evaluation.

19. There are more details in my "Hard-Won Lessons in Program Evaluation" in *New Directions in Program Evaluation* (Summer 1993, whole issue) and still more in the latest edition of the Key Evaluation Checklist, online at michaelscriven.info.

20. Some more details on the logical issues in the logic of evaluation (i.e., on the contents of this paragraph rather than the previous one) will be found in an article on valuing in a forthcoming issue of *New Directions in Evaluation*, edited by George Julnes. A further claim of great importance is mentioned there, the claim that ethics itself must be classified as a subarea of evaluation and would, therefore, become part of the social sciences in R3 (probably as part of normative social psychology along with game theory and decision theory).

13

COST-EFFECTIVENESS EVALUATION IN EDUCATION

H. M. Levin

Cost-effectiveness analysis has a long history as an approach to making decisions. As Quade (1971), a pioneer in establishing cost-effectiveness as a decision tool at the Rand Corporation states, "The practice of cost-effectiveness started when man first realized his resources were limited." Given the limited resources, the goal of cost-effectiveness analysis was to seek the least costly methods of reaching particular objectives. The initial governmental applications of the technique were designed to allocate Department of Defense budgets to weapons systems that would optimize military objectives for any given resource constraint. The Rand Corporation was the principal developer of cost-effectiveness tools as an extension of its operations research division. A typical type of problem for cost-effectiveness analysis was whether the Department of Defense should use its budget to develop and purchase relatively small numbers of highly sophisticated and costly fighter planes or a much larger number of more basic and cheaper fighter planes to confront enemy air forces. Using actual data from the Vietnam War and computer simulations, the two strategies were analyzed under a variety of different assumptions, with the conclusion that a swarm of cheaper aircraft was more effective in aerial warfare than a much smaller number of highly advanced craft.

As an analytic tool for allocating resources, cost-effectiveness analysis followed from the much earlier development of cost–benefit analysis. Cost-effectiveness analysis compares the costs and results of different options for meeting a specified objective or level of performance, such as an increase in reading scores or graduation rates. It is assumed that multiple alternatives are available to address an objective, each with different levels of potential effectiveness and different costs. The costs and estimated effects of the different alternatives are compared to see which is the most cost-efficient in terms of achieving a particular objective or gaining the largest effectiveness. In contrast, cost–benefit analysis compares the monetary value of both costs and benefits according to their market worth (Layard & Glaister, 1994; Prest, 1965). Cost–benefit criteria were first used under the Water Resources Act of 1936 to assess diverse alternatives, such as hydroelectric dams, flood control, expansion of harbors, canals, and increases in potable water, very diverse goals that could be encompassed by federal investments under the act. Since the different projects and outcomes had purposes that were incommensurable, their projected outcomes were converted into dollar values. In this way, their benefits could be compared with anticipated costs so that projects with very different objectives could be compared for their investment returns.

COST-EFFECTIVENESS IN EDUCATION

There are many fields in which cost-effectiveness has not been systematically implemented. My interest, in particular, is in education, an area that enjoys a thin history of systematic use of cost-effectiveness in making decisions. Most educational alternatives do not have outcomes that can be converted to monetary measures, with the exception of those that are designed to directly increase labor market productivity, income, and employment. Usually, resource allocation in education is designed to address specific educational objectives where both the costs and the educational outcomes are pertinent to the decision. When both costs and results are taken into account, one has information to undertake a cost-effectiveness comparison. Typically, this comparison is expressed in terms of cost-effectiveness ratios, the cost per unit of educational effects, such as the cost of achieving given test gains or rises in graduation rates or modes of providing instruction of equal quality (e.g., classroom instruction or online). The overall goal is to consider not only effectiveness but also how it can be achieved at a lower cost. Alternatives with lower cost per outcome or higher outcome per unit of cost are given preference. The selection of more cost-effective strategies frees up resources to provide additional education services or resources for other important social uses.

Elementary and secondary education command a very large portion of our national, state, and local resources. The total expenditure on elementary and secondary education in 2006–2007 was about $562 billion, of which almost half came from the states and about 44% from local governments. The federal government provided about 8% of the total, mainly for special educational functions or low-income populations. Of course, there is strong justification for ample financial support for education, given its contribution to national prosperity, technical and cultural advancement, enhanced health, and preparation for productive citizenship and democracy (Oreopoulos & Salvanes, 2011; Psacharopoulos & Patrinos, 2004). But there is still the issue of how to provide an effective system without wasting resources.

Whatever the cost was in the past, it is inexorably higher today. The expenditure per student in 1959–1960 was about $2,703 in constant (2006–2007) prices; by 2006–2007, it had risen to $10,720, quadrupling in cost over this period. The main rises in costs seem to be associated with the inability or unwillingness of the educational system to improve productivity through new technologies, greater use of capital, and methods of substituting less costly personnel for more costly labor—that is, to use more cost-effective approaches.

In the most productive segments of the economy, there is competitive pressure to raise productivity as a means to contain costs. This has meant that in most industries there is a persistent search for ways to improve the production of goods and services through new technologies that raise productivity as well as substitution of lower-cost methods for producing the same or better outcomes. But elementary and secondary schooling does not reflect this dynamic, and it is not mere neglect or lack of competition according to William Baumol (1996), a distinguished economist.

Baumol (1996) has referred to the problem as a cost disease that is inherent in labor-intensive endeavors that cannot be easily altered without modifying the character of the activity. According to Baumol, the economy can be divided into two sectors, one a dynamic and increasingly productive sector and the other stagnant in terms of productivity. In the productive sector, there is a constant attempt to find new ways of improving productivity through new technologies, substitution of capital for labor, and substitution of labor with lower skills for workers with higher and more expensive qualifications. The result of these continual improvements means that labor productivity in this sector is rising, with concomitant increases in wages and salaries that compensate for the greater output.

But in the nonprogressive sector, of which education is a part, the production of the good or service does not change substantially. Cuban (1993) found that over a period of almost a century, the organization and activities of schools and classrooms remained remarkably similar. Education is labor intensive, with a traditional production technology of teachers instructing students of given class sizes and alterations only at the margins of instruction, such as the addition of computers as an instructional tool. It has been estimated that about 80% of the cost of education is linked to personnel costs that have persisted through different educational reforms. Technologies have not been used extensively for the core functions of education or shown to be productive as substitutes for teacher labor, but they have been used as adjuncts to traditional instruction. Although online instruction might be the ultimate solution, this is far from proven by the evidence on effectiveness or cost-effectiveness.

A systematic search for more cost-effective approaches to education needs to be marshaled to yield greater efficiency in the use of educational resources. In this respect, cost-effectiveness analysis is an extension of traditional forms of educational evaluation. If there are high-quality evaluation studies of alternative interventions for addressing particular educational objectives with reliable effectiveness results, one can add the cost information to construct cost-effectiveness comparisons. Costs must be measured systematically with the same attention to method and detail that is used for determining effectiveness. But to the degree that evaluators consider costs at all, they are rarely estimated in a systematic way. Although the What Works Clearinghouse (WWC) of the U.S. Department of Education follows careful evaluative procedures in considering evidence of educational effectiveness, it often simply lists no cost figure or one provided by the developer of the educational intervention, with no attention to the veracity, source, or method of the cost figure.

Clune (2002) concluded that *cost-effectiveness* is typically a meaningless term when used in education. About a decade ago, he located more than 9,000 studies in the Education Resources Information Center database that used *cost-effectiveness* as descriptors. Restricting the sample to the years 1991 to 1996 revealed 1,329 titles, of which he found 541 that seemed to refer to instructional interventions. Using abstracts and full publications, he sought to determine the extent to which the term was based on actual evidence on cost-effectiveness analysis. Clune found that 83% of the studies used the term only as a rhetorical device or "marketing" claim for advancing an educational intervention with no supporting analysis or evidence. Less than 2% of the articles and reports showed even a minimally plausible attempt to do a cost-effectiveness evaluation. The other 15% showed a partial analysis that was incomplete and flawed. Although cost-effectiveness analysis is used widely as an evaluation method in other social fields, such as health and medicine (e.g., Gold, 1996), it is rarely used in any systematic or rigorous way in education. More generally, Rice (2002) found that publications evaluating interventions in public policy fields more generally pay considerably greater attention to costs than those in educational policy.

FRUSTRATED EFFORTS TO ADVANCE THE FIELD

I once thought that my own career would serve to advance the nascent field considerably. I received my PhD in economics in 1966 with a specialization in government finance. For the following 2 years, I was a research staff member of the Economic Studies Department of Brookings Institution, undertaking research in the new field (at that time) of economics of education. The Coleman Report had just been published, and I had been using the data from that study to understand teacher labor markets and to also raise concerns on the methods used in that report (Bowles & Levin, 1968). With the escalation of the Vietnam War during that period, I desired to get out of Washington and sought an academic position. Fortunately, I received an appointment at Stanford University and arrived there in 1968 with a joint appointment in the School of Education and Department of Economics. Economics of education was not an established subject in schools of education in those days, so I sought to find an academic role that I might play. Based on my work with the Coleman data and the obvious absence of economics in educational evaluation and policy, I decided to focus on cost-effectiveness in education. Indeed, I saw this as a pioneering challenge to develop the field and make it an integral component of educational evaluation, policy, and resource allocation.

I was particularly distressed by the capacity of educational evaluation to draw policy conclusions without concern about costs. Because of my interest in educational technology, a distinguished Stanford colleague of mine, Patrick Suppes, sent me a copy of an article that he had just published in the prestigious journal *Science* (Suppes & Morningstar, 1969). Using a rough experimental design with treatment and control schools in a school district, the authors found that 7 minutes/day of computerized drill and practice in arithmetic for disadvantaged youngsters produced mathematics scores greater than those from standard classroom instruction. Given the difficulty in finding compensatory educational interventions that promised success, the finding was impressive, and the article concluded that computer-assisted instruction (CAI) had come of age and should be adopted.

Although the article said nothing about the cost of CAI or alternatives, it did have information that might be useful in making a cost-effectiveness comparison. In one of the control schools, the teachers had devoted 25 minutes a day to "additional" drill and practice and had obtained results comparable with those of the CAI. With assistance from Suppes's staff, I estimated the costs of the CAI and that of 25 minutes a day of teacher time. Had the schools adopted the CAI and paid for it themselves rather than having it provided at no cost by a research project funded by the National Science Foundation, it would have added about 25% to per-student costs for the 7-minutes/day instruction. In contrast, the additional teacher time would have produced a similar effect for about a 6% increase in student costs or about 3% if the drill could be done by training classroom aides. Even though computer costs declined dramatically in the next decade and a half, a further study in 1984 found that it was still not as cost-effective as the alternatives (Levin, Glass, & Meister, 1987).

Using Coleman data, I published my first article on the subject, "A Cost-Effectiveness Analysis of Teacher Selection" (Levin, 1970). This article compared the cost-effectiveness in raising student achievement by hiring teachers with greater experience versus teachers with greater verbal ability, using the Coleman verbal test for teachers. Costs were based on incorporating these variables into earnings functions of teachers, and effectiveness was obtained from estimates of educational production functions. The work found that hiring teachers with greater verbal ability was 5 to 10 times as cost-effective as hiring teachers with greater experience. This article received positive feedback, not only from economists but also from evaluators. At this point, my colleague Lee Cronbach saw promise in this approach and invited me to join his evaluation seminars, where I learned much more about issues surrounding educational evaluation. I followed up this work with publications on the cost-effectiveness of educational technologies and more sophisticated versions of educational production functions, including linear programming models and those estimating simultaneous equations for multiple educational outputs.

Despite these efforts, cost-effectiveness approaches were not catching on in the literature on educational evaluation or even among my own colleagues, whose specializations and interests were elsewhere. I concluded that the problem was a lack of familiarity of the evaluation fraternity with the methods, so I began to construct a methodology that could be understood and embraced even by nonspecialists. My colleague, Lee Cronbach, took enough interest that he recommended to the editors of the first *Handbook on Evaluation Research* that they incorporate a chapter by me on cost-effectiveness. For this purpose, I constructed a method that I believed could be followed by knowledgeable evaluators in education, criminal justice, health, and other areas, requiring only minimal guidance or assistance from economists. This method was built around connecting intervention treatments and processes to a series of steps that were recorded on a financial spreadsheet. Fortunately, the advent of personal computers a decade later facilitated this approach by providing user-friendly electronic spreadsheets such as EXCEL. The *Handbook* and chapter (Levin, 1975) were published in 1975, and I received many invitations to speak at evaluation conferences and colloquia to discuss my analysis. The evaluation consortium at Stanford welcomed my active participation. My colleagues and I gave short courses in cost-effectiveness analysis. I was also elected president of the Evaluation Research Society (now the American Evaluation Association) in 1982 and worked actively within the society to promote my specialized field. Encouraged by this reception, I thought that the approach would gain momentum. To provide a more ambitious and comprehensive source on cost-effectiveness for educational evaluators, I published a book on the subject (Levin, 1983).

The approach at the heart of these endeavors is known as the ingredients method and is described in detail in Levin and McEwan (2001). The usual path that is taken by those who lack familiarity with cost accounting is to ask a business manager what the costs are of an intervention or to seek a statement of expenditures or budget to infer costs. Unfortunately, this approach will almost invariably give the wrong answers because it will not take into account those costs that are not found in budgets or expense statements. Moreover, the accounting principles and categories used to construct such documents were designed for purposes other than generating accurate costs of programs, interventions, or services. Accordingly, the approach that we designed had to build on evaluators' understanding of the details of the treatment or intervention and use that knowledge to construct direct estimates of costs. This process built on three main steps to ascertain accurate and consistent measures of costs. The underlying rationale and procedures for all three steps and their applications are found in Levin and McEwan (2001).

Only alternatives with similar objectives are compared for costs and effectiveness because we are concerned with comparisons of alternatives that have similar criteria of effectiveness. We assume that acceptable comparisons of these alternatives are available using experimental or quasi-experimental methods. Thus, the attempt is to develop cost information that can be matched to effectiveness results. First, the ingredients or particular resources required for each intervention must be specified in detail. For example, the precise types and amounts of personnel are listed and described according to their qualification and time commitments. A similar exercise is carried out for facilities, equipment, and other program inputs as well as for client resources. Details on ingredients are obtained from three sources: (1) descriptive reports, (2) observations, and (3) interviews. All ingredients are identified and specified, regardless of how or by whom they were financed. The reason is that we wish to identify all required resources that make up the total cost, regardless of who provided or paid for them.

Second, once the ingredients are set out, it is possible to place values on them. To as great an extent as possible, market prices are derived for each and used to value or "cost" them. In many cases, the ingredients may not be obtained through a market transaction, such as space in a building that is owned by the sponsoring entity or in-kind resources such as volunteers. In those cases, so-called shadow prices are used—the estimated value of the resources based on an alternative procedure, for example, if a market did exist. Although some of these costs can be obtained from expenditure information based on market transactions, much of that information will be incomplete or inappropriate, so one must be exceedingly cautious in ascertaining precisely how expenditures are accounted for by these sources. But for each ingredient category, there are accepted methods for determining their costs.

Third, once the costs of individual ingredients are obtained, they can be summed to estimate the total cost of each alternative. In education, these are normally measured on a per-student or per-participant basis (average cost) to compare effectiveness per unit of cost among alternatives.

It is important to follow this costing by analyzing the distribution of the burden of costs among different sponsoring entities as well as clients to find out who pays the costs for each alternative. Cost information is combined with effectiveness measures to make overall cost-effectiveness comparisons along with the distribution of the burden of costs for any particular decision-making entity, such as different levels of government. For guiding decisions, preference is given to those alternatives with the lowest cost relative to effectiveness, even though other criteria may also be taken into account.

Using the ingredients approach, my colleagues and I continued to do studies of cost-effectiveness in education, such as comparing four interventions for raising student achievement in reading and mathematics in the elementary school grades (Levin et al., 1987). Since the primer on cost-effectiveness published in 1983 sold well, we thought that it would only be a matter of time before cost-effectiveness became a regular part of the evaluator toolkit in education and beyond. Although the primer went through 13 printings in 16 years, it appears that it sat on bookshelves rather than being used as a source of training or undertaking studies. Very few studies were published on cost-effectiveness in education, and the preoccupation with effectiveness and the absence of costs continued to predominate in evaluation research. We have also used the cost-analytic design to undertake cost–benefit studies in both education and health areas (e.g., Levin, 1986; Levin, Belfield, Muenning, & Rouse, 2007). In 2001, we came out with a second edition of the book, a much expanded version with more examples, including some in noneducational areas, and with greater inclusion of effectiveness methods and their integration with costs. We had the hope that this extended presentation would generate more applications. In addition, we continued to produce studies of costs of educational interventions and capitalize on their findings.

For example, we studied the costs of adolescent literacy programs, finding that the costs could vary considerably from site to site depending on implementation. This was a warning that cost-effectiveness studies (and effectiveness ones) should limit their generic claims in favor of site-specific ones and search for generalization only over replications. We found a high variance in costs among sites with different resource implementation (Levin, Catlin, & Elson, 2010). Furthermore, we found that from a cost-effectiveness perspective, meta-analysis should be used cautiously. Schools adopt a particular application of an intervention, not a meta-analytic average, and costs also make little sense from a meta-analytic perspective because any cost would be some "average" of the costs of many different applications rather than the cost of a single and well-defined adoption and implementation. It is the latter that is necessary for a valid cost calculation. We also found large cost-effectiveness differences among different approaches to common objectives such as increasing high school graduation when measured in terms of costs for producing an additional graduate (Levin, Belfield, Muenning, & Rouse, 2007).

THE BIG PUZZLE

Given the compelling case for using cost-effectiveness analysis in educational evaluation, why is it rarely used? And when it is "used," why is it done so poorly in so many cases? A widely accepted methodology is available, one that is similar to that used regularly in the areas of health, medicine, transportation, and other public policy topics. I have found three hypotheses that might be used to account for the lack of significant development of cost-effectiveness evaluation in education. Two address the supply side of evaluation and evaluators (Levin, 2001). The first is the lack of apparent capability and training in the field. This hypothesis has support in the dearth of cost-effectiveness analysis in training programs and textbooks used to prepare personnel in the field of educational evaluation. The second supply-side explanation is the lack of acceptable studies that show educational effects. This phenomenon is so ubiquitous that the WWC sponsored by the U.S. Department of Education has found relatively few interventions with adequate evidence on effectiveness, and many evaluators even refer to the WWC as the "Nothing-Works Clearinghouse." Without good evidence of effectiveness, cost estimates seem superfluous.

But I am convinced that the main problem is the lack of demand by government decision makers for cost-effectiveness information. Unlike in the health care sector, there is little concern for cost-effectiveness guidance. Both sectors face runaway costs, but the literature on health care shows a preoccupation with costs—even though one could argue that not all of the knowledge is used to guide practice in a world where health and medicine have their own organizational and political obstacles that undermine efficient resource use. The big difference is that educational decision makers seem to show no concern for cost-effectiveness and seem to prefer subjective judgments to any cost information that might reduce their latitude in making educational decisions. To the extent that sound cost-effectiveness studies have met rigorous professional standards and provided guidance for decisions, those findings have rarely been followed. For example, Levin et al. (1987) found that increasing school time is relatively inefficient in cost-effectiveness relative to other interventions. Nevertheless, most states and school districts have increased the minimum length of the school year and established more extended day and after-school programs at great cost and with little to show for it. Forty years after finding that teachers with higher verbal ability are more cost-effective than those with more experience (Levin, 1970), salary incentives for teachers are heavily dominated by experience and rarely reflective of teachers' academic ability. If educational policy at all levels required cost-effectiveness information, more expertise would be demanded in the field. This change would be communicated quickly to evaluation training programs, textbooks, and practitioners and would likely expand the incorporation of cost-effectiveness in these fields. To this point, the roots of cost-effectiveness in education have been well developed, and the foliage has grown and budded. But the blooms have rarely emerged.

REFERENCES

Baumol, W. (1996). Children of performing arts, the economic dilemma: The climbing costs of health care and education. *Journal of Cultural Economics, 20,* 183–206.

Bowles, S., & Levin, H. M. (1968). The determinants of scholastic achievement: An appraisal of some recent evidence. *Journal of Human Resources, 3*(1), 3–24.

Clune, W. H. (2002). Methodological strength and policy usefulness of cost-effectiveness research. In H. M. Levin & P. J. McEwan (Eds.), *Cost-effectiveness and educational policy* (pp. 55–70). Larchmont, NY: Eye on Education.

Cuban, L. (1993). *How teachers taught: Constancy and change in American classrooms 1880–1890* (2nd ed.). New York, NY: Teachers College Press.

Gold, M. (1996). *Cost-effectiveness in health and medicine.* New York, NY: Oxford University Press.

Layard, R., & Glaister, S. (Eds.). (1994). *Cost–benefit analysis* (2nd ed.). New York, NY: Cambridge University Press.

Levin, H. M. (1970). A cost-effectiveness analysis of teacher selection. *Journal of Human Resources, 5*(1), 24–33.

Levin, H. M. (1975). Cost-effectiveness in evaluation research. In M. Guttentag & E. Struening (Eds.), *Handbook of evaluation research 2* (pp. 89–122). Beverly Hills, CA: Sage.

Levin, H. M. (1983). *Cost-effectiveness analysis: A primer.* Beverly Hills, CA: Sage.

Levin, H. M. (1986). A benefit–cost analysis of nutritional programs for anemia reduction. *The World Bank Research Observer, 1*(2), 219–245.

Levin, H. M. (2001). Waiting for Godot: Cost-effectiveness analysis in education. *New Directions for Evaluation, 90,* 55–68.

Levin, H. M., Belfield, C. R., Muennig, P., & Rouse, C. E. (2007). The public returns to public educational investments in African-American males. *Economics of Education Review, 26*(6), 699–708.

Levin, H. M., Catlin, D., & Elson, A. (2010). *Adolescent literacy programs: Costs of implementation.* New York: Carnegie Corporation of New York. Retrieved from http://carnegie.org/publications/search-publications/pub/199/

Levin, H. M., Glass, G. V., & Meister, G. R. (1987). Cost-effectiveness of computer-assisted instruction. *Evaluation Review, 11*(1), 50–72.

Levin, H. M., & McEwan, P. J. (2001). *Cost-effectiveness analysis: Methods and applications* (2nd ed.). Thousand Oaks, CA: Sage.

Oreopoulos, P., & Salvanes, K. G. (2011). Priceless: The non-pecuniary benefits of schooling. *Journal of Economic Perspectives, 25,* 159–184.

Prest, A. R. (1965). Cost–benefit analysis: A survey. *The Economic Journal, 75*(300), 683–735.

Psacharopoulos, G., & Patrinos, H. (2004). Returns to investment in education: A further update. *Education Economics, 12*(2), 111–134.

Quade, E. (1971). *A history of cost-effectiveness* (P-4557). Santa Monica, CA: Rand Corporation. Retrieved from http://www.rand.org/pubs/papers/2006/P4557.pdf

Rice, J. K. (2002). Cost analysis in education policy research: A comparative analysis across fields of public policy. In H. M. Levin & P. J. McEwan (Eds.), *Cost-effectiveness and educational policy* (pp. 21–36). Larchmont, NY: Eye on Education.

Suppes, P., & Morningstar, M. (1969). Computer-assisted instruction. *Science, 166,* 343–350.

14

RESPONSIVE EVALUATION IV

Robert E. Stake

In the last few months, I have reflected on what is important about educational program evaluation, and how responsive evaluation fits into the practice of professional evaluators. I am especially concerned about the tendency to see informal and formal evaluation as worlds apart.

Education is infused with evaluation. Social service is infused with evaluation. All professional work is infused with evaluation. It is not a matter of choice. One cannot do one's work without sensing the quality of things (Persig, 1974; Eiseley, 1971).

Improvement in the quality of teaching and learning—and quietly thinking—requires refinement, refinement in the recognition of merit and shortcoming (Scriven, 1967). Some of an evaluating person's refinement comes naturally with age, and with challenge and commitment, but unfortunately, just as naturally, come *distortion* and *diminution* of skill. With good meta-evaluation, i.e., with good management of evaluation, the eye becomes sharper and the will becomes stronger. We can train ourselves to be better evaluators. But ever and ever, some judgments go awry.

Formal evaluation is the conscious disciplining of judgment. We train ourselves better to see value. Each conscious step taken to manage, to refine, to validate judgment extends its formalization. Formalization is disciplined thinking, often a way of making thinking impersonal and artificial. We become more exact in identifying the things we evaluate, the *evaluands*. Soon we have styles, protocols, models, and mechanisms to refine our formalizations, and we argue about which are the better. Personally I look for ways to be responsive to the situation, empathic with stakeholders. I do not worry much about "going native."

Author's note: Three earlier papers on responsive evaluation are Stake 1974, Stake, 2004, and Stake and Abma, 2005. "Evaluand" is evaluator jargon for the thing being evaluated. Reprinted by permission of author.

Formal and informal evaluation are part of the same act. People who become professional evaluators, or experts in any way, or arbiters or leaders, formalize their ways of recognizing quality. They rely still on the informal, as well as the formal. The boundary between formal and informal is indistinct, the mix is a gradation of refinement. In the ubiquity of evaluation, only some refinement will be apparent. It should be more apparent in the work of those of us who see evaluation as a skill to be sharpened and sensitized to complication, resistant to simplification.

Student: What is the meaning of "going native?"

Mentor: Researchers go out with expectations reflecting their culture and discipline. As they become more familiar with the schools being studied, some become more empathic and protective, drifting toward support of local views and standards, thus, as the anthropologists have called it, "going native."

BEING EVALUATED

People expect to have educational things evaluated; they do it all the time. People grade teaching as quickly as learning. When it comes to getting evaluated *themselves* and the things they do, people are apprehensive. They do not want to be seen as simple. They want high marks and they do not want low marks. Mothers, administrators, and other stakeholders want high marks. They often do not think of evaluation time as an opportunity to make things better. Theirs is summative more than formative evaluation.

When marked low in quality, people often think that the evaluator is using inappropriate criteria or standards. They often think that the evaluator has less than full comprehension of what is being evaluated. They have good reason for thinking so. The evaluator is often insensitive to that person's standards, preferring those professionally made explicit. Evaluators often think that measurement of an easy criterion will represent the quality of the whole. Evaluation puts people at risk.

Of course, the experts and authorities in general agree some but not fully. They see different aspirations and implications. They see the evaluand differently. They see formal evaluation having purposes in addition to informing the highest-standing stakeholder. Regularly, evaluators have their own purposes to serve in giving high and low marks, such as displaying their expertise, furthering self-employment, and trying to upgrade the organization. Many evaluators are highly ethical, but they are not indifferent to their own well being (House, 1973; MacDonald, 1999).

The formal evaluation scene is often a political scene (Cronbach, 1977). The well being of the organization, community, and state are, to some extent, also at risk. An evaluation finding may strengthen or weaken working relationships and endorsements. It may cause shudders in power relations, sometimes more than shudders. But not usually, because the administrators somehow constrain the design of evaluation to limit institutional risk. Questions of management of the evaluand often are not included in the study. Many administrators think that competence for evaluating the evaluand is different from competence for evaluating administration. And administrators are skilled at putting a promotional interpretation on the findings.

VALUES NOT INTRINSIC

The value of something is created by humans. Horses crave water and moths crave light, but it is the value set by humans by which we judge the quality of quenching and beckoning. Health and safety are important to all creatures, but people concentrate their attention on the value placed by people. There may be a comfort for horses that horses know, but the comfort for horses we know is a human conceptualization. For teaching and learning, timeliness and usefulness are not intrinsic qualities; schooling is valued because humans find it so.

People do not value an object the same all the time. Food is less valuable after dinner; safety is less valuable in the absence of threat. The voice of a tenor is more cherished singing before the diva soprano than after. The obligation of an evaluator includes description and interpretation of the situation. The merit and worth of the evaluand depend on it.

Appetite for evaluation often diminishes. By the time an evaluator gathers evidence of value, the commissioner of the evaluation and the chief stakeholders, (the students, the teachers, the managers) often find themselves busy with other matters. Even the evaluator has different perceptions of his or her data as the study moves along. Quality is a market quotation, fluctuating over time and place.

RESPONSIVE EVALUATION

Not only is evaluation a vital part of human activity, it follows human sensitivity to changing circumstances, stresses and values. When formal evaluation focuses on the here and now, that is, on the merit of a particular evaluand in a particular situation, it is reasonable to think that it should be designed to respond to current problems, decisions to be made, and values needing protection (Stufflebeam, 1968). Responsive evaluation is the term sometimes used to emphasize that immediacy, that localization, that particularity of educational quality (Stake, 2004).

Responsive evaluation uses the methods of informal evaluation: getting personally acquainted with the evaluand, observation of activities, interviewing people in different ways familiar with the evaluand, searching documents that reveal what happened in the past or somewhere else. But also, it asks for sustained and disciplined effort to know quality and insufficiency.

Approaches different from responsive evaluation are called evaluation research, policy evaluation, and program theory evaluation, where the emphasis is on extending understanding of evaluands to those *not studied,* generalizing to further uses and contexts, and making policy. The mindset and methods for generalizing from evaluative research are far from the particularity of responsive evaluation. Actually, there is generalizing from responsive studies, however weakly warranted, coming from variation within the evaluand, relating it to other studies, and by interpreting quality in terms of common processes and settings. But responsive design is not oriented to nomothetic generalization. As with generalizing informally, seldom can a level of confidence be enumerated.

Responsive evaluation is a process of becoming personally well acquainted with the evaluand, examining closely its activities, communities, and commitments. Usually, much depends on the perceptions and judgment of participants. Sometimes there are qualities or troubles of which no one knows and the evaluator needs to find them, and to pick and choose among the interpretations. The evaluator is responsible for reporting local interpretations, found judgments of quality, as well as his or her own.

All evaluation is responsive in some ways, responsive to some form of criteria and standards, responsive to history and politics, responsive to people and governance. But only a few evaluators have chosen to use the term. In use, responsive evaluation has come to focus on local interests more than systemic, on immediate stakeholders more than societal, on relative values more than generic, and on experience more than measurement.

Mentor: "Responsive" is a point of view for looking more than a method for looking.

Student: I see its point of view as one of favoring methods that engage the personal experience of the evaluator.

REMEDIATION

Evaluation has been classified in many ways (Scriven, 1967; Alkin, 2006; Monnier, 2007). None has been more common than as formative versus summative evaluation—formative aiming to further develop and remediate the evaluand, summative aiming to declare its quality as it stands. The difference may be difference in when the evaluation is done, in production or after consumption, but it usually is a difference in questions asked. The conductor and the craftsman tend to seek formative evaluation. The judge at court and the consumer in the market tend to seek summative evaluation. But many practitioners and audiences want to know both how good is it and what parts need be made better.

Plans for remediation depend on how much needs to be known about evaluand quality before taking action, before beginning overhaul. The wait is partly a matter of personality. Activists want to get busy making changes, figuring the flaws are clear enough. They mix evaluation with change making. Cautious people want to know the complexity of the problem, tailoring changes to that complexity. They tend to keep evaluation and change-making separate.

I am a responsive evaluator personally advocating finishing the evaluation before designing change (Stake, 2004). My Dutch colleague Tineke Abma (1996, 2005, 2006) is a responsive evaluator advocating helping to make evaluand changes along the way. In the real world, such changes are made all the while, not awaiting formal evaluation. In the real world, waiting until the problems are thoroughly understood sometimes means little remediation will happen.

CRITERIA

An evaluand is usually complex, having multiple criteria by which its quality can be recognized. An evaluation study itself might be judged as to its timeliness, its integrity, its usefulness, and its sensitivity to political issues. Of course each criterion could be defined in different ways. One of the largest responsibilities of the evaluator is to identify criteria of primary importance. These can be quantitative or qualitative (Stake, 2004).

Many evaluation designs invest heavily in good measurement of one or only a few criteria. It is often supposed that the findings on multiple criteria will be correlated, so that good measurement of one criterion will provide good approximation of the over-all quality of the evaluand. That simplicity appeals to many administrators, who sometimes claim having a single standard will be fair.

Given a single evaluand, responsive evaluation anticipates many criteria worthy of attention. The budget allows close examination of only a few, but others are alluded to. Just as a child wordlessly expressed appreciation for attention, any stakeholder may wordlessly express appreciation for an evaluand. The responsive evaluator uses words and pictures to discern the implicit criteria attended to (Polanyi, 1966). Formally identifying the criteria sometimes will be seen as too simplifying, too formalistic, but, in the absence of definition, more of the complex quality might be overlooked.

Mentor: When I grade your work, am I unfair if I do not tell you in advance my criteria?

Student: You would have been unfair had you not made me aware of works of which you think highly and poorly.

STANDARDS

Evaluation can be defined as comparing the perceived quality of the evaluand to the quality desired. The level of desired quality is called a *standard*. Being best in the class is a standard, a weak standard because it depends on the happenstance of other people present. Pleasing yourself is a standard, often a good one, depending mostly on yourself. It is difficult to be fully explicit about standards; some remain covert.

The standard may change from time to time and, at any given time, different people will have different standards for the same evaluand. Responsive evaluation tries to honor a diversity of stakeholders by describing the goodness of the evaluand and indicating separately how well it meets standards abiding in different points of view.

Standards are often presumed better if the same standard is applied to all, often it is said to be fairer. In school, when a common standard is used, competition is created, a common teacher ploy. But most of the work of education needs to be judged less comparatively, more individually, taking into account the individualistic circumstances, and contributing formatively to individual improvement. Responsive evaluation often challenges over-reliance on common-standards-for-all and any cult of standardization (Stake, 2004). Evaluation cannot happen without standards, but they need be neither explicit nor uniform.

LANGUAGE OF GENERALIZATION

Generalization is part of the heredity of evaluation. The word "teacher" implies the existence of other teachers; the word "grading" somehow stands for grading elsewhere. Implication of the general lies in words throughout the language. People who want to can find at least the hint of generalization in any thinking that evaluators do, certainly in planning, data collecting, and reporting.

It is easy to presume that, at some level, all evaluation aims at providing nomothetic generalization to guide practice (Mejía, 2010; Bullough, in press). Much evaluation does seek assertions of this form: this action had this effect in this situation. From that, a practitioner may hypothesize a more causal generalization: this kind of action will have this kind of effect in this kind of situation, and users try to decide if their idiographic situation is of that kind. This language of generalization has a tricky grammar.

The language of responsive evaluation is the language of events, experiences, and episodes—time and place bound, with many contexts and many experiential accounts of human activity. The descriptions may lead practitioners in their situations to decide to take similar action to try to get similar effects. Their thinking might be mediated by the language of causal generalization. But responsive evaluation offers a vicarious experience that needs, neither in writing nor reading, the language of cause and effect.

Student: How much do evaluators want the evaluation study to contribute to general understanding about teacher training or community values?

Mentor: It varies, of course. Some evaluation predispositions, methods, and contracts press toward resolution of important educational issues. It is common in responsive evaluation to pay attention to issues swaying the evaluand, but pursuing such issues can capsize any particular search for merit and shortcoming.

PARTICULARIZATION

Responsive evaluation concentrates on the particular evaluand, seeing its action in its own particular contexts, with its own particular stakeholders. The evaluator's intent is to come to know that evaluand in a close, personal, and empathic (and partly critical) way. That does not mean the responsive evaluator is uninterested in the general nature of evaluands, or uninterested in their future well-being, but the emphasis is on quality at the present time.

Parents, counselors and action researchers tend to be interested in particular persons, for example, their children and students, or in their own particular work spaces. It seems our society has pushed them to compare their individuals to other individuals, as if competition were the main way to understand people and places. Responsive evaluation pushes people to understand the learning, idle time, and long living that the evaluand does, to evaluate it itself more than for its standing among others.

EXPERIENCE

Nothing is more important to the responsive evaluator than embracing the evaluand experientially, against a personal history, with dialogue, in personal context. The embrace comes partly through capturing the experience of others from interviews and documents. It includes portraying experience in such a way that the readers of evaluation reports may have vicarious experience. The view is subjective, scoured some of sympathy and posturing via triangulation, balanced somewhat with contradiction, including objectivity, but not bounded by it. The presence of the evaluator remains in the telling of the story (Abma, 2005, Kushner, 2000).

M: (leaning back) So, what do you make of responsive?

S: (upending the soda to take the last swallow) It seems a little catch as catch can. Like hanging out. You may happen to see and hear some good things, but will a skeptic find the report credible?

M: Measurements have panache?

S: I don't want to think so. (pausing) But how can the boss tell that I really worked to find a deeper meaning?

M: I think Stake would say that if you dig deeply you will find issues that haven't been visible to others, new complexities about the quality of the program.

S: Finding complexity isn't the same as finding credibility.

M: Well said. (pausing) But you haven't mentioned triangulation. Won't the boss be persuaded by a redundancy of evidence? Of course, you may be persuaded by the replication but others may not.

S: You're saying triangulation is more a matter of becoming convinced than of compiling pertinent data?

M: Actually, what I am thinking is that, if the boss is like most people, she already has an idea of how good the program is. She may not be open-minded. She may be looking for support. If the report is well developed and supports management's view, she will be persuaded. If it doesn't support that view, probably no amount of triangulation will turn her around.

S: (throwing the can in the bin) That's pretty discouraging. But let me see if I can guess Stake's rationalization. Readers (clients) look for what they can use. If a responsive evaluation report claims to show new complexities, chances are the reader has had some similar thought like that before, and it gets elevated "on the chart." Yes, the boss may not change her plans, but soon is heard claiming that next year's program will take a more comprehensive approach, maybe meaning some of the complexity reported has become part of the plan.

UTILITY

Good evaluation studies are comprehensive, honest, triangulated and useful. Many evaluation writers give high priority to making evaluation work useful (Braskamp, Brown and Newman, 1978; Patton, 2010). A study is easily seen useful if it leads to a decision or change in policy. It should also be seen as useful merely if it adds understanding of how the thing works (Stake, 2010). The study may be useful if it protects a good program from excessive criticism. Just having carried out an evaluation gives the appearance of administrative responsibility. And these three do not exhaust the uses made of formal evaluation studies.

Some studies are enhanced by recommendations. Some recommendations are hortatory, such as: the personnel policy should be reviewed. Some are self-serving: evaluation should be made routine throughout the organization. During the study, the evaluator hears recommendations from stakeholders and tries them out on others. Recommendations seldom flow directly from interpretation of the data. Recommendations are sometimes a requirement of the contract and, in a great number of cases, bolster the position of the administration (Simons, 1987; MacDonald, 1999).

Responsive evaluation tries to provide a comprehensive description of activity, interpretation of issues, and display of merit and shortcoming. Some words carry invitation to action. Tacit exhortation is not uncommon. But explicit recommendation of action is problematic. Alternative courses of action are seldom available for study and a budget including such exploration is uncommon. Not knowing the implication of an alternative course of action, the prudent evaluator limits assertions to the goodness and badness of action studied.

RESPONSIVITY

Any individual doing action research or any agency doing mandated assessment can design their work to be responsive to the activity, the contexts, and the need for stakeholders to know the quality of what they are doing. Quality of management and operations are only weakly comprehensible in terms of "indicator variables," such as student test scores, market surveys, such as value added, and organizational climate. The work of the evaluand is more comprehensibly represented by carefully selected description of activity and critical analysis of operations.

Understanding the integrity and problem resolution of the evaluand greatly needs observation of choice-making situations, repetitive interviewing of diverse players, and document analysis. Responsive evaluation offers an up close and personal look at these data. More objective and statistical emphases and more collaborative approaches are sometimes needed, particularly for policy study and remediation. But excellent measurement does not provide proof of quality. An enthusiastic collaboration of stakeholders seldom attends to the range of stakeholder concerns. Responsive evaluation emphasizes a diversity of perspectives and an experiential portrayal of evaluand quality.

What is worthy of response to the quality of an evaluand will vary with the circumstances, the purposes for the evaluation, and the audiences to whom it is directed. As I advised in my first evaluation paper, data can speak of antecedents, transactions and outcomes (Stake, 1967). Informal evaluation needs to be included. Still, the picture will ever be incomplete. Important facts will fail to reach the report. Whatever the goals, the problems, and the potential utility, the responsive evaluator and the responsive reader will recognize descriptions, dialogues and issues that enhance understanding of the merit and shortcoming of the evaluand.

REFERENCES

Abma, T. (1996). *Responsief evalueren, Discoursen, controversen en allianties in het postmoderne [Evaluating responsively, discourses, controversies and alliances with/in the postmodern]*, dissertation, Delft, Eburon.

Abma, T. (2006). The Practice and Politics of Responsive Evaluation. *American Journal of Evaluation, 27*, 1, 31–43.

Abma, T. (2005). The practice and politics of responsive evaluation. *The American Journal of Evaluation,* 27(1): 31–43.

Alkin, M. C. (2006). *Evaluation roots: Tracing theorists' views and influences.* Thousand Oaks, CA: Sage.

Braskamp, L. A. (1982). Studying Evaluation Utilization through Simulations. *Evaluation Review, 6,* 1, 114–26.

Braskamp, L. Brown, R. and Newman, D. (1978). Studying evaluation utilization through simulations. *Evaluation Review, 6,* 1, 114–126.

Bullough, R. B. (in press). Against best practice: Uncertainty, outliers, and local studies in educational research. *Journal of Education for Teaching.*

Cronbach, L. (1977). Remarks to the new Society. *Evaluation Research Society,* 1.

Eiseley, L. C. (1971). "The Mind as Nature," in his *The Night Country,* 195–226. New York: Scribner.

House, E. R. (1973). *School evaluation: The politics and process.* Berkeley, CA: McCutchan Pub. Corp.

Kushner, S. (2000). *Personalizing evaluation.* London: Sage.

MacDonald, B. (1999). Statement on occasion of his investiture as Doctor Honoris Causa, University of Vallodolid, Spain.

Mejía, A. (2010). The general in the particular. *Journal of Philosophy in Education, 44,* 1, 93–107.

Monnier, E. (2007). Un sistema pluralista y participativo: Coproducir la evaluación con la sociedad civil. Madrid: Instituto Madrileño de Administración Pública.

Patton, M. Q. (2010). *Developmental evaluation: Applying complexity concepts to enhance innovation and use.* New York: Guilford Press.

Persig, R. M. (1974). *Zen and the art of motorcycle maintenance.* New York: William Morrow and Company.

Polanyi, M. (1966). *The tacit dimension,* Garden City, NY: Doubleday.

Scriven, M. (1967). The methodology of evaluation. In Stake, R. E., ed., *Perspectives of curriculum evaluation.* Chicago: Rand McNally. .

Simons, H. (1987). *Getting to know schools in a democracy, The politics and process of evaluation.* Social Research and Educational Studies Series, 5. London: Falmer Press.

Stake, R. E. (1967). The countenance of educational evaluation. *Teachers College Record, 68, 7,* 523–540.

Stake, R. E. (1974). Program evaluation, particularly responsive evaluation. New Trends in Evaluation. Gothenburg, Sweden: Institute of Education, University of Gothenburg. Report No. 35, 1–20.

Stake, R. E. (2004). *Standards-based and responsive evaluation.* Thousand Oaks, CA: Sage.

Stake, R. E. (2010). *Qualitative research: Studying how things work.* New York: Guilford Press.

Stake, R. E. and Abma, T. (2005). Responsive evaluation. In Mathison, S., ed. *Encyclopedia of Evaluation.* Thousand Oaks, CA: Sage.

Stufflebeam, D. L. (1968). *Evaluation as enlightenment for decision-making.* Columbus, OH: Evaluation Center, Ohio State University.

15

WORK MEMOIR

Ideas and Influences

Ernest R. House

In 1967, I was sitting in a university office talking to Gene Glass, my statistics instructor, when Bob Stake walked in. Glass said, "Do you know Ernie House?" Stake said, "He doesn't know I know him, but I know who he is." Glass said, "Ernie has a gold mine here, a big evaluation project." Thus began my evaluation career. I was finishing graduate study at the University of Illinois and had been asked to evaluate the statewide Illinois Gifted Program.

How did I get here? I began by trying to change education, convinced by my experiences that there was something amiss in the education system. My scholarly career has been marked by two themes: educational innovation and evaluation, including the processes, politics, policies, and values of both. The two merge in evaluating education innovations. Gradually, I moved more into evaluation.

The purpose of this chapter is to identify the influences on my ideas. Memory is a biased instrument, not balanced in this case by other accounts of events. To approach the task, I have outlined my career activities and identified what influenced them at that time. It's one way of putting distance between now and then, to reduce the danger of rewriting history by projecting current ideas backward. The approach hasn't been as successful as I had hoped. In a multidecades career, you interact with hundreds of people, engage in dozens of projects, and write far too many papers. My first draft wasn't very readable—too many names, too many places, too many ideas. The early version did prove one thing: The influences were numerous, varied, and complex. To make this chapter more readable, I have omitted many, and there is much that I regret leaving out.

Author's Note: Thanks to Steve Lapan and Gene Glass for helpful comments on this chapter.

I have identified several types of influences. First, there are those scholars a generation or so ahead of me in the field. Second, there are scholars from other disciplines, especially philosophy, political science, history, and economics. Third, there are a few friends and colleagues who shaped my ideas by reviewing my work in the early drafts. Fourth, there are colleagues I met a few times a year and had productive exchanges with. Fifth, there are the diffuse effects of spending time in other countries.

During my career, the social context—indeed, society itself—changed greatly. Evaluation gained its impetus in 1965 with passage of the Great Society legislation, which mandated evaluation for some education programs for the first time. Through the 1960s and 1970s, the role of evaluation was to legitimate government activities by evaluating them. ("We aren't sure this will work, but we will evaluate it to see.") In the 1980s, Reagan reversed 50 years of the New Deal and Great Society by privatizing, deregulating, and discrediting government endeavors. The private sector could do things better, he maintained. In the 1990s, these trends continued, with Clinton trying to convert government's role to managing rather than producing services. In the new century, Bush embarked on even more radical privatizing and deregulating of policies. Hence, while evaluation began in 1965 by serving the public interest, by 2010, evaluation itself was being privatized to serve private interests in some cases.

These are remarkable changes, against which my career played out. To simplify the analysis, I have divided the era into four periods corresponding roughly to the decades, each period typified by a different ethos.

LEARNING THE CRAFT AND CREATING NEW IDEAS (1967–1980)

In 1967, I prepared for the Illinois evaluation by putting all the evaluation papers I could find in a cardboard box and reading them in a month. There wasn't much. I established an advisory panel, including Stake, Egon Guba, and Dan Stufflebeam. Their advice proved invaluable. I used Stake's (1967) "countenance" model of evaluation to plan the study. In 4 years, I learned evaluation from the bottom up, aided by a talented team consisting of Steve Lapan, Joe Steele, and Tom Kerins. We worked with program managers, hundreds of school districts, including Chicago, the state education agency, and the Illinois legislature. These interactions convinced me that evaluation was highly political, not a common idea at the time. Following that, Stufflebeam, Wendell Rivers, and I conducted a review of the Michigan Accountability Program, touted as a national model. This reinforced my sense of the ubiquity of politics.

In fact, I asked myself, was it all politics? The possibility disturbed me. Surely, there must be a way to adjudicate what evaluators did. I saw a review of Rawls's (1971) work on social justice. Maybe this was what I needed. If politics was about who got what, an ethical framework might help evaluators grapple with the politics. I wrote an article on justice in evaluation. It's difficult to imagine the incredulity of people in the field. What could justice possibly have to do with evaluation? The two terms didn't belong in the same sentence. Some did see the relevance. Don Campbell sent for copies, and Glass included the article in the first *Annual* (Glass, 1976).

Rawls's theory hypothesizes an "original position" in which people decide what principles of justice they should adopt. He arrives at one principle securing basic civil liberties and another stipulating that if inequalities are allowed, these inequalities should benefit the least advantaged. This conception was more egalitarian than the dominant utilitarian view. I discussed how the principles might apply to evaluation. The import was to bring social justice into consideration. Even if evaluators disagreed with Rawls, they needed to think about how what they were doing affected others, particularly the disadvantaged. Evaluation was more than politics.

During the 1970s, the quantitative–qualitative debate heated up. Along with others, I defended the legitimacy of qualitative studies. Again, I looked for a broader perspective and found a work reviving the classical discipline of rhetoric (Perelman & Olbrechts-Tyteca, 1969). I conceived that evaluations were arguments in which evaluators presented evidence for and against and that in making such arguments they might use both quantitative and qualitative data. Evaluation was more than methods. These ideas gained quick acceptance. I received personal messages from Lee Cronbach and Guba that the ideas had changed their thinking. Cronbach recast the validation of standardized tests as arguments, and Guba advanced naturalistic evaluation much further in work with Lincoln.

Meanwhile, our innovative center at Illinois, led by Stake and Tom Hastings, was experimenting with case studies, influenced by Barry MacDonald at East Anglia. In the Illinois evaluation, we had collected 40 different kinds of information on a stratified random sample of local gifted programs. How should we put that together? Bob encouraged us to combine these data into "portrayals." After writing some cases, I gave a folder of data to a colleague, who said, "From what angle do I write this?" I said you don't need an angle, just read the material and put it together. The result was incoherent. I realized you must have a point of view to make sense.

The framework this time was to see evaluations as using voice, plot, story, imagery, metaphor, and other literary elements, based on ideas from literary theory, linguistics, and cognitive science. I applied these concepts to case studies and scientific studies. Even scientific studies tell a story. One example was a sociological analysis of research on drunk driving, showing how the studies had changed the image of drunk drivers from those who have one drink too many to that of falling down habitual drunks. This change in image prompted strong legislation. Such elements I called "the vocabulary of action." They motivate people to act. The deeper idea is one of coherence and meaning, of conveying powerful, shared values through metaphors, images, and nonliteral means. Evaluation is more than literal truth.

In the 1970s, the field expanded rapidly. There were at least 60 evaluation models. Examining them, I saw that they were similar. I posited eight basic approaches and analyzed how these differed in methods and assumptions. From there, I critiqued the approaches with the criteria—meta-evaluation. I included all these papers in my 1980 validity book, generalizing that truth, beauty, and justice were three broad criteria by which evaluations could be judged (House, 1980). Evaluations should be true, coherent, and just. Untrue, incoherent, and unjust evaluations are invalid. You need adequacy in all three areas. In each case, I had encountered a practical problem and looked to other disciplines to provide insights.

What about change in education? The Illinois Gifted Program was a complex, very effective innovation. In 1974, I published a book on the politics of educational innovation, drawing on the

Illinois study and on quantitative geography about how innovations spread (House, 1974). Educators do not respond to new ideas as rationalistic research and development models of change anticipate. Teachers blend new ideas with old practices, heavily influenced by colleagues around them. The distinction is between reforms that enhance teacher skills and replacing teacher practices with techniques from authorities—craft versus technology. Adding to the craft perspective, Lapan and I wrote a book of advice for teachers (House & Lapan, 1978). In our view, the key to educational innovation was to influence teacher thinking and, through that, teacher practice. It wasn't advisable to ignore how teachers conceive their work.

In those early years, I participated in several projects that influenced me in the long term. One was a study of change in a Chicago school by a team that included Dan Lortie and Rochelle Mayer. This study deepened my insights about how complex school social structures are and how that affects reform. Another project was a 4-month visit to East Anglia, where I established connections with MacDonald and his colleagues, who were working on democratic evaluation via case studies. A third was a critique of the Follow Through program evaluation with Glass, Decker Walker, and Les McLean. Our panel concluded that the Follow Through findings depended on how closely programs fit narrowly defined outcome measures rather than broader criteria. Our conclusion: There was no simple answer as to which early childhood program was the best. Our critique dealt a blow to the presumption that government could conduct large evaluations to determine definitive answers for everyone everywhere. Evaluation findings don't generalize that easily.

META-EVALUATION: CRITIQUING POLICIES AND PRACTICES (1980–1990)

After his election in 1980, Reagan began privatizing and deregulating many government functions. Concern about the public interest began giving way to private interests, backed by claims that the private sector would be more effective. I began the 1980s by conducting two high-profile meta-evaluations. The New York City mayor's office asked me to "audit" the evaluation of their controversial Promotional Gates Program, in which students were retained at grade level if they did not achieve prescribed scores on standardized tests. Those doubting the program's efficacy insisted on an outside audit of the school district's evaluation. Political pressures were intense. As I testified at a city council meeting, "No one in New York City seems to trust anyone else." Bob Linn, Jim Raths, and I wrote confidential reports for the chancellor and mayor's offices. The district evaluation had problems like failing to account for regression to the mean, thus claiming test gains when there were none. After a few rocky encounters, the district administrators decided that we were trying to help, and the evaluators corrected the errors. Eventually, the *Village Voice* obtained our confidential reports and featured them in a front-page story.

The second meta-evaluation was a critique of the evaluation of Jesse Jackson's PUSH/Excel program. Eleanor Farrar and I thought that the evaluators imposed an inappropriate program model on PUSH/Excel that was too rationalistic for a motivational enterprise. PUSH/Excel was like a church or coaching program, featuring loosely connected inspirational activities. Indeed, athletic teams rely heavily on similar motivational activities. (Also, the headlines generated by the evaluation—Jesse Jackson took government money and did not do what he said—did not match the findings.) I later wrote a book about the PUSH/Excel program, emphasizing the central issue of race (House, 1988).

The chief evaluator for PUSH/Excel was Charles Murray, who published *Losing Ground* (Murray, 1984) a few years later. This work claimed that Great Society programs made their beneficiaries worse off rather than better. Murray estimated the effects of Great Society programs by comparing before and after data in several areas. Unfortunately, Murray's data analyses were badly flawed. In the education analysis, I discovered that he had used nonstandardized means for his critical measures, an egregious error. Bill Madura and I demonstrated that his analysis of unemployment was incorrect and misleading, accomplished by leaving out key employment data. Murray's analyses seemed shaped to fit his message rather than the other way around. In spite of severe scholarly shortcomings, the book's message attracted raves among neoconservatives and a White House eager to discredit the Great Society efforts.

Losing Ground set the tone for the coming decades of ideological studies purporting to be scholarly. Neoconservatives found that they could publish findings that did not meet rigorous standards in political journals and that the media would interpret these findings as social science—especially if the studies had lots of numbers. Journalists did not have the capacity to assess the statistics. Privately funded conservative think tanks became major sources of reform ideas. Education reforms became increasingly punitive, imposed on teachers and students and justified by pseudo–social science.

During the 1980s, I extended the craft perspective by writing papers on teacher thinking, teacher appraisal, and how to improve the insights of teachers as they direct their classrooms, coauthored with Lapan, Sandra Mathison, and Robin McTaggert. Cronbach (1982) influenced how we construed the validity of teacher inferences. Ultimately, I did not extend this work as far as intended, which was to integrate the craft perspective with evaluation thinking. Seeking educational improvement through enhancing teacher skills was being supplanted. Coercing teachers with standardized test scores became the reform focus for the next several presidents.

Looking back on the 1980s, perhaps I spent too much time fighting neoconservative ideas. In retrospect, many of these scholars were not influenced by rational argument. Rather, they were funded to produce certain findings, and they did. Ideological positions are not affected by discordant data. The privatizing, deregulating, and de-professionalizing policies they supported are taking their toll now in financial crises, a deteriorating infrastructure, and increasing social discord and stratification. Sometimes you have to take a stand even when you know your view won't prevail.

EXPLORING EVALUATION FRONTIERS (1990–2000)

During the Clinton years, privatization and deregulation continued—for example, repealing the Glass–Steagall Act separating investment banking from other banking activities and refusing to regulate the burgeoning derivatives trade—which led directly to a financial crisis in 2008

(Roubini & Mihm, 2010; Stiglitz, 2010). Clinton and Gore also tried "reinventing" government by making it the manager rather than the producer of social services. In such a scheme, evaluators would supply information to managers.

During this decade, I explored the institutional nature of evaluation. I spent 3 months in Spain, a culture different from any I had experienced. Curiosity led to the *Annale* historians, particularly Braudel's (1981, 1982, 1983) history of capitalism as an institution developing over centuries. These ideas provided a map across time and societies in which I could place my own society and evaluation. I portrayed evaluation as a developing social institution in *Professional Evaluation* (House, 1993). My idea was that at some stage of capitalist development, government activities must be further justified and that professional evaluation emerges to play a legitimating role (which is how mandated evaluation of Great Society programs began).

In 1993, Sharon Rallis and Chip Reichart attempted to end the quantitative–qualitative dispute and asked me to talk on this at the American Evaluation Association (AEA). I had used scientific realism as a framework for integrating approaches (Bhaskar, 1975; House, 1991). If there is a substantive real world (and not just different perceptions), quantitative and qualitative inquiries must be ways of looking at the same thing and hence compatible at some level. There is no reason to claim the superiority of one method over another. Methods of inquiry depend on which aspect of reality one is investigating. Methods differ depending on the substance explored, but there is one complex reality of which evaluators are a part. Being immersed in that reality affects how people think about it. Indeed, actively participating enables people to think about it.

A new adventure began when Ken Travers at the National Science Foundation asked me to assist his research and evaluation unit. I considered the National Science Foundation the best federal agency and was not disappointed. I served on committees, interviewed staff, and became a participant observer of how evaluation works inside the agency. In addition to its own evaluations, the unit oversaw the first review of science, math, and technology education across all federal departments. Practical problems like finding contractors led to transaction cost economics as an explanation for how evaluation markets function. I developed a framework to appraise prospective innovations by using factors that characterize transaction costs in some markets, bounded rationality, opportunism, and asset specificity, based on Williamson's (1985) work, which won a Nobel Prize in 2008 (House, 1998).

At the end of the decade, I concentrated on values and democratic evaluation. During the 1990s, Ove Karlsson spent considerable time in Colorado discussing evaluation politics. Continued contacts in Sweden and Norway reinforced Scandinavian egalitarian ideas. In 1999, Ken Howe and I published a book on values in evaluation, bringing together ideas on social justice, the Karlsson Scandinavian egalitarianism, the pragmatism of Dewey and Quine, the British ideas of MacDonald, and work on deliberative democracy by political scientists and philosophers (House & Howe, 1999). Among evaluators, Scriven's (1976) influence was particularly strong regarding the objectivity of value judgments. Many evaluators view value judgments as subjective. In our conception, evaluators can arrive at (relatively) unbiased evaluative conclusions by including the views, perspectives, and interests of relevant stakeholders; conducting a dialogue with them; and deliberating together on the results. Evaluative findings can be "objective" in the sense of being relatively free of biases, including stakeholder biases as well as more traditional biases.

An additional rationale for the approach derives from considering hundreds of years of racism in the United States. Racism has not gone away; it has gone underground. In my experience, in a racist democracy racism takes disguised forms because citizens do not want to admit discrimination even to themselves. Treating minority students as explicitly "different" is no longer acceptable in most places. What happens is that policies and programs are promulgated that purport to help the students but, in fact, disadvantage them further. At some level, they are treated as different in ways that are damaging. In other words, there is considerable self-deception. One remedy is to have minority interests represented in evaluations to guard against such possibilities.

SEMIREFLECTING IN SEMIRETIREMENT (2000–2010)

In the new century, Bush pushed through even more radical privatizing and deregulating policies. Attention to private interests, rather than the public interest, became paramount. In education, privatization, deregulation, and de-professionalization crossed new boundaries. Private foundations and other agents of concentrated wealth promoted and sponsored many of these changes. As income and wealth distribution became increasingly unequal, those with power found it important to differentiate education to match an increasingly stratified social class structure. Even evaluation began to be privatized and controlled by private entities for their own ends (for additional influences, see Glass, 2008).

I began the century at the Center for the Advanced Study in the Behavioral Sciences, introducing evaluation to colleagues there by explaining how changing conceptions of causes, values, and politics had shaped the field. I handled causes and values analytically, but I presented politics in a case study, a storytelling technique I transformed into fiction by writing a novel about evaluation politics (House, 2007). I portrayed the political and ethical challenges evaluators face in what I call an educational novel, fiction deliberately constructed to educate students on substantive issues while entertaining them.

My major evaluation project of the decade was monitoring the Denver bilingual program. Denver schools were under federal court order to provide Spanish language services for 15,000 immigrant children who did not speak English. Judge Matsch needed someone to monitor the implementation of the program agreed to by the school district and the plaintiffs—the Congress of Hispanic Educators and U.S. Justice Department. I anticipated an intensely political evaluation that might employ deliberative democratic principles.

I established a committee representing the contending parties. As I collected data from schools, I fed this information to the committee. We discussed progress in implementing the program, and when we had significant disagreements, we collected more data to resolve them. As evaluators, we insisted on standards for data collection and analysis, but the stakeholders shaped the evaluation in part. In my view, the findings should be more accurate since we tapped the knowledge of those in and around the program, as well as traditional data sources.

During the study, acrimony among stakeholders lessened, and implementation proceeded in an orderly manner, albeit slower than planned. At the end, there were still disagreements, but we also had a successful implementation informed by data.

For a few years, I had been considering semiretirement so that I could spend more time overseas, do other writing, and focus more on financial investing. I began investing in the early 1990s, when I first thought about retirement (following a long meeting in which faculty members complained about not being appreciated). There are remarkable similarities between evaluation and investing, and I have derived many insights about evaluation from the finance and economics literature. Like evaluation, investing requires controlling emotions and evaluating situations in which there is overwhelming yet incomplete information. (I also wanted to leave something for my descendants other than several filing cabinets of reprints.)

At the same time, the evaluation community was important to me. It had shaped my working and social life. Staying involved with a few articles, speeches, and activities helped me stay in touch. Each year, I spend several months overseas—for example, northern winters in Australia, a place I admire for its egalitarianism, levelheadedness, and laid-back lifestyle.

In 2006, Gary Henry and Mel Mark asked me to talk at AEA about the consequences of evaluation. I had been wondering about the frequent renunciations of findings from pharmaceutical drug evaluations. What was wrong with these studies? On investigation, I discovered that drug companies had gained control over many aspects of the evaluations and used their influence to produce findings favorable to their drugs, sometimes producing incorrect findings. Conflict of interest of the evaluators had become a threat—in fact, a serious threat to the field. This was another effect of privatization and unrestrained self-interest.

At the end of the decade, Leslie Cooksy, president of AEA, chose the quality of evaluation as the 2010 conference theme, citing my 1980 validity book on truth, beauty, and justice. The occasion enticed me to look back at work I had done over the years, reflections I have elaborated here. Truth, beauty, and justice are still appropriate as criteria for judging the validity of evaluations, even drug evaluations done 30 years later, though the social context has changed and the meaning of truth, beauty, and justice has shifted.

LOOKING BACK AND LOOKING AHEAD

Looking back, what influenced my ideas? I built directly on the ideas of some scholars, both those within evaluation, like Stake and Scriven, and those outside, like Rawls, Braudel, and Williamson. A few friends and colleagues shaped my ideas by reacting directly to my work, notably Glass, Lapan, and Howe, my Colorado colleague, and on occasion MacDonald and Karlsson overseas. The sociologist Dave Harvey, a hometown friend, provided valuable guidance over the years by reminding me where I came from. The influence of these people is greatly underestimated in this account. My work would have been much worse without questions like "This doesn't make sense," even if some of it still does not make sense. There were also useful discussions with certain colleagues, including Marv Alkin, editor of this volume (for a sample, see Alkin, 1990). And there was the influence of spending time overseas, especially in England, Spain, Sweden, and Australia.

As I become older, I find it important to listen to younger scholars. Having a long career means that you have made many mistakes, learned many lessons, and solved many problems. However, as the social context changes, these lessons become less relevant. This effect is noteworthy in finance. Having learned the secrets of investing success in a U.S.-centric world, investing gurus are having a difficult time adjusting to a global economy focused on Asia. Cronbach (1982) said that generalizations decay. The trouble is you're not sure which ones.

One of my traits has been a strong interest in new ideas, especially new concepts that explain puzzling phenomena, and arranging those concepts into coherent patterns. Seeking coherence in explanations, in the meaning of phenomena, and in the meaning of life has been a driving motive. How do these things fit together? What do they mean? Once found, I tend to lose interest and move on (not a good scholarly trait). These tendencies are matters of personality as much as mind.

Introducing me at the Canadian Evaluation Society in 2004, Alan Ryan said, "Throughout his long and distinguished career, Ernest House has continuously stressed the moral responsibility of evaluators. His social activist perspective has time and again alerted us to the dangers of being seduced by the agendas of those in power." This personality trait comes from my family. My mother was the best person I ever knew. My father and his four brothers were the toughest. Sometimes I see things others don't see and will say things others are afraid to say.

Of course, as we know, being outspoken comes at a cost. Keynes (1936/1997) wrote, "Worldly wisdom teaches that it is better for reputation to fail conventionally than to succeed unconventionally" (p. 158). Career risk is a major vulnerability of professionals. Professionals fear damaging their careers by taking stands different from their colleagues or contrary to those wielding power. I have been threatened with lawsuits and loss of my job and offered thinly veiled bribes. No doubt I would have won more prizes, had better jobs, and made more money if I had played along. But that's not who I am.

As I look at those colleagues who shaped evaluation in its early decades, many have been people similarly willing to risk their careers by exploring uncharted ideas and, most important, taking a principled stand against those subverting evaluation's integrity. Looking ahead to an ethically challenged era in which private interests trump the public interests, the pressures to compromise evaluations will intensify. Defending the integrity of the field will require more than intellect; it will require character.

REFERENCES

Alkin, M. C. (1990). *Debates on evaluation.* Newbury Park, CA: Sage.

Bhaskar, R. (1975). *A realist theory of science.* Sussex, England: Harvester Press.

Braudel, F. (1981, 1982, 1983). *Civilization and capitalism: 15th-18th century.* New York, NY: Harper & Row.

Cronbach, L. J. (1982). *Designing evaluations of educational and social programs.* San Francisco, CA: Jossey-Bass.

Glass, G. V. (Ed.). (1976). *Evaluation studies review annual* (Vol. 1). Beverly Hills, CA: Sage.

Glass, G. V. (2008). *Fertilizers, pills, and magnetic strips.* Charlotte, NC: Information Age.

House, E. R. (1974). *The politics of educational innovation.* Berkeley, CA: McCutchan.

House, E. R. (1980). *Evaluating with validity.* Beverly Hills, CA: Sage. (In Spanish, *Evaluacion, etica y poder*, 1994, Madrid, Spain: Morata, 1994. Reprinted 2010, Charlotte, NC: Information Age)

House, E. R. (1988). *Jesse Jackson and the politics of charisma: The rise and fall of the PUSH/Excel program.* Boulder, CO: Westview Press.

House, E. R. (1991). Realism in research. *Educational Researcher, 20*(5), 21–26.

House, E. R. (1993). *Professional evaluation: Social impact and political consequences.* Newbury Park, CA: Sage.

House, E. R. (1998). *Schools for sale: Why free market policies won't improve America's schools and what will.* New York, NY: Teachers College Press.

House, E. R. (2007). *Regression to the mean: A novel of evaluation politics.* Charlotte, NC: Information Age.

House, E. R., & Howe, K. R. (1999). *Values in evaluation and social research.* Thousand Oaks, CA: Sage.

House, E. R., & Lapan, S. G. (1978). *Survival in the classroom.* Boston, MA: Allyn & Bacon.

Keynes, J. M. (1997). *The general theory of employment, interest, and money.* Amherst, NY: Prometheus Books. (Original work published 1936)

Murray, C. (1984). *Losing ground: American social policy 1950–1980.* New York, NY: Basic Books.

Perelman, C., & Olbrechts-Tyteca, L. (1969). *The new rhetoric: A treatise on argumentation.* Notre Dame, IN: University of Notre Dame Press.

Rawls, J. (1971). *A theory of justice.* Cambridge, MA: Harvard University Press.

Roubini, N., & Mihm, S. (2010). *Crisis economics.* New York, NY: Penguin Books.

Scriven, M. (1976). Evaluation bias and its control. In G. V. Glass (Ed.), *Evaluation studies review annual* (pp. 119–139). Beverly Hills, CA: Sage.

Stake, R. E. (1967). The countenance of educational evaluation. *Teachers College Record, 68,* 523–540.

Stiglitz, J. E. (2010). *Freefall.* New York, NY: W. W. Norton.

Williamson, O. E. (1985). *The economic institutions of capitalism: Firms, markets, and relational contracting.* New York, NY: Free Press.

16

MAKING THE WORLD A BETTER PLACE THROUGH EVALUATION

Jennifer C. Greene

How did I get interested and involved in evaluation? What commitments and aspirations do I have for my evaluation practice? What is my evaluation story? In the next few pages, I have the distinct privilege and honor of answering these questions through considered self-reflection and autobiographical narrative.

TWO SNAPSHOTS FROM THE PRESENT

Snapshot 1

With the superb collaboration of several cohorts of graduate students,[1] I am currently (spring of 2011) finishing 7 years of research on a particular way of thinking about and doing evaluation. This research was funded by the U.S. National Science Foundation and included an initial 2-year conceptual phase and then several years of field testing our ideas in contexts involving the evaluation of science, technology, engineering, and mathematics (STEM) educational programs. We awkwardly label this constellation of evaluation ideas a "values-engaged, educative" approach to evaluation, which has no catchy acronym.[2] An excerpt from our synthesis of this work follows (Greene et al., 2011, pp. 3–5):

> Our work addresses . . . the need for evaluation approaches and strategies that can meaningfully contribute to the enhancement of STEM educational excellence *and* equity. Our response to this need is a values-engaged, educative approach to STEM education evaluation. This approach draws from responsive (Stake, 1973, 2004) and democratic (House & Howe, 1999) traditions in evaluation and, as such, it emphasizes particular evaluative purposes, commitments, processes, and evaluator roles, rather than particular designs and methodologies.
>
> Distinctively, our values-engaged, educative evaluation approach foregrounds explicit attention to the values that permeate all evaluation contexts, with particular attention to the *inclusion* of multiple perspectives and interests in a given STEM education project and to the project's success in advancing *equity* of access, experience, and accomplishment for all learners, particularly those from underrepresented groups. All evaluation approaches serve to promote some set of values, as evaluation is inherently about making judgments of value based on selected criteria of quality. We believe evaluative value commitments in evaluation should be explicit. And following others in the democratic tradition of evaluation, we believe that evaluation can most justifiably promote an engagement with democratic values, specifically in this approach, inclusiveness of multiple and diverse stakeholder views, and equity of participant access, experience, and accomplishment. Our commitment to engaging with equity is offered in direct support of NSF's longstanding commitment to diversity.
>
> This approach also privileges the evaluative purpose of learning, in this case, learning by diverse stakeholders about the logics, underlying assumptions, values, and plurality of experiences that are engaged in the project being evaluated. This educative purpose well complements our focus on values-engagement.

Snapshot 2

I am currently (2011) serving as the president of the American Evaluation Association (AEA), a once-in-a-lifetime honor and experience. The theme I have identified for the year and the conference is "values and valuing in evaluation." This theme is described in the February 2011 president's newsletter column, offered below with minor editing.

> Greetings AEA colleagues,
>
> What does evaluation have to do with momentous world events? Actually, a lot in my view. I believe that most evaluators are committed to making our world a better place. With quiet insistence, we work for the critical role of data and reason in
>
> *(Continued)*

> (Continued)
>
> decision making. With steady persistence, we search for quality and meaning in the policies and programs we assess. And with these shared values, we strive for a presence at the decision table.
>
> The call for proposals for AEA 2011 is now out, and the theme is *Values and Valuing in Evaluation!* Please do submit a proposal and join me in continuing conversations about our values, both shared and distinct, in Anaheim next fall. As suggested by this theme, I believe that values permeate the practical work of evaluators, and they do so in at least three major ways. First, the contexts in which we work—in particular, the socio-political, economic, and cultural diversity of stakeholder interests and perspectives—are rich in varied value commitments. These varied values get incorporated into our work through such evaluation components as the purpose and audience for the evaluation, the key questions to be addressed, and *especially* the criteria to be used to make judgments of program quality. Second, our technical evaluation designs and methodologies themselves carry along particular values, as do different evaluation approaches—for example, contrast the values advanced in a utilization-focused evaluation and an accountability-oriented evaluation. Third, the role of evaluation in society, and the evaluator's responsibilities for that role, offer further opportunities and challenges related to values and valuing in our work. These dimensions of values in evaluation practice are all transmitted, of course, through each of our own value systems and evaluation commitments. Self-reflection and respectful dialogue with others are key means by which we gain insight and purpose into our own thinking.
>
> The major values shaping our conversations in Anaheim will be civility and respect. So send in your proposals by March 18th (almost springtime)!
>
> With appreciation,
>
> Jennifer Greene

Where did my current evaluation commitments to values-engagement and to evaluation as an educative practice come from? What are their roots? Next, I will offer my best insights about critical formative influences on my thinking, beginning with my profound commitment to evaluation as an opportunity for meaningful, catalytic, consequential learning.

EDUCATION: FAMILY, FREIRE, THE 1960s, AND LEE CRONBACH

My commitment to education as a force for good *and* as the most powerful catalyst for democracy and social change in the world is rooted in my parents' beliefs and actions. School was a top priority in my family's life as far back as my memory permits. Many dinner conversations were devoted to "interesting things" that had happened at school that day. My father was president of the town's school board when I was in high school. And school increasingly became the epicenter of *my* life as I moved through adolescence and beyond.

I studied psychology in college, a major filled with midnight shifts on a chick imprinting study and endless hours of operant conditioning of pigeons to peck a key on cue. More significantly, I was studying these remnants of behaviorism in the midst of the revolutionary 1960s in the United States, a time of protest against war and corporate greed (aka, the military industrial complex) and a time of social movements for civil rights and a healthy planet. (Who else remembers Rachel Carson's *The Silent Spring*, 1962?) My political conscience was awakened during this heady time of social unrest and personal disequilibrium, and it has barely snoozed since then. I became committed to a life of some consequence, anchored in the activist Eldridge Cleaver's mantra: "If you are not part of the solution, then you are part of the problem."[3]

I decided to pursue an advanced degree, mainly because I so very much enjoyed being a student, which had been a safe and secure identity for me since childhood. But studying more psychology did not excite the passion I needed to succeed (or even persist) in graduate school. My understanding of psychology at that time did not encompass the real-world consequentiality I was beginning to require of my life's work. Then, I read Paulo Freire's *Pedagogy of the Oppressed* (1970), the now foundational bible of liberation educational philosophy. "Of course!" I realized, also remembering my parents. Being an educator offers profound opportunities to make a difference in the world, albeit on a slow timeline. And off I went to more years as a student, studying educational psychology.

It was in graduate school that I first bumped into the field of evaluation. I had the incredible privilege of taking two evaluation courses with Lee Cronbach, one a theory course and one a practicum in which the class evaluated an on-campus interdisciplinary program in "values, technology, and society." As the world knows, Cronbach was a brilliant thinker, at the leading edge of many methodological developments in the latter part of the 20th century, including internal consistency reliability, construct validity, generalizability theory, and envisioning evaluation as a fundamentally educative practice. In a book that was published after I completed my graduate studies—but that has since become embedded in my evaluation soul—Cronbach and his associates (1980) positioned evaluation as a practice by which society could learn about the character of its most persistent problems *and* about promising ideas to address them. Of the book's 95 theses, 3 are as follows:

1. The evaluator is an educator; his (or her) success is to be judged by what others learn.

2. Program evaluation is a process by which society learns about itself.

3. Program evaluation should contribute to enlightened discussion of alternative plans for social action.

(Please also see the chapter "The Educative Evaluator: An Interpretation of Lee J. Cronbach's Vision of Evaluation" by Jennifer C. Greene, this volume.)

These are then the roots of my commitment to evaluation as a fundamentally educative practice, as an opportunity for data-informed reflections on the sensibility of a program's logic and the power of its design to reach desired outcomes. Among the multiple legitimate roles and purposes for evaluation in society today presented in Table 16.1, my educative roots are best captured by the middle row, representing Cronbach's influential legacies. I also position myself in the final two rows, a story to which I will now turn.

Table 16.1 Major Evaluation Purposes and Audiences

Purpose	Key Audiences
Inform policy and decision making	Policy and decision makers
Provide accountability	Funders (taxpayers), managers
Learn more about persistent social problems and how best to address them → enlighten the policy conversation	The "policy-shaping community" (Cronbach & Associates, 1980)
Enhance contextual program understanding, improve the program, and contribute to organizational learning	On-site program administrators and staff
Democratize decision making	Program beneficiaries and their communities

BECOMING VALUES-ENGAGED: A CHRONICLE OF ENLIGHTENMENT

As revealed in the opening snapshots of this chapter, in the present, I am fully committed to surfacing and meaningfully engaging with the values that permeate evaluation contexts and evaluation practice. But this wasn't always so. In fact, I started in a very different place.

At the Beginning

My first tenure-track professorial job was at Cornell University in the early 1980s. My very first doctoral advisee was Bessa Whitmore, known to the evaluation community for her many contributions to our thinking about participatory evaluation (Whitmore, 1998). Bessa, just about 10 years my senior, is now retired from her professorship of social work at Carleton University in Ottawa, Ontario, Canada. She was then, and remains so today, deeply committed to social justice and to being and working in the world in service of greater justice. One of her retirement pursuits, for example, is membership in the Raging Grannies (http://raginggrannies.org/).

For her dissertation, Bessa wanted to do a participatory evaluation with youth. She wanted to do this to give youth a voice in matters pertaining to their own lives and also to study the potentialities of participatory evaluation for youth empowerment. Bessa's thinking about participatory inquiry was influenced by the participatory action research (PAR) traditions originating in international development research.[4] My initial reaction to Bessa's dissertation ideas was something like the following: "Well, if you are really interested in empowerment, then you should go on over to community development and urban studies. They do empowerment work over there. The field of study in this department is about evaluation. And evaluation is mostly about good method, defensible inferences, and learning something worthwhile from the study." This characterization came directly from my graduate studies, which had emphasized the central role of good method in educational research, and I had transferred that lesson to my evaluation thinking and practice. More broadly, evaluation was at that time—and arguably remains so today, at least in the United States—a method-driven field. Although today we have a rich repertoire of legitimate approaches to evaluation, we seem to find it hard to give up our methodological quarrels.

But Bessa is nothing if not determined and persistent, and persist she did, with me trailing along behind. Bessa conceptualized and implemented a very fine local participatory evaluation with youth, related to changing some rules and regulations at the high school, as I recall. The youth got to present their work to the principal of the school, which was in and of itself an empowering experience. And among the most significant of Bessa's findings was the importance of the unintended effects of this experience for the youth, effects in the social and relational domains so central to adolescence.

I was indeed a follower in my very first doctoral research supervisory experience. But the seeds were sown. I, perhaps grudgingly, learned that good method and social justice are not inherently in tension (although see Greene, 1990). And I began to ponder the implications of this insight for my own work.

The ideas of two additional senior evaluation scholars were also significant influences on the evolution of my evaluative thinking about values in evaluation.

Thank You to Egon Guba

Egon Guba is well-known in the evaluation and qualitative research communities for his revolutionary advancement of the legitimacy of constructivist methodologies in the social sciences and his ideologically motivated responsive evaluation theory, both developed in partnership with his wife, Yvonna Lincoln. Guba died a few years ago, and I wish to make my points about his influence on the evolution of my evaluative thinking about values by sharing a few excerpts (with a few minor edits) from one tribute I wrote for him on his death (Greene, 2008), titled "Tribute to Egon Guba: Memories of a Novice, Learning From a Master."

> Egon was a pivotal influence on my own development as a scholar. During my critically formative years as a scholar-practitioner in the field of evaluation, I met Egon Guba, who I knew as a leader in the advancement of qualitative methods. At that time, I was an avid observer of the "great qualitative-quantitative debate" and was struggling to make sense of it and to learn enough to participate. Recall that most social and educational inquirers in my generation learned only about the "proper methods properly applied." So all of the fuss about alternative methods and about these mysterious scientific paradigms was not obviously sensible or understandable to young inquirers like me. Egon took some interest in me and strongly encouraged me to pursue serious learning of qualitative methods. Egon encouraged my own exponential growth in qualitative methodologies most powerfully by asking me to participate in two conferences on qualitative methods.
>
> *(Continued)*

> (Continued)
>
> One was Egon's "paradigm dialogue" conference, held in San Francisco in 1989.[5] This conference was in an important sense Egon's farewell to the field—he retired shortly thereafter. It was organized around three paradigms—post-positivism, constructivism, and critical theory. There were keynote speakers for each paradigm—Dennis Phillips, Yvonna Lincoln, and Tom Popkewitz, respectively. Then, there were about 10 issue papers, on topics like criteria for judging quality, implementation, values, and ethics, presented by a selected speaker with one or two selected discussants. Egon asked me to do the issue paper on knowledge accumulation. I said I didn't know enough to do that. He assured me I did. I assured him I did not. He didn't back down, however, and I eventually agreed to do it, but only with enormous trepidation and anxiety and hours and hours and hours of work. But I did write and present the paper and was present at the conference.
>
> And this was an enormously influential event in my own career trajectory. The conference was wonderfully dynamic and exciting, full of talk of realism and idealism, objectivity, and subjectivity, emic and etic perspectives. The issues engaged were ones I hadn't really studied in graduate school, again because there was only one methodology to learn at that time. And I loved learning about these issues. I struggled to understand them in their philosophical form, but especially liked thinking about them in their practical form, in terms of how these new ways of thinking about inquiry, knowledge, and values could work in my own inquiry practice.
>
> The encouragement and guidance of Egon Guba were indeed pivotal in my career, for which I feel profoundly grateful and deeply indebted. I think we all routinely underestimate the importance of our mentors along the way. Thank you, Egon.

So the qualitative revolution and the actuality of a values-committed stance for evaluators—a stance in which values are prominent and important—were enormous influences on my own intellectual development and evaluative thinking. I was still quite uncertain about how to do this, or when and where to do it, but a vast arena of possibilities had opened up with these revolutions in thought among major leaders of the field.

And Then, Along Comes Ernie House

Ernest House's contributions to the field of evaluation, and to the development of my own evaluation thinking, are just as deep and profound as those of my earlier mentors—Cronbach and Guba—though experienced from a greater distance. For a number of years, I knew Ernie only through his books and articles, but his ideas about the politics of evaluation and of methodology resonated well with my growing understanding of evaluation as a social and political, and not just technical, practice.

Ernie's contributions to evaluation have long championed social justice, based on John Rawls's justice theory. In his early 1980 book, *Evaluating With Validity*, Ernie arrayed extant evaluation approaches in a table, along a core vertical dimension of who was the primary evaluation audience and what were the values associated with an evaluation project that addressed the interests of that audience. At the top of the table were audiences of policy and decision makers, with associated values of efficiency and utility. At the bottom of the table were audiences of program participants, their families and communities, and associated values of social justice. The table thus offered a continuum of democratization for arraying evaluation approaches, and Ernie was one of the first evaluation theorists to imagine and then advocate for democratic approaches to evaluation (House, 1980).

Ernie continued his advancement of a democratic form of evaluation with a marvelous chapter on "Methodology and Justice" in his book *Professional Evaluation* (House, 1993). In this chapter, Ernie used historical examples to argue that values also penetrate our methodological choices and the data they generate. In social science, Ernie maintained, value neutrality is an illusion (House, 1993). Specifically in these works and those that followed (including the seminal book on democratic values in evaluation coauthored with the philosopher Kenneth Howe—House & Howe, 1999), Ernie has argued thus:

- Facts and values are not so neatly divided into separate piles, but rather, both are constitutive of most social phenomena.
- Values are an inevitable strand of social inquiry because social inquiry is a human activity. Values do not reside outside the domain of science but, rather, are inevitably integral to it—both in the substance of what is studied and in the method used.
- Values are particularly inherent in evaluation, as the central task of evaluation is judgment.
- So social research and evaluation inevitably advance some values and not others.
- Those most justifiably advanced are those of democracy—justice, equity, and inclusion.

These ideals and arguments appealed greatly to my own 1960s coming-of-age years and political sensibilities. They provided a direction for my emerging values-committed stance for evaluation. And they provided a challenge to my methodological training—where indeed do values show up in our methods? My adoption of the ideals and arguments of Ernie has only strengthened over time. And I have come to believe, paraphrasing Bob Dylan, "you are gonna have to serve somebody."

Ernie made one other argument that has been very influential in my thinking—one I probably repeat at least once a week in my classes and conversations with students. The argument is as follows. Evaluation is clearly influenced by its context, as the context shapes evaluation priorities, foci, resources. But evaluation, in turn, by its very character, serves to reconstitute that context in particular ways. These may be ways that maintain the status quo, or they may be ways that challenge the dominant thinking. Either way, there is a reciprocal influence between evaluation and its context, not just a one-way influence. So who are *you* gonna serve?

Reprise

From my very first doctoral student to major revolutionary theorists in our field, my journey of becoming a values-engaged and even values-committed evaluator has taken a long time. These influences serve to locate my evaluative thinking in the final row of Table 16.1, in which evaluation is explicitly positioned as a force for democracy. I now turn to one additional set of important influences on how I understand and practice evaluation, all related to the fourth row of Table 16.1.

RESPONSIVENESS, CULTURE, AND CONTEXT

Threaded throughout both my commitments to evaluation as an educative practice and to evaluation as a force for democracy is the central importance of context. Unlike most other social sciences, evaluation *only* takes place in the real world of people going about their business and their lives; there is no laboratory form of evaluation. So evaluation is importantly a *social* practice (Schwandt, 2005), in that it is enacted through interactions and relationships among particular people in particular contexts. And context matters. The character and impact of a given program differ from context to context. Moreover, an educative and democratic agenda for evaluation invokes the importance of responsiveness to context—attending to the specific character of the program in particular contexts and to the concerns and issues stakeholders in each context may have about the program and its evaluation.

I started learning about the importance of context before I learned much else (beyond graduate school) about evaluation. My first post-PhD job was in a small research and evaluation center at the University of Rhode Island, where much of our work constituted state-level programs funded by grants authorized by the federal Elementary and Secondary Education Act. I was the evaluator on a number of Title I (supplementary instruction in reading and math) and Title IV (innovative programs) grants. The state at that time had highly prescribed evaluation guidelines, including three reports a year (initial, implementation, and outcome), and standardized questions to address and metrics for reporting. As I traveled around this tiny state, I increasingly found the state's evaluation expectations not only overbearing but also of little sense, even for the same Title I program implemented in the small community of Woonsocket and in the larger and more urbanized Cranston. What I found much more meaningful and rewarding than the state's evaluation prescriptions was to meet the challenge of understanding, even if in just some small way, the unique educational character of each community in which I worked.

Responsive evaluation, in all of its countenances, thus constitutes another influence on my evaluation thinking and practice—but one that is more intertwined with the others than distinctively or separately demarcated in my mind. For example, inclusion is a democratic value advanced in Ernie's democratic evaluation theory. Inclusion is also valued in responsive evaluation, though more as populist pluralism than as advocacy for those on the margins. As another example, my embracing of interpretive and constructivist traditions for evaluation (alongside my continued regard for postpositivist traditions) gets confounded with support for responsive evaluation, as Bob Stake has advanced interpretivist case study methodology precisely as a means of being responsive in evaluation practice. Clearly, the substantial work of Stake—first remotely and now up close as a colleague—has permeated my evaluation thinking, from its values pluralism to its fundamental contextual responsiveness. I have further had the distinct privilege of having colleagues and friends among the developers and advocates of culturally and contextually responsive evaluation, notably including Melvin Hall, Stafford Hood, Rodney Hopson, and Veronica Thomas. Though still challenged to fully understand the cultural dimensions of context, I have come to believe that culture and context are fully intertwined and interlaced. So my continued ambition to understand context also requires a companion ambition to understand culture.

AND SO...

Thanks to all my mentors along the way, all those mentioned herein and all those not. This reflective adventure has been educative in itself, as well as a journey through time, geography, and friendships. My thanks to all who have been a part of this journey. What a ride!

NOTES

1. These include Jeehae Ahn, Ayesha Boyce, Amarachuku Enyia, Jori Hall, Jeremiah Johnson, Ezella McPherson, Maurice Samuels, and, for the conceptual phase, my colleague Lizanne DeStefano.
2. Earlier on, we named our approach an "educative, values-engaged" way of thinking about evaluation, which does have the catchy acronym of EVEN, an acronym that also substantively represents core commitments of the approach to the democratic ideals of equity and inclusion. But it became clear that the more distinctive feature of this evaluation approach is its values-engagement, so that is now placed first, but we are stuck with the awkward label until another catchy acronym appears.
3. This saying is often attributed to Cleaver, though the historical record is not completely clear on this.
4. At that time, this research was advanced by Orlando Fals-Borda and Rajesh Tandon, among others, and more currently by Robert Chambers and Irene Guijt, also among others.
5. These conference proceedings were edited by Guba and published in a 1990 book called *The Paradigm Dialog*.

REFERENCES

Carson, R. (1962). *The silent spring*. Boston, MA: Houghton Mifflin.

Cronbach, L. J., & Associates. (1980). *Toward reform of program evaluation*. San Francisco, CA: Jossey-Bass.

Freire, P. (1970). *Pedagogy of the oppressed*. New York, NY: Continuum International.

Greene, J. C. (1990). Technical quality versus user responsiveness in evaluation practice. *Evaluation and Program Planning, 13*, 267–274.

Greene, J. C. (2008). Memories of a novice, learning from a master. *American Journal of Evaluation, 29*(3), 322–324.

Greene, J. C., Ahn, J., Boyce, A., Hall, J. M., Johnson, J., & Samuels, M. (2011). *A values-engaged, educative approach to evaluating STEM education projects*. Urbana: University of Illinois at Urbana-Champaign.

Guba, E. G. (Ed.). (1990). *The paradigm dialog*. Newbury Park, CA: Sage.

House, E. R. (1980). *Evaluating with validity*. Beverly Hills, CA: Sage.

House, E. R. (1993). *Professional evaluation: Social impact and political consequences*. Newbury Park, CA: Sage.

House, E. R., & Howe, K. R. (1999). *Values in evaluation and social research*. Thousand Oaks, CA: Sage.

Schwandt, T. A. (2005). The centrality of practice to evaluation. *American Journal of Evaluation, 28*(1), 95–105.

Stake, R. E. (1973). *Program evaluation, particularly responsive evaluation*. Keynote presentation at a conference on "New Trends in Evaluation" at the Institute of Education at Göteborg University, Goteborg, Sweden. Retrieved from http://www.ed.uiuc.edu/circe/Publications/Responsive_Eval.pdf

Stake, R. E. (2004). *Standards-based and responsive evaluation*. Thousand Oaks, CA: Sage.

Whitmore, E. (Ed.). (1998). *New directions for evaluation: Vol. 80. Understanding and practicing participatory evaluation*. San Francisco, CA: Jossey-Bass.

☙ 17 ❧

THE ROOTS OF FOURTH GENERATION EVALUATION

Theoretical and Methodological Origins

Yvonna S. Lincoln and Egon G. Guba

As Alkin and Christie point out in their opening chapters to this volume, any classification schema of necessity emphasizes some characteristics and downplays others. This is true with virtually all of the classification and category systems that attempt to deal with evaluation models, theories, and paradigms (Madaus, Scriven, & Stufflebeam, 1983; Shadish, Cook, & Leviton, 1991; Stufflebeam, Madaus, & Kellaghan, 2000; Worthen & Sanders, 1987). Thus, we might argue that while some models are classified as accountability models and others as social inquiry models, each of these classifications relies heavily on definitions, that is, the question of to whom one is accountable or the question of whether all evaluation, focused as it is around social programs (in this instance, at least), is not a form of social inquiry. Thus, any given classification scheme relies heavily on definitions and theories regarding meaning. The meaning of terms—whether generalizability, use, users, stakeholders, decision makers, knowledge, values and valuing, effects, causes, even programs—is, as the poststructuralists, linguists, and philosophers tell us, constantly in play, constantly contested.

Since the meaning one adopts for terms is heavily dependent on the social theory or theories that guide the use of those terms, even those who use the same term, for example, *accountability*, may find that they imply very different standards for that accountability, vastly different audiences

---

Source: Excerpted from Lincoln, Y. S. & Guba, E. G. (2004). The roots of fourth generation evaluation: Theoretical and methodological origins. In M. C. Alkin (Ed.), *Evaluation roots*. Thousand Oaks, CA: Sage Publications.

(or an expanded sense of audiences), radically different political contexts (e.g., local, neighborhood contexts vs. national policy and funding contexts), and may be implying very different sorts of information needs and wishes for the different audiences. Consequently, the adoption of terms is a fragile, unstable, and highly value-laden enterprise in and of itself. Putting boundaries around terms is part and parcel of the utilization of a given model. Furthermore, since the last time we wrote in any extended way about evaluation as model, set of practices and discourses, or theoretical perspective, the evaluation world has become far more complex and more sophisticated (as well as more populous), and efforts to trace evaluation's historical antecedents, as well as capturing its lineages, have become a more ambitious undertaking for any author.

At the same time, the social sciences themselves (program evaluation included) have been shaped by the debates spilling over from literary theory and the arts, especially the critiques of the limits of knowledge, the criticisms of experimental science's appropriateness for social research, and political assaults on the gendered, classed, colonial, and perhaps raced nature of the scientific enterprise as practiced by Western scientists. As a result of these new theoretical and critical lenses, and their impact on the social sciences more broadly, we will try to demonstrate in a much clearer way than we have undertaken previously to show the roots of fourth generation, or constructivist, evaluation, and to make clear—to ourselves and to readers—what we believe to be our own roots.

As it turns out, this was a less facile task than we imagined when we agreed to the assignment. As we reread our own work (in the context of the work of others), we are struck with what we call "foreshadowing." Only dimly intuiting the meaning of this or that work, we nevertheless appear to have sensed its importance for the phenomenological and constructivist project. And so we ask ourselves, "Did we really say that? My, wasn't that smart!" It is, of course, impossible to know, at this distance, whether we were smart, more attuned to other theorists' work than we realized, or, more likely, part of a growing wellspring of interest in and theorizing about this critical social inquiry activity, one of many sources of fresh new ideas, practices, and discourses. Whatever the case, we now see linkages between our work and that of others that we were unable to see at the time or perhaps have interactively come into existence since that time.

In the same vein, we would firmly argue that fourth generation evaluation is equally about use, particularly who might use evaluation results and how users might deploy findings to effect change; about methods—at least to the extent that while we have never omitted quantitative methods from the arsenal of tools available to evaluators, we have contended strongly that an expanded repertoire of methods, including qualitative methods, serves evaluation practitioners more flexibly (Guba & Lincoln, 1981, 1989; Lincoln & Guba, 1985); and about valuing—especially the pluralistic values that different stakeholders bring to social and educational programs and the necessarily political context in which both programs and evaluations are mounted.

In fact, it is this multifocus approach that counteracts the somewhat narrower predelictions of some models (for instance, those that believe the only adequate way to test for effects is randomized controlled experimentation), whether their focus is decision makers and decision making, generalizability ("the production of knowledge," itself a value-laden phrase), causation, prediction, control, or accountability. That said, the basic outlines of fourth generation evaluation can be limned.

FOURTH GENERATION EVALUATION THEORY

Fourth generation, or constructivist, evaluation, builds upon the three previous eras of evaluation (Guba & Lincoln, 1989), incorporates elements of all three eras (e.g., description, judgment, an expanded range of stakeholders), and shifts the philosophical model that serves as the basis for evaluation practice. In this shift, the ontological base for conducting evaluation inquiry is expanded from that which is considered to be real in conventional inquiry (the physical, the tangible, the countable, and the numbers that abstractly represent those entities). Constructivist evaluation focuses equally strongly on the socially constructing, meaning-making, and meaning-deriving activities of stakeholders, based on the well-recognized principle of Gestalt psychologists that individuals will not act on what they are *told* is real, but on what they themselves believe to have personal or social meaning. The rebalancing of the ontological scales to include not only the tangible and the measurable but also the ascriptive meanings of stakeholders takes account of a major lacuna in social science philosophy since the early 20th century.

Constructivist evaluation (and inquiry more broadly; see Lincoln & Guba, 1985) also addresses, at the paradigmatic level, multiple questions in epistemology, particularly the issues of the subject-object dualism (and concomitant threats to validity so comprehensively outlined by Campbell & Stanley, 1963); the role of causality and the forms of causal statements possible in social science; the nature of possible truth statements; and the role of multiple ways of knowing—that is, experiencing—the world brought on by race, class, gender, historical, and embodied variations in human life.

The Subject-Object Conundrum

The epistemological concern labeled by philosophers the "subject-object dualism" (Hesse, 1980) has, quite simply, caused fits for social scientists who apply the methods of the natural, or hard, sciences to social inquiry for over a century. What is to be done with all those thinking, contemplating, scheming, possibly lying, and assuredly confused human subjects? How can we get them to tell the truth, the whole truth, and nothing but the truth? Deception, containment, isolation (in laboratories, for example), correction, deep familiarity with the seemingly endless threats to validity, and reliability estimates seemed the major ways around the possibility that humans were unable to give social scientists straight answers to serious scientific questions. The phenomenological and hermeneutic metaphysics of constructivism answered the problem more straightforwardly for those willing to abandon conventional research axioms in evaluation practice. Rather than constructing respondents and stakeholders as deceptive and/or confused, fourth generation evaluators approach stakeholders as though they engage in meaning-making, sense-making (Weick, 1995) activities as a part of daily life, and that furthermore, those sense-making activities themselves are of deep interest to program evaluators, since they shape and maintain behaviors and activities.

Thus, rather than see the interaction effects of human dialogue as threats to validity, fourth generation evaluators take the interactions as opportunities to observe and understand how individuals and groups of stakeholders make meaning of their "lived experience" (Turner & Bruner, 1986) and, possibly, why. In an expanded epistemology (to which we would now assent), the roles of teacher and learner are constantly intertwined in the evaluation process. Evaluators teach stakeholders what kinds of information needs are critical to the evaluation effort from the perspective of program managers and funders; subsequently, stakeholders teach evaluators which kinds of claims, concerns, and issues are most critical for their needs to be met. This trading of roles may continue for most of the evaluation effort, as data are collected, analyzed, and assessed for their appropriateness in answering the questions and addressing the issues of all stakeholders.

Causality: The Chains That Bind

Since the putative object of scientific inquiry is the acquisition of sufficient empirical knowledge of some phenomenon to be able to predict and control its behavior accurately, questions of causality and causal inferences dominate discussions of program evaluation. Particularly in the arena of school reform, "What works?" becomes a paramount theme in the struggle to create a new kind of school that can virtually guarantee "success for all." The imputation of causal chains, however, suggests a stability of social circumstance, an invariability of necessarily shifting social landscapes, that are virtually impossible to achieve. Because of the problems inherent with applying linear causality concepts to nonlinear human dynamics, constructivists typically opt for a concept borrowed from physics, biological ecology, and catastrophe mathematics: mutual causality. Things happen *in the presence of* certain other events, but not necessarily *on account of* those things, events, and so on. Mutual causation suggests that events or persons are not linked sequentially, but rather are interpenetrating and arrayed in a dynamic, changing complex that may be altered via any number of actors exhibiting intentionalities of one sort or another. The metaphor often preferred for this more circular form of causal theory is the spiderweb, a multiuse organic vehicle for signaling danger, capturing food, staking out territory, and managing reproduction. Put more simply, mutual causality (or causation) implies that events transpire in the neighborhood of other, related events, but that linear causality is therefore not a necessary conclusion; rather, the sufficient conclusion is that events may be related within some complex pattern. Causality itself is not assumed, but when ascriptions are made, causality need not be temporally precedent with an event or circumstance; it may be simultaneous or antecedent to the event.

For the practicing evaluator, the implication is that the search for the causes of particular outcomes will always remain problematic, uncertain, and lacking in any meaningful reliability statistic.

What Is Truth?

Constructivists concern themselves with truth statements as systematically as conventional evaluators but are much more cautious about how those truth statements are framed. The search for generalizability—some set of law-like principles that contribute to the project of prediction and control—is largely thought to be a unicorn hunt for the constructivist. Even Lee J. Cronbach (1975), in his presidential address to the American Psychological Association, suggested that the possibility of meaningful generalizability in social and human inquiry might be a profitless venture and offered instead the more realistic proposal that inquiry around social life produce a set of "working hypotheses." These working hypotheses should be considered more time bound, change imminent, and culture conditioned than any generalization could be. Consequently, the constructivist fourth generation evaluator offers findings frequently parried with cautions about how these findings may not be generalizable or meaningful outside this context. Truth is taken directly from stakeholder experience (with evaluator experience, of course, through which it may be filtered) and assumes some of the evanescence and transitoriness of all human experience. In the minds of constructivist evaluators, truth is greatly constrained by the time, context, and particular experiences of the stakeholding community that generated it.

This does not mean, of course, that we have no knowledge worth having or that it is impossible to "translate" what is learned in one context to another, similar context. Knowledge is delightfully portable as well as transportable. What it does mean, however, is that isomorphism—the one-to-one correspondence between contexts or populations that permits generalization—is likely a lost cause; there is little hope of finding two social contexts that are exactly, precisely the same in every respect or even sufficiently to assure that in toto transport of a program will work. Since the "template" (blueprint, cookie-cutter) model of social experimentation is so vulnerable to local adaptation, generalization becomes a weak, rather than a robust, goal of program evaluation. Findings coupled with intense, deep, "thick" description better serve the purposes of science when stakeholders will simply not refrain from making a good program work better *in their own particular, unique, and local contexts.*

Do Different "Knowers" "Know" Differently?

There is a growing body of evidence to suggest that science is, at best, a classed activity and at worst, an expression of gender concerns, race consciousness, and (judging from the critiques of scholars of developing and formerly colonized nations) perhaps even a uniquely "colonial" activity. Feminist theorists, race and ethnic studies theorists, postcolonial theorists, critical theorists, postmodern and poststructural theorists, border/*la frontera*/liminal theorists, and other critics of the sociology and philosophy of science have advanced a number of trenchant arguments surrounding what is loosely called the "modernist project." Chief among the criticisms is that scientific method dreams of a disembodied knower, transcendentally disinterested, factually objective, undisturbed by the mundane concerns of gender, race, class, or bodily experience of the world. Such an individual, these theorists argue, has never been born on this earth.

Rather than a disembodied epistemology being attached to the science project, these theorists suggest, would we not be clearer about the claims and aims of research if we conceded that our epistemologies proceed from *standpoints?* These standpoints represent the largely hidden, but still critical, influences of our social locations: our races, our genders, our class statuses, our ethnicities, linguistic experiences, educational backgrounds—in short, our identities.

Constructivist evaluators recognize and honor the process by which stakeholders speak from their social locations and try to make transparent their own social locations as well as the concerns and issues that bring them to this particular evaluation effort, this particular contract, this particular funding opportunity, this unique program. Even though we cannot have perfect knowledge and should be extremely suspicious of those who claim to have it or to be able to produce it, the partial perspectives of our situated epistemologies and standpoints are still extremely worthwhile (Richardson, 2000). The recognition that among other things, race, socioeconomic class, educational status, gender, and national origin or extraction shape what it is we know, how we know it, and how we frame that knowledge when we share it with others is part and parcel of the experience of a more limited and fallible, but also more realistic, program evaluation theory.

Fourth generation evaluation is equally clear about its axiological position in the metaphysics of phenomenology. While conventional inquirers and evaluation practitioners claim to engage in scientific activity that is value-free, constructivist evaluators recognize that science is not an inerrant command of some invisible hand. It is, rather, a distinctly human project and consequently infused with human values. (Indeed, as many philosophers of science like to point out, the claim to value-freedom is itself a values statement [see, for instance, Hesse, 1980], the purpose of which is to obscure the values and social locations and standpoints that lie behind the choice of a problem, the choice of a paradigm, the choice of guiding theory, the choice of research site, and the choice of methods, among other expressions of values.) The possibility of scientific objectivity has undergone extensive critique (Brodbeck, 1968; Dahrendorf, 1973; MacIntyre, 1971; Myrdal, 1970; Rex, 1970) and been largely dismissed by serious philosophers and sociologists of science; what remains of the claims appears to represent a kind of scientific "security blanket" for what Knorr-Cetina (1999) has termed "the sacerdotal priesthood of science," a group of knowledge-producing elites who use such claims to establish dominance and legitimacy in the "knowledge industry."

A calm acceptance of the assertion that doing science is a human activity permits the realization that the likelihood is that it is also permeated with human values, expressed in many different ways (see, for instance, Lincoln & Guba, 1985, for a catalogue of the more conscious value decisions that social scientists and evaluators make with every project undertaken). Constructivist evaluators take these values as historical givens, to be explored for their logical means and ends and to be recreated in more thoughtful, sophisticated, and informed ways via the collection and analysis of data in an evaluation effort. That is, value allegiance should, as a result of a constructivist evaluation conducted fairly, thoroughly, and openly, become more conscious and more deliberative as a consequence of the inputs of data and interpretations from all stakeholders.

Constructivists, finally, are more self-conscious regarding the methodological and design strategies they employ. Methodology, like ontology, epistemology, and axiology, joins an integrated set of foundational assumptions (a philosophy, a paradigm, a model) regarding how best to proceed to garner the knowledge deemed most valuable and most worth having. While some kinds of data are best gathered through measuring, surveying, counting, or weighing, other kinds of data can be accessed only via qualitative tools. The social constructions—the sense-making mechanisms humans use to order their existence—can only be collected via observational, documentary, and interviewing tools. We will not know in any accurate, rigorous, or reasonably thorough sense what people think or how they make sense of programs, personnel, or activities until we ask them to tell us about their thinking and meaning-imputing processes.

As a consequence, the constructivist evaluator relies as heavily on qualitative methods as on quantitative methods. Please notice that while some individuals think that constructivist evaluation or research is *about* qualitative methods or utilizes *only* qualitative methods, this is quite simply not true, at least as we have "constructed" the paradigm or understood phenomenology. Naturalistic and constructivist evaluators utilize whatever methods best collect the data that answer one or another specific question. Sometimes, that question may require qualitative methods, as when we wish to know how people make sense of programs mounted on their behalf. Other times, we may need to know pre- and posttest scores, as when we are evaluating the efficacy of various elementary school mathematics curricula. It is our contention that constructivist evaluation utilizes whatever data have authentic meaning for the question at hand, whether qualitative or quantitative. The real differences in models are in the set of beliefs which evaluators bring to the project about what are "real" data, what are "hard" data, and what are "meaningful" data. Depending on the question which is being posed, either qualitative or quantitative data may provide the best insight into the answer. But neither method is superior or "better science" than the other.

Procedures for Conducting Fourth Generation, Constructivist Evaluations

Because constructivist evaluators begin with a different set of assumptions from conventional evaluators, they proceed, in a design sense, slightly differently. Rather than generate a priori and rather inflexible designs (that are frequently adhered to even when the assumptions cannot any longer be met), constructivist evaluators assume that they do not know everything that they do not know. Consequently, it is appropriate to "leave space" in the design for a highly exploratory stage, where purposive, theoretical sampling of the *maximum variation* variety is deployed, to discover the full range of constructions around a program from as large a range of stakeholders as can be solicited to join the evaluation effort. Once theoretical saturation—redundant information begins to show up, and no new information is uncovered—is achieved, then evaluators can be fairly certain they can "map" the full range of claims, concerns, and issues. At this point, a hermeneutic, dialectic process is engaged that permits evaluators to lay out for all stakeholders the full range of issues, point out the value conflicts that inhere in some of those issues (i.e., these issues are positions about which perfectly reasonable people might disagree), and prepare for some nomination from all stakeholding groups of which issues are likely the most critical to pursue. Please note, however, some or all of these same issues may or may not be responsive to the *objectives* of the program.

If evaluating along the domains of the objectives is critical to funders or program managers, the evaluation team will need to point that out to all stakeholding groups from the start. The "mapping" process, however, is designed to uncover those "unintended side effects" of which

Scriven (1973) spoke so forcefully. It is what we (personally) term the "Westinghouse Head Start" problem: Evaluating solely along the domains of objectives permits blindness to other critical social goals being sought or achieved.

Once nominations are sought for the top critical concerns or issues (since rarely can an evaluation effort manage the time or money to consider all the issues and concerns raised), then additional illuminative data are sought on those specific issues; and once data gaps have been filled, stakeholders are brought back into the loop to make determinations about changes in the program, redirections that appear to be important, midcourse corrections, and/or abandonment of the program in favor of something more successful. Virtually without exception, some of the data will involve value conflicts between stakeholder groups, and these value conflicts must be negotiated (sometimes by an evaluator, sometimes by other skilled negotiators and mediators outside the evaluation effort), often before final decision making about programs can take place.

During the evaluation effort, all stakeholder groups are kept informed about the claims, concerns, and issues nominated by other groups. Using what Stake called "portrayals," various aspects of the program are displayed, explained, explored from multiple perspectives, and stakeholders invited to comment or elaborate upon, correct, amend, extend, or otherwise make more accurate or precise the information, data, or interpretations. Unlike the situation in many conventional evaluations, there is no closely guarded set of findings; rather, stakeholders have access to a wide variety of information types and a rich array of interpretations and meanings that they and other stakeholders attach to the data. This access to information and to interpretations from other stakeholding groups creates a strong information base for all participants and, in so doing, permits more sophisticated and informed, as well as more highly participatory, decision making around some program or evaluand. Openness and transparency in evaluation processes prevents the synoptic, "managerially cozy" contracts where many or most stakeholding groups are primarily kept in the dark regarding findings, whether positive or negative.

The constant interaction around data is what makes this model hermeneutic. Such interaction creates new knowledge, and permits old or taken-for-granted knowledge to be elaborated, refined, and tested. The dialectic of this evaluation model is the focus on carefully bringing to the fore the conflict inherent in value pluralism. Unlike more conventional models of evaluation, constructivist, fourth generation evaluation assumes that social life is rife with value pluralism and, therefore, conflict. A critical part of the evaluation effort within this model involves getting at core values of participants and stakeholders, so that when decisions are made, the value commitments that those decisions represent are clear, negotiable, and negotiated between and among stakeholders.

OLD FRIENDS, BOOKENDS: INFLUENCES AND BUILDING BLOCKS

It is not always possible to see precisely where, and when, or even how, one's ideas shifted. In some instances, ideas shifted, leaned, edged toward some attractive and interesting idea. In other instances, ideas from others came like thunderbolts, changing thinking overnight. It is nearly impossible to assess, even at this distance, the power—intellectual and conceptual power—or the influence of two groups early on the development of evaluation models: the May 12th group and the Evaluation Network. The May 12th group met around that date every year. Its membership was a "floating crapshoot," consisting of whomever the individual who agreed to be host decided to invite, although the program evaluation community was so small in the late 1960s and early 1970s that virtually everyone who was writing about evaluation could be invited and accommodated comfortably. The ideas shared informally during that 2- to 3-day period shaped, we expect, all of us in ways we have never sorted out.

In the same way, the earliest professional evaluation groups—the Evaluation Network and the Evaluation Research Society (which later merged membership to become the American Evaluation Association)—were also crucibles for new ideas, new proposed models, and new ways of undertaking evaluation activities. In those two settings, problems were proposed, advice was offered, and when the Network was still young and small, many informal groups coalesced to discuss particular interests, experiences, and evaluation settings.

The major contributors to fourth generation's development came from those groups and those interactions. Stake's push beyond program funders and managers to suggest that "stakeholder" needed to be more broadly defined provided one defining moment in this development. It was a clearly liberal principle, deeply rooted in democratic ideals of community decision processes and procedures. When combined with the stinging critique of Michael Scriven's "managerial coziness," it helped pave the way to an enlargement of the audiences and aims of evaluation practice. Barry MacDonald's writing on democratic evaluation, along with the work of the East Anglia CARE group, when coupled with Malcolm Parlett's early writing on illuminative evaluation, gave some focus to the growing conception that evaluation processes should be open, available, data- and description-rich, as accessible to ordinary stakeholders as it was to managers and funders. The notion of democracy playing out in the evaluation arena as much as it should in everyday civic life was seen—and still is, in some quarters—as an odd if not treacherous principle for a form of social inquiry, the modernist roots of which suggest disinterest rather than serious considerations of political theory or philosophy.

Additional and more recent influences to our evaluation theorizing include the profound theoretical tides of literary theory, postmodernism, poststructuralism, critical theory, and identity politics, as well as feminist, race and ethnic, border/liminal, postcolonial, and identity politics critiques of social science. Like waves breaking on a beach, these critiques wash over the domain of conventional Western social science, slowly erasing its dominance for women, for persons of color, and for indigenous peoples. These powerful new criticisms of conventional social science and new formulations for conducting more socially meaningful inquiry and evaluation permit increased sensitivity to the concerns of those traditionally left voiceless in Western social science. The criticisms themselves portend both a more pluralistic and socially aware evaluation practice and, at the same time, a succession of models more inclusive, more democratic, than those deployed by traditional experimental practitioners. We would make this prediction despite the National Research Council's recent report advocating "evidence-based research," which is coded text for experimental and largely (although not exclusively) quantitative methods.

In any event, the newer theoretical formulations have influenced our work and the work of others in both implicit and explicit ways, and have moved some practitioners to rethink practices that enhance social justice and practices that serve to limit it.

A final comment is appropriate here. We have likely misunderstood to no small extent the manner in which evaluation practice is pursued today, but it would appear to us that there are two communities engaged in evaluation at the current moment. One community, which early on declared itself the true scientists, continues to deploy experimental and quasi-experimental designs and to treat whole groups of citizens as control groups in vast social experiments. In some instances, for example, medicine or epidemiology, this might well be appropriate. Another group, however, practices alongside this group. In the second community of evaluation specialists, practitioners attempt to remain conscious of the value pluralism that marks American life, and they tend to engage larger questions of political and social theory in their practice, particularly with respect to issues of social justice, democratic values, and the equitable distribution of goods and services. The second community will continue to practice evaluation informed by democratic social theory and a Western liberal tradition, we would suspect, even as the first community will continue claiming they are the only true practitioners of real science. The evaluation community more broadly might be considerably informed by a serious and more authentic dialogue between these two communities of practice, although such a dialogue seems in the far future. Meanwhile, consumers and contractors of evaluations have many choices among models and practices. Choosing a contractor might well be as problematic as living with evaluation findings.

REFERENCES

Abma, T. A. (1997). Sharing power, facing ambiguity. In R. E. Stake & L. Mabry (Eds.), *Advances in program evaluation: Evaluation and the postmodern dilemma* (pp. 105–120). Greenwich, CT: JAI.

Brodbeck, M. (Ed.). (1968). *Readings in the philosophy of the social sciences.* New York: Macmillan.

Campbell, D. T. (1988). *Methodology and epistemology for social science: Selected papers.* E. Samuel Overman (Ed.). Chicago: University of Chicago Press.

Campbell, D. T., & Stanley, J. C. (1963). *Experimental and quasi-experimental design for research.* Chicago: Rand McNally.

Cronbach, L. J. (1975). Beyond the two disciplines of scientific psychology. *American Psychologist, 30,* 116–127.

Dahrendorf, R. (1973). *Homo sociologicus.* Dusseldorf, Germany: Westdeutscher Verlag.

Greene, J., Lincoln, Y., Mathison, S., Mertens, D., & Ryan, K. E. (1998). Advantages and challenges of using inclusive evaluation approaches in evaluation practice. *Evaluation Practice, 19*(1), 101–122.

Guba, E. G., & Lincoln, Y. S. (1981). *Effective evaluation.* San Francisco: Jossey-Bass.

Guba, E. G., & Lincoln, Y. S. (1989). *Fourth generation evaluation.* Newbury Park, CA: Sage.

Hamilton, D., MacDonald, B., King, C., Jenkins, D., & Parlett, M. (Eds.). (1977). *Beyond the numbers game: A reader in educational evaluation.* Berkeley, CA: McCutcheon.

Hesse, M. (1980). *Revolutions and reconstructions in the philosophy of science.* Bloomington: Indiana University Press.

House, E. R., & Howe, K. R. (2000). Deliberative democratic evaluation in practice. In D. L. Stufflebeam, G. F. Madaus, & T. Kellaghan (Eds.), *Evaluation models: Viewpoints on educational and human services evaluation* (pp. 409–421). Boston: Kluwer.

House, E. R., & Howe, K. R. (2003). Deliberative democratic evaluation. In T. Kellaghan, D. L. Stufflebeam, & L. Wingate (Eds.), *International handbook of educational evaluation, Part One* (pp. 79–101). Dordrecht, Netherlands: Kluwer.

Kaplan, A. (1964). *The conduct of inquiry: Methodology for behavioral science.* Scranton, PA: Chandler.

Knorr-Cetina, K. (1999). *Epistemic cultures: How the sciences make knowledge.* Cambridge, MA: Harvard University Press.

Lincoln, Y. S. (2003a). Constructivist knowing, participatory ethics and responsive evaluation: A model for the 21st century. In T. Kellaghan, D. L. Stufflebeam, & L. A. Wingate (Eds.), *International handbook of educational evaluation, Part One* (pp. 69–78). Dordrecht, Netherlands: Kluwer.

Lincoln, Y. S. (2003b). Fourth generation evaluation in the new millennium. In S. I. Donaldson & M. Scriven (Eds.), *Evaluating social programs and problems: Visions for the new millennium* (pp. 77–90). Mahwah, NJ: Erlbaum.

Lincoln, Y. S., & Guba, E. G. (1985). *Naturalistic inquiry.* Beverly Hills, CA: Sage.

MacIntyre, A. (1971). *Against the self-images of the age.* London: Duckworth.

Madaus, G. F., Scriven, M., & Stufflebeam, D. L. (Eds.). (1983). *Evaluation models: Viewpoints on educational and human services evaluation.* Boston: Kluwer-Nijhoff.

Mertens, D. M. (2003). The inclusive view of evaluation: Visions for the new millennium. In S. I. Donaldson & M. Scriven (Eds.), *Evaluating social programs and problems: Visions for the new millennium* (pp. 91–108). Mahwah, NJ: Erlbaum.

Myrdal, G. (1970). *Objectivity in social research.* London: Duckworth.

Rex, J. (1970). *Key problems of sociological theory.* London: Routledge & Kegan Paul.

Richardson, L. (2000). Writing as a method of inquiry. In N. K. Denzin & Y. S. Lincoln (Eds.), *Handbook of qualitative research* (2nd ed., pp. 923–948). Thousand Oaks, CA: Sage.

Schwandt, T. A. (1997). Whose interests are being served? Program evaluation as a conceptual practice of power. In R. E. Stake & L. Mabry (Eds.), *Advances in program evaluation: Evaluation and the postmodern dilemma* (Vol. 3, pp. 89–104). Greenwich, CT: JAI.

Scriven, M. (1973). Goal-free evaluation. In E. R. House (Ed.), *School evaluation: The politics and process* (pp. 319–328). Berkeley, CA: McCutcheon.

Shadish, W. R. Jr., Cook, T. D., & Leviton, L. C. (1991). *Foundations of program evaluation: Theories of practice.* Newbury Park, CA: Sage.

Stufflebeam, D. L., Madaus, G. F., & Kellaghan, T. (Eds.). (2000). *Evaluation models: Viewpoints on education and human services evaluation* (2nd ed.). Boston: Kluwer.

Turner, V. W., & Bruner, E. M. (Eds.). (1986). *The anthropology of experience.* Urbana: University of Illinois Press.

Weick, K. E. (1995). *Sensemaking in organizations.* Thousand Oaks, CA: Sage.

Worthen, B. R., & Sanders, J. R. (1987). *Educational evaluation: Alternative approaches and practical guidelines.* White Plains, NY: Longman.

18

SOCIAL TRANSFORMATION AND EVALUATION

Donna M. Mertens

My theoretical position reflects a number of different philosophical and theoretical strands that focus on providing a framework for understanding issues of power, discrimination, and oppression. As an evaluator, I struggle with the definition of the evaluator's role as it relates to influencing social change. I recognize that many of the programs that we are asked to evaluate focus on the needs of persons who are marginalized in society. As many evaluators do, I feel the frustration that results when program evaluations do not yield the changes hoped for. My lifework is reflected in the development of the transformative paradigm, a philosophical framework that offers a metaphysical umbrella that brings together the various philosophical and theoretical strands applicable to addressing the diverse needs of people who experience discrimination and oppression. Relevant theoretical strands include, but are not limited to, feminist theories, critical theory, critical race theory, disability rights theory, indigenous rights theory, queer theory, and deafness rights theory.

In this chapter, I explore personal experiences that influenced the development of my perspective as well as historical influences in broader society and the work of other evaluation theorists that guided my thinking. Through sharing the roots of my work, I provide a picture of the transformative paradigm and its application in evaluation that offers one framework for addressing social injustice.

PERSONAL EXPERIENCES

At an early age, I had a strong sense of privilege and inequity in the world. I first became aware of this when my family moved from Washington State to Kentucky in the early 1960s.

In Washington, I had only seen people who looked like me—white, middle class, able-bodied, and English speaking. In Kentucky, it became immediately obvious that there was a division by race and class in terms of access to privileges associated with housing, schooling, and recreation. I saw that black people did not go to my school, live in my neighborhood, or go to my swimming pool. When I asked my teacher why there were no black people at my school, she patted me on the head and said, "Honey, they prefer to be with their own kind." Although I did not know the word for what I was feeling at that time, I was experiencing cognitive dissonance. How could black people prefer to live in the inner-city slum, where it was hot and humid, and not prefer to attend the nice suburban school or swim at the private country club like I did?

The feeling that "something was not right with this picture" stayed with me and served as my motivation to explore what was being done in the broader society to address social inequities. My experience of cognitive dissonance coincided with the civil rights movement in the United States, which probably explains why my initial concern about inequities was based on racial discrimination. Even at that young age, I found myself thinking like an evaluator, mulling over questions such as "What were the effects of the civil rights movement?" and "How is the war on poverty improving living conditions for the poor people in our country?" I found inspiration in the writings of historical greats such as Martin Luther King Jr., Eleanor Roosevelt, Nelson Mandela, and Paulo Freire. As I read more widely and experienced the broader world, I became aware of multiple bases of discrimination and oppression beyond race, such as disability, immigrant status, political conflicts, sexual orientation, poverty, gender, age, and a multitude of other characteristics that are associated with less access to social justice.

PROFESSIONAL EXPERIENCES

As luck would have it, I graduated with a bachelor's degree in psychology just as evaluation was emerging as a field with employment opportunities for people with research skills. I worked at the University of Kentucky's College of Medicine, supporting faculty in the evaluation of their teaching. At this time, I was primarily influenced by Ralph Tyler's approach to evaluation, in which learning objectives were stated and then data were collected to determine if those objectives had been achieved. I was also asked to evaluate the predictors of success in medical school. Not surprisingly, undergraduate science grades and high scores on MCAT (Medical College Admission Test) predicted success in medical school. In writing up the results of this study, I raised the question "Are there other, more humanistic qualities that need to be attended to in the selection of future doctors?" Thus, as a nascent evaluator, I was serving in the role of asking provocative questions. This is an essential part of the role of a transformative evaluator.

While working on my PhD, I served as the coordinator of evaluation for a federally funded program that used one of NASA's (National Aeronautics and Space Administration [USA]) first satellites to provide continuing education in a high-poverty region. At that time, I benefited from Daniel Stufflebeam's CIPP (*c*ontext, *i*nput, *p*rocess, *p*roduct) model of evaluation. The CIPP model consisted of four components to encourage evaluators to think beyond outcomes (products), broadening evaluation efforts to consider the project's context in order to set appropriate goals through needs sensing, evaluate the inputs to determine the adequacy of resources, and provide information about the quality of program implementation. I found it useful to analyze contextual variables in the remote rural areas of Appalachia, the resources available in terms of personnel and equipment as it was a technology-based project, the quality of the process as the programs were implemented for various stakeholder groups, and the outcomes of the continuing-education programs. However, I worked under constraints that limited the amount of time I could spend in the field. Consequently, the majority of my evaluation work consisted of surveys that were sent to participants to complete, which were then sent back to me for analysis. I felt that the influence of my work could have been enhanced if I had the opportunity to become more immersed in the daily experiences of the intended audiences.

On completion of my doctoral degree, I was hired at the Ohio State University National Center for Research in Vocational Education as a policy analyst. In this position, I was responsible for analyzing data on the effectiveness of vocational education for the purpose of informing congressional policymakers. I was aware of and influenced by Michael Patton's utilization-focused evaluation. He recommended that evaluators identify the primary intended user and then direct their efforts to meeting the information needs of that user, based on the rationale that there are a limited number of stakeholders who care about the results and are in a position to act on them. I did know who in the Congress cared about the legislation that governed funding for vocational education. However, I grew increasingly concerned because of what seemed to me a lack of representation of the voices of students who were experiencing limited opportunities by virtue of being placed in vocational programs that were discriminatory with regard to gender, race, class, or disability. The legislation under which the center was funded precluded the collection of original data for policy analysis purposes. Hence, we made use of national longitudinal data that were collected by other organizations. My feeling of discomfort was strengthened because of this lack of connection with the people most affected by the programs. I began to search in earnest for the position in which I could respectfully enter a community composed of marginalized people to test my hypothesis that by working together, we could enhance the possibility of social change.

It was with this in mind that I answered an ad in the Washington Post for an assistant professor position at Gallaudet University to teach research and evaluation methods. Gallaudet University is the only university in the world with the primary mission of serving deaf students. When I walked into my classroom for the first time, I experienced culture shock at multiple levels. First I was teaching through an interpreter because I had not yet acquired the skills of using sign language; all professors at Gallaudet are required to teach using American Sign Language (ASL). Second, when I started lecturing, the deaf students did not lower their heads to start taking notes the way hearing students do. They have to keep their eyes on the teacher (or the interpreter), or they will not know what is being said. Third, the substance of research and evaluation that I was taught, and therefore what I was teaching, did not have relevance for the deaf students in my courses. Rather, the students told me stories of being the subjects in research studies conducted by hearing people, the results of which, they felt, many times misrepresented their group and its culture.

Such culture shock served as the stimulus for action on my part. I began learning ASL and passed the necessary competency tests in ASL for faculty; I recognized my limitations because

I am not a native signer. I adjusted my teaching methods to be much more interactive in order to provide me with feedback as to what the students actually understood. And I critically examined the material that I was teaching. This led me to revisit those theoretical perspectives that had guided me in my earlier examination of inequities. As I tentatively introduced the ideas that have been expressed by feminist theorists about power differentials in research and evaluation contexts, I found that the deaf students understood their relevancy when discussed within the context of living in the hearing-dominated world. As I reflected on their responses to bringing issues of power and discrimination into the research and evaluation context, I felt an affirmation that bolstered my determination to continue to pursue the role of research and evaluation in an unequal world.

EVALUATION INFLUENCES

As I consciously journeyed through the territory where evaluation and social justice intersect, I found the work of several evaluators quite insightful. In particular, the work of Ernie House and Ken Howe, Jennifer Greene, and Karen Kirkhart provided me with insights into this complex terrain. Robert Stake's writings about case studies as a way of capturing complex realities were useful. Veronica Thomas and Henry Frierson's writings about critical race theory also helped elucidate my thinking. Fiona Cram and Bagele Chilisa added to my thinking through their explication of the implications of an indigenous, rights-based approach to evaluation. The work of Rodney Hopson and Stafford Hood has been especially useful in terms of their development of culturally responsive approaches to evaluation. Raychelle Harris and Heidi Holmes challenged me to bring the Deaf perspective into transformative thinking.

PARADIGMS AND EVALUATION

The pieces of the puzzle that portray a picture of evaluation focused on issues of human rights and social justice are quite complex. I found Egon Guba and Yvonna Lincoln's (2005) writings about paradigms to be particularly helpful in organizing my thinking around the major topics related to an evaluation stance that focuses on human rights and social justice. Guba and Lincoln described paradigms as sets of philosophical assumptions that describe an evaluator's worldview. They defined the constitution of paradigms in evaluation as including four basic assumptions:

1. Axiological assumption—the nature of ethics
2. Ontological assumption—the nature of reality
3. Epistemological assumption—the nature of knowledge and the relationship between the researcher and the community
4. Methodological assumption—the nature of systematic inquiry

Given the multiple dimensions of diversity that have been and are used as a basis for discrimination, an approach to thinking about evaluation is needed that provides an overarching umbrella that encompasses the complexity within marginalized communities. The transformative paradigm offers such an overarching framework.

THE TRANSFORMATIVE PARADIGM

The transformative paradigm (Mertens, 2009, 2010; Mertens & Wilson, 2012) is made up of these four philosophical assumptions, with priority placed on the axiological assumption that explicitly places value on the pursuit of social justice and the furtherance of human rights. The transformative paradigm is based on recognition of human rights as they are articulated by the United Nations and as it is understood in the targeted communities. The United Nations (1948) passed a universal declaration of human rights in the 1940s. It would seem that a universal declaration would mean that the rights of people from all walks of life would be protected. However, the United Nations acknowledges that specific groups of people have not had their rights protected and enforced; therefore, they undertook to recognize those constituencies by passing resolutions that recognize the rights of racial minorities (1969), women (1979), children (1990a), migrant workers (1990b), people with disabilities (2006a), and indigenous peoples (2006b). This gives us a partial listing of subgroups whose rights need to be consciously addressed in evaluations that are conducted with an awareness of the diversity within these communities. Dimensions of diversity are contextually dependent; different dimensions will be of relevance in different evaluation contexts.

TRANSFORMATIVE AXIOLOGICAL ASSUMPTION

The axiological belief is the first-listed of the transformative assumptions because it has a critical influence on the character of the subsequent assumptions. Evaluators might ask themselves questions such as the following: What are the ethical principles that guide my work? What is the connection between those ethical principles and issues of social justice? How do the ethical principles reflect issues of culture and power differences? How can this evaluation contribute to social justice and human rights? If I accept that this is a desirable goal for evaluation, what would I do differently in terms of methodology?

To conduct an ethical transformative evaluation study, evaluators need to be able to identify the cultural norms and beliefs that are present in the communities in which we work. If we are to act respectfully, then we need to include mechanisms for entering communities that permit the identification of these cultural norms and beliefs and to understand the implications of those norms for either supporting the pursuit of human rights or sustaining an oppressive system. Such an ethical assumption calls on us to be proactive in the identification of cultural beliefs and norms and to be interactive with community members to solicit their understanding of how those norms and beliefs influence their lives. For evaluations to be inclusive of a variety of beliefs and norms, evaluators need also to be aware of relevant cultural groups in the context of the inquiry and the cultural norms associated with those groups.

In practice, awareness of cultural norms and beliefs can be addressed in a number of ways, such as engaging diverse members of the community as evaluators, forming teams of evaluators that represent the dominant and nondominant cultural groups, or forming advisory bodies that represent appropriate dimensions of diversity. In an evaluation of a federally funded teacher preparation program, we used the strategies of establishing an evaluation team that was reflective of diverse members of the community and of forming relationships with important community gatekeepers. For example, Mertens, Harris, Holmes, and Brandt (2007) formed a team to evaluate a program that was designed to recruit and support teachers who were deaf or hard of hearing in order to increase the number of teachers who reflect the same characteristics as deaf students. Hearing applicants were also accepted into the program. The program was focused on the preparation of teachers to teach deaf students who have an additional disability.[1] We developed the team with one hearing evaluator, two culturally deaf native users of ASL, and one deaf evaluator who uses a cochlear implant and knows ASL but is not a native user. Thus, the team represented the variety of cultural groups that were taking part in the program, which allowed it to match with the communication preferences of the participants during the collection of data. Deaf ASL users were interviewed by the two deaf ASL evaluators working together. The hearing participants were interviewed by the team made up of the hearing evaluator and the evaluator who used a cochlear implant.

Another aspect of the transformative axiological assumption raises questions about focusing on negative versus positive qualities in targeted communities. As evaluators, it is easy to focus only on problems; however, such a focus ignores their strengths and resilience. Rather than painting a picture of a downtrodden, victimized people, evaluators should be aware of the community members' strengths and make sure that those are brought to visibility along with the challenges that the members experience. In addition, evaluators should be cognizant of the history of evaluators taking information from communities without giving anything in return. There is a need to consider how the findings of the evaluation can be used to sustain change in the community when the evaluators leave—or how to give proactive attention to issues of sustainability. At the same time, evaluators have an ethical obligation to clearly communicate the limitations of their work in terms of being realistic about the potential for changes.

The transformative methodological assumption is discussed later in this chapter. However, each of the transformative assumptions has implications for methodological decisions and criteria for determining if the assumptions have been realized. For example, the transformative axiological assumption suggests that evaluators ask questions such as the following to critically examine the consistency of their ethical beliefs and their methods choices:

- To what extent is the evaluator able to identify cultural norms within communities that are supportive of or deleterious to the pursuit of social justice and human rights?
- How do evaluators demonstrate that they have taken action to support those norms that support human rights and social justice and challenge those that sustain an oppressive system?

- How do evaluators demonstrate that they are leaving the community better off than when they began the evaluation—in terms of increased knowledge, capacity, or changes in policies or practices?
- In what ways was the evaluation framed to take into account the expertise, knowledge, and strengths of the community in order to provide a platform for authentic engagement between the evaluator and the community?
- How does the evaluation address the sustainability of the changes in the community that provide for the possibility of taking action to enhance social justice and human rights after the evaluator leaves the community?

TRANSFORMATIVE ONTOLOGICAL ASSUMPTION

The logical connection between the axiological and ontological assumptions is clear. If some cultural norms and beliefs support the enhancement of social justice and human rights and some do not, then the evaluator needs to design the evaluation so that it can reveal those different versions of reality and needs to understand the dimensions of diversity that influence which versions of reality are given privilege. The evaluator also needs to build in mechanisms to reveal versions of reality that sustain oppressive systems and those that have the potential to further human rights. These beliefs and their implications for methodological decisions lead to questions that assess the quality of evaluation studies, including the following:

- To what extent did the evaluator reveal different versions of reality?
- How did the evaluator determine those versions of reality that have the potential to either support or impede progress toward social justice and human rights?
- What were the consequences of identifying these versions of reality?
- How did this evaluation contribute to the change in the understanding of what is real?

The transformative ontological assumption calls on the evaluator to proactively plan how to gain insights into diverse perspectives and to analyze those perspectives to reveal their potential to contribute to or impede social justice. For example, in Mertens et al.'s (2007) evaluation of the teacher training program, the evaluators captured and made visible different versions of reality with respect to the teachers' expectations for their students in the schools where they taught. These participant comments illustrate this point:

> I feel teachers in the mainstream resist our students, especially students with multiple disabilities. (Graduate, Field Notes, May 2007)

> When I graduated, I thought I was ready to teach. Then the principal gave me my list of students and my classroom and just washed his hands off me. You're on your own. The principal did not require me to submit weekly plans like other teachers because he thought I'd only be teaching sign language. But I told him, I'm here to really teach. We (my students and I) were not invited to field day or assemblies. That first year really hit me—what a challenge and a WOW at the same time. So I changed schools and this one is definitely better. Now I'm in a school where people believe that deaf students can learn. (Graduate, Field Notes, May 2007)

Low expectations have long been recognized as an impediment to academic progress. The contrast of these two realities—resistance and low expectations from other school personnel alongside the new teacher's determination to really teach—makes visible pathways with the potential to either impede or facilitate the realization of the right of all children to an education.

TRANSFORMATIVE EPISTEMOLOGICAL ASSUMPTION

The transformative epistemological assumption explores the nature of knowledge and the relationship between the knower and that which would be known or, in evaluation parlance, between the evaluator and the stakeholders. For evaluators to design and implement evaluation studies that are commensurate with the assumptions that have been explained previously, they need to establish an interactive link between themselves and the full range of stakeholders. Taking the word of the most powerful about the viewpoints of the least powerful can result in evaluation that does not address the most important concerns of the least powerful. Thus, criteria for quality in methods related to the transformative epistemological assumption include the following:

- What is the nature of the relationship between the evaluator and the stakeholders?
- What evidence is there that the evaluator explicitly addressed issues of power differentials and that the voices of the least powerful are accurately expressed and acted on?
- How did the evaluator establish a trusting relationship with the stakeholders?

Evaluators need to understand appropriate strategies for entering cultural groups in order to establish relationships that have the potential to contribute to social transformation. When evaluators attempt to enter cultural groups that are not reflective of their own backgrounds, they need to investigate and make use of appropriate strategies for entry by reading and consulting with members of the community. For example, when I entered the Deaf community as a hearing professor at Gallaudet University, I had to learn ASL and Deaf culture. After almost 30 years in that environment, I am comfortable communicating and interacting with members of the Deaf community who use ASL. However, I still describe myself as a learner because ASL is not my native language and the Deaf community is not my home culture. I also know that the ASL Deaf group represents only one portion of the deaf population. To interact with other people who are deaf, I need to consult with members of these other deaf subgroups. For example, if deaf people lip-read and use assistive listening devices, it is very important to face the person and to speak distinctively in order to provide appropriate information for communication.

Evaluators who are not working in their native language or in their home culture may not have 30 years to establish their credibility in communities. Therefore, other strategies might be needed when circumstances present themselves in shorter time frames. Importantly, evaluators need to present themselves and their backgrounds in ways that make clear their strengths and limitations in terms of their knowledge and life experiences. This positioning allows the evaluator to acknowledge the need to work together with people from the community who have a stronger understanding of cultural and social issues.

Cultural awareness also contributes to the evaluator being cognizant of relevant dimensions of diversity within a particular context. For example, the evaluation team in the teacher preparation program was aware of the dimensions of diversity within the Deaf community that needed to be recognized in order to capture the complexity of less powerful voices. For example, the new teachers raised concerns about their abilities to address the needs of deaf students who came to school with no language or using a communication system other than ASL; those with learning disabilities, autism, or behavioral problems; as well as those who came from non–English-speaking homes. The participants' comments illustrate these dimensions of diversity:

> My biggest challenge was when the home language is Spanish and the kid has very limited language and no sign, no English. I contacted Gallaudet and they had limited resources. Now I have a student who is deaf with another disability, from another country. (Graduate Interview, May 2007)

> My students are under 5 years old and they come with zero language and their behavior is awful. They can't sit for even a minute. Kids come with temper tantrums and run out of the school building. I have to teach these kids language; I see them start to learn to behave and interact with others. My biggest challenge is seeing three kids run out of school at the same time. Which one do I run after? One kid got into the storm drain. I'm only one teacher and I have an assistant, but that means there is still one kid we can't chase after at the same time as the other two. (Graduate Interview, May 2007)

> They use three different methods of communication: sign, oral, and cued speech. I tried to explain in sign, but the other kids don't understand. I learned cued speech—it took me a long time but it is required for two students. (Graduate, Field Notes, May 2007)

TRANSFORMATIVE METHODOLOGICAL ASSUMPTION

The transformative methodological assumption does not mandate the use of any particular method. However, it does provide the rationale for choosing to use mixed methods in order to be consistent with the other transformative assumptions within the context of community responsiveness. Evaluators need qualitative/dialogic moments in the beginning of their planning to ascertain the cultural context in which they are working. And the use of qualitative and quantitative data facilitates responsiveness to different stakeholders and issues. Mixed methods can also be used to capture the contextual complexity and provide pluralistic avenues for appropriately engaging with diverse cultural groups in the evaluation. To this end, criteria for quality related to the transformative methodological assumption include the following:

- How was a cyclical design used to make use of interim findings throughout the study?
- To what extent did evaluators engage with the full range of stakeholders to gather qualitative data that enhance their understandings of the community?
- How were data collection methods used to be responsive to the needs of diverse stakeholders?

- To what extent were the methods used responsive to the specific needs of the different stakeholder groups?
- How were the methodologies designed to enhance use of the evaluation findings to support the pursuit of social justice and human rights?

In the Mertens et al. (2007) evaluation, the evaluation team began by reading documents from the previous 7 years of the project, such as the original proposal that was funded, the project annual reports, and curriculum materials from the program. They treated these documents as qualitative data sources and identified themes that arose in them as a starting point for decisions about the next steps in data collection. The evaluators noted that the project planned a reflective seminar for the graduates, inviting everyone to the university campus for 3 days. They asked the project director if they could observe the first 2 days of the seminar and then interview the participants on the last day; he agreed to that strategy. All four evaluators observed each day; at the end of each day, they compared notes as to what issues were emerging. They identified issues related to successes and challenges in the classroom that were associated with the graduates' positions in the schools in which they worked and how they interacted with their students based on diverse characteristics. From these observations, the evaluators developed interview questions for the participants that focused on their experiences as they entered their new schools and the characteristics of their students that were relevant to their feelings of competence or frustration. The evaluation team analyzed the data from the interviews and found that the new teachers were frustrated by their marginalization in their schools, which they perceived to be associated with low expectations for their students and lack of awareness of the capability of students who are deaf and have a disability on the part of the other teachers and administrators in their schools.

Only some of the project graduates were able to attend the reflective seminar. The evaluators proposed using the data gathered from the participants to develop a web-based quantitative survey that could be sent to all the program graduates as a way of determining how the larger group perceived their successes and challenges. The data from both the qualitative and the quantitative data collection strategies were used to craft interview questions for the university faculty and the teachers at the cooperating schools that had hosted the project participants for student-teaching experiences. The evaluators took comments from the qualitative data and combined them with participant responses to the quantitative survey and then asked the faculty and cooperating teachers to respond to the data.

When presented with the data, one faculty member commented as follows:

> I would have liked to see a mentoring type relationship that would pair them with a teacher the first year and develop a mentorship—even if it was for first and second year of teaching. That would really help—especially for the first year of teaching. That would have been another piece that would have been really nice. The students need to be able to remain in contact with each other . . . We should also teach them that it is their responsibility to mentor younger teachers. (Faculty, June 2007)

This particular faculty member subsequently started a virtual discussion group for the program graduates, where they could share their frustrations and experiences with each other, the faculty at the university, and more experienced teachers. This is one change that resulted from the program. In addition, the evaluators made a presentation at the professional association for faculty who prepare teachers of the deaf across the United States and Canada. This presentation also included the data that were used in the faculty and cooperating teachers' interviews. During the presentation, faculty from across the two countries began a discussion about the increase in the number of deaf students with disabilities and how they might address this population's needs as a professional community. They agreed to work through a virtual discussion board found at www.deafed.net—a website that was established specifically for this professional community about 10 years earlier and that was available to host this type of activity.

This example illustrates how a cyclical approach can be used to be responsive to emerging understandings of the effectiveness of a program and how it can also stimulate transformational change. Even though the grant that stimulated the need for the evaluation was coming to an end, the evaluation was designed to contribute to transformational change that could address the ongoing needs of students who are deaf with disabilities. Each step of the evaluation informed subsequent methodological decisions. The data were used to stimulate change on the part of the faculty who prepare such teachers across the broader professional community. The evaluators consciously chose to share the results in multiple ways through multiple channels and to monitor the actions that were stimulated by the sharing of the results over time.

CONCLUSION

The idea of using research and evaluation to address social inequities is not new territory. We can think back to Donald Campbell's call for an experimenting society as one road to social improvement. However, in the ensuing years since Campbell wrote his treatise on using research (and presumably evaluation) as a tool for social betterment, the dream has not been realized. Numerous voices, many noted in this chapter, have been raised that suggest that another perspective needs to be brought to the world of evaluation that situates the struggle in the lives of those who are in less powerful positions due to a legacy of discrimination and oppression. The transformative paradigm is one framework for thinking about the intersection of social justice and evaluation based explicitly on recognizing the need to address issues of power. The theorizing about this approach is not complete. I am encouraged by the number of evaluators around the world who find value in this framework. I look forward to bearing witness to additional developments along this frontier.

NOTE

1. Members of the Deaf community view themselves as a cultural group who have their own languages, values, and shared behavior patterns. They do not view themselves as having a disability. Therefore, if persons who are deaf have a disability such as blindness or cerebral palsy, they describe themselves as deaf with a disability.

REFERENCES

Guba, E. G., & Lincoln, Y. S. (2005). Paradigmatic controversies, contradictions, and emerging confluence. In N. K. Denzin & Y. S. Lincoln (Eds.), *The SAGE handbook of qualitative research* (3rd ed., pp. 191–215). Thousand Oaks, CA: Sage.

Mertens, D. M. (2009). *Transformative research and evaluation.* New York, NY: Guilford Press.

Mertens, D. M. (2010). *Research and evaluation in education and psychology: Integrating diversity with quantitative, qualitative, and mixed methods* (3rd ed.). Thousand Oaks, CA: Sage.

Mertens, D. M., & Wilson, A. T. (2012). *Program evaluation theory and practice*: A comprehensive guide. New York, NY: Guilford Press.

Mertens, D. M., Harris, R., Holmes, H., & Brandt, S. (2007). *Project SUCCESS: Summative evaluation report.* Washington, DC: Gallaudet University.

PART IV

USE

19

THE CIPP EVALUATION MODEL

Status, Origin, Development, Use, and Theory

Daniel L. Stufflebeam

The CIPP evaluation model is an apt topic for this book's review of the evaluation field's roots. In the mid-1960s, I tried and largely rejected that period's orthodox evaluation approaches (objectives based, experimental design, and standardized testing); then I began developing a new, decision/accountability-oriented approach designed to work in the real world. The CIPP model (Stufflebeam, 1966a, 1967b) and other conceptualizations of the 1960s era—especially those created by Stake (1967) and Scriven (1967)—have over the past 45 years evolved and significantly influenced the theory and practice of evaluation. In this update of my chapter in Marvin Alkin's (2004) *Evaluation Roots*, I describe the CIPP model's 2011 status, origin, development, uses, and main theoretical underpinnings.

THE CIPP MODEL, CA. 2011

The CIPP evaluation model is a comprehensive framework for guiding formative and summative evaluations of projects, programs, personnel, products, institutions, and systems. The model is configured for guiding organizations' internal evaluations, self-evaluations conducted by project teams and individual service providers, and contracted or mandated external evaluations. The model is intended for use and has been applied in a wide range of disciplines and service areas in many countries.

Context, Input, Process, and Product Evaluations

The model's core concepts are denoted by the acronym CIPP, which stands for evaluations of an entity's *c*ontext, *i*nputs, *p*rocesses, and *p*roducts. *Context evaluations* assess needs, problems, assets, and opportunities, as well as relevant contextual conditions and dynamics, to help decision makers define goals and priorities and to help the broader group of users judge goals, priorities, and outcomes. *Input evaluations* serve program planning by helping identify and then assess alternative approaches, competing action plans, staffing plans, and budgets for their feasibility and potential cost-effectiveness to meet targeted needs and to achieve defined goals. Decision makers use input evaluations to identify and choose among competing plans, write funding proposals, allocate resources, assign staff, schedule work, and ultimately help others judge an effort's plans and budget. *Process evaluations* assess the implementation of plans to help staff carry out activities and later to help the broad group of users judge program implementation and expenditures and also interpret outcomes. *Product evaluations* identify and assess costs and outcomes—intended and unintended, short term and long term—both to help a staff keep focused on achieving important outcomes at a reasonable cost and, ultimately, to help the broader user group gauge the effort's cost-effectiveness in achieving defined goals and meeting targeted needs.

In the formative case—where evaluation helps guide an effort—context, input, process, and product evaluations ask the following questions, respectively: What needs to be done? How should it be done? Is it being done? Is it succeeding? The evaluator submits interim reports addressing these questions to keep stakeholders informed about findings, to help guide and strengthen decision making and staff work, and to maintain an accountability record.

In finalizing a summative report, the evaluator refers to the store of context, input, process, and product information and obtains additionally needed information. The evaluator uses the information obtained to address the following questions, respectively: Was the program (or other evaluand) keyed to clear goals based on assessed beneficiary needs? Was the effort guided by a defensible design, staffing plan, and budget? Was the service design executed competently and efficiently and modified as needed? Did the effort succeed?

Partitioning the Product Evaluation Component. In summing up long-term evaluations, the product evaluation (Did it succeed?) component may be divided into assessments of impact, effectiveness, sustainability, and transportability. These product evaluation subparts ask the following: Were the right beneficiaries reached? Were their targeted needs met? Were the beneficiaries' gains sustained? Did the processes that produced the gains prove transportable and adaptable for effective use elsewhere?

Focus on Improvement. The CIPP model emphasizes that evaluation's purpose is not only to prove but also to improve. Evaluation is thus conceived primarily as a functional activity oriented in the long run to stimulating, aiding, and abetting efforts to strengthen enterprises. However, the model also posits that some programs or other services will prove unworthy of attempts to improve them and should be terminated. By helping stop unneeded, corrupt, overly expensive, or hopelessly flawed efforts, evaluations serve an improvement function by assisting organizations to free resources and time for worthy enterprises.

Proactive and Retrospective Applications of the CIPP Model. Consistent with its improvement orientation, the CIPP model assigns priority to guiding the planning and implementation of development efforts. The model's intent is thus to supply evaluation users—including policy boards, government officials, foundation presidents and staff members, project directors and staffs, school administrators, curriculum developers and specialists, city planners, military leaders, teachers, and counselors—with timely, valid information for use in identifying an appropriate area for development; in taking account of relevant contextual conditions and dynamics; in formulating sound goals, activity plans, and budgets; in carrying out work plans efficiently and successfully; in communicating project progress and accomplishments to constituents; in deciding periodically whether and, if so, how to repeat or expand an effort; and in meeting accountability requirements.

The CIPP model also provides for conducting retrospective, summative evaluations to serve a broad range of stakeholders. Potential consumers need summative reports to help assess the quality, cost, utility, and competitiveness of products and services. Other stakeholders might want evidence on what their tax dollars or other types of support yielded. If evaluators effectively conduct, document, and report formative evaluations, they will have much of the information needed to produce a defensible summative evaluation report. Such information will also prove invaluable to outsiders engaged in conducting a summative evaluation.

Table 19.1 summarizes the uses of the CIPP model for both formative and summative evaluations. The matrix's eight cells encompass much of the evaluative information required to guide enterprises and to produce summative evaluation reports. Beyond context, input, process, and product evaluations—set in both formative and summative contexts—the CIPP model includes several other key features.

The Values Component. Figure 19.1 summarizes the basic elements of the CIPP model in three concentric circles and portrays the central importance of defined values. The inner circle and the one-directional arrows denote the core values that should be defined and used to ground a given evaluation. The wheel surrounding the values is divided into four evaluative foci associated with any program or other endeavor: goals, plans, actions, and outcomes. The outer wheel indicates the type of evaluation that serves each of the four evaluative foci (i.e., context, input, process, and product evaluation). Each two-directional arrow represents a reciprocal relationship between a particular evaluative focus and a type of evaluation.

These relationships are made functional by grounding evaluations in core values, referenced in the scheme's inner circle, including the ideals held by a society, group, or individual. The values provide the foundation for deriving and/or validating particular evaluative criteria. These, in turn, provide the basis for selecting/constructing the evaluation instruments and procedures, accessing existing information, and defining interpretive standards. Also, a values framework provides a frame of reference for detecting unexpected defects and strengths. The bottom line values intended for use with the CIPP model are those found in the U.S. Constitution and its preamble, especially equality

Table 19.1 The Relevance of Four Evaluation Types to Formative and Summative Evaluation Roles

Evaluation Roles	Context	Input	Process	Product
Formative evaluation: prospective application of CIPP information to assist decision making and quality assurance	Guidance for determining areas for improvement and for choosing and ranking goals (based on assessing needs, problems, assets, and opportunities, plus contextual dynamics)	Guidance for choosing a program strategy (based on identifying and assessing alternative strategies and resource allocation plans) Examination of the work plan	Guidance for implementing the operational plan (based on monitoring and judging activities and delivering periodic evaluative feedback)	Guidance for continuing, modifying, adopting, or terminating the effort (based on assessing outcomes and side effects)
Summative evaluation: retrospective use of CIPP information to sum up the effort's merit, worth, probity, equity, feasibility, efficiency, safety, cost, and significance	Comparison of goals and priorities with assessed needs, problems, assets, opportunities, and relevant contextual dynamics	Comparison of the program's strategy, design, and budget with those of critical competitors and with goals and targeted needs of beneficiaries	Full description of the actual process and record of costs Comparison of the designed and actual processes and costs	Comparison of outcomes and side effects with goals and targeted needs and, as feasible, with the results of competitive programs Interpretation of results against the effort's assessed context, inputs, and processes

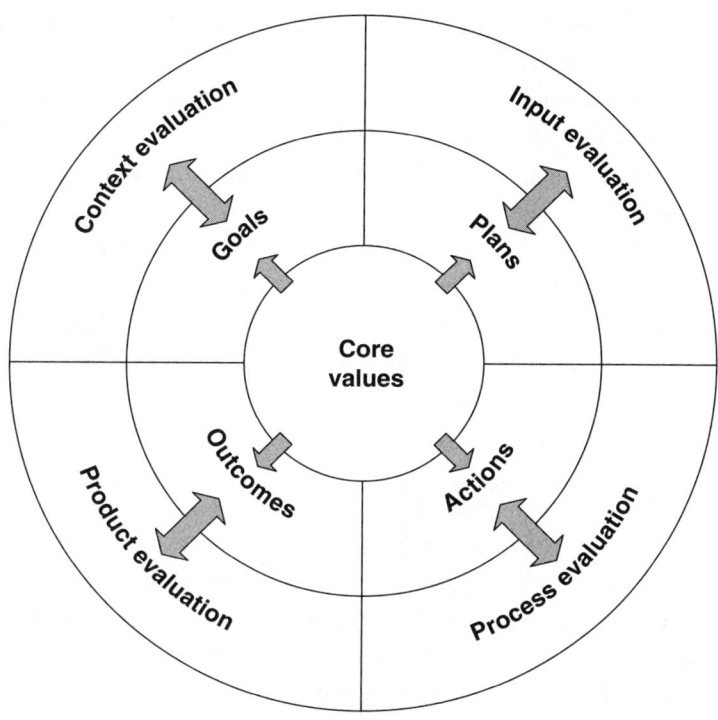

Figure 19.1 Key Components of the CIPP Evaluation Model and Associated Relationships With Program Components and Core Values

and the freedoms of religion, speech, the press, and assembly. Typical more specific criteria concern the evaluand's merit, worth, probity, equity, feasibility, efficiency, safety, cost, and significance.

Standards for Evaluations. The bases for judging CIPP evaluations are pertinent professional standards, especially including the Joint Committee on Standards for Educational Evaluation (1981, 1994, 2011) standards for evaluations of programs, personnel, and students. These require evaluations to meet conditions of utility (serving the information needs of intended users), feasibility (keeping evaluation operations realistic, prudent, diplomatic, and frugal), propriety (conducting evaluations legally, ethically, and with due regard for the welfare of participants and those affected by results), accuracy (revealing and conveying technically sound information about the features that determine the evaluand's value), and evaluation accountability (documenting the evaluation work and subjecting it to internal and external meta-evaluations).

ORIGIN AND DEVELOPMENT OF THE CIPP EVALUATION MODEL

Now let's consider why and how the CIPP model was developed and how it acquired its current configuration, including key practical, methodological, and theoretical influences. Work on this model began in 1965 because U.S. public schools could not meaningfully and feasibly evaluate their federally supported projects using the (then) gold standard for program evaluations: controlled, variable-manipulating, comparative experiments (Guba, 1966; Stufflebeam, 1966a, 1967b). Since its humble beginnings, the CIPP model has been extensively developed and widely applied (e.g., see Candoli, Cullen, & Stufflebeam, 1997; Guba & Stufflebeam, 1968; Stufflebeam, 1969, 1997, 2003a, 2003b; Stufflebeam et al., 1971; Stufflebeam & Shinkfield, 1995; Stufflebeam & Webster, 1988).

My present view of evaluation was derived not from conceptualizing in university ivory towers but from working in evaluation's "school of hard knocks." My beliefs about evaluation are based on learning by doing and on an ongoing effort to identify and correct mistakes made in evaluation practice plus a fundamental commitment to the tenets of a free society and grounding in the basics of sound empirical research.

My Quite Accidental Entry Into Evaluation

In 1965, when I was directing The Ohio State University (OSU) Test Development Center, Dr. John Ramseyer (head of OSU's School of Education) entered my office and said, "Dan, you're going into the evaluation business." He stated that the federal government had offered huge school improvement grants to U.S. school districts under the Elementary and Secondary Education Act of 1965 (ESEA) and that Ohio's schools needed funds to improve the education of disadvantaged students but couldn't meet the ESEA evaluation requirements. As Ohio's flagship university, he said OSU had to help the schools.

Although I had never taken a course labeled "evaluation," I was in a good place to start an evaluation career. Ralph Tyler—widely acknowledged as the father of educational evaluation—had created an evaluation reputation for OSU, especially through directing the famous Eight-Year Study of progressive schools (Smith & Tyler, 1942). Maybe he would help me, since he still came to OSU occasionally to visit his brother Keith. Moreover, Dr. Ramseyer made a $10,000 travel fund available for me to visit and study sites of suspected evaluation activity (like the federally funded UCLA Center for the Study of Evaluation being ably assisted by the then young assistant professor Dr. Marvin Alkin). My educational background included substantial work in statistics, experimental design, psychometrics, and clinical assessment. In addition, I was developing many standardized achievement tests, researching matrix sampling (Cook & Stufflebeam, 1967; Owens & Stufflebeam, 1964), and testing the Program Evaluation and Review Technique (Stufflebeam, 1967a). Moreover, I had been given leave to attend the 1965 eight-week University of Wisconsin summer institute on experimental design and statistics, led by Julian Stanley and Donald Campbell.

How could I fail in my new evaluation assignment? I could dust off Ralph Tyler's (1942) "General Statement on Evaluation," use it to help schools write behavioral objectives, construct achievement tests keyed to the objectives, follow the Campbell and Stanley (1963) advice in assisting schools to conduct randomized experiments, administer the achievement tests following project cycles, conduct analyses of variance and appropriate a posteriori tests for identifying and investigating statistically significant project outcomes, and report methodologically defensible findings.

Although from 1958 to 1961 I had taught school in rural Iowa and Chicago, I had since become engrossed in "gullible's travels" at graduate school and other venues. Obviously, I had forgotten that dynamic school settings typically are not amenable to laboratory research controls and that disadvantaged students have needs and problems that vary widely in kind and amount and are not sensitively measured by standardized tests. My initial thinking about evaluating the schools' "War on Poverty" projects would prove to make little sense.

Start-Up of the Evaluation Center

Despite my initial unrealistic approach to evaluating school projects, I took some steps in my new assignment that over time worked out pretty well. Dr. Ramseyer approved my recommendation to start a new evaluation center. The Evaluation Center's mission became then—and nearly 50 years later is—to advance the theory, practice, and utilization of evaluation. Since no center could directly serve the evaluation needs of all Ohio schools, I projected that we would conduct a few representative evaluation projects; use these as research and training laboratories; produce models, methods, and tools that schools could adopt and adapt; graduate some well-trained evaluation master's and doctoral students; and help set up a few exemplary school district–based evaluation offices as demonstration sites. The new Ohio State center would conduct and (now at Western Michigan University [WMU]) continues to conduct research, development, dissemination, training, and leadership in the context of its evaluation service projects. (See Stufflebeam, 2002, for a checklist that reflects lessons related to developing and directing successful university-based R&D centers.)

Evaluation of Elementary and Secondary Education Act (ESEA) Projects

The Evaluation Center's first project was for the Columbus, Ohio, public schools. In 1965, the 110,000-student district potentially was entitled to receive $6.6 million for 3-year, ESEA, Title I projects (targeted at economically disadvantaged students). However, according to the superintendent, the district had no staff member who could write acceptable evaluation plans. I projected that The Evaluation Center could help the district meet the evaluation requirements but only under certain conditions keyed to The Evaluation Center's mission. These included (1) contracting for 9% of the ESEA project budgets; (2) our writing the needed evaluation plans and supervising their execution; (3) staffing the evaluation with school district personnel; (4) providing the school district evaluators with on-the-job training and graduate degree programs; (5) an intent by the district to fund, staff, and install its own office of evaluation at the end of 3 years; and (6) allocation of 2% of the 9% of contracted evaluation funds to study and document the experience. Superintendent Eibling agreed to the basic approach but objected to Conditions 3 to 5. I noted that the new center's aim was to try to work ourselves out of jobs and help create institutional models of school district–based evaluation that other districts could study and possibly emulate. Otherwise, I was convinced that the center's staff would fail to advance evaluation theory and practice and would make little impact on districts' long-term evaluation capacities. Dr. Eibling reluctantly agreed to my conditions, and off I went on a well-intentioned but partly misguided effort.

Consultants had helped Columbus educators complete essentially fill-in-the-blanks proposals, and I added the evaluation plans. Following basically "rubber stamp" funding by the government, members of my team engaged focus groups of project staff in a time-consuming process to clarify each project's objectives. Subsequently, we intended to develop or select the needed achievement tests and other instruments. We gave up early on randomly assigning disadvantaged students to the Title I projects and control groups, because this clearly was not feasible and likely was illegal. Also, we soon found that existing achievement tests were poor matches to the widely varying developmental needs of the targeted students and that project evaluators could not wait the 2 or more years required to design, construct, pilot test, revise, norm, and validate new achievement tests.

Out of the Armchair and Into the Schools

When I became bored with watching project leaders writing behavioral objectives, I decided to visit schools to find out what was happening in the funded projects. Confusion was evident wherever I went. Nothing like the proposals' intended activities was happening. Those responsible for carrying out the projects had not helped write the proposals, many had not seen the plan they were supposed to be implementing, promised project resources had not been delivered, and the needs and problems in classrooms often seemed critically important but unrelated to the procedures in the proposals and the objectives being worked out at the central office. For good reason, teachers and principals often were upset with the situation.

Rejection of the 1960s Evaluation Orthodoxy

A light bulb went on. Here was an opportunity to improve evaluation theory, if only to discredit the prevalent views. Many evaluation plans that appeared in proposals were true to the (then) evaluation orthodoxy that evaluations should employ methods of experimental design, behavioral objectives, and objective testing to determine whether project objectives had been achieved. This conceptualization was wrong for the situations I found in Columbus classrooms. At best, following this approach could only confirm schools' failures to achieve (dubious) objectives. Such evaluations would not help schools get projects on track and successfully meet the education needs of poor kids.

After I decided to criticize current ideas about evaluation and call for a reconceptualization of evaluation, a relevant opportunity emerged. In January 1966, the Michigan Department of Education engaged me to give the keynote address at a statewide conference on evaluation of projects under Title I of ESEA. At the conference (Stufflebeam, 1966b), I said that I had learned just enough in my evaluation of such projects to reject basically everything I had thought necessary for evaluating educational projects, including behavioral objectives, experimental designs, and standardized tests.

Orienting Evaluation to Decision Making

Instead, I advised educators to key evaluations to provide information for decision making. I identified key types of decisions as those day-to-day choices involved in making projects work and the annual decisions about whether to retain, expand, or discontinue a project. For these implementation and recycling decisions, I suggested that schools concentrate on conducting and reporting process and product evaluations, respectively.

Overall, the Michigan educators disliked what I said. As staunch supporters of local control of schools, most seemed averse to federally mandated evaluations and (possibly as supporters of the Michigan Wolverines and determined enemies of the Buckeyes from the state to the south) not receptive to advice from an Ohio State professor. However, three influential people strongly supported my analysis and asked me to assist their evaluation efforts. They were Stuart Rankin and Robert Lankton, the heads of evaluation and testing in the Detroit Public Schools, and a representative of the U.S. Office of Education.

An Opportunity to Develop and Test a New Approach to Evaluation

A few days after returning to Columbus, Dr. Ramseyer informed me that a U.S. Office of Education official had requested that OSU release me so I could devote my entire time in Washington to leading the federal evaluation of Titles I and III of ESEA. (This was a dubious decision since in Michigan I had essentially said that everything I knew about evaluation wouldn't work in the ESEA program.) Dr. Ramseyer said that he had rejected the request but, instead, committed me to work on the assignment Mondays and Tuesdays in Washington. For the next 2 years, I spent 2 days a week in Washington chairing the government committee on evaluation of the ESEA Titles I and III programs and the subsequent 3 days in Columbus directing The Evaluation Center.

Early Reflections on the Lessons Being Learned

Through the related but different assignments, I gained an appreciation of the problem of orienting evaluations to the very different information requirements of local, state, and national audiences. Largely to appease school personnel throughout the country, the U.S. Office of Education had allowed each school district to submit an annual evaluation report, choosing its own evaluation questions, methods, and instruments. The 14,000-plus school districts subsequently flooded the U.S. mail system with tens of thousands of idiosyncratic evaluation reports not amenable to storage, retrieval, and reading, let alone data aggregation and summarization. The official charged with developing the report for Congress futilely attacked the impossible task of pulling the information together to answer pointed questions of Congress until he suffered a stress-induced heart attack. A lesson? An old one from information science: *Investigators must specify questions in advance and standardize data requirements at each administrative level at which an audience requires answers.*

Soon after beginning the weekly trips to Washington, D.C., at the request of some OSU faculty members, I presented at a university-wide symposium on the issues in evaluating ESEA projects. The attendees readily agreed that laboratory research methods wouldn't work well in school-based development projects; that evaluations should be functional, as in assisting decision making; and that evaluators should assess the process as well as the product. However, some attendees asserted that process and product evaluations are not enough. They stressed that I had failed to address the key need to evaluate project goals.

These critics were correct. Projects could go very wrong if guided by unclear or bad goals, and I had seen that happening in several ESEA projects. In keeping with my new view that evaluations should inform decisions, I decided that goal setting was critically important and should be guided by context evaluations—that is, assessments of needs, problems, assets, opportunities, and environmental dynamics.

The CIPP Model Takes Shape

At this point, the basic structure of the CIPP model was nearly complete. It included context evaluation to guide goal setting, process evaluation to guide project implementation, and product evaluation to guide recycling decisions. I subsequently added input evaluation to aid in planning projects, for example, proposal writing (Stufflebeam, 1967b).

An Invitation to Test the CIPP Model

After I had presented the model at a national conference in Florida (Stufflebeam, 1968), Edwin Hindsman, the then director of the Southwest Educational Laboratory in Austin, Texas, invited me to test the model on one of the lab's major projects. His lab had been assigned to mount and evaluate a $10 million program for meeting the educational needs of migrant children. It was agreed that Egon Guba, Robert Hammond, and I would use the CIPP model to help the lab evaluate the migrant education program. Among the lessons learned from this rich experience were that the CIPP model has to be applied flexibly (e.g., what Stake, 1983, terms "responsively"); active members of the migrant community provided more cogent information on the needs of migrant kids than did experts who had been studying migrant children; and ongoing face-to-face reporting and exchange with project stakeholders was more effective than simply issuing periodic, carefully produced printed reports. We also gained insights into input evaluation. To guide the needed input evaluation, we invented the advocate teams technique (see Reinhard, 1972), through which competing teams develop proposals for meeting a set of targeted needs (e.g., the strongest possible program for addressing the needs of migrant students). Evaluators then assess the alternatives' merits on predetermined criteria.

The Phi Delta Kappa International Book

In 1969, Phi Delta Kappa International (PDK) engaged me to head a national study committee on evaluation, which culminated in the book *Educational Evaluation and Decision Making*

(Stufflebeam et al., 1971). That book sharply criticized the traditional views of educational evaluation, analyzed the evaluative information needs in decision making, and elaborated the CIPP model. The book also suggested that criteria for judging evaluations should include utility and feasibility as well as technical adequacy. We noted that evaluations can go very wrong if keyed exclusively to criteria of technical adequacy, such as the requirements for internal and external validity then being promulgated for judging experiments (Campbell & Stanley, 1963). (The PDK book's division of criteria for guiding and judging evaluations into relevance, importance, timeliness, clarity, credibility, and technical adequacy was a precursor of the work done by the Joint Committee on Standards for Educational Evaluation [1981] to identify and define standards for an evaluation's utility, feasibility, propriety, and accuracy.)

The Model Training Program in Evaluation

The PDK book garnered much interest and support and was undoubtedly a major factor in The Evaluation Center winning a major competitive federal grant, over 10 other universities, in excess of $1 million in 1971 to establish a model graduate training program in evaluation. A consortium of universities, school districts, state education departments, and educational research, development, and dissemination organizations operated the program. An underlying goal was to help some of the participating organizations institutionalize systematic evaluation, especially through staffing their evaluation systems with well-trained evaluation specialists.

In its first 2 years, the program was highly successful. It contributed to strengthening evaluation operations in organizations such as the public schools of Dallas, Texas; Detroit, Lansing, and Saginaw, Michigan; and Cincinnati, Columbus, and Xenia, Ohio. It also helped institutionalize evaluation in the federally funded OSU Center for Vocational and Technical Education; regional educational laboratories in Texas and Oregon; and the state education departments in Michigan and Ohio. Among this project's products and those of early Evaluation Center training were dozens of graduates who would successfully apply evaluation in their careers and help shape the evaluation profession.[1]

Debacle at OSU

Simultaneously, however, storm clouds appeared on the home front. The Evaluation Center had grown into a relatively large, nationally visible organization, with substantial external funding. Its organizational location in Ohio State within a small educational development department proved debilitating to the center's progress and its national leadership activities. After university officials promised but didn't follow through to locate the center in a viable location, I resigned and moved the center to WMU. A lesson I took with me is that a university-based center should report to a dean or vice president. Key reasons are to avoid debilitating politics and natural conflicts of interest at the departmental level (especially concerning the possible allocation of external grant funds to meet unrelated department needs) and instead to provide a home where a center can draw participation from and make contributions across the university's array of disciplines and avoid threats to its fiscal viability and integrity.

The Work in Michigan

The center's work prospered at WMU, and a number of center involvements influenced my further development of the CIPP model.

1. Through a long collegial relationship with Michael Scriven and assignments to conduct several external evaluations, I strengthened the CIPP model's attention to summative evaluation and affirmed and explained its objectivist orientation (see Stufflebeam & Shinkfield, 2007, p. 331).

2. As founding chair of the Joint Committee on Standards for Educational Evaluation, I learned firsthand the virtues and difficulties of engaging a diverse group of evaluators and evaluation users to collaborate in defining what is meant by "sound evaluation."

3. While I learned to value diverse perspectives in the course of an evaluation, I also learned that after conducting what Cronbach et al. (1981) referred to as "evaluation's divergent stage," the evaluator should skillfully lead evaluation participants to converge on a conclusion about an evaluand's soundness.

4. I have been fortunate over the years to interact and work with leading evaluation theorists and methodologists. These relationships helped me clarify where my views of evaluation agree with and differ from others' views (e.g., see Stufflebeam, 2001a; Stufflebeam, Madaus, & Kellaghan, 2000; Stufflebeam & Shinkfield, 2007).

5. Through contentious meta-evaluations conducted on the Michigan Educational Assessment Program (House, Rivers, & Stufflebeam, 1974) and on the National Assessment of Educational Progress (Stufflebeam, Jaeger, & Scriven, 1992), I asserted and demonstrated the importance of negotiating a clear, sound contract before proceeding with an evaluation (Stufflebeam, 2000; Stufflebeam & Shinkfield, 2007, chap. 24).

6. As the designer and director of the National Center for Research on Educational Accountability and Teacher Evaluation (CREATE), I extended the CIPP model for use in evaluating teachers, superintendents, and other school personnel (Candoli et al., 1997; Shinkfield & Stufflebeam, 1995).

7. In leading an evaluation of the Marine Corps system for evaluating officers and enlisted personnel, I gained greater insights into the roles that clients can play as evaluation-oriented leaders in securing the use of evaluation findings and, based on that experience, developed with Arlen Gullickson the feedback workshop procedure (Gullickson & Stufflebeam, 2001).

8. After expanding The Evaluation Center's work to a range of disciplines, WMU's president and I determined that the center would function best as a university-level unit—drawing from the university's full range of disciplines. The relocation of the

center was a key factor in my being able to lead the collaboration among the center and WMU's colleges of arts and sciences, education, engineering, and health and human services, which culminated in WMU's interdisciplinary PhD program in evaluation (Coryn, Stufflebeam, Davidson, & Scriven, 2010; Stufflebeam, 2001b).

9. Because I have become quite sensitized to the real-world politics of evaluation, I employ a range of measures to help preserve an evaluation's political viability. These include negotiating advance contracts, grounding evaluations in professional standards, engaging stakeholder panels to review evaluation plans and draft reports,[2] obtaining independent meta-evaluations, and, when feasible, having a third party fund the meta-evaluation (see Finn, Stevens, Stufflebeam, & Walberg, 1997).

10. Throughout my career, I have sought to develop practical evaluation tools (e.g., see www.wmich.edu/evalctr/checklists).

APPLICATIONS OF THE CIPP MODEL

In a comprehensive search for relevant literature on the CIPP model to support a forthcoming book on the model, my coauthor for that book, Dr. Guili Zhang, identified about 500 CIPP-related evaluation studies, journal articles, and doctoral dissertations across nations, disciplines, and service areas. She found that the model had been applied in at least 134 doctoral dissertations that were completed at 81 universities and applied in 39 disciplines. She also cited a sample of 55 published studies that employed the model in disciplines such as agriculture, aviation, business, communication, education, evaluation, health care, law, the military, psychology, religion, and sociology.

Application to a Community Development and Self-Help Housing Project

An instructive application of the CIPP model occurred in an 8-year evaluation of the Consuelo Foundation's Ke Aka Ho'ona Self-Help Housing Project for low-income families. This application is described and analyzed in Stufflebeam and Shinkfield (2007, chaps. 12–18). Before The Evaluation Center undertook this evaluation, the foundation had already conducted what could be labeled as both context and input evaluations. The context evaluation had helped the then new foundation decide on conducting a project to help meet the acute housing needs of the working poor on Oahu's crime-ridden and highly depressed Waianae Coast. After visiting and studying housing projects for low-income families in California and reviewing the relevant literature, the foundation's staff selected self-help housing as its basic approach. It then creatively designed a project through which, over a period of 7 years, 75 families would, under supervision, construct their own houses (at a pace of between 6 and 17 houses each year) on a 14-acre plot and together build a values-based community (oriented especially to the healthy development of the residents' children in a peaceful, supportive environment).

At the outset of the construction process, the foundation contracted The Evaluation Center to apply the CIPP model both formatively and summatively. Our ensuing 8-year evaluation periodically updated information on housing and community development needs in the local environment, monitored and assessed the project's ongoing planning, monitored construction and associated processes, and used the foundation's mandated values to assess the project's side effects, as well as its success in producing houses and a viable, values-based community. The study was grounded in the Joint Committee's (1994) *Program Evaluation Standards*. Key procedures included interviews of stakeholders, an on-site resident observer, site visits, document/records analysis, periodic environmental analyses, and case studies. Ultimately, we produced a final report for foundation decision makers and interested outside parties (Stufflebeam, Gullickson, & Wingate, 2002). The final report recapped the project's background, described its structure and procedural plan, described its actual implementation, and noted and assessed its accomplishments. Roughly, the report's outline mirrored Stake's (1967) countenance evaluation model, which calls for describing and judging a project's antecedents, transactions, and outcomes. At the end of the report's different sections, pictures were presented to depict the project's environment and show what the residents had achieved in constructing their houses, landscaping their properties, providing play areas for children, and developing a sense of community. Our summative assessment presented data-based judgments of the program's goals, plans, implementation, reach to the targeted beneficiaries, effectiveness, sustainability, and transportability.

Throughout the study, the evaluators regularly employed a feedback process to keep the foundation's leaders and project staff informed about the findings. The foundation's president assigned a panel to review, react to, and make use of the succession of reports produced throughout the evaluation. The evaluators sent draft reports to the panel about 10 days in advance of each feedback workshop, in which the evaluators and panel met to discuss the findings.

The final evaluation report included the evaluators' attestation of the extent to which the evaluation met professionally defined standards for utility, feasibility, propriety, and accuracy. Overall, the evaluation found the project to be highly successful in helping 75 families construct their own high-quality houses; work together to develop an attractive, safe, functional community; effectively protect, educate, and nurture their children; meet their mortgage and land lease payments; and keep their houses and properties well maintained. The foundation's president affirmed that the evaluation was instrumental in assisting the program to succeed and communicate its process and success to interested parties. Readers of this chapter are encouraged to access and study the full final report of this evaluation, titled *The Spirit of Consuelo*, at www.wmich.edu/evalctr (Stufflebeam, 2002).

THEORETICAL UNDERPINNINGS OF THE CIPP MODEL

The CIPP model reflects prolonged effort and a modicum of progress to achieve the still distant goal of developing a sound evaluation theory, that is, *a coherent set of conceptual, hypothetical, pragmatic, and ethical principles forming a general framework to guide the study and practice of evaluation* (see Stufflebeam & Shinkfield, 2007, chap. 2). The model's theoretical underpinnings are evident in its concepts as summarized earlier in this chapter, its grounding in professionally defined standards as explained earlier in the chapter, and its fundamental definition of evaluation and objectivist orientation (addressed below).

Evaluation Defined

According to the CIPP model, evaluation is the systematic process of delineating, obtaining, reporting, and applying descriptive and judgmental information about an object's value—for example, its merit, worth, probity, equity, feasibility, efficiency, safety, cost, and significance. The result of an evaluation process is an evaluation as product. The main uses of evaluations are to guide and strengthen enterprises, issue accountability reports, help disseminate effective practices, and, as appropriate, make decision makers, stakeholders, and consumers aware of enterprises that proved unworthy of further use. Evaluation is a ubiquitous process that applies across national boundaries and to all disciplines and service areas. Systematic evaluation is a fundamental responsibility of professionals and organizations in their ongoing efforts to examine and strengthen services.

Objectivist Orientation

The CIPP model's epistemological orientation is objectivist (Stufflebeam & Shinkfield, 2007, p. 331), not relativist. Objectivist evaluations posit that moral good is objective and independent of personal or merely human feelings. They are grounded in ethical principles, such as the U.S. Bill of Rights; strive to control bias, prejudice, and conflicts of interest that may threaten an evaluation's integrity; invoke and justify appropriate technical standards; obtain and validate findings from multiple sources; search for the best answers; set forth and justify the best available conclusions; report findings honestly, fairly, and as circumspectly as necessary to all right-to-know audiences; subject the evaluation process and findings to independent assessments; and identify needs for further investigation. Fundamentally, objectivist evaluations are intended over time to lead to conclusions that are correct—not correct or incorrect relative to an evaluator's or other party's predilections, position, preferences, or point of view. The model contends that when different evaluations are focused on the same object in a given setting, are keyed to fundamental principles of a free society and agreed-on criteria, meaningfully engage all stakeholder groups in the quest for answers, and conform to the evaluation field's standards, different, competent evaluators will arrive at fundamentally equivalent, defensible conclusions.

Pragmatic Guidelines for Conducting Successful Evaluations

According to the CIPP model, an evaluation is judged successful when it fulfills requirements defined by the evaluation profession for utility, feasibility, propriety, accuracy, and evaluator accountability (Joint Committee on Standards for Educational Evaluation, 2011). To achieve success across all five dimensions, the CIPP model posits—based on long and widespread experience in applying the model—that both the evaluator and the evaluation client can and should carry out certain actions in planning, organizing, and implementing the evaluation. Lists of such actions are delineated in the CIPP Evaluation Model Checklist, which may be accessed at www.wmich.edu/evalctr.

SUMMATION

The CIPP model treats evaluation as an essential concomitant of improvement and accountability within a framework of appropriate values and a quest for clear, unambiguous answers. It responds to the reality that evaluations of innovative, evolving efforts typically cannot employ controlled, randomized experiments. The model is configured to enable and guide comprehensive, systematic examination of efforts that occur in the dynamic conditions of the real world. Fundamentally, the model sees evaluation as essential to societal progress and well-being.

The model employs multiple methods, is based on a wide range of applications, is keyed to professional standards for evaluations, is supported by an extensive literature, and is buttressed by practical procedures, including a set of evaluation checklists (www.wmich.edu/evalctr/checklists). Clearly, the CIPP model and its history of development and use constitute a part of the roots of the current evaluation discipline. It cannot be overemphasized, however, that the model is and must be subject to continuing assessment, research, and further development.

NOTES

1. The OSU Model Training Program's legacy is evident in its having provided the basic pattern for the current WMU Interdisciplinary PhD Program in Evaluation.

2. I have found review panels extremely useful. Persons who serve on such panels can make valuable contributions by critiquing evaluation plans and reports from their different perspectives. However, I have an aversion to calling such groups "advisory panels." Assigning such a label seems to cause persons with no special qualifications in evaluation generally or in the content of the specific study to feel perfectly comfortable and assertive in saying how problems seen in the evaluation should be solved. Usually, such determinations are best directed to appropriately qualified experts and those with responsibility for carrying out the evaluation.

REFERENCES

Alkin, M. (2004). *Evaluation roots: Tracing theorists' views and influences.* Thousand Oaks, CA: Sage.

Campbell, D. T., & Stanley, J. C. (1963). Experimental and quasi-experimental designs for research on teaching. In N. L. Gage (Ed.), *Handbook of research on teaching* (pp. 171–246). Chicago, IL: Rand McNally.

Candoli, I. C., Cullen, K., & Stufflebeam, D. L. (1997). *Superintendent performance evaluation: Current practice and directions for improvement.* Boston, MA: Kluwer.

Cook, D. L., & Stufflebeam, D. L. (1967). Estimating test norms from variable size item and examinee samples. *Educational and Psychological Measurement, 27,* 601–610.

Coryn, C. S., Stufflebeam, D. L., Davidson, E. J., & Scriven, M. (2010). The Interdisciplinary Ph.D. in Evaluation: Reflections on its development and first seven years. *Journal of Multidisciplinary Evaluation, 6*(13), 118–129.

Cronbach, L. J., Ambron, S. R., Dornbusch, S. M., Hess, R. D., Hornick, R. C., Philips, D. C., . . . Be Wemmer. (1981). *Toward reforms of program evaluation.* San Francisco, CA: Jossey-Bass.

Finn, C. E., Stevens, F. I., Stufflebeam, D. L., & Walberg, H. (1997). A metaevaluation. *International Journal of Educational Research, 27*(2), 159–174.

Guba, E. G. (1966, October). *A study of Title III Activities: Report on evaluation* [Mimeo]. National Institute for the Study of Educational Change, Indiana University, Bloomington.

Guba, E. G., & Stufflebeam, D. L. (1968). Evaluation: The process of stimulating, aiding, and abetting insightful action. In R. Ingle & W. Gephart (Eds.), *Problems in the training of educational researchers.* Bloomington, IN: Phi Delta Kappa.

Gullickson, A., & Stufflebeam, D. (2001, December). *Feedback workshop checklist.* Retrieved from Western Michigan University Evaluation Center website: http://www.wmich.edu/evalctr/checklists/

House, E. R., Rivers, W., & Stufflebeam, D. L. (1974). An assessment of the Michigan accountability system. *Phi Delta Kappan, 60*(10), 663–699.

Joint Committee on Standards for Educational Evaluation. (1981). *Standards for evaluations of educational programs, projects, & materials.* New York, NY: McGraw-Hill.

Joint Committee on Standards for Educational Evaluation. (1994). *The program evaluation standards.* Thousand Oaks, CA: Corwin Press.

Joint Committee on Standards for Educational Evaluation. (2011). *The program evaluation standards* (3rd ed.). Thousand Oaks, CA: Sage.

Owens, T. R., & Stufflebeam, D. L. (1964). An experimental comparison of item sampling and examinee sampling for estimating test norms. *Journal of Educational Measurement, 6*(2), 75–83.

Reinhard, D. (1972). *Methodology development for input evaluation using advocate and design teams* (Unpublished doctoral dissertation). Ohio State University, Columbus.

Scriven, M. (1967). The methodology of evaluation. In R. Tyler, R. Gagne, & M. Scriven (Eds.), *Perspectives on curriculum evaluation* (pp. 39–83; AERA Monograph Series on Curriculum Evaluation, No. 1). Skokie, IL: Rand McNally.

Shinkfield, A. J., & Stufflebeam, D. L. (1995). *Teacher evaluation: Guide to effective practice.* Boston, MA: Kluwer.

Smith, E. R., & Tyler, R. W. (1942). *Appraising and recording student progress.* New York, NY: Harper.

Stake, R. (1967). The countenance of educational evaluation. *Teachers College Record, 68,* 523–540.

Stake, R. (1983). Program evaluation, particularly responsive evaluation. In G. Madaus, M. Scriven, & D. Stufflebeam (Eds.), *Evaluation models.* Boston, MA: Kluwer-Nijhoff.

Stufflebeam, D. L. (1966a). A depth study of the evaluation requirement. *Theory Into Practice, 5*(3), 121–133.

Stufflebeam, D. L. (1966b, January). *Evaluation Under Title I of the Elementary and Secondary Education Act of 1967.* Address delivered at evaluation conference sponsored by the Michigan State Department of Education, Lansing.

Stufflebeam, D. L. (1967a). *Applying PERT to a test development project.* Paper presented at the annual meeting of the American Educational Research Association, Chicago, IL.

Stufflebeam, D. L. (1967b). The use and abuse of evaluation in Title III. *Theory Into Practice, 6,* 126–133.

Stufflebeam, D. L. (1969, January). *Evaluation as enlightenment for decision-making.* Paper presented at the Association for Supervision and Curriculum Development Conference on Assessment Theory, Sarasota, FL.

Stufflebeam, D. L. (1997). A standards-based perspective on evaluation. In R. E. Stake & L. Mabry (Eds.), *Advances in program evaluation: Vol. 3. Evaluation and the postmodern dilemma* (pp. 61–88). Greenwich, CT: JAI Press.

Stufflebeam, D. L. (2000). Lessons in contracting for evaluations. *American Journal of Evaluation, 21*(3), 293–314.

Stufflebeam, D. L. (2001a, Spring). Evaluation models. *New Directions for Evaluation, 89,* 7–99.

Stufflebeam, D. L. (2001b). Interdisciplinary Ph.D. programming in evaluation. *American Journal of Evaluation, 22*(3), 445–455.

Stufflebeam, D. L. (2002). *CIPP evaluation model checklist.* Retrieved from www.wmich.edu/evalctr/checklists

Stufflebeam, D. L. (2003a). The CIPP model for evaluation. In T. Kellaghan & D. L. Stufflebeam (Eds.), *The international handbook of educational evaluation* (pp. 31–62). Boston, MA: Kluwer.

Stufflebeam, D. L. (2003b). Institutionalizing evaluation in schools. In T. Kellaghan & D. L. Stufflebeam (Eds.), *The international handbook of educational evaluation* (pp. 775–806). Boston, MA: Kluwer.

Stufflebeam, D. L., Foley, W. J., Gephart, W. J., Guba, E. G., Hammond, R. L., Merriman, H. O., & Provus, M. M. (1971). *Educational evaluation and decision making.* Itasca, IL: Peacock.

Stufflebeam, D. L., Gullickson, A. R., & Wingate, L. A. (2002). *The spirit of Consuelo: An evaluation of Ke Aka Ho'ona.* Kalamazoo: Western Michigan University Evaluation Center. Retrieved from www.wmich.edu/evalctr/checklists

Stufflebeam, D. L., Jaeger, R. M., & Scriven, M. (1992, April 21). *A retrospective analysis of a summative evaluation of NAGB's pilot project to set achievement levels on the national assessment of educational progress.* Paper presented at the annual meeting of the American Educational Research Association, San Francisco, CA.

Stufflebeam, D. L., Madaus, G. F., & Kellaghan, T. (2000). *Evaluation models: Viewpoints on educational and human services evaluation.* Boston, MA: Kluwer.

Stufflebeam, D. L., & Shinkfield, A. J. (1995). *Teacher evaluation: Guide to effective practice.* Boston, MA: Kluwer.

Stufflebeam, D. L., & Shinkfield, A. J. (2007). *Evaluation theory, models, & applications.* San Francisco, CA: Jossey-Bass.

Stufflebeam, D. L., & Webster, W. J. (1988). Evaluation as an administrative function. In N. Boyan (Ed.), *Handbook of research on educational administration* (pp. 569–601). White Plains, NY: Longman.

Tyler, R. W. (1942). General statement on evaluation. *Journal of Educational Research, 36,* 492–501.

20

USING EVALUATION TO IMPROVE PROGRAM PERFORMANCE AND RESULTS

Joseph S. Wholey

MY VIEWS ON EVALUATION

My interest is in program evaluation: a retrospective assessment of the performance of programs (policies, programs, projects, and processes) that have been implemented by public and nongovernmental organizations. The purposes of program evaluation are to increase transparency, strengthen accountability, improve program performance, and support resource allocation and other policy and management decision making. In my view, the primary purpose of evaluation is to improve program performance and results.

Within program evaluation, my focus is on evaluation utilization—use of information from performance measurement systems or evaluation studies, either of which can produce judgments about the value or worth of programs (Scriven, 1980). I am therefore interested in the planning and design of evaluations that provide credible, useful information—and in the monitoring and evaluation of the evaluation process (U.S. Department of Health, Education, and Welfare, 1980; Wholey, 1979, 1983, 1998, 2006). To enhance the likelihood that evaluation will be used to improve program performance, I am especially interested in approaches that help develop agreement on program goals and that focus evaluation efforts on criteria that key stakeholders consider relevant. In recent years, I have become interested in approaches for overcoming political and bureaucratic challenges to the use of evaluation (Wholey, 2010b).

While recognizing the importance of randomized experiments and quasi-experiments designed to estimate the extent to which program activities cause intended or unintended outcomes, I have long been concerned that evaluation may be costly and yet yield little by way of useful information (see Horst, Nay, Scanlon, & Wholey, 1974). I am therefore particularly interested in evaluability assessment and rapid-feedback evaluation: two low-cost exploratory evaluation approaches that can be used to help key stakeholders get better value from the expenditure of evaluation resources. Evaluability assessments are exploratory evaluation studies that assess whether programs are ready for useful evaluation—and help key stakeholders and evaluators come to an agreement on realistic program goals, information needs, evaluation criteria, and specific intended uses for evaluation information (see Horst et al., 1974; Nay & Kaye, 1982; Schmidt, Scanlon, & Bell, 1979; Wholey, 1979, 1983, 1987, 2004, 2010a). Evaluability assessment is a six-step process: (1) involve intended users and other key stakeholders, (2) clarify the program design, (3) explore program reality, (4) assess the plausibility of the program (the likelihood that program activities will lead to intended outputs and outcomes), (5) reach agreement on any needed changes in program design or program implementation, and (6) reach agreement with intended users on the focus and intended use of any further evaluation.

Rapid-feedback evaluations are pilot studies designed to estimate program effects, indicate the range of uncertainty in the estimates, and produce tested designs for more definitive evaluation efforts (see Wholey, 1979, 1983, 2010a). Rapid-feedback evaluation is a five-step process: (1) collect existing data on program performance in terms of agreed-on program goals; (2) collect limited amounts of new data on program performance in terms of the agreed-on goals; (3) estimate program effectiveness and state the range of uncertainty in the estimates (e.g., uncertainty due to conflicting evidence or small sample sizes); (4) develop options for more definitive evaluation, and analyze those options in terms of their feasibility, cost, and likely usefulness; and (5) reach agreement with intended users on the design and intended use of any further evaluation. Use of either evaluability assessment or rapid-feedback evaluation yields useful evaluation findings and provides a foundation for more extensive evaluation efforts. Evaluability assessment is especially useful in large, decentralized programs in which policymaking and management responsibilities are dispersed, evaluation criteria are unclear, and program results are not readily apparent; rapid-feedback evaluation helps determine the likely value of future evaluation efforts.

Performance measurement systems and program evaluation studies can and should be mutually reinforcing. Evaluation studies should be more feasible, less costly, and more useful when performance criteria have been clarified and performance data have been collected on a regular basis. And the demand for and supply of evaluation studies are likely to increase after agencies begin to measure program inputs, process, outputs, and outcomes. When policymakers and managers are regularly provided information on a program's outcomes, they are likely to want to know why the outcomes have occurred (what difference the program has made) and how performance can be improved. Such interest is likely to stimulate evaluation studies to answer such "why" and "how" questions (Hatry, Wholey, & Newcomer, 2010; Wholey, 2003).

Rarely will a single performance measurement system or evaluation study meet the needs of all key stakeholders. Learning organizations use many types of information to inform policy formulation and program improvement (Weiss & Morrill, 1998). Performance information may come from performance measurement systems, process evaluations, or impact evaluations. It will usually be necessary to develop hierarchies of performance measures to meet information needs at different levels (see U.S. General Accounting Office, 1996).

INFLUENCES ON MY VIEW OF EVALUATION

My interest in program evaluation began with policy analysis, systems analysis, cost-effectiveness analysis, and cost–benefit analysis in the U.S. Department of Health, Education, and Welfare (now the Department of Health and Human Services), under the guidance of two premier policy analysts (both economists): Assistant Secretary William Gorham and Deputy Assistant Secretary Alice Rivlin. As we searched for cost-effective solutions to social problems, we recognized and began to help meet the need for program evaluation studies that would support federal policy decision making (see Rivlin & Wholey, 1969; U.S. Department of Health, Education, and Welfare, 1966, 1968; Wholey, 1969).

At the Urban Institute, under the guidance of President William Gorham, those of us in the program evaluation group evaluated the federal government's ability to evaluate the impact of federal programs—with a dual focus on the development of social policies and the improvement of social programs—and suggested how federal evaluation efforts might be improved (Wholey, Scanlon, Duffy, Fukumoto, & Vogt, 1970). In subsequent years, in a growing group of Urban Institute evaluators, my primary focus turned to formative evaluations that could help program managers and policymakers redirect and improve programs. We became concerned, however, that the costs of evaluation too often outweighed its value (see Horst et al., 1974). The evaluation approach that we developed—sequential purchase of information—uses evaluability assessment, rapid-feedback evaluation, performance measurement systems, and impact evaluation studies to produce successive increments of information on program promise and performance (see Shadish, Cook, & Leviton, 1991; Wholey, 1979, 1983, 2010a). Given the information resulting from initial evaluation efforts, program managers and policymakers may maintain or change program activities or objectives in an effort to improve performance—and may or may not decide to purchase additional evaluation information.

My experiences as a policymaker and evaluation user have also influenced my views on the conditions under which evaluation can affect decision making. Encouraged by Urban Institute president William Gorham, I combined my years at the Urban Institute with service on the Arlington County Board and on the Washington Metropolitan Area Transit Authority (Metro) Board of Directors. With the support of colleagues on both boards, I led efforts to use strategic planning, program evaluation, and a simplified form of zero-base budgeting to support policy decision making and improve government efficiency and effectiveness (see Wholey, 1978).

In my second tour in the Department of Health and Human Services, under the guidance of Secretary Joseph Califano and Under Secretary Hale Champion, our evaluation staff focused on the use of "exploratory evaluation" (evaluability assessment), "short-term evaluation" (rapid-feedback evaluation), and performance measurement systems to improve program performance and on efforts to monitor and enhance the utilization of evaluation findings (see Abramson & Wholey, 1981; Strosberg & Wholey, 1983; U.S. Department of Health, Education, and Welfare, 1980; Wholey, 1983).

At the University of Southern California, as I learned more about—and taught—policy analysis, research methods, policy evaluation, program evaluation, and philosophy of science as a professor of public administration, I fell under the subtle but real influence of a broader set of mentors: evaluation theorists (see Campbell & Stanley, 1963; Cook & Campbell, 1979; Joint Committee on Standards for Educational Evaluation, 1994; Lincoln & Guba, 1985; Patton, 1997; Scriven, 1991; Shadish et al., 1991; Vedung, 1997; Yin, 1984, 1993) and colleagues who joined me in monthly brown-bag sessions at the University of Southern California's Washington Public Affairs Center, made conference presentations, and then published (see Wholey, Newcomer, & Associates, 1989). I have also been influenced by efforts to use evaluation to improve the performance of nonprofit organizations (see Hatry, 2006; United Way of America, 1996a, 1996b; Wholey, 2002) and to communicate the value of programs to policymakers (Wholey, 1984, 1986a, 1986b).

The most recent influences on my thinking in the evaluation arena have come from my involvement in efforts to effectively implement strategic planning, performance measurement systems, performance management, and performance budgeting in federal agencies under the Government Performance and Results Act, the Bush administration's Budget and Performance Integration initiative, and the Obama administration's efforts to improve the use of performance and related information in resource allocation and other policy decision making (see Government Performance and Results Act, 1993; Panel on Improving Government Performance, 1998; U.S. Office of Management and Budget, 2001, 2003, 2010; Wholey, 1999a, 1999b, 2001, 2002, 2003, 2010b). Especially influential have been insights gained from the often daily interaction with colleagues at the U.S. Office of Management and Budget and the U.S. Government Accountability Office and with Harry Hatry and Kathryn Newcomer, with whom I have worked closely over many years.

CONCLUSION

Looking back at the evolution of my views on evaluation over a span of more than 40 years of involvement in evaluation and policy-making efforts in public and nonprofit organizations, I thank my mentors and colleagues for their influence and support. I thank Marv Alkin for the opportunity to reflect on those insights and experiences.

REFERENCES

Abramson, M. A., & Wholey, J. S. (1981). Organization and management of the evaluation function in a multilevel organization. In Evaluation of complex systems [Special issue]. *New Directions for Program Evaluation, 1981*(10), 31–48.

Campbell, D. T., & Stanley, J. C. (1963). Experimental and quasi-experimental designs for research on teaching. In N. L. Gage (Ed.), *Handbook of research on teaching* (pp. 171–246). Chicago, IL: Rand McNally.

Cook, T. D., & Campbell, D. T. (1979). *Quasi-experimentation: Design and analysis issue for field settings*. Boston, MA: Houghton Mifflin.

Government Performance and Results Act of 1993, Pub. L. No. 103–62107, Stat. 285 (1993).

Hatry, H. P. (2006). *Performance measurement: Getting results* (2nd ed.). Washington, DC: Urban Institute Press.

Hatry, H. P., Wholey, J. S., & Newcomer, K. E. (2010). Evaluation challenges, issues, and trends. In J. S. Wholey, H. P. Hatry, & K. E. Newcomer (Eds.), *Handbook of practical program evaluation* (3rd ed., pp. 668–679). San Francisco, CA: Jossey-Bass.

Horst, P., Nay, J. N., Scanlon, J. S., & Wholey, J. S. (1974). Program management and the federal evaluator. *Public Administration Review, 34*(4), 300–308.

Joint Committee on Standards for Educational Evaluation. (1994). *The program evaluation standards* (2nd ed.). Thousand Oaks, CA: Sage.

Lincoln, Y. S., & Guba, E. G. (1985). *Naturalistic inquiry.* Beverly Hills, CA: Sage.

Nay, J., & Kaye, P. (1982). *Government oversight and evaluability assessment.* Lexington, MA: D. C. Heath.

Panel on Improving Government Performance. (1998). *Effective implementation of the Government Performance and Results Act.* Washington, DC: National Academy of Public Administration.

Patton, M. Q. (1997). *Utilization-focused evaluation* (3rd ed.). Thousand Oaks, CA: Sage.

Rivlin, A. M., & Wholey, J. S. (1969). Education of disadvantaged children. *Socio-Economic Planning Sciences, 2*(2–4), 373–380.

Schmidt, R. E., Scanlon, J. W., & Bell, J. B. (1979). *Evaluability assessment: Making public programs work better* (Human Services Monograph Series). Rockville, MD: U.S. Department of Health, Education, and Welfare, Office of the Secretary Office of the Assistant Secretary for Planning and Evaluation.

Scriven, M. (1980). *The logic of evaluation.* Iverness, CA: Edgepress.

Scriven, M. (1991). *Evaluation thesaurus* (4th ed.). Newbury Park, CA: Sage.

Shadish, W. R., Jr., Cook, T. C., & Leviton, L. C. (1991). *Foundations of program evaluation.* Newbury Park, CA: Sage.

Strosberg, M. A., & Wholey, J. S. (1983). Evaluability assessment: From theory to practice in the department of health and human services. *Public Administration Review, 43*(1), 66–71.

United Way of America. (1996a). *Focusing on program outcomes.* Alexandria, VA: Author.

United Way of America. (1996b). *Measuring program outcomes.* Alexandria, VA: Author.

U.S. Department of Health, Education, and Welfare. (1966). *Maternal and child health care programs.* Washington, DC: Office of the Assistant Secretary for Program Coordination.

U.S. Department of Health, Education, and Welfare. (1968). *Child development: Summary of the child development task force report.* Washington, DC: Author.

U.S. Department of Health, Education, and Welfare. (1980). *Evaluation utilization in the Department of Health, Education, and Welfare.* Washington, DC: Author.

U.S. General Accounting Office. (1996). *Executive guide: Effectively implementing the Government Performance and Results Act.* Washington, DC: Author.

U.S. Office of Management and Budget. (2001). *President's management agenda.* Washington, DC: Author.

U.S. Office of Management and Budget. (2003). *Performance and management assessments: Budget of the United States government, fiscal year 2004.* Washington, DC: Author.

U.S. Office of Management and Budget. (2010). *Performance and management: Budget of the United States government, fiscal year 2011.* Washington, DC: Author.

Vedung, E. (1997). *Public policy and program evaluation.* New Brunswick, NJ: Transaction Books.

Weiss, H. B., & Morrill, W. A. (1998, April). *Useful learning for public action.* Paper presented at the American Society for Public Administration National Conference, Seattle, WA.

Wholey, J. S. (1969). The absence of program evaluation as an obstacle to effective public expenditure policy. In *The analysis and evaluation of public expenditures: The PPB system; a compendium of papers submitted to the Subcommittee on Economy in*

Government of the Joint Economic Committee, Congress of the United States (pp. 451–471). Washington, DC: U.S. Government Printing Office.

Wholey, J. S. (1978). *Zero-base budgeting and program evaluation.* Lexington, MA: D. C. Heath.

Wholey, J. S. (1979). *Evaluation: Promise and performance.* Washington, DC: Urban Institute Press.

Wholey, J. S. (1983). *Evaluation and effective public management.* Boston, MA: Little, Brown.

Wholey, J. S. (1984). Executive agency retrenchment. In G. B. Mills & J. L. Palmer (Eds.), *Federal budget policy in the 1980s* (pp. 295–332). Washington, DC: Urban Institute Press.

Wholey, J. S. (1986a). The job corps: Congressional use of evaluation findings. In J. S. Wholey, M. A. Abramson, & C. Bellavita (Eds.), *Performance and credibility* (pp. 271–283). Lexington, MA: D. C. Heath.

Wholey, J. S. (1986b). WIC: Positive outcomes for a demonstrably effective program. In J. S. Wholey, M. A. Abramson, & C. Bellavita (Eds.), *Performance and credibility* (pp. 245–255). Lexington, MA: D. C. Heath.

Wholey, J. S. (1987). Evaluability assessment: Developing program theory. *New Directions for Program Evaluation, 33,* 77–92.

Wholey, J. S. (1998). Assessing performance measurement systems. *The Public Manager, 27*(3), 23.

Wholey, J. S. (1999a). GPRA: Progress, challenges, and prospects. *The Public Manager, 28*(3), 20.

Wholey, J. S. (1999b). Performance-based management: Responding to the challenges. *Public Productivity & Management Review, 22*(3), 288–307.

Wholey, J. S. (2001). Managing for results: Roles for evaluators in a new management era. *American Journal of Evaluation, 22,* 343–347.

Wholey, J. S. (2002). Making results count in public and nonprofit organizations. In K. Newcomer, E. T. Jennings Jr., C. Broom, & A. Lomax (Eds.), *Meeting the challenges in performance-oriented government* (pp. 13–36). Washington, DC: American Society for Public Administration.

Wholey, J. S. (2003). Improving performance and accountability: Responding to emerging management challenges. In S. I. Donaldson & M. Scriven (Eds.), *Evaluating social programs and problems* (pp. 43–61). Mahwah, NJ: Lawrence Erlbaum.

Wholey, J. S. (2004). Evaluability assessment. In J. S. Wholey, H. P. Hatry, & K. E. Newcomer (Eds.), *Handbook of practical program evaluation* (2nd ed., pp. 15–39). San Francisco, CA: Jossey-Bass.

Wholey, J. S. (2006). Quality control: Assessing the accuracy and usefulness of performance measurement systems. In H. P. Hatry (Ed.), *Performance measurement: Getting results* (2nd ed., pp. 267–286). Washington, DC: Urban Institute Press.

Wholey, J. S. (2010a). Exploratory evaluation. In J. S. Wholey, H. P. Hatry, & K. E. Newcomer (Eds.), *Handbook of practical program evaluation* (3rd ed., pp. 81–99). San Francisco, CA: Jossey-Bass.

Wholey, J. S. (2010b). Use of evaluation in government: The politics of evaluation. In J. S. Wholey, H. P. Hatry, & K. E. Newcomer (Eds.), *Handbook of practical program evaluation* (3rd ed., pp. 651–667). San Francisco, CA: Jossey-Bass.

Wholey, J. S., Newcomer, K. E., & Associates. (1989). *Improving government performance.* San Francisco, CA: Jossey-Bass.

Wholey, J. S., Scanlon, J. S., Duffy, H. D., Fukumoto, J. S., & Vogt, L. M. (1970). *Federal evaluation policy.* Washington, DC: Urban Institute Press.

Yin, R. K. (1984). *Case study research: Design and methods.* Beverly Hills, CA: Sage.

Yin, R. K. (1993). *Applications of case study research.* Newbury Park, CA: Sage.

21

EVALUATION PURPOSES, PERSPECTIVES, AND PRACTICE

Eleanor Chelimsky

The question Professor Alkin has posed—about my views on evaluation and how I came to hold them—sounds simple enough, but in fact, like almost all evaluation questions, it's a challenging one. It forces me to make painful decisions, of the "Sophie's Choice" variety, about which cherished ideas are important and which aren't, to recollect long-forgotten trails of influence in order to figure out how the "important" ones developed, to incorporate all this selective complexity into a reasonably comprehensible but authentic picture of where I stand today, and to do it all in 25 pages or less. Obviously, the challenge is real. But it's also a cognitive luxury, an opportunity to consider subterranean passages that I never would have explored otherwise, burrow far, far down into the past, come up for air only when necessary, and then finally return to the 21st century with a couple of observations and suggestions. So, Dickensian beginnings aside, let me start with my first job as an evaluator.

PROFESSIONAL INFLUENCES, EXPERIENCE, AND IDEAS

An International Setting for Evaluation: The North Atlantic Treaty Organization

My first evaluations were done at the North Atlantic Treaty Organization (NATO). I worked initially as an economist/statistician in 1960s' Paris, and then in Brussels, on defense and foreign policy questions. Some of the issues I dealt with involved the relative effectiveness of the various (often extremely costly) components of NATO's deterrent force, the appropriateness of each country's budgetary commitment in terms of both its own possibilities and NATO burden sharing as a whole, changes in the long-term trends in three budgetary sectors (capital expenditures, operations and maintenance, and personnel costs), and the reasons for the success or failure of recruitment efforts in individual nations. My users were the defense and foreign ministers of 15 NATO countries (first and foremost, the U.S. Department of Defense [DOD] and the State Department), all of them with different agendas, histories, political commitments, and axes to grind within NATO. For me, it was a baptism of fire with respect to the use of findings because these sponsors were often in conflict, more apt to hide than to reveal information, and quite overwhelming in their ability to suppress findings and conclusions (or even footnotes) that they didn't like.

NATO's data systems naturally reflected this disinterest in accurate information. I found missing data everywhere, definitions that were different across nations and could change in mysterious ways from year to year, and quality control that was virtually inexistent. I would sometimes discover a published version of one of my own evaluation reports from which important sections had been deleted (without any discussion with me), changing both the import and the credibility of the findings. However, in other cases—when it happened that the findings fit the NATO Alliance's conventional wisdom or felicitously supported a popular position—the reports were not only presented correctly but also well received and well used.

Evaluation Purpose

My experiences at NATO, influenced by the guidance of mentors like Harlan Cleveland, Tim Stanley, Gerald Sullivan, Andre Vincent, and Serge Michelson (and especially by the writings of Max Weber on *Entzauberung*—or demystification—and the role of analysis in government), convinced me that evaluation had enormous potential in a political environment for clarifying the world of spin that I was discovering (Aron, 1967; Freund, 1966). I came to see evaluation as a means not only to improve individual policies and programs but also to serve the public good, through policy and data analysis that proceeded from carefully researched and accurate information. Jefferson's ideas on the importance of knowledge for keeping freedom alive and well in a democracy had always resonated deeply with me, and Weber's writing on the need to carefully investigate the various myths presented as the bases and rationales for government initiatives greatly reinforced the Jeffersonian concept. Still, I realized that Weber's own advice to Generals Ludendorff and von Hindenburg in 1916 had gone unheeded by the German government, and this raised the question for me of how evaluation's small, sober voice could ever be expected to make itself heard across the din of power politics. I started thinking about the need for evaluative expertise, experience, and credibility (to stand up to the kind of politically inspired criticism I had already seen); some real independence for the evaluation team (to protect them from political lobbying and interference); high morale and courage on the part of evaluators (to keep them targeted on their efforts, whatever the odds); and reliable dissemination methods for informing the public.

Credibility and Good Data

With respect to the evaluation process itself, NATO taught me the importance of high-quality data for (a) monitoring trends and programs, (b) performing stronger evaluations, and (c) reinforcing the technical expertise and credibility needed for evaluators' voices to be heard (and their findings used) in a political environment. I noticed that evaluators were a lot more persuasive in questioning conventional wisdom when their opponents knew they had good data to support their case. So I focused heavily on data improvements at NATO—first, because they could, in and of themselves, bring a better basis for understanding what was happening in the NATO Alliance; second, because, used longitudinally, they could help determine the effectiveness of a specific policy intervention; third, because missing data—which could signify the exclusion of voices presenting the other side of an argument—had the potential to invalidate both analyses and conclusions; and fourth, because improving data systems was in fact feasible—something I could get international staff analysts from all 15 nations to support. Incidentally, it was in doing this work that I first came to see the importance, for credibility, of presenting all voices relevant to an evaluation, not just those that are the most powerful, loudest, or easiest to access.

Understanding Context

The experience of evaluating NATO activities in a diversity of nations showed me the need to integrate past history and politics into the blood and bones of an evaluation. In a number of cases, doing this enabled me to interpret findings that would have been difficult to analyze with the data alone. For instance, understanding the social role that Turkey's enormous army played in the life of that country was crucial for explaining issues of recruitment and maintenance there. Indeed, I found that by integrating the past and present context of a policy question into an evaluation, there was less chance of error, a better foundation for applying case studies in a targeted way, and, overall, a greater likelihood of use. Incorporating past history and politics into an evaluation also helps the evaluator by warning about potential obstacles. As Faulkner said, "The past is never dead; it isn't even past" (Morris, 1989).

Importance of the Evaluation Question

Finally, at NATO I grasped the structural nature of the evaluation question and the leverage it has to determine and constrict almost everything in the evaluation process that comes with it. This, of course, made me much more careful in defining, analyzing, and accepting an evaluation question. A few failures taught me to negotiate obstinately until a question was researchable methodologically, targeted to an important aspect of the subject (Weber again), and likely to produce findings of interest either to someone in government who could do something about them or to the public, which needed to know of their existence.

In short, on returning to the United States in 1970, I'd say I brought back with me

- some understanding of at least one among the different kinds of political environments in which evaluation may be embedded;
- the conviction that a major purpose of evaluation was to work on behalf of a sometimes invisible public (if not as a seeker after truth at least as a demolisher of myths and a source of sound information about governmental activities);
- a belief in the importance of independence, expertise, and credibility for influencing the consideration and use of evaluative findings;
- some experience of the benefits accruing to a study of the past history, politics, and general context of an evaluation subject; and
- an awareness of the determinative power of an evaluation question.

An Executive-Branch Setting for Evaluation: The Think Tank

My second job was in Virginia, with a not-for-profit think tank called the MITRE Corporation. There I worked on criminal justice, health care, and welfare policy evaluations, along with studies of economic productivity, returns to investment in R&D, and research on evaluation. This was a change not only in subject matter but also in the evaluation setting, since all my work was now done for agencies of the executive branch and—to my great relief—on behalf of only two users: MITRE and the executive agency sponsor of a particular evaluation (as opposed to the 15 nations I had had to deal with at NATO).

Subject Matter Change and New Influences

With respect to subject matter, the new evaluation questions were, of course, very different from the ones at NATO, deriving from shifting social theories (Moynihan, 1969) rather than from the logic, strategy, and tactics of deterrence (Kissinger, 1969). This new concentration on social problems led me first to a re-reading of Don Campbell (1969) and then to a circle of evaluators who were raising various concerns that were new to me. Some were questioning the appropriateness and fit of certain methodologies (especially the experimental design) with respect to the typical settings in which social programs were implemented and evaluated (Guttentag, 1973; Weiss & Rein, 1970). Some were debating the value of a summative versus a formative approach to evaluation (Cronbach, 1964; Scriven, 1972). Still others had become concerned about the limited application of evaluation findings by the sponsors who had commissioned them and were reconsidering both the evaluative concept of use and how to maximize it (Weiss, 1972; Wholey, 1973). Finally, a number of evaluators were trying to better understand and describe the relationships existing between social program evaluations and the formulation of public policy (Marris & Rein, 1967; Mosteller, 1977; Rossi & Williams, 1972).

I owe an inestimable debt to all these people, especially Peter Rossi, who when consulted on an early evaluation of mine at MITRE, suggested a whole repertoire of methods to be used in conjunction with one another, spent time listening to my problems with sponsors, and educated me on the evaluative zeitgeist in America. Indeed, in directing my first major evaluation at MITRE (the Law Enforcement Assistance Administration's $160 million "High-Impact Anti-Crime Program"), it was Rossi's influence that led me to use a witch's brew of mixed methods to learn about participant and practitioner views; differences in service delivery modes and efficacy (across eight program sites); the economic, social, political, and geographical attributes of cities that are relevant to the outcomes of anticrime programs; and so on. I ended up borrowing methods from anywhere and everywhere, according to the type of analysis needed.

Technological Versus Social Program Evaluation

Despite the social orientation of my work at MITRE, I was able to keep up with the latest developments in defense, transportation, and environmental evaluations, since these were being done elsewhere at MITRE, and I got to review them occasionally too. Looking at the two kinds of evaluations together (i.e., technological and human service evaluations) was a useful experience in two ways. First, I noticed that the evaluation of technology seemed to pose fewer problems to evaluators from an external-validity viewpoint than did human service evaluations. This was because a technological program that had been through developmental and operational testing could be expected to perform more or less the same way everywhere, whereas human service programs, which depended for their delivery on program staff and a whole set of particular contextual variables, might well perform differently at different sites. That is, the dissimilarities across sites in these complex delivery systems, along with dissimilarities in program beneficiaries, history, local politics, and other place-related factors, meant that a social program that was effective in one place might not be so in another. I drew from this the conclusion that, for social programs, methods establishing internal validity (such as the experimental design) needed to be integrated with other methods, including case studies, to measure those critical site-specific variables if we wanted to generalize effects from one site to others. For technological evaluations, however, I thought the effort needed to be directed toward the issue of sustainable use rather than transferability.

Second, in looking carefully at MITRE's technological evaluations, I could see that many of them would have benefited from the use of certain methodological techniques employed in the evaluation of social programs. So, since the same issues of definition, design, measurement, comparison, and data collection applied to both types of evaluation, it seemed like a better idea to bring these kinds of evaluations together, for cross-fertilization purposes, than to separate them, as was usually the case for most evaluation shops in the 1970s. At MITRE, some of the managers (Walter Yondorf, Bob Everett, Fred Holland, and Warren McCabe) and, especially, my boss and mentor, Charlie Zraket, gave me a remarkable opportunity to do that.

Disappointed Expectations About Use

At NATO, the evaluators and analysts I'd worked with seemed generally to have taken the usual social-scientific position about the purpose of their work: that the important thing was that it be right (and, especially, replicable). Although use of the findings in policy was, of course, devoutly to be wished, it was viewed as a somewhat secondary issue. In the United States, however,

> many evaluators had naively anticipated that their results would be routinely used as the central input into policy decisions, but experience taught them that decisions are not so easily made in the political world. This led to a crisis in evaluation: if the field could not be justified in terms of instrumental usage, how could it be justified? (Cook, 1997, pp. 40–41)

So, in America, a major issue of the 1970s was how to improve on what everyone agreed seemed to be an inadequate use of evaluation findings. But there was some disagreement among evaluators about why that use was inadequate. Some questioned whether the problem wasn't really one of definition (perhaps "instrumental" use of findings by government was too much to expect, and perhaps there were other forms of use that were occurring that we didn't know about). Others felt that the problem was simply poor quality in the evaluative work.

A Symposium on the Use of Evaluation Findings by Agencies and the Congress

Since most of the literature on use reflected the thoughts and concerns of evaluators, it seemed as if it might be a good idea to query governmental program managers and policymakers themselves about their views on the subject. So I asked MITRE to support a symposium that would bring together evaluators, government managers, and policymakers to explore the question directly. This symposium, held in 1976, included evaluators from universities, from government, from think tanks, and from private consulting firms; program managers from a variety of agencies evaluating both technological and human service programs; and policymakers from the Office of Management and Budget, the Law Enforcement Assistance Administration, and the Congress. We discovered in the first hour of the first day's proceedings that the issue of use was conceived very differently by evaluators and by government officials (Chelimsky, 1977).

Dialogues About Questions and Answers

Many evaluators at the symposium approached the problem entirely in terms of the technical excellence and conclusiveness of the work performed, assuming that the use of the findings was uniquely a function of evaluative quality. But agency people and congressional staff talked much more about the lack of relevance, timeliness, breadth of analysis, and responsiveness in the work than about excellence or conclusiveness. Although nearly everyone agreed that methodological weakness was a problem, they minimized the issue of rigor in design or of inconclusiveness in findings as factors in the use (or nonuse) of those findings. On the contrary, the general assessment was that "purifying" the methodology and increasing the statistical "hardness" of evaluations would neither increase the use of findings by agencies nor help answer the policy questions posed by decision makers. It was pointed out repeatedly that the most important factors in ensuring the use of evaluation findings were (a) the match between the sponsor's (or agency's) question and the evaluator's answer and (b) the existence of a particular decision maker committed to using the findings and familiar enough with evaluation to know how to use them well (Chelimsky, 1977).

This, of course, pointed up the importance of a clear understanding by evaluators of exactly what a sponsor needed to know, as well as a willingness, on the evaluators' part, to try to produce that information and not some other information of interest to the evaluators (a common occurrence, according to a number of agency managers at the symposium). It also showed a clear need to ensure the spread of an evaluative culture and its relevant capabilities to the various agencies if evaluation findings were to be understood, considered, and used in government (Chelimsky, 1978).

Three Evaluation Perspectives

Moreover, different dialogues at the symposium revealed that evaluators as well as users held some quite distinct perspectives on evaluation and that, depending on who held which, the opportunities for mismatch between, say, a sponsor's question and an evaluator's answer could be almost infinite. In an analysis I did of the symposium proceedings in 1977, I described three of these perspectives and characterized them as focused on (1) accountability, (2) the acquisition of knowledge, and (3) management/development (i.e., program improvement *and* the related capability to understand and use evaluation within agencies). This last perspective thus had two strands: (1) enlisting managers in the evaluative effort to make their programs more effective and (2) developing evaluation capabilities among agency staff, managers, and policymakers (see Note 1).

Looking at the three perspectives from the viewpoint of use helped explain why a manager searching for ways to improve a troubled program might not be interested in the findings of an evaluation that brought new knowledge about the social problem being addressed by the program, important though that may have seemed to the evaluator (and perhaps also to the public) (Chelimsky, 1981).

Two Evaluation Purposes

The identification of these different perspectives, the mismatch between question and answer, and the sense that evaluators and users were each wrapped in the individual cocoons of their preoccupations and experience also helped in reexamining the concept of use as the single purpose of evaluation. Like my colleagues at NATO, I had believed that the basic purpose of evaluation was its ability to "speak truth to power" (or at least to demolish political inaccuracies and disinformation in the service of truth) and that use was a desirable but not always essential component of the equation. Now, in light of the three-perspective discussion, it became clear that both of these concepts of purpose were viable, albeit not in all cases. Use *had* to be the purpose of the management/development perspective because without it that enterprise would fail. However, the achievement of accountability and the acquisition of knowledge don't require use to succeed, and in fact, use may be virtually impossible in some cases, depending on the issues and political passions involved (Chelimsky, 1997).

The Importance of Perspective With Respect to Use

Indeed, the search for knowledge or accountability often engenders questions that are profoundly important to ask from the viewpoint of the public good but whose answers and findings are not likely to be used or even get a hearing in government. (Examples here would be evaluations about the short- and long-term social costs of the one-child-per-family policy in China, about the issues of public accountability and open government raised by classification of information in the United States, about civil liberties in Iran, or about freedom of dissent almost anywhere.) This nonuse may occur because the governmental structure does not provide for civil liberties or, when it does, the political climate is "wrong"; the subject falls outside normal bureaucratic boundaries; the findings evoke intense opposition from political groups in the electorate; or some other reason. Yet it is critically important for evaluation's role in government, especially a democratic government, that evaluators answering accountability or knowledge questions have the discretion, when needed, to bypass a requirement for use. There are three reasons for this: first, if these evaluators are obliged to rely on the immediate acceptability of their findings, the most important questions may be choked off at the planning stage because of their controversial nature; second, too much concern for use can induce dependence on the favor and good graces of sponsors, as well as concomitant distortion in the findings; and, finally, too much emphasis on the "client" or the "policy-shaping community" can mean (and has meant in the past) that relevant views, other than those of users, may be ignored in the evaluation.

In short, the multiple-perspective idea is helpful in that it illuminates what "purpose" means for the different kinds of evaluations and also how various criteria apply, depending on the perspective. For example, such attributes as independence, credibility, and nonpartisanship are clearly necessary for accountability and knowledge evaluations if they are to stand up to the barrages of criticism that often attend unpopular findings or subjects. But for evaluators working from a development or management perspective, gaining the trust of agency staff, to work with them effectively, is what counts. And loyalty, discretion, and technical expertise may be more important in gaining trust than independence or nonpartisanship in the evaluator.

To sum up, then, the NATO/MITRE experience allowed me to bring to my next job in government a clearer understanding of the political constraints on accountability and knowledge evaluations, as well as a recognition of the need for independence and credibility in those evaluations. I also developed some familiarity with the management of large, costly evaluations of social programs; a preference for a question-centered approach to the determination of appropriate methodology; a belief in two basic purposes of evaluation, depending on the evaluation perspective involved; and the sense that technological and human service evaluations belong together, that mixed methods provide great flexibility for answering evaluative questions, and that an important facilitator of use is the closeness of the match between a sponsor's question and an evaluator's answer.

A Congressional Setting for Evaluation: The Legislative Agency

When I moved to the Government Accountability Office (GAO) in 1980, it was at the invitation of Elmer Staats, who was then the U.S. Comptroller General. He had asked me to create an evaluation unit at GAO with a dual mission: to perform evaluations for the Congress and also teach evaluation skills and develop an evaluation culture at GAO. In one fell swoop, then, I became a practitioner of all three evaluation perspectives: doing accountability and knowledge evaluations for the Congress, on the one hand, and developing evaluation capabilities at the GAO, on the other.

The evaluation unit I would run was first known as the Institute for Program Evaluation, but later it became the Program Evaluation and Methodology Division. Over a period of 14 years at GAO (1980–1994), I would direct nearly 300 evaluations for the Congress and also discover the joys and miseries of the development perspective. For me, the new legislative environment (as opposed to the international and executive-branch settings I had known) would combine with the new work experience under the congressional oversight function to bring me (a) an expanded appreciation of the relation between politics and evaluation, (b) some changes in thinking about the evaluation process as it occurred in different settings, (c) a new set of strategies and tactics for improving evaluation performance at GAO, and (d) some confirmations of views I already held.

A Different Role for Evaluation in Government

After a year or so at GAO, I came to realize that evaluation was not really a discretionary function, as I had thought previously, but rather one that was a fundamental part of those checks-and-balances aspects of a democratic government that serve as protections against usurpation of power by any one branch. I now saw evaluation as an enabler of the separation-of-powers structure, with its legitimacy derived from the dual ability to perform the studies needed by each of the three branches to fulfill their individual functions (i.e., oversight, judicial review, and accountability) and to satisfy the public need for sound information about its government's activities. This is, of course, a grounded rather than a discretionary role for evaluation, which implicates it explicitly in the workings of our separated branches of government and their relationships.

Policy Questions and the Legislative Setting

Working with the Congress, I soon learned that the legislative setting would induce new and different kinds of evaluation questions. We were asked not only to conduct evaluations but also to help committees with legislative planning and evaluation language for use in upcoming bills. We had to develop some new methods—the Evaluation Synthesis, and the Prospective Evaluation Synthesis—for doing that, and these then turned out to be useful for other evaluations as well (Chelimsky, 1987; Chelimsky & Morra, 1984; U.S. General Accounting Office, Program Evaluation and Methodology Division, 1989). Also, based on a large number of requests to examine the quality of incoming studies received by members and senators, I developed the Methodological Review, which brought to legislative users some sense of the confidence they could have in an academic or executive-branch study and which we would turn around in 5 days or less. (An example of this kind of question was a request from Congressman Mike Synar asking us to explain how it could be that four different studies estimating the annual U.S. production of hazardous waste used different samples—one about a quarter the size of another—and different approaches and yet all arrived at the same mystical total of 260 million metric tons [Chelimsky, 1986].)

Again, with respect to the evaluation setting, I found that working for a legislative body requires substantive knowledge in a large number of fields, and we had to develop some capability in all of them. This is, of course, quite different from working with an executive agency that specializes in one subject, no matter how vast, and I was concerned about potential superficiality with respect to subject matter and about all the evaluative uncertainties and weaknesses that can flow from that. (I resolved this by creating subject matter teams within the Program Evaluation and Methodology Division, so that the staff and I could accumulate knowledge over time, and also by developing a network of experts in all of our substantive fields.) Over the years, we did evaluations in the areas of defense, health care, education, public assistance, transportation, agriculture, the environment, energy, immigration, housing, and criminal justice (among others). As might be expected, we found great disparities in evaluation capabilities among the agencies responsible for the programs and policies we looked at, and this often led us into a developmental mode in agencies where little evaluation had been or was being done.

Caution With Respect to the Policy or Evaluation Question

The legislative setting also meant that knowledge and accountability questions were often posed to support the oversight function (e.g., the question asked by Senator Daniel Patrick Moynihan: What theory or theories should underlie a legislative policy for dealing with teenage pregnancy? or by Congressman James Oberstar: What effects have construction grants programs had on water pollution?). Here, I soon learned that before agreeing to perform one of these evaluations, it was necessary to do a great deal of background work: (a) to understand the history, politics, and general context of the evaluative subject matter; (b) to look at past studies and evaluations on the issue; (c) to know the state of the evaluation art (and of data systems) in the programming agency; (d) to judge whether the time was right to ask a cause-and-effect question in, say, a new or underfunded program area (and if not, whether a simpler, more basic question could also produce information meeting the legislative sponsor's needs); and then, (e) to look at the potential methodological choices available given a specific time constraint.

This work enabled us to either move forward with the original question or renegotiate it, as I had done at NATO, until it made sense in terms of past experience and was feasible to perform. Thus, although we did many accountability and knowledge studies for the Congress in almost every imaginable subject area, there were at least as many examples of evaluations for development as for knowledge and accountability. Also, many of our studies had multiple perspectives or else grew one from another (as in the case of accountability evaluations that had to be followed by knowledge or development evaluations to remedy some of the gaps or answer some of the questions that couldn't be resolved). However, the usual case was that a particular perspective would dominate a particular evaluation (Chelimsky, 2006).

The Kinds of Questions Typically Posed

With regard to the types of questions legislators asked, I observed that, whether the governmental purpose in asking evaluation questions was oversight, policy making, expansion of knowledge, agency mission, or something else, those questions all tended to fall into no more than four categories: (1) descriptive, (2) normative, (3) cause-and-effect, or (4) knowledge questions. Since each of these types carries inferences with respect to methods choice, and any type can arise in any branch or level of government, this turned out to be helpful for evaluation planning because an evaluation question can then be more quickly understood as, say, premature, improperly targeted, or infeasible methodologically simply by examining the type of question posed in the context of the program or policy to be evaluated (Chelimsky, 2007). Also, evaluators are able to move faster (and with more certainty) in identifying the array of methods potentially useful for a new evaluation. This not only improved our response times—a matter of great importance to the Congress—but also allowed us earlier and better preparation for renegotiating the evaluation question when necessary.

Politics, Pressure Groups, and the Evaluation Process

Again, the legislative setting brought a new understanding of the vulnerability of accountability and knowledge evaluations to political interference in the evaluation process: at the planning stage, during implementation, when the draft final report is being prepared, and at publication (Chelimsky, 2008). This interference was often both forceful and sophisticated, certainly more brutal than anything I had previously seen either in international or executive-branch work. Our reaction to this was to use the evaluation-planning stage to try and foresee the likely size and shape of possible political problems, and to build in defenses, throughout the evaluation process, to bolster credibility, avoid perceptions of partisanship, and develop the arguments needed for standing up to potential intimidation.

An Initiation Into Capacity Building

Trying to develop an evaluation culture at GAO turned out to be a long, hard struggle. There were many reasons for this, of course, but two of them predominate, as I think back. First, the auditors at GAO didn't believe they had anything to learn from evaluation, even though congressional criticism of their work had been both loud and persistent (e.g., Congressman Jack Brooks' Committee took public exception to single case studies being generalized to the universe based on "auditor judgment," to findings of effectiveness reported without comparisons to support them, to the inappropriate use of normative methods to report program effects, and so on) (House Select Committee on Congressional Operations, 1978). And because we were becoming increasingly successful in the work we were doing on the Hill (as part of our other mission to perform evaluations for the Congress), the auditors saw us as competitors, which made it difficult to build trust in our development role.

To try to deal with both the mission and its obstacles, I elaborated a 10-pronged plan for building a culture of evaluation at GAO that, over time, did seem to improve the quality of the general evaluation work (Chelimsky, 1990, 2009b). However, this effort may have taught us evaluators more than it taught the auditors. For example, to do an effective job of teaching evaluation to auditors, we had to learn auditing; the papers we targeted at auditors on the applications of evaluation methods were used by evaluators more than by auditors; and the staff transfers I was eventually forced to make, when progress in capacity building appeared to be moving too slowly, were helpful in bringing to us a better understanding of the merits of auditor thinking, attitudes, and methods. Indeed, this learning process stood me in good stead as I expanded our development work in evaluation to agencies of the executive branch, legislative staff, and Members of Congress; the Office of Management and Budget; some international audit agencies (e.g., those of France, Great Britain, China, Poland, and Sweden); and two legislative bodies (the Canadian and French parliaments).

Some Old Ideas Reconsidered

Some of my early views about evaluation were, in fact, confirmed in light of the legislative setting. First among these was the idea that asking skeptical questions about conventional wisdom could be very important, especially when that wisdom was packaged for the purpose of receiving extensive appropriations from the Congress. An example of our continuing work in this vein is a set of accountability evaluations we did of the DOD's chemical warfare program, which exposed a highly selective presentation of facts and opinion by the DOD to the Congress. The House Committee on Foreign Affairs held numerous hearings on our studies; Members of Congress actually read them, despite their length and technicality; the entire program was eventually de-funded because of our findings; and the State Department made use of them in negotiating the U.S.-Soviet bilateral chemical weapons agreement (Fascell, 1990). An interesting point here is that because these evaluations were of the Entzauberung or demystification variety, I hardly expected their findings to be used, and yet it is now 20 years since Dick Cheney was forced to decommission all chemical weapons facilities in the United States because of those findings. So Entzauberung, yes, but also use.

A second confirmed idea was to take advantage of the evaluation planning or design stage to build a thick, rich, nourishing paste of all the factors likely to be important in the evaluation. Although I had found at NATO that the beginning of an evaluation was a good place for considering all contextual issues relevant to the subject matter, it would have been possible, given the leisurely pace of work there, to do that at some other point in the study process. Working with the Congress, however, it turned out to be the only feasible point: That is, at the planning stage, we had not yet agreed to do the evaluation, we felt free to look openly at anything even remotely related to it, we were not yet bogged down by methodological constraints, we knew that what we uncovered could be critical in the decision to either do the evaluation or renegotiate the question, and given the timeliness expected in work for the Hill, there simply would not be another point in a study as propitious for understanding context.

Another view that strengthened over time had to do with the need for independence, credibility, and nonpartisanship in accountability or knowledge evaluations, especially those that were likely to come under political fire. We tried to make absolutely sure that we had captured, to the degree possible, all voices relevant to an evaluation; that we could not be perceived as advocates for any individual group; and that we did not succumb to the various subtle or overt pressures that were often brought to influence our work. In addition, I had recruited a stellar Board of Advisors (these included social scientists—psychologists, sociologists, economists, and political scientists—engineers, physicists, statisticians, auditors, retired heads of evaluation offices, and a former member of Congress) and developed a checklist of indicators that together helped us focus hard on the prerequisites for credibility (Chelimsky, 1996).

So much, then, for the slow process of influence, experience, and idea development that I've tried to evoke here. As I look back, it seems to me that, over time, I learned a lot more from failure than from success and also that my evaluative voyage as a whole was peculiarly precarious. I was always having to outwit Cyclops, it appeared, while simultaneously teetering dangerously between Scylla and Charybdis. These were not the temperate joys of contemplative analysis that I had anticipated. I believe this may have been largely because I had to spend so much time, energy, and concentration in that "other" world of politics, with all its ferocity and unpredictability, quite distant from the evaluation process itself. I infer from this that there may remain today not one but two unfinished agendas in the field of evaluation: a first that faces inward and seeks to consolidate, improve, and further routinize the public performance of evaluation—its thinking, processes, and methods, for example—and a second that faces outward, addressing the relationship between evaluation and public policy.

SOME CONCLUDING OBSERVATIONS

Re-reading this account of my own evaluative development over several decades, I wonder if I haven't drawn too rosy a picture, downplaying, perhaps, the difficulties inherent in conducting evaluations. Of course, this may well be because any linear narration of idea development necessarily gives short shrift to practical dilemmas and to the external circumstances of the work. Yet almost nothing in evaluation is ever simple, or black and white, whether it be inside or outside the evaluation enterprise. The choices I've described here reflect a cumulative, long-term effort to rationalize and advance evaluation practice, to grapple in an orderly way with the processes of evaluation performance and with the political, bureaucratic, and other systems that surround it. Unfortunately, nothing says that these systems will stand still so that we can grapple with them. In addition, there always remains a certain innate messiness and inelegance about the evaluation process itself: for example, the typical vagueness and imprecision about how a program is expected to work; our own muddy path from cause to effect; the often unmeasurable differences in the delivery of program services from site to site; our inability to hold things in place "while political priorities, administrations, budgets and policy debates are all changing around us" (Rivlin, 1974); and the plain honest muddling through that accompanies searches for truth in government. These are the day-to-day realities of our work, and although we can try to deal with them "in an orderly way," as I've suggested, it seems that we are always confronting alien systems that may be severely intimidating, are always in motion, and rarely within our control. As evaluators, we have to live with that, but nothing prevents us from developing tools and arguments for coping with those systems.

If we see evaluation as critical to maintaining the structure and transparency of democratic government, then the task is clearly to develop an evaluation process that is inclusive of context and other relevant complexities but can nonetheless be routinely used to answer questions in government in a timely manner. This is what my work has been about. Of course, some of the concerns I've described may be less important for evaluators working in settings other than government (or, within government, for evaluators pursuing a management or capacity-building perspective). In particular, capacity builders may not find that independence is an issue, and academics already have at least some independence, because of their university setting. On the other hand, academics may be more isolated from decision makers than evaluators working in government, which adds to their difficulties in achieving use. But in general, I believe that many of the ideas and evaluation processes I developed at NATO, MITRE, and the GAO should be transferable, with some modifications, to quite different settings (Chelimsky, 2006).

I'm less sanguine about our ability to work easily and smoothly within our political environment. We will need to get a better grasp of evaluation's relations with policymakers and politics if we want to maximize our value to a democratic society. The American Evaluation Association, in creating its Evaluation Policy Task Force, has taken a first step in addressing this issue. But this Task Force has been mostly focused on educating legislative and executive agency staff and policymakers on the how-tos and essentials of evaluation processes and organization, whereas the problem of evaluation's small voice and inability to be heard remains, in many cases, unexamined (Chelimsky, 2009a).

Evaluators, like scientists generally—whether hard or soft, theoretical or applied, quantitative or qualitative—make up a weak political constituency. We live and work in a world of politics, but in some ways, we are as powerless as Job, in Muriel Sparks's description—arguing the problem of suffering and suffering the problem of argument. Indeed, Roland Tharp (2007) thinks we're more like Sisyphus, "eternally rolling evaluations uphill against politicians pushing them back down again." So we need to think more carefully about how to increase our presence and our power, perhaps by joining with other groups, making coalitions with other disciplines, and doing more to achieve regular dissemination of our reports.

The point here is that we need an outward-facing coherence that is as strong as the one we've developed with respect to inward-looking issues like process and methods. That is, we have to sharpen our understanding of how the policy world works, how evaluation can best fit into that world, and how we can increase our power to deal with it. Developing relationships with other similar disciplines and associations may be one way to become stronger. Lewis Thomas (1982) reminds us that

> successful species have always made a lot of friends and we must learn from those species. We should go warily into the future, looking for ways to be more useful, listening more carefully for signals, watching our step, and having an eye out for partners.

Of course, evaluation isn't easy, and of course, it can't always bring clear answers to policy questions. But for me, its great attraction is the combination of humility and skeptical judgment contained in its two purposes—to be useful and to search for truth. And no matter how incomplete that truth is or how closely it can ever approximate real "truth," in the

Platonic sense, it's the act of striving for it, I think, using all our experience, shrewdness, and courage to get at it, that makes evaluation noble, beautiful, and always interesting.

NOTE

1. I described the stances, or intentions, of these perspectives as follows, (a) An accountability perspective seeks to measure value and merit related to funds expended, to assess the logic and accuracy of statements made by government officials about the rationale for the program or policy, to examine fidelity of implementation and participation with respect to the legislative intent, to determine costs, to assess efficiency, and so on. (b) A knowledge perspective seeks to generate insights about public problems, policies, programs, and processes; to bring evidence from past research with regard to what is known about the application of theory to practice or about the effectiveness of particular programs or policies; to develop new methods; to critique old ones; and so on. (3) A management/development perspective seeks to strengthen institutions, to improve programs and policies, and to build agency or organizational capacity in evaluation (Chelimsky, 1997).

REFERENCES

Aron, R. (1967). *Main currents in sociological thought: Max Weber* (pp. 281–317). Paris, France: Gallimard.

Campbell, D. T. (1969). Reforms as experiments. *American Psychologist, 24*, 409–429.

Chelimsky, E. (1977). *Proceedings of a symposium on the use of evaluation by federal agencies* (Vols. 1–2). Washington, DC: National Institute of Law Enforcement and Criminal Justice.

Chelimsky, E. (1978). Differing perspectives of evaluation. *New Directions for Program Evaluation, 2*, 1–18.

Chelimsky, E. (1981, October). *Designing backward from the end-use.* Presidential address to the Evaluation Research Society, Austin, TX.

Chelimsky, E. (1986, September). *The condition of information on hazardous waste.* Statement by the Director of the Program Evaluation and Methodology Division (GAO) before the Committee on Government Operations, House of Representatives. Washington, DC: Center for Program Evaluation and Performance Measurement, Bureau of Justice.

Chelimsky, E. (1987). The politics of program evaluation. *New Directions for Program Evaluation, 34*, 5–21.

Chelimsky, E. (1990). Expanding GAO's capabilities in program evaluation. *The GAO Journal, 8*, 43–52.

Chelimsky, E. (1996). Producing credible evaluations of federal health programs. *Evaluation & the Health Professions, 19*(3), 264–279.

Chelimsky, E. (1997). The coming transformations in evaluation. In E. Chelimsky & W. R. Shadish (Eds.), *Evaluation for the 21st century* (pp. 1–26). Thousand Oaks, CA: Sage.

Chelimsky, E. (2006). The purposes of evaluation in a democratic society. In I. F. Shaw, J. C. Greene, & M. M. Mark (Eds.), *The SAGE handbook of evaluation* (pp. 33–55). Thousand Oaks, CA: Sage.

Chelimsky, E. (2007). Factors influencing the choice of methods in federal evaluation practice. *New Directions for Evaluation, 113*, 13–33.

Chelimsky, E. (2008). A clash of cultures: Improving the fit between evaluative independence and the political requirements of a democratic society. *American Journal of Evaluation, 29*(4), 400–415.

Chelimsky, E. (2009a). Integrating evaluation units into the political environment of government: The role of evaluation policy. *New Directions for Program Evaluation, 123*, 51–66.

Chelimsky, E. (2009b). Oral history, the professional development of Eleanor Chelimsky. *American Journal of Evaluation, 30*(2), 238–239.

Chelimsky, E., & Morra, L. (1984). Evaluation synthesis for the legislative user. *New Directions for Program Evaluation, 24,* 75–89.

Cook, T. D. (1997). Lessons learned in evaluation over the past 25 years. In E. Chelimsky & W. R. Shadish (Eds.), *Evaluation for the 21st century* (pp. 40–41). Thousand Oaks, CA: Sage.

Cronbach, L. J. (1964). Evaluation for course improvement. In R. J. Heath (Ed.), *New curricula* (pp. 231–248). New York, NY: Harper & Row.

Fascell, D. (June 14, 1990). *Chair, House Committee on Foreign Affairs, One Hundred First Congress* [Letter to Eleanor Chelimsky]. Washington, DC.

Freund, J. (1966). *Sociologie de Max Weber* [The sociology of Max Weber] (pp. 205–206, 211–212). Paris, France: Presses Universitaires de France.

Guttentag, M. (1973). Evaluation of social intervention programs. *Annals of the New York Academy of Science, 218,* 3–13.

House Select Committee on Congressional Operations. (1978). *General Accounting Office services to the Congress: An assessment.* Washington, DC: U.S. Government Post Office.

Kissinger, H. (1969). *Nuclear weapons and foreign policy.* New York, NY: W. W. Norton.

Marris, P., & Rein, M. (1967). *Dilemmas of social reform.* London, England: Routledge & Kegan Paul.

Morris, W. (1989). Faulkner's Mississippi. *National Geographic, 175*(3), 339.

Mosteller, F. (1977). Assessing unknown numbers: Order of magnitude estimation. In W. W. Fairley & F. Mosteller (Eds.), *Statistics and public policy* (p. 163). Reading, MA: Addison–Wesley.

Moynihan, D. P. (1969). *Maximum feasible misunderstanding.* New York, NY: Free Press.

Rossi, P. H., & Williams, W. (1972). *Evaluating social programs: Theory, practice and politics.* New York, NY: Seminar Press.

Scriven, M. (1972). The methodology of evaluation. In C. H. Weiss (Ed.), *Evaluating action programs: Readings in social action and education* (pp. 123–136). Boston, MA: Allyn & Bacon.

Tharp, R. (2007). A developmental process view of inquiry and how to support it. *New Directions for Evaluation, 113,* 124.

Thomas, L. (1982). *Things unflattened by science.* Commencement address at Williams College, Williamstown, MA.

U.S. General Accounting Office, Program Evaluation and Methodology Division. (1989). *Prospective evaluation methods: The prospective evaluation synthesis.* Washington, DC: Author.

Weiss, C. H. (1972). Utilization of evaluation: Toward comparative study. In C. H. Weiss (Ed.), *Evaluating action programs* (pp. 318–326). Boston, MA: Allyn & Bacon.

Weiss, R. S., & Rein, M. (1970). The evaluation of broad-aim programs: Experimental design, its difficulties, and an alternative. *Administrative Science Quarterly, 15*(1), 97–109.

Wholey, J. (1973). Contributions of social intervention research to government practices. *Annals of the New York Academy of Sciences, 218,* 31–42.

22

CONTEXT-SENSITIVE EVALUATION

Marvin C. Alkin

W*ell, here I am again.*

I hadn't planned on being part of the evaluation theory tree on this go-round. As I said in an interview that Jean King conducted in 2008, which was published in the *American Journal of Evaluation*, "I should say that I really don't view myself any longer as a prescriptive theorist... In fact, on the next revision of the theory tree, I am going to take myself off of the tree" (King, Shanker, Miller, & Mark, 2010, pp. 268–269).

You see, I am very serious about this business of making distinctions between "theorists" and evaluation writers, researchers, and the like. So what happened? What happened is that after many years of doing research on use, conceptualizing theory categories, and other writing, I rediscovered my prescriptive theory voice. I started writing an evaluation text, *Evaluation Essentials* (Alkin, 2011), and found that I did have some things to prescribe, to suggest that one might do to conduct a "proper" evaluation by my standards. Writing the book forced me to reconceptualize my dormant prescriptive utterings (see Alkin, 1972, 1991).

What is the essence of this theoretic prescriptive voice? As indicated by the title of this chapter, it is the intense sensitivity to the context in which the evaluation takes place. I, and many others, have pointed out the major distinction between "research" and "evaluation." For me, that distinction rests heavily on the difference between producing generalizable knowledge and providing information that will be helpful in improving specific programs. In prior writings I have expressed my basic commitment to trying to improve the usefulness and subsequent use of evaluation information. But attentiveness to utilization alone does not lead to program and organizational improvement.

The evaluation information—to be useful—cannot be produced without a clear understanding of the program being evaluated and the context in which it operates. I allude here to things such as gaining understanding of the stakeholders, organizational/social/political contexts, exact characteristics of the program, rationale for program activities and sequence, and questions of interest and concern to stakeholders.

The specified purpose of a program and its organizational arrangements and complexities differ from one situation to the next. Political settings certainly vary. The evaluator must be cognizant of each of these and be certain that they are made visible and are reflected within the evaluation. In my view, the evaluator must aggressively adapt the evaluation procedures based on the particular context to ensure, to the greatest extent possible, that the actions taken are in the best interests of enhancing the possibility of evaluation use occurring.

HOW I GOT HERE

We are all molded by our experiences, whether they be educational experiences (formal or informal), events, or interactions with people. I acknowledged this when I wrote a chapter for the National Society for the Study of Education (NSSE) Yearbook on the topic of evaluation (1991) reflecting on what had led to changes in my views on evaluation over a 25-year period. My roots, however, shaped not only my changes at any particular point but also my initial thoughts on evaluation as well as the various changes over time.

Early Academic Training

Academic training is a starting point. My bachelor's degree in mathematics and subsequent teaching of math at the high school and community college levels started me out thinking quantitatively about evaluation. My master's degree in counseling and guidance and brief service as a high school counselor sensitized me to dealing with others in nonthreatening, understanding ways. This further added to my future evaluation repertoire. As an evaluator, I am very attentive to the need for the evaluator to use a variety of social skills that put stakeholders at ease while patiently and forcefully reaching a reasonable conclusion. This has strengthened the way that I work with users in framing an evaluation.

The Center for the Study of Evaluation

Circumstances shape receptiveness to new ideas. As a new assistant professor, I participated in the development of the proposal for the Center for the Study of Evaluation. Major federal funding was to be made available for creating research centers in education. The dean of the UCLA School of Education, frustrated over several years by the full professors fighting about the focus of a research center proposal, appointed a committee of assistant professors. We were instructed to write a proposal not to our interests but one that provided a basis for broad faculty participation. We selected "evaluation" as the proposal topic, enabling a broad spectrum of research topics covering organizational context, personal characteristics, measurement, statistics, and so on. There was no one at UCLA who had national recognition in evaluation or who had shown much interest in the field. The proposal captured the evaluation concept with 31 quite diverse projects, which encompassed the many particular interests of the faculty.

To prepare for the site visit, I prepared vitae about each of the site visitors and enlisted knowledgeable faculty from other parts of the campus to "role-play" the site visitors in two successive simulated site visits with a debriefing between the two. Subsequently, the actual site visit team was awed by the way these diverse projects showed such strong interrelationships. The Center for the Study of Evaluation was funded over competing proposals (on other topics) from the University of Chicago, MIT, and John Hopkins University. The die was cast for me to be an evaluator—but I didn't realize it.

I was appointed associate director of this center and, because of the absence and lack of interest of the codirectors, essentially ran the center for 2 years while still an assistant professor. In that role, I was content to continue my writing in the area of my formal training (educational administration with emphasis on cost–benefit and other economic issues). However, when appointed somewhat reluctantly as the director of the center 2 years later, I felt the necessity to really focus on thinking about evaluation theory and framing my own views.

Evaluation Experience

Experience counts. I am among the group of theorists who have had substantial experience actually conducting evaluations. These evaluations encompass a broad array of topic areas and programs, including a state's juvenile detention facilities, a psychiatric residence training program, compensatory education in schools and school districts, a state's 106 community college articulation programs, agricultural extension in eight Caribbean countries, a program for empowering campesinos in a South American country, and a school for the blind. Each of these varied experiences provided opportunities that made me acutely aware of the need to fully understand and be sensitive to context—*all* dimensions of context.

Individuals, Ideas, and Interactions

As noted in my NSSE chapter (1991), one source of influence on the development of evaluation points of view are the insights of colleagues, whose ideas we sort, filter, and refine until they fit our conceptual mind-set. My initial general conceptualizations of evaluation were in part shaped by the early evaluation work of Bob Stake and Michael Scriven. Yet the theorists whose views were most akin to my way of thinking at that time were Daniel Stufflebeam and Malcolm Provus. Their orientation fit with some of my earlier doctoral studies, which focused on administrative theory.

Another area of influence noted in my NSSE article (1991) is "one's own research." Stimulated by Carol Weiss's (1972) call for the study of evaluation utilization, I read authors in the knowledge utilization field (e.g., Nathan Caplan, Robert Rich) and, over a number of years, conducted a good deal of research and engaged in conceptualization on evaluation utilization (e.g., Alkin & Coyle, 1988; Alkin, Daillak, & White, 1979; Alkin, Kosecoff, Fitz-Gibbon, & Seligman, 1974; Alkin & Taut, 2003). The work on utilization obviously influenced my evaluation theoretic views and drew me away from what had been referred to in the literature as the "evaluation and decision-making" point of view. Fortuitously, at about the same time, I met Michael Patton while we were both consulting in Ecuador. We shared views on evaluation utilization. Several years later, I was the first publisher's reviewer of his book *Utilization-Focused Evaluation*. Clearly, Michael and I each gained insights from our initial and continuing communication and interchange.

Over time, the views of other evaluation theorists struck responsive chords and filtered their way into my thinking about evaluation. It is very difficult to be precise about how a particular evaluation conception, procedure, or way of thinking had influence. So many ideas are first propounded by one theorist and repeated or elaborated by others that it is often not possible to identify the idea's originator. Interaction with others conducting research on evaluation utilization had an impact—in particular Jean King and, subsequently, Brad Cousins. As my views evolved, notions about stakeholder participation in evaluation (as articulated by Stake and many others) became mingled with the idea of differentiating intended users (e.g., Patton). The idea of "evaluability assessment" (as described by Wholey) developed in me an awareness about situations in which evaluation is or is not feasible. Work on logic modeling seemed like a fruitful addition to my thinking.

Ideas that one does not fully accept nonetheless have influence; they direct attention to the necessity for pondering why they are *not* to be included in an evaluator's theoretic perspective. Thus, in some circuitous way, writers whom I disagreed with had an impact on my theoretic views through my criticism of particular points that they might have made. Ongoing conversations over the years with Ernie House led both to ideas I disagreed with and to others that stimulated my thinking.

Evaluation Theory Category Systems

Classification or category systems can also be an important source for modification of views. As my views emerged and became more oriented toward the evaluator trying to make his work relevant and to have an impact on program change, classification systems that had placed me in the "evaluation and decision-making" category made me uncomfortable. The category implied that evaluators worked only for decision makers—implicitly those who commissioned the evaluation. The implicit lack of recognition of the role of other stakeholders troubled me. This led to the need for me to clarify and explain my views more fully.

Beyond this, however, my examination of evaluation theories and, in particular, the study of comparisons between evaluation theories (Alkin & Christie, 2004; Christie & Alkin, 2008) have led me to appreciate the necessity of making modifications to what I might consider a starting point to an ideal approach and then adapting it to the situation. Many differences in the evaluation theories that I have studied are attributable to the way theorists view the context for their evaluation work.

Teaching

Teaching. I love to teach, and I learn from my teaching. Over the years, simulations and role playing have become an important part of the way I teach evaluation—especially in my theory course (Alkin & Christie, 2002). My views on evaluation have been sharpened by many interchanges with Stake, Scriven, House, and the panoply of writers represented in this volume.

I have also learned and been influenced by interactions with my 60 or so doctoral student advisees. In particular, I reflect on those students with whom I have written: Carol Taylor Fitzgibbon, Jacqueline Kosecoff, Richard Daillak, Brian Stecher, Joan Ruskus, Karen Coyle, Carolyn Hofstetter, Sandy Taut, Tina Christie, Kara Crohn, Nicole Eisenberg, Tarek Azzam, Tanner Le Baron Wallace, Anne Vo, and many others.

MY GENERAL ORIENTATION TO EVALUATION

My theoretic perspective is not "top down." It does not start with a particular epistemological perspective and then intuit the steps to be taken. Rather, my set of prescriptions (theory) is "bottom up," based on over 40 years of experience conducting evaluations, tempered by my research on evaluation and study of evaluation theory and theorists. My goals in doing evaluation are modest. I don't set out to change the world—or directly achieve social betterment—but I do hope that society improves. I don't necessarily set as a prime goal improving individuals in a project, but I do hope that through the process of evaluation, they will gain understandings and thereby become empowered to make change. I don't set as an agenda trying to ensure social justice—or my interpretation of what is just—although I do care about resolving inequity. What I want to do in conducting an evaluation is to conduct a sound, context-sensitive evaluation. Hopefully, such an evaluation is responsive to all aspects of the context, including the diverse stakeholders. I want my evaluations to be so relevant that the results (as well as the process) will be used to make positive change and thereby improve programs.

I am an incrementalist. I believe that I can have influence by making small improvements in programs. I am hopeful that many such program changes will lead to major improvements in society. I believe also that my doing a careful job and paying close attention to understanding the context and building relationships will lead to strengthening of the institutions with which I work. I hope that the organizations that I serve, and the individuals within them, will benefit, learn, and be affected by the evaluation.

What is the evaluator? In my conception of evaluation, the evaluator is a specialist in group processes who helps potential evaluation users identify important aspects of their program and particular concerns that they have. The evaluator is a specialist in examining the many aspects of the evaluation context. The evaluator is a specialist in identifying a broad array of potential means of acquiring information about programs and in implementing systems to obtain those data. The evaluator is a specialist in analyzing a broad array of types of information. The evaluator is a specialist in developing ways to help users themselves specify the means of valuing data and identifying the potential action implications of valued findings. The evaluator is a change agent helping potential users to see opportunities for improving their programs through the use of evaluation information.

Some further thoughts on my general orientation to evaluation. What I am *not*! Generally, I do not believe in granting particular powers to the evaluator, such as being a spokesperson for a particular belief or for particular groups. I do not believe that it is appropriate for me to empower myself in that way. Nor do I believe that the evaluator should be inserting his or her own value system into a process by personally making judgments about findings. Furthermore, I do not believe that the evaluator should act as a program consultant in recommending program revisions (other than as specifically derived from the evaluation data collected). I am troubled by the expanded role that many evaluators have taken onto themselves. I strongly believe that evaluations must be stakeholder directed to meet program needs.

With these beliefs, perceptions, attitudes, and biases as a background, let me now comment on some specific activities. My preferred framework for conducting evaluation is comparable with the steps followed in many (if not most) other schemes. The approach, perhaps, has a few unique twists. I will focus the discussion on five general areas of evaluation activity:

1. Framing the questions and use context

2. Negotiating agreement on acceptability of design, measures, and procedures

3. Establishing a framework for judging results

4. Data collection and reporting

5. Interpretation and facilitation of use

An important element of the evaluation approach is *framing the evaluation questions and use context*. Of necessity, the framing begins with the report commissioners (those who hire the evaluator). The evaluator needs to understand what those who hired him or her believe to be the purpose of the evaluation and the intent of what is to be accomplished. The evaluator must probe deeply on the uses that the evaluation *might* lead to. Are there decisions that might be made? Are there attitudes that might be influenced? In essence, what are the potential instrumental and conceptual uses of the evaluation findings as well as potential uses that might evolve from the evaluation process itself?

Another important aspect of the discussions with evaluation report commissioners is the broadening of the potential user base. The evaluator must seek to extend the "framing group" to other primary users. The evaluator should continually probe about whether there are other individuals who might have an interest (or stake) in the program and are likely to want to make use of the findings. There is a need to actively pursue the issue of who might have a voice in making use of the evaluation findings. Once these other evaluation users are identified, a round of discussions needs to take place with this intended primary user group or their representatives.

Not to be neglected is the larger stakeholder audience. It is my belief that the evaluator cannot be attentive to the full involvement of all stakeholders; to do so makes the process unmanageable and overwhelming. Instead, the evaluator must seek to interview and understand the viewpoints of these other stakeholder audiences and to interject their views and concerns into the negotiations that take place during discussions with report commissioners and others in the primary intended user group.

A second major phase of the evaluation is *negotiating agreement on the acceptability of design measures and procedures.* I pointedly use the term *negotiate* because that is literally what the process involves. It is not simply a presentation of a design and measures that the evaluator plans to use but a reached agreement that these are acceptable in satisfying information needs. I like to subject users to a reality test in considering the acceptability of measurements (data/ information) and procedures. I do this by framing scenarios involving proposed measures and asking whether information on potential outcome areas would be sufficiently persuasive in instrumental (making decisions) or conceptual (changing attitudes) ways. If not, I probe about the kind of information that would be satisfactory.

Having agreed on measures and procedures, I have, for many years, made it a practice to work with intended primary users in establishing a *framework for judging results.* As noted earlier, I do not believe that it is the role of the evaluator to impose his or her value judgments on the data collected. Again, the use of scenarios helps in negotiating this framework for judging results. On quantitative measures, I would ask the users to consider what would be satisfactory results, and I would present hypothetical possible findings and ask what the implications for action would be. A variety of outcome scenarios are posed to delimit the judging framework. ("Suppose I found X outcome—what would it mean in terms of possible changes in your program?") With descriptive or qualitative information to be gathered, I inquire as to what they think we will find—what they would consider to be a positive result in descriptive or qualitative terms. I would then use these initial descriptions and conceptions not only as a basis for refining the questions and measures but also as a standard or guideline for subsequent comparison (valuing).[1]

When establishing a framework for judging results is not feasible, I try to confine my evaluation results and reporting to descriptive data that can be assessed and judged by the various stakeholders. I would subsequently work with stakeholders as a "guide" in developing criteria for judging.

Data collection and reporting is the fourth stage of evaluation. This is more or less a standard kind of thing. In most evaluations, obviously, one would want to involve primary users in the process to the greatest extent possible. To do so is to add to the credibility of the process and to increase the primary users' subsequent acceptance (and use) of findings. With respect to reporting, I try to be particularly sensitive to viewing reporting as an ongoing activity. Furthermore, information should be cast in a user-friendly manner suitable for review by multiple stakeholders. In large part this is aided by contextualizing the findings—presenting information that provides an insight into the program context. I do not generally favor making recommendations, preferring to allow them to evolve from a discussion of findings.

The final aspect of an evaluation involves *interpretation and facilitation of use*. The evaluator has a responsibility for going beyond simple reporting and should be able and willing to respond to questions about the meaning of the data, while being careful not to impose his or her own value system or program priorities. A process of intense interaction with intended primary users should lead to a discussion of the meaning of the evaluator-presented findings and possible explanations for why they were what they were. The evaluator should engage in discussions with primary users about the possible uses of the information. At the outset, this discussion focuses on the priorities initially established, but beyond that there are issues and insights derived from the joint interaction. I care about process use, and when it occurs, I am delighted, but I do not explicitly direct activities to attain process use that I believe will be beneficial. I believe that this gives too much authority to the evaluator and goes against the spirit of stakeholder-directed evaluation.

The evaluation prescriptions just specified have commonalities present in many other approaches. Two of the most distinct features relate to determining the appropriateness and relevance of the evaluation questions and establishing a framework for assigning values to findings. Each is done through the creation of mini-simulations (scenarios) as a guide for, in one instance, developing more appropriate questions and, in the other, establishing a valuing framework prior to data collection. Another area that perhaps differs from other concerns is the emphasis on utilization, but with limits on evaluator directiveness in attempting to attain process use.

THE ROLE OF CONTEXT

In real estate, it's location, location, location. The evaluation counterpart is *context, context, context.*

Beyond this general approach to evaluation, I recognize the vital importance of attempting to fully understand context as an influence on the evaluation. What are the components of evaluation context? Clearly, important elements of the context are the various stakeholders—program managers, staff, participants, funders, and so on. An understanding of who these stakeholders are and, to a certain extent, how they perceive the program is critically important. Another element of the context is the various questions and issues to be addressed. I have discussed each of these two context components in the earlier section where I indicated my preferred framework for conducting evaluations.

Let me now focus on the program and what I will call the *program context*. What is the program? First, one must understand the program intentions. What do the stakeholders believe about the program? What do they think is to be accomplished? Who is to be served? What services are to be provided? Who and what are the program materials required to implement the program? What is the program logic or theory of action, often (but not always) depicted in a logic model? Also, what is *not* in the program? Frequently, there is overlap with other programs. Several programs might have similar goals and, indeed, overlapping staff. When the program is part of a larger program, it is important to know which features are designed as supplements. Needless to say, program intentions are not always program actualities. Thus, adjustments in one's understanding of the context take place throughout the process of conducting the evaluation.

Another element of context I refer to as organizational context—of which there are numerous aspects. One of these aspects is the formal and informal reporting line both within the program and to the larger organization in which it might be encompassed. I also consider the program's history as an important aspect of context. Programs happen over time. In this history, decisions are made by those within the program or outside it. Similar comments can be made about the *social context*. And by this I mean the program as it relates to the larger community. Further understanding of the nature of the community, the people, and the value system are important elements of context to which the evaluator must be sensitive.

Finally, multiple evaluators (most notably Carol Weiss, 1993) have indicated that all evaluations are political—have a *political context*. Evaluation is inherently political. Decisions about programs are the views and preferences of individuals, and when they are adopted, there are winners and losers. But first let me make this clear: Politics as such is not all negative. Programs themselves are created through a political process. Political mechanisms include the attainment of the political consensus that led to the creation of the program. Apart from the evaluation purpose being political, the evaluation process is political as well. What is being tested by the evaluator is the viability of a program's goals and the logic perceived to be relevant in attaining them.[2] The evaluator must recognize the political reality of evaluation. It exists: Be sensitive to it but unbiased in your work.

I recognize that in addition to the above areas of eval*uation* context (the characteristics of the evaluation situation and its participants and surroundings), there is also an eval*uator* context. As an evaluator, I have views about how an evaluation should be conducted. I must be aware of and explicitly recognize this evaluator context—those beliefs that I previously discussed—so that I can account for them throughout the evaluation and adapt to the evaluation context where necessary. If unable to do so because differences are too great, I prefer to decline performing the evaluation.

My job as an evaluator is not only to adapt the evaluation procedures based on the particular context but also to ensure, to the greatest extent possible, that the actions taken are in the best interests of enhancing the possibility of evaluation use occurring. I am convinced that use and program improvement will not occur without acute sensitivity to context.

REALITY CHECK

Once past the reverie of idealism, reality announces itself. I can't always do as I prescribe. The constraints imposed by context sometimes (often?) preclude doing the "perfect evaluation." Money is usually a problem, especially in small-scale evaluations. Bureaucracy and conflicting expectations frequently raise their head. We each determine our own tolerable limits of variance from our ideal.

NOTES

1. My student Mark Hansen recently pointed out that this is also a way of establishing accountability for use on the part of these primary stakeholders.

2. A further discussion of some of these contextual areas is to be found in Alkin (2011): Stakeholders (Section D), Questions and Issues (Sections I and N), Program Context (Sections G and H), Organizational, Social, and Political Contexts (Section F).

REFERENCES

Alkin, M. (1972). Evaluation theory development. In C. Weiss (Ed.), *Evaluating action programs: Readings in social action and education* (pp. 105–117). Boston, MA: Allyn & Bacon.

Alkin, M. (1991). Evaluation theory development. In M. McLaughlin & D. C. Phillips (Eds.), *Evaluation and education: At quarter-century* (90th yearbook of the National Society for the Study of Education, Part II; pp. 91–112). Chicago, IL: University of Chicago Press.

Alkin, M. (2011). *Evaluation essentials: From A to Z.* New York, NY: Guilford Press.

Alkin, M., & Christie, C. (2002). The use of role-play in teaching evaluation. *American Journal of Evaluation, 23*(2), 209–219.

Alkin, M., & Christie, C. (2004). An evaluation theory tree. In M. Alkin (Ed.), *Evaluation roots: Tracing theorists' views and influences.* Thousand Oaks, CA: Sage.

Alkin, M., & Coyle, K. (1988). Thoughts on evaluation utilization, misutilization, and nonutilization. *Studies in Educational Evaluation, 14,* 331–340.

Alkin, M., Daillak, R., & White, P. (1979). *Using evaluations: Does evaluation make a difference?* (Sage Library of Social Research, Vol. 76). Beverly Hills, CA: Sage.

Alkin, M., Kosecoff, J., Fitz-Gibbon, C., & Seligman, R. (1974). *Evaluation and decision making: The Title VII experience* (CSE Monograph No. 4). Los Angeles: University of California–Los Angeles, Center for the Study of Evaluation.

Alkin, M., & Taut, S. (2003). Unbundling evaluation use. *Studies in Educational Evaluation, 29,* 1–12.

Christie, C., & Alkin, M. (2008). Evaluation theory tree re-examined. *Studies in Educational Evaluation, 34,* 131–135.

King, J. A., Shanker, V., Miller, R. L., & Mark, M. M. (2010). The oral history of evaluation: The professional development of Marvin C. Alkin. *American Journal of Evaluation, 31*(3), 268–269.

Weiss, C. (1972). The utilization of evaluation: Toward a comparative study. In C. Weiss (Ed.), *Evaluating action programs: Readings in social action and education.* Boston, MA: Allyn & Bacon.

Weiss, C. (1993). Politics and evaluation: A reprise with mellower overtones. *Evaluation Practice, 14*(1), 107–109.

23

THE ROOTS OF UTILIZATION-FOCUSED EVALUATION

Michael Quinn Patton

Utilization-focused evaluation begins with the premise that evaluations should be judged by their utility and actual use; therefore, evaluators should facilitate the evaluation process and design any evaluation with careful consideration of how everything that is done, from beginning to end, will affect use. Use concerns how real people in the real world apply evaluation findings and experience the evaluation process. Therefore, the focus in utilization-focused evaluation is on *intended use by intended users*. Since no evaluation can be value-free, utilization-focused evaluation answers the question of whose values will frame the evaluation by working with clearly identified, primary intended users who have the responsibility to apply evaluation findings and implement recommendations.

Utilization-focused evaluation is highly personal and situational. The evaluation facilitator develops a working relationship with intended users to help them determine the kind of evaluation they need. This requires negotiation in which the evaluator offers a menu of possibilities within the framework of established evaluation standards and principles.

Utilization-focused evaluation does not advocate any particular evaluation content, model, or method—including qualitative methods. Nor does utilization-focused evaluation advocate a particular kind of use. Rather, it is a process for helping primary intended users select the most appropriate content, model, methods, theory, and uses for their particular situation. Situational responsiveness guides the interactive process between evaluator and primary intended users. A utilization-focused evaluation can include any evaluative purpose (formative, summative, developmental), any kind of data (quantitative, qualitative, mixed), any kind of design (e.g., naturalistic, experimental), and any kind of focus (processes, outcomes, impacts, costs, and cost–benefit, among many possibilities). *Utilization-focused evaluation is a process for making decisions about these issues in collaboration with an identified group of primary users focusing on their intended uses of the evaluation.*

A psychology of use undergirds and informs utilization-focused evaluation: Intended users are more likely to use evaluations if they understand and feel ownership of the evaluation process and findings; they are more likely to understand and feel ownership if they've been actively involved; by actively involving primary intended users, the evaluator is training users in use, preparing the groundwork for use, and reinforcing the intended utility of the evaluation every step along the way.

ROOT INFLUENCES

Peace Corps in Africa

One of the early and lasting influences on my perspective can be traced to the years in the 1960s when I served as a Peace Corps volunteer in eastern Burkina Faso among the Gourma people. We were community development generalists working in very poor, rural villages where farmers engaged in subsistence agriculture, growing primarily millet and sorghum. Soils were poor. Water was scarce. Infant mortality was high. Infectious diseases were common and debilitating. Markets were underdeveloped. Resources were few. We were young, idealistic, hopeful, and clueless.

We began by talking with the villagers, listening to their stories, gathering their histories, learning about their experiences, and working to understand their perspectives. Gradually, as we learned the language, engaged with the people, and began to understand the local setting, project possibilities emerged: well-digging projects, building one-room schools, introducing cash crops, new approaches to cultivation, organizing cooperatives, and initiating education efforts. But our role was always more one of facilitation than of actual doing. We figured out shared interests, helped organize groups for action, and helped them find resources. Our efforts were highly pragmatic, just trying to find something that would work, that might create a little leverage that could be used to gather insights into and start to address larger problems. In the grand scheme of things, our efforts were very modest.

I learned how to figure out what someone cared about, how to bring people together to identify shared interests, and how to match initiatives and resources to those shared interests. I learned to ground my change efforts in the perspectives, values, and interests of those with whom I worked, the indigenous people who were there before I came and would be there after I left. I learned to appreciate and honor local villagers and farmers as the primary stakeholders in change and to see my role as facilitating their actions, not letting my interests and values drive the process but rather deferring to and facilitating their interests and values. In that way, I tried to make myself useful to people struggling to survive in a harsh environment.

My approach to evaluation grew out of those seminal community development experiences in Africa. From the very beginning, it was clear to me that I was not going to be the primary user of the evaluation findings. My niche would be facilitating use by others. I could apply what I had learned about how to figure out what someone cared about, how to bring people together to identify shared interests, and how to match evaluation designs and resources to those shared interests. I drew on what I had learned about how to ground my Peace Corps efforts in the perspectives, values, and interests of those with whom I had worked then by grounding my evaluation efforts in the perspectives, values, and interests of those with whom I now worked: that is, the indigenous program participants, staff, administrators, lenders, and other decision makers who were involved with the program before I came and would be there after I left. I learned to appreciate and honor these people as the primary stakeholders in program improvement efforts and to see my role as facilitating their actions, not letting my interests and values drive the process but rather deferring to and facilitating their interests and values. In that way, I tried to make myself useful to people struggling to survive in harsh, demanding, and volatile human services, education, social change, and public policy environments.

Sociological Influences

My university studies, from undergraduate work at the University of Cincinnati through my doctorate at the University of Wisconsin, Madison, gave me a solid grounding in quantitative methods, theory construction, philosophy of science, and sociology of knowledge, all of which have influenced my evaluation thinking and practice. Substantively, three particular sociological specializations have influenced my evaluation perspective: (1) diffusion of innovations, (2) sociological perspectives on power and conflict, and (3) organizational sociology, which examines how people behave in institutions and organizations, much of which transfers to behavior in programs, the primary arena of evaluation studies.

The diffusion of innovations literature and scholarship in organizational sociology that focused on the characteristics of innovative organizations provided the frameworks that informed my first empirical inquiry into evaluation use, an inquiry that was the basis for the first edition of *Utilization-Focused Evaluation* (Patton, 1978). We basically did case studies of evaluations to find out what characteristics were associated with use, about which I will discuss more later.

Another root sociological influence has been a theory of power that I have found instructive in helping me appreciate what evaluation offers stakeholders and intended users. Understanding this has helped me explain to intended users how and why their involvement in a utilization-focused evaluation is in their own best interest. It provides a basis for understanding how knowledge is power and led me to the following premise: *Use of evaluation will occur in direct proportion to its power-enhancing capability.* Power-enhancing capability is determined as follows: *The power of evaluation varies directly with the degree to which the findings reduce the uncertainty of action for specific stakeholders.* This view of the relationship between evaluation and power is derived from the classic organizational theories of Michael Crozier (1964) and James Thompson (1967).

For example, Thompson (1967) theorized that organizations are open systems that need resources and materials from outside and that "with this conception the central problem for complex organizations is one of coping with uncertainty" (p. 13). He found that assessment and evaluation are used by organizations as mechanisms for reducing uncertainty and enhancing their control over the multitude of contingencies with which they are faced. *Information for prediction is information for control—thus the power of evaluation.* To be power laden, information must be relevant and in a form that is understandable to users. Crozier (1964) recognized this qualifier in linking power to reduced uncertainty: "One should be precise and specify *relevant* uncertainty. People and organizations will care only about what they can recognize as affecting them and, in turn, what is possibly within their control" (p. 158).

Systems Thinking and Complexity Concepts: Developmental Evaluation

Organizational sociology laid the foundation for attention to the application of systems thinking and complexity concepts to evaluation, and the identification of what I've called *developmental evaluation* as a specific niche in utilization-focused evaluation (Patton, 2010). Developmental evaluation supports innovation *development* to guide adaptation to emergent and dynamic realities in complex environments. Innovations can take the form of new projects, programs, products, organizational changes, policy reforms, and system interventions. A complex system is characterized by a large number of interacting and interdependent elements in which there is no central control; self-organizing and emergent behaviors based on sophisticated information processing generate learning, evolution, and development. Complex environments for social interventions and innovations are those in which one is uncertain about what to do to solve problems and key stakeholders are in conflict about how to proceed. Informed by systems thinking and sensitive to complex nonlinear dynamics, developmental evaluation supports social innovation and adaptive management. Evaluation processes include asking evaluative questions, applying evaluation logic, and gathering real-time data to inform ongoing decision making and adaptations. The evaluator is often part of a development team whose members collaborate to conceptualize, design, and test new approaches in a long-term, ongoing process of continuous development, adaptation, and experimentation, keenly sensitive to unintended results and side effects. The evaluator's primary function in the team is to infuse team discussions with evaluative questions, thinking, and data and to facilitate systematic data-based reflection and decision making in the developmental process.

Developmental evaluation as a distinct niche emerged in response to one of my client's questions and needs. I had a standard 5-year contract with a community leadership program that specified 2½ years of formative evaluation for program improvement, to be followed by 2½ years of summative evaluation that would lead to an overall decision about whether the program was effective, a common design and sequence. The leadership program served small, rural communities throughout Minnesota. During the formative evaluation, major changes were made in many aspects of how the program operated. Recruitment processes were expanded. Program activities were adjusted based on feedback from participants. New curriculum elements and small-group exercises were added and fine-tuned. Follow-up interviews with graduates led to new support initiatives after program completion. Formative evaluation focuses on improving a model, and this program team was hungry for feedback and eager to make improvements, which was done willingly and enthusiastically. Then came the time to close this highly creative phase of formative evaluation and move to summative evaluation.

The program leadership and staff resisted standardizing the program for summative evaluation. They wanted to keep developing the program, not just improving it to get it ready for summative evaluation but also providing for ongoing development in response to changing conditions and complex contextual dynamics. Thus, my two evaluation colleagues and I became part of the leadership program's design team to support ongoing development. Our evaluation role was to bring evaluative thinking and data to bear as the team conceptualized, developed, and tried out new approaches for new groups, including immigrants, Native Americans, people from distressed rural communities, elected officials, and young people. The program developed new approaches in light of new federal and state policies affecting rural communities. The ongoing decline in many rural communities led to a more regional focus. As more than one cohort from a community went through the program, the issue of how to connect different cohorts arose. New funding opportunities opened up to support follow-up projects by program graduates. New staffing needs arose. The developmental relationship lasted for more than 6 years and involved different evaluation designs each year, including participant observation, several different surveys, field observations, telephone interviews, face-to-face interviews, focus groups, case studies of individuals and communities, cost analyses, theory of change conceptualizations, and training participants to do their own community-based evaluations. Each year the program changed in significant ways, and new evaluation questions emerged. Program goals and strategies evolved. The evaluation evolved. No summative evaluation was ever conducted. No final report was ever written. The program continues to evolve and develop.

Getting to Maybe

The development of developmental evaluation was significantly propelled forward by opportunities in the late 1990s to work with two Canadian scholars deeply involved in studying social innovations through the lens of complex adaptive systems. Collaborating with Frances Westley and Brenda Zimmerman, including participating in a 2-year think tank they organized on these issues, led to our writing a book titled *Getting to Maybe: How the World Is Changed* (Westley, Zimmerman, & Patton, 2006). That book led directly to and set the stage for *Developmental Evaluation: Applying Complexity Concepts to Enhance Innovation and Use* (Patton, 2010).

The points I would emphasize here, from a roots perspective, are (a) the influence of responding and adapting to emergent client and user information needs as an impetus for new directions in evaluation and (b) the importance of collegial relationships in thinking through and conceptualizing these responses and adaptations to clients, users, and other stakeholders.

For example, my recent work on evaluating *strategy* as the focus for evaluation (strategy as the *evaluand*) came in direct response to the needs and interests of presidents of philanthropic foundations and the demands of their boards of directors to focus on evaluating strategy (Patrizi & Patton, 2011). Being utilization and user focused has opened up new arenas for evaluation practice and theory.

UNLEARNING SOCIOLOGY: THE PERSONAL FACTOR

While sociology has constituted my intellectual foundation, the breakthroughs in developing utilization-focused evaluation, and subsequently developmental evaluation, came from unlearning and thinking beyond the sociological perspective into which I had been socialized in graduate school. The dominant Weberian perspective in organizational sociology posits that organizations are made up of and operate based on positions, roles, and norms such that the individuality of people matters little because individuals are socialized to occupy specific roles and positions and behave according to specific learned norms, all for the greater good of the organization's goal attainment. Thus, I had been schooled in the notion that organizations are an impersonal collection of hierarchical positions. What I had to learn was that *people, not organizations, use evaluation information.* I learned this by studying actual evaluation use.

In the mid-1970s, as evaluation was emerging as a distinct field of professional practice, I undertook a study with colleagues and students of federal health evaluations to assess how their findings had been used and to identify the factors that affected varying degrees of use. We interviewed the evaluators and those for whom the evaluations were conducted. We asked respondents to comment on how, if at all, factors extracted from the literature on diffusion of innovations and evaluation utilization had affected use of their study. Finally, we asked the respondents to pick out the single factor that each one felt had the greatest effect on how this study was used.

From this long list of questions, only two factors emerged as consistently important in explaining utilization: (1) political considerations and (2) a factor we called "the personal factor." This latter factor was unexpected, and its clear importance to our respondents had, we believed, substantial implications for the use of program evaluation. The personal factor is the presence of an identifiable individual or group of people who personally care about the evaluation and the findings it generates. Where such a person or group was present, evaluations were used; where the personal factor was absent, there was a correspondingly marked absence of evaluation impact. Use is not simply determined by some configuration of abstract organizational dynamics; it is determined in large part by real, live, caring human beings. Sociology had not prepared me for that understanding. Once understood, this became the foundation of utilization-focused evaluation. Thus, the challenge of increasing use consists of two parts: (1) finding and involving those who are, by inclination, information users and (2) training those not so inclined.

Humanistic Values

One of the seminal experiences that I believe prepared me for the importance of the personal factor was the 2 years I spent doing dissertation research at the New School for Behavioral Studies in Education at the University of North Dakota with Vito Perrone, to whom I dedicated the first edition of *Utilization-Focused Evaluation* (1978). His philosophy of open education emphasized the importance and value of each individual child, which was part of the reason why Vito preferred rich case studies to standardized tests when examining student learning. Vito was the core of the North Dakota Study Group on Evaluation, where I first became involved in the qualitative–quantitative paradigm debate, which led to my first evaluation publication, *Alternative Evaluation Research Paradigms* (Patton, 1975). Having never had a course in qualitative methods in the highly quantitative department of sociology at the University of Wisconsin, I learned qualitative methods from Vito and his colleagues while doing an evaluation of open classrooms throughout North Dakota (basically learning by doing). I also learned the politics of methods. The North Dakota stakeholders were interested only in the rich qualitative data from classroom observations and interviews with teachers, parents, and students. My dissertation committee was interested only in linear regression analysis. As a result, I produced two separate documents, a qualitative evaluation for North Dakota users and, having coded the qualitative data to permit regression analysis, an entirely statistical dissertation for my doctorate. The North Dakota stakeholders never saw the statistical analysis, and my doctoral committee never saw the qualitative evaluation. Thus, I experienced firsthand the implications of working with people who value different methods and the need to adapt to the interests and perspectives of different users.

Evaluation Training

In 1973, the year I completed my doctorate, the National Institute of Mental Health (NIMH) funded a handful of evaluation methodology training programs at major universities, one of which was the University of Minnesota, where I went as the program's first postdoctoral fellow in evaluation methodology. The program was highly interdisciplinary, involving professors from 17 different departments across the university. A year later, I became director of the program and established the Minnesota Center for Social Research as a place where participants in the program could conduct actual evaluations. We made the study of evaluation use the focus of the program, and it was the participants in this program who conducted the utilization study that led to our discovery of the personal factor. Here are some of the things I learned directing that program.

As the program participants undertook real evaluations in local settings, we found much of our traditional methodological training to be irrelevant. We learned that evaluators need skills in building relationships, facilitating groups, managing conflict, walking political tight ropes, and effective interpersonal communication to capitalize on the importance of the personal factor. We learned that a particular evaluation may have multiple levels of stakeholders and therefore need multiple levels of stakeholder involvement. Technical skills and social science knowledge, while critical, are not sufficient to get evaluations used. People skills are critical. Evaluators without the savvy and skills to deal with people and politics will find their work largely ignored or, worse yet, used inappropriately.

We also learned that the national funders at NIMH didn't value what we were learning and doing. The three national site visitors who evaluated the program criticized it for not teaching large-scale experimental designs for national studies. The site visit team dismissed as unimportant the 80 local evaluations we had conducted and the fact that we had placed graduates in important positions in local government, philanthropic foundations, nonprofits, and training units of corporations. They also dismissed the research we had conducted on evaluation use, noting that the sample size of 20 cases was insignificant. They were unimpressed with the publication of *Utilization-Focused Evaluation*, and the very fact that we pointed to our utilization research as the centerpiece of the training program demonstrated to them that the program was not fulfilling its purpose (sophisticated methodological training, in their judgment). The program therefore was not renewed, lost NIMH funding, and subsequently lost University of Minnesota support. (For more details about this experience and its effects, as well as other critical personal turning points not covered in this chapter, see King & Patton, 2007.)

EARLY ENCOUNTERS WITH EVALUATION LUMINARIES

While the national NIMH site visitors found little of value in our work on utilization-focused evaluation, that work had attracted the attention of two of the luminaries in evaluation, Carol Weiss, who is credited with first making evaluation use a priority in the emerging field of evaluation, and Marv Alkin, who had founded and was still directing UCLA's Center for the Study of Evaluation. Carol Weiss published our utilization study in her important book on using social research for policy making (Patton et al., 1977; Weiss, 1977). When we received word that she had accepted the chapter, we had a boisterous party (well, boisterous by Minnesota standards).

Meanwhile, Sage Publications had sent the draft manuscript for *Utilization-Focused Evaluation* to Marv Alkin for review. His supportive and helpful review led not only to publication (occasion for yet another boisterous celebration) but also to an invitation to participate in an extraordinary gathering with other evaluators at UCLA. For 3 days, with Marv's facilitation, we discussed evaluation utilization (see Alkin, 1990). The participants included Ross Connor, Ernie House, Michael Kean, Jean King, Susan Klein, Alex Law, Milbrey McLaughlin, and Carol Weiss. Those discussions and the long-term relationships formed have had a lasting impact on my work. In complexity theory terms, those 3 days of butterfly wings flapping created a tempest that energized the study of evaluation use and set the agenda for issues that continue to challenge the field.

The preface to the fourth edition of *Utilization-Focused Evaluation* (Patton, 2008) includes an acknowledgment of a lengthy list of colleagues who have influenced my work, contributed to my understandings, and nurtured my evaluation practice. My evaluation roots are intricately entangled with the roots of others on the theory tree, both the use branch and other branches, and beyond the tree to the vibrant and growing forest of practitioners and scholars that is the global evaluation community.

DISCOVERING PROCESS USE

When I established the Minnesota Center for Social Research in the mid-1970s, I began the practice of following up every evaluation we conducted to find out how it was used. Those evaluations are the basis for many of the stories in my writings. Part of my preparation for doing each new edition of *Utilization-Focused Evaluation* is reviewing client feedback from evaluations and workshops. When, in the mid-1990s, I went to prepare the third edition of the book and began reflecting on what had happened in the field in the 10 years since the last edition, I was struck by something that my own myopia had not allowed me to see before. When I have followed up my own evaluations over the years, I have enquired from intended users about actual use. What I would typically hear was something like this: "Yes, the findings were helpful in this way and that, and here's what we did with them." If there had been recommendations, I would ask what subsequent actions, if any, followed. But beyond the focus on findings and recommendations, what they almost inevitably added was something to the effect that "it wasn't really the findings that were so important in the end; it was going through the process." In reflecting on that feedback, I came to realize that *the entire field had narrowly defined use as use of findings*. We have thus not had ways to conceptualize or talk about what happens to people and organizations as a result of being involved in an evaluation process: what I have come to call "process use" (Patton, 1997, 1998, 2007).

This idea of process use draws our attention to individual changes in thinking and behavior among those involved in evaluation as a result of the learning that occurs during the evaluation process. Changes in program or organizational procedures and culture may also be manifestations of process use.

Process use includes helping those we work with learn to think evaluatively. Evaluative thinking is often alien to nonevaluators. Evaluative thinking includes the value we place on clarity, specificity, and intentionality; being systematic and making assumptions explicit; operationalizing program goals; distinguishing inputs and processes from outcomes; valuing empirical evidence; and separating statements of fact from interpretations and judgments. When we take people through a process of evaluation, at least in any kind of stakeholder involvement or participatory process, they often learn how to think in these ways.

Process use is distinct from use of the substantive findings of an evaluation. It's equivalent to the difference between learning how to learn versus learning substantive knowledge about something. Learning how to think evaluatively is learning how to learn. This kind of process impact has become increasingly valued because the capacity to engage in evaluative thinking can have more enduring value than a delimited set of findings, especially for organizations interested in becoming what has come to be popularly called "learning organizations." Findings have a very short "half-life," to use a physical science metaphor. They deteriorate very quickly as the world changes rapidly. In contrast, learning to think and act evaluatively can have a lasting impact on how program staff think, on their openness to reality testing, and on how they view the things they—and we—do.

GLOBAL INFLUENCES

In the past few years, I've had extraordinary opportunities to be part of evaluation conferences and professional associations throughout the world. Evaluation has become a global profession, as the expanded international chapters in this book illustrate. Our colleagues from around the world are infusing the profession with new energy as we learn different ways of looking at what we do and face challenges about how to translate some of what we do for the rest of the world. I find myself challenged to think more deeply about the cultural values and biases of Western approaches to evaluation and to include attention to cultural diversity and sensitivity as important factors affecting evaluation quality and use.

HALCOLM

How we communicate with nonevaluators affects their openness to use. I've had a long-standing interest in increasing the effectiveness of my communications. My writings are infused with metaphors and stories, especially Sufi tales, which represent the tradition of stories with morals. Stories and metaphors are especially important for cross-cultural communications.

I found that I needed a wise character, a kind of Sufi master, to express evaluation wisdom in my books, so I created the character of Halcolm (pronounced "how-come," as in "why?"). Writing Halcolm stories became an outlet for that part of me that wanted and needed to do creative writing and storytelling. I've long studied good writing and storytelling and have attempted to incorporate what I've learned in my writings, including a creative nonfiction book about my efforts to pass on the evaluation perspective to my eldest son as part of his initiation into adulthood (Patton, 1999). Here, as an example, is Halcolm's interpretation of the personal factor: "There are five key variables that are absolutely critical in evaluation use. They are, in order of importance: *people, people, people, people*, and *people* [italics added]" (opening quote in Patton, 1997, p. 39).

This insight is not evident to everyone. I sometimes get feedback from students that they become impatient with my stories about people with whom I've worked closely, people deeply involved in innovation and evaluation who have influenced my approach to evaluation. "*Enough with the stories already. Get to the point*," they admonish. I appreciate the frankness of this feedback. And it gives me a chance to explain to my students that *the stories are the point*. The people in the stories, what they do and how they think, are the point. If you skip the stories and the people, you will have missed the point. Here's why. People matter. Relationships matter. Evaluation is not just about methods and data.

The *personal factor* matters. My evaluation roots are grounded in places where I've worked, ideas I've encountered, theories I've studied, research I've undertaken, and evaluations I've conducted, but most of all, my roots are grounded in relationships with the people I've encountered along the way. To all of them I offer my deepest thanks.

REFERENCES

Alkin, M. (Ed.). (1990). *Debates on evaluation.* Newbury Park, CA: Sage.

Crozier, M. (1964). *The bureaucratic phenomenon.* Chicago, IL: University of Chicago Press.

King, J., & Patton, M. Q. (2007). History of evaluation: Oral history interview with Michael Quinn Patton. *American Journal of Evaluation, 28*(1), 102–114.

Patrizi, P., & Patton, M. Q. (Eds.). (2011). *Evaluating strategy* (New Directions for Evaluation, No. 128). San Francisco, CA: John Wiley.

Patton, M. Q. (1975). *Alternative evaluation research paradigms.* Grand Forks: University of North Dakota, North Dakota Study Group on Evaluation.

Patton, M. Q. (1978). *Utilization-focused evaluation* (1st ed.). Beverly Hills, CA: Sage.

Patton, M. Q. (1997). *Utilization-focused evaluation: The new century text* (3rd ed.). Thousand Oaks, CA: Sage.

Patton, M. Q. (1998). Discovering process use. *Evaluation, 4*(2), 225–233.

Patton, M. Q. (1999). *Grand Canyon celebration: A father–son journey of discovery.* Amherst, NY: Prometheus Books.

Patton, M. Q. (2007). Process use as usefulism. *New Directions for Evaluation, 116,* 99–112.

Patton, M. Q. (2008). *Utilization-focused evaluation* (4th ed.). Thousand Oaks, CA: Sage.

Patton, M. Q. (2010). *Developmental evaluation: Applying complexity concepts to enhance innovation and use.* New York, NY: Guilford Press.

Patton, M. Q., Grimes, P. S., Guthrie, K. M., Brennan, N. J., French, B. D., & Blyth, D. A. (1977). In search of impact: An analysis of the utilization of federal health evaluation research. In C. Weiss (Ed.), *Using social research in public policy making* (pp. 141–164). Lexington, MA: D. C. Heath.

Thompson, J. D. (1967). *Organizations in action.* New York, NY: McGraw-Hill.

Weiss, C. (Ed.). (1977). *Using social research in public policy making.* Lexington, MA: D. C. Heath.

Westley, F., Zimmerman, B., & Patton, M. Q. (2006). *Getting to maybe: How the world is changed.* Toronto, Ontario, Canada: Random House Canada.

24

EMPOWERMENT EVALUATION

Learning to Think Like an Evaluator

David M. Fetterman

Since its inception in 1994, empowerment evaluation has become a part of the landscape of evaluation.[1] It is being used from remote Amazonian regions to the corporate offices of Hewlett-Packard in Silicon Valley. Empowerment evaluation is currently being applied in more than 14 countries.

In the past, empowerment evaluation has been used by NASA/Jet Propulsion Laboratory to educate youth about the prototype Mars Rover, in townships in South Africa to create sustainable community health initiatives, by the U.S. Department of Education's Office of Special Education and Rehabilitation Services to foster self-determination, and with Native American tribes to build technological and economic infrastructures on reservations. Likewise, it has branched out to many new areas, including schools in academic distress (Fetterman, 2005a), accreditation in higher education (Fetterman, 2001, 2011), minority tobacco prevention (Fetterman & Wandersman, 2007), and medical education (Fetterman, 2009; Fetterman, Deitz, & Gesundheit, 2010). That said, empowerment evaluation's greatest growth has been conceptual and methodological, as a result of rigorous critique and practice.

This discussion highlights the definition, theories, principles, concepts, and steps of empowerment evaluation. These are sequentially ordered conceptual building blocks. Once defined, they begin with the macrolevel or highest level of abstraction—theories—and end at the microlevel—the specific steps of empowerment evaluation. This serves to place the steps in a theoretical and conceptual context, much the same as other theories, models, and concepts are used to place the steps of alternative approaches in context. The sequence is designed to help practitioners understand and implement empowerment evaluation practice.

DEFINITION AND OVERVIEW

Empowerment evaluation is the use of evaluation concepts, techniques, and findings to foster improvement and self-determination (Fetterman, 1994a). An expanded definition is as follows: "Empowerment evaluation is an evaluation approach that aims to increase the likelihood that programs will achieve results by increasing the capacity of program stakeholders to plan, implement, and evaluate their own programs" (Wandersman et al., 2005, p. 27).

Empowerment evaluation is guided by empowerment and self-determination theories. It is also informed by specific evaluation theories, including process use and theories of use and action. In turn, these theories help me define 10 overarching principles that provide empowerment evaluation with an explicit direction and purpose, beginning with improvement and continuing to accountability. Key concepts that help define empowerment evaluation primarily include critical friends, cultures of evidence, cycles of reflection and action, communities of learners, and reflective practitioners.

There are many ways by which to implement an empowerment evaluation. However, one of the most popular approaches is a three-step model.[2] These steps help further explicate the nature of empowerment evaluation. These theories, principles, concepts, and steps are interrelated and reinforcing. The theories provide a 30,000-foot view of the approach, while the steps provide turn-by-turn insights. Together they provide a rich and layered map of the dynamic terrain of empowerment evaluation.

THEORIES

The theories behind this simple process are surprisingly complex. These theories are the underpinnings of this approach. An exploration into the theories guiding empowerment practice will help illuminate the integral relationship between method and use in empowerment evaluation. The most pertinent theories guiding empowerment evaluation are empowerment theory, self-determination theory, process use, and theories of use and action. *Empowerment theory* is divided into processes and outcomes. This theory has implications for the role of the empowerment evaluator or facilitator, which differs from that of a traditional evaluator. *Self-determination* is one of the foundational concepts underlying empowerment theory, and it helps detail the specific mechanisms or behaviors that enable the actualization of empowerment. *Process use* represents much of the rationale or logic underlying empowerment evaluation in practice, because it cultivates ownership by placing the approach in the hands of community and staff members. Finally, the alignment of *theories of use and action* explains how empowerment evaluation helps people produce the desired results.

Empowerment Theory

Writings in community psychology have developed an area called empowerment theory. Empowerment theory is about gaining control, obtaining resources, and understanding one's social environment. It is also about problem solving, leadership, and decision making. It operates on many levels, and distinguishing between empowering processes and outcomes is critical. According to Zimmerman (2000),

> empowerment processes are ones in which attempts to gain control, obtain needed resources, and critically understand one's social environment are fundamental. The process is empowering if it helps people develop skills so they can become independent problem solvers and decision makers. Empowering processes will vary across levels of analysis. For example, empowering processes for individuals might include organizational or community involvement, empowering processes at the organizational level might include shared leadership and decision making, and empowering processes at the community level might include accessible government, media, and other community resources. (pp. 47–48)

Similar to the distinctions between process and outcome in evaluation, empowerment theory processes contribute to specific outcomes. Linking the processes to outcomes helps draw meta-level causal relationships or at least a chain of reasoning. When specified outcomes are achieved, it is possible to retrace the steps to determine which processes were the most effective. Similarly, when specific processes are implemented poorly, it is easy to see the causal relationship or at least the contributing factors associated with the failure to achieve specified outcomes. Zimmerman (2000) provides additional insight into the outcome level of analysis to further explicate empowerment theory:

> Empowerment outcomes refer to operationalization of empowerment so we can study the consequences of citizen attempts to gain greater control in their community or the effects of interventions designed to empower participants. Empowered outcomes also differ across levels of analysis. When we are concerned with individuals, outcomes might include situation-specific perceived control, skills, and proactive behaviors. When we are studying organizations, outcomes might include organizational networks, effective resource acquisition, and policy leverage. When we are concerned with community level empowerment, outcomes might include evidence of pluralism, the existence of organizational coalitions, and accessible community resources. (pp. 52–53)

Role

Zimmerman's (2000) characterization of the community psychologist's role in empowerment activities is easily adapted to the empowerment evaluator. It also demonstrates the impact of theory on practice, shaping every dimension of the approach, including the evaluator's role.

> An empowerment approach to intervention design, implementation, and evaluation redefines the professional's role relationship with the target population. The professional's role becomes one of collaborator and facilitator rather than expert and counselor. As collaborators, professionals learn about the participants through their cultures, their worldviews, and their life struggles. The professional works *with* participants instead of advocating *for* them. The professional's skills, interest, or plans are not imposed on the community; rather, professionals become a resource for a community. This role relationship suggests that what professionals do will depend on the particular place and people with whom they are working, rather than on the technologies that are predetermined to be applied in all situations. (pp. 44–45)

An eloquent literature on empowerment theory by Zimmerman (2000), Zimmerman, Israel, Schulz, and Checkoway (1992), Zimmerman and Rappaport (1988), and Dunst, Trivette, and LaPointe (1992) also informs empowerment evaluation.

Self-Determination[3]

The theoretical level of empowerment processes and outcomes requires mechanisms to link it to action. Dennis Mithaug's (1991, 1993) extensive work with individuals with disabilities to explore the concept of self-determination provided additional theoretical inspiration and guidance. The concept of self-determination details the specific mechanisms that help program staff members and participants implement an empowerment evaluation. Self-determination was one of the foundational concepts in the study that informs empowerment evaluation today.

Self-determination is defined as the ability to chart one's own course in life. It consists of numerous interconnected capabilities, such as the ability to identify and express needs; establish goals or expectations and a plan of action to achieve them; identify resources; make rational choices from various alternative courses of action; take appropriate steps to pursue objectives; evaluate short- and long-term results, including reassessing plans and expectations and taking necessary detours; and persist in the pursuit of those goals. A breakdown at any juncture of this network of capabilities—as well as various environmental factors—can reduce a person's likelihood of being self-determined.[4]

Dennis and I, as part of an American Institutes for Research team, completed a 2-year grant funded by the Department of Education on self-determination and individuals with disabilities. We conducted research designed to help both providers for students with disabilities and the students themselves become more empowered. We learned about self-determined behavior and attitudes and environmentally related features of self-determination by listening to self-determined children with disabilities and their providers.

Process Use

One of the most significant problems facing the field of evaluation is inadequate knowledge utilization. Evaluation reports often sit and gather dust. Decisions are made without the benefit of information from evaluation findings. Empowerment evaluation is designed to be used by people. It places evaluation in the hands of community and staff members. The more people are engaged in conducting their own evaluations, the more likely they are to believe in them, because the evaluation findings are theirs. In addition, a by-product of this experience is that they learn to think evaluatively. This makes them more likely to make decisions and take actions based on their evaluation data. This way of thinking is at the heart of process use.[5]

According to Patton (2002),

> helping people learn to think evaluatively by participating in real evaluation exercises is what I've come to call "process use" (Patton, 1997a, 1998). I have defined process use as relating to and being indicated by individual changes in thinking and behaving that occur among those involved in evaluation as a result of the learning that occurs *during the evaluation process*. (p. 189)

In an empowerment evaluation, thinking evaluatively is a product of guided immersion. This occurs when people conduct their own evaluation as guided by an empowerment evaluator. Teaching people to think evaluatively is like teaching them to fish. It can last a lifetime and is what evaluative sustainability is all about—internalizing evaluation (individually and institutionally).

Empowerment evaluation invites, if not demands, participation. Participation or immersion is a form of experiential education. Being guided, this immersion helps people see the world through an evaluative lens. Participation also creates an authentic, credible, and almost palpable sense of ownership. It is this combination of evaluative thought and ownership, through immersion, that makes empowerment evaluation work, improving knowledge utilization in the process.

Theories of Use and Action

Once the groundwork is laid with empowerment theory, self-determination theory, and process use theories, conceptual mechanisms become more meaningful. Theories that enable comparisons between use and action are essential. The approach works when the pieces are in place. When things go wrong, which is normal in life, it is possible to compare and identify the areas needing attention.

Empowerment evaluation relies on the reciprocal relationship between theories of action and use at every step in the process. A *theory of action* is usually the espoused operating theory about how a program or organization works. It is a useful tool, generally based on the views of program personnel. This theory of action is often compared with a theory of use. The theory of use is the actual program reality, the observable behavior of stakeholders (see Argyris & Schon, 1978; Patton, 1997b). People engaged in empowerment evaluations create a theory of action at one stage and test it against the existing theory of use at a later stage. Similarly, they create a new theory of action as they plan for the future. Because empowerment evaluation is an ongoing and iterative process, stakeholders test their theories of action against theories in use during various microcycles to determine whether their strategies are being implemented as recommended or designed. The theories go hand in hand in empowerment evaluation.

These theories are used to identify gross differences between the ideal and the real. For example, communities of empowerment evaluation practice compare their theory of action with their theory of use to determine whether they are even pointing in the same direction. Three common patterns that emerge from this comparison include *in alignment*, *out of alignment*, and *alignment in conflict* (see Figure 24.1). In alignment is when the two theories are parallel or pointed in the same direction. They may be distant or close levels of alignment, but they are on the same general track. Out of alignment occurs when actual practice is divergent from the espoused theory of how things are supposed to work. The theory of use is not simply distant or closely aligned but actually off target or at least pointed in another direction. Alignment in conflict occurs when the theory of action and use are pointed in diametrically opposite directions. This signals a group or organization in serious trouble or self-denial.

Chapter 24. Empowerment Evaluation

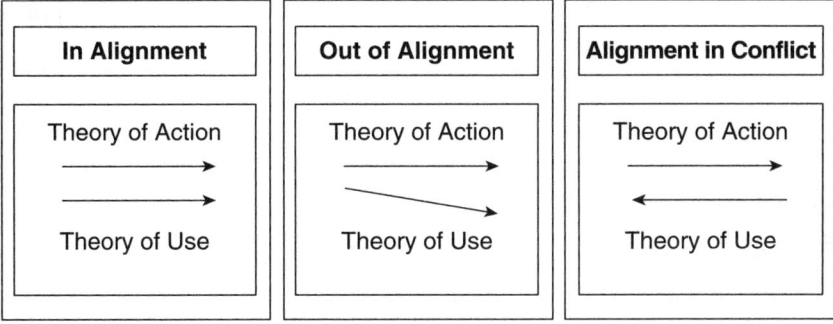

Figure 24.1 Contrasting Patterns of Alignment
Source: © 2001 by Fetterman and Eiler. Reprinted from Fetterman and Eiler (2001).

After making the first-level comparison, a gross indicator, to determine whether the theories of action and use are even remotely related to each other, communities of empowerment evaluation practice compare their theory of action with their theory of use in an effort to reduce the gap between them. This assumes that they are at least pointed in the same direction. The ideal progression is from distant alignment to close alignment between the two theories. This is the conceptual space where most communities of empowerment evaluation practice strive to accomplish their goals as they close the gap between the theories (see Figure 24.2).

The process of empowerment embraces the tension between the two types of theories and offers a means of reconciling incongruities. This dialectic in which theories of action and use are routinely juxtaposed in daily practice creates a culture of learning and evaluation.

PRINCIPLES

The foundations of empowerment evaluation theoretically lead to specific principles to instruct practice. Empowerment evaluation principles provide a sense of direction and purposefulness

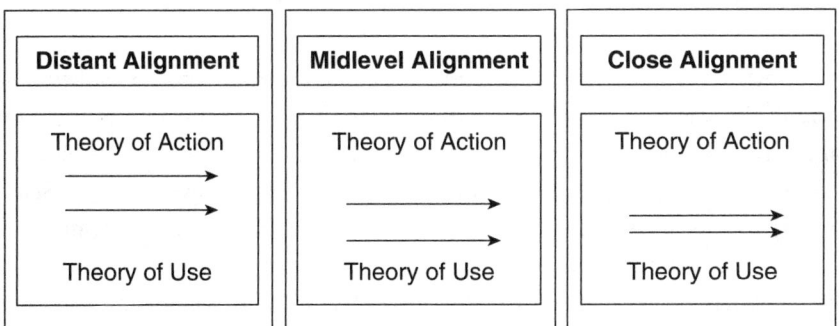

Figure 24.2 Aligning Theories of Action and Use to Reduce the Gap
Source: © 2001 by Fetterman and Eiler. Reprinted from Fetterman and Eiler (2001).

throughout an evaluation. Empowerment evaluation is guided by 10 specific principles (see Fetterman & Wandersman, 2005, pp. 1–2, 27–41, 42–72):

1. *Improvement:* Empowerment evaluation is designed to help people improve program performance; it is designed to help people build on their successes and reevaluate areas meriting attention.

2. *Community ownership:* Empowerment evaluation values and facilitates community control; use and sustainability are dependent on a sense of ownership.

3. *Inclusion:* Empowerment evaluation invites involvement, participation, and diversity; contributions come from all levels and walks of life.

4. *Democratic participation:* Participation and decision making should be open and fair.

5. *Social justice:* Evaluation can and should be used to address inequities in society.

6. *Community knowledge:* Empowerment evaluation respects and values community knowledge.

7. *Evidence-based strategies:* Empowerment evaluation respects and uses the knowledge base of scholars (in conjunction with community knowledge).

8. *Capacity building:* Empowerment evaluation is designed to enhance stakeholders' ability to conduct an evaluation and to improve program planning and implementation.

9. *Organizational learning:* Data should be used to evaluate new practices, inform decision making, and implement program practices; empowerment evaluation is used to help organizations learn from their experience (building on successes, learning from mistakes, and making midcourse corrections).

10. *Accountability:* Empowerment evaluation is focused on outcomes and accountability; empowerment evaluations functions within the context of existing policies, standards, and measures of accountability; did the program accomplish its objectives?

Empowerment evaluation principles help evaluators and community members make decisions that are in alignment with the larger purpose or goals associated with capacity building and self-determination. The principle of inclusion, for example, reminds evaluators and community members to include rather than exclude members of the community, even though fiscal, logistic, and personality factors might suggest otherwise. The capacity building principle reminds the evaluator to provide community members with the opportunity to collect their own data even though it might initially be faster and easier for the evaluator to collect the same information. The accountability principle guides community members to hold one another accountable. It also situates the evaluation within the context of external requirements and credible results or outcomes. (See Fetterman, 2005b, p. 2.)

CONCEPTS

Empowerment evaluation concepts provide a more instrumental view of how to implement the approach. Key concepts include critical friends, cultures of evidence, cycles of reflection and action, communities of learners, and reflective practitioners.[6] Critical friends are evaluators who facilitate the process and steps of empowerment evaluation. They believe in the purpose of the program but provide constructive feedback. They help ensure that the evaluation remains organized, rigorous, and honest.

Empowerment evaluators help cultivate a culture of evidence by asking people why they believe what they believe. They are asked for evidence or documentation at every stage, so that it becomes normal and expected to have data to support one's opinions and views. Cycles of reflection and action involve ongoing phases of analysis, decision making, and implementation, based on evaluation findings. It is a cyclical process. Programs are dynamic, not static, and require continual feedback as they change and evolve. Empowerment evaluation is successful when it is institutionalized and becomes a normal part of the planning and management of a program.

Empowerment evaluation is driven by a group process. It is a community of learners. The group members learn from one another, serving as a peer review group and as critical friends, resources, and norming mechanisms for one another. Individual members of the group hold each other accountable concerning progress toward stated goals. Finally, empowerment evaluations help create reflective practitioners. Reflective practitioners use data to inform their decisions and actions in their daily lives. This produces a self-aware and self-actualized individual who has the capacity to apply this worldview to all aspects of his or her life. As individuals develop and enhance their own capacity, they improve the quality of the group's exchange, deliberation, and action plans.

STEPS

There are many ways by which to implement an empowerment evaluation. In fact, empowerment evaluation has accumulated a warehouse of useful tools. The three-step approach to empowerment evaluation is one of the most popular tools in the collection (Fetterman, 2001). It includes helping a group (1) establish its mission, (2) take stock of its current status, and (3) plan for the future. The popularity of this particular approach is in part a result of its simplicity, effectiveness, and transparency.

Mission

The group members come to a consensus concerning their mission or values. This gives them a shared vision of what's important to them and where they want to go. The empowerment evaluator facilitates this process by asking participants to generate statements that reflect their mission. These phrases are recorded on a poster sheet of paper (and may be projected on an LCD projector depending on the technology available). These phrases are used to draft a mission statement (crafted by a member of the group and the empowerment evaluator). The draft is circulated among the members of the group. They are asked to approve it and/or suggest specific changes in wording as needed. A consensus about the mission statement helps the group think clearly about its self-assessment and plans for the future. It anchors the group in common values (see Figure 24.3).

Taking Stock

After coming to a consensus about the mission, the group members evaluate their efforts (within the context of a set of shared values). First, the empowerment evaluator helps them generate a list of the most important activities required to accomplish organizational or programmatic goals. The empowerment evaluator gives each participant five dot stickers and asks the participants to place them by the activities they think are the most important to accomplish programmatic and organizational goals (and thus the most important to evaluate as a group from that point on). They can put one sticker on five different activities or all five on one activity if they are concerned that activity will not get enough votes. The top 10 items with the most dots represent the results of the prioritization part of taking stock (see Figure 24.4). The 10 activities represent the heart of Part 2 of taking stock: rating.

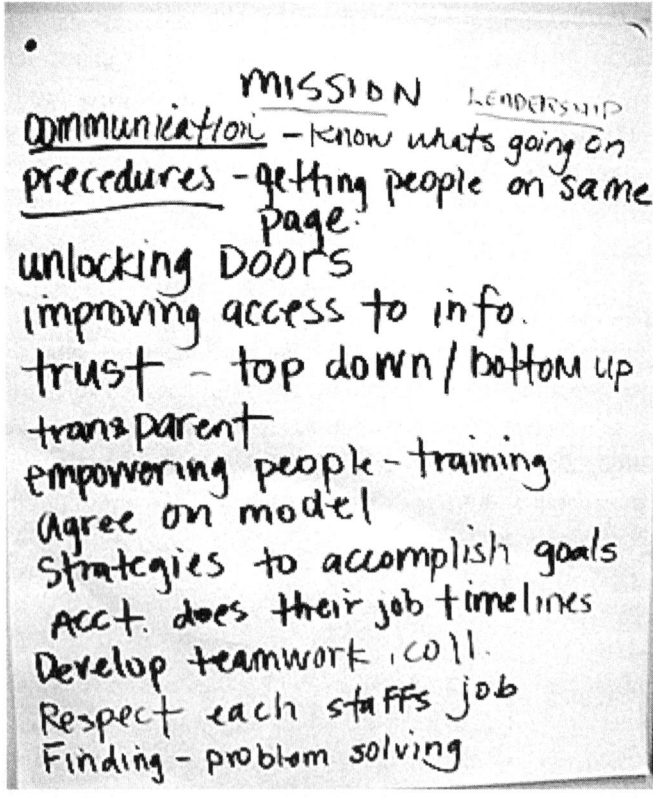

Figure 24.3 Mission: Notes Reflecting the Mission of the Group

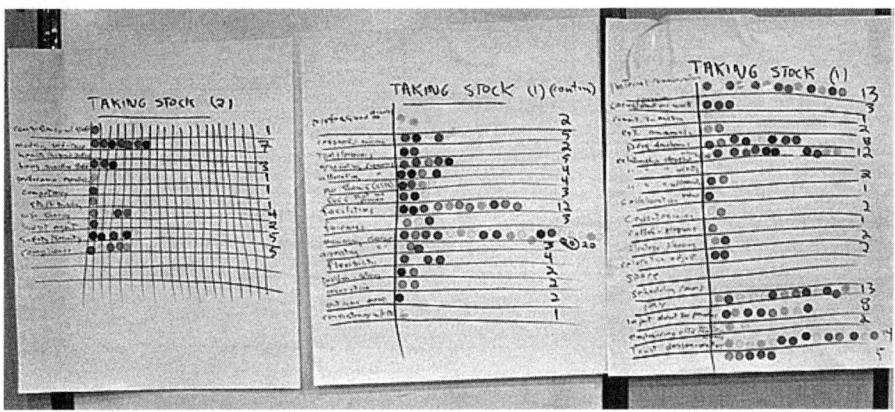

Figure 24.4 Taking Stock: Part 1 (Using Dots to Prioritize the List of Activities to Evaluate)

The empowerment evaluator asks participants in the group to rate how well they are doing concerning each of the activities selected, using a scale of 1 (*low*) to 10 (*high*). The columns are averaged horizontally and vertically. Vertically, the group can see who is typically optimistic or pessimistic. This helps the group calibrate or evaluate the ratings and opinions of each individual member. It helps the group establish norms. Horizontally, the averages provide the group with a consolidated view of how well (or poorly) things are going. The empowerment evaluator facilitates a discussion and dialogue about the ratings, asking participants why they gave a certain activity a 3 or a 7.

The dialogue about the ratings is one of the most important parts of the process. In addition to clarifying issues, evidence is used to support viewpoints, and "sacred cows" are surfaced and examined during the dialogue. Moreover, the process of specifying the reason or evidence for a rating provides the group with a more efficient and focused way of identifying what needs to be done next, during the planning for the future steps of the process. Instead of generating an unwieldy list of strategies and solutions that may or may not be relevant to the issues at hand, the group can focus its energies on the specific concerns and reasons for a low rating that were raised in the dialogue or exchange (see Figure 24.5).

Planning for the Future

Many evaluations conclude at the taking-stock phase. However, taking stock is a baseline and a launching-off point for the rest of the evaluation. After rating and discussing programmatic activities, it is important to do something about the findings. It is time to plan for the future. This step involves generating goals, strategies, and credible evidence (to determine if the strategies are being implemented and if they are effective). The goals are directly related to the activities selected in the taking-stock step. For example, if communication was selected, rated, and discussed, then communication (or improving communication) should be one of the goals. The strategies emerge from the taking-stock discussion, as well, as noted earlier. For example, if communication received a low rating and one of the reasons was that

	Individual Initials			Activity Averages	
TAKING STOCK II: RATINGS					
ACTIVITIES	BC	DD	RR	DS	AVG
Respectful Workplace	6	7	8	7.0	7.1
Generating Resources	5	8	8	7.0	6.9
Modeling Self-care	4	6	7	5.7	5.75
Safety & Security	5	6	6	5.7	5.7
Pay	5	6	6	5.7	5.6
Managing Change	4	6	6	5.3	5.4
Facilities	4	5	7	5.3	5.2
Trusting Decision Makers	3	4	8	5.0	5.1
	4.5	6.0	7.0	5.8	5.8

Individual Averages — Program Average

Figure 24.5 Taking Stock: Part 2 (Initial Baseline Taking Stock Ratings—Abbreviated Example)

the group never had an agenda for its meetings, then preparing agendas might become a recommended strategy in the "planning for the future" exercise (see Figure 24.6).

Monitoring the Strategies

Many programs, projects, and evaluations fail at this stage for lack of individual and group accountability. Individuals who spoke eloquently and/or emotionally about a certain topic should be asked to volunteer to lead specific task forces to respond to identified problems or concerns. They do not have to complete the task. However, they are responsible for taking the lead in a circumscribed area (a specific goal) and reporting the status of the effort periodically at ongoing management meetings. Similarly, the group should make a commitment to reviewing the status

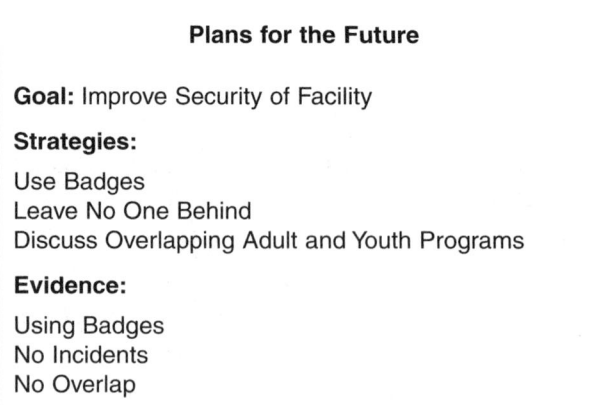

Plans for the Future

Goal: Improve Security of Facility

Strategies:
Use Badges
Leave No One Behind
Discuss Overlapping Adult and Youth Programs

Evidence:
Using Badges
No Incidents
No Overlap

Figure 24.6 Planning for the Future: Goals, Strategies, and Evidence (Abbreviated Example)

of these new strategies as a group (and be willing to make midcourse corrections if they are not working). Conventional and innovative evaluation tools are used to monitor the strategies, including online surveys, focus groups, interviews, as well as the use of a quasi-experimental design (if appropriate). In addition, program-specific metrics are developed, using baselines, benchmarks, and goals (as deemed useful and appropriate). For example, an empowerment evaluation of a minority tobacco prevention program in Arkansas has established the following:

1. Baselines (the number of people using tobacco in the community)

2. Goals (the number of people the program plans to help stop using tobacco by the end of the year)

3. Benchmarks (the number of people the program expects to help stop using tobacco each month)

These metrics are used to help a community monitor program implementation efforts and enable program staff and community members to make midcourse corrections and substitute ineffective strategies with potentially more effective ones as needed. These data are also invaluable when the group conducts a second taking stock exercise (3–6 months later) to determine if it is making progress toward its desired goals and objectives. Additional metrics enable community members to compare, for example, their baseline assessments with their benchmarks or expected points of progress, as well as their goals (see Figure 24.7).

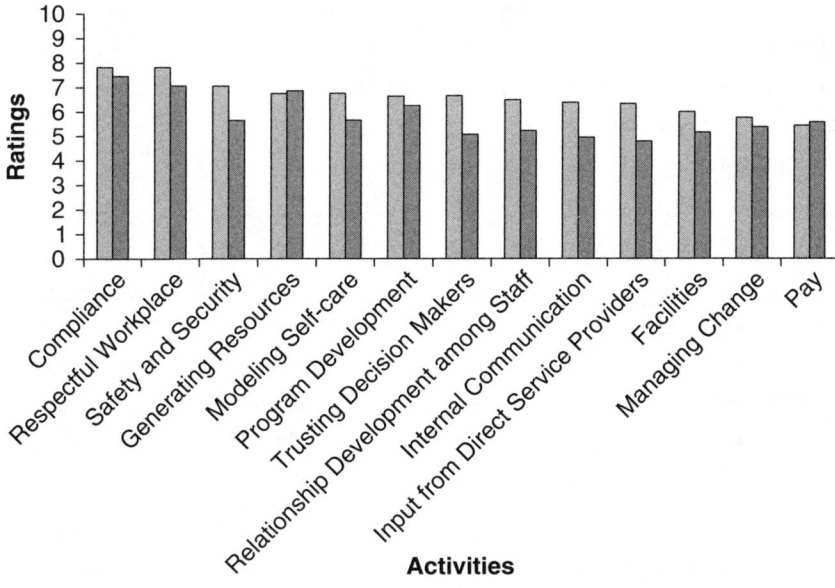

Figure 24.7 Comparing Initial Taking Stock Ratings With Second Taking Stock Ratings

Source: The figures and data used to illustrate many of the points in this presentation are based on the Family and Children Services and Minority Initiative Sub-Recipient Grant Office Tobacco Prevention empowerment evaluations.

CLARIFYING EMPOWERMENT EVALUATION ISSUES

Now that we have presented a theoretical, conceptual, and step-by-step road map for empowerment evaluation, additional clarity is gained by peeling away layers of potential misunderstandings and misconceptions about empowerment evaluation. These range from the locus of control to the politics of empowerment evaluation and are briefly discussed below.

1. *Empowerment:* A common misconception about empowerment evaluation is that it empowers either individuals or groups. Empowerment evaluation can't empower anyone. People empower themselves. Empowerment evaluation simply provides the tools and environment conducive to empowering oneself.

2. *Objectivity and advocacy:* The question of whether empowerment evaluation is objective or promotes advocacy is a legitimate concern. However, science and, specifically, evaluation have never been neutral. Likewise, evaluation is not free from political, social, cultural, or economic influences. In contrast, empowerment evaluation is transparent, brings bias to the surface, and generates meaningful data to inform decision making. These findings should be used by staff, community members, and other relevant parties to advocate for their programs or communities as the data merit.

3. *Consumer focus:* Though evaluators and donors should be an integral part of empowerment evaluation, consumers (community members, program staff, and participants) are the driving force.

4. *Internal verses external evaluation:* Empowerment evaluation (internal evaluation) and traditional forms of evaluation (typically external evaluation) are not mutually exclusive. In fact, they can be mutually reinforcing. However, external evaluations should be rooted in internal concerns, otherwise they may be irrelevant or may divert program staff, participants, and resources from the most relevant issues given the organization's stage of development.

5. *Purpose:* There are multiple purposes for evaluation, including development, accountability, and knowledge. Empowerment evaluation's most significant contribution is to development. However, it makes a strong contribution to accountability by cultivating internal accountability. Such a contribution remains long after an episodic and often anticipated external examination. All forms of evaluation potentially add to the compilation of knowledge; however, time is required to accumulate thorough case examples and enough wisdom to make a credible impact on knowledge development. (See Chelimsky & Shadish [1997] concerning the multiple purposes of evaluation.)

6. *Bias:* Internal evaluations are often seen as biased and self-serving. This has not been found to be the case in empowerment evaluations. On the contrary, empowerment evaluations are typically more critical of their own programs than external examinations (which are concerned about being asked to return for a follow-up or extended engagement).

Empowerment evaluations provide people with a window of opportunity to address long-standing issues of dysfunction and inefficiency in their own organizations. Empowerment evaluations are not about individual inadequacies. Hence, this is the organization's chance to "make things work." In addition, the process is inclusive and transparent, open to critique and review, and makes it difficult to keep people from publicly "speaking their truth."

7. *Outcomes:* One of the 10 principles guiding empowerment evaluations is accountability. Empowerment evaluations are highly collaborative and participatory in nature. However, the bottom line remains, Did you produce the desired results? Empowerment evaluations are conducted within the context of what people are already being held accountable for in their communities or workplaces. This makes the entire process more credible and authentic.

8. *Political or psychological:* Empowerment evaluation has a political dimension. However, the richness of this approach is found in the psychological arena. E. Glass (personal communication, 1977) was one of the first evaluators to observe this dimension. He explains, "For people who know you, empowerment evaluation is first and foremost a psychological phenomenon, much more than a political act." Some colleagues have argued that empowerment evaluation should be limited to the disenfranchised. Empowerment evaluators, however, believe that everyone can benefit from being more empowered. The very nature of empowerment evaluation rejects the assumption that people can't take control of their lives, particularly from a perspective of positive psychological growth.

These points about conceptual clarity, as well as additional information[7] about methodological specificity and outcomes, are discussed in greater detail in the literature (Fetterman, 2001; Fetterman & Wandersman, 2005, 2007).

ROLE OF BACKGROUND AND EXPERIENCE

My background and various experiences in conducting empowerment evaluations have helped inform and refine the approach. In addition to the theoretical influences cited earlier, my personal roots in the field of ethnography and the myriad experiences I have had have shaped the empowerment evaluation approach.

A cursory review of my previous scholarly activity documents this powerful ethnographic influence shaping the development of empowerment evaluation. For example, I had written a popular methodological textbook, *Ethnography: Step by Step* (Fetterman, 1989),[8] by the time empowerment evaluation was introduced. I had also written or edited substantial collections specifically in the area of qualitative and ethnographic evaluation.[9] My book *Qualitative Approaches to Evaluation in Education: The Silent Scientific Revolution* (Fetterman, 1988) consisted of chapters by the founders or prominent proponents of the major qualitative approaches at the time, including Patton (generic or sociological qualitative approach), Guba and Lincoln (naturalistic inquiry), Eisner (connoisseurship and criticism), and Miles and Huberman (qualitative analysis), in addition to my ethnographic evaluation. I had also published methodological contributions in encyclopedias, handbooks, and journals.[10]

To provide an insight into how ingrained my ethnographic persona and training had become at that time, I share a brief family exchange. Many years ago, at my cousin's wedding, I remember explaining to my aunt what I did for a living. I told her I was a methodologist, as that is how I thought of myself and my work, specifically in the areas of ethnography and ethnographic evaluation. Her response in retrospect was predictable: "Does this mean you aren't Jewish anymore?" I clarified my explanation, reaffirmed my religious and cultural commitments, and apologized for the confusion. This level of methodological socialization does not fade as a result of maturing and evolving intellectual interests. Instead, they influence and transfer to, in this case, empowerment evaluation. For example, the roots of empowerment evaluation's commitment to community ownership and respect for community knowledge are in ethnography. The same applies to community psychology, with an emphasis on democratic participation and social justice (see also Fetterman, 2003b; House & Howe, 2000). This discussion underscores the importance of surfacing methodological roots.[11] It also helps explain, in part, who we are as empowerment evaluators.

CONCLUSION

The test of any good empowerment evaluation is whether it works in practice. Stanford University's School of Medicine provides a case in point. They used an empowerment evaluation approach to inform curricular decision making (Fetterman et al., 2010). The process was placed in the hands of faculty, students, staff members, and administrators to help them participate in system changes. (Patients were involved in the courses to enhance the clinical dimension.) Empowerment evaluation provided them with a method for gathering, analyzing, and sharing data about their academic program and its outcomes. Process use, as applied to this example, assumed that the more closely stakeholders are involved in conducting their own evaluations and reflecting on their data, the more likely they are to take ownership of the results and to guide curricular decision making and reform. One test of process use is measuring outcomes. Did it have any impact? Applying process use, as part of an empowerment evaluation model, to curriculum evaluation at Stanford contributed to improvements in course and clerkship ratings. In comparing evaluation results before and after stakeholders began using this approach (and in essence took control of their own evaluation), we found that the average student ratings for required courses improved significantly ($p = .04$; Student's one-sample t test). The use of empowerment evaluation, and specifically process use, fostered greater institutional self-reflection, led to an evidence-based model of decision making, and expanded opportunities for students, faculty, and support staff to work collaboratively to improve and refine the medical school curriculum.

Empowerment evaluation is firmly rooted in the field of evaluation. Now it is time to nurture it, improve its practices, and help it grow. Admittedly, there is much work ahead. However, as Thomas Edison said, "Opportunity is missed by most people because it is dressed in overalls, and looks like work." We, on the contrary, are eager to seize this opportunity to continue to work with communities and colleagues as coequals, as we all expand our understanding and insight into empowerment evaluation.

NOTES

1. A sample of the literature that helps situate empowerment evaluation in the field of evaluation is in the reference list below (Alkin & Christie, 2004; Altman, 1997; Brown, 1997; Cousins, 2005; Donaldson, 2005; Fetterman, 1995, 1997a, 2001; Fetterman et al., 2010; Fetterman, Kaftarian, & Wandersman, 1996; Fetterman & Wandersman, 2005, 2007; Patton, 1997a, 2005; Scriven, 1997, 2005; Sechrest, 1997; Stufflebeam, 1994; Wild, 1997).

2. There is also an equally popular 10-step approach referred to as "Getting to Outcomes," developed by Chinman, Imm, and Wandersman (2004).

3. Mithaug's work in this area is typically referred to as self-regulation theory, with self-determination as a guiding concept in his work. For the purposes of clarity and as it relates to instructing empowerment evaluation, self-determination is being used as the umbrella term in this discussion.

4. See also Bandura (1982) for more detail on issues related to self-efficacy and self-determination.

5. There is a substantial literature concerning the use of evaluation. However, most of it is devoted to lessons learned after the evaluation. The discussion of process use in this context focuses on use during an evaluation.

6. These concepts are influenced by traditional organizational development and transformation theorists, including Argyris and Schon (1978) and Senge (1990), as well as evaluators associated with organizational learning (Preskill & Torres, 1999).

7. Christie (2001, 2003) has also revealed a unique contribution empowerment evaluation has made to the field and how to differentiate its contribution from that of similar approaches (see also Fetterman, 2003b).

8. This book focuses on anthropological concepts, methods, and techniques, as well as equipment, analysis, writing, and ethics. See also the second (Fetterman, 1998a) and third (Fetterman, 2010) editions.

9. See *Using Qualitative Research in Institutional Research* (Fetterman, 1991); *Perennial Issues in Qualitative Research* (Fetterman, 1987); *Educational Evaluation: Ethnography in Theory, Practice, and Politics* (Fetterman & Pitman, 1986); and *Ethnography in Educational Evaluation* (Fetterman, 1984a).

10. See the *Encyclopedia of Social Science Research* (Fetterman, 2003a), *Handbook of Applied Social Research Methods* (Fetterman, 1997b), *Evaluation Studies Review Annual* (Fetterman, 1984b), and *The International Encyclopedia of Education* (Fetterman, 1994b). Numerous methodological contributions were published as chapters and in journals such as *Educational Researcher, American Journal of Evaluation, Educational Evaluation and Policy Analysis, Human Organization, Practicing Anthropology, Anthropology & Education Quarterly*, and the *Canadian Journal of Evaluation*.

11. I branched out further into the methodological area of auditing (Fetterman, 1986, 1990) and quantitatively oriented issues of reactivity and differential attrition while studying the use of experimental design in a national evaluation (Fetterman,1982). This gave me an appreciation and more critical understanding of the limitations and assumptions that need to be met to apply an experimental design to an empowerment evaluation. Similarly, the use of technology in empowerment evaluation is in part a result of my previous work in educational technology, ranging from virtual classrooms (Fetterman, 1996a, 1998b) to videoconferencing on the Internet (Fetterman, 1996b, 1998c).

REFERENCES

Alkin, M., & Christie, C. (2004). An evaluation theory tree. In M. Alkin (Ed.), *Evaluation roots: Tracing theorists' views and influences* (pp. 381–392). Thousand Oaks, CA: Sage.

Altman, D. (1997). Review of the book *Empowerment evaluation: Knowledge and tools for self-assessment and accountability*, by Fetterman, Kaftarian, & Wandersman. *Community Psychologist, 30*(4), 16–17.

Argyris, C., & Schon, D. A. (1978). *Organizational learning: A theory of action perspective.* Reading, MS: Addison-Wesley.

Bandura, A. (1982). Self-efficacy mechanism in human agency. *American Psychologist, 37,* 122–147.

Brown, J. (1997). Review of the book *Empowerment evaluation: Knowledge and tools for self-assessment and accountability*, by Fetterman, Kaftarian, & Wandersman. *Health Education & Behavior, 24*(3), 388–391.

Chelimsky, E., & Shadish, W. R. (1997). *Evaluation for the 21st century: A handbook.* Thousand Oaks, CA: Sage.

Chinman, M., Imm, P., & Wandersman, A. (2004). *Getting to outcomes: Promoting accountability through methods and tools for planning, implementation, and evaluation.* Santa Monica, CA: RAND Corporation. Retrieved from http://www.rand.org/pubs/technical_reports/TR101/

Christie, C. A. (2001). *What guides evaluation? A study of how evaluation practice maps onto evaluation theory* (Doctoral thesis). University of California, Los Angeles.

Christie, C. A. (2003). *The practice–theory relationship in evaluation* (New Directions for Evaluation, No. 97). San Francisco, CA: Jossey-Bass.

Cousins, B. (2005). Will the real empowerment evaluation please stand up? A critical friend perspective. In D. M. Fetterman & A. Wandersman (Eds.), *Empowerment evaluation principles in practice* (pp. 183–208). New York, NY: Guilford Press.

Donaldson, S. (2005). Review of the book *Empowerment evaluation principles in practice*, by Fetterman & Wandersman. Retrieved from http://www.amazon.ca/Empowerment-Evaluation-Principles-Practice-Fetterman/dp/1593851146

Dunst, C. J., Trivette, C. M., & LaPointe, N. (1992). Toward clarification of the meaning and key elements of empowerment. *Family Science Review, 5,* 111–130.

Fetterman, D. M. (1982). Ibsen's baths: Reactivity and insensitivity (A misapplication of the treatment–control design in a national evaluation). *Educational Evaluation and Policy Analysis, 4*(3), 261–279.

Fetterman, D. M. (1984a). *Ethnography in educational evaluation.* Beverly Hills, CA: Sage.

Fetterman, D. M. (1984b). Guilty knowledge, dirty hands, and other ethical dilemmas: The hazards of contract research. In R. F. Conner (Ed.), *Evaluation studies review annual* (Vol. 9, pp. 214–224). Beverly Hills, CA: Sage.

Fetterman, D. M. (1986). Operational auditing in a teaching hospital: A cultural approach. *Internal Auditor, 43*(2), 48–54.

Fetterman, D. M. (Ed.). (1987). Perennial issues in qualitative research. *Education and Urban Society, 20*(1), 3–8.

Fetterman, D. M. (Ed.). (1988). *Qualitative approaches to evaluation in education: The silent scientific revolution.* Albany: SUNY Press.

Fetterman, D. M. (1989). *Ethnography: Step by step.* Newbury Park, CA: Sage.

Fetterman, D. M. (1990). Ethnographic auditing. In W. G. Tierney (Ed.), *Assessing academic climates and cultures* (New Directions for Institutional Research; pp. 19–34). San Francisco, CA: Jossey-Bass.

Fetterman, D. M. (Ed.). (1991). *Using qualitative research in institutional research.* San Francisco, CA: Jossey-Bass.

Fetterman, D. M. (1994a). Empowerment evaluation. *Evaluation Practice, 15*(1), 1–15.

Fetterman, D. M. (1994b). Ethnographic evaluation in education. In T. Husen & T. N. Postlethwaite (Eds.), *The international encyclopedia of education.* Oxford, England: Pergamon Press.

Fetterman, D. M. (1995). Response to Dr. Daniel Stufflebeam's empowerment evaluation, objectivist evaluation, and evaluation standards: Where the future of evaluation should not go, where it needs to go, October, 1994, 321–338. *American Journal of Evaluation, 16,* 179–199. Retrieved from http://www.davidfetterman.com/dfresponsetostufflebeam.pdf

Fetterman, D. M. (1996a). Ethnography in the virtual classroom. *Practicing Anthropology, 18*(3), 2, 36–39.

Fetterman, D. M. (1996b). Videoconferencing on-line: Enhancing communication over the Internet. *Educational Researcher, 25*(4), 23–27.

Fetterman, D. M. (1997a). Empowerment evaluation: A response to Patton and Scriven. *American Journal of Evaluation, 18,* 253–266.

Fetterman, D. M. (1997b). Ethnography. In L. Bickman & D. Rog (Eds.), *Handbook of applied social research methods* (pp. 473–507). Thousand Oaks, CA: Sage.

Fetterman, D. M. (1998a). *Ethnography: Step by step* (2nd ed.). Thousand Oaks, CA: Sage.

Fetterman, D. M. (1998b). Teaching in the virtual classroom at Stanford University. *The Technology Source.* Retrieved from http://technologysource.org/article/teaching_in_the_virtual_classroom_at_stanford_university/

Fetterman, D. M. (1998c). Webs of meaning: Computer and Internet resources for educational research and instruction. *Educational Researcher, 27*(3), 22–30.

Fetterman, D. M. (2001). A high-stakes case example: Documenting the utility, credibility, and rigor of empowerment evaluation in a high-stakes arena—Accreditation. In D. M. Fetterman (Ed.), *Foundations of empowerment evaluation* (pp. 75–86). Thousand Oaks, CA: Sage.

Fetterman, D. M. (2003a). Ethnography. In M. Lewis-Beck, A. Bryman, & T. Futing Liao (Eds.), *Encyclopedia of social science research* (p. 248). Thousand Oaks, CA: Sage.

Fetterman, D. M. (2003b). Fetterman-House: A process use distinction and a theory. In C. A. Christie (Ed.), *New directions for evaluation: Vol. 97. The practice–theory relationship* (pp. 47–52). San Francisco, CA: Jossey-Bass.

Fetterman, D. M. (2005a). Empowerment evaluation: From the digital divide to academic distress. In D. M. Fetterman & A. Wandersman (Eds.), *Empowerment evaluation principles in practice* (pp. 107–122). New York, NY: Guilford Press.

Fetterman, D. M. (2005b). A window into the hearth and soul of empowerment evaluation: Looking through the lens of empowerment evaluation principles. In D. M. Fetterman & A. Wandersman (Eds.), *Empowerment evaluation principles in practice* (p. 2). New York, NY: Guilford Press.

Fetterman, D. M. (2009). Empowerment evaluation at the Stanford University School of Medicine: Using a critical friend to improve the clerkship experience. *Ensaio, 17*(63), 197–204.

Fetterman, D. M. (2010). *Ethnography: Step by step* (3rd ed.). Thousand Oaks, CA: Sage.

Fetterman, D. M. (2011). Empowerment evaluation and accreditation case examples: California Institute of Integral Studies and Stanford University. In C. Secolsky & D. B. Denison (Eds.), *Handbook on measurement, assessment, and evaluation in higher education.* New York, NY: Routledge.

Fetterman, D. M., Deitz, J., & Gesundheit, N. (2010). Empowerment evaluation: A collaborative approach to evaluating and transforming a medical school curriculum. *Academic Medicine: Journal of the Association of American Medical Colleges, 85*(5), 813–820.

Fetterman, D. M., & Eiler, M. (2001). *Empowerment evaluation and organizational learning: A path toward mainstreaming evaluation.* St. Louis, MO: American Evaluation Association.

Fetterman, D. M., Kaftarian, S., & Wandersman, A. (1996). *Empowerment evaluation: Knowledge and tools for self-assessment and accountability.* Thousand Oaks, CA: Sage.

Fetterman, D. M., & Pitman, M. A. (1986). *Educational evaluation: Ethnography in theory, practice, and politics.* Beverly Hills, CA: Sage.

Fetterman, D. M., & Wandersman, A. (2005). *Empowerment evaluation principles in practice.* New York, NY: Guilford Press.

Fetterman, D. M., & Wandersman, A. (2007). Empowerment evaluation: Yesterday, today, and tomorrow. *American Journal of Evaluation, 28*(2), 179–198.

House, E. R., & Howe, K. R. (Eds.). (2000). *Deliberative democratic evaluation* (New

Directions for Evaluation, No. 85, pp. 3–12). San Francisco, CA: Jossey-Bass.

Mithaug, D. E. (1991). *Self-determined kids: Raising satisfied and successful children.* New York, NY: Macmillan.

Mithaug, D. E. (1993). *Self-regulation theory: How optimal adjustment maximizes gain.* New York, NY: Praeger.

Patton, M. Q. (1997a). Toward distinguishing empowerment evaluation and placing it in a larger context. *Evaluation Practice, 15*(3), 311–320.

Patton, M. Q. (1997b). *Utilization-focused evaluation: The new century text.* Thousand Oaks, CA: Sage.

Patton, M. Q. (2002). *Qualitative research and evaluation methods.* Thousand Oaks, CA: Sage.

Patton, M. Q. (2005). Toward distinguishing empowerment evaluation and placing it in a larger context: Take two. *American Journal of Evaluation, 26,* 408–414.

Preskill, H., & Torres, R. T. (1999). *Evaluative inquiry for learning in organizations.* Thousand Oaks, CA: Sage.

Scriven, M. (1997). Empowerment evaluation examined. *Evaluation Practice, 18*(2), 165–175. Retrieved from http://www.davidfetterman.com/scrivenbkreview1997.pdf

Scriven, M. (2005). Review of the book *Empowerment evaluation principles in practice*, by Fetterman & Wandersman. *American Journal of Evaluation, 26*(3), 415–417.

Sechrest, L. (1997). Review of the book *Empowerment evaluation: Knowledge and tools for self-assessment and accountability*, by Fetterman, Kaftarian, & Wandersman. *Environment & Behavior, 29*(3), 422–426.

Senge, P. (1990). *The fifth discipline: The art and practice of organizational learning.* New York, NY: Doubleday.

Stufflebeam, D. (1994). Empowerment evaluation, objectivist evaluation, and evaluation standards: Where the future of evaluation should not go and where it needs to go. *Evaluation Practice, 15*(3), 321–338. Retrieved from http://www.davidfetterman.com/stufflebeambkreview.pdf

Wandersman, A., Snell-Johns, J., Lentz, B., Fetterman, D. M., Keener, D. C., Livet, M., . . . Flaspohler, P. (2005). The principles of empowerment evaluation. In D. M. Fetterman & A. Wandersman (Eds.), *Empowerment evaluation principles in practice* (pp. 27–41). New York, NY: Guilford Press.

Wild, T. (1997). Review of the book *Empowerment evaluation: Knowledge and tools for self-assessment and accountability*, by Fetterman, Kaftarian, & Wandersman. *Canadian Journal of Program Evaluation, 11*(2), 170–172.

Zimmerman, M. A. (2000). Empowerment theory: Psychological, organizational, and community levels of analysis. In J. Rappaport & E. Seldman (Eds.), *Handbook of community psychology* (pp. 43–64). New York, NY: Kluwer Academic/Plenum Press.

Zimmerman, M. A., Israel, B. A., Schulz, A., & Checkoway, B. (1992). Further explorations in empowerment theory: An empirical analysis of psychological empowerment. *American Journal of Community Psychology, 20*(6), 707–727.

Zimmerman, M. A., & Rappaport, J. (1988). Citizen participation, perceived control, and psychological empowerment. *American Journal of Community Psychology, 16*(5), 725–750.

25

THE TRANSFORMATIONAL POWER OF EVALUATION

Passion, Purpose, and Practice

Hallie Preskill

It's all connected. This has become my mantra over the past few years, and with each passing day, I believe it more strongly. One benefit of growing older is that you have the opportunity to reflect on why you do what you do and how you got to where you are. For me, this has meant reflecting on my passion for evaluation—when it started, why I made certain educational and professional choices, and why I still think, after more than 25 years in the field, that evaluation remains an exciting, challenging, and worthwhile enterprise.

It all began with a course on evaluation I was taking as part of a Certificate of Advanced Study (post-master's) in 1979 at the University of Vermont. I had been a special education teacher for 4 years and was taking courses for no other reason than that I liked learning new things. I had always enjoyed doing research as part of my coursework and wanted to become a "researcher." However, not having any mentors or particularly effective career guidance up to that point, I was totally unaware of how one actually got a job doing research. Though I enjoyed teaching, I knew there was something else out there for me, but I just didn't know what it was—that is, until I took a course on educational program evaluation, in which I read the work of Ralph Tyler, James Popham, Michael Scriven, Robert Stake, Barry MacDonald, Rob Walker, Ernie House, and Elliot Eisner. After only a few weeks, I knew my calling was evaluation. It was as if a whole new world had suddenly opened up to me.

By the end of the course, I had applied for and been accepted to do an internship at the University of Vermont's Center for Policy Research and Evaluation with Dr. Robert Carlson.

I left my teaching job and gained invaluable experience working with veteran evaluators on several evaluations. During my year at the center, Dr. Robert Stake was invited to consult on an evaluation Carlson was conducting. I had recently read Stake's 1978 article, "The Case Study Method in Social Inquiry," published in the *Educational Researcher*. I was profoundly affected by his view of inquiry; his approach to evaluation resonated deeply with my developing sense of what evaluation could or should be. More specifically, Stake taught me how case studies could be used to provide readers with a vicarious experience of life in the program and how important it is to communicate the nuances of program participants' experiential understandings. I found Stake's discussion of tacit knowledge, naturalistic generalizations, and the notion that truth lies in the particulars both enlightening and inspiring.

Before leaving Vermont, Bob Stake offered me an opportunity to become a doctoral student at the University of Illinois (Urbana-Champaign), with an assistantship in the Center for Instructional Research and Curriculum Evaluation. That invitation and my subsequent studies and evaluation experiences at the University of Illinois constituted a major turning point in my professional life. Since finishing my graduate work in 1984, I have practiced evaluation in a variety of settings, as both an internal and an external evaluator. For 22 years, I taught graduate-level courses in evaluation, training, and organizational learning at three universities, and now I serve as the executive director of the Strategic Learning and Evaluation Center at FSG, a non-profit strategy, evaluation, and research organization with offices around the world. Being able to update my original chapter is a wonderful gift; moving from an academic position to one where I am working directly with clients who are committed to social change has allowed me to learn and grow in ways I could never have expected. In this chapter, I hope to take the reader along with me on my continuing journey.

AN EVOLVING THEORY OF EVALUATION

My point of view, my evaluation theory, can best be described as dynamic and as one that is continuously evolving, much like a house that is constantly being redecorated as new ideas, colors, patterns, and textures are selected. While my foundational beliefs about evaluation have remained fairly stable over the years, I have nevertheless changed the ways in which my approach to evaluation looks on the inside. I've painted the walls, rearranged the furniture, and even tried to bring a greater aesthetic sense to the house, so much so that this house has become my home. Thus, while my fundamental interest in evaluation has always been on making evaluation useful and meaningful, my theory has evolved to encompass a deep commitment to learning from evaluation processes and findings and to ensure that evaluation is strategic, systems oriented, responsive, flexible, and timely.

My theory of evaluation is based on several critical assumptions concerning the purpose of evaluation, the nature of evaluation practice, the context of evaluation work, and how we communicate and report evaluation processes and findings. These assumptions have developed over the years as a result of (a) conducting evaluations in a wide variety of nonprofit and for-profit organizations; (b) implementing various evaluation research studies; (c) engaging in conversations with colleagues, students, and clients; and (d) reading the research literature in the fields of evaluation, adult learning, training, and organizational learning, change, and development.

Assumptions Regarding the Purpose of Evaluation

My assumptions about the purpose of evaluation are based on the belief that evaluation is a learning process that should result in findings that are useful and actionable.

- Evaluation is a catalyst for individual, group, and organizational learning. As such, it is change oriented and constitutes an intervention at whatever levels it is conducted.
- Evaluations should be conducted only when there is an intention to use the findings. Such use might reflect any type of use: for example, instrumental, conceptual–enlightenment–knowledge, and political–symbolic–persuasive.
- Evaluations should focus on questions that matter; they should reflect the strategic information needs of the organization or community and should be designed to inform decision making and potential actions.
- Expected use of evaluation processes and findings should guide an evaluation's design and implementation.

Assumptions About the Nature of Evaluation Practice

My assumptions about evaluation practice are embedded in a belief that evaluation is most effective, meaningful, and useful when it is conducted using collaborative, participatory, learning-focused, and systems-oriented approaches.

- When a wide range of stakeholders are involved in various phases of an evaluation, they will not only learn more about evaluation, themselves, the evaluand, and the organization but will also be more likely to use the evaluation's findings.
- Involving a wide range of stakeholders increases the likelihood that multiple perspectives and values will guide the evaluation's design as well as the interpretation of the data, thus resulting in more representative findings.
- Involving stakeholders in evaluation processes contributes to building their own capacity to do future evaluation work. This capacity building helps develop and sustain internal and external communities of evaluation practice.
- The use of dialogic processes enhances stakeholders' learning throughout the evaluation.
- The most effective evaluator role is that of facilitator, guide, educator, mentor, critical friend, and consultant.
- Evaluators who use collaborative, participatory, and learning-oriented approaches to evaluation will be more effective if they understand the concepts of team development, group dynamics, systems theory, trust and power, organizational change and culture, self-efficacy, multicultural competence, and adult learning. They will also be more successful if they are able to facilitate meetings effectively, provide feedback, listen actively, mediate conflict, and negotiate compromise.

Assumptions About the Context of Evaluation Work

My assumptions here reflect the belief that evaluation occurs within dynamic, changing, and volatile environments. As such, evaluators need to recognize the political and value-laden nature of their work, as well as how an organization's culture, systems and structures, and leadership influence evaluation practice and the use of findings.

- Evaluation is inherently a political activity. Consequently, evaluators must consider the political influences and environment when negotiating, designing, and implementing an evaluation. Among other things, these considerations might affect the involvement of certain stakeholders, possible ethical conflicts, and/or the potential use or misuse of evaluation processes and findings.
- How an organization is structured, how individuals' jobs are designed, how supportive the organization's culture is of evaluative inquiry, the extent to which the leadership models and supports learning and inquiry, and how information is distributed and accessed strongly influence the extent to which and the ways in which evaluation is successful.
- Not all organizations or units within organizations are ready to engage in, learn from, or act on an evaluation's process and findings. As such, it is often beneficial to determine the organization's readiness for evaluation by conducting some kind of evaluability assessment using interviews or diagnostic instruments (e.g., Preskill & Torres, 2000b).

Assumptions About Communicating and Reporting Evaluation Findings

My assumptions about communicating and reporting evaluation processes and findings suggest that how we share the progress and outcomes of an evaluation matters. It matters with regard to the ways in which and the extent to which evaluation information is used and how organization members learn and grow from the evaluation experience.

- Different formats for communicating and reporting evaluation processes and findings are essential for enhancing audiences' understanding of the information and the extent to which it is useful and used.
- Various audiences have different information needs and therefore require different forms of communication.
- The ways in which evaluation processes and findings are shared can significantly affect the ways in which audiences learn and grow from evaluation practice.

In sum, these assumptions stem from my deep-seated concern for and commitment to evaluation use.

EVALUATIVE INQUIRY FOR LEARNING IN ORGANIZATIONS

Each of the assumptions just described are implicitly represented in my work over the years, but they are perhaps most explicit in the approach Rosalie T. Torres and I developed a number of years ago (Preskill & Torres, 1999; see Figure 25.1).

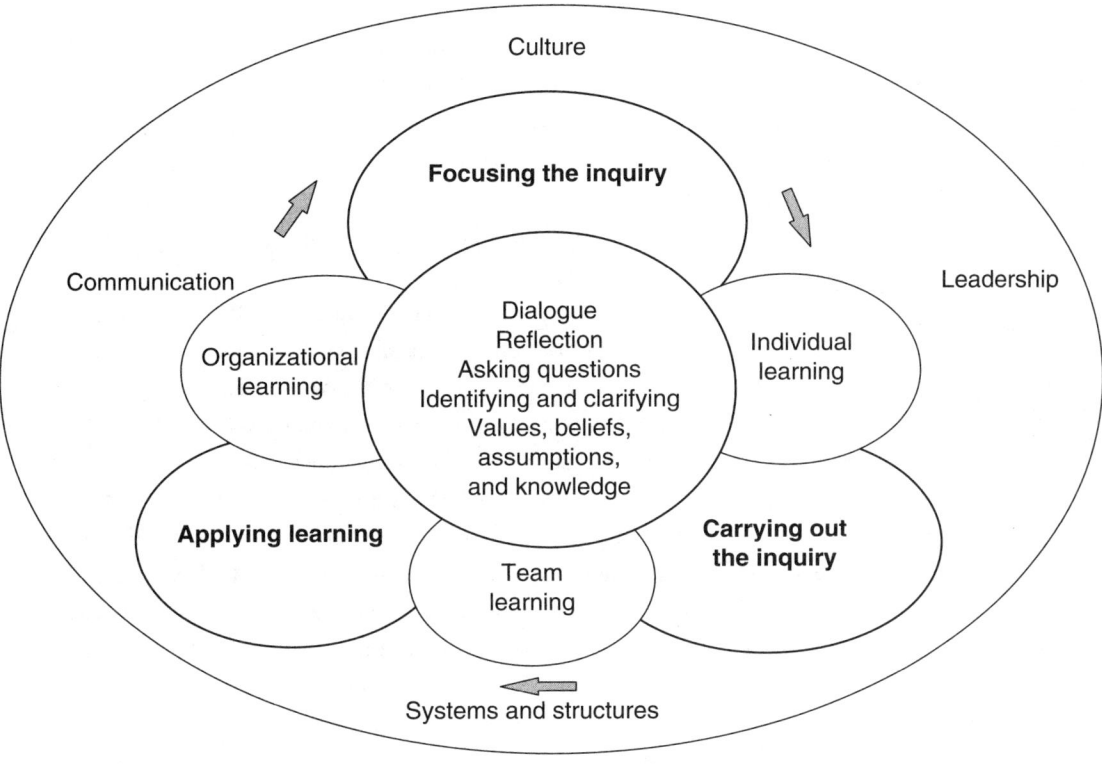

Figure 25.1 Evaluative Inquiry for Learning in Organizations

Source: Preskill and Torres (1999).

In general, our vision for evaluation is grounded in a desire for evaluation to play an expanded and more productive role *within* organizations. We envision evaluative inquiry as an ongoing process for investigating and understanding critical organizational issues. This approach is fully integrated with an organization's work practices and, as such, engenders (a) organization members' interest and ability in exploring critical issues using evaluation logic, (b) organization members' involvement in evaluative processes, and (c) the personal and professional growth of individuals within the organization (Preskill & Torres, 1999, pp. 1–2).

While several elements of the EILO (evaluative inquiry for learning in organizations) approach are similar to other stakeholder and collaborative evaluation approaches, there are somewhat unique aspects that we believe push the boundaries of evaluation theory and practice. These include the following:

- *Evaluation should be ongoing, reflexive, and embedded in organizational practice:* We view evaluative inquiry as an open-ended, continuous process that should be integrated into the everyday work of organization members. As such, it does not constitute an event, nor is it product driven. Instead, it seeks to address critical organizational issues and questions as they arise in the course of one's work. This means that all organization members are responsible for thinking evaluatively, that is, for understanding the role of evaluation and how and when it might be used to gather information for decision making and action.

- *Evaluators should work with stakeholders to apply their learning from the evaluation processes and findings:* Most evaluation studies end with the delivery of a final report or verbal presentation and executive summary of the findings. However, the EILO approach adds another phase to traditional evaluation practice (see Figure 25.1). This phase, called "Applying Learning," suggests that the evaluator work with individuals and groups within the organization to plan how and by whom the findings can be used. The evaluator might (a) facilitate action planning or debriefing sessions with various stakeholders, (b) assist with some of the work to be done, or (c) be a resource for locating other individuals to help with implementing the evaluation's recommendations or action plans. The emphasis here is on optimizing the use of the results. Both internal and external evaluators know all too well that once a report is delivered, if the findings are not disseminated, considered, or used in a timely fashion, it is unlikely they ever will be. How large this window of opportunity is depends on the political climate of the organization, the timing of the evaluation, the perceived need for the information generated by the evaluation, and the substance or content of the evaluation.

- *Learning from the evaluation process is an important goal:* The EILO approach assumes that stakeholders will be involved in various phases of the evaluation process. While the scope and breadth of their involvement will vary from one evaluation to another, it is hoped that their participation will build their capacity not only to think evaluatively but also to be proactive in supporting future evaluations. To foster this, the EILO approach uses *four learning processes*: (1) asking questions; (2) engaging in dialogue; (3) identifying and challenging values, beliefs, and assumptions; and (4) reflection (both public and private). The basic premise is that when stakeholders come together to review and discuss various aspects of the evaluation process and intentionally use these learning processes, they will come to understand the evaluation, the evaluand, the organization, themselves, and each other that much better.

- *EILO acknowledges that evaluation occurs within a complex system and is influenced by the organization's infrastructure:* This infrastructure consists of (a) the organization's culture (e.g., the degree of risk taking and trust among organization members, the attitudes and practices regarding collaboration and problem solving, and the extent to which the organization supports participatory decision making), (b) the organization's systems and structures (e.g., the extent to which there is an open and accessible work environment, the organization's rewards and recognition systems and practices, the relationship of one's work to the organization's goals, and how organization members' jobs are designed), (c) the organization's communication systems (e.g., availability of information and how information is disseminated), and (d) the leadership's vision, mission, and support of learning, inquiry, and change.

The success or failure of evaluative inquiry is often mediated by the presence or absence of these elements.

Ultimately, we believe that when evaluation is collaborative, reflective, and dialogic, it can be a mechanism for creating communities of evaluation practice that may result in individual, team, and organizational transformation (Preskill & Torres, 2000a).

INFLUENCES ON MY POINT OF VIEW

I have learned so much from so many over the years. In fact, I think that one of the reasons I am still passionate about evaluation is that it has always stimulated me to keep on learning. Conducting a wide variety of evaluations, teaching evaluation, mentoring evaluation students, conducting research on evaluation, and, now, working with philanthropic, corporate, and nonprofit organizations seeking to make evaluation meaningful always raise new questions and issues that continue to shape my evaluation point of view. At the same time, there is little doubt that several scholars in various fields have significantly influenced my theory of evaluation.

From Bob Stake, I learned about the importance of responding to stakeholders' information needs, the value of representing the multiple realities of program participants, and the art of the case study. The early works of Marv Alkin, Michael Q. Patton, Jean King, and Carol Weiss on evaluation use not only helped me focus my dissertation research but also paved the way for making evaluation use the center of my long-term research agenda and consulting practice. And Patton's more recent work on developmental evaluation and process use has motivated me to explore new ways of thinking about the evaluator's role and how evaluation can facilitate individual, team, and organizational learning.

Many individuals have influenced my belief in the value of participatory, collaborative, and empowerment approaches to evaluation. Jennifer Greene's candid and reflective writings on the realities of participatory evaluation have forced me to be more truthful and honest about the realities of involving stakeholders in evaluation work. Brad Cousin's work (with Lorna Earl, Lyn Shulha, and Elizabeth Whitmore) has helped me understand the nuances of participatory evaluation and the challenges individuals face in doing such work.

Though my approach to evaluation doesn't necessarily address the politics of evaluation explicitly, I am always aware of the political nature of evaluation and the issue of power (with regard to position, class, gender, race, ability, culture, and resources) that is inherent in participatory and collaborative evaluation approaches. The political uses of evaluation, social justice, and democratic deliberation, as Carol Weiss, Ernie House, and Sandra Mathison have explored, respectively, always seem to be at the back of my mind. Their work has kept me from being too idealistic and naive while still remaining hopeful and optimistic.

As my work increasingly took on an organizational learning focus, I read the work of Chris Argyris, Donald Schon, Peter Senge, Karen Watkins, and Victoria Marsick. Their writings affirmed the idea that evaluation, being an approach to organizational inquiry, could help an organization resolve critical issues and grow from the collective experience of its members. I found that the approaches to team and organizational learning, which were based on social constructivism, were also related to participatory and collaborative forms of evaluation.

And from the organizational learning literature, I learned about Appreciative Inquiry (AI). As I explored this philosophy and approach to organization, community, and social change, I was inspired to find ways to bring it into the evaluation field, and my work specifically; I am greatly indebted to Tessie Catsambas, who was willing to share her rich insights and experiences that culminated in our book, *Reframing Evaluation Through Appreciative Inquiry* (Preskill & Catsambas, 2006). AI is a process that inquires into, identifies, and further develops the best of "what is" in organizations. It is best described as an approach, framework, or mind-set that focuses on illuminating and affirming personal success factors or forces within an organization, to be used with existing organizational development interventions such as strategic planning, organizational design or restructuring, and project evaluations (Watkins & Mohr, 2001). Shifting from the deficit-based model and language that reflect most evaluation work to a more appreciative, positive-based model and language is extremely appealing. The work of David Cooperrider, who developed this approach in the 1980s along with others, including Diana Whitney, Jane Watkins, and Bernard Mohr, helped us connect AI's philosophy and practice with participatory, collaborative, and learning-oriented evaluation approaches. Finally, I've learned an inestimable amount from Rosalie T. Torres, with whom I've written several articles and books. Our book *Evaluation Strategies for Communicating and Reporting* (Torres, Preskill, & Piontek, 1996) was instrumental in connecting evaluation use to learning from evaluation.

THE NEXT STAGE IN MY EVOLVING POINT OF VIEW

My long-term goal is to make evaluation more understandable, relevant, and useful for organizations. To this end, I will continue searching for ways to maximize the ways in which evaluation can enhance use and increase learning. Developing the EILO approach with Rosalie T. Torres was a significant step in this journey (Preskill & Torres, 1999). In the past 5 years, my evolving theory and practice has focused on three areas: (1) process use, (2) evaluation capacity building, and (3) strategic evaluation. Believing that evaluation is a mechanism for learning, I have been interested in the construct of process use and how it occurs. Though I am convinced that process use must be intentional from the very beginning of an evaluation, how it is developed and sustained is clearly a complex undertaking. From a study that my colleagues and I conducted, we learned that when studying individual and group learning, it is necessary for organization members to think deeply about their evaluation experiences and the learning that may have resulted from these experiences. From a research perspective, this requires (a) innovative questioning techniques, (b) the ability of interviewees to remember their involvement in the study, (c) the ability of the interviewees and the evaluator to differentiate between what was learned specifically from the evaluation process and what was learned from other experiences, and (d) helping the interviewees discover their learning through dialogue and reflection. With little time devoted to thinking about our practice within the work environment, we often do not know that we have learned something until we are asked to use this learning. Even then, we might remain unaware of when or where this learning was attained. Furthermore, because learning is often tacit, it can be difficult to distill evidence of this learning after the fact (Preskill, Zuckerman, & Matthews, 2003). I have come to believe that process use—or learning from and about evaluation—needs to be intentional and deliberately built into an evaluation's design and implementation.

The second area that continues to interest me, and one that remains ripe for further research and practical insights, is evaluation capacity building (ECB). With the goal of helping others learn and appreciate evaluation, Shanelle Boyle and I undertook a research study in an effort to understand what was happening in the name of ECB and to develop an integrated framework that could guide those who are designing and implementing capacity-building experiences for a range of audiences. This work culminated in a "multidisciplinary model" and the following definition:

> ECB involves the design and implementation of teaching and learning strategies to help individuals, groups, and organizations, learn about what constitutes effective, useful, and professional evaluation practice. The ultimate goal of ECB is sustainable evaluation practice—where members continuously ask questions that matter, collect, analyze, and interpret data, and use evaluation findings for decision-making and action. For evaluation practice to be sustained, participants must be provided with leadership support, incentives, resources, and opportunities to transfer their learning about evaluation to their everyday work. Sustainable evaluation practice also requires the development of systems, processes, policies, and plans that help embed evaluation work into the way the organization accomplishes its mission and strategic goals. (Preskill & Boyle, 2008, p. 444)

We are heartened by the fact that this topic is being studied in serious ways; understanding how people learn and develop new ways of thinking and behaving and what motivates them to engage in effective evaluation practice is essential for the future of the field.

The third and most recent evolution of my thinking has been the result of moving from academia to providing full-time support to clients interested in designing and conducting evaluations, developing evaluation systems, and building evaluation capacity. While I always thought that evaluation should be strategic, and that it should inform strategy, being part of a strategy consulting firm has helped me reflect on, clarify, and articulate just what this means. As such, I am now deeply committed to ensuring that evaluation and strategy are fluid and reinforcing concepts and practices (see Figure 25.2).

Not very different from other kinds of evaluation, the focus of strategic evaluation is on questions of critical importance to the organization's mission and goals, and it positions evaluation as a means for collecting relevant, credible, and useful evaluation information for strategic decision making and action. However, strategic evaluation is primarily concerned with a set of questions that often differs from many program-level evaluations:

- To what extent are we making the right strategic choices?
- What are we learning about how well our programs are making progress on implementing our strategy?
- What else should we be doing? How should we refine our strategy for going forward?

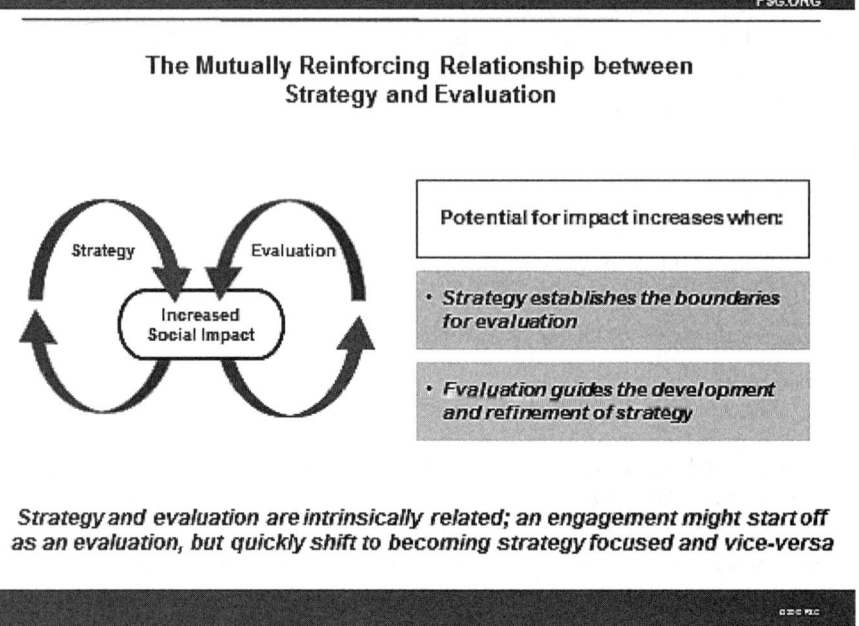

Figure 25.2 The Mutually Reinforcing Relationship Between Strategy and Evaluation
Source: Hallie Preskill, Executive Director, FSG.org.

And while most program evaluations are geared toward use by program staff, strategic evaluations should also serve senior-level leaders as they consider the future of the program or initiative and course corrections, refinements, and/or enhancements to the organization's strategy(ies). Ultimately, strategic evaluation promises to lead to social change and improvements in the conditions of target populations, organizations, and systems. Finally, I continue to believe that the most informative and useful evaluations are those that are adaptive, flexible, nimble, responsive, real time, collaborative, and systems oriented. As organizations and communities strive to find new ways to solve social problems, evaluators must also evolve and grow in their approaches to increase not only the quality of the data and findings they deliver but also the ways in which they do their work. Waiting 6 months or a year to learn about what's happening, who is being affected and how, and if something is working and why or why not is simply not acceptable any longer.

PARTING THOUGHTS

As always, writing a chapter such as this provides a special and rare opportunity to reflect on where one has been and where one wants to go. It has allowed me to reflect deeply on my values, experiences, hopes, and desires for evaluation. Writing about my evaluation journey has enabled me to reaffirm my convictions about the value of evaluation, my passion for evaluation, and the possibilities of evaluation, topics near and dear to my heart and mind. Yet I also realize that putting such thoughts on paper has its downside. It seems to fix things in time, when in reality, theories of any kind are always in progress, always being tested and revised, as Alkin and Christie remind us. Though aspects of my evaluation point of view will likely shift in the coming years, I do know that I will always be committed to making evaluation processes and outcomes useful and will do everything I can to enhance what may be learned from evaluation practice.

REFERENCES

Preskill, H., & Boyle, S. (2008). A conceptual model of evaluation capacity building: A multidisciplinary perspective. *American Journal of Evaluation, 29*(4), 443–459.

Preskill, H., & Catsambas, T. (2006). *Reframing evaluation through appreciative inquiry.* Thousand Oaks, CA: Sage.

Preskill, H., & Torres, R. T. (1999). *Evaluative inquiry for learning in organizations.* Thousand Oaks, CA: Sage.

Preskill, H., & Torres, R. T. (2000a). The learning dimension of evaluation use. *New Directions for Evaluation, 88,* 25–38.

Preskill, H., & Torres, R. T. (2000b). *Readiness for organizational learning and evaluation instrument (ROLE).* Retrieved from http://www.fsg.org/Portals/0/Uploads/Documents/Impact Areas/ROLE_Survey.pdf

Preskill, H., Zuckerman, B., & Matthews, B. (2003). An exploratory study of the variables affecting process use. *American Journal of Evaluation, 24*(4), 423–442.

Stake, R. E. (1978). The case study method in social inquiry. *Educational Researcher, 7*(2), 5–8.

Torres, R. T., Preskill, H., & Piontek, M. E. (1996). *Evaluation strategies for communicating and reporting.* Thousand Oaks, CA: Sage.

Watkins, J., & Mohr, B. (2001). *Appreciative inquiry: Change at the speed of imagination.* San Francisco, CA: Jossey-Bass/Pfeiffer.

26

GETTING PEOPLE INVOLVED

The Origin of Interactive Evaluation Practice

Jean A. King

This chapter has two sections: (1) a rough chronology of influences on my evaluation practice and (2) a brief explication of what some might call my evaluation theory. Let me begin by noting that I did not have a childhood ambition to become a program evaluator. Like many in the field, I fell into the role for a number of reasons and over the course of many years.

My father, who became a science teacher in the 1930s, was a key influence in my professional life. Ever the empiricist, Dad celebrated the idea of research applied to educational practice and was fortunate to study at Teachers College, Columbia University at the height of progressive education. The notion of studying his own practice, first as a teacher and then as a building administrator, gave him a tool for continuous improvement. When he became principal of the toughest elementary school in his district in upstate New York, he set a personal goal that the school's test scores would not remain the district's lowest. To his great pride, after several years of persistent attention and targeted instruction, the test scores rose dramatically. That was in the 1950s. Years later when I studied to become a junior high school teacher, Dad gave me his dog-eared copies of Dewey's writings, full of his marginal comments, and we talked about how a teacher could collect classroom data to improve student learning. That was in the early 1970s, and this evaluative idea was firmly rooted.

My father encouraged me to become an educational researcher, something World War II had prevented him from doing. During my doctoral study at Cornell University in the late 1970s, I was fortunate to connect with Jason Millman, who specialized in measurement and statistics. Even though he wasn't my formal advisor (I was a student of curriculum and instruction), he became my mentor and friend. It was Jay who brought me to the field of program evaluation.

As part of a course, I organized a simple study of one component of my school's grammar curriculum and did a comparative evaluation of two methods for teaching adverbs. Despite the small sample size, the results were statistically significant—to Jay's amazement—and I felt more secure about how to teach at least one part of speech. I also saw how data collected purposefully could answer a question about practice and provide support for a decision. That lesson stuck.

Through example, Jay also taught me about building community through self-directed collaboration. I was one of a group of graduate students in education that he supported in organizing a do-it-yourself program evaluation course using Worthen and Sanders' new edited text. In another colloquium, I compiled a bibliography of Michael Scriven's writing, extensive even then. And I distinctly remember a visit Jay organized from Dan Stufflebeam, who was barnstorming the country during the development of the Program Evaluation Standards. (I remember he wore cowboy boots.) At Jay's invitation, my first professional evaluation project was in the Elmira, New York schools, where I was the token classroom teacher on an evaluation team; since I can't remember the program we studied, I certainly must have played a cameo role.

When I moved to New Orleans, Louisiana, to assume a professorship in teacher education at Tulane University, I was again fortunate to make an important professional and personal connection. Early on I met Ellen Pechman, head of evaluation and testing for the Orleans Parish schools, a practitioner with two master's degrees, a doctorate in educational psychology, and an indefatigable commitment to using data to improve practice. Because of my background, she invited me to participate in a National Institute of Education–funded project to study the process of evaluation use in her district, tracking the efforts of her and her staff within a large, politicized bureaucracy over time. Collaborating on that first grant with Ellen and Bruce Thompson (then at the University of New Orleans) and on a second grant project solely with Ellen, I immersed myself in the literature and the practice of evaluation use. Studying the elusive way in which data made their way through an organization fascinated me. This was the small classroom-specific process writ large, and the political variables that wreaked havoc on the evaluation endeavor shattered any remaining innocence I might have had.

It was at this time that I first read Michael Quinn Patton's *Utilization-Focused Evaluation* (the 1978 edition), and my professional life changed forever. I can distinctly remember reading the book cover to cover in a day, chuckling at the Halcolm comments, reflecting on the Sufi stories, and feeling immense relief at finding someone who had captured what I had been struggling to articulate. As an evaluator I had grown up professionally with the Big Bang theory of evaluation use—the decision maker breathlessly awaiting an evaluation report, reading it cover to cover on its arrival, deducing the action implications of the content, making the "right" decisions based on them, and then—ta dah—taking appropriate action. In our New Orleans study, the instances had rarely been Big Bang–like—except in the one case where a decision maker had used the initial results as an excuse to cut an expensive program, a move that clearly had little to do with the data.

Patton's notions of the personal factor and intended use by intended users pointed to a key flaw in the Big Bang thinking: It was the *users*, not the report, who played a critical role in the evaluation process. With that insight, the dots suddenly connected. Building on interpersonal connections, my understanding of personally meaningful evaluation practice blossomed. The implications for action were clear, and from that point on, I was hooked on utilization-focused evaluation. (Having majored in English earlier, I did wonder whether we could drop *utilization* in favor of the equally apt but simpler term *use*, but it was too late; utilization-focused evaluation was already a brand.) I should also note that, thanks to the National Institute of Education projects, I met Marv Alkin from the UCLA Center for the Study of Evaluation and found a warm connection to a scholar who shared my interest in evaluation use.

My move upriver from New Orleans to St. Paul, Minnesota, created an opportunity to bring practical evaluation to life in schools. In 1989, I became the founding director of the Center for Applied Research and Educational Improvement at the University of Minnesota, a collaboration of Minnesota school districts and the University's College of Education and Human Development with a mission to use research to improve practice in the schools. Shortly before moving north, I briefly met Louis Smith, one of my heroes, over lunch. His grounded theory studies of classroom instruction and school change had shown me how to derive knowledge from an extended engagement with practice. As I was eating a corned beef sandwich, he asked if I had ever heard of something called action research. I pulled the term from a far recess of my mind—it had been mentioned in a classic curriculum text that I cited during my doctoral orals. But beyond that, I was unfamiliar with the idea. He suggested that it might make sense in my new center.

When I arrived in Minnesota, I read everything I could find on action research—its American roots, its British and Australian proponents, its theory and practice. Through a number of activities, I then worked collaboratively to bring this process to life in schools, supported by central office staff and teachers in more than 30 districts. Ever fortunate, I connected with colleagues at the college's professional practice school (PPS), Patrick Henry High School in north Minneapolis, then in its formative stages. Three people in particular—Linda Trevorrow, the school's PPS coordinator; Louise Sundin, president of the Minneapolis Federation of Teachers; and Principal Mike Huerth—understood the importance of a viable evaluation process that could work in the school over time and provided ongoing support. It was Mike who once noted the error of giving lack of time as a reason for not doing action research. "People will make time for things they consider important," he told me. "The real question is how to get them to consider this work important." That idea reframed my thinking about institutionalizing the process. I should note, too, the challenge of bridging a research-like practice in academia and public schools. On campus, eyes would roll when I said I was engaged in *action* research; in the schools, I got the same reaction when I said I was engaged in action *research*. Such a deal: The phrase got me in trouble in each community but for different reasons.

At the university, my action research study group consisted of Rob Orton, a philosopher/math educator who died tragically in his early 40s, and R. D. (Dick) Nunneley, Jr., our resident pragmatist philosopher, who also died, sadly, 13 years later at the age of 56. We used to drink espresso at a nearby coffee shop while reading our way through key texts. Despite continuing challenges, I became increasingly convinced that if we could only figure out how to sustain them, evaluation processes could increase organizations' ability to learn from data over time, hence increasing their ability to improve practice. I started working with schools and other organizations to do just that, what I would now call building their capacity to do evaluation. Involving people through active participation, that is, using participatory evaluation methods, became a mechanism for capacity building.

During these years, I also served as a faculty member in the revised Bush Educators' Program (BEP), a selective professional development program for roughly two dozen Minnesota educators each year. John Mauriel, the program director, wanted participants to experience a real-world evaluation project in preparation for their own change efforts, and I was brought on to facilitate that activity. For each of 4 years, a school district leader volunteered his or her site, and BEP participants spent 2 full weeks collecting and analyzing data and preparing a formal report for the district staff. That description belies the complexity of the task. The massive volume of data, the challenge of 24 people working together in concert, and the inevitability of the clock ticking toward the presentation deadline were comparable, one superintendent told us, to his experiences as a helicopter pilot behind enemy lines in Vietnam. But what a learning experience! This was an interactive evaluation process that demanded flexibility and interpersonal skills of the highest order. You simply couldn't plan all the details beforehand, and I learned to coach novice evaluators under extreme pressure.

Although I remained on the faculty of the University of Minnesota throughout, my BEP experience led me to wonder what it would be like to work as an internal evaluator, someone who intentionally sought to institutionalize evaluation processes in an educational bureaucracy. As luck would have it, I was able to take a 2-year leave of absence to work full-time as a large district's coordinator of research and evaluation from 1999 to 2001, and for well over a decade now, I have continued to conduct evaluations and work on evaluation capacity building in what has become Minnesota's largest school district, Anoka-Hennepin ISD #11. Since 2009, I have served as evaluation coach to Johnna Rohmer-Hirt, the district's Director of Research, Evaluation, and Testing, collaborating on evaluations of the many special-education programs, the program for English-language learners, and the middle school program, among others, as we work to create a sustainable evaluation process for the district. Much of what I describe below as my current evaluation theory has been informed by these collaborative efforts to create a sustainable evaluation infrastructure for this large district, which continually faces financial challenges.

Two other important connections stemming from the late 1990s began in a colloquium I gave on professional development for evaluators. Three doctoral students (now alumnae)—Gail Ghere, Jane Minnema, and Laurie Stevahn—approached me after a session that explored the reasons why program evaluation had no formal competency statements and suggested that we give competency development a try. Educators all, each was familiar with a set of professional competency statements (special education, early childhood, and teacher education), and they found the assertion that program evaluators could never agree on competencies unlikely to be true. And thus began a multiyear process with an intrepid team of collaborators—never funded externally—that led eventually to the Essential Competencies for Program Evaluators (King, Stevahn, Ghere, & Minnema, 2001; Stevahn, King, Ghere, & Minnema, 2005), which are now the basis of the Canadian Evaluation Society's Professional Designation Program.

That colloquium was also the beginning of a long-term collaboration with Laurie Stevahn, a longtime professional development trainer and social psychologist who was finishing her PhD in the Department of Educational Psychology. My practical experiences across 20 years had shown me the importance of interpersonal interactions in the successful conduct of program evaluation. Beginning in that class, Laurie taught me the research base that documented how and why certain procedures work better than others. Our connection has resulted in a productive collaboration that a decade later will result in a coauthored book on interactive evaluation practice.

A final source of influence on my evaluation practice came from my mother and father, mentioned last because it is central to what I do. My parents instilled in me the practice of good deeds done quietly, the notion that every person is responsible for giving back to the community and striving always to help people in need. At their deaths just 3 weeks apart in 2002, the list of organizations they had been involved in—the Boy Scouts, the Girl Scouts, their church, a sheltered workshop, the Hospital Guild, the Farm and Garden Club, the city recreation board, and more—documented lifetimes devoted to making the world a better place, not in earth-shaking or headline-grabbing ways but with unfailing constancy of purpose over time. My mother, in particular, was rarely in the limelight, although she was named Woman of the Year by one civic organization following her selfless behind-the-scenes commitment to her city's bicentennial celebration. They were role models who instilled in me the importance of civic engagement. No matter what your role in a community, it is your job throughout your life to work to improve it. I choose to do this in large part through acts of evaluation, teaching people skills they can use to learn about and improve programs and, hopefully over time, their situations.

As retirement edges ever closer, my commitment to the field remains. Having turned 60 two years ago, I unavoidably have more experiences with illness (a bout with Lyme disease and accompanying Bell's palsy in 2004, which taught me powerful lessons about physical appearance) and with death (three relatives and two friends died within a few months in 2005; two close friends, far too young, died within 3 weeks of each other in 2010). Thankfully, I have been fortunate in recent years to travel the world professionally (including trips to Israel, England, New Zealand, Japan, Sweden, South Africa, and Singapore) and broaden my understanding of the evaluation process in diverse places. On reflection, my path to program evaluation appears inexorable; in reality, it was marked by twists and turns. I twice made a conscious decision to leave the field to work in curriculum—twice unsuccessful, I note with a smile. My professional evolution was, however, always grounded in four ideas that remain integral to my practice: (1) creating an evaluation process that people actually use in practice, (2) the notion of its continuing application, (3) the value and joy of working with others, and (4) the importance of community, both in its immediate and in its broader sense.

MY EVALUATION "THEORY"/POINT OF VIEW

Having traced the influences on my practice, let me now explain what some might call my evaluation *theory*. I fear that word is far grander than the content to be presented. Our field contrasts the so-called prescriptive theory of evaluation practitioners with more traditional forms of social science theory, labeled descriptive theory (Alkin & House, 1992). Using that standard, this section will outline a prescriptive theory of sorts, but with an important cautionary note: I would never insist—which the term *prescriptive* implies to me—that anyone use these ideas in settings where they do not fit. At its best, program evaluation is context specific, and the "theory" that I describe fits well in certain contexts and not in others. Like most program evaluators, I imagine, my evaluation practice includes a variety of different kinds of projects. As we learn in basic research design classes, the methods must match the questions at hand. I have calculated a regression or two in my day, but I am happiest in evaluation projects that are long-term engagements with the extensive involvement of groups of collaborators—hence my interest in participatory evaluation and an interactive theory that highlights involvement.

In my introductory evaluation class, my Day 1 lecture begins with three grounding ideas. First, everyone is an evaluator, which means that our job is to make systematic a process that people engage in routinely—for example, every time they see a movie, buy an appliance, or work in an educational or social program. Second, people have differing values, which means that different clients can see the same program as either good or bad. Third, context is key, which leads us to the classic evaluation response: "It depends." And it really does. I have long since believed that there is no one ideal approach to conducting program evaluations. Evaluations are the outcome of extensive interactions based on context-specific details, such as the values and preferences of intended users, the resources available, political factors, ethical issues, and measurement challenges. To my mind, context is everything. Grounded in four principles, the ideas that guide my evaluation theory relate directly to my commitment to fostering use by specific people in specific settings.

First, the evaluator should accept responsibility for facilitating use. There are surely no guarantees—it would be arrogant to say that an evaluator can *ensure* use in every case. However, if I lead an evaluation process and its results are not useful to anyone, I must be willing to take personal responsibility for the failure of that process. The connection to utilization-focused evaluation is both obvious and direct. The organizations that I have worked in over the past quarter-century have never had money to spare, and I believe firmly that the results of my work should be worth the resources required to get them, a commitment Michael Scriven proposed long ago. In my opinion, evaluators should make use their problem, even while acknowledging Michael Patton's oft-repeated quip that evaluation use is too important to be left to evaluators.

Second, program evaluators must have excellent interpersonal skills. Relationships matter. I concluded a while ago that *all* evaluation is "participatory" because in every case an evaluator must interact with someone, at least minimally, to frame the evaluation task. In ongoing work, Laurie Stevahn and I have presented a number of frameworks for analyzing interactive evaluation practice, including the interactive-participation quotient, the evaluation capacity building continuum, and the dual-concerns model from social psychology. Each of these allows an evaluator to make sense of a specific situation in interpersonal terms and to then respond appropriately.

Third, given my instructional bent, I believe that participation in program evaluation should be a learning experience for those who take part, including the evaluator. By accepting the role of teacher, an evaluator can not only provide information but also provide support and enthusiasm for the evaluation process and directly teach people (aka primary intended users) how to use that information. The framework that surrounds my work is Joseph Schwab's commonplaces of a learning experience: a teacher (the evaluator); learners (the primary intended users); the curriculum, that is, what you are teaching (the process and results of the evaluation); and what Schwab calls the milieu, the context in which the evaluation takes place (King & Thompson, 1983). This notion of the evaluator as teacher supports my commitment to building organizational evaluation capacity.

Fourth, for me the highest form of evaluation is one that lives independently in an organization. I call this, only slightly tongue in cheek, free-range evaluation—a collaborative evaluation process that lives freely in the world, that is more viable when it survives (and it often does not) because it lives in a natural setting and reproduces itself in its organizational context. It is longitudinal, it encompasses both process and product use, and it focuses on building individuals' capacity to engage in evaluation. My evaluation teaching expands its curriculum from the specifics of a given study to more general habits of thinking, what I call "bringing evaluation to life." This is evaluation capacity building, the creation of an evaluation community within an organization. What I am referencing is a paraphrase of the classic aphorism (entirely appropriate for a Minnesotan) that if you give someone a fish, you feed her or him for a day, but if you teach the person to fish, you feed her or him for a lifetime.

These four principles, then—commitments to fostering and facilitating use, to high-quality interpersonal skills, to teaching evaluation to participants, and to building evaluation capacity over the long term—form the basis both for my work as a program evaluator and for my evaluation theory. They can be clearly traced to my upbringing, to my experiences conducting evaluations, and to my pragmatic hope that I will make a difference in this world. The catch is, of course, that, to the extent that an evaluator has any influence with intended users, it is an indirect influence. An evaluator can't make anyone (except herself or himself) *do* anything with the results. The evaluator's job, instead, is to encourage and cajole and to set up situations where people will interact with evaluation in helpful ways. As I remind my students, even though people think that evaluators wield power, in reality we often do not. This detail is coupled, of course, with the fact that we evaluators always have to be nice; no other parties in an evaluation context are required to be so, which can make our job a challenge.

I find the role of external evaluator, parachuted into an organization for a brief period of time, difficult, much preferring to work in an organization over time, learning the organizational culture firsthand, and becoming aware of—and even a part of—its evaluation history. Having said that, for many reasons, evaluators often do not have the privilege of a lengthy engagement, which is why what my coauthor Laurie Stevahn and I call interactive evaluation practice applies to all program evaluations. As noted previously, even the most nonparticipatory, evaluator-directed evaluation requires interactions to ensure that the resulting evaluation will meet the needs of those who are commissioning the study. I should note, too, that a recent National Science Foundation–funded research study on multisite evaluations found that involving secondary-level users in a large-scale program evaluation increased the likelihood of their using the results (King & Lawrenz, 2011). Because involvement and relationships matter, an evaluator's ability to ask good questions, structure meaningful interactions, and manage or resolve conflict are important skills that can lead to an effective evaluation process. By establishing an environment of strong interactions and trust, an evaluator can build relationships that are able to weather the challenges that inevitably occur.

As I have developed my evaluation practice over time, I have sought to integrate ideas from Donna Mertens's, Jennifer Greene's, and Rodney Hopson's ongoing commitment to inclusive practice; Michael Patton's utilization-focused evaluation; Hallie Preskill's and Rosalie Torres's notion of organizational learning; my colleagues Karen Seashore's and Sharon Kruse's work on professional community; and the concept of evaluation capacity building initially presented by Michael Baizerman, Don Compton, and Stacey Stockdill. I, therefore, seek to develop structures that create a professional community in which evaluation can thrive. What I'm talking about here might be called organizational learning, the idea that an organization—like a person—can, over time, learn things to benefit itself. One thing I have learned, however, is that it's a lot easier to *talk* about evaluation capacity building than to do it, especially in large organizations. I often remind myself that if this capacity building is such a good thing, why aren't more organizations effectively engaged in it? The question for me, then, is extremely practical: What can I do as an evaluator to create an environment in an organization to support an ongoing process of evaluation and the integral use of its results?

What I have learned is that if you are serious about using evaluation information over time, then an evaluator, working with program staff, should put structures in place that will build both the technical and the personal means to foster use. The brief version of the rationale is that adults learn by constructing meaning from what is around them and that they can learn well in collaborative settings where they value both the task to be completed (i.e., the work of the organization) and their relationships with their colleagues. The idea of building a professional community to foster evaluation use builds on these well-proven psychological principles.

What does it take to build the capacity to support evaluation efforts in an organization? In Schwab's commonplace terms, I realize that much of this relates to milieu (context), both in an organizational (macro) sense and in a program-specific (micro) sense, and even in an individual sense (mini-micro). What I am suggesting is work in three areas (Volkov & King, 2007) to create an evaluation community over time:

1. *Organizational context:* The first component speaks to the atmosphere, both internal and external, in which the evaluation will take place. First, trust and respect must exist among the group of people the evaluation will touch. If positive relationships do not exist, they must be created before you can think about capacity building, because without them the free-range evaluation process cannot survive. This is an extremely idealistic claim, but it is also unavoidably practical. Second, people engaged in the evaluation must individually and collectively have an open mind, that is, be willing to "think outside the box" about how to use the evaluation process itself as an intervention and then how to use the information gathered for improving the program. Third, we have recognized the importance of power and politics in evaluation for at least 20 years, but beyond saying, "Avoid them," there has been little practical writing about what to do. Power surges or power spikes and the clout factor, terms I use, can make an evaluator's life miserable.

What can an evaluator do about this? You must identify supportive leadership that will at best participate visibly in the evaluation process and commit publicly to using its outcomes or that will, at least minimally, not block its activities or ignore its results. In addition, your intended users must have sufficient autonomy (they must be "empowered") to do two things: (1) to set evaluation activities in place and act on their results and (2) to take on any and all important issues they believe require evaluative attention. The final contextual component is an organization's external environment, which can either support or hinder efforts at building evaluation capacity. Evaluators should work to understand the specifics of each case.

2. *Evaluation capacity building structures:* Of the components, this is the easiest for evaluators to attend to directly because they can work purposefully to create structures—mechanisms within the organization—that foster the development of evaluation capacity. Paying attention to the structural conditions for creating evaluation capacity involves four areas: (1) developing and implementing a purposeful long-term evaluation capacity building plan for the organization, (2) building and reinforcing infrastructure to support specific components of the evaluation process and communication systems, (3) introducing and maintaining purposeful socialization into the organization's evaluation process, and (4) building and expanding peer learning structures.

3. *Access to resources:* To build evaluation capacity, an organization must make evaluation resources available and use them. My experience suggests that you must not ignore this final component because, even if the leadership and professional climates are fine and even if the infrastructure is in place, an organization that cannot support evaluation activities over time cannot successfully institutionalize the process. People must have access to expertise, not only about evaluation but also about the program content. It is important to provide and continuously expand access to evaluation resources and further to secure sources of support for program evaluation in the organization.

I once hoped that as I got grayer, challenging evaluation events would become less common. But I have learned that I still *practice* evaluation just as I practice the piano. Let me close, then, with two continuing struggles in my evaluation practice. The first is a contradictory realization. On the one hand, evaluators should remember that the earth rarely moves as a result of an evaluation because evaluation information is only one input into an often complex system. People may fear that we have power, but in reality our power is at best indirect. We must remember that evaluation's Big Bang theory was long ago exploded. The question for me is how to enrich ongoing discussions with evaluation information and how to encourage people other than me to advocate the use of that information. On the other hand, meaningful evaluation and real change can be a risky business, and people sometimes do get hurt. I once participated in a symposium where I was asked the question "What are the barriers to evaluation?" I would rephrase it to ask, instead, "What *aren't* the barriers to evaluation?" Although people are constantly making judgments, formal program evaluation seems an unnatural act in most settings I've encountered. The acronym MORT (money, ownership, rigor, and time) beautifully captures the key reasons why program evaluation doesn't thrive in social and educational program settings (Gomez & Goldstein, 1996). And if program evaluation itself struggles to survive, what can we hope for the use of its results?

My second struggle is a personal dilemma I continue to face, which I've written about elsewhere (King, 1998). I call it the "Mother Teresa versus Princess Diana" problem. As I mentioned above, my ultimate goal as a professional evaluator is to make the world a better place, *tikkun olam*—literally, "to heal the world." That was the goal of Mother Teresa, who chose to live a life of poverty and work directly with the people who struggled so desperately. But that was also a goal of Lady Diana, who committed herself to good causes, raising millions, sponsoring benefits, and going to Africa and Bosnia in the name of land mine reform. She, however, unlike Mother Teresa, lived a life of incredible privilege even as she did amazing acts of good. And I feel more like Lady Di than Mother Teresa—a white, middle-class, privileged evaluator who makes good money in her participatory practice. Wouldn't it be better to simply work in the organizations we're evaluating if we really want to make a difference? Can we really believe that this work we do will improve the world? My current view of evaluation, then, surely builds on my practice of more than 30 years, but given these continuing conflicts, it will just as surely continue to evolve.

REFERENCES

Alkin, M., & House, E. (1992). Evaluation of programs. In M. Alkin (Ed.), *Encyclopedia of educational research*. New York, NY: MacMillan.

Gomez, C. A., & Goldstein, E. (1996). The HIV prevention evaluation initiative: A model for collaborative and empowerment evaluation. In D. M. Fetterman, S. J. Kaftarian, & A. Wandersman (Eds.), *Empowerment evaluation: Knowledge and tools for self-assessment and accountability* (pp. 100–122). Thousand Oaks, CA: Sage.

King, J. A. (Winter, 1998). Making sense of participatory evaluation practice. *New Directions for Evaluation, 80,* 57–67.

King, J. A., & Lawrenz, F. (Eds.). (2011). Multisite evaluation practice: Lessons and reflections from four cases. *New Directions for Evaluation, 129.* Hoboken, NJ: Wiley.

King, J. A., Stevahn, L., Ghere, G., & Minnema, J. (2001). Toward a taxonomy of essential evaluator competencies. *American Journal of Evaluation, 22*(2), 229–247.

King, J. A., & Thompson, B. (1983). Research on school use of program evaluation: A literature review and research agenda. *Studies in Educational Evaluation, 9,* 5–21.

Stevahn, L., King, J. A., Ghere, G., & Minnema, J. (2005). Establishing essential competencies for program evaluators. *American Journal of Evaluation, 26*(1), 43–59.

Volkov, B., & King, J. A. (2007). *A checklist for building organizational evaluation capacity.* Retrieved from http://www.wmich.edu/evalctr/archive_checklists/ecb.pdf

☆ 27 ☆

PRIVILEGING EMPIRICISM IN OUR PROFESSION

Understanding Use Through Systematic Inquiry

J. Bradley Cousins

I am honored and privileged to be invited to contribute this chapter to the second edition of the *Roots* compendium, and I certainly appreciate the recognition of our contributions over the years. I say "our contributions" because in my professional career I have long held a commitment to collaborative work. That commitment developed early in my career, and I will attribute it to Professor Ken Leithwood, my doctoral thesis supervisor and mentor. Many of the articles, chapters, and books that I have offered up have been coproduced with colleagues (including Leithwood), students, or both. Their valuable insights have helped shape my own thinking in ways that are hard to capture, and for that I am grateful.

In considering any domain of inquiry, I find it useful to distinguish among three levels of abstraction. At one end of the spectrum is theory, which is usually abstract and often elegant, coherent, and lofty. At the other end is practice, which can be sophisticated, harmonic, skillful, and reflective but which is most often messy, complex, ill defined, problem laden, and challenging. An important function of theory—there are many—is to inform practice in insightful, helpful, and enduring ways. Practice, too, if properly captured and understood, can profitably inform theory. "There is nothing as theoretical as good practice," to put a spin on Kurt Lewin's time-honored adage. But the bridge between theory and practice is a slippery one, and crossing that bridge can be treacherous. In my mind, a third level of abstraction—empirical research—can assist enormously in traversing the chasm between theory and practice. I am not saying that empirical inquiry is *the* bridge between theory and practice, but I am firm in the conviction that research is a force that has the potential to foster safe passage, whether from theory to practice or vice versa. "Research on evaluation," first and foremost, is where I would choose to locate my professional identity.

Another dimension of my professional identity, I would say, is a sustained interest in evaluation utilization. Over the trajectory of my career, this interest has evolved considerably. In my doctoral work, it served as the direct focus of inquiry of my research, leading to a serious review and integration of empirical research (ultimately published in Cousins & Leithwood, 1986) and a qualitative study followed by a quantitative reanalysis of extant data (ultimately acknowledged as a Canadian national award-winning thesis, Cousins, 1988). As a young academic, I developed an interest in what has now come to be known as practical participatory evaluation (P-PE), mostly through evaluation practice and experiences in the Ontario school system. P-PE turned out to be a great approach to enhance interest in, and the use of, evaluation in schools and school districts. Eventually, our work evolved into a concentration on evaluation capacity building (ECB) and the integration of evaluation into organizational cultures. We pushed hard on the concept of building not just the capacity to *do* evaluation but also the capacity to *use* it. I will return to this career trajectory in due time but first a comment on my epistemological leanings and my perspective on evaluation.

WAYS OF KNOWING

I don't really have a label for my approach to systematic inquiry and ways of knowing, but I suppose if I were pushed, I would frame it as "logical empiricism." That perspective, too, has evolved over time. I can say that with two degrees in psychology, one certainly develops a strong grounding in traditionalistic social sciences and quantitative methods. When I began my doctoral studies, I was a complete neophyte in the domain of qualitative inquiry, but I quickly recognized its value and proceeded to develop my knowledge and skills in this area. I suppose I've considered myself to be "methodologically eclectic" for quite a while now.

I always liked Michael Huberman's approach to qualitative research (Miles & Huberman, 1984), which I followed pretty closely because he also had a strong interest in evaluation and research use (e.g., Huberman, 1989). I suppose a defining feature would be the development, in advance of data collection, of a solid, defensible conceptual framework, which ultimately guides data collection, analysis, and interpretation while remaining open to unanticipated, unexpected, or otherwise new discoveries. This, of course, is juxtaposed (and, I suppose, at some level, opposed) with naturalistic, relativistic perspectives that lead to the development of new conceptualizations or emergent theoretical perspectives through iterative conversations with data. Huberman really helped shape my early thinking about inquiry. Partly from his contributions, I learned about the inevitable and important role of context in understanding research findings. Like him, I would argue that knowledge (as opposed to information) can be packaged up and transported (i.e., removed from context) to the benefit of others; yet when received by others, it is interpretation within the local context that defines the validity of such knowledge (Huberman, 1994).

MY PERSPECTIVE ON EVALUATION

I have come to learn over the years that there is considerable diversity in thinking about and defining evaluation, and I am persuaded that this will continue to be so. Yet I think that, at some level, we all settle on a definition that works for us and use it to guide our work. For me, evaluation is the use of systematic inquiry to make judgments about program merit, worth, and significance and to support program decision making. Key to this definition is the term *judgment*. Judgment in evaluation requires the comparison of systematically gathered observations against some basis. The basis for comparison, in the case of program evaluation, can be standards of program performance, the performance of other programs (or the performance of others in the absence of a program), or the performance of the program in question at an earlier point in time. Few, I believe, would argue with these ideas. However, what is not explicit here, yet is pivotal I think, is the answer to the question "Whose judgment?"

Even in my days as a graduate student, I was uncomfortable with an answer to this question, which elevates the role of the evaluator to judge, decider, and/or arbiter of program disposition. There is something deeply arrogant about that scenario that never did quite sit with me. I see evaluation as essentially a service industry—those with training, experience, and/or expertise working to construct (or co-construct) knowledge to support program decision making and development. Program decision making, however, should be mostly in the hands of program community members, those with intimate knowledge about the program's logic and content and the context in which the program is located. To the extent that evaluation ultimately factors into typically nonrational or political program decision making, it is useful. To the extent that it is useful, it has a viable future as a powerful means of social change.

And so, it is my view that the locus of judgment about program merit, worth, and significance should lie with *nonevaluator* stakeholders (henceforth, "stakeholders") located within the program community. A pivotal role for evaluators, then, is to foster informed judgment making on the part of stakeholders. And now I return to reflections on my career trajectory and why an interest in evaluation use seems to have woven its way through it.

THE PROBLEM OF NONUSE AS A TRIGGERING EXPERIENCE

Early on I completed a master's degree at Lakehead University in Ontario in experimental psychology and subsequently accepted a research post at the University of British Columbia in the Faculty of Commerce and Business Administration. I worked on a research project on risk in business decision making, but on the side, I took on an extended consulting responsibility with a multidisciplinary clinic for the treatment of chronic pain. Privately owned and funded by a venture capitalist, the clinic had on staff some 35 care professionals, including psychiatrists, psychologists, biofeedback specialists, physiotherapists, social workers, physicians, and other health care workers. My role was to work with these many and varied professionals to develop and establish a database and an ongoing data collection mechanism to be used for monitoring, research, and evaluation. I spent my time seeking input from the staff on important and valid process and outcome indicators and to develop instrumentation for ongoing routine data collection, storage, and analysis. After working part-time for about a year on this project, I departed for Toronto to begin my doctoral studies, leaving behind a well-oiled and fully functional data-gathering and management mechanism that had apparent ownership by all concerned. Checking in some 3 months later, much to my dismay, I learned that our collaborative creation had been swept away like a house of cards in a sea breeze.

I wondered how a system so carefully structured and founded on such inclusive input could have had such a complete and hasty demise. I wondered what it would take to develop a system that would actually not only be perceived as useful but would, in fact, be used. It dawned on me that I had identified a suitable domain of inquiry for my dissertation research, one for which I felt considerable passion and empathy. Are evaluation data used? If so, how and what factors and conditions influence their use? And off I went, delving deeper and deeper into a burgeoning literature shaped by the likes of Weiss, Alkin, Patton, and King, to name a few.

Working with Leithwood had a profound intellectual impact on me. In his own work at the time of my doctoral studies, he toyed with interests in evaluation, but his scholarship was primarily located in planned school change and educational leadership. Through my interactions with him, I developed a deep appreciation of the explanatory power of empirical research and commitments to scholarly field development and methodological eclecticism. I learned that understanding practice in both informal and systematic ways is pivotal to research and, ultimately, theory development. I mentioned above the survey article that we published (Cousins & Leithwood, 1986). The skills I learned on that project—skills of synthesizing and integrating empirical research in a particular domain—are ones that I have developed and used extensively throughout my career. With colleagues and students, I have published several reviews over my career in diverse yet related domains of inquiry such as organizational learning (Cousins, 1996), evaluation and organizational culture (Cousins, Goh, Clark, & Lee, 2004), cross-cultural evaluation (Chouinard & Cousins, 2007, 2009), process use of evaluation (Amo & Cousins, 2007), and, of course, participatory evaluation (Cousins, 2003; Cousins & Chouinard, 2010, in press). In addition to helping chart the field in a given domain, I learned that there is great personal/professional value in undertaking such integrative work. Of course, it fits hand in glove with logical empiricist commitments, or what Huberman might call "soft-nosed logical positivism" (Miles & Huberman, 1984); it provides the fodder from which preordinate conceptual frameworks emerge. Over the years, research integrations have played a strong role in helping me develop such frameworks and use them in the pursuit of research funding.

PARTICIPATION AND USE

One way for evaluators to overcome the problem of evaluation nonuse would be to engage stakeholders with the evaluation. Many possibilities exist; indeed, a number of them are represented in this volume. I mentioned above an approach that I have found—through experience, observation, and systematic inquiry—to be particularly potent in this regard, namely, P-PE. I define participatory evaluation as evaluative inquiry carried out in a partnership between members of the evaluation community and stakeholders. Evaluators bring to the partnership their knowledge of and expertise in evaluation logic, methods, and standards of practice; stakeholders contribute their knowledge of program logic and context. I reiterate that participatory evaluation is but one way to engage stakeholders. The choice to invoke this approach depends very much on the evaluation questions asked. I would claim that formative, improvement-oriented contexts provide the best platform for this approach.

P-PE, the particular approach that I most often practice (there are certainly others), involves a limited number of primary stakeholders (those with a vital stake in the program or its evaluation); it is characterized by control of technical evaluation decision making that is balanced between evaluators and stakeholders, and it engages stakeholders quite directly in many, if not all, of the technical activities associated with evaluative inquiry. It is primarily concerned with program problem solving (e.g., fostering learning about program functioning and providing support for decision making for program improvement) and can lead to ECB at the individual, group, and organizational—and even community—levels. Developing understanding about the nature and consequences of participatory evaluation and the conditions and factors supporting its implementation has provided a focus for our research for some time. But my interest in participatory evaluation ultimately emerged from evaluation practice.

Following my doctorate, I accepted a tenure-stream post with the Ontario Institute for Studies in Education/University of Toronto, in one of its satellite field centers. Our primary function was field development, working with about 10 school districts in the east-central Ontario region to address curriculum development, leadership, in-service, and evaluation needs. That role provided me with several opportunities to work in partnership with educators in planning and implementing school- or district-based systematic inquiry (e.g., needs assessment, school improvement monitoring, program and curriculum evaluation). I found this approach—working in partnership—to be particularly effective in producing evaluation products that people actually paid attention to and, in some way, shape, or form, *used*. It was highly responsive, in my estimation, to the information needs of stakeholders.

Within my first few years in the role, I had occasion to connect with my colleague Lorna Earl about a classroom assessment project. At the time, Lorna was director of a research and evaluation unit in a large school district in metropolitan Toronto. She had a staff of about three or four full-time project directors who handled a very large number of evaluation-related projects in any given year. Over coffee, we traded stories about our mutual interest in program evaluation and quickly discovered that we subscribed to similar approaches: that is, working in partnership with educators not particularly well versed in evaluation logic or methods. Her project directors would routinely coordinate and engage teams of principals, department heads, teachers, and/or educational consultants in planning and implementing systematic inquiry. More often than not, the resulting support for program-level decision making was, in her view, quite remarkable. I shared similar experiences with the school districts in which I worked. Our discussion soon revealed that we knew of other Canadian educational evaluators adopting similar modes of inquiry. We decided over that coffee that we ought to try to systematically capture and analyze these partnering experiences and began to plan a panel session for the 1993 American Educational Research Association annual meeting featuring a set of empirical papers and discussant remarks by Alkin and Huberman. Ultimately, with encouragement from Marv Alkin, we compiled and published these papers (and a few others) in an edited volume (Cousins & Earl, 1995). We referred to the approach as "participatory evaluation" and examined its consequences and supporting conditions and influences through evaluation utilization and organizational learning lenses. My own contributions to this volume were linked to an ongoing funded research program that was to extend over a considerable period of time and ultimately involved graduate student thesis research. Even now, we continue to work in this domain (Cousins & Chouinard, 2010, in press).

THE MANY MODES OF PARTICIPATORY EVALUATION

Through personal communications and interactions, Jennifer Greene enhanced my awareness and sharpened my understanding of the breadth and scope of approaches that had come to be labeled participatory evaluation. Indeed, Huberman (1995) had raised similar issues in his analysis of our set of empirical studies mentioned above. There exists, mostly in the context of monitoring and evaluation in the developing world, a long-standing tradition of participatory inquiry variously labeled participatory evaluation, participatory action research, participatory rural appraisal, and the like. Such approaches are deeply rooted in principles of equity, emancipation, and transformation and are normative in form and function. Evaluation and inquiry serve as educative tools, the use of which would help enlighten typically oppressed peoples as to the forces at play in their own circumstances and foster self-determination among them. The ideals and the vision of those working in this milieu are a far cry from our own approach to participatory evaluation.

As a consequence, I felt the need to clarify our own use of the term *participatory evaluation* in our published work. Over time, I became increasingly concerned about the highly variable and inconsistent use of the term in the literature; our strategy of defining up front what we mean by it, if effective, was not one typically adopted by many, or even most, other writers in the field. The abundance of meanings and uses of the term were leading to considerable confusion in the literature, I believed. Bessa Whitmore provided me with the impetus to address this issue in a direct way. She compiled a volume for *New Directions in Evaluation* on participatory evaluation (Whitmore, 1998) and invited me to develop with her a conceptual piece as an introductory chapter (Cousins & Whitmore, 1998). In that chapter, we depicted two streams of participatory evaluation, each with distinct yet overlapping justification. We labeled the stream aligned with ameliorative approaches to issues of social inequity and injustice "transformative participatory evaluation," its counterpart being P-PE. In that article, Whitmore and I also developed a three-dimensional conceptual device for differentiating among important process dimensions (control, stakeholder selection, and depth of participation) as a way to better understand the form and function of participatory and collaborative inquiry. It would seem that that contribution really captured the attention and interest of many; ultimately, it was acknowledged as one of the top 10 publications in *New Directions for Evaluation* in a 20th-anniversary special edition edited by Mathison (2007).

As our work progressed, I developed an interest in ECB. I realized that P-PE and other approaches that privilege use (e.g., Patton, 2008, 2009) might be thought of as *indirect* approaches to ECB, as opposed to the more direct coursework, workshop, and/or formal training/educational options.

EVALUATIVE INQUIRY AND CULTURAL CHANGE IN ORGANIZATIONS

Much of our research on participatory evaluation has pointed to conditions and factors associated with organizational context and culture as being essential in explaining the extent to which the approach is effective in leading to desirable practical consequences. Linkages between evaluative inquiry and organizational change have captured the imagination of several of my colleagues over the years. Among them, I would include Preskill and Torres (1998), with their contributions on evaluative inquiry and organizational learning, and Owen and his colleagues on evaluation and administrative and leadership functions (Owen & Lambert, 1995). To be sure, organizational context has figured in the work of many scholars interested in evaluation use over the years (Cousins & Leithwood, 1986). Certainly, such considerations have been prominent in the work of Alkin and colleagues (Alkin, Daillak, & White, 1979) and in Patton's delineation of the principles of utilization-focused evaluation (2008) and developmental evaluation (2009). More recently, a doctoral thesis written by Katherine Seiden (2000) revisited some earlier work on the cultural construct of "organizational readiness for evaluation." Her thesis is a testament to the increasing attention to issues of culture at the organizational level and the role of evaluation in developing it.

Our current work is moving very much in this direction. Our recent research is focusing on understanding evaluation as an organizational learning system in the context of the organizational culture of a variety of Canadian organizations. Guided by the initial integration of research (Cousins et al., 2004), our first interest was in describing variation within and between schools in organizational readiness for evaluation and linkages between evaluative inquiry and the learning capacity of schools (Goh, Cousins, & Elliott, 2006). This we accomplished through quantitative inquiry using a hybrid instrument that builds on prior work of Goh (2000), Preskill and Torres (1998), and Seiden (2000). Our next step was to explore in rich detail schools that are relatively far along on these dimensions (Cousins, Goh, & Clark, 2005). That project was really the basis for the formulation of a working hypothesis that has undergirded our work in ECB for the past few years. Specifically, our conjecture is that "data use leads to data valuing." From that point, we developed an ECB conceptual framework that highlights not only the capacity to *do* evaluation but also the capacity to *use* it. The framework has guided a broader look at the organizational capacity for evaluation, again with quantitative (Cousins et al., 2008) and qualitative inquiry. We did a pan-Canadian survey of internal evaluators as well as a multiple case study involving government organizations, foundations, nongovernmental organizations (NGOs), and higher-educational organizations (soon to be published).

Although describing organizations that have developed cultures of readiness for evaluation and learning capacity, or have shown an interest in doing so, is no doubt worthy of study, it is, in my view, ultimately the first step in a line of inquiry committed to understanding how organizations can develop such a capacity. From where I sit, interventionist, longitudinal, multimethod empirical work in this stream holds great potential to advance evaluation theory, particularly theory about evaluation use, in significant and enduring ways.

At the time of writing, I am on sabbatical leave in Dakar, Senegal, leading a series of ECB workshops with more than 70 participants from multiple sectors, including government, NGOs, multilateral agencies, and universities. The overarching framework for this series reflects a commitment to doing evaluation that is ultimately useful. I am delighted to say that our participants consist of a balanced mix of evaluators (supply side) and managers and decision makers/policymakers (demand side). Many members of this latter group likely will never do evaluation, but they do seek to understand it at deeper levels and its implications for their organizations. It is the demand-side group from which I think we can learn much about integrating evaluation into organizational culture, perhaps by somehow getting them to experience successful use, that is, to test the working hypothesis that "data use leads to data valuing." And that just may be the theme for another proposal for research funds.

REFERENCES

Alkin, M. C., Daillak, R., & White, P. (1979). *Using evaluations: Does evaluation make a difference?* Beverly Hills, CA: Sage.

Amo, C., & Cousins, J. B. (2007). Going through the process: An examination of the operationalization of process use in empirical research on evaluation. In J. B. Cousins (Ed.), *New Directions for Evaluation: Vol. 116. Process use in theory, research, and practice* (pp. 5–26). San Francisco, CA: Jossey-Bass.

Chouinard, J. A., & Cousins, J. B. (2007). Culturally competent evaluation for Aboriginal communities: A review of the empirical literature. *Journal of Multidisciplinary Evaluation, 4*(8), 40–57.

Chouinard, J. A., & Cousins, J. B. (2009). A review and synthesis of current research on cross-cultural evaluation. *American Journal of Evaluation, 30*(4), 457–494.

Cousins, J. B. (1988). *Principals' use of appraisal data concerning their own performance* (Unpublished doctoral dissertation). University of Toronto, Toronto, Ontario, Canada.

Cousins, J. B. (1996). Understanding organizational learning for educational leadership and school reform. In K. Leithwood, J. Chapman, D. Corson, P. Hallinger, & A. Hart (Eds.), *International handbook of educational leadership and administration* (pp. 589–652). Boston, MA: Kluwer Academic.

Cousins, J. B. (2003). Utilization effects of participatory evaluation. In T. Kellaghan, D. L. Stufflebeam, & L. A. Wingate (Eds.), *International handbook of educational evaluation* (pp. 245–265). Boston, MA: Kluwer Academic.

Cousins, J. B., & Chouinard, J. (2010). *A review and integration of empirical research on participatory evaluation.* Invited paper for the Virtual Conference on Methodology in Programme Evaluation, University of Witswatersrand, Johannesburg, South Africa. Retrieved from http://wpeg.wits.ac.za/

Cousins, J. B., & Chouinard, J. A. (Eds.). (in press). *Participatory evaluation up close: An integration of research based knowledge.* Charlotte, NC: Information Age.

Cousins, J. B., & Earl, L. M. (Eds.). (1995). *Participatory evaluation in education: Studies in evaluation use and organizational learning.* London, England: Falmer Press.

Cousins, J. B., Elliott, C., Amo, C., Bourgeois, I., Chouinard, J. A., Goh, S., & Lahey, R. (2008). Organizational capacity to do and use evaluation: Results of a pan-Canadian survey of evaluators. *Canadian Journal of Program Evaluation, 23*(3), 1–35.

Cousins, J. B., Goh, S., & Clark, S. (2005). Data use leads to data valuing: Evaluative inquiry for school decision making. *Leadership and Policy in Schools, 4,* 155–176.

Cousins, J. B., Goh, S., Clark, S., & Lee, L. (2004). Integrating evaluative inquiry into the organizational culture: A review and synthesis of the knowledge base. *Canadian Journal of Program Evaluation, 19*(2), 99–141.

Cousins, J. B., & Leithwood, K. A. (1986). Current empirical research on evaluation utilization. *Review of Education Research, 56*(3), 331–364.

Cousins, J. B., & Whitmore, E. (1998). Framing participatory evaluation. In E. Whitmore, Ed., *Understanding and practicing participatory evaluation* (New Directions in Evaluation, pp. 3–23). San Francisco: Jossey Bass.

Goh, S. (2000). Towards a learning organization: The strategic building blocks. *SAM Advanced Management Journal, 63*(2), 15–22.

Goh, S., Cousins, J. B., & Elliott, C. (2006). Organizational learning capacity, evaluative inquiry, and readiness for change in schools: Views and perceptions of educators. *Journal of Educational Change, 7,* 289–318.

Huberman, M. (1989). Predicting conceptual effects in research utilization: Looking with both eyes. *Knowledge in Society, 2*(3), 6–24.

Huberman, M. (1994). Research utilization: The state of the art. *Knowledge and Policy, 7*(4), 13–33.

Huberman, M. (1995). The many modes of participatory evaluation. In J. B. Cousins & L. M. Earl (Eds.), *Participatory evaluation in education: Studies in evaluation utilization and organizational learning* (pp. 103–111). London, England: Falmer Press.

Mathison, S. (Ed.). (2007). *Enduring issues in evaluation: The 20th anniversary of the collaboration between NDE and AEA* (New Directions for Evaluation, No. 114). San Francisco, CA: Jossey-Bass.

Miles, M., & Huberman, A. M. (1984). *Qualitative data analysis: A sourcebook of methods.* Beverly Hills, CA: Sage.

Owen, J. M., & Lambert, F. C. (1995). Roles for evaluation in learning organizations. *Evaluation, 1*(2), 237–250.

Patton, M. Q. (2008). *Utilization-focused evaluation* (4th ed.). Thousand Oaks, CA: Sage.

Patton, M. Q. (2009). *Developmental evaluation.* New York, NY: Guilford Press.

Preskill, H., & Torres, R. (1998). *Evaluative inquiry for organizational learning.* Thousand Oaks, CA: Sage.

Seiden, K. (2000). *Development and validation of the "organizational readiness for evaluation" survey instrument* (Unpublished doctoral dissertation). University of Minnesota, Minneapolis.

Whitmore, E. (Ed.). (1998). *Participatory evaluation approaches* (New Directions in Evaluation, No. 80). San Francisco, CA: Jossey-Bass.

PART V

EVALUATION ROOTS

A Wider Perspective

28

A EUROPEAN EVALUATION THEORY TREE

Nicoletta Stame

This chapter is devoted to European evaluation theorists, not to European evaluation (institutions and traditions[1]). Evaluation theorists—according to Marvin Alkin's definition—are "individuals who are definitely associated with a particular evaluation theoretical position" (Alkin, 2004, p. 6). It is therefore based on people who have influenced the evaluation discourse in Europe, by reflecting on experiences of evaluation, and who have focused in their theoretical prescriptions on *valuing*, on *methodology*, and on enhancing the possibilities of *use:* The branches of Alkin's metaphorical tree are all from the United States, but they are valid all over the world.

In considering European evaluation theorists, we need to locate them in their cultural tradition and political system, which may differ from country to country. The field of evaluation has indeed been opened by U.S. thinkers and practitioners, and the European evaluation community has grown, even purposely (see the first editorial of the journal *Evaluation*), in a dialogue with the other side of the Atlantic. This is also a key to its vitality: European evaluators are proud of heralding a new way of looking at the old state. Indeed in Europe, there have been influential thinkers in the field of evaluation who were policy analysts, not evaluators: Michel Crozier (1988) in France, Bruno Dente (1982) in Italy, and Hans-Ulrich Derlien (1990) in Germany.

In some European countries, a long-established pragmatic political culture has, for a long time, provided a suitable ground for evaluation theories to develop. In the United Kingdom, the evaluation of education has been a field of evaluation methodological attention since the 1970s. In Sweden and other Scandinavian countries, evaluation has been an attribute of a democratic state since the 1960s.

In the past two decades, some original contributions to the field, like "realist evaluation" and "systematic reviews," have been provided by prominent European evaluation theorists.

More recently, with greater international communication, the European evaluation community has started an intense dialogue with theorists abroad, as is witnessed by its participation in evaluation association conferences, articles in evaluation journals, teaching programs, and so on. Hence, European evaluators have contributed to the debate about almost all approaches that have been prominent: to name a few, Peter Dahler Larsen on constructivist evaluation, Tineke Abma on dialogue and participatory evaluation, Frans Leeuw on theory-based evaluation, Alberto Martini on counterfactual analysis, Giandomenico Majone on evolutionary implementation, Christopher Pollitt and Helmut Wollmann on the relationships between new public management and evaluation, Rheinard Stockman on sustainability, and Richard Hummelbrunner on systems theory and complexity.

However, the scene would not be complete if we did not mention another kind of contributor. Alkin has distinguished evaluation thinkers from evaluation interpreters and teachers, who "having written evaluation textbooks, while not specifically expounding a new theory, provide an important resource for teaching about evaluation," and has decided not to locate this group on his tree. Beyond the latter category, which is of course well inhabited also in Europe, here we may identify another type who sit in between thinkers and interpreters, whom I would call *developers* (or *theory weavers*[2]), people who have shaped the evaluation discourse, like the editor of the journal *Evaluation* and the authors of the *Guides for the Evaluation of Structural Funds*.

In this chapter, I will review the contributions by those I consider original theorists and *theory weavers* and will end with some considerations on the development of European evaluation, with reference to its internal differences and to its relationships with its U.S counterpart.

ILLUMINATIVE, DEMOCRATIC, AND PERSONALIZED EVALUATION

Back in 1972, European authors contributed to the development of evaluation theory in a dialogue with the other side of the Atlantic—actually, with a criticism of mainstream evaluation. Parlett and Hamilton's "illuminative evaluation" of innovative educational programs was even developed through Parlett's experience with two innovative undergraduate programs at MIT in the aftermath of the 1968 movement. It was then elaborated at Edinburgh University and was very influential in U.K. circles.

Illuminative evaluation stands as an alternative to the "'classical' or 'agricultural-botany' paradigm, which—by studying students like plants receiving a fertilizer and yielding a crop—utilizes a hypotetico-deductive methodology derived from the experimental and mental-testing traditions in psychology" (Parlett & Hamilton, 1977, p. 10). Illuminative evaluation relates to social anthropology, psychiatry, and participant observation research in sociology. Its main concern is description and interpretation rather than measurement and prediction; it studies how the program operates, how it is influenced by the school situation in which it is applied, and what those directly concerned regard as advantages and disadvantages. It should "enlighten" the innovator and the academic community "by clarifying the processes of education" and by helping "identify those procedures, those elements in the educational effort which seem to have had desirable results" (Parlett & Hamilton, 1977, p. 10).

The new paradigm rejects the experimental one on the following bases: the logic of randomization (large samples, strictly controlled) reduces individuals and institutions to parameters and factors, divorcing the study from the complex real world; it assumes that innovative programs undergo little or no change during the period of study; it is insensitive to local perturbations and unusual effects; it fails to articulate the concerns of different interest groups; and in effect, it "diverts attention away from questions of educational practice towards more centralized bureaucratic concerns" (Parlett & Hamilton, 1977, p. 9).

To contrast these limitations, illuminative evaluation is based on two main concepts: (1) the instructional system and (2) the learning milieu. An instructional system is not just composed of the new pedagogic assumptions, syllabus, techniques, and equipment, but "when adopted it undergoes modifications that are rarely trivial," since "technicians and students interpret and reinterpret the instructional system for their particular setting" (Parlett & Hamilton, 1977, p. 11). In fact, these actors (with their specific characteristics and preoccupations) work in a particular social-psychological and material environment composed of work styles, constraints on the organization of teaching, and operating assumptions. Thus, the innovative program cannot be seen as an independent system but as something that sets off a chain of repercussions, unintended consequences included, throughout the learning milieu. Another consequence of such a way of conceiving the program is that it takes into consideration the intellectual experience of students and the interdependence of learning and teaching: "Students do not respond merely to presented content and to tasks assigned. Rather, they adapt to and work within the learning milieu taken as an interrelated whole" (Parlett & Hamilton, 1977, p. 11).

Not knowing in advance what will happen but aiming at understanding what will be the effects deemed desirable by the people involved, Parlett and Hamilton describe their procedure—which could not be charted in advance—as composed of three stages according to the following activities performed: (1) observing the day-to-day reality of the setting, familiarizing with the complex scene; (2) inquiring further on those topics ("issues," à la Stake), being more systematic and directive; and (3) seeking the general principles underlying the organization of the program, spotting patterns of cause and effect. As can be easily understood, this sequence implies also the use of appropriate research techniques for each task (observation, interviews, questionnaires, tests), which will amount to a triangulation approach.

Parlett and Hamilton's (1977) article strikes the contemporary reader for its enduring relevance in current debates. In presenting their alternative approach, not only did the authors provide a criticism of randomized controlled trials (RCTs) that is currently echoed against a revitalization of the botanic approach under the guise of a medical metaphor, but they also answer the criticism that randomistas may level against them. Against the criticism of subjectivism: Any study involves judgments on the data collected and the need to use different techniques to cross-check them, for which the interpretive human insight is needed; moreover, since any research creates disturbance, evaluators should develop interpersonal skills in the relationship with the evaluee. Regarding the criticism of being limited in scope: During the three stages of the evaluation, one passes from small sample studies to large-scale inquiries by way of comparisons. In fact, "despite their diversity, learning milieus share many characteristics" that provoke familiar reactions in teaching, learning, and innovating. This understanding, however, requires a specific method of developing "abstracted summaries, for shared terminology and for insightful concepts," which can serve as aids to communication and to facilitate theory building.

In sum, Parlett and Hamilton's illuminative evaluation stands as a clear opponent of traditional, experimental evaluation—at the beginning of the paradigm war. However, they are not relativist/subjectivist against objectivists. They are on the same wavelength as Stake's responsive evaluation, supporters of the comparative case study, and even proponents of something that can anticipate theory-based evaluation.

Working in a similar vein of purporting case studies as the most suitable tool for educational evaluation,[3] Barry MacDonald is dissatisfied with the usual opposition between two different ways of doing research (quantitative and qualitative), each responding to the rules and standards of its own academic communities. That way of doing fails to recognize that "case-study research in education takes the researcher into a complex set of politically sensitive relationships" (MacDonald & Walker, 1977). In choosing his or her approach to evaluation, the evaluator needs to answer the question "Who controls the pursuit of the new knowledge, and who has access to it?" This political dimension defines three types of evaluation:

1. It is *bureaucratic evaluation* when the evaluator accepts the values of those who hold office and acts as a management consultant who tries to satisfy his client, who finally owns the report. The techniques utilized must be credible to the policymakers, who are mainly concerned with "utility" and "efficiency." Its key justificatory concept is the "reality of power."

2. It is *autocratic evaluation* when the evaluator offers external validation of policy in exchange for compliance with his recommendations. The evaluator is aware of the constitutional and moral obligations of the bureaucracy, but at the same time his techniques of study need the validation provided by the academic research community. The key concepts are "principle" and "objectivity." Its key justificatory concept is "the responsibility of office."

3. It is *democratic evaluation* when the evaluator collects definitions of, and reactions to, the program, recognizes value pluralism, and acts as a broker in exchanges of information between different groups of informed citizens. The report must be accessible to nonspecialist audiences and should not contain recommendations. The key concepts are "confidentiality," "negotiation," and "accessibility." The key justificatory concept is "the right to know" (MacDonald, 1977).

MacDonald believed that existing studies of the first two types had been dominant and that it was time to develop a third one, which he saw as "an emergent model, not yet substantially realised." In so doing, he has certainly paved the way to further developments, most notably "deliberative democratic evaluation" by Ernest House and empowerment evaluation by David Fetterman and Abe Wandersman.

Following in the same tradition, Saville Kushner has recently proposed to "personalize" evaluation to invert the "conventional relationship between individual and program," influenced by the forms of thinking of program managers and "intolerant of others' rights to meaningfulness." Rather than document the program and read the lives of the individuals in that context, it is necessary to document the lives and work of people and to use that as a context within which to read the significance and meaning of programs. In fact, "programs can only work through their participants," and the core of evaluation methodology is to know "how they arrive at judgements, how those judgements are mediated through their association with others, and are prejudiced or favoured by the way individuals relate to power." And the case study methodology comes to service to study "individuals in their institutional and political contexts . . . [and] individual experience as an element in the interaction of institutional cultures" (Kushner, 2000, p. 12).

POLICY TOOLS AND EVALUATION

From within the Swedish political culture, favorable as it is to public intervention in social policies, and keen on its improvement, an important contribution to evaluation theory was offered by Evert Vedung's elaboration on policy tools and their relation to evaluation.

Evert Vedung is the author of perhaps the first European textbook on evaluation (Vedung, 1997), which starts with this striking phrase "unintended effects of intentional action fascinate" and goes on to maintain that the insight into the reverse consequences "has been a major force behind the shaping of mechanisms for result-oriented analysis and information feed-back in the public sector" (p. xvii), like evaluation, which has been promoted in democratic states since the 1960s. The link between evaluation and democracy has been constant in Vedung's evaluation theory, until a recent article in which he suggests integrating theory-based approaches with a stakeholder approach to create a plurality of voices and make theory reconstructions heard (Hansen & Vedung, 2010).

From his own experience with the evaluation of instruments for nuclear energy policy, Vedung became concerned with the centrality of policy tools. He notes that with classic administrative theory, which deems that means (not ends) are up for discussion, the choice of means is dictated by the efficiency criterion only. But is this criterion sufficient to evaluate the choice of instruments? Other criteria are important, such as democracy and legality; moreover, it is necessary to take into consideration the political culture, sector, and so on.

Vedung's main contention is that "the theoretical merit of evaluations will be augmented" if they "permit the extrapolation of findings to other contexts"; in this, he is reminiscent of Cronbach's plea for devising methods for generalizing evaluation results to different situations (a special type of external validity) (see Stame, 2010). Such extrapolation may happen if evaluands are considered in a general light, like the one provided by looking at the policy instruments that they embody. To this aim, he works out the tripartite typology of "sticks, carrots and sermons,"[4] which in policy parlance are regulations, economic means (incentives), and information (Vedung, 1997):

> Regulations (sticks) are measures undertaken by government units to influence people by means of verbally formulated rules and directives, which mandate the receivers to act in accordance with what is ordered in these rules and directives. . . . the purported relationship between the governor and the governed is authoritative in the sense that the latter are thought to be obligated to comply . . . regulations are associated with threats of negative sanctions such as fines, imprisonment and other types of punishment.
>
> Economic policy instruments (carrots) involve either distributing or taking away material resources. They make it cheaper or more expensive to pursue certain actions. However, addressees are not ordered to take the measures involved . . . Economic tools always leave subjects of governance a certain leeway within which to choose by themselves whether to take an action or not.
>
> Information (sermons), or "moral suasion" . . . covers attempts at influencing people through the transfer of knowledge, communication of reasoned argument, and persuasion. The information dispensed may . . . concern the nature of the problem at hand, how people are actually handling the problem, measures that can be taken to change the prevailing situation, and reasons why these measures ought to be considered and adopted by the addressees. (pp. 124–125)

The importance for evaluation of this typology can be understood in the following aspects.

The three types of tools are put on a scale from more authoritative (regulations) to less (information). Each tool has its rationale that helps choose which one to adopt. That distinction might also constitute the criterion against which the evaluation is conducted, in connection to the way the different tools are implemented and the policies enforced.

Then, many variations may occur within each tool and in the way they are combined: vertical, horizontal, or chronological. "In vertical packaging, one policy instrument is used to promote or restrain another. Horizontal packaging implies the use of two or more instruments for the same purpose." Chronological packaging implies a sequence of tools (Bemelmans-Videc, Rist, & Vedung, 1998). In this way, Vedung has anticipated the need for evaluation to deal with complexity.

DIALOGUE IN EVALUATION

Another important contribution to evaluation coming from within the Scandinavian democratic tradition is that of the critical dialogue proposed by Ove Karlsson. Being aware of the strict relationship between evaluation and politics (Palumbo, 1987) and of the need to include the voices of the different stakeholders in the evaluation process, as had been proposed by the "stakeholder approach" (Stake, 1989), Karlsson (1996, p. 406) thought that to achieve "increased justice within the evaluation," what was needed was an interaction between the stakeholders, to be reached through a critical, "Socratic" dialogue. Such a dialogue does not aim at reaching a compromise, which may hide asymmetrical power positions, nor at reaching a consensus, which may be too idealistic. Instead, what Karlsson aims at is a reciprocal understanding among the different stakeholders, changing perspectives, seeing things from another point of view, or even "casting one's skin" (p. 412), so that the stakeholders "reach a greater insight and clarity of the foundations on which one's own and others' judgements are based" and "become a more enlightened and active participant in the evaluation." This also has implications for the role of the evaluator, who is seen as a critical inquirer, someone who helps "develop a deeper understanding of what the program means for different stakeholders in terms of limitations and possibilities, especially for disadvantaged groups in society" (Karlsson, 2001, pp. 223–224), knowing that "there are seldom any simple answers or unambiguous results when evaluating social and pedagogical activities" (p. 223).

In an interesting "dialogue" coordinated by Tineke Abma (2001), Karlsson showed how critical dialogue evaluation brought participatory evaluation methods forward, and he described the process that he underwent in the evaluation of the program for after-school centers. In the first (dialogue to judge what program to develop) and second (dialogue to evaluate the program in practice) phases, he developed intensive dialogues with one stakeholders group at a time (politicians, bureaucrats, professionals, families, and children) to try to get as power-free a situation as possible. Metaphors were worked out to illuminate the possible values attached to the program. Then, in the third phase (dialogue for deliberation and learning), he presented a "discussion theater": four actors, representing the different stakeholders groups, were engaged in critical incidents illustrating the potential conflicts among stakeholders. This elicited the participants' reactions and exchange of opinions and helped them see things from a new perspective.

THE TURN OF THE 1990s

In the 1980s and 1990s, evaluation practices expanded to different policy domains, from education to social and welfare policies to public sector reforms. Any kind of approach was imported from the United States, often in isolation from each other, each approach being dominant in one policy domain irrespective of what was going on in the other one. Evaluation was considered as a technique.

The 1990s brought important novelties. On the one side, with the journal *Evaluation*, an attempt was made at creating a locus of horizontal exchange across different approaches, irrespective of disciplinary or policy sector boundaries. On the other side, realist evaluation defined itself as a third option between positivism and nominalism (constructivism) and became very popular. Unexpectedly, positivist approaches then broke in with the evidence-based movement, gaining a prominence they had never enjoyed before.

REALIST EVALUATION

Realist evaluation is the European version of theory-based evaluation, and its ontological stance puts it clearly as a third, "realist" way opposed to both the positivist-experimentalist and the nominalist-constructivist traditions in evaluation. Against the positivist tradition, it criticizes the empiricist view that only what can be based on direct observation can be known; in evaluation, this means a concept of the program as a treatment of a target, of which one can measure the status of the concerned variables before and after (sequential causality) without knowing why (black box). On the contrary, realism assumes that one can study the development of underlying processes by uncovering the hidden mechanisms that make it work (generative causality). It criticizes the nominalist tradition that everything is contingent; in evaluation, this means that there are no possible regularities. On the contrary, realism assumes the existence of demi-regularities (middle-range theories).

Concepts taken from the realist[5] kit help redefine the object of the evaluation exercise and its process. Programs are defined as social systems of interaction between individuals and institutions—micro and macro processes. They are opportunities offered to people embedded in a stratified situation, who may choose whether to take advantage of the new ideas introduced into their context. Hence, programs work when the hidden mechanism (the "resourced, directed, and constrained choices made by social actors") interacting with the context (i.e., the existing social relationships) is able to produce an outcome (generative causality). This is expressed in the CMO (*c*ontext, *m*echanism, *o*utcome) configuration, which is represented as C + M = O.

Evaluation answers the question "What (*mechanism*)[6] works better (*outcome*), where, for whom, in what circumstances (*context*), and why (*causality*)?" The evaluator works with hypotheses, the kind of middle-range theories,[7] or midregularities and tries to test them in different contexts. His methods are taken from all the available research techniques, but they are, so to speak, put under the dominance of the realist interview, a way in which the evaluator works as a theorist formulating hypotheses and the informant (interviewee, evaluee), as his research assistant (Pawson & Tilley, 1997, p. 164).

Pawson and Tilley (1997) have mainly worked in the evaluation of social policies, originally with criminal justice programs (the famous example of the CCTV in the parking lot). But their approach has been applied in many fields.

Realist evaluation has become very popular in Europe. However, its original grip (*presa*) on the evaluation discourse has become parallel to the emergence of a new trend of a positivist flavor—that of evidence-based policy and systematic reviews (see below). And it is precisely against this that realist evaluation has taken its new twist of realist syntheses.

Pawson has a spontaneous bent toward methods that compare different studies, and he has often used them for enucleating his own theories (mechanisms). Thus, it is only natural that he is interested in the new trend of systematic reviews. But he is at the same time critical of how they work. In the same way as he is opposed to the language of variables, the CMO configuration based on the language of generative mechanisms, so also he has come to criticize the logic of meta-analysis, which is based on a cumulation of results obtained by what are considered "robust" studies and by replication, and has maintained that the only thing that can be compared are families of mechanisms (Pawson, 1989), by refutation (Pawson, 2006). In so doing, he develops a strand of evolutionary epistemology that goes back to Campbell and his idea of eliminating rival explanations.

SYNTHESES AND THE EVIDENCE-BASED MOVEMENT

One of the main issues of evaluation studies is the degree to which it is possible to validate the results of a single program or to infer a conclusion from single studies and apply it to other situations. It concerns the methodology used for single studies (Campbell's [1969] threats to internal and external validity) but also the limits of single studies—hence the need to accumulate knowledge from many studies dealing with the same, or similar, program in order to get better evidence. This is the rationale for synthesis.

The practice of syntheses of evaluation studies goes back to the intuition of Gene Glass, a statistician who invented meta-analyses. It was well established in the United States (General Accounting Office, 1992) by the end of the 1980s and has continued ever since. But it has had a special impulse in the United Kingdom in the 1990s under the Labour government's thrust for an evidence-based policy, linked to the perennial question "What works?"

The road had been paved by Cochrane and the movement for evidence-based medicine. The Cochrane Collaboration has worked out a way of synthesizing the results of different studies on medical practice by providing a protocol for the choice of studies involved that was mainly concerned with methodologies: a preference for RCTs and the "need for collating and updating evidence from different studies, in order to arrive to the most reliable estimate of effects" (Oakley, Gough, Oliver, & Thomas, 2005). Hence, the idea came of expanding the systematic reviews to social policies, by the Campbell collaboration, the Evidence for Policy and Practice Information and Coordinating Center (EPPI) Center, and so on.[8] These groups differ on the policy that is the object of analysis (crime, education, health, welfare), but they follow a similar logic. Since the rule of thumb at the basis of the exercise is the replicability of the procedures and controllability of the results, what constitutes the kernel of this kind of study is setting protocols that should be followed by whoever wants to join the exercise of particular reviews. Protocols establish how to define questions and the scope of the reviews, criteria for inclusion of studies, criteria for search of studies, how to appraise the studies (quality assurance), how to synthesize the evidence, and how to disseminate it.

The theorists whom we meet here are methodologists, people who discuss the robustness of designs and credibility of evidence: According to Petticrew and Roberts (2006), systematic reviews are another research method that is not based on single studies but on many studies (like surveys). They have contributed to establishing institutions and research centers with good technological infrastructures, which support their work. These competing centers, however, employ different methods, from more orthodox meta-analyses to a more eclectic mixing of meta-analyses with narrative reviews.

Ann Oakley is perhaps the author most involved in advocating experimental methods from an epistemological standpoint. Having herself once embodied the link between feminist and qualitative research, she has come to oppose the feminist rejection of experimental methods as positivist, rational, masculine and to advocate a reversal of the current constructivist, postmodern approaches to knowledge and of the related naturalistic and theory-driven approaches to evaluation (Oakley, 2000). Therefore, she exposes the narrow-minded academics,[9] who end up being jealous of their findings and are hardly transparent, and supports the democratic attitude of those who engage in systematic reviews, who make their judgments explicit "in the choice of question, the selection and appraisal of literature, and the interpretation of the findings, and their efforts to involve others in making these judgements" (Oakley et al., 2005, p. 23). She sees in the synthesis movement a development of the experimental methodology and considers this a step forward in the experimenting society advocated by Campbell as a way of having a more democratic, better-informed, active, and innovating society (Oakley, 2000).

A different attitude is that of Petticrew, who together with Helen Roberts has written a practical guide, *Systematic Reviews in the Social Sciences* (2006). This is an effort at pluralism (mixed methods) in systematic reviews, in so far as it deals with different types of reviews (meta-analyses, narrative reviews, and other, less systematic reviews) using not only quantitative but also qualitative research methods. Petticrew is keen on treating qualitative research on an equal footing as quantitative research and strives to be objective in assessing the merit of each method: "Systematic reviews allow challenge to the paradigm to occur—a challenge permitted by close examination of the underpinning evidence" (Petticrew & Roberts, 2006, p. 20). It all depends on the question answered. And, as he reminds us, it is not only a question of "what works," that is, of effectiveness, which would require quantitative methods, but maybe of any other kind, such as estimates of risks, the meaning of an intervention for the beneficiaries, and so on, which require qualitative methods. Thus, he uses the delicate concept of a "hierarchy of evidence," trying to neutralize it by saying that there is no single hierarchy (meaning the usual one that goes from the top level of RCTs to the bottom level of ethnographic studies) but that each question answered implies its own hierarchy of evidence.

In his pluralist attitude, Petticrew is concerned with the limitations of syntheses when confronted with complex programs that require a complex set of evidence: "Reviews of complex social interventions are themselves often complex, extensive and expensive, because of the need to locate and review very heterogeneous types of evidence" (Petticrew & Roberts, 2006, p. 29). As we have seen above, this movement has even stimulated a complete reversal of the way the same idea of synthesis can be upheld, which is the realist synthesis by Pawson that places complexity as its starting point.

EVALUATION: THE INTERNATIONAL JOURNAL OF THEORY AND PRACTICE

Most of what can be said about European evaluation theories has a point of reference in the work that has been done through the years by Elliot Stern, the editor of *Evaluation*, as coordinator of a group of devoted referees but mainly as the author of the editorials that appear in each issue and that constitute the thread of the evolution of evaluation thinking in Europe.

Evaluation is not only a repository of articles by mainly European authors, it has also been a "terrain for exchange of a learned discourse" that has nurtured, oriented, and even shaken the

European theorists and has thus contributed to shaping a pluralist and democratic identity of European evaluation. The journal has a subtitle: *The International Journal of Theory and Practice*. The word *international* stands for being open to a vast authorship and audience: On the one hand, it is open to dialogue with the U.S. evaluation community, and on the other, it is open to dialogue with all the European evaluation communities and not limited to a U.K.–U.S. dialogue. This has been one of its strengths: New approaches coming from the United States have been immediately received, and innovative European approaches have also been discussed by non-European authors. See, for example, the review of *Realistic Evaluation* by Feinstein (1998) and the note on realism by Julnes, Mark, and Henry (1998).

The original purposes of the journal (Stern, 1995) have been the following:

1. Overcoming gaps, for instance, by opening the journal to new domains—the evaluation of health services, innovation programs, laws, and so on—and by giving voice to the national evaluation communities

2. Creating bridges
   - *between theory and practice (see the subtitle):* for instance, by dealing with theoretical issues (cross-cutting themes, e.g., generalization, causality, etc.) analyzed within specific cases and contexts (practice);
   - *between approaches (multimethod):* the journal has allowed all approaches to be presented, even in a contentious way, but it favors articles that compare the strengths and weaknesses of different methods for a given object; and
   - *across disciplines and policy domains:* the general assumption is that evaluation theories and methodologies are valid across policy domains, irrespective of disciplinary boundaries (a notable exception is represented by economists' contributions, given their rarity)

Through the subsequent editorials, Stern has been able to shape a terrain for the continuity of debates. In the beginning, it was for fourth-generation evaluation, and later, it was for realist evaluation, complexity, participatory evaluation, the evidence-based movement, and impact evaluation. In all these cases, the aim was to gain further knowledge, either by the refinement of methods, as with syntheses (from new ideas to be better accepted to the need for building on them), or by shaping a new framework, as with the case of complexity (in the beginning acknowledged by Ian Sanderson, then addressed by Patricia Rogers, then becoming a taken-for-granted terrain of inquiry).

In creating the conditions for these fruitful debates, Stern has always been able to push for sound and theoretically based arguments, as when he invoked the need to be more critical in endorsing fourth-generation evaluation and invited more balanced contributions or when he has backed instances for putting more theory in the European Union (EU) evaluations (see Pollitt, 1998). And when he has reinvested in well-trodden paths (e.g., in EU structural funds), it was because new aspects had been disclosed that could have favored advancement.

NOT ONLY GUIDES

One of the main drivers of European evaluation has been the request to evaluate EU programs. This has also been a great challenge for the whole evaluation community, interested in the opening of an evaluation market as well as motivated by the opportunity of spreading good evaluation practices on a continental scale.

However, the task was not simple. Although the EU had imported from the United States the practice of social programs, whose goals were established in Brussels but were articulated and implemented at the state and local levels, the EU administration had been forged according to a different model, reminiscent of the French centralized bureaucracy: Regulations for evaluation are issued from above, as they are for any other administrative procedure. The tension between centralism and localism (some would say federalism) has been prominent in the making of an evaluation culture in EU (Stame, 2006).

Thus, the ordinary relationship between the EU administration and the local implementers is much more of the regulatory type than of the reflective one. Nonetheless, two main documents promoted by the Directory General on Regional Policies to evaluate structural funds programs (i.e., the tools of the cohesion policy, aimed at socioeconomic development and at a territorial re-equilibrium between European regions, what represented one third of EU expenditure) have attempted at spreading a reflective attitude in these administrative bodies and stand as important milestones in the creation of an EU evaluation culture.

The MEANS (Methods for Evaluating Actions of a Structural Nature) Guide was issued in 1999, and it is the result of a specific program.[10] It was aimed at managing people and performing evaluation and has provided a new awareness of the broad scope that research could have for policy making by directly addressing the evaluation problems of specific programs and by introducing from the start the idea that socioeconomic development programs were complex (multiple objectives, a partnership dimension, multisectoral components) and that evaluation should adopt tools from many disciplines (economics, sociology, management, geography, etc.).

For better or worse, the MEANS Guide is responsible for the diffusion of an evaluation culture and a proper language in Structural Funds (SF), and even wider, circles. The link between evaluation and programming cycles, the logical framework, the definition of evaluation criteria, the timing of the evaluation (ex ante, in itinere, ex post), the operationalization of objectives, the quality standards, the use of indicators, all these have become common currency, thanks to MEANS. The figure of the "main evaluation criteria" (European Community, 1999, p. 71, Box 12, Vol. 1), which shows the relationship between the three levels of society (needs, outcomes), program (objectives, inputs, outputs), and evaluation (relevance, efficiency, effectiveness, utility), has been the most popular representation of the evaluation exercise in the EU for at least a decade.

The EVALSED (Evaluation of Socio-Economic Development) Guide[11] followed 4 years later. It updated the MEANS Guide in many respects, mostly because of policy changes: Following the Lisbon agenda,[12] there was greater attention to the role of human and social capital, the information society, and the knowledge economy, which has changed the content of many programs. Moreover, the accession of new member states required a greater stress on capacity-building needs. From the methodological side, there has been a development of new evaluation tools of a participatory kind and a greater role for theory in evaluation (program theory, theories about the practice of evaluation, theories of implementation and change, policy-specific theories) (sec. 1.3).

What characterizes the EVALSED Guide is its pluralistic stance and flexible approach. Its pluralism—it builds on three main philosophical traditions (positivism, constructivism, realism) that could be combined depending on the circumstances of the evaluation. Its flexibility (some could call it pragmatism)—it insists on the "constant need to learn about different contexts and how best to combine different measures most effectively" (sec. 1.2) and different methodologies used for evaluation purposes (Box 1.3), on determining the implications for evaluation of the characteristics of different socioeconomic development programs and their theoretical underpinning, and on learning how to choose among methods and techniques when designing an evaluation.

Its main asset is in the attempt at writing a guide that is instructive but not prescriptive, which for any topic states as "golden rules" to be aware of the alternatives between which choices have to be made.

DISCUSSION

The relationship with U.S. evaluation is everywhere a point of reference, in two ways.

In the first place, although evaluation had existed in Europe for many years, notably in education, it is in the United States that evaluation acquired the status of a new field of research, if not a discipline: So U.S. evaluation had established a standard against which any new thinker had to compare, and it was a partner in a dialogue that has never been interrupted. In some cases, this has meant even the desire for European evaluators to outsmart their U.S. counterparts in a specific expertise, as in the case of evidence-based policy.

In the second place, in certain policy domains, European evaluators claimed their identity as opponents of mainstream approaches created in the United States. This is particularly the case with Parlett and Hamilton's illuminative evaluation, which was presented as opposed to U.S. experimental designs and quantitative methods, and MacDonald's democratic evaluation, as opposed to bureaucratic evaluation, although these same authors were closely connected with other U.S. evaluators, specifically Stake and House.

In fact, European evaluators stand on all sides in the *paradigm war* between positivist and constructivist that raged among U.S. evaluators. There are authors who clearly share the constructivist (as the illuminative, democratic, personalized) versus others who share the positivist (as in the synthesis movement) position. But there is also a strong group of people who take a pluralist stance and advocate mixed methods, such as Petticrew and the theory weavers. Perhaps, only realist evaluation stands alone on a terrain that overcomes this division.

The Institutional Context. We have seen the importance of different institutional contexts in the development of European evaluation theories. This may work within two different temporal dimensions. In a short-term perspective, the syntheses are a response to the Blair government's evidence-based movement.

From a long-term perspective, what matters most is the relationship to the welfare state. First of all, there is a commonality among European states that is different from the United States. Karlsson and Petersson have analyzed it this way: The United States is a market economy where it is necessary to show that there is a need for state intervention and where evaluations are outsourced to external evaluators; in Europe, the state intervention enjoys greater legitimacy, evaluations are done to improve state performance, and they are conducted by public institutions. This also explains national differences. European states can be classified according to two main institutional traditions: (1) states of a Napoleonic centralistic administrative tradition (France, Italy, Spain, and also the EU administration) and (2) states characterized by a more pragmatic, sometimes federal, tradition. People living in the former are used to receiving instructions from above, to which they have to comply; they have greater difficulty in innovating because there is supposed to be just one way of doing things, evaluation included (Karlsson & Petersson, 2006). It is by no accident that most of the original thinkers we have talked about did not come from these situations. And this also shows the merits of the theory weavers, who have helped the European evaluation community engage in a cross-European dialogue that could benefit people irrespective of their institutional context, leaving them to adapt the new thinking to their situations.

NOTES

1. The origin of this chapter is a debate held in Stockholm (June 2006) and later in London at the European Evaluation Society (EES) conference (October 2006) under the coordination of Ove Karlsson and Gustav Petersson, with the participation of Marvin Alkin, Christina Christie, Frans Leeuw, Jan Eric Furubo, Reinhard Stockmann, Evert Vedung, and myself. The debate hinged on the question of what a European evaluation tree would look like: Some participants, maintaining that Europeans are more importers than exporters of ideas, suggested that beyond a branch called "discourse" (which would have looked like the American one but less populated), there should be two other branches: (1) "institutions for evaluation" and (2) "evaluation practices."

2. Thanks to Barbara Befani for coining this term.

3. MacDonald and Walker (1977) in their plea for the case study add to the usual advantages and concerns an interesting note on the case study as art, in the sense of "the artist, who achieves greatness when, through the portrayal of a single instance locked in time and circumstance, he communicates enduring truths about the human condition" (p. 182).

4. Vedung (1998) traces this typology back to Etzioni's distinction between coercive, remunerative, and normative power.

5. Pawson and Tilley consider themselves scientific realists and refer to authors such as Bashkar and Harrè. Julnes et al. (1998), while being appreciative of their application of realism to evaluation, contend that they could have utilized other brands of realism, namely, critical realism.

6. Among the examples of mechanisms, Pawson also includes Vedung's policy instruments.

7. Pawson (2010) builds on Merton's middle-range theories.

8. For a story of this movement, from Cochrane onward, see Oakley et al. (2005). References to the many centers working in this field are also provided by Petticrew and Roberts (2006).

9. "Academic culture supports the proliferation of small-scale research projects that are often strikingly parochial and lack international vision and any sense of connectedness with one another" (Oakley et al., 2005, p. 21).

10. The program lasted a few years, with presentations at EES conferences and ad hoc meetings organized by the DG Regio. It was realized by the Centre for European Evaluation Expertise (C3E) under the direction of Eric Monnier and Jacques Toulemonde, who are the authors of the Guide. It was supervised by Philippe Goybet and Angel Benito Alonso of DG Regio.

11. The EVALSED Guide has been prepared by the Tavistock Institute, in association with GHK and Istituto per la Ricerca Sociale (IRS); its main author is Elliot Stern. It is available online (http://ec.europa.eu/regional_policy/sources/docgener/evaluation/evalsed/index_en.htm) and is open to further additions. A new chapter on evaluation tools has been added in 2010: The author is Alberto Martini.

12. The Lisbon agenda set the goals for 2010, stating that Europe should have become "the most competitive and dynamic knowledge-based economy in 2010, capable of sustainable economic growth, with more and better jobs and greater social cohesion."

REFERENCES

Abma, T. (Ed.). (2001). Special issue: Dialogue in evaluation. *Evaluation, 7*(2), 155–280.

Alkin, M. (2004). *Evaluation roots.* Thousand Oaks, CA: Sage.

Bemelmans-Videc, M. L., Rist, R., & Vedung, E. (1998). *Carrots, sticks and sermons.* New Brunswick, NJ: Transaction Books.

Campbell, D. (1969). Reforms as experiments. *American Psychologist, 24,* 409–429.

Crozier, M. (1988). *Comment réformer l'Etat? Trois pays, trois stratégies: Suède, Japon, Etats-Unis.* Paris, France: La documentation française.

Dente, B. (1982). L'analisi dell'efficacia delle politiche pubbliche: Problemi di teoria e di metodo. *Rivista Trimestrale di Scienza dell'Amministrazione, 3–4,* 3–43.

Derlien, H.-U. (1990). Genesis and structure of evaluation efforts. In R. Rist (Ed.), *Program evaluation and the management of government* (pp. 146–176). New Brunswick, NJ: Transaction Books.

European Community, DG Regional Policy. (1999). *The MEANS guide.* Luxembourg: Author.

Feinstein, O. (1998). Review of *Realistic Evaluation. Evaluation, 4*(2), 243–246.

General Accounting Office. (1992). *Evaluation syntheses.* Washington, DC: Author.

Hansen, M. B., & Vedung, E. (2010). Theory-based stakeholder evaluation. *American Journal of Evaluation, 31*(3), 295–313.

Julnes, G., Mark, M. M., & Henry, G. T. (1998). Promoting realism in evaluation: Realistic evaluation and the broader context. *Evaluation, 4*(4), 483–504.

Karlsson, O. (1996). A critical dialogue in evaluation: How can the interaction between evaluation and politics be tackled? *Evaluation, 2*(4), 405–416.

Karlsson, O. (2001). Critical dialogue: Its value and meaning. *Evaluation, 7*(2), 211–227.

Karlsson, O., & Petersson, G. (2006). *Evaluation roots in the USA and in Europe. Tracing traditions?* Stockholm, Sweden: Mälardalen Evaluation Academy.

Kushner, S. (2000). *Personalizing evaluation.* London, England: Sage.

MacDonald, B. (1977). A political classification of evaluation studies in education. In D. Hamilton, D. Jenkins, C. King, B. MacDonald, & M. Parlett (Eds.), *Beyond the numbers game: A reader in educational evaluation* (pp. 224–227). London, England: Macmillan.

MacDonald, B., & Walker, R. (1977). Case-study and the social philosophy of educational research. In D. Hamilton, D. Jenkins, C. King, B. MacDonald, & M. Parlett (Eds.), *Beyond the numbers game: A reader in educational evaluation* (pp. 181–189). London, England: Macmillan Education.

Oakley, A. (2000). *Experiments in knowing*. New York, NY: New Press.

Oakley, A., Gough, D., Oliver, S., & Thomas, J. (2005). The politics of evidence and methodology: Lessons from the EPPI-Centre. *Evidence and Policy, 1*(1), 5–31.

Palumbo, D. J. (Ed.). (1987). *The politics of program evaluation*. London, England: Sage.

Parlett, M., & Hamilton, D. (1977). Evaluation as illumination: A new approach to the study of innovatory programs. In D. Hamilton, D. Jenkins, C. King, B. MacDonald, & M. Parlett (Eds.), *Beyond the numbers game: A reader in educational evaluation* (pp. 6–22). London, England: Macmillan.

Pawson, R. (1989). *A measure for measures*. London, England: Routledge.

Pawson, R. (2006). *Evidence-based policy: A realist perspective*. London, England: Sage.

Pawson, R. (2010). Middle range theory and program theory evaluation: From provenance to practice. In J. Vaessen & F. L. Leeuw (Eds.), *Mind the gap: Perspectives on policy evaluation and the social sciences* (pp. 171–202). New Brunswick, NJ: Transaction Books.

Pawson, R., & Tilley, N. (1997). *Realistic evaluation*. London, England: Sage.

Petticrew, M., & Roberts, H. (2006). *Systematic reviews in the social sciences*. Oxford, England: Blackwell.

Pollitt, C. (1998). Evaluation in Europe: Boom or bubble? *Evaluation, 4*(2), 214–224.

Stake, R. (1989). *Quieting reform*. Urbana-Champaign: University of Illinois Press.

Stame, N. (2006). The European project, federalism and evaluation. *Evaluation, 14*(2), 115–138.

Stame, N. (2010). What does not work? Three failures and many answers. *Evaluation, 16*(4), 1–17.

Stern, E. (1995). Editorial. *Evaluation, 1*(1), 5–9.

Tavistock Institute, in association with GHK and IRS. (2003). *The evaluation of socio-economic development*. Retrieved from http://ec.europa.eu/regional_policy/sources/docgener/evaluation/evalsed/guide/index_en.htm

Vedung, E. (1997). *Public policy and program evaluation*. New Brunswick, NJ: Transaction Books.

Vedung, E. (1998). Policy instruments: Typologies and theories. In M. L. Bemelmans-Videc, R. Rist, & E. Vedung (Eds.), *Carrots, sticks and sermons* (pp. 21–58). New Brunswick, NJ: Transaction Books.

29

AUSTRALIAN AND NEW ZEALAND EVALUATION THEORISTS

Patricia J. Rogers and E. Jane Davidson

Australia and New Zealand have a long and rich history of evaluation theory and practice. Drawing eclectically from evaluation theory from across the world, evaluation theorists have developed original new theories about how evaluation can and should be undertaken, which have been described as a "distillation of the old, wellspring of the new" (Kemmis, McTaggart, & Caulley, 1991). While many of the major Australasian evaluation theorists have studied or worked in the United States or the United Kingdom, many have drawn from European philosophers and theorists, and from Australasian thinking more generally. From these roots, and from their evaluation practice, a rich variety of evaluation theories have developed—more than can be included in this chapter. Other theoretical developments can be found in publications and conference proceedings of the Australasian Evaluation Society (AES; http://www.aes.asn.au) and the Aotearoa New Zealand Evaluation Association (anzea; http://www.anzea.org.nz) and in specific books and articles (e.g., Lunt, Davidson, & McKegg, 2003; Ryan, 2003; Trotman, 2003).

In this chapter, we have focused on three areas where the theories developed in Australia and New Zealand might be particularly useful for a broader audience. In terms of use, we discuss theories that conceptualize evaluation as an ongoing system of processes rather than as a discrete event. This incorporates theories about how practitioners can incorporate evaluative inquiry into their work and how evaluation can support ongoing program delivery and management, including using program theory. In terms of values, we discuss theories about how to articulate, negotiate, and include the different values that stakeholders bring to an evaluation. This includes theories about putting the values of the intended beneficiaries at the heart of an evaluation, incorporating Indigenous values in an evaluation, and ensuring evaluative synthesis in an evaluation. Many theories about methods flow on from these positions on use and values. In addition, we explore how concepts and methods from systems theory can be incorporated into evaluation, how diverse evidence from multiple evaluations can be synthesized, how rigorous impact evaluation needs to address multiple aspects of evaluation, and how evaluators can negotiate with stakeholders about appropriate methods.

HISTORICAL AND SOCIAL CONTEXT

There are particular reasons why Australia and New Zealand have been the origins of theories in these areas. Whereas in the United States, evaluation "grew up in the projects," as Michael Patton (1994) puts it, with most evaluations focused on evaluating federally funded projects to test models of delivery for upscaling, in Australia and New Zealand, evaluation "grew up in the programs," focused on evaluating ongoing programs and seen as a fundamental component of the corporate management and program-budgeting reforms in public administration in the 1980s.

This does not mean Australasian evaluation began in the 1980s. In Australia, evaluation dates back at least to a Royal Commission (government-appointed independent "blue ribbon" panel of inquiry) into public expenditure in 1918–1921. Evaluation had a clear role in program planning in state governments in the 1950s and 1960s, the first regular university course was established in 1971, and a community of practice had produced the first issue of the Australian Evaluation Newsletter in 1979 (Sharp, 2004). However, the 1988 Evaluation Strategy of the Australian federal government embedded evaluation in management practice. It emphasized management responsibility for ongoing programs rather than for short-term pilots and required all major programs to be evaluated every 5 years with published results. In New Zealand, evaluation was also an important component of public administration reforms, in particular the move during the 1980s to the contracting and outsourcing of services previously provided by government departments. This shift in government focus from outputs to outcomes fueled the demand for evaluation, particularly in the form of comparative performance information (Hawkins, 2003).

Cultural and structural reasons have increased the emphasis on the use of evaluation by service deliverers and program clients. In Australia and New Zealand, decision making is often devolved to frontline professionals, and egalitarianism is an avowed value. Frontline delivery staff are likely to have considerable control over their work—for example, teachers may develop curriculum for their classes rather than following a prescribed textbook. The credentials and status of evaluators, policymakers, and senior managers are not enough to convey credibility or ensure use. This creates a demand for evaluation that is done by staff for their own use, and many of the theoretical developments have focused on ways of undertaking this type of evaluation and ways of creating the organizational structures to support it.

This approach is strengthened by the Australasian emphasis on participation. Studies of what "quality" means have shown that, whereas in other countries this is usually understood in terms of perfection, meeting specifications, or being achieved by those with credentials, for Australasians quality is perceived "primarily in terms of the relationship they have with those around them and the organisations with which they are involved. It is more about 'who' they are than 'what' they do" (Innovation & Business Skills Australia, 2010, p. 8).

This culturally driven understanding of quality means that inclusive and participatory approaches to evaluation are more important here—not just for utilization reasons but also for validity and credibility reasons, because stakeholders will judge both the validity and the credibility of the evaluation partly in terms of the relationships with those involved and whether their own priorities and values are reflected.

The AES (which covers both countries) and the Aotearoa New Zealand Evaluation Association do not operate as industry associations of external evaluators. Along with evaluators, they have members who manage and commission evaluation, service deliverers whose professional practice includes evaluation as a responsibility rather than as a core professional identity, as well as internal and external evaluators. Many of the issues discussed at their conferences relate to evaluation as an ongoing process and as something to inform local decisions.

Both New Zealand and Australia have seen significant attention devoted to the development of evaluation approaches appropriate for working with Indigenous populations—Māori (in New Zealand) and Aboriginals and Torres Strait Islanders (in Australia). The AES has recently made it a priority to focus on Indigenous evaluation (Wehipeihana, 2008). However, important contextual issues have led to quite different approaches and advancements in each country.

In New Zealand, the Treaty of Waitangi requires all government agencies to adhere to the principles of the Treaty as the legal founding document for the country. This has led to a significant expansion of evaluation theories and approaches that align with Indigenous ways of connecting with people and developing understandings, as well as applying core concepts from the Treaty to evaluation design and evidence interpretation.

New Zealand now has a critical mass of Māori evaluators, which allows for significant practice of evaluation by Māori, for Māori, with Māori. It is no longer considered acceptable for non-Māori evaluators to lead evaluations of culturally based programs designed specifically for (or by) Māori communities. In New Zealand, the Treaty of Waitangi and the more recent concept, developed by Sir Mason Durie (2005), of "as Māori" participation have provided a unique opportunity for Māori evaluators to develop clear conceptions of what "as Māori" participation looks like as it applies to policy and programming—and to evaluate in those terms (e.g., Cram, 1997; Pipi, Wehipeihana, & McKegg, 2010). In Australia, with smaller numbers of Indigenous evaluators, the emphasis has been more on how non-Indigenous evaluators can work in culturally responsive ways (e.g., National Health and Medical Research Council, 2003; Scougall, 1997, 2006; Taylor, 2003).

We turn now to 11 particular Australasian evaluation theorists.

USE

Stephen Kemmis

In addition to completing a master's and a doctorate in education at the University of Illinois at Urbana-Champaign, Stephen Kemmis spent time in the 1970s working with the

University of Illinois at Urbana-Champaign and the Centre for Applied Research in Education at the University of East Anglia on the development of case study methods in evaluation and on democratic evaluation.

Stephen's work has focused particularly on how evaluation can be used by program staff to improve their own work. This has led to considerable development of methods that support iterative learning and doing, including participatory action research in education and management and communicative evaluation. His most frequently cited works include *Becoming Critical* (Carr & Kemmis, 1986), *The Action Research Planner (Action Research & the Critical Analysis of Pedagogy)* (Kemmis & McTaggart, 1981/1982/1988), and a chapter on "Communicative Action and the Public Sphere" (Kemmis & McTaggart, 2000, 2005).

The seven principles he developed for program evaluation in curriculum development and innovation (Kemmis, 1986) illustrate how use has been defined in terms of informed debate among interested parties rather than as an instrumental use of a finding. These principles were based on a definition of evaluation as:

> the process of marshalling information and arguments which enable interested individuals and groups to participate in the critical debate about a specific programme . . . evaluation consists in harnessing and refining the ubiquitous processes of individual and public judgment, not in resolving or replacing them with a technology of judgment. (p. 118)

In line with this definition, even formally commissioned external evaluations ought not to be intended for use solely by the sponsor:

> The evaluation of a project or programme should be regarded as a cooperative venture, not as an information service for a sponsor's own exclusive use. Sponsors should recognize that they will "co-own" the information generated by an evaluation study with other participants; and that their own role in shaping a programme is relevant in evaluating it. (Kemmis, 1986, p. 126)

Stephen's colleague Robin McTaggart has explored the difficulties of actually implementinïg this democratic approach to evaluation within the confines of government evaluation contracts (McTaggart, 1991; McTaggart & Blackmore, 1990).

Jerome A. Winston

Originally from Iowa, with undergraduate studies at MIT and graduate studies at Tufts in science and systems theory, Jerome moved to Australia in the 1960s, teaching research methods and then evaluation in human services.

During the 1980s, Jerome was seconded to the Department of Finance as they developed guidance for program managers on developing the performance indicators required, both for internal use for management and for external reporting to policymakers and funding decision makers. As enthusiasm for evaluation and for performance monitoring increased in the 1980s, Jerome came to play a cautionary role, warning of the misuse of monitoring and evaluation and the potential negative consequences (Winston, 1993, 1999).

In addition to data corruption, Jerome warned of the risks of goal displacement and gaming. Goal displacement occurs when managers and staff change their behavior in ways that achieve a stated target at the cost of actually achieving a goal—for example, selecting easier cases so that performance targets can be more easily attained. Gaming involves defining targets in ways that make it easier to achieve them—for example, timing waiting time from when an application begins to be processed rather than from when it is submitted. To address these risks, Jerome called for an end to simple reporting of univariate performance indicators as a basis for decision making and a move to incorporate evaluation questions, multiple indicators and multivariate analysis of them, commentary, and discussion (Winston, 1993, 2010). Burt Perrin (2002, 2006), a Canadian evaluator, drew on many of these issues and examples in reports Burt subsequently produced for the Organization for Economic Co-operation and Development.

Sue C. Funnell

Sue Funnell completed studies in psychology, followed by graduate studies in education (University of Sydney), including time studying with Robert Stake at the University of Illinois at Urbana-Champaign. In the mid-1980s, she was a key member of a group introducing the use of program theory (logic models) in the state government in New South Wales.

Through presentations at AES conferences in the 1980s and 1990s, her work was influential in the development of program theory in Australia and New Zealand and was picked up by an international audience when it was published in the AES magazine (Funnell, 1997) and in the American Evaluation Association's *New Directions in Evaluation* (Funnell, 2000).

One of Sue's particular contributions was developing the "program logic matrix"—a framework for helping incorporate evaluative logic into program theory. Instead of a linear version of program theory in the form of "inputs → processes → outputs → outcomes → impacts," she advocated representing program theory as a series of outcomes, each of which could have direct actions. The matrix helps articulate, for each of the outcomes in the chain of results, a description of what success looks like, program factors and nonprogram factors that are assumed to affect the outcomes, outputs and throughputs, activities, and resources. The matrix was intended to be used pragmatically rather than slavishly:

> The matrix is a thinking tool rather than an end in itself. Applying the principles discussed in this chapter and incorporated in the matrix is far more important than filling in the boxes of the matrix ... With practice, application of the principles becomes a natural part of the way of thinking about programs, and the matrix can become redundant. (Funnell & Rogers, 2011, p. 237)

To improve the quality of the theories used in program theory evaluation, Sue also developed a set of "program archetypes," or templates for different types of interventions (e.g., direct service, case management, and incentives programs), which could be used as the basis for developing specific program theories for individual programs (Funnell, 1997; Funnell & Rogers, 2011).

John M. Owen

With an original disciplinary background in physics, John Owen came to evaluation through an interest in improving science education, completing a Masters of Education and then a PhD (Monash University) studying the diffusion of education innovation.

From his experiences of explaining to students and to evaluation clients the different options for evaluation, John developed a classification framework of evaluation forms, which became the basis of his popular book on program evaluation, *Program Evaluation: Forms and Approaches* (Owen, 1993, 1999, 2006). In this book, John classified the types of knowledge produced by evaluations into five epistemological clusters, based on different purposes, (1) proactive, (2) clarificative, (3) interactive, (4) monitoring, and (5) impact, and described a number of different methods that could be used for each of these. This framework provided a helpful way for evaluation clients to better understand the match, or the lack of one, between the type of evaluation they needed and the methods being proposed by the evaluator.

The need to plan and implement evaluation to support the different uses made of it by different stakeholders has led to some new theoretical developments in terms of the role of the evaluator. John set out three key considerations in developing "a theory of negotiation" that addresses processes for identifying key players, determining what is negotiable and when negotiation should take place, and establishing reasons for negotiation (Owen, 1998). Anne Markiewicz (2005) and Diane McDonald (2008) have further developed these ideas by drawing explicitly on the research literature on mediation and conflict resolution.

VALUES

Fiona Cram

After a PhD in social and developmental psychology, leading Māori evaluator Fiona Cram (Ngāti Kahungunu)[1] built on the groundbreaking work of Linda Tuhiwai Smith, whose book *Decolonizing Methodologies: Research and Indigenous Peoples* (1999) challenged traditional research methodologies with its taking for granted of Māori language, culture, and values in research design. Fiona's work has been influential not just in New Zealand but also among Indigenous evaluators (and other evaluators working with Indigenous programs) in Hawai'i, mainland United States, and Canada.

Building on Linda Smith's *Community-Up Model*, Fiona showed how Māori concepts can be incorporated into evaluation theory and practice (Cram, 2001, 2009; Kennedy & Cram, 2010). These concepts included *Whanaungatanga* (building and maintaining relationships in the Māori context), *Manaakitanga* (respect for hosts, generosity, and genuine sharing in the research process), *Aroha* (treating people with respect on their own terms), Māhaki (sharing knowledge with humility), *Mana* (taking care to respect people's dignity), *Titiro, whakarongo . . . korero* (taking care to observe and listen before, and maybe instead of, speaking), and *Kia Tupato* (being culturally safe, politically astute, aware of their insider/outsider status, and alert to how the research or evaluation process can unravel unexpectedly).

Nan Wehipeihana

Nan Wehipeihana (Ngāti Porou, Te Whānau-a-Apanui, and Ngāti Tukorehe) came to evaluation from a marketing research background, where she primarily used quantitative methods and worked with large databases. Since moving into evaluation, Nan's work has spanned the full range, from "flax-roots" (the New Zealand term for *grassroots*) community programs through to high-level strategic policy evaluation for central government and from culturally based programs designed specifically for Māori to general population initiatives. As such, her contributions to the theory and practice of evaluation in New Zealand have reflected this ability to conceptualize evaluation using multiple levels/layers and perspectives. Her most powerful contributions to thinking and practice have been in evaluation design for Māori contexts and in the translation of policy into practice and practice into policy—primarily but not exclusively in Māori settings (Wehipeihana & McKegg, 2008).

What distinguishes Nan from many of the other evaluators working internationally in the Indigenous space is her relatively tough stance on what constitutes quality evaluation and how direct one should be about communicating findings. Nan taps into Māori communities' high expectations and aspirations for themselves and is uncompromising in her insistence that sights not be lowered nor the results softened once the findings are in, lest the sense of urgency and the aspiration to realize Māori potential be diluted.

Nan's views of who should be doing/leading evaluation with and within Māori, other Indigenous, and minority communities reflects the earlier-mentioned Australasian emphasis on the "who" being at least as important as the "what": "It is not a question of who can—theoretically all evaluators can/could—but it is a question around what is right ethically and methodologically. I believe that evaluation in Māori communities should be led by Māori" (Wehipeihana, Davidson, McKegg, & Shanker, 2010, p. 187). Nan also emphasizes the importance of cultural capital for evaluation validity, not just for credibility:

> There are some things that can't be learnt, known or explored except from within the culture. Therefore, for me it is in the sense-making process that there is no substitute for the cultural capital (understanding, knowledge, and intuit) that comes from being of the culture. (Wehipeihana et al., 2010, pp. 187–188)

E. Jane Davidson

Jane's disciplinary roots are in chemistry, astrophysics, and industrial and organizational psychology, followed by a PhD in organizational psychology (with an emphasis on evaluation). She is known for challenging the absence of the essential "evaluative judgment" component in much of evaluation work and for providing very practical ways of explicitly and defensibly incorporating values in evaluation via stepping through a conscious, inclusive, and values-driven process (Davidson, 2007, 2009, 2010).

An important implication of Jane's work is the emergence of evaluative practices that make the "values" much more clearly visible and the evaluative reasoning more systematic and transparent, in particular through the use of evaluative rubrics. In her first book, *Evaluation*

Methodology Basics (Davidson, 2004), Jane set out practical ways in which evaluative rubrics could be used to make the underlying values explicit and then to synthesize them with performance evidence to draw evaluative conclusions. This approach has now been widely used in a range of settings, including evaluations across multiple programs within a policy (Davidson & Wehipeihana, 2011; Wehipeihana & Davidson, 2010).

Evaluative rubrics and related evaluation-specific methodologies have become particularly widely used in the participatory mode. The resulting work might be termed *participatory plus*. Stakeholders have a high level of involvement in and influence on the evaluation, particularly in defining "quality" and "value" for the particular context, but the work is centered on a very clear process and methodology that help ensure that defensible conclusions are reached and evaluative capacity is built among those participating. The application of rubrics and other values-driven methods and approaches to capture Indigenous values has been spearheaded by Nan Wehipeihana and Kataraina Pipi (Pipi et al., 2010). A key emphasis of this work has been evaluation by Māori, for Māori, with Māori.

METHODS

Yoland Wadsworth

Yoland Wadsworth's disciplinary background is in sociology, including a PhD studying sociologists at work in academic and social policy–oriented settings. She began her research undertaking quantitative social surveys in the suburban areas of Melbourne but has become better known for her contributions to collaborative and participatory approaches to evaluation.

Her first book, *Do It Yourself Social Research* (Wadsworth, 1997, 2011a), set out methods that even small community groups and nongovernmental organizations could use to plan, undertake, and use social research, including evaluative needs assessment, before a program begins. Her second book, *Everyday Evaluation on the Run* (Wadsworth, 1998, 2011b), focused more specifically on evaluation and on the enduring gap in evaluation theory, which is mostly about external evaluators undertaking a discrete evaluation. Yoland described how organizations could build in the ongoing internal evaluative processes needed for effective programs and organizations. She argued that these processes needed to be embedded within the reiterative spiral of planning, delivering, reporting, and continuous quality improvement and built into the rhythms of the organization. A comprehensive program of built-in evaluation (Wadsworth, 1998, p. 57) comprises opportunities for daily informal personal reflection, the reflections spanning each week; special-effort evaluations of particular aspects of practice or activities; monthly collective problem-pooling sessions; annual "what-have-we-achieved" and "where-are-we-heading-next" workshops; and comprehensive program "stock-takes" every 3 to 10 years or more.

Program recipients are often not considered as potential users of evaluation, but they can make use of evaluation processes and findings to inform their selection of services (or decision about whether or not to engage in a service where they don't have a choice of provider) and to inform their actions as cocreators of practice. In a 10-year project of consumer evaluation that began in a single ward of an acute psychiatric hospital, and eventually extended to all mental health services across the state of Victoria (Wadsworth & Epstein, 1994, 1996a, 1996b, 2001), working with some of the most marginalized consumers of human services, Yoland developed methods to put the values of the "critical reference group" (the intended beneficiaries) at the center of an evaluation and to meet their needs for evaluation findings and processes. The project not only gathered consumer feedback but also engaged consumers in supporting dialogue between staff and consumers to make sense of the feedback and to work toward making the consequent, relevant, and appropriate changes to hospital practices. At the heart of these changes was co-inquiry by consumers and staff—"getting to know each other and each other's purposes and intentions. Only when this basic mutual knowing existed could trust become a basis for effective shared action" (Wadsworth, 2010, pp. 15–16).

In her third book, *Building in Research and Evaluation: Human Inquiry for Living Systems* (Wadsworth, 2010), Yoland brought together these different strands to set out methods for both studying change and helping to bring about change by using methods that take account of the personal, social, and organizational systems in which inquiry and action occur. The book outlined four strategies needed to build in research and evaluation in organizations:

1. Enhance everyday inquiry capabilities.

2. Create concrete ways for person/people systems to meet and inquire together as critical inquirers.

3. Ensure ways to collect and share information, reflect, and generate new knowledge.

4. Continue inquiring through action and facilitate learning about how to inquire ever more deeply and widely.

Adrienne Alton-Lee

Adrienne Alton-Lee's key intellectual influences were from her studies of the philosophy of science, particularly the realist philosophy of science.

Adrienne is the chief education advisor for the New Zealand Ministry of Education's Best Evidence Synthesis (BES) program, a series of systematic reviews and syntheses of the evidence about a range of educational interventions (Alton-Lee, 2004, 2007). The BES methodology has gained international recognition for its ability to include the full range of credible and relevant research and evaluation evidence—as expressed in this quote from Luke and Hogan (2006) in the *World Yearbook of Education*:

> What is distinctive about the New Zealand approach is its willingness to consider all forms of research evidence regardless of methodological paradigms and ideological rectitude, and its concern in finding contextually effective, appropriate and locally powerful examples of "what works." Its focus is on capturing and examining the impact of local contextual variables (e.g., population, school, community, linguistic and cultural variables). (p. 174)

The BES methodology provides guidance for planning and then scoping a BES "iteration" (a synthesis completed at one point in time but destined to be revised and updated over time), ensuring transparency of approach, identifying and retrieving relevant evidence, evaluating and then analyzing the evidence, synthesizing the evidence, and then writing up the synthesis. To date, a total of eight BES iterations have been completed, each following the same transparent methodology and presented with user-friendly language that is accessible to a broad audience.

A key feature of the BES process is that iterations are developed not just by academics and content experts. When looking in particular at synthesizing findings relevant to Māori and Pasifika learners, a "partnership model" pairs academic experts with those who have deep cultural and contextual expertise and an experiential knowledge of what works in practice for those learners.

Bob Williams

Originally trained in ecology and systems thinking in the United Kingdom, Bob's distinction between "evaluation capacity" (stored resources) and "evaluation capability" (stored resources and an ability to deploy them) has been very influential in Australasia. "All the skills, knowledge, technical expertise and experience in the world won't help an evaluation if the capability of the program, community, organisation or environment cannot sustain and nurture those skills, and abilities" (Williams, 2001, p. 1). The major focus of Bob's work has been on linking systems science and evaluation, building on the earlier work of Jerome Winston, Yoland Wadsworth, and Keith Linard. He was instrumental in establishing the AEA "Systems in Evaluation" Topical Interest Group, which brought together a critical mass of people interested in exploring these methods. Bob then bridged the two communities of systems and evaluation, bringing systems researchers into evaluation publications and sessions at AEA conferences and introducing many evaluators to their ideas.

The W. K. Kellogg Foundation funded the development of a book on systems methods in evaluation, edited by Bob Williams and Iraj Iman (2007) and published by the AEA. In addition to the individual chapters on specific methods, the project brought together the authors to discuss common issues across systems approaches. At this meeting, they built on Gerald Midgley's overview chapter on three waves of systems approaches and identified three concepts—interrelationships, perspective, and boundaries.

In later work, Bob added evaluation questions to the principles and methods, developing a framework that makes systems approaches both relevant and accessible (Williams & Hummelbrunner, 2010). Bob developed a list of questions, each of which related to particular systems approaches (Williams, 2008):

- Interrelationships

  What is the structure of the interrelationships within a situation?

  What are the processes between the elements of that structure?

What is the nature of the interrelationships (e.g., strong, weak, fast, slow, conflicted, collaborative, direct, or indirect)?

What are the patterns that emerge from these interrelationships in action and with what consequences and for whom?

Why does this matter? To whom? In what context?

- Perspectives

Who or what are the key stakeholders within the situation?

What are the key stakes within a situation?

What are the different ways in which a situation can be framed?

How are these different framings going to affect the way in which stakeholders act within a situation, especially when things go wrong from their perspective?

- Boundaries

Which interrelationships are privileged, and which are marginalized? With what effect and on whom?

Which perspectives (i.e., stakeholders, stakes, framings) are privileged and which are marginalized? With what effect and on whom?

How can the ethical, political, and practical consequences of these decisions be managed, especially those decisions that cause harm or have the potential to cause harm because of the exclusion of an interrelationship or perspective?

Patricia J. Rogers

Patricia's original disciplinary background was in political sociology (and medieval European languages), followed by a PhD in evaluation, developing a conceptual and methodological framework for evaluating approaches to program evaluation, and a postdoctoral fellowship with Carol Weiss at Harvard University.

Her research has focused on developing and selecting methods suitable for the particular purposes and situation of an evaluation. She has highlighted the assumptions that underpin different evaluation methods about how organizations work (Rogers & Hough, 1995), discussed how different evaluation methods would be appropriate for different types of development interventions and evaluation purposes (Rogers, 2009), and suggested how organizations can develop their capabilities to engage in appropriate types of evaluation (McDonald, Rogers, & Kefford, 2003).

Much of her work has focused on the use of program theory (logic models) in evaluation. Most recently, she has explored how program theory can be used for evaluation in ways that address the complicated and complex aspects of programs. Distinguishing between what is complicated (having many components) and what is complex (emergent and adaptive), she has discussed implications for program theory and evaluation, generally covering seven issues: (1) governance, (2) focus, (3) consistency, (4) sufficiency, (5) necessariness, (6) change trajectory, and (7) unintended outcomes (Funnell & Rogers, 2011; Rogers, 2008).

NOTE

1. As is customary in New Zealand, we have listed tribal affiliations for key Māori theorists.

REFERENCES

Alton-Lee, A. (2004). *Guidelines for generating a Best Evidence Synthesis iteration.* Wellington, New Zealand: Ministry of Education. Retrieved from http://www.educationcounts.govt.nz/topics/BES

Alton-Lee, A. (2007). The iterative best evidence synthesis programme: Collaborative knowledge building and use across research, policy and practice in education. In *Evidence in education: Linking research and policy.* Paris, France: Organisation for Economic Co-operation and Development.

Carr, W., & Kemmis, S. (1986). *Becoming critical: Education, knowledge and action research.* Lewes, DE: Falmer Press.

Cram, F. (1997, Spring). Developing partnerships in research: Päkeha researchers and Mäori researchers. *SITES, 35,* 44–63.

Cram, F. (2001). Rangahau Māori: Tona Tika, Tona Pono. In M. Tolich (Ed.), *Research ethics in Aotearoa* (pp. 35–52). Auckland, New Zealand: Longman.

Cram, F. (2009). Maintaining Indigenous voices. In D. M. Mertens & P. E. Ginsberg (Eds.), *The handbook of social research ethics.* Thousand Oaks, CA: Sage.

Davidson, E. J. (2004). *Evaluation methodology basics: The nuts and bolts of sound evaluation.* Thousand Oaks, CA: Sage.

Davidson, E. J. (2007). Unlearning some of our social scientist habits. *Journal of Multidisciplinary Evaluation, 4*(8), iii–vi.

Davidson, E. J. (2009, November). *Improving evaluation questions and answers: Getting actionable answers for real-world decision makers.* Paper presented at the 2009 Conference of the American Evaluation Association, Orlando, FL. Retrieved from http://comm.eval.org/EVAL/EVAL/Resources/ViewDocument/Default.aspx?DocumentKey=e5bac388-f1e6-45ab-9e78-10e60cea0666

Davidson, E. J. (2010). "Process values" and "deep values" in evaluation. *Journal of Multidisciplinary Evaluation, 6*(13), 206–208.

Davidson, E. J., & Wehipeihana, N. (2011, February). *Credible evidence of effectiveness for Māori learners: An introduction to the Measurable Gains Framework and related rubrics.* Paper presented at the National PLD Facilitator Training, Auckland, New Zealand.

Durie, M. (2005). *Ngā Tai Matatū: Tides of Māori endurance.* Melbourne, Victoria, Australia: Oxford University Press.

Funnell, S. C. (1997). Program logic: An adaptable tool for designing and evaluating programs. *Evaluation News and Comment, 6*(1), 5–12.

Funnell, S. C. (2000). Developing and using a program theory matrix for program evaluation and performance monitoring. In P. J. Rogers, A. J. Petrosino, T. Hacsi, & T. A. Huebner (Eds.), *New Directions for Evaluation: Vol. 87. Program theory in evaluation: Challenges and opportunities.* San Francisco, CA: Jossey-Bass.

Funnell, S. C., & Rogers, P. J. (2011). *Purposeful program theory.* San Francisco, CA: Jossey-Bass.

Hawkins, P. (2003). Contracting evaluation: A tender topic. In N. Lunt, C. Davidson, & K. McKegg (Eds.), *Evaluating policy and practice: A New Zealand reader* (pp. 48–57). Auckland, New Zealand: Pearson.

Innovation & Business Skills Australia. (2010). *Australian cultural imprints at work: 2010 and beyond.* Retrieved from http://www.ibsa.org.au/Portals/ibsa.org.au/docs/Project%20Related/Business%20Services/leadership%20and%20produtivity%20reports/IBSA%20REPORT%20-%20Cultral%20Imprints.pdf

Kemmis, S. (1986). Seven principles for programme evaluation in curriculum development and innovation. In E. R. House (Ed.), *New directions in educational evaluation* (pp. 117–142). Oxford, England: RoutledgeFalmer.

Kemmis, S., & McTaggart, R. (1981/1982/1988). *The action research planner* (1st/2nd/3rd ed.). Geelong, Victoria, Australia: Deakin University Press.

Kemmis, S., & McTaggart, R. (2000). Participatory action research: Communicative action and the public sphere. In N. Denzin & Y. Lincoln (Eds.), *Handbook of qualitative research* (2nd ed., pp. 567–607). Thousand Oaks, CA: Sage.

Kemmis, S., & McTaggart, R. (2005). Participatory action research: Communicative action and the public sphere. In N. Denzin & Y. Lincoln (Eds.), *Handbook of qualitative research* (3rd ed., pp. 559–604). Thousand Oaks, CA: Sage.

Kemmis, S., McTaggart, R., & Caulley, D. (1991). Evaluation traditions in Australia: Distillation of the old, wellspring of the new. *Evaluation and Program Planning, 14,* 122–130.

Kennedy, V., & Cram, F. (2010). *Ethics of researching with Whānau Collectives* (MAI Review 3). Retrieved from http://review.mai.ac.nz/index.php/MR/article/view/381/560

Luke, A., & Hogan, D. (2006). Steering educational research in national contexts: The Singapore model. In D. Coulby, J. Ozga, T. Popkewitz, & T. Seddon (Eds.), *World yearbook of education: Educational research and policy* (pp. 170–184). Edinburgh, Scotland: Edinburgh University Press.

Lunt, N., Davidson, C., & McKegg, K. (Eds). (2003). *Evaluating policy and practice: A New Zealand reader.* Auckland, New Zealand: Pearson Education.

Markiewicz, A. (2005). A balancing act: Resolving multiple stakeholder interests in program evaluation. *Evaluation Journal of Australasia, 4*(1–2), 13–21.

McDonald, B., Rogers, P. J., & Kefford, B. (2003). Teaching people to fish? Building the evaluation capability of public sector organizations. *Evaluation, 9*(1), 9–29. Retrieved from http://www.stes-apes.med.ulg.ac.be/Documents_electroniques/EVA/EVA-GEN/ELE%20EVA-GEN%207568.pdf

McDonald, D. E. (2008). Revisiting a theory of negotiation: The utility of Markiewicz' (2005) proposed six principles. *Evaluation and Program Planning, 740, 31*(3), 259–265.

McTaggart, R. (1991). When democratic evaluation doesn't seem democratic. *Evaluation Practice, 12*(1), 9–21.

McTaggart, R., & Blackmore, J. (1990). Government control of evaluation research. *Evaluation Journal of Australasia, 2*(3), 29–40.

National Health and Medical Research Council. (2003). *Values and ethics: Guidelines for ethical conduct in Aboriginal and Torres Strait Islander research.* Retrieved from http://www.nhmrc.gov.au/guidelines/publications/e52

Owen, J. M. (1993). *Program evaluation: Forms and approaches* (1st ed.). St Leonards, New South Wales, Australia: Allen & Unwin.

Owen, J. M. (1998). Towards a theory of negotiation in evaluation. *Evaluation News and Comment, 7*(2), 32–35.

Owen, J. M. (1999). *Program evaluation: Forms and approaches* (2nd ed.). St Leonards, New South Wales, Australia: Allen & Unwin.

Owen, J. M. (2006). *Program evaluation: Forms and approaches* (3rd ed.). St Leonards, New South Wales, Australia: Allen & Unwin.

Patton, M. Q. (1994). Developmental evaluation. *American Journal of Evaluation, 15,* 311–319.

Perrin, B. (2002). *Implementing the vision: Addressing challenges to results-focused management and budgeting.* Paris, France: Organisation for Economic Co-operation and Development.

Perrin, B. (2006). *Moving from outputs to outcomes: Practical advice from governments around the world*. Washington, DC: IBM Center for the Business of Government. Retrieved from http://siteresources.worldbank.org/CDFINTRANET/Resources/PerrinReport.pdf

Pipi, K., Wehipeihana, N., & McKegg, K. (2010). *Grappling with uncertainty in innovative and complex settings: Weaving quality in developmental evaluation*. Paper presented at the American Evaluation Association conference, San Antonio, TX. Retrieved from http://comm.eval.org/multiethnicissuesinevaluation/resources/viewdocument/?DocumentKey=ed18dee1-6d66-46f9-83eb-8d5e1df8fc70

Rogers, P. J. (2008). Using programme theory for complicated and complex programmes. *Evaluation, 14*(1), 29–48. Retrieved from http://www.rismes.it/pdf/rogers_complex.pdf

Rogers, P. J. (2009). Matching impact evaluation design to the nature of the intervention and the purpose of the evaluation. *Journal of Development Effectiveness, 1*(3), 217–226.

Rogers, P. J., & Hough, G. (1995). Improving the effectiveness of evaluations: Making the link to organizational theory. *Evaluation and Program Planning, 18*(4), 321–332.

Ryan, B. (2003). Death by evaluation? Reflections on monitoring and evaluation in Australia and New Zealand. *Evaluation Journal of Australasia, 3*(1), 6–16.

Scougall, J. (1997). Giving voice: The conduct of evaluation research in Aboriginal contexts. *Evaluation Journal of Australasia, 9*(1–2), 53–60.

Scougall, J. (2006). Reconciling tensions between principles and practice in indigenous evaluation. *Evaluation Journal of Australasia, 6*(2), 49–55.

Sharp, C. A. (2004). Development of program evaluation in Australasia and the Australasian Evaluation Society: The early decades. *Evaluation Journal of Australasia, 3*(2), 6–16.

Smith, L. T. (1999). *Decolonizing methodologies: Research and indigenous peoples*. London, England: Zed Books.

Taylor, R. (2003). An indigenous perspective on evaluations in the inter-cultural context: How far can one throw a Moree boomerang? *Evaluation Journal of Australasia, 3*(2), 44–52.

Trotman, I., (2003). Evaluation in New Zealand: A founder's reflection. In N. Lunt, C. Davidson, & K. McKegg (Eds.), *Evaluating policy and practice: A New Zealand reader* (pp. 21–26). Auckland, New Zealand: Pearson.

Wadsworth, Y. (1997). *Do it yourself social research* (1st ed.). St Leonards, New South Wales: Allen & Unwin.

Wadsworth, Y. (1998). *Everyday evaluation on the run* (1st ed.). St Leonards, New South Wales, Australia: Allen & Unwin.

Wadsworth, Y. (2010). *Building in research and evaluation: Human inquiry for living systems*. St Leonards, New South Wales, Australia: Allen & Unwin.

Wadsworth, Y. (2011a). *Do it yourself social research (3rd ed.)*. St Leonards, New South Wales: Allen & Unwin.

Wadsworth, Y. (2011b). *Everyday evaluation on the run* (3rd ed.). St Leonards, New South Wales, Australia: Allen & Unwin.

Wadsworth, Y., & Epstein, M. (1994). *Understanding and involvement: Vol. 1. Consumer evaluation of acute psychiatric hospital practice: A project begins*. Melbourne, Victoria, Australia: Victorian Mental Illness Awareness Council.

Wadsworth, Y., & Epstein, M. (1996a). *Understanding and involvement: Vol. 2. Consumer evaluation of acute psychiatric hospital practice: A project unfolds*. Melbourne, Victoria, Australia: Victorian Mental Illness Awareness Council.

Wadsworth, Y., & Epstein, M. (1996b). *Understanding and involvement: Vol. 3. Consumer evaluation of acute psychiatric hospital practice: A project concludes*. Melbourne, Victoria, Australia: Victorian Mental Illness Awareness Council.

Wadsworth, Y., & Epstein, M. (2001). *The Essential U&I: A one-volume presentation of the findings of a lengthy grounded study of whole systems change towards staff-consumer collaboration for enhancing mental health services.* Carlton South, Victoria, Australia: VicHealth.

Wehipeihana, N. (2008). Indigenous evaluation: A strategic objective of the Australasian evaluation society. *Evaluation Journal of Australasia, 8*(1), 40–44.

Wehipeihana, N., & Davidson, E. J. (2010, May). *Strategic policy evaluation: Answering macro-level cross-project questions.* Paper presented at the anzea Wellington Regional Symposium, Wellington, New Zealand. Retrieved from http://realevaluation.com/strategic-policy-evaluation-anzea-session-handout/

Wehipeihana, N., Davidson, E. J., McKegg, K., & Shanker, V. (2010). What does it take to do evaluation in communities and cultural contexts other than our own? *Journal of MultiDisciplinary Evaluation, 16*(13), 182–192.

Wehipeihana, N., & McKegg, K. (2008). *Indigenous values: Adding value to evaluation practice.* Paper presented at the Australasian Evaluation Society Conference, Perth, Western Australia, Australia.

Williams, B. (2001). *Building evaluation capability.* Retrieved from http://www.bobwilliams.co.nz/Works_in_Progress_files/capability%233.pdf

Williams, B. (2008). *Using systems concepts to navigate complexity.* Paper presented at Wageningen University. Retrieved from http://users.actrix.co.nz/bobwill/Systems_Intro.pdf

Williams, B., & Hummelbrunner, R. (2010). *Systems concepts in action: A practitioner's toolkit.* Stanford, CA: Stanford University Press.

Williams, B., & Imam, I. (2007). *Systems concepts in evaluation: An expert anthology.* Point Reyes, CA: EdgePress/American Evaluation Association.

Winston, J. (1993). Performance indicators: Do they perform? *Evaluation News and Comment, 2*(3), 22–29.

Winston, J. (1999). Performance indicators–promises unmet: A response to Perrin. *American Journal of Evaluation, 20*(1), 95–99.

Winston, J. (2010). *Reflecting on goal displacement and gaming.* Paper presented at the Conference of the Australasian Evaluation Society, Wellington, New Zealand. Retrieved from http://www.aes.asn.au/conferences/2010/Presentations/Winston,%20Jerome.pdf

※ 30 ※

EVALUATION THEORY

A Wider Roots Perspective

Marvin C. Alkin, Christina A. Christie, and Anne T. Vo

In this chapter, we will start with the evaluation theory tree presented in Chapter 2 and seek to introduce a wider perspective to the evaluation theory tree. We will do this by incorporating theorists from Europe and Australasia. In Chapter 28, Nicoletta Stame has presented an excellent description of the underlying themes of evaluation in Europe and those who have prominently participated in defining and elaborating evaluation there. Likewise, in Chapter 29, Patricia Rogers and Jane Davidson have presented a description of major evaluation writers in Australia and New Zealand.

Many distinguished evaluation writers have been identified in these two excellent chapters, and in most instances, the authors have attempted to portray the potential location of each of the authors on the evaluation theory tree. Indeed, the authors have presented us with a bit of a dilemma by the thoroughness of their work. Many evaluation writers have been identified, and we have to be judicious in determining who is to be included on the theory tree. Again, we return to the distinction presented in Chapter 1 about our definition of "theorists." As the reader will recall, we distinguished between individuals who had contributed to basic research methodology related to evaluation—whom we defined as "methodologists"—and other evaluation writers who had written cogently about particular evaluation issues or topics—whom we considered as "evaluation issue analysts"—and those individuals whom we considered "evaluation interpreters and teachers." We reserved the category of "theorists" for those who had presented a full and unique theoretical exposition of prescribed evaluation practice—namely, a prescriptive theory of evaluation.

It is within these guidelines that we have analyzed the European and Australasian chapters to select individuals for inclusion on the evaluation theory tree. In the remainder of this chapter,

---

Authors' Note: The authors thank Ernest House and Michael Patton for their helpful comments.

we will discuss European and Australasian theorists whom we have chosen to include on the tree, indicate their placement on a branch of the tree, and provide our rationale for choosing to include them. Some note will be made of those whom we have chosen not to include and the rationale for our decision.

As a further note, we offer an additional insight into our inclusion criteria. We readily admit to not being expert analysts of European or Australasian evaluation theorists and their theories. Thus, while there may be other individuals potentially worthy of being represented on the tree, we have used the authors identified in the two preceding chapters as our starting point and then applied the above-noted inclusion criteria. For the most part, we will not attempt to replicate the description of the theorists' work that is presented in the two preceding chapters.

Furthermore, as in Chapter 2, the decision about placement of theorists is enormously difficult. In some cases, we made the decision quite easily. For other individuals, we engaged in extended debate over many hours to reach a placement decision. This was especially true for some theorists for whom we could make a case for placement on either the Use or the Valuing branch of the tree.

EUROPE

There are many early roots of evaluation theory development in Europe. As Nicoletta Stame has noted, these writings were particularly evident in the United Kingdom and in Sweden and other Scandinavian countries. In the Scandinavian countries, these earlier writings about evaluation emanated from the strong democratic traditions of those countries. Early theoretical work in the United Kingdom reflected both a democratic vision of evaluation and, somewhat later, a philosophical realist point of view.

Let us start first with a consideration of the early democratic writings from the United Kingdom, which originated from criticism of so-called mainstream evaluation. This criticism and reaction to the traditional, "scientific" orientation to evaluation mirrored the counterpart theory development within the United States. As Nicoletta Stame has described, its main concern is description and interpretation, and it is intended to enlighten by clarifying the processes of evaluation. Parlett and Hamilton's procedures of observing, inquiring further, and then seeking general principles are in many ways comparable with Stake's responsive evaluation. Thus, we would emphatically place Malcom Parlett and David Hamilton's "illuminative evaluation" as a prescriptive theory appropriate for inclusion on the Valuing branch of the evaluation theory tree (see Figure 30.1).

A similar early effort at democratizing evaluation was propounded by Barry MacDonald. MacDonald recognizes the multiplicity of perspectives held by stakeholders and believes that the evaluator's duty is to present the values of differing stakeholders. MacDonald distinguishes between what he calls "types" of evaluation and advocates for the use of democratic evaluations as a means of portraying multiple realities with "justice and truth." We have placed MacDonald on the Valuing branch of the tree.

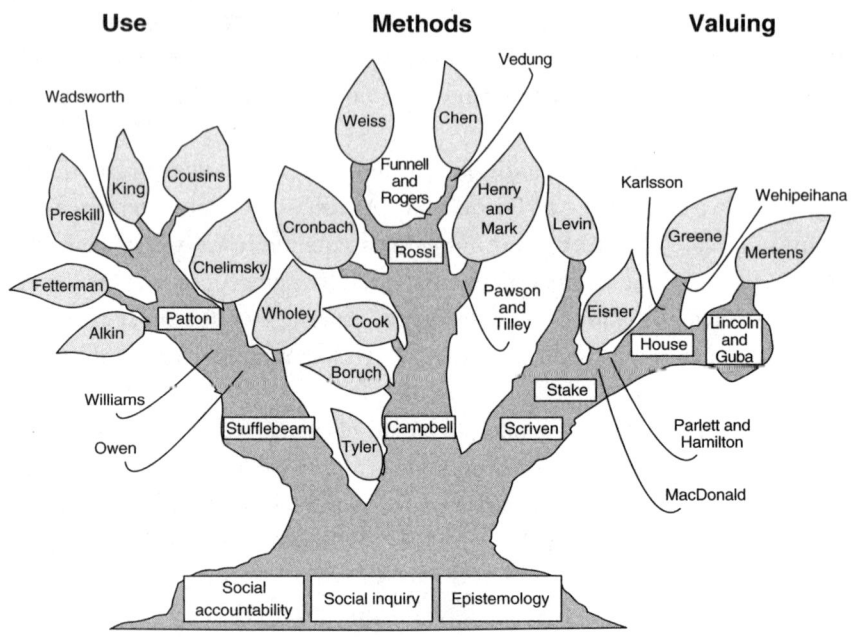

Figure 30.1 Evaluation Theory Tree: A Wider Perspective

Ove Karlsson (1996), out of a concern for allowing the voices of evaluation stakeholders to be heard in a more socially just way, developed dialogue procedures to be employed in the conduct of evaluations. The idea of critical dialogue is not in and of itself a theory, but we feel that the elaboration and description of three distinct phases approached a prescription (Karlsson, 2001). We have placed Karlsson on the Valuing branch.

Another Swedish writer, Evert Vedung, is credited by Nicoletta Stame as being the author of perhaps the first European evaluation text. Vedung is concerned about policy evaluation and has expounded about the multiple instruments at hand for conducting policy evaluation. Vedung's work focuses on methods and "the extrapolation of findings to other contexts," primarily enhanced by the use of program theory. He complements this by recognizing the role of stakeholders in the process, which is in line with Swedish democratic traditions (Hansen & Vedung, 2010). We have placed Vedung on the Methods branch, with a reflection of his values orientation shown by his sub-branch, pointed in the direction of the Valuing branch.

Likewise, on the Methods branch is the work of Ray Pawson and Nick Tilley. Their realist evaluation is described by Stame as "the European version of theory-based evaluation" and, indeed, constitutes some of the earliest work in this area. Thus, like theory-based evaluation in the United States and in Australasia, their work is concerned with uncovering the underlying processes (or mechanisms) that lead to particular outcomes and the circumstances in which that occurs.

Nicoletta Stame, in her chapter, has discussed the role that European writers have played in considering syntheses of evaluation studies. She points out the relationship of such studies to the meta-analysis procedures originally devised by Gene Glass. Certainly, the work of the Cochrane Collaboration in synthesizing studies of medical practice has been of monumental importance to understandings in the health field. In many ways, however, we consider this a methodological work rather than a prescriptive evaluation procedure. In a similar manner, we have not classified the Campbell Collaboration in education as a prescriptive theory. Furthermore, Stame has commented on Ann Oakley's (2000) work in the analysis of evaluation syntheses and in discussing the synthesis movement as a platform for evaluation. Also, the writings of Petticrew and Roberts (2006) have been cited in this regard, but as Stame has noted, these are primarily methodologies rather than prescriptive evaluation theories. Thus, we have chosen not to include these authors on the theory tree.

We now address a somewhat more complicated situation. The creation of the Structural Funds program within the European Union provided the stimulus for considering the nature of evaluation. This program distributed resources to various countries within the European Union. In many ways, this was comparable to the stimulus to evaluation provided by the Great Society programs of the 1960s in the United States. As Stame has noted in the early writings related to evaluation of the structural funds activities, a document called the MEANS (Methods for Evaluating Action of a Structural Nature) Guide was produced. In our view, this was primarily a teaching document and not a prescriptive theory per se. That is, it mainly provided an awareness of the broad scope of what constituted evaluation and how it might be performed. The update to the MEANS Guide produced 4 years later, the EVALSED (Evaluation of Socio-Economic Development), was more prescriptive in nature. It placed greater stress on capacity building and participatory evaluation within a European multicountry context while recognizing the constraints (and opportunities) inherent in different contexts. Designation of this work as a "theory" is a bit of a problem. First, there have been multiple authors involved in producing each of these documents. Indeed, we were in a bit of a quandary as to whether these procedures constituted an evaluation theory. Light dawned when we heard a presentation by Gary Henry (2011) at an evaluation symposium on "Evaluation Use and Decision Making in Society." Henry discussed the evaluation guidelines developed by the Institute of Education Sciences for the No Child Left Behind (NCLB) Act in the United States. He noted that the procedures were developed by committees or by individuals who are government officials. He noted that the closest thing to a "theorist" for this prescriptive evaluation would be George Bush. That idea is easily rejected. Thus, while NCLB and Structural Funds evaluations are sets of prescriptions for conducting an evaluation, they are not evaluation theories. Theories require the presence of a specific theorist who has promulgated the concept.

The chapter on Europe (Chapter 28) makes a cogent point about the role of Elliot Stern and the journal *Evaluation* in nurturing and otherwise contributing to the evaluation debate in Europe. This role of helping shape the development of prescriptive views on evaluation in Europe is noteworthy. Stame refers to Stern as a "theory weaver." We agree and want to acknowledge Sterns' contribution and its important role in the European scene. It is, however, not a theory per se.

On a related note, we cannot help but mention Nicoletta Stame's role as that of one who has conceptualized evaluation within the European context. We regret her modesty in not citing her own work more thoroughly. In many ways, the conceptualization of the nature of evaluation as it relates to Europe is, if not a prescriptive evaluation theory, at least a precursor to prescribing appropriate evaluation in a European context (see Stame, 2006). She likewise is a "theory weaver" of a sort.

AUSTRALIA AND NEW ZEALAND

Patricia Rogers and Jane Davidson have carefully articulated the history and nature of evaluation theory and practice in Australia and New Zealand (Chapter 29). They astutely observe that unlike evaluation in many countries, which focused on externally funded projects, evaluation in Australia and New Zealand focused primarily on the evaluation of ongoing programs. This impetus led to viewing evaluation as closely integrated with management practice conducted by frontline professionals. In turn, this led to a greater drive for improved understanding of programs (program theory) and more well-defined outcome measures (performance indicators). Moreover, the greater integration of evaluation into local programs aligned well with participatory evaluation approaches. An extension of this participatory emphasis is to be found in New Zealand, where the treaty of Waitangi required, or led to, the development of evaluation approaches aligned with indigenous (Māori) concepts. New definitions of what constitutes Māori participation and values have led to the definition of a unique evaluation prescriptive theory. These various themes form the context for identifying evaluation theories in Australia and New Zealand.

We have noted the way in which a concern for program theory derives naturally from the nature of evaluation in Australia. Sue Funnell is readily acknowledged as the leader in introducing program theory concepts into the country. Her work has drawn much international attention as well. The authors of the previous chapter cite in particular her development of the "program logic matrix" as a unique contribution. This matrix depicts the program theory as a series of outcomes, which in turn lead to other actions. She, along with Patricia Rogers, conceives of the matrix as a "thinking tool rather than an end in itself" (Funnell & Rogers, 2011, p. 237).

Patricia Rogers has written about a variety of evaluation topics. These are noted in the preceding chapter. But these papers, as such, do not constitute a prescriptive theory. It is only in her recent work on program theory that we see a prescriptive model. Her exploration of how program theory may be used in complicated and complex programs is noteworthy. Likewise, her participation with Sue Funnell in a recent book more fully depicts a systematic evaluation procedure (Funnell & Rogers, 2011). In light of this collaborative effort, we have chosen to jointly list them on the Methods branch of the theory tree.

Rogers and Davidson have ably described a case for Bob Williams's inclusion on the evaluation theory tree. His training in systems thinking has been applied broadly in evaluation. The areas in which his participative approach may have been highly influential include organizational change, development, and learning. The book with Iraj Imam (Williams & Imam, 2007) laid out general principles; however, it was a later publication (Williams & Hummelbrunner, 2010) that spelled out evaluation questions. His application of systems thinking in practice and his publications, together, provide added specificity and indeed fulfill the promise of a prescriptive theory. We have placed Williams on the Use branch of the tree.

John Owen has been a leading figure in evaluation ever since the introduction of his first book on program evaluation in the early 1990s. Owen is concerned about the one-size-fits-all nature of most prescriptive evaluation theories. He believes that philosophical perspectives should be adapted depending on the goals, aims, and contexts of each evaluative situation. Owen's book *Program Evaluation*, now in its third edition (Owen, 2007), highlights the need for the evaluation procedures employed to reflect the particular "what" and "why" of each situation. Owen identifies five distinct "epistemological clusters," which he refers to as "forms." These are (1) proactive (e.g., needs assessment, best practices), (2) clarificative (e.g., logic development), (3) interactive (e.g., particular involvement in examining adequacy of implementation), (4) monitoring (e.g., documenting the program in operation), and (5) impact (e.g., the effects of a program). Each of these forms has relevant methods and key approaches associated with it. Owen clearly must be represented on the Use branch of the theory tree.

The authors of the Australasian chapter identify Yoland Wadsworth as best known in evaluation for her work on collaborative and participatory approaches. Wadsworth's work is cognizant of the Australian context, as we have previously discussed it. Namely, we refer to the strong emphasis on evaluation that is conducted in ongoing programs and by online professionals. Wadsworth has developed evaluation procedures that build onto these internal program processes. She describes, quite specifically, activities to be engaged in daily, weekly, monthly, and annually (Wadsworth, 2011). In some ways, this seems to us to be akin to Cousins's and King's capacity-building approaches.

More recently, Wadsworth has expanded her evaluation ideas to consider ways in which program recipients' views could become a more central part of evaluations. She has a strong interest in ensuring that their values and voices are seriously considered throughout the evaluation process. The tools that she uses to accomplish this task include transformative social research and methods that facilitate open dialogue among different stakeholder groups. These are views that hearken back to Greene's work around dialogue and inclusion. Taken in its totality, we opt to include Wadsworth on the Use branch but pointing to the left to reflect a tendency toward the Valuing branch.

The work done in New Zealand on indigenous evaluation has been at the forefront of thinking about sensitivity to culture and values. Smith and Cram's (2001) book spoke about this issue with reference to research methodology. Generally, Fiona Cram's work has continued the refinement of Māori concepts as they might apply to the conduct of research or evaluation, but it does not constitute a prescriptive theory. Nan Wehipeihana (2008) has more specifically directed her work toward expanding on the nature of evaluation in the Māori way. Others (especially Kate McKegg) have been involved as well in the broadening of Māori evaluation concepts. We readily admit to not being experts on evaluation in New Zealand and must, out of necessity, rely on the evaluation writers identified by Rogers and Davidson. While acknowledging the contribution of many, we have chosen to place Nan Wehipeihana as a representative of Māori evaluation.

Her placement on the theory tree is not an easy decision (indeed many are not). Clearly, Wehipeihana in addressing the Māori context is interested in use. However, the theorists on the Use branch seem to consider the values and value systems of those in the program being evaluated in an effort to be responsive and to attain use. While Wehipeihana is interested in use, she seems more driven by the need to give voice to the Māori and their views in decision-making contexts—that is, situations from which they have traditionally been excluded and in which their interests have not been considered. She shares with the North American theorists on the Valuing branch, such as House and Greene, an emphasis on her own perceptions of what is right and fair. We have placed her on the Valuing branch, angled to the right toward the Use branch.

While recognizing the high quality of their work, we nonetheless have chosen not to include Adrienne Alton-Lee, E. Jane Davidson, Stephen Kemmis, and Jerome Winston on the evaluation tree.

In Alton-Lee's instance, we see the case for inclusion on the theory tree as similar to the discussion in the previous section related to systematic reviews and syntheses. Best Evidence Synthesis is essentially a methodology designed to consider broad-based research evidence to reach conclusions. Just as the Campbell Collaboration, the Cochrane Collaboration, and review panels that examine research for evidence of "best practice" are not included on the tree, so too with Alton-Lee.

Jane Davidson has done truly outstanding work in providing ways to integrate systematic valuing procedures into evaluation practice. However, we believe that the valuing principles that she outlines are primarily a furtherance of Michael Scriven's work. As such, it is a superb example of the evaluation category defined as "evaluation interpreters and teachers" in Chapter 1 of this volume.

Stephen Kemmis has been active in Australian evaluation circles since the 1980s. His publications at that time addressed topics such as participatory action research and discussion of expanded definitions of evaluation use that were founded on critical theory principles. More recent work has not further defined a specific prescriptive theory.

Jerome Winston has prepared important guidelines for the development of performance indicators and cautionary notes as to their proper use. This is an important contribution to evaluation in Australia. However, we do not consider this work to be a fully developed prescriptive theory.

We thank the authors of the two previous chapters for their identification of potential theorists on their continent. Our selection from among those names presented is solely based on our interpretation of the way they fit within the inclusion criteria previously mentioned—most certainly not on the quality of their work.

REFERENCES

Funnell, S. C., & Rogers, P. J. (2011). *Purposeful program theory*. San Francisco, CA: Jossey-Bass.

Hansen, M. B., & Vedung, E. (2010). Theory-based stakeholder evaluation. *American Journal of Evaluation, 31*(3), 295–313.

Henry, G. (2011, June). Educational evaluation and use since NCLB: The golden age or awed by fool's gold? *Issues in Evaluation Use and Decision Making in Society*. Program evaluation symposium conducted at the University of California–Los Angeles, Los Angeles.

Karlsson, O. (1996). A critical dialogue in evaluation: How can the interaction between evaluation and politics be tackled? *Evaluation, 2*(4), 405–416.

Karlsson, O. (2001). Critical dialogue: Its value and meaning. *Evaluation, 7*(2), 211–227.

Oakley, A. (2000). *Experiments in knowing*. New York, NY: The New Press.

Owen, J. (2007). *Program evaluation: Forms and approaches* (3rd ed.). San Francisco, CA: Allen & Unwin.

Petticrew, M., & Roberts, H. (2006). *Systematic reviews in the social sciences*. Oxford, England: Blackwell.

Smith, L. T., & Cram, F. (2001). *Community-up model*. Retrieved from http://www.rangahau.co.nz/ethics/166/

Stame, N. (2006). The European Project, federalism and evaluation. *Evaluation, 14*(2), 115–138.

Wadsworth, Y. (2011). *Everyday evaluation on the run* (3rd ed.). San Francisco, CA: Allen & Unwin.

Wehipeihana, N. (2008). Indigenous evaluation: A strategic objective of the Australasian Evaluation Society. *Evaluation Journal of Australasia, 8*(1), 40–44.

Williams, B., & Hummelbrunner, R. (2010). *Systems concepts in action: A practitioner's toolkit*. Stanford, CA: Stanford University Press.

Williams, B., & Imam, I. (2007). *Systems concepts in evaluation: An expert anthology*. Point Reyes, CA: EdgePress/American Evaluation Association.

AUTHOR INDEX

Abma, T., 34, 35, 192, 195, 361
Abramson, M. A., 263
Ai, X., 34
Albarracin, D., 145
Alkin, M., ix, 6, 7, 14, 26, 28, 34, 41, 44, 49, 63, 73, 97, 140, 141, 144, 151, 205, 243, 283, 286, 287, 300, 329, 336, 339, 349, 350, 355, 356
Allison, P., 79
Alton-Lee, A., 379, 392
Ambron, S. R., 254
Amo, C., 347, 350
Argyris, C., 308, 329
Aron, R., 268
Astin, A., 50
Atkin, M., 8
Ayers, L. P., 158
Azzam, T., 287

Ballou, F., 158
Bamberger, M., 5
Baumol, W., 182
Belfield, C. R., 186
Bell, J. B., 262
Bemelsmans-Videc, M. L., 360
Berk, R., 21, 108
Bhaskar, R. A., 153, 203
Bickman, L., 113
Birkeland, S., 26, 138
Bjorndahl, A., 74
Blackmore, J., 374
Bloom, B., 30, 159, 163
Blyth, D., 45, 141, 300
Borgotta, E., 70
Boruch, R., 20–21, 70, 78, 79, 108, 154
Bourgeois, I., 350
Bowles, S., 183
Bowsher, C., 75

Boyle, S., 331
Brandt, S., 234, 235, 238
Braskamp, L., 195
Braudel, F., 203, 205
Brennan, N., 45, 141, 300
Brodbeck, M., 223
Brown, R., 195
Bruner, E. M., 221
Bryk, A., 5

Campbell, A., 75
Campbell, D. T., 5, 6, 18, 19, 20, 22, 24, 25, 28, 35, 61–65, 70–71, 73, 74, 77, 78, 81, 82, 84, 85, 87, 92–95, 101, 108, 112, 114, 119, 120, 140, 141, 153, 154, 160, 220, 248, 264, 270, 363
Campbell, R., 146, 152
Candoli, I. C., 248, 254
Caplan, N., 70, 73, 286
Caracelli, V. J., 124, 150
Carey, R., 5
Carey, R. G., 113
Carlson, R., 323, 324
Carr, W., 374
Carson, R., 211
Catlin, D., 186
Catsambas, T., 330
Caulley, D., 371
Chalmers, I., 74
Chambers, O., 21
Chang, K., 67
Checkoway, B., 307
Chelimsky, E., 8, 40, 43, 75, 148, 272, 273, 275, 276, 277, 278, 279, 280, 316
Chen, H. T., 3, 13, 20, 25, 27–28, 113, 114, 117, 118, 120, 121, 122, 124, 125, 126, 127
Chilisa, B., 232
Chinman, M., 122
Chouinard, J. A., 347

Christie, C., 4, 7, 8, 17, 28, 41, 47, 63, 97, 119, 123, 141, 144, 286, 287
Christie, T., 287
Clark, S., 47, 347, 350
Clinton, B., 203
Clune, W. H., 183
Cochran, W., 108
Colosi, L., 127
Connell, J. P., 113, 115
Conner, R., 300
Cook, D. L., 248, 263, 264
Cook, T. C., 5, 6, 12, 18, 22–23, 24, 25, 26, 27, 32, 33, 61, 62, 63, 81, 82, 86, 91, 92, 93, 95, 108, 114, 119, 121, 125, 141, 146, 154, 218, 264
Cook, T. D., 272
Cooksey, L., 205
Cooperrider, D., 330
Cordray, D., 154
Coryn, C. L. S., 113, 255
Courtis, S. A., 158
Cousins, J. B., 4, 8, 46–47, 150, 345, 347, 349, 350
Coyle, K., 286, 287
Cram, F., 232, 373, 376, 391
Crohn, K., 287
Cronbach, L. J., 7, 8, 19, 20, 23–24, 25, 28, 35, 81–95, 97–105, 108, 114, 121, 140, 157, 158, 184, 190, 200, 202, 206, 211, 222, 254, 270, 359
Crozier, M., 295, 296, 355
Cuban, L., 182
Cullen, K., 248, 254

Dahrendorf, R., 223
Daillak, R., 286, 287, 350
Datta, L. E., 5, 142
Davidson, C., 371
Davidson, E. J., 255, 377–378, 390, 391, 392
Davidson, J., 8
Dawes, R., 76
Deitz, J., 304, 318
Deming, W. E., 78
DeMoya, D., 21
De Moya, D., 74
Dente, B., 355
Dentler, B., 140
Derlien, H.-U., 355
Diesing, P., 12
Donaldson, S., 5, 115, 119, 123
Donaldson, S. L., 113
Dornbusch, S. M., 254

Duffy, H. D., 263
Dunst, C. J., 307
Durie, M., 373
Durkheim, E., 15
Dwass, M., 71

Earl, L., 4, 46–47, 349
Easley, J., 34
Ebener, P., 122
Eiseley, L. C., 189
Eisenberg, N., 287
Eisner, E., 8, 35–36, 318, 323
Ellett, F., Jr., 6, 7
Elliot, E. C., 158, 350
Elliott, C., 350
Elson, A., 186
Englehart, D., 30
Epstein, R., 62, 379
European Community, 366

Farrar, E., 201
Fascell, D., 278
Feinstein, O., 365
Fetterman, D. M., 7, 45–46, 49, 50, 151, 304, 305, 310, 317, 318, 359
Finn, C. E., 255
Fisher, R., 68
Fiske, D. W., 64, 68, 87, 160
Fiske, S. T., 145
Fitz-Gibbon, C., 3, 286, 287
Fitzpatrick, J., 5
Flaspohler, P., 305
Fleischer, D. N., 17
Fletcher, J., 76
Foley, W. J., 248, 253
Freeman, H., 8, 24, 25, 26, 108, 109, 111, 113, 114, 140
Freire, P., 211
French, B., 45, 141, 300
Freund, J., 268
Frierson, H., 232
Fukumoto, J. S., 263
Fulbright-Anderson, K., 113, 115
Funnell, S. C., 375, 382, 390
Furst, E., 30

Gandhi, A., 26
Garbe, P., 118, 119, 122, 127
Geertz, C., 16
Gephart, W. J., 248, 253
Gesundheit, N., 304, 318
Ghere, G., 337

Ginsburg, A., 76
Glaister, S., 181
Glass, E., 317
Glass, G. V., 6, 8, 140, 184, 186, 187, 199, 204, 205
Glennan, T., 70
Gleser, G. C., 87, 99
Goh, S., 47, 347, 350
Gold, M., 183
Goldstein, E., 342
Gomez, C. A., 342
Gore, A., 203
Gosset, W. S., 114
Gough, D., 363, 364
Granger, B., 76
Greenberg, D., 153
Greene, J., 7, 8, 31, 38, 97, 124, 208, 211, 213, 232
Grimes, P., 45, 141, 300
Gruder, C., 23
Guba, E., 13, 35, 39–40, 120, 140, 141, 200, 213–214, 219, 220, 223, 232, 248, 252, 253, 264, 318
Gullickson, A., 254, 256
Guthrie, K., 45, 141, 300
Guttentag, M., 270

Hall, G. S., 158
Hall, M., 216
Hamilton, D., 8, 356–358, 387
Hammond, R. L., 30, 248, 252, 253
Hansen, M. B., 113, 359
Hanushek, E., 76
Harris, R., 232, 234, 235, 238
Harvey, D., 205
Harvey, O. J., 154
Hasci, T. A., 113
Hastings, T., 8
Hatry, H. P., 42, 76, 262, 264
Hawkins, P., 372
Henry, G., 4, 8, 14, 28–29, 41, 141, 144, 145, 147, 149, 150, 151, 152, 153, 205, 365, 389
Herzog, E., 140
Hess, R. D., 254
Hesse, M., 220, 223
Hill, W., 30
Hofstetter, C., 34, 287
Hogan, D., 379
Hollister, R., 70, 71
Holmes, H., 232, 234, 235, 238
Holtzman, E., 72–73
Hood, S., 216, 232

Hood, W. R., 154
Hopkins, T., 140
Hopson, R., 216, 232
Hornick, R. C., 254
Horst, P., 262, 263
Hough, G., 381
House, E., 6, 7, 31, 34, 35, 36–38, 37, 40, 49, 104, 125, 151, 190, 198, 200, 201, 202, 203, 204, 209, 214–215, 232, 254, 287, 300, 318, 323, 329, 339, 359, 367
House Select Committee on Congressional Operations, 277
Howe, K. R., 31, 37, 38, 104, 151, 203, 205, 209, 215, 232, 318
Huberman, M., 5, 8, 318, 345, 347, 349
Huebner, T. A., 113
Huffman, D., 123
Hume, D., 31
Hummelbrunner, R., 380, 390
Hunter, S. B., 122
Hyman, H., 140

Imam, I., 380, 390
Imm, P., 122
Innovation & Business Skills Australia, 373
Israel, B. A., 307

Jackson, J., 201–202
Jaeger, R. M., 254
Johnson, B. T., 145
Joint Committee on Standards for Educational Evaluation, 247, 258, 264
Judd, C. H., 158
Julnes, G., 8, 14, 28–29, 144, 145, 149, 150, 153, 365

Karlsson, O., 203, 205, 360–361, 368, 388
Kaye, P., 262
Kean, M., 300
Keener, D. C., 305
Kefford, B., 381
Kellaghan, T., 218, 254
Kemmis, S., 371, 374, 392
Kempthorne, O., 68, 69, 79
Kennedy, V., 376
Kerins, T., 199
Keynes, J. M., 206
King, J. A., 48–49, 141, 283, 300, 329, 337, 340, 341, 343
Kirkhart, K., 5, 29, 41, 150, 232
Kissinger, H., 270
Klein, S., 300

Knorr-Cetina, K., 223
Kosecoff, J., 286, 287
Krathwohl, D., 30
Kubisch, A. C., 113, 115
Kupermintz, H., 98, 103
Kushner, S., 195, 359

Lahey, R., 350
Lakoff, G., 83
Lambert, F. C., 350
Lapan, S., 199, 201, 202, 205
LaPointe, N., 307
Law, A., 300
Lawrenz, F., 123, 340
Layard, R., 181
Lazarsfeld, P. F., 107, 108
Lee, L., 347, 350
Leithwood, K. A., 150, 345, 347, 350
Lentz, B., 305
Levin, H., 8, 33–34, 108
Levin, H. M., 13, 183, 184, 185, 186, 187
Leviton, L., 6, 12, 18, 24, 25, 26, 27, 32, 33, 61, 62, 63, 91, 95, 119, 121, 125, 146, 154, 218, 263, 264
Lincoln, Y., 35, 39–40, 120, 213, 219, 220, 223, 232, 264, 318
Lindblom, C. E., 140
Linn, B., 201
Linnan, L., 50
Lippmann, W., 78
Lipsey, M., 26, 74, 109, 113, 114, 144, 151
Little, R., 79
Livet, M., 305
Lorenz, K., 62
Lortie, D., 201
Luke, A., 379
Lunt, N., 371
Lyall, C., 108

Mabry, L., 5
MacDonald, B., 51, 190, 196, 200, 201, 205, 226, 323, 358, 387
MacDonald, G., 74
MacIntyre, A., 223
Madaus, G., 29, 30, 158, 159, 161, 162, 218, 254
Madura, B., 202
Mager, R. F., 159
Mandell, M., 153
Mark, M., 4, 8, 14, 28–29, 41, 101, 119, 123, 141, 144, 145, 149, 150, 151, 152, 153, 154, 205, 283, 365
Markiewicz, A., 376

Marris, P., 270
Marsick, V., 329
Marx, K., 15
Masia, B., 30
Mathison, S., 16, 202, 329, 350
Matthews, B., 331
Mayer, R., 201
McDonald, B., 381
McDonald, D., 376
McEwan, P. J., 33, 185
McKegg, K., 371, 373, 377, 378
McLaughlin, M., 300
McLean, L., 201
McTaggart, R., 202, 371, 374
Meehl, P. E., 87, 99
Meister, G. R., 184, 186, 187
Mejia, A., 194
Merriman, H. O., 248, 253
Mertens, D., 8, 40, 233, 234, 235, 238
Metfessel, N., 30
Michael, W., 30
Mihm, S., 203
Miles, M., 5, 318, 345, 347
Miller, R. L., 146, 152, 283
Minnema, J., 337
Mithaug, D., 307
Mohr, B., 330
Monnier, E., 192
Morell, J., 5
Morningstar, M., 183
Morra, L., 275
Morrill, B., 75
Morrill, W. A., 262
Morris, L., 3
Morris, M., 5
Morris, W., 269
Moses, L., 76, 79
Mosteller, F., 21, 74, 75, 78, 108, 270
Moynihan, D. P., 270
Muenning, P., 186
Murphy-Graham, E., 26, 138
Murray, C., 202
Myrdal, G., 223

Nader, R., 103
Nanda, H., 87, 99
National Health and Medical Research Council, 373
Nay, J. N., 261, 262
Newcomer, K., 42, 262
Newman, D., 195
Noakes, L. A., 113
Nowakowski, J. R., 159, 160, 161

Oakley, A., 363, 364, 389
Olbrechts-Tyteca, L., 8, 200
Oliver, S., 363, 364
Onstott, M., 153
Oreopoulos, P., 181
O'Sullivan, R., 5
Owen, J., 51, 350, 376, 391
Owen, T., 51
Owens, T. R., 248

Paddock, S. M., 122
Palumbo, D. J., 360
Parlett, M., 226, 356–358, 387
Patrinos, H., 181
Patrizi, P., 298
Patton, M. Q., 44–45, 49, 113, 141, 146, 148, 153, 174, 195, 231, 264, 286, 295, 296, 297, 298, 299, 300, 301, 302, 307, 308, 318, 329, 335, 350, 372
Pawson, R., 113, 362, 388
Perelman, C., 8, 200
Perrin, B., 375
Petersson, G., 368
Petrosino, A., 26, 113
Petticrew, M., 363, 364, 367, 389
Philips, D. C., 254
Piontek, M. E., 330
Pipi, K., 373, 378
Pitman, M., 50
Polanyi, M., 62, 193
Pollitt, C., 365
Popham, W., 4, 6, 30, 140, 159, 323
Popper, K., 62
Posavac, E. J., 113
Posevac, E., 5
Powers, E., 140
Pratt, J. W., 70
Preskill, H., 47–48, 151, 326, 327, 329, 330, 331, 350
Prest, A. R., 181
Provus, M., 51, 285
Psacharopoulos, G., 181
Putnam, H., 154

Quade, E., 180
Quine, W. V., 62

Rajaratnam, N., 87, 99
Rallis, S., 203
Ramseyer, J., 248, 251
Rappaport, J., 307
Raths, J., 201

Rawls, J., 37, 199, 200, 205, 214
Reichardt, C., 154, 203
Rein, M., 270
Reinhard, D., 252
Reiss, A., 72, 78
Rex, J., 223
Rice, J. K., 183
Rice, J. M., 158
Rich, R., 286
Richardson, L., 223
Riecken, H., 70, 74, 76
Rist, R., 360
Rivers, W., 254
Rivlin, A., 263, 279
Roberts, H., 363, 364, 389
Rodriguez-Campos, L., 5
Rog, D. J., 145
Rogers, P. J., 8, 113, 375, 381, 382, 390, 391
Rossi, P. H., 13, 20, 24–26, 27, 28, 70, 72, 74, 78, 106–112, 113, 114, 124, 140, 141, 270
Roubini, N., 203
Rouse, C. E., 186
Rousseau, J.-J., 26
Rubin, D., 79, 154
Rugh, J., 5
Ruskus, J., 287
Ryan, A., 206
Ryan, B., 371

Sacks, J., 71
Sage, 175
Salvanes, K. G., 181
Sanders, J., 5, 6, 218, 335
Scanlon, J. S., 261, 262, 263
Schmidt, R. E., 262
Schon, D. A., 308, 329
Schorr, L. B., 113
Schoter, D., 113
Schubert, A. L., 159, 160
Schubert, W., 159, 160
Schulz, A., 307
Schwandt, T., 5, 151, 216
Scougall, J., 373
Scriven, M., 3, 8, 12, 24, 27, 31, 32–33, 35, 36, 102, 140, 141, 152, 159, 189, 192, 203, 205, 218, 225, 226, 243, 254, 255, 261, 264, 270, 285, 287, 323, 335
Sechrest, L., 71, 73, 79
Seiden, K., 350
Seligman, R., 286
Senge, P., 329

Shadish, W., 5, 6, 8, 12, 18, 24, 25, 26, 27, 32, 33,
    61, 62, 63, 81, 82, 91, 95, 114, 119, 121,
    125, 141, 146, 154, 218, 263, 264, 316
Shanker, V., 283, 377
Sharp, C. A., 372
Shavelson, R. J., 22, 76
Sheldon, E., 70
Sherif, C. W., 154
Sherif, M., 154
Shinkfield, A. J., 248, 254, 255, 257
Simons, H., 196
Singer, E., 138
Smith, E. R., 248
Smith, L. T., 376, 391
Smith, M., 73
Smith, N., 5
Snell-Johns, J., 305
Snow, D., 100, 108
Snow, R., 24
Snyder, B., 21
Soydan, H., 74
Staats, E., 75
Stake, R., 4, 8, 12, 16, 31, 34–35, 38, 141, 191,
    192, 193, 196, 198, 199, 205, 209, 216, 232,
    243, 252, 256, 285, 287, 323, 324, 360, 367
Stame, N., 359, 366, 388–389, 390
Stanley, J. C., 5, 18, 19, 20, 22, 24, 61, 62, 64,
    101, 108, 114, 119, 120, 141, 220, 248, 264
Starch, D., 158
Stecher, B., 287
Steckler, A., 50
Steele, J., 199
Stern, E., 365
Stevahn, L., 49, 337
Stevens, F. I., 255
Stiglitz, J. E., 203
Stillman, L., 122
Strosberg, M. A., 263
Stufflebeam, D., 8, 13, 14, 29, 30, 40, 41–42, 44,
    140, 158, 159, 161, 162, 218, 230, 243, 248,
    249, 250, 252, 253, 254, 255, 256, 257,
    285, 335
Suchman, E., 19–20, 24, 118, 140, 141
Suppes, P., 183

Taba, H., 161
Tashakkori, A., 16, 124
Taut, S., 41, 286, 287
Taylor, R., 373
Taylor, S. E., 145
Teddlie, C., 16, 124
Tharp, R., 280

Thomas, J., 363, 364
Thomas, L., 280
Thomas, V., 216, 232
Thompson, B., 340
Thompson, J., 295, 296
Thorndike, E. L., 158, 159
Tilley, N., 362, 388
Tilly, N., 113
Torres, R. T., 47–48, 151, 326, 327, 329, 330, 350
Towne, L., 22
Travers, K., 203
Trivette, C. M., 307
Trochim, B., 154
Trotman, I., 371
Turner, V. W., 220, 221
Tyler, R. W., 3, 8, 23, 29–31, 140, 157–163, 230,
    248, 323

United Way of America, 264
U.S. Department of Health, Education,
    and Welfare, 261, 263
U.S. General Accounting Office, 262, 275, 363
U.S. Office of Management and Budget, 264

Vedung, E., 113, 264, 359, 360, 388
Vo, A., 287
Vogt, L. M., 263
Volkov, B. B., 48, 341
Vonnegut, K., 79

Wadsworth, Y., 378–379, 391
Wagner, R. B., 14
Walberg, H., 255
Walker, D., 75, 201
Walker, R., 323, 358
Wallace, T. L. B., 287
Wandersman, A., 122, 304, 305, 310, 317, 359
Watkins, J., 330
Watkins, K., 329, 330
Watts, H., 70
Weber, M., 15, 171
Webster, W. J., 248
Weeks, H. A., 140
Wehipeihana, N., 373, 377, 378, 391–392
Weick, K. E., 220
Weiss, C. H., 7, 8, 13, 20, 25, 26–27, 70, 79, 103,
    113, 115, 138, 146, 151, 154, 285, 291, 300,
    329, 381
Weiss, H. B., 262
Weiss, R. S., 270
Weizenbaum, R., 8
Westine, C. D., 113

Westley, F., 297
White, B. J., 154
White, E. E., 158
White, P., 286, 350
Whitehurst, G., 74
Whitmore, E., 212, 349
Whitney, D., 330
Wholey, J., 13, 24, 42–43, 113, 140, 141, 261, 262, 263, 264, 270
Whyte, W., 141
Williams, B., 380, 390–391
Williams, J., 6
Williams, W., 70, 270
Williamson, O. E., 203, 205
Willinsky, J., 104
Wilson, A. T., 233
Wingate, L. A., 256
Winston, J., 374–375, 392
Witmer, H., 140
Witte, O., 21
Wolf, R., 51
Wolins, L., 68
Worthen, B., 5, 6, 140, 218, 335
Wortman, P., 154
Wright, C., 140
Wright, S., 25

Yin, R., 5, 73, 264

Zanna, M. P., 145
Zhang, G., 255
Zimmerman, B., 297, 307
Zimmerman, M. A., 306
Zuckerman, B., 331

SUBJECT INDEX

Accuracy standards, 41
Action, theory of, 308–309
Action model in theory-driven evaluation, 115–116
Action research, 336
Action Research Planner, The, 374
Administrative criteria, 20
Advocacy, 316
Alignment, 308–309
Alkin, M. C.
   experiences and training, 284–287
   general orientation to evaluation, 287–290
   reality check, 291
   role of context, 290–291
Alpha discipline, evaluation as the, 172–175
Alternative Evaluation Research Paradigms, 299
Alton-Lee, A., 379–380
American Council on Education (ACE), 69
American Evaluation Association (AEA), 144–145, 185, 203, 205, 209–210, 226, 375
American Institutes for Research, 77, 307
American Journal of Evaluation, 283
American Psychological Association, 222
American Sign Language (ASL), 231–232, 234, 236
Anthropology, 16
Aotearoa New Zealand Evaluation Association, 371
Appraising and Recording Student Progress, 159
Appreciative Inquiry (AI), 330
Aptitude-treatment interactions (ATIs), 100
Aroha, 376
Assessment
   authentic or alternative, 160
   evaluability, 42
   holistic, 117

Assisted sensemaking, evaluation as, 145–146
Australia and New Zealand, evaluation in, 371–372
   A. Alton-Lee, 379–380
   B. Williams, 380–381
   BES program, 379–380
   capacity and capability, 380–381
   community groups, 378–379
   democratic, 374
   E. J. Davidson, 377–378
   evaluative rubrics, 377–378
   F. Cram, 376
   forms, 376
   goal displacement and, 375
   historical and social context, 372–373
   J. A. Winston, 374–375
   J. M. Owen, 376
   Maori people, 376–377
   methods, 378–382
   N. Wehipeihana, 377
   P. J. Rogers, 381–382
   program logic matrix, 375
   program theory, 381–382
   roots, 390–392
   S. C. Funnell, 375
   S. Kemmis, 373–374
   use, 373–376
   values, 376–378
   Y. Wadsworth, 378–379
Autocratic evaluation, 358

Basic Principles of Curriculum and Instruction, 159, 161, 163
Becoming Critical, 374
Behavioral processes, 151
Belief systems, 17
Best Evidence Synthesis (BES) program, 379–380

Between-study improvements and causal
    generalizations, 94–95
Bias, 17
    empowerment evaluation and, 316–317
Boruch, R., 20–22, 66, 78–80
    evaluation firms, 77
    foundations work, 76
    postgraduate roots, 69–71
    publications, 77–78
    statistics, modeling, and theory graduate
        education, 67–69
    theory and experiments in engineering, 66–67
    transcending academic disciplines, bureaucratic
        boundaries, and geopolitical jurisdictions,
        71–76
Bottom-up versus top-down approaches for
    advancing validity, 121–124
*Building in Research and Evaluation: Human
    Inquiry for Living Systems,* 379
Bureaucratic evaluation, 358
Bush Educators' Program (BEP), 337

Campbell, D., 18–19
    construct validity applied to persons and
        settings, 88–89
    construct validity as an alternative model for
        causal generalization, 86–88
    evaluation point of view, 61–63
    on evolutionary epistemology, 62
    four interconnected domains, 82
    generalization tasks, 83–85
    limited reach of formal sampling theory, 85–86
    personal influences on career of, 63–65
    practical methods to extend causal
        generalization, 92–95
    principles of construct validity applied to all
        ways of framing external validity, 90–91
Campbell Collaboration, 76, 363
Canadian Evaluation Society, 206
Capability, evaluation, 380–381
Capacity building, evaluation, 331, 337,
    350–351
    access to resources and, 342
    Australia and New Zealand, 380–381
    organizational context and, 341–342
    structures, 342
Case Studies in Science Education, 34
"Case Study Method in Social Inquiry,
    The," 324
Category systems, 6–7, 286
Causal relationships
    between-study improvements and, 94–95

    construct validity and, 86–92
    four interconnected domains and, 82
    fourth generation evaluation and, 221
    generalization tasks, 83–85
    limited reach of formal sampling theory and,
        85–86
    practical methods to extend, 92–95
    within-study improvements and, 93–94
Center for Study of Evaluation, 284–285
Center for the Advanced Study in the Behavioral
    Sciences, 204
Center for the Study of Evaluation (CSE) model,
    6, 44
Change model in theory-driven evaluation, 115
Characteristic causal chain, 32
Chelimsky, E., 43, 279–281
    MITRE Corporation work, 270–274
    North Atlantic Treaty Organization (NATO)
        work, 267–270
    professional influences, experience, and ideas,
        267–279
    U.S. Government Accountability Office work,
        274–279
CIPP model. *See* Context-input-process-product
    (CIPP) model
Clientism, 37
Cochrane Collaboration, 74
Cognitive and affective processes, 151
Cognitive dissonance, 230
Communicating and reporting evaluation
    findings, 326
Community development projects, 255–256,
    378–379
Community-Up Model, 376
Competitive elaboration, 29
Computer-assisted instruction (CAI), 184
Consequences, evaluation, 151
Constructing Achievement Tests, 158–159
Constructivism, 16, 17, 18, 221–222, 361,
    367–368
    knowing differently and, 222–224
    methodology and, 223–224
    procedures for conducting fourth generation
        evaluation, 224–225
Construct validity, 86–88
    applied to all ways of framing external validity,
        90–91
    applied to persons and settings, 88–89
    See also Validity
Consuelo Foundation, 255
Consumer focus of empowerment
    evaluation, 316

Consumer Reports, 32
Content of Children's Minds, The, 158
Context
  of evaluation work, 326
  importance of, 216, 269, 290–291
  organizational, 291, 341–342
  political, 291
  program, 290–291
Context evaluations, 41, 244
  See also Context-input-process-product (CIPP) model
Context-input-process-product (CIPP) model, 6, 14, 41–42, 230, 243
  application, 255–256
  core concepts, 244–247
  evaluation of Elementary and Secondary Education Act (ESEA) projects, 249–250
  focus on improvement, 244–245
  origin and development, 247–255
  proactive and retrospective applications, 245
  standards for evaluations, 247
  theoretical underpinnings, 256–258
  values component, 245–247
Context-sensitive evaluation, 283–284
Contextualized program understanding and L. J. Cronbach, 99–101
Contextual support, 116
Contractualism, 37
Cook, T., 22–23, 81–82, 95
  See also Campbell, D.
Cooperative test construction, 160
Cost analyses, 33–34
"Cost-Effectiveness Analysis of Teacher Selection, A," 184
Cost-effectiveness evaluation
  in education, 181–183
  efforts to advance the field of, 183–186
  origins, 180–181
  reasons for underutilization of, 186–187
Countenance model of evaluation, 199
"Countenance of Educational Evaluation, The," 31, 34
Cousins, J. B., 46–47, 344–345
  evaluative inquiry and cultural change in organizations, 350–351
  many modes of participatory evaluation, 349–350
  participation and use, 347–349
  perspective on evaluation, 346
  problem of nonuse as a triggering experience, 346–347
  ways of knowing, 345

Cram, F., 376
Credible evidence, 125–126, 269
Critical reference group, 379
Criticism, 35–36
Cronbach, L. J., 23–24, 97–98, 211
  commitment to contextualized program understanding, 99–101
  evaluation as education in service of more democratic society and, 103–104
  evaluators as educators and, 102–103
  generalizability theory, 99
  legacy of, 102–103
  method, 98–99
  theory of evaluation, 98–99
Curriculum and evaluation, 160–162

Data
  collection and reporting, 289
  good, 269
Davidson, E. J., 377–378
Decision accretion, 27
Decision facilitation, 6, 23
  CIPP model and, 251
Decision management, 6
Decolonizing Methodologies: Research and Indigenous Peoples, 376
Deconstructing questions, 177
Definition of evaluation, 170–171, 257
Deliberative justification, 38
Democratic evaluation, 215, 358–359, 374, 387–388
Descriptive model, 4
Determinants in change model, 115
Developmental evaluation, 45, 296–297
Developmental Evaluation: Applying Complexity Concepts to Enhance Innovation and Use, 296
Dialogue in European evaluation, 360–361
Discovery, principled, 29
Diversity, 40
Do It Yourself Social Research, 378
Domains of evaluation, 23–24
  four interconnected, 82
  See also UTOs and *UTOs
Down and Out in America, 109
Dualism, subject-object, 220–221

Ecological context in action model, 116
Education
  cost-effectiveness evaluation, 181–183
  evaluation, experience in, 194–195
  evaluation criteria, 192–193

evaluation standards, 193
formal evaluation in, 189–190
importance of evaluation in, 189
language of generalization, 193–194
origin and development of CIPP model and, 247–255
particularization and, 194
remediation and, 192
responsive evaluation, 191–192, 196
STEM, 208–209
utility in, 195–196
values in, 191
See also Context-input-process-product (CIPP) model
Educational connoisseurship, 35
Educational evaluation, 30, 103–104
Educational Evaluation and Decision Making, 252–253
Educators, evaluators as, 102–103
Effectiveness evaluation, 120–121
Effectuality, intervention, 121, 125–126
Effectual validity, 120
  RCTs and, 125
Eight Year Study, The, 3–4, 160–161, 163
Elaboration, competitive, 29
Elementary and Secondary Education Act (ESEA) projects, 249–250, 251–252
Emergent realist evaluation (ERE), 28–29
Empirical theory, 4
Empiricism, logical, 345
Empowerment evaluation, 45–46, 304
  applications, 304
  concepts, 311
  definition and overview, 305
  group mission, 311–312
  issues clarification, 316–317
  monitoring strategies in, 314–315
  planning for the future in, 313–314
  principles, 309–310
  process use, 307–308
  psychologist's role in, 306–307
  self-determination and, 307
  steps, 311–315
  taking stock in, 312–313
  theories, 305–309
  theories of use and action, 308–309
Empowerment theory, 305–307
Engineering education, 66–67
Epistemology, 11, 16–18
  evolutionary, 62
Ethnographies, 16
Ethnography: Step by Step, 317

European evaluation theory tree, 355–356
  demographic evaluation and, 387–388
  dialogue in, 360–361
  discussion on relationship with U.S. evaluation, 367–368
  European Union programs and, 366–367
  Evaluation: The International Journal of Theory and Practice, 364–365
  illuminative, democratic, and personalized evaluation, 356–359
  policy tools and, 359–360
  realist evaluation, 361–362
  roots of, 387–390
  syntheses and the evidence-based movement, 363–364
  turn of the 1990s, 361
  See also Evaluation theory tree
European Union, 366–367, 389
EVALSED (Evaluation of Socio-Economic Development) Guide, 366–367, 389
Evaluability assessment, 42
Evaluating with Validity, 214
Evaluation
  acknowledging the limits of, 133
  as the alpha discipline, 172–175
  as art, 168
  as assisted sensemaking, 145–146
  capability, 380–381
  capacity building (ECB), 331, 337, 341–342, 350–351, 380–381
  category systems, 6–7, 286
  communicating and reporting findings of, 326
  consequences, 151
  context, 41, 244
  defined, 170–171, 257
  democratic, 215, 358–359, 374, 387–388
  developmental, 45, 296–297
  domain of, 23–24
  early writing on, 3–4
  educational, 30, 103–104
  effectiveness, 120–121
  "Eight-Year Study" of progressive education and, 3–4
  emergent realist (ERE), 28–29
  as enmeshed in politics, 133–134
  evidence cumulation, 136
  forms, 376
  foundational roots, 11, 14–18
  fourth generation, 39
  goal-free, 33
  illuminative, 356–359
  inclusive/transformative model of, 40

influence, alternative pathways to, 150–153
institutional nature of, 203
intensive, 43
interpreters and teachers, 5
issue analysts, 5
judgments and, 110
multiple purposes of, 148–150
objectives-oriented, 30
as the paradigm discipline, 175–178
participatory, 46–47
as political activity, 26–27, 103–104
practice, nature of, 325
practice of theory-driven, 27–28
primary aim of, 110
as professional practice, 132–133
program theory and, 134–136
quality control, 172–173
question, nature of, 269–270, 276–277
rapid-feedback, 43, 262
as research, 169–170
responsive, 191–192, 196, 216
review panel (ERP), 76
revolution in thought about, 170
rubrics, 377–378
scientific legitimacy of, 171–172, 174
as seeking objectivity, 131–132
social betterment through, 146–148, 287
social policy and, 109–112
as social research applied to policy-oriented questions, 110
technological versus social program, 271
theories, 4–5
theorists, 5–6
type A and type B failures in, 168–169
utility, 136–138
variety of perspectives in, 130–131
   See also Cost-effectiveness evaluation; Education; Empowerment evaluation; Fourth generation evaluation; Practical participatory evaluation (P-PE); Purposes of evaluation; Revolutions in evaluation; Theory-driven evaluation
Evaluation: A Systematic Approach, 24–25, 108, 109
Evaluation: The International Journal of Theory and Practice, 364–365
Evaluation Center (Stufflebeam), 249–250, 253, 254
Evaluation Essentials, 283
Evaluation Forms and Approaches, 376
Evaluation Methodology Basics, 377–378
Evaluation Network, 226

Evaluation Research, 26, 140, 141
Evaluation Research Society, 226
Evaluation Roots, 8–9
Evaluation Strategies for Communicating and Reporting, 330
Evaluation theory tree, 7–8, 12 (figure), 49–51, 386–387
   Australian and New Zealand roots, 390–392
   central branch, 12
   epistemology in, 11, 16–18
   European roots, 387–390
   foundational roots, 11, 14–18, 386–387
   objectivist arm, 13
   relational nature of, 13
   research methodology in, 12, 18–31
   social accountability in, 11, 14–15
   social inquiry in, 11, 15–16
   subjectivist arm, 13
   use branch, 13, 40–49
   valuing branch, 12, 31–40
   See also European evaluation theory tree
Evaluative inquiry
   and cultural change in organizations, 350–351
   for learning in organizations, 326–329
Evaluative Research, 19–20
Evaluative rubrics, 377–378
Evaluators
   as educators, 102–103
   external, 340–341
   facilitating use, 339
   interpersonal skills, 339
   learning from evaluation, 339–340
   role in empowerment evaluation, 306–307
   specialization by, 168
   variety of methods of, 131
Everyday Evaluation on the Run, 378
Evidence
   for action, 137
   as ammunition, 137
   -based research, 226–227, 363–364
   credible, 125–126, 269
   culture of, 311
   cumulation of evaluation, 136
   as a warning, 137
Evidence for Policy and Practice Information and Coordinating Center (EPPI), 363
Evidence Matters : Randomized Trials in Education Research, 21
Evolutionary epistemology, 62
Experimental and Quasi-Experimental Designs for Generalized Causal Inference, 81

Experimental and Quasi-Experimental Designs for Research, 18, 21, 22
Experimental designs, 18–19, 25, 61
External validity
  principles of construct validity applied to all ways of framing, 90–91
  as robust replication, 84–85
  See also Validity

Failures in evaluation, 168–169
Feasibility standards, 41–42
Fetterman, D., 45–46, 317–318
  See also Empowerment evaluation
Formal evaluation in education, 189–190
Formal sampling theory, 85–86
Formal theory-based interventions, pros and cons of, 126–127
Formative dimension to evaluation, 44, 246 (table)
Forms, evaluation, 376
Fourth generation evaluation, 39, 218–219
  causality and, 221
  influences and building blocks, 225–227
  knowing differently and, 222–224
  procedures for conducting, 224–225
  subject-object conundrum in, 220–221
  theory, 220–225
  truth and, 221–222
Fourth Generation Evaluation, 39
Framework for judging results, 289
Funding, top-down versus bottom-up approaches for advancing validity and, 123–124
Funnell, S. C., 375

General influence processes, 151
Generalizability theory, 99
Generalization, language of, 193–194
"General Statement on Evaluation," 247
Getting to Maybe: How the World Is Changed, 296
Goal(s)
  accountability, 14
  displacement, 375
  -free evaluation, 33
  and outcomes in change model, 115
Government Performance and Results Act, 264
Greene, J. C., 38
  American Evaluation Association (AEA) and, 209–210
  becoming values-engaged, 212–215
  current research, 208–209
  education of, 210–211, 212 (table)

responsiveness, culture, and context, 216
snapshots from the present, 208–210
Guba, E., 39–40, 213–214
  See also Fourth generation evaluation
Guides for the Evaluation of Structural Funds, 356

Halcolm, 302–303
Handbook of Applied Social Research Methods, 175
Handbook of Applied Social Science, 171
Handbook of Practical Program Evaluation, 171
Handbook on Evaluation Research, 184
Henry, G. T., 28–29, 144–145, 154–155
  alternative pathways to evaluation influence, 150–153
  epistemological roots, 153
  evaluation as assisted sensemaking, 145–146
  influences on, 154
  multiple purposes of evaluation, 148–150
  social betterment through evaluation, 146–148
Hewlett-Packard, 304
Holistic assessment, 117
House, E. R., 36–38, 198–199, 214–215
  exploring evaluation frontiers, 202–204
  learning the craft and creating new ideas, 199–201
  looking back, 205–206
  meta-evaluation, 201–202
  semireflecting in semiretirement, 204–205
Housing projects, 255–256

Illuminative evaluation, 356–359
Implementing organization in action model, 115
Inductive logic, 17
Industrial/organization (I/O) psychology, 176
Influence process model, 150–153
Input evaluations, 41, 244
  See also Context-input-process-product (CIPP) model
Institute for Program Evaluation, 275
Integrative validity model, 118–121
Intensive evaluation, 43
Intent-to-treat analysis (ITT), 79
Interactive evaluation practice (IEP), 48–49
Interpretation of Cultures, The, 16
Interpretivism, 17
Intervention(s)
  effectuality, 121, 125–126
  or treatment in change model, 115

revision and improvement in real world before finalization, 122
and service delivery protocols in action model, 116
usefulness to stakeholders, 122
viability, 121, 125–126

Joint Committee on Standards for Educational Evaluation, 247, 254
Journal of Aesthetic Education, 35
Judgment role in evaluation, 20
Justice theory, 37

Kemmis, S., 373–374
King, J. A., 48–49, 334–338
  evaluation "theory"/point of view, 338–343
  See also Interactive evaluation practice (IEP)
Knowledge construction, 12

Learning
  evaluative inquiry for, 326–329
  transformational, 47–48
Levels of analysis, 150–151
Levin, H. M., 183–186
Lincoln, Y. S., 39–40
  See also Fourth generation evaluation
Logical empiricism, 345
Logic of Evaluative Argument, The, 8
Losing Ground, 202

Macrolevel contextual support, 116
Manaakitanga, 376
Managerialism, 37
Manpower Development Research Corporation, 77
Maori people, 376–377, 390, 391–392
Marginalized groups, 40
Mark, M. M., 28–29, 144–145, 154–155
  alternative pathways to evaluation influence, 150–153
  epistemological roots, 153
  evaluation as assisted sensemaking, 145–146
  influences on, 154
  multiple purposes of evaluation, 148–150
  social betterment through evaluation, 146–148
Mathematica Policy Research, 77
Maximum variation, 224
MEANS (Methods for Evaluating Actions of a Structural Nature) Guide, 366, 389
Mertens, D. M., 40
  evaluations influences, 232
  paradigms and evaluation, 232–233

personal experiences, 229–230
professional experiences, 230–232
transformative axiological assumption, 233–235
transformative epistemological assumption, 236–237
transformative methodological assumption, 237–239
transformative ontological assumption, 235–236
transformative paradigm, 233
Meta-analysis, 136
Meta-evaluation by E. R. House, 201–202
Methodologicalism, 37
Methodology, research, 5, 12
  Australia and New Zealand, 378–382
  Carol Weiss, 26–27
  Donald Campbell, 18–19
  Edward Suchman, 19–20
  European roots of evaluation and, 388–389
  Gary Henry and Melvin Mark, 28–29
  Huey T. Chen, 27–28
  Lee J. Cronbach, 23–24
  Peter Rossi, 24–26
  Ralph Tyler, 29–31
  Robert Boruch, 20–22
  Thomas Cook, 22–23
  See also individual evaluators
"Methodology of Evaluation, The," 167
"Methods for the Experimenting Society," 62
Michigan Educational Assessment Program, 254
Microlevel contextual support, 116
Minnesota Center for Social Research, 301
Mission statements, 311–312
MITRE Corporation, 270–274
Models, prescriptive and descriptive, 4
Modus operandi (MO), 32
Motivational processes, 151

NASA/Jet Propulsion Laboratory, 304
National Academy of Sciences (NAS), 70, 73, 76
National Center for Research on Educational Accountability and Teacher Evaluation (CREATE), 254
National Institute of Education, 335
National Institute of Mental Health (NIMH), 299
National Opinion Research Center (NORC), 107–108
National Research Council, 226

National Science Foundation, 203, 208
Nature of evaluation practice, 325
Needs, 33
Negotiation of agreement on acceptability of design measures and procedures, 289
New Directions for Evaluation, 28, 113, 349, 350
New Zealand. *See* Australia and New Zealand
No Child Left Behind, 22, 389
Nominalism, 361
North Atlantic Treaty Organization (NATO), 267–270

Objectives-oriented evaluation, 30
Objectivism
 arm in evaluation theory tree, 13
 CIPP model, 257
Objectivity
 empowerment evaluation and, 316
 evaluation as seeking, 131–132
Organizational context, 291, 341–342
Organization for Economic Cooperation and Development (OECD), 109
Outcome(s)
 accountability, 14
 empowerment evaluation, 317
Owen, J. M., 376

Paradigms, 16–17, 232–233
 discipline, evaluation as the, 175–178
 transformative, 233
Participatory action research (PAR), 212
Participatory evaluation. *See* Practical participatory evaluation (P-PE)
Particularization in education evaluation, 194
Patton, M. Q., 44–45, 293–294
 discovering process use, 301–302
 early encounters with evaluation luminaries, 300–301
 global influences, 302
 Halcolm character, 302–303
 influences on, 294–298
 unlearning sociology, 298–300
Peace Corps, 294–295
Pedagogy of the Oppressed, 211
Peer organizations/community partners in action model, 116
Peer review, 174
Performance
 evaluation for improving, 261–262
 rapid-feedback evaluations of, 43, 262
Performance monitoring, 43
Personalized evaluation, 359

Phi Delta Kappa International (PDK), 252–253
Pluralism/elitism, 37
Policy analysis, 263–264, 276–277
Policy tools and European evaluation, 359–360
Political context, 291
Politics
 educational innovation, 199–200
 empowerment evaluation and, 317
 evaluation as, 26–27, 103–104, 215
 evaluation enmeshed in, 133–134
Positivism, 15, 17, 361, 367–368
Postpositivism, 16–17
Practical participatory evaluation (P-PE), 46–47, 348
 modes of, 349–350
Pragmatism, 16, 17–18, 38
 CIPP model, 257–258
Prescriptive model, 4, 339
Preskill, H., 47–48, 323–324
 evaluative inquiry for learning in organizations, 326–329
 evolving theory of evaluation, 324–326
 influences on point of view, 329–330
 next stage in evolving point of view, 330–332
 parting thoughts, 332–333
Primary intended users, 44
Principled discovery, 29
Process accountability, 14
Process evaluations, 41, 244
 See also Context-input-process-product (CIPP) model
Process use, 301–302, 307–308
Product evaluations, 41, 244
 See also Context-input-process-product (CIPP) model
Professional Evaluation, 215
Professional practice, evaluation as, 132–133
Program context, 290–291
Program Evaluation, 391
Program Evaluation, Particularly Responsive Evaluation, 34
Program Evaluation Standards, The, 41, 256
Program implementers in action model, 115
Program logic matrix, 375
Program theory
 Australia and New Zealand, 381–382
 conceptual framework of, 114–116
 evaluation and, 134–136
 usefulness of, 116–118
Propriety standards, 41
Psychology, 15
 experimental, 16
 industrial/organizational, 176

Psychology of Arithmetic, 159
Purposes of evaluation, 268, 273, 325
  empowerment, 316
  multiple, 148–150
PUSH/Excel program, 201–202

Qualitative Approaches to Evaluation in Education: The Silent Scientific Revolution, 317
"Qualitative Knowing in Action Research," 62, 64
Quality control, evaluation, 172–173
Quasi-experimental designs, 18–19, 22, 61–62
Questions, evaluation, 269–270, 276–277
  framing, 288

Racism, 204
Rand Corporation, 180
Randomized controlled trials (RCTs), 120–121, 357
  effectual validity and, 124
  social betterment and, 148
Randomized field experiments, 20–22
Rapid-feedback evaluation, 43, 262
Realism, 153
Realist evaluation, 361–362
Realistic Evaluation, 365
Reductionism, 127–128
"Reforms as Experiments," 62
Reframing Evaluation Through Appreciative Inquiry, 330
Relativism, 17, 31, 37
Remediation in evaluation, 192
Reporting and communicating evaluation findings, 326
Research, evaluation as, 169–170
Responsive evaluation, 191–192, 196, 216
Revolutions in conceptualizations of evaluation, 167–168
Revolutions in evaluation, 170–171
  evaluation as the alpha discipline and, 172–175
  evaluation as the paradigm discipline, 175–178
  scientific legitimacy and, 171–172
Robert Wood Johnson Foundation, 76
Robust replication, 84–85
Rogers, P. J., 381–382
Rossi, P. H., 24–26
  MITRE Corporation and, 270–271
  origins and influences, 106–109
  on what is evaluation, 109–112
Rubrics, evaluative, 377–378

Scientific legitimacy of evaluation, 171–172, 174
Scientific Research in Education, 22
Self-determination, 307
Self-help housing projects, 255–256
Sensemaking, evaluation as assisted, 145–146
Sequential purchase of information, 43
Silent Spring, The, 211
Social accountability, 11, 14–15
Social betterment through evaluation, 146–148, 287
Social inquiry, 11, 15–16
Social policy and evaluation, 109–112
Sociology, 298–300
Spouse Assault Replication Program (SARP), 72
Stake, R. E., 34–35, 189–196
Stakeholders, 23, 34
  delineation of strategy to consider views and interests of, 117
  evaluative inquiry for learning in organizations and, 328
  fourth generation evaluation and, 225
  integrative validity model and, 118–119
  involvement, 38, 39–40, 347–349
  nonevaluator, 346
  representative panels, 42
Standards
  CIPP evaluations, 247
  education evaluation, 193
  professional, 41–42
Standpoints, 222–223
Statistical Methods for Utilizing Personal Judgments to Evaluate Activities for Teacher-Training Curricula, 158
STEM education, 208–209
Stock-taking in empowerment evaluation, 312–313
Structural Funds, European Union, 366–367, 389
Stufflebeam, D., 41–42, 243
  See also Context-input-process-product (CIPP) model
Subjective belief systems, 17
Subjective meaningfulness, 12
Subjectivism, 13, 31, 34
Subject-object dualism, 220–221
Summative dimension to evaluation, 44, 246 (table)
Syntheses of evaluation studies, 363–364
Systematic Reviews in the Social Sciences, 364
Systematic social inquiry, 11, 15–16
  See also Cousins, J. B.
Systems thinking, 127–128, 296–297

Target group in action model, 116
Taxonomy of Educational Objectives, The, 159, 163
Technological evaluations, 271
Technological scientism, 35
Theories, evaluation, 4–5
    category systems and, 6–7, 286
    empowerment, 305–307
Theorists, evaluation, 5–6
Theory-Driven Evaluation, 13
Theory-driven evaluation, 13, 27–28
    action model in, 115–116
    as an integrated perspective, 125–128
    change model in, 115
    conceptual framework of program theory and, 114–116
    concurrent validity approaches, 124
    integrative validity model and, 118–121
    literature on, 113
    providing balanced view on credible evidence, 125–126
    providing contingency perspective on methods, 125
    recognizing the pros and cons of formal theory/stakeholder, 126–127
    roots of, 113–114
    synthesizing reductionism versus fluid complexity's program view, 127–128
    top-down versus bottom-up approaches for advancing validity in, 121–124
    usefulness of program theory and, 116–118
Theory tree, evaluation. *See* Evaluation theory tree
Thick description, 34
"Thick Description: Toward an Interpretive Theory of Culture," 16
Top-down versus bottom-up approaches for advancing validity, 121–124
Toward Reform of Program Evaluation, 23
Transferable validity, 120
Transformational learning, 47–48
Transformative axiological assumptions, 233–235
Transformative epistemological assumptions, 236–237
Transformative methodological assumption, 237–239
Transformative ontological assumptions, 235–236
Transformative paradigm, 233
Tree, evaluation theory. *See* Evaluation theory tree

Truth and fourth generation evaluation, 221–222
Tyler, R. W., 29–31, 162–163
    curriculum and evaluation by, 160–162
    early work, 158
    Eight Year Study and, 3–4, 160–161
    legacy of, 157
    testing and evaluation by, 158–160
Type A and type B failures in evaluation, 168–169

Urban Institute, 263
U.S. Department of Defense, 180, 268, 278
U.S. Department of Education, 72–73, 182, 187
U.S. Department of Health and Human Services, 263
Use
    Australia and New Zealand, 373–376
    branch in evaluation theory tree, 13, 40–41
    Daniel Stufflebeam and, 41–42
    David Fetterman and, 45–46
    Eleanor Chelimsky and, 43
    empowerment evaluation in, 45–46
    evaluability assessment in, 42
    Hallie Preskill and, 47–48
    importance of perspective with respect to, 274
    interactive evaluation practice (IEP) and, 48–49
    J. Bradley Cousins and, 46–47
    Jean King and, 48–49
    Joseph Wholey and, 42–43
    Marvin Alkin and, 44
    Michael Patton and, 44–45
    participatory evaluation in, 46–47
    professional standards in, 41–42
    transformational learning in, 47–48
    user oriented approach in, 44
    utilization-focused evaluation (UFE) and, 44–45
    See also individual evaluators
U.S. Government Accountability Office (GAO), 15, 43, 73, 75, 264, 274–279
Using Social Research in Public Policy Making, 141
U.S. Office of Education, 251
U.S. Office of Management, 264
Utilitarianism, 36–37
Utility
    in resonsive evaluation, 195–196
    standards, 41
Utilization-Focused Evaluation, 286, 295, 299, 300, 301, 335
Utilization-focused evaluation (UFE), 44–45, 293–294

UTOs and *UTOs, 23–24, 85–86
    between-study improvements and, 94–95
    construct validity and, 90–91
    Cronbach framework of, 101
    external validity and, 84–85
    generalizing to, 83–85
    generic methods for extending external validity understood as generalizing to, 91–92
    limited reach of formal sampling theory and, 85–86
    See also Domains of evaluation

Validity, 19, 25, 61
    concurrent approaches, 124
    construct, 86–91
    effectual, 120
    model, integrative, 118–121
    as robust replication, external, 84–85
    top-down versus bottom-up approaches for advancing, 121–124
    transferable, 120
    viable, 119–120
Valuing in evaluation, 12, 31–32
    Australia and New Zealand, 376–378
    cost analyses and, 33–34
    criticism and, 35–36
    Donna Mertens and, 40
    Egon Guba and Yvonna Lincoln and, 39–40
    Elliott Eisner and, 35–36
    empowerment evaluation and, 312–313
    Ernest House and, 36–38
    Henry Levin and, 33–34
    inquiry, 147
    Jennifer C. Greene and, 38
    justice theory and, 37
    Michael Scriven and, 32–33
    Robert Stake and, 34–35
    subjectivism in, 13
    utilitarianism and, 36–37
    See also individual evaluators
Viability, intervention, 121, 125–126
Viable validity, 119–120

W. K. Kellogg Foundation, 380
Wadsworth, Y., 378–379
Wehipeihana, N., 377
Weiss, C. H., 26–27, 130–131, 141–142
    acknowledging the limits of evaluation, 133
    cumulation of evaluation evidence, 136
    evaluation and program theory, 134–136
    evaluation as enmeshed in politics, 133–134
    evaluation as professional practice, 132–133
    evaluation as seeking objectivity, 131–132
    evaluation use, 136–138
    influences on, 139–141
Whanaungatanga, 376
What Works Clearinghouse (WWC), 74–75, 182, 187
Wholey, J. S., 42–43
    influences on view of evaluation, 263–264
    views on evaluation, 261–262
Why Families Move, 107
Williams, B., 380–381
Winston, J. A., 374–375
Within-study improvements and causal generalization, 93–94

Youthful Offenders at Highfields, 140

ABOUT THE EDITOR

Marvin C. Alkin is an emeritus professor in the Social Research Methods Division of the Graduate School of Education and Information Studies at the University of California, Los Angeles (UCLA). He has written extensively on evaluation utilization and comparative evaluation theory. He is the author of *Debates on Evaluation*, *Using Evaluations*, and *A Guide for Evaluation Decision Makers* (all Sage publications). He was editor of *Educational Evaluation and Policy Planning*, was executive editor of the *Encyclopedia of Educational Research* (sixth edition), and for more than 30 years was associate editor of *Studies in Educational Evaluation*. He is currently co–section editor of the Teaching Evaluation section of the *American Journal of Evaluation*. Alkin has been a consultant to six national governments and has conducted more than 85 evaluations of a variety of educational, governmental, and foundation programs. He founded and directed the UCLA Center for the Study of Evaluation. Alkin is a winner of the American Evaluation Association's Lazarsfeld Award for Evaluation Theory.

ABOUT THE CONTRIBUTORS

Robert F. Boruch is University Trustee Chair Professor at the University of Pennsylvania in the Graduate School of Education and the Statistics Department of the Wharton School and is a member of the graduate groups for the School of Social Policy and Practice and Criminology Department. He is the author or coauthor of more than 200 articles in peer-reviewed journals and author and editor of a dozen books and special editions of peer-reviewed journals. He contributes frequently to committees and panels of the National Academy of Sciences and of professional organizations. Boruch is an elected Fellow of the American Academy of Arts and Sciences, the American Educational Research Association, the American Statistical Association, and the Academy for Experimental Criminology. He has received awards from the Policy Studies Organization, the American Educational Research Association, the American Evaluation Association, and the Campbell Collaboration. He is a founding member of the Evaluation Research Society, a progenitor of the American Evaluation Association, and the international Campbell Collaboration. He has served on advisory boards and panels of governmental agencies at the U.S. Department of Education, the U.S. Government Accountability Office, the National Institutes of Health, and the National Science Foundation and on multinational groups for the World Bank, World Health Organization, and others. Boruch has served on the board of trustees for the William T. Grant Foundation and currently serves on the board of directors of the American Institutes for Research and the Society for Research in Educational Effectiveness.

Eleanor Chelimsky is currently a consultant in evaluation methodology, practice, and policy. She has worked with the Rockefeller Foundation, the U.S. Environmental Protection Agency, the Department of Health and Human Services, the World Bank, the National Science Foundation, the Robert Wood Johnson Foundation, and many others. At present, she also serves as a member of the American Evaluation Association's Evaluation Policy Task Force. She was the Assistant Comptroller General of the U.S. Government Accountability Office for Evaluation and Methodology and, for 14 years, ran a division of about 100 social scientists who performed evaluations for the Congress in a very wide variety of subject areas. She had been a Fulbright scholar in Paris, France, and an economic and statistical analyst at the North Atlantic Treaty Organization and has been president of the Evaluation Research Society (1981) and the American Evaluation Association (1995). In 1991, she received the Government

Accountability Office's top honor, the Comptroller General's Award for Excellence, and in 1994, she received the Donald Campbell Award for Methodological Innovation in Public Policy Studies.

Huey T. Chen is Director of the Center for Research and Evaluation on Education and Human Services and Professor of Health and Nutrition Sciences at Montclair State University. Previously, he was a senior evaluation scientist at the Centers for Disease Control and Prevention (CDC). He has written extensively on program theory, theory-driven evaluation, integrative validity model, and bottom-up approach. He is the author of several evaluation books. His book *Theory-Driven Evaluations* (1990, Sage) is seen as one of the landmarks in program evaluation. His book *Practical Program Evaluation: Assess and Improve Program Planning, Implementation, and Effectiveness* (2005, Sage) provides a systematic conceptual framework and strategies that benefit evaluation practitioners in understanding the trade-offs among evaluation options at different program stages and how to choose an option as a basis for designing an evaluation that best serves stakeholders' needs. Recently, he was a coeditor of *Advancing Validity for Outcome Evaluation: Theory and Practice* (2011, Volume 130, *New Directions for Evaluation*). The volume discussed the limitations of applying the existing framework in addressing validity issues in the context of program evaluation and proposed alternative perspectives and approaches for dealing with the problems. He serves on the editorial advisory boards of *New Directions of Evaluation* and *Evaluation and Program Planning*. He is a winner of the American Evaluation Association's Lazarsfeld Award for Evaluation Theory. He also received the Senior Biomedical Service Award from CDC for his evaluation work.

Christina A. Christie is Associate Professor and Division Head, Social Research Methodology, at the Graduate School of Education and Information Studies, University of California, Los Angeles. Christie's research on evaluation practice is designed to strengthen our understanding of evaluation as a method for facilitating social change by contributing to an empirical knowledge base of the factors and conditions that influence evaluation practice. Her theoretical scholarship intends to advance frameworks for understanding evaluation models with the goal of refining practice. Christie was the 2004 recipient of the American Evaluation Association's Marcia Guttentag Early Career Award and was recently elected to serve on the board. She served as a section editor of the *American Journal of Evaluation* (2004–2009) and serves on the editorial board of *Studies in Educational in Evaluation*. She is the editor of *Exemplars of Evaluation Practice* (with Jody Fitzpatrick and Mel Mark; Sage, 2008) and *What Counts as Credible Evidence in Evaluation and Evidence-Based Practice?* (with Stewart Donaldson and Mel Mark; Sage, 2008).

Thomas D. Cook is John Evans Professor of Sociology at Northwestern University, with appointments also in Psychology and Education and Social Policy.

J. Bradley Cousins is Professor of Program Evaluation and Organizational Studies at the Faculty of Education, University of Ottawa. His main academic interests are in program evaluation, including participatory and collaborative approaches, utilization issues, and evaluation capacity building. He is the author of several articles, chapters in international handbooks, and books on evaluation-related topics, including *Participatory Evaluation in Education* (1995, coedited with Lorna Earl), *The Sage International Handbook of Educational Evaluation* (2009, coedited with Katherine Ryan), and *Participatory Evaluation Up Close: A Review and Integration of the Research Base* (in press, with Jill Chouinard). Cousins recently received from the American Evaluation Association the prestigious Paul F. Lazarsfeld Award 2008 for contributions to evaluation theory. Recognized by his University of Ottawa peers in 2004 for excellence in research, he is the 2007 recipient of the Canadian Evaluation Society's (National Capital Chapter) Karl Boudreau Award for Leadership in Evaluation. He also received the Canadian Association for the Study of Educational Administration's 1989 Doctoral Dissertation Award and, in 1999, the Contributions to Evaluation in Canada award from the Canadian Evaluation Society. He was editor of the *Canadian Journal of Program Evaluation* from 2002 to 2010 and served as program cochair for the Canadian Evaluation Society–American Evaluation Association joint conference held in Toronto in October 2005. Cousins received his PhD in educational measurement and evaluation from the University of Toronto in 1988.

E. Jane Davidson is the director of Real Evaluation Ltd., an evaluation consulting business based in Auckland, New Zealand. Jane Davidson returned home to Aotearoa (New Zealand) in 2004 from the United States, where she served as the associate director of the internationally recognized evaluation center at Western Michigan University. There, she launched and directed the world's first fully interdisciplinary PhD in evaluation, spanning the Colleges of Arts & Science, Education & Human Development, Engineering & Applied Sciences, and Health & Human Services. She currently runs a successful evaluation consulting business, working across a range of domains, including leadership development, human resources, health, education, and social policy. Her work includes evaluation training and development, facilitated self-evaluation and capacity building, independent evaluation, and formative and summative meta-evaluation (advice, support, coaching, and critical reviews of evaluation plans or evaluations). Jane has presented numerous keynote addresses and professional development workshops internationally, including those for the American Evaluation Association, the UK Evaluation Society, the Australasian Evaluation Society, the Evaluators' Institute (United States), the Aotearoa/New Zealand Evaluation Association, and the University of South Africa. Jane is author of *Evaluation Methodology Basics: The Nuts and Bolts of Sound Evaluation* (2004, Sage), which is used internationally as a graduate text and practitioners' guidebook. In 2005, she received the American Evaluation Association's Marcia Guttentag Award, awarded to a promising new evaluator within 5 years of completing their doctorate. Jane received her PhD from Claremont Graduate University (California) in organizational behavior with substantial emphasis on evaluation.

David M. Fetterman is the president and chief executive officer of Fetterman & Associates, an international evaluation consulting firm. He is concurrently a professor of education at the University of Arkansas at Pine Bluff and director of the Arkansas Evaluation Center. He has 25 years' experience at Stanford University, including serving as Director of Evaluation in the School of Medicine and Director of the MA Policy Analysis and Evaluation Program in the School of Education. He is a past president of the American Evaluation Association (AEA) and the American Anthropological Association's Council on Anthropology and Education. He is the cochair of AEA's Collaborative, Participatory, and Empowerment Evaluation (CP&EE) Division. His contributions to ethnography, ethnographic evaluation, and empowerment evaluation are widely recognized. He conducts evaluations throughout the United States and internationally. (Details are available at Dr. Fetterman's website; see below.) He received the Paul Lazarsfeld Award for Outstanding Contributions to Evaluation Theory and the Myrdal Award for Cumulative Contributions to Evaluation Practice. He also received a Mensa Education and Research Foundation Award for Excellence. Fetterman teaches online and maintains AEA's CP&EE website (http://www.davidfetterman.com) and the Empowerment Evaluation blog (http://eevaluation.blogspot.com). He has consulted for government agencies, foundations, corporations, and academic institutions. He is the author of 14 books, including *Empowerment Evaluation Principles in Practice*, *Ethnography: Step by Step* (third edition), *Qualitative Approaches to Evaluation in Education: The Silent Scientific Revolution*, *Excellence and Equality: A Qualitatively Different Perspective on Gifted and Talented Education*, and *Ethnography in Educational Evaluation*. He received his PhD from Stanford University.

Jennifer C. Greene is Professor of Educational Psychology at the University of Illinois at Urbana-Champaign. Her work focuses on the intersection of social science methodology and social policy and aspires to be both methodologically innovative and socially responsible. Greene's methodological research has concentrated on advancing qualitative and mixed methods approaches to social inquiry as well as democratic commitments in evaluation practice. Greene has held leadership positions in the American Evaluation Association and the American Educational Research Association. She has also provided editorial service to both communities, including a 6-year position as coeditor-in-chief of *New Directions for Evaluation*. Her own publication record includes a coeditorship of the recent *The SAGE Handbook of Evaluation* and authorship of *Mixed Methods in Social Inquiry*. Greene is the 2011 president of the American Evaluation Association.

Egon G. Guba, now deceased, was Professor Emeritus at Indiana University. He had been a contributor to evaluation theory since the 1960s, beginning with contributions to the CIPP model of evaluation, and proceeding to naturalistic evaluation and fourth generation evaluation. He was the coauthor (with Yvonna Lincoln) of *Effective Evaluation, Naturalistic Inquiry,* and *Fourth Generation Evaluation,* and the editor of *The Paradigm Dialog,* as well as author of numerous chapters on the paradigm revolution and its impact on evaluation theory and practice. He was the recipient of the Paul Lazarsfeld Prize for Contributions to Evaluation Theory (1985).

Gary T. Henry holds the Duncan MacRae '09 and Rebecca Kyle MacRae Professorship of Public Policy, directs the Carolina Institute for Public Policy, and holds an appointment in Frank Porter Graham Institute for Child Development at University of North Carolina (UNC) at Chapel Hill. Formerly, he held the William Neil Reynolds Distinguished University Visiting Professorship at UNC. He has served as a professor in the Andrew Young School of Policy Studies, Department of Political Science, and the Department of Education Policy Studies at Georgia State University; and the Department of Public Policy at Georgia Institute of Technology. He previously served as

Director of Evaluation and Learning Services for the David and Lucile Packard Foundation. Henry has evaluated a variety of policies and programs, including North Carolina's Disadvantaged Student Supplemental Fund, Georgia's Universal Pre-K, public information campaigns, and the HOPE Scholarship as well as school reforms and accountability systems. He is the author of *Practical Sampling* (Sage, 1990) and *Graphing Data* (Sage, 1995) and coauthor of *Evaluation: An Integrated Framework for Understanding, Guiding, and Improving Policies and Programs* (Jossey-Bass, 2000). He received the Outstanding Evaluation of the Year Award from the American Evaluation Association in 1998 and the Joseph S. Wholey Distinguished Scholarship Award in 2001 from the American Society for Public Administration and the Center for Accountability and Performance along with Steve Harkreader. Henry serves as a principal member of the Standing Committee for Systemic Reform, Institute of Education Sciences, U.S. Department of Education.

Ernest R. House is Professor Emeritus at the University of Colorado, Boulder, where he was a professor of education, specializing in evaluation and policy, from 1985 to 2001. Previously, he was a professor of education at the Center for Instructional Research and Curriculum Evaluation at the University of Illinois, Urbana (1969–1985). He has been a visiting scholar at the University of California, Los Angeles; Harvard University; University of New Mexico; Center for Advanced Study in the Behavioral Sciences, Stanford; and universities in England, Australia, Spain, Sweden, Austria, and Chile. He has published many books, including *The Politics of Educational Innovation* (1974), *Survival in the Classroom* (with S. Lapan, 1978), *Evaluating With Validity* (1980), *Professional Evaluation* (1993), *Schools for Sale* (1998), *Values in Evaluation and Social Research* (with K. Howe, 1999), *Regression to the Mean* (an evaluation novel, 2007), and *Cherry Street Alley* (a childhood memoir). He is a recipient of the Harold E. Lasswell Prize (with W. Madura, 1989), presented by Policy Sciences, and the Paul F. Lazarsfeld Award for Evaluation Theory (1990), presented by the American Evaluation Association.

Jean A. King is a professor and director of Graduate Studies in the Department of Organizational Leadership, Policy, and Development at the University of Minnesota. She received her bachelor's, master's, and doctoral degrees from Cornell University and taught middle school English in upstate New York before moving to New Orleans, Louisiana, to become a professor at Tulane University. In 1989, she moved upriver to the University of Minnesota as the founding director of the Center for Applied Research and Educational Improvement in the College of Education and Human Development, a position she held for 4 years before working collaboratively to revitalize program evaluation instruction in the college. King founded the Minnesota Evaluation Studies Institute in 1996 and currently serves as its director. With more than 30 years of experience conducting evaluations, she has taught many evaluation courses and mentored numerous graduate students. A sought after presenter and longtime writer on evaluation, she is the author of many articles, chapters, and reviews and retains an abiding interest in participatory evaluation and evaluation capacity building. With Laurie Stevahn, she is currently completing *Interactive Evaluation Practice: Mastering the Interpersonal Dynamics of Program Evaluation* (to be published by Sage in 2012).

H. M. Levin is the William Heard Kilpatrick Professor of Economics and Education and director of the National Center for the Study of Privatization in Education (NCSPE), and codirector of the Center for Benefit-Cost Studies in Education. He is also the David Jacks Professor of Higher Education, Emeritus, at Stanford University, with a joint appointment in the School of Education and Department of Economics. Levin is the founding director of the Accelerated Schools Project, a national school reform that reached about 1,000 schools in 41 states and Hong Kong. Levin has been a Fulbright scholar in Barcelona and Mexico, visiting professor at Beijing University and the Chinese University of Hong Kong, visiting scholar at the Russell Sage Foundation, and fellow at the Center for Advanced Studies in Behavioral Sciences. He has also been president of the Palo Alto, California, school board, the Comparative and International Education Society, and the American Evaluation Association. He is an elected member of the National Academy of Education and is the author of about 300 articles and author or editor of 20 books. Professor Levin is a specialist in the economics of education, educational finance, and school reform. His latest books are *Cost-Effectiveness Analysis: Methods and Applications Second Edition* (2001), *Privatizing Education* (2001), *Cost-Effectiveness Analysis and Educational Policy* (2002), *Privatizing Educational Choice: Consequences for Parents, Schools, and Public Policy* (2005), and *The Price We Pay: Economic and Social Consequences of Inadequate Education* (2007).

Yvonna S. Lincoln holds the Ruth Harrington Chair of Educational Leadership and is University Distinguished Professor of Higher Education at Texas A&M University. She is a former President of the American Evaluation Association and has been an evaluation practitioner and consultant for over 25 years. She is the coauthor of *Effective Evaluation, Fourth Generation Evaluation,* and numerous chapters and journal articles on evaluation practice and ethics in evaluation. Her interests lie in democratic, inclusionary, participative, and social justice issues in evaluation and public policy formulation.

Jason K. Luellen is Senior Statistical Analyst for Centerstone Research Institute (CRI), a not-for-profit organization dedicated to improving mental health care through research and information technology. He splits his efforts between the Research Analytics and Program Evaluation departments. For Research Analytics, he works with CRI's award-winning data warehouse and business intelligence solutions summarizing electronic health record and operational data and applying predictive analytics to facilitate business and clinical decision making. For Program Evaluation, he is responsible for contributing to study design, database management, statistical analyses, and dissemination for multiple federally funded evaluation projects. Prior to CRI, he was an Institute for Education Sciences' postdoctoral fellow for Vanderbilt University's Experimental Education Research Training (ExpERT) program. He received a doctoral degree in research design and statistics from The University of Memphis and a master's degree in clinical psychology from Middle Tennessee University. His personal program of research has focused largely on causal inference, especially understanding and improving the estimates of treatment effects from quasi-experiments given the problem of selection bias.

George F. Madaus is currently the Boisi Professor of Education and Public Policy at Boston College. He was named as the recipient of the 2003 E.F. Lindquist award, presented by AERA and ACT to a distinguished research scientist for "Significant contributions to the field of educational measurement." He is the former director of BC's Center for the Study of Testing, Evaluation, and Educational Policy, and the former Executive Director of the National Commission on Testing and Public Policy. He has been the Vice President of AERA Division D and a past President of NCME. He served on the 1974 and the 1985 Joint AERA, APA, and NCME Test Standards Committee, and on the 1981 Joint Committee on Standards for Educational Evaluation. He was Cochair of the APA, AERA, and NCME *Joint Committee on Testing Practices,* and served on the subcommittee that drafted the *Code of Fair Testing Practices in Education.* He has been a visiting Professor at the Harvard Graduate School of Education and St. Patrick's College, Dublin, and is a member of the National Academy of Education. In addition, he has been a Fellow at the Center for Advanced Studies in the Behavioral Sciences.

Melvin M. Mark is Professor and Head of Psychology at the Pennsylvania State University. He has served as president of the American Evaluation Association and as editor of the *American Journal of Evaluation* (for which he is now Editor Emeritus). Mark's interests include the theory, methodology, and practice of program and policy evaluation, as well as the application of social psychology. Among his books are *Evaluation: An Integrated Framework for Understanding, Guiding, and Improving Policies and Programs* (Jossey-Bass, 2000; with Gary Henry and George Julnes) and the coedited volumes *Evaluation Studies Review Annual, Volume 3* (1978), *Social Science and Social Policy* (1985), *Multiple Methods in Program Evaluation* (1987), *Realist Evaluation* (1998), *The SAGE Handbook of Evaluation* (2006), *What Counts as Credible Evidence in Applied Research and Evaluation Practice* (2009), *Evaluation in Action: Interviews With Expert Evaluators* (2008), *Evaluation Policy and Evaluation Practice* (2009), *Social Psychology and Evaluation* (2011), and *Advancing Validity in Outcome Evaluation* (2011). He received his PhD from Northwestern University.

Donna M. Mertens, PhD, is a professor in the Department of Educational Foundations and Research at Gallaudet University, where she teaches advanced research methods and program evaluation to deaf and hearing students. She also serves as editor for the *Journal of Mixed Methods Research.* The primary focus of her work is transformative mixed methods inquiry in diverse communities that prioritizes the ethical implications of research in the pursuit of social justice. Her recent books include *Program Evaluation Theory to Practice: A Comprehensive Guide*; *Transformative Research and Evaluation*; *The Handbook of Social Research Ethics*; *Research and Evaluation in Education and Psychology: Integrating Diversity With Quantitative, Qualitative, and Mixed Methods* (third edition); *Research and Evaluation Methods in Special Education*; and *Parents and Their Deaf Children: The Early Years.* She is widely published in the *Journal of Mixed Methods Research, American Journal of Evaluation, American Annals of the Deaf,* and *Educational Evaluation and Policy Analysis.*

Michael Quinn Patton is an independent program evaluation and organizational development consultant. He is a former president of the *American Evaluation Association* (AEA). He is the author of six major evaluation books: *Utilization-Focused Evaluation*, *Developmental Evaluation: Applying Complexity Concepts to Enhance Innovation and Use*, *Qualitative Research and Evaluation Methods*, *Creative Evaluation*, *Practical Evaluation,* and *How to Use Qualitative Methods in Evaluation*. He is a recipient of both the Alva and Gunnar Myrdal Award for Outstanding Contributions to Useful and Practical Evaluation Practice and the Paul F. Lazarsfeld Award for Lifelong Contributions to Evaluation Theory from AEA. He teaches regularly in The Evaluators' Institute, the International Programs for Development Evaluation Training, and AEA preconference professional development workshops.

Hallie Preskill is the executive director of FSG's Strategic Learning & Evaluation Center. In her role as a senior advisor, she works on a wide variety of strategic evaluation and learning projects with foundations, nonprofits, corporations, and government organizations. Prior to joining FSG, Hallie spent more than 20 years in academia, teaching graduate-level courses in program evaluation, training design and development, organizational learning, appreciative inquiry, and consulting. Her research has focused on evaluation capacity building, transfer of learning/training, evaluation use, and evaluation as a catalyst for individual, team, and organizational learning. Hallie's books include *Reframing Evaluation Through Appreciative Inquiry* (2006), *Building Evaluation Capacity: 72 Activities for Teaching and Training* (2005), and *Evaluation in Organizations: A Systematic Approach to Enhancing Learning, Performance, and Change* (2001, 2009). Dr. Preskill was the 2007 president of the American Evaluation Association. She received the American Evaluation Association's Alva and Gunnar Myrdal Award for Outstanding Professional Practice in 2002 and the University of Illinois Distinguished Alumni Award in 2004. Over the years, she has provided consulting services and workshops on various evaluation and training-related workshops and has conducted evaluations in the areas of education, economic development, public and mental health, media and information, the environment, poverty, and global development. Hallie holds a PhD from the University of Illinois at Urbana-Champaign.

Patricia J. Rogers is Professor of Public Sector Evaluation at RMIT University (Royal Melbourne Institute of Technology), Melbourne, Australia. Patricia has worked in public sector evaluation and research for more than 25 years, across a wide range of program areas (including agriculture, community development, criminal justice, early childhood, education, health promotion, and Indigenous housing) and levels of government (national, state, and local). In addition to her work in Australia with federal, state, and local governments, she has worked on projects with government and nongovernmental organizations in New Zealand, South Africa, the United Kingdom, the United States, Malaysia, South Africa, Japan, and Singapore; presented keynote addresses at conferences of evaluation societies and associations in Australasia, Aotearoa/New Zealand, Europe, the United Kingdom, South Africa, and Sweden; and taught short courses in Australia, New Zealand, France, Japan, Malaysia, Singapore, South Africa, and the United States. She has been awarded the American Evaluation Association's Myrdal Award for Evaluation Practice, the Australasian Evaluation Society's

(AES's) Evaluation Training and Services Award for outstanding contributions to the profession of evaluation, the AES Caulley-Tulloch Prize for Pioneering Literature in Evaluation, and led the team that was awarded the AES 2007 Best Evaluation Study award. Her publications include *Purposeful Program Theory: Effective Use of Theories of Change and Logic Models* (with Sue Funnell) and chapters in the *Handbook of Practical Program Evaluation*, the *Encyclopedia of Evaluation*, and *The SAGE Handbook of Evaluation*. Patricia lives with her family in the Australian bush on the edge of Melbourne.

Peter H. Rossi, now deceased, was Stuart A. Rice Professor Emeritus of Sociology and Director Emeritus of the Social and Demographic Research Institute at the University of Massachusetts at Amherst. He had been on the faculties of Harvard University, the University of Chicago, and Johns Hopkins University and was director from 1960 to 1967 of the National Opinion Research Center at the University of Chicago. He was past president (1980) of the American Sociological Association and was the 1985 recipient of the Common Wealth Award for lifetime contributions to sociology. He received awards from the Evaluation Research Society, the Eastern Evaluation Research Society, and the Policy Studies Association for his contributions to evaluation research methodology. His most recent books include *Evaluation: A Systematic Approach* (with Mark Lipsey and Howard Freeman, 7th ed., 2004); *Of Human Bonding* (with Alice S. Rossi, 1990); *Down and Out in America* (1989); *Just Punishments* (with R. A. Berk, 1997); and *Feeding the Poor* (1998). He served as editor of the *American Journal of Sociology* and *Social Science Research*. He had been elected a Fellow of the American Academy of Arts and Sciences and of the American Association for the Advancement of Science.

Michael Scriven is a professor of psychology at Claremont Graduate University and a senior research associate at the Evaluation Center, Western Michigan University. He took his bachelor's and master's degrees from the honors school of mathematics at Melbourne University, Australia, and his first two jobs were in mathematical physics. He went on to do a doctorate in philosophy at Oxford for a thesis on the logic of explanations in science and history. His 50 years of teaching have been in departments of mathematics, philosophy, psychology, the history and philosophy of science, law, evaluation, and education, and as university professor; most of this was done at the Universities of Minnesota, Indiana, California (Berkeley), Western Australia, and Auckland, as well as Swarthmore, Harvard, and San Francisco. His 450+ publications have been mainly in the fields of his appointments and in computer science, informal logic, cosmology, international philanthropy, and technology studies. He has held a Whitehead fellowship at Harvard and been a fellow at the Center for Advanced Study in the Behavioral Sciences at Stanford, has served as president of the American Educational Research Association and the American Evaluation Association, and has been on the editorial or review boards of 42 journals. His publications are mainly in the philosophy of science, evaluation, ethics, computer studies, philosophy of technology, historiography, and educational research. Some of his recent articles are in the online *Journal of MultiDisciplinary Evaluation*, which he founded and coedits (jmde .com), and in *New Directions in Evaluation* (Summer 2008), a special issue on the evaluation of research/researchers/research institutes in all disciplines.

William R. Shadish is Professor and Founding Faculty, University of California, Merced, where he is also Chair of Psychological Sciences. His current research interests include experimental and quasi-experimental design, the empirical study of methodological issues, and the methodology and practice of meta-analysis. He is author of *Experimental and Quasi-Experimental Designs for Generalized Causal Inference* (with T. D. Cook and D. T. Campbell, 2002) and *Foundations of Program Evaluation* (with T. D. Cook and L. C. Leviton, 1991). He was the founding Secretary-Treasurer of the Society for Research Synthesis Methodology (2005–2010). He is winner of numerous awards for research, including the 1994 Paul F. Lazarsfeld Award for Evaluation Theory from the American Evaluation Association, the 2002 Donald T. Campbell Award for Innovations in Methodology from the Policy Studies Organization, the 2009 Frederick Mosteller Award for Lifetime Contributions to Systematic Reviews from the Campbell Collaboration, and the 2011 Ingram Olkin Award for Lifetime Contributions to Systematic Reviews from the Society for Search Synthesis Methodology.

Robert E. Stake is one of several educational researchers who created theory and practice for educational program evaluation in the 1960s. He became in 1975, and remains, director of CIRCE at the University of Illinois. His approach, *"responsive evaluation"* emphasizes the study of classroom experience, personal interaction, institutional processes and contexts, often in the form of case studies. Among the evaluative studies he has directed have been works in science and art education, model programs and conventional teaching, and special education and gender equity. Stake authored *Quieting Reform,* a book on Charles Murray's evaluation of Cities-in-Schools and four earlier books on research methodology: *Standards-Based and Responsive Evaluation; Evaluating the Arts in Education; The Art of Case Study Research;* and *Multiple Case Study Analysis.* For his evaluation work, in 1988, he received the Lazarsfeld Award from the American Evaluation Association and, in 2007, the President's Citation from the American Educational Research Association, and in 2011, a Lifetime Achievement award from the International Congress of Qualitative Research. He holds honorary doctorates from the University of Uppsala and the University of Valladolid.

Nicoletta Stame teaches social policy at the University "La Sapienza," Rome. She was a cofounder and the president of the Italian Evaluation Association. She is a past president of the European Evaluation Society. She is a member of the International Evaluation (Inteval) network. Nicoletta is interested in the theory and methods of evaluation. She is the author of *L'esperienza della valutazione* (The Evaluation Experience, 1998), editor of *Classici della valutazione* (Classics in Evaluation, 2007), coeditor (with Ray Rist) of *From Studies to Streams* (2006), and author of many essays in books and journals. She is associate editor of *Evaluation, the International Journal of Theory, Research and Practice.* Her professional background includes research on socioeconomic development, industrial policies, family business, and political participation. She has evaluated programs of enterprise creation, aid to small and medium enterprises, and social integration at local and national levels; she has been a member of evaluation panels of European Union Framework Programs 6 and 7. Her work aims at enhancing the evaluation capacities of public administrators, program implementers, and beneficiaries.

Daniel L. Stufflebeam retired in 2007 from Western Michigan University (WMU) as Distinguished University Professor and McKee Professor of Education. His degrees include Bachelor of Music (1958) from the University of Iowa and MS in counseling (1962) and PhD with specializations in statistics, experimental design, and clinical and objective measurement (1964) from Purdue University. In 1965 he founded The Evaluation Center at The Ohio State University (OSU), directed it there until 1973 (when he moved it to WMU), and then directed it at WMU until 2002. He developed the CIPP evaluation model, directed the construction of more than 100 standardized achievement tests (including eight forms of the General Educational Development [GED] tests), led the development of the Joint Committee professional standards for program and personnel evaluations, developed about a dozen evaluation checklists, helped establish the Evaluation Network, conducted numerous evaluations and consultations in the United States and abroad, and taught and advised many doctoral students who became leading evaluation practitioners and scholars. His publications include 25 books and monographs and more than 100 journal articles and book chapters. Among his awards are the AEA Paul Lazarsfeld Prize, the WMU Distinguished Faculty Scholar Award, the inaugural CREATE Jason Millman Award, and induction into The Ohio State University College of Education Hall of Fame. His recent books are *Evaluation Models* (with Madaus and Kellaghan, 2000, Kluwer), *International Handbook of Educational Evaluation* (with Kellaghan, 2003, Kluwer), and *Evaluation Theory, Models, & Applications* (with Shinkfield, 2007, Jossey-Bass).

Anne T. Vo is a doctoral student of the Social Research Methodology Division in the Graduate School of Education and Information Studies at the University of California, Los Angeles. She is also coeditor of the *American Journal of Evaluation*'s section on Teaching Evaluation and codirector of the Southern California Evaluation Association. Her research interests include comparative evaluation theory, evaluation context, and teaching of evaluation. Her practice has centered on evaluation capacity building and the evaluation of academic preparation and enrichment programs that serve underrepresented populations in the K-20 educational pipeline.

Carol Hirschon Weiss is Beatrice B. Whiting Professor in the Graduate School of Education at Harvard University. She received her doctorate in sociology at Columbia University. She has written, edited, or coedited 11 books and has published more than 225 articles, book chapters, and reviews. Her work has been translated into Spanish, German, French, Portuguese, Thai, Lithuanian, Hungarian, and Ukrainian. She pioneered the development of program theory as a basis for evaluation; she was one of the originators of empirical study of the uses of evaluation in policy and practice, a subject on which she continues to write; she initiated the study of the politics of evaluation, the topic of her current research. She has consulted for dozens of public, private, and nonprofit organizations both in the United States and abroad, including the U.S. Department of Education, the Department of Housing and Urban Development, the National Institutes of Health, the Canadian International Development Centre, World Bank, and Witwatersrand University in South Africa. She has been a fellow at the Center for Advanced Study in the Behavioral Sciences, fellow of the American Association for the Advancement of Science, member of 11 panels of the National Academy of Sciences,

Guest Scholar at Brookings Institution, senior fellow at the Department of Education, and recipient of the 2009 presidential citation of the American Educational Research Association.

Joseph S. Wholey is Professor Emeritus at the University of Southern California's School of Policy, Planning, and Development. He received his BA in mathematics from Catholic University and his MA in mathematics and PhD in philosophy from Harvard University. His work focuses on the use of strategic planning, performance monitoring, and program evaluation to improve the performance and accountability of public and nonprofit organizations. He is the author of many journal articles and author, coauthor, editor, or coeditor of eight books. Wholey served as senior advisor for performance and accountability at the U.S. Government Accountability Office and as senior advisor to the deputy director for management at the U.S. Office of Management and Budget. Before coming to the University of Southern California, he was deputy assistant secretary for planning and evaluation at the U.S. Department of Health and Human Services and director of program evaluation studies at the Urban Institute. Wholey is a fellow of the National Academy of Public Administration. He received the Elmer B. Staats Award from the American Society for Public Administration, National Capital Area Chapter and the Gunnar and Alva Myrdal Prize from the Evaluation Research Society. In 1999, he was the first recipient of the Joseph Wholey Distinguished Scholarship Award from the American Society for Public Administration.

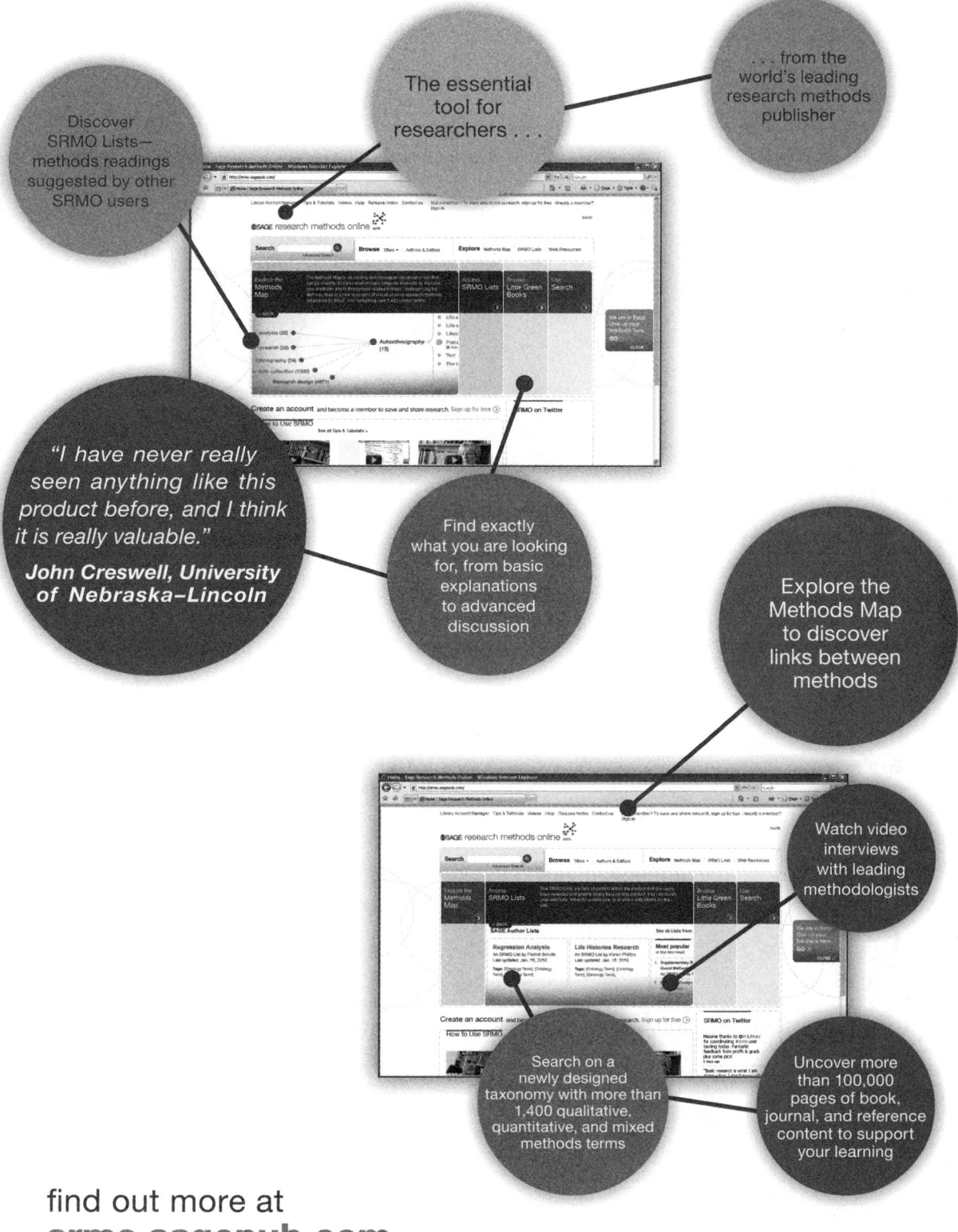